Disembodied Voices

Disembodied Voices

Music and Culture in an Early Modern Italian Convent

❧

Craig A. Monson

UNIVERSITY OF CALIFORNIA PRESS

Berkeley   Los Angeles   London

Publication of this book was made possible
by a generous grant from the
National Endowment for the Humanities.

University of California Press
Berkeley and Los Angeles, California

University of California Press, Ltd.
London, England

Library of Congress Cataloging-in-Publication Data

Monson, Craig (Craig A.)
  Disembodied voices : music and culture in an early modern Italian
  convent / Craig A. Monson.
    p.   cm.
  Includes bibliographical references (p.   ) and index.
  ISBN 0-520-08875-1 (alk. paper)
    1. Music in convents—Italy—Bologna.   2. Church music—Italy—
  Bologna—16th century.   3. Church music—Italy—Bologna—
  17th century.   4. Santa Cristina della Fondazza (Convent : Bologna,
  Italy) I. Title.
  ML3033.8.B65M66   1995
  780'.945'4109031—dc20   94-28823
                                                            CIP
                                                            MN

Printed in the United States of America
9 8 7 6 5 4 3 2 1

The paper used in this publication meets the minimum requirements
of American National Standard for Information Sciences—Perma-
nence of Paper for Printed Library Materials, ANSI Z39.48–1984.

To Susan, Temma, and other friends
from the National Humanities Center

CONTENTS

ILLUSTRATIONS AND TABLES

FIGURES

TABLES

MUSICAL EXAMPLES

ACKNOWLEDGMENTS

It would have proved impossible to piece together this history of Lucrezia Orsina Vizzana and Santa Cristina della Fondazza from widely scattered scraps of documentary information without the assistance of numerous archives and libraries. Over many years I have enjoyed regular access to the rich archival and bibliographical collections of Bologna, which are of primary importance to this work. The staffs of the Archivio di Stato and the Biblioteca Universitaria have been courteous, cooperative, and tolerant. At the Biblioteca Comunale dell'Archiginnasio, dottoressa Anna Maria Scardovi took a particular interest, readily shared her knowledge of that impressive collection, and helped in innumerable ways. At the Archivio Generale Arcivescovile, dott. Mario Fanti responded patiently to many requests, despite the imprecision of my references and of my Italian. I am especially grateful to dott. Francesco Cavazza for generously permitting me repeated access to the Fondo Paleotti in the Archivio Isolani-Lupari. Signora Luisa Laffi of the Archivio Opera Pia Davia-Bargellini was especially solicitous in helping me to gain access to artwork in that collection. Giorgio Piombini and the staff of the Civico Museo Bibliografico Musicale extended to me the same unequaled courtesy and hospitality that have endeared them to countless foreign scholars who regularly consult that extraordinary library.

I have likewise benefited from the opportunity to consult collections elsewhere in Italy, such as the Archivio del Duomo in Vercelli and the Biblioteca Civico Correr in Venice. A. Ugo Fossa, prior and librarian of the monastery of Camaldoli (Arezzo) went out of his way to be sure I could make full use of important sources from the monastery library. Clearly, this research would have been impossible without access to the Biblioteca Apostolica Vaticana and the Archivio Segreto Vaticano. Other scholars who have worked there will recognize the extent and particular nature of my appreciation to their staffs.

Closer to home, I have enjoyed not only the use of the library of the Camaldolese Hermitage of the Immaculate Heart, Big Sur, California, but also the hospitality of Fr. Robert Hale and the other monks, and their abiding interest in the progress of my work. I am indebted to the library system of Washington University in Saint Louis, particularly to the staff of the interlibrary loan department, without whom I could have accomplished little. The rich theological holdings and microfilm collections of the Pius XII Library at Saint Louis University significantly reduced my need to rely on interlibrary loan.

This work would also have been impossible without the support and encouragement of many other institutions and innumerable individuals over the past eight years. The research was made possible in part by an NEH summer stipend and research grants and leaves from Washington University. I completed some of the preliminary work during my term as Joseph E. and Grace W. Valentine Visiting Professor in the Music Department at Amherst College in 1990. I drafted and revised the text as an NEH fellow at the National Humanities Center in 1992–93, an opportunity that changed not only the book but my scholarship generally.

Many have contributed in diverse ways and helped to get the work this far, including Jane Bernstein, Franca Camiz, Giampiero Cammarota, Katherine Gill, Celestino Grossi, James Haar, Jeffrey Hamburger, Jeffrey Kurtzman, James Ladewig, Luciano Malossi, William Matheson, Dolores Pesce, Lucio Riccetti, Ann Roberts, Margaret Ann Rorke, Colin Slim, Howard Smither, Richard Spear, Susan Strocchia, Carolyn Valone, Elissa Weaver, and Carolyn Wood. The late Jerome Roche kindly searched for many texts in his motet database. Marilane Bergfelt drafted the plan of the convent of Santa Cristina (fig. 4). Patrizia Bittini and Beatrice Asper struggled valiantly with the vagaries of my Italian, while Naomi Gold fulfilled a similar role with my Latin. Nevertheless, I must bear responsibility for all unattributed translations.

I am scarcely the first to have been influenced by the impressive scholarship of Gabriella Zarri or to have benefited from her generosity, hospitality, and friendship. Dott. Oscar Mischiati, who in the very beginning took an interest in my work on convent music, has continued to share his wide-ranging knowledge and expertise, as well as his own discoveries, and offered useful reactions to the draft. Carlo Vitali likewise provided a wealth of advice, suggestions, and corrections over the years, and particularly in the final stages. Count Gian Ludovico Masetti Zannini, the first to write about Bolognese nuns' music, generously shared his expertise, made available copies of his extensive writings, and offered me hospitality in both Bologna and Rome. Roberta Zucchini and Ugo Capriani kindly made available copies of their theses on Santa Cristina, from which I have benefited greatly, gave me permission to publish some of their photographs, and were generous with their time, help, and good company. Monsignor Niso Albertazzi, abate parroco di San Giuliano, and signor Gianluigi Panzacchi afforded me repeated access to the church of Santa Cristina, and indulged my enthusiasms for the convent and its history. I am particularly grateful to Candace Smith and Bruce Dickey for their frequent hospitality and for sharing their knowledge of Bolognese and convent music, convincingly brought to life by their performances, including *Canti nel Chiostro: Musiche nei monasteri femminili del '600 a Bologna* (Tactus, TC 60001), which presents works by Lucrezia Vizzana and other composers discussed below; and to Dafne Dickey for lending her own particular perspective.

Many others substantially helped along the process of getting the book down on paper and into final form by their encouragement and advice. Believing that turnabout is fair play, Antonia Banducci helped me recognize many organizational lapses and syntactical quagmires. Robert Kendrick took pleasure not only in our common interests but also in generously and constantly sharing his wide knowledge of the field, as well as many, many discoveries he could have kept to himself. Emma Kafalenos assumed the role of the (extremely) intelligent nonspecialist reader and offered an admirably candid appraisal of my attempts to capture the character of some particularly unmemorable Italian verse in my poetic translations ("bad translations of cheap poetry")—an appraisal I ignore at my own peril. As readers for the University of California Press, Suzanne Cusick and Ann Matter tried to recognize what might be good about the book and to help me recognize what could be better. Anne Schutte lavished on the manuscript the sort of meticulous reading and evaluation at all levels of discourse that one always secretly hopes for but knows it is unreasonable ever to expect. Dore Brown, Peter Dreyer, and Doris Kretschmer of the University of California Press taught me a lot about consistency, clarity, and style with patience, tact, and diplomacy.

The book would have been very different had it not been written at the National Humanities Center. The center's staff created an atmosphere that was both congenial and extraordinarily conducive to hard work. Its library staff took on what seemed impossible challenges, made them seem ordinary, and almost invariably conquered them. A number of fellows played particularly important roles as interested and critical readers and as mentors. Elizabeth Kirk quietly slipped into my hand or mailbox references, articles, or books she thought might be useful—and they invariably were. Edward Muir genially let me lure him repeatedly into the paleographic thickets and tangled syntax of intractable archival documents, which only he, it seemed, could clarify, and then shared my own fascination and his own insights about them. Susan Porter Benson suggested new historical approaches, sent me off into labor history and work culture, then labored over whatever I slipped under her door, always with wit, good humor, and healthy cynicism. Temma Kaplan, in the marginalia she scattered over chapter after chapter, in her own writings, and in her concerns with gender studies, history, and the academy, shared on damp late winter walks, showed me the way to write what I wanted to write.

Much of chapter 3 has appeared under the title "The Making of Lucrezia Orsina Vizzana's *Componimenti musicali* (1623)" in *Creative Women in Medieval and Early Modern Italy: A Religious and Artistic Renaissance,* edited by E. Ann Matter and John Coakely (Philadelphia, 1994), and I thank the University of Pennsylvania Press for permission to reuse the material here. The music in the examples is published with permission of the Civico Museo Bibliografico Musicale, Bologna.

DRAMATIS PERSONAE

A genealogy of the Vizzani and Bombacci families is provided in table 1, at the end of the Dramatis Personae.

Adda, Ferdinando [Borromeo] d'. Cardinal, official protector of the Camaldolese order, and papal legate in Bologna (1698–1707). Interceded on behalf of the nuns of Santa Cristina over the Sacra in 1698.

Allè, Maria Caterina (1624–1707). Mother superior at Santa Cristina. Active in rallying outside noble support to the nuns' cause in the suit over the Sacra in 1698.

Azzolini, Maria Elisabetta Ermenegilda (1637–1708). Bursar, prioress, and mistress of novices at Santa Cristina for twelve years, then abbess during the suit against Giacomo Boncompagni in 1704 over nuns' music.

Bardelloni, Desiderio. Camaldolese visitor who participated in the first pastoral visitation to Santa Cristina in 1622–23.

Bernardo da Venezia (d. 1630). Camaldolese monk, curate of San Damiano in Bologna. Declined under duress to serve as confessor extraordinary to the nuns of Santa Cristina during the Jubilee of 1629.

Bianchi, Cecilia (c. 1576–c. 1630?) (*al secolo* Irenea). Musical rival of Emilia Grassi and chief fomenter of the crises at Santa Cristina in the 1620s; removed from the convent in 1629 to San Michele in San Giovanni in Persiceto. Daughter of Stefano di Giovanni Battista Bianchi.

Bolognetti, Camillo. Mediator for the nuns of Santa Cristina in their suit before the Congregation of Bishops in 1704 over nuns' music.

Bolognetti, Lucidaria (d. c. 1662). Ally of Cecilia Bianchi in the struggles of the 1620s at Santa Cristina. Removed from the convent to San Bernardino in 1629.

Bolognetti, Count Paolo. Former secular administrator for the convent of Santa Cristina. The nuns' particular advocate in the suit over the Sacra in 1698.

Bolognini, Maria Giuditta Ginevra (1680–1762) (*al secolo* Teodora Maria). Entered the novitiate at Santa Cristina in 1695, professed in 1696, was consecrated in 1699, and sang on the feast of Saint Christina in 1704, in violation of Giacomo Boncompagni's ban on convent music. Subsequently served three years as bursar, six as mistress of novices, fifteen as prioress, and nine as abbess. Still remembered every January in the Camaldolese menology.

Bombacci, Camilla (1571–1640) (*al secolo* Laura). Nun at Santa Cristina from 1587. Served as organist, mistress of novices, and abbess during the struggles of the 1620s, when she led the revolt against Archbishop Ludovico Ludovisi. Daughter of Giovanni Bombacci and Camilla Luchini.

Bombacci, Flaminia (1563–1624) (*al secolo* Lodovica). Nun at Santa Cristina from 1578. Served as abbess at least twice, and was the spiritual leader at the convent in the early 1620s. Daughter of Giovanni Bombacci and Camilla Luchini. Still remembered every September in the Camaldolese menology.

Bombacci, Giovanni di Antonio (d. 1604). Father of Isabetta, Camilla, Flaminia, and Ortensia; grandfather of Lucrezia Orsina Vizzana.

Bombacci, Isabetta (1560–98). Daughter of Giovanni Bombacci and Camilla Luchini, wife of Ludovico Vizzani, mother of Lucrezia Orsina and Isabetta Vizzani.

Bombacci, Ortensia (1565–1631) (*al secolo* Isabella). Nun at Santa Cristina from 1580, where she was one of the least active members of her family, and apparently a recluse in her last years. Daughter of Giovanni Bombacci and Camilla Luchini.

Boncompagni, Giacomo (1653–1731). Second in succession to his uncle Cardinal Archbishop Girolamo Boncompagni as archbishop of Bologna (1690). His reforming interests included substantial restrictions on convent music and two clashes with the nuns of Santa Cristina.

Boncompagni, Girolamo (1622–1684). Cardinal archbishop of Bologna from 1651 to 1684.

Boncompagni, Ippolita Ludovisi. Interceded with Archbishop Giacomo Boncompagni on behalf of the nuns of Santa Cristina after the confrontation of 1704. Wife of Gregorio Boncompagni, sister-in-law of Giacomo Boncompagni, and the last survivor of the Ludovisi line.

Bondini, Giovanni (known as "don Gioanino"). The apparently corrupt Bolognese vicar of nuns under Archbishop Ludovico Ludovisi.

ABBREVIATIONS

AAB	Archivio Generale Arcivescovile, Bologna
ASB	Archivio di Stato, Bologna
ASV	Archivio Segreto Vaticano
ASV, VR	Archivio Segreto Vaticano, Sacra Congregazione dei Vescovi e Regolari
BAV	Biblioteca Apostolica Vaticana
b.c.	basso continuo
BCB	Biblioteca Comunale dell'Archiginnasio, Bologna
BUB	Biblioteca Universitaria, Bologna
Gozz.	Gozzadini
JAMS	*Journal of the American Musicological Society*
ks	key signature
ML	*Music and Letters*
MQ	*Musical Quarterly*
posiz.	posizione
Reg. episc.	Regestum episcoporum
Reg. monial.	Regestum monialium
Reg. regular.	Regestum regularium
sez.	sezione
ten.	tenor
⟨⟩	words omitted in a redaction of pre-existent text
£	Italian lire (1 scudo = approximately £5 in seventeenth-century Bologna)

Bonsignori, Lorenza (d. 1629). Twice abbess of Santa Cristina, the second time during the pastoral visitation of 1622–23.

Bordino (or Bardino), Giusto. Camaldolese monk. Mauro Ruggeri's successor as confessor to the nuns of Santa Cristina in the 1620s, a job for which he was apparently unqualified.

Bovio, Carlo. Successor to Angelo Gozzadini as suffragan bishop of Bologna under Archbishop Ludovico Ludovisi. Led the second pastoral visitation to Santa Cristina in 1626 and the subsequent takeover of the convent.

Caprara, Alessandro. Bolognese prelate in Rome who surreptitiously supported the nuns of Santa Cristina in the suit over the Sacra in 1698.

Carrati, Colomba (1629–1702). Abbess of Santa Cristina during the suit over the Sacra in 1698.

Cavazza, Christina Teresa Prudenza Deodata (c. 1679–1751). Music-loving nun, consecrated in 1699, who sang in violation of Giacomo Boncompagni's ban on convent music in 1704. Caught leaving the cloister in disguise to attend the opera in 1708.

Colloredo, Leonardo. Cardinal appointed *ponente* for the suit over the Sacra in the Congregation of Sacred Rites in 1698, and again for the suit over nuns' music in the Congregation of Bishops in 1704.

Colonna, Girolamo (1603–66). Cardinal archbishop of Bologna, 1632–45.

Fabbri, Ludovica (d. 1633). A *conversa* at Santa Cristina, and Cecilia Bianchi's ally in the troubles of the 1620s. Less deeply implicated than Maria Gentile Malvasia and Lucidaria Bolognetti, she was never removed from the convent.

Fagnani, Prospero (d. 1678). Secretary of the Sacred Congregation of Bishops and Regulars in the 1620s and an ally of Archbishop Ludovico Ludovisi in the takeover of Santa Cristina; subsequently an important advisor to Pope Alexander VII.

Gargallante (Gargalini). Agent of Cardinal Ferdinando d'Adda and a papal lobbyist in Rome. Presented the petition of the nuns of Santa Cristina over the Sacra to Innocent XII in 1697.

Gozzadini, Angelo. Suffragan bishop of Bologna under Archbishop Ludovico Ludovisi in the early 1620s. Led the first pastoral visitation to Santa Cristina in 1622–23.

Gozzadini, Ulisses Joseph. Professor of canon law in Bologna, papal secretary of briefs, and eventually a cardinal. Lent surreptitious support to the nuns of Santa Cristina in the suit over the Sacra in 1698.

Grassi, Emilia (d. 1633). Leading musician, patron of the arts, twice abbess, and a protagonist in the intramural rivalries at Santa Cristina in the

1620s. Chief enemy of Cecilia Bianchi. Illegitimate daughter of the Grassi family.

Leoni, Adeodata (d. 1655). Important mediator, political figure, abbess in the 1640s, and patron of music at Santa Cristina.

Luchini, Camilla (d. 1612). Daughter of Filippo Luchini, wife of Giovanni Bombacci, grandmother of Lucrezia Orsina Vizzana.

Luchini, Ortensia (d. 1576). Nun at Santa Cristina. Possibly the sister of Camilla Luchini Bombacci.

Ludovisi, Alessandro (1554–1623). Archbishop of Bologna (1612–21) and Pope Gregory XV (1621–23). Supported Ludovico Ludovisi's early efforts to bring Santa Cristina under archdiocesan control.

Ludovisi, Ludovico (1595–1632). Cardinal nephew to Pope Gregory XV and cardinal archbishop of Bologna (1621–32). Took the convent of Santa Cristina from Camaldolese jurisdiction and subjugated it to archdiocesan control.

Ludovisi, Niccolò Albergati (1608–87). Cardinal archbishop of Bologna from 1645 to 1651. Opposed the nuns of Santa Cristina in the matter of secular confessors in 1646–47. A cousin of Ludovico Ludovisi's, he assumed the Ludovisi name after being accepted as a brother by Prince Niccolò Ludovisi, duke of Fiano and prince of Venosa and Piombino.

Malatendi, Francesca (d. 1643). A *conversa* at Santa Cristina for forty years. Confessed before her death to having spread rumors about the possible pregnancy of another *conversa* in the 1620s. Her confession helped to provoke the nuns' renewal of their campaign for reunion with the Camaldolese.

Malvasia, Maria Gentile (d. 1647). One of the three troublemakers who fomented the crises of the 1620s at Santa Cristina; a chief ally of Cecilia Bianchi's. Removed from the convent to Sant'Agostino in 1629.

Muzzi, Maria Diletta Vittoria (1678–1748) (*al secolo* Livia). Consecrated in 1699, sang in violation of Giacomo Boncompagni's ban on convent music in 1704, served three times as abbess, and was a convent patron of the arts.

Narici, Giovanni Battista. Roman lawyer for the nuns of Santa Cristina in their suit before the Congregation of Bishops in 1704 over nuns' music.

Orsi, Ludovico Maria. Prior of the Camaldolese hermitage of San Benedetto di Ceretola near Bologna. Played a primary role as advisor and mediator for the nuns of Santa Cristina in the suit over the Sacra of 1699. Brother of Luigia Orsina.

Orsi, Luigia Orsina (1632–1720). Joined Santa Cristina in 1648, served as prioress and abbess, and oversaw the suit over the Sacra of 1699. Sister of Ludovico Maria Orsi.

Paleotti, Alfonso (1531–1610). Distant cousin, coadjutor, and successor to Gabriele Paleotti; the only Bolognese archbishop never made a cardinal.

Paleotti, Gabriele (1522–97). Cardinal and first archbishop of Bologna. Strongly committed to the implementation of the decrees of the Council of Trent.

Pini, Bernardo. Nuns' vicar to Cardinal Archbishop Giacomo Boncompagni in Bologna during the first two decades of the Settecento.

Ranuzzi, Angelo Maria (1626–89). Cardinal archbishop of Bologna from 1688 until his death. Never set foot in his diocese.

Ruggeri, Mauro (d. 1660). Prior general of the Camaldolese order in the 1630s, titular abbot and confessor to the nuns of Santa Cristina in the early 1620s. An eyewitness to the convent's struggles, which he described in his manuscript "Caduta di Santa Cristina."

Sabbatini, Giovanni Battista. Protégé of Ludovico Maria Orsi. Served as procurator in Rome for the nuns of Santa Cristina in the suit over the Sacra in 1699.

Spada, Bernardino. Cardinal and papal legate in Bologna (1627–29, 1630) during the later stages of the crisis at Santa Cristina. Acted as emissary for the curia with Camilla Bombacci and the nuns in 1628.

Ubaldini, Uberto (or Roberto). Cardinal and papal legate in Bologna (1623–27) during the crises of the 1620s at Santa Cristina. Led the notorious third visitation to the convent in 1626.

Vizzani, Angelo Michele di Dioniggio (b. 1620). Natural son of Dioniggio di Ludovico and Anna Veneta, nephew of Lucrezia Orsina; legitimized in 1628 and made heir to the estate of Ludovico di Obizzo.

Vizzani, Dioniggio di Ludovico (1584–1628). Brother of Lucrezia Orsina and Isabetta, father of Angelo Michele.

Vizzani, Isabetta (1587–1653) (*al secolo* Verginia). Entered Santa Cristina in 1598. An important political figure at the convent from c. 1624 to 1653. Daughter of Ludovico Vizzani and Isabetta Bombacci, sister of Lucrezia Orsina.

Vizzani, Lucrezia Orsina (1590–1662) (*al secolo* Lucrezia). Entered Santa Cristina c. 1598. Composer of *Componimenti musicali* (1623). Daughter of Ludovico Vizzani and Isabetta Bombacci.

Vizzani, Ludovico di Obizzo (d. 1628). Father of Lucrezia Orsina, Isabetta, and Dioniggio.

Vizzani, Maria Clorinda (1618–95) (*al secolo* Valeria). Member of Santa Cristina from c. 1639, where she served as prioress in her last years; (illegitimate?) daughter of Dioniggio di Ludovico, sister of Angelo Michele, niece of Lucrezia Orsina and Isabetta.

Vizzani, Obizzo di Pirro (d. 1581). Corrector of acts to the Bolognese college of notaries. Father of Ludovico and grandfather of Lucrezia Orsina.

Vizzani, Teresa Pompea (1618–84) (*al secolo* Elena). Abbess and important patron of music and art at Santa Cristina. Daughter of Costanzo di Giasone Vizzani, distant cousin of Lucrezia Orsina.

Zanelli, Scipione. Roman lawyer of the nuns of Santa Cristina in their suit over the Sacra of 1699.

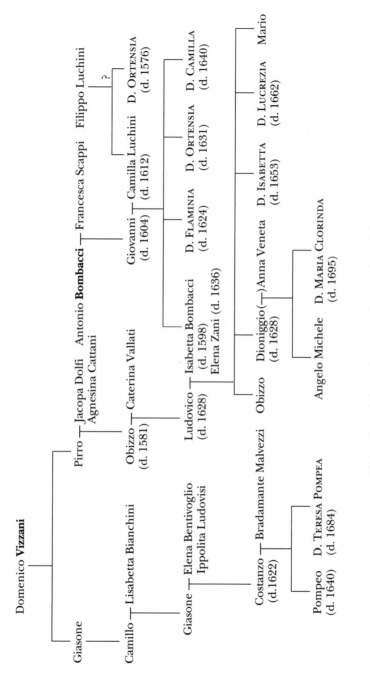

TABLE 1. The Vizzani and Bombacci Families (abbreviated)

Domenico **Vizzani**

Giasone

Camillo ┬ Lisabetta Bianchini

Pirro ┬ Jacopa Dolfi
      Agnesina Cattani

Antonio **Bombacci** ┬ Francesca Scappi   Filippo Luchini

Obizzo ┬ Caterina Vallati
(d. 1581)

Giovanni ┬ Camilla Luchini
(d. 1604)   (d. 1612)

D. ORTENSIA
(d. 1576)

Ludovico ┬ Isabetta Bombacci
(d. 1628) │ (d. 1598)
           └ Elena Zani (d. 1636)

D. FLAMINIA
(d. 1624)

D. ORTENSIA
(d. 1631)

D. CAMILLA
(d. 1640)

Giasone ┬ Elena Bentivoglio
        Ippolita Ludovisi

Obizzo

Dioniggio (┬) Anna Veneta
(d. 1628)

D. ISABETTA
(d. 1653)

D. LUCREZIA
(d. 1662)

Mario

Costanzo ┬ Bradamante Malvezzi
(d.1622)

Angelo Michele

D. MARIA CLORINDA
(d. 1695)

Pompeo   D. TERESA POMPEA
(d. 1640)   (d. 1684)

NOTE: In capitals are the names of nuns at Santa Cristina

INTRODUCTION
The Singing Nuns of Bologna

What shall I say of the virgins of Bononia . . . at one time they resound in spiritual song [*canticis spiritualibus personant*], and at another they provide their sustenance by their labors and seek similarly to provide the material of their charity with the work of their hands.[1]

Saint Ambrose, c. 392 A.D.

It is intriguing to encounter a reference to the music of Bologna's sacred virgins at such an early date, and to discover that Saint Ambrose counted singing among their good works. For twelve hundred years later, when nuns' music in Bologna began more regularly to provoke local comment, the opposite opinion flourished among Saint Ambrose's successors within the church hierarchy.

It still comes as something of a surprise to historians of the early modern period that nuns' music loomed as large as it did in the minds of many nuns, their religious superiors, and the public beyond the convent wall. Nuns are the prime example of women cultivating music in a private sphere, one that external forces—the paternalistic church authorities—strove to keep as private as possible. It is not surprising that we have remained largely unaware of most nun musicians and their musical activities or accomplishments. Although it is true that the Catholic church "employed no women musicians in any capacity"[2] in the public sphere beyond the walls of the cloister, within the convent, the situation was entirely different. In the post-Tridentine period, thousands of organists, singers, and composers can be traced in the records of Italian nunneries. The more talented of these sacred divas may have been out of sight, but they were regularly on the minds of music lovers, as this book seeks to show.

For young women trained as musicians during the sixteenth and seventeenth centuries, the cloister was probably the most obvious milieu in which to practice that profession in its various respectable aspects. If they were accepted as convent organists, these young women might also save their parents hundreds—indeed thousands—of lire. In an era when providing for several daughters was perceived as a potential financial burden to their families, the development of a daughter's musical gifts with an eye toward the nunnery thus proved a very sound investment. She could be sent to a convent with a much smaller dowry than a potential husband required, and if she were accepted as an organist, her basic nun's dowry could be further reduced by anywhere from 25 to 100 percent. For a poor or orphaned girl, musical talent offered the means to rise above the convent servant class (the *converse*), appropriate to a modest dowry, to the upper, governing class (the *professe* or *coriste*).[3]

For parents or guardians of prospective nun musicians, dowry reductions made convent musical careers attractive. For nun musicians, a musical career within the cloister offered the chance to perform, and perhaps to achieve a certain musical prominence in a realm associated with "celestial harmony," without the taint commonly attributed to the public stage. In convents, early modern women musicians could reach an appropriate "public" and still retain respectability—at least in the eyes of the nobility and upper classes, whom the nuns courted as an audience, if not in those of their ecclesiastical superiors. Indeed, the nun musician, performing in pseudo-privacy from behind the grated windows of the convent's inner church to her audience in the adjoining outer, public church, found a way around the genteel suspicion of musical professionalism and public performance extending from Aristotle to Castiglione, and beyond.

In post-Tridentine Italy during the heyday of convent music, Bologna's musical nuns and their singing were not atypical or unusual. The singing nuns of San Vito in Ferrara were probably better known. And the nun musicians of both Bologna and Ferrara were eclipsed by the nuns of Milan, where more cloistered composers ventured into print and their sisters enjoyed a musical renown or notoriety that was truly international.[4]

A majority of Bolognese convents practiced music to some degree. More than half a dozen, including San Lorenzo, Santi Naborre e Felice, Santi Vitale et Agricola, San Guglielmo, Santa Margherita, and especially Santa Cristina della Fondazza, fostered outstanding musical traditions, which attracted audiences from Bologna and farther afield. At least a dozen composers dedicated published collections of music to nuns of Bologna, testifying both to the nuns' musical talents and to their patronage of the arts.

The musical nuns of Bologna are particularly interesting because they maintained their musical traditions in the face of strong and persistent opposition from the local episcopate. The severe restrictions on Bolognese convent music imposed promptly after the Council of Trent (1545–63) by the reforming bishop Gabriele Paleotti continued unabated under the comparably antipathetic Alfonso Paleotti and Ludovico Ludovisi. In the last decade of the Seicento, that old severity was revived by Cardinal Archbishop Giacomo Boncompagni. Even in the intervening periods, Bologna's nun musicians never enjoyed the artistic encouragement of a pastor such as Archbishop Federico Borromeo of Milan.[5] The history of the musical nuns of Bologna is thus one of artists working against the odds, finding ways to maneuver around barriers regularly erected by their diocesan superiors.

THE HISTORICAL AND SOCIAL BACKGROUND

Bolognese convent music came to prominence at a time of comparative peace, prosperity, and tranquility for the city, following centuries of disruptions. In a quick backward glance at the first fifteen hundred years of the Christian era in Bologna, periods of relative stability that in fact lasted from a generation to over a century can appear deceptively brief amid the dozens of changes in governmental control. Bolognese history before 1500 gives the impression of perpetual political ferment.

Bolognese liked to date the first of half a dozen periods of republican government to as early as 385 A.D., around the time Saint Ambrose remarked upon the singing of the city's sacred virgins. The last republican era, beginning in 1276, coincided with a time of prosperity and commercial expansion. Bologna's situation at the foot of the Apennines, at the intersection of routes to Rome, Florence, Milan, Ravenna, and Venice, made the city a major economic hub and center of commerce. Many of its leading families grew wealthy in banking and trading, particularly in hemp, which supported some twelve thousand workers by the late Cinquecento. The city also specialized in finished wool and silk goods. In the spinning and weaving of silk, Bologna claimed to have few rivals. There were more than three hundred silk mills, staffed by some three thousand laborers, along the city's canals by the late Cinquecento, and as many as six thousand other silk-workers wove the thread into fabric.[6] Bologna's other primary economic resource was, of course, its famous university, which for centuries attracted large numbers of foreign students to the city. A favorite explanation for a characteristic feature of the Bolognese cityscape, the deep porticoes that shade most sidewalks, was the influx of thousands of these university students, who supposedly found in the abundant arcades along the city streets a useful public extension of their generally tiny private living spaces.[7]

In the same period, and in part because of the flourishing university, Bologna became an increasingly significant focus of Catholicism. The city had been subjected briefly to direct church government as early as 756, when Pépin the Short, king of the Franks, donated Bologna to the pope.

Close papal affiliation revived time and again, alternating with resurgences of republicanism and local despotism. Saint Dominic, who resided in Bologna off and on in 1219–21, held the first two Dominican general chapters in the city and because of the university's particular strength in canon law made the Bolognese Dominican monastery one of the two principal houses of his order of friars preachers. Dominic died in Bologna in 1221 and is interred in the church of San Domenico.

Anthony of Padua founded the Franciscan *studium* in Bologna shortly thereafter. The Augustinians and Servites followed not long after midcentury. In the sixteenth and seventeenth centuries, members of regular orders, who remained especially numerous in the city because of their many colleges and centers of study there, came to exercise something of a monopoly on pastoral care.

Women's religious orders in Bologna also achieved their greatest expansion during the spiritual ferment and renewal of the thirteenth century. Scarcely more than half a dozen convents date from before 1200, but by the later decades of the thirteenth century, the number reached three dozen, the highest of any period.[8]

The apogee of Bolognese republicanism in 1276, roughly corresponding to the dramatic expansion of the textile industry, the growth of religious orders, and the expansion of female monasticism, was disrupted within a decade by burgeoning civil strife between the Guelph faction, led locally by the Geremei family, and the Ghibellines, under the Lambertazzi. Bologna passed back and forth among the ascendant Bentivoglio clan, other powerful families, and the church until 1434, when the Bentivoglio family gained the upper hand, which it largely retained for eighty years.

In 1506, Pope Julius II, Giuliano della Rovere, former bishop of Bologna, entered the city in full armor at the head of his troops, having driven out Giovanni II Bentivoglio. After a last paroxysm or two during the next two decades, by 1526, papal rule had settled in firmly and to stay. "Recognizing that [papal rule] permitted it [Bologna] to live merrily and pleasantly, without the disruptions of war or sedition, [the city] devoted and dedicated itself to it completely, valuing life in the lap of the church as a true and steady liberty, as in effect it is"[9]—thus the Bolognese academic Camillo Baldi, writing in the early Seicento, somewhat cynically characterized Bologna's abandonment of liberty and any republican aspirations in favor of a more comfortable and less disruptive papal domination a century before his time. Baldi's view of civil decline promoted by comfortable, ostentatious living, is echoed, of course, by any number of commentators in other cities and centuries.[10] Subsequent Bolognese historiography suggests that the city's acceptance into the bosom of the church ushered in a relatively trouble-free period that contrasted with the regular disruptions of earlier centuries. In the history of the city that opens his *Cronologia delle famiglie nobili di Bologna* of 1670, for example, Pompeo Dolfi requires twenty-four pages to pick through the thicket of earlier historical events and political convulsions leading up to 1506, then devotes barely two pages to the next 165 years of papal domination nearer his time. Giuseppe Guidicini's schematic chronology of Bolognese government, published in 1869, records a confusing tangle of eighty epochal dates before 1506, cataloguing four dozen political changes just between "the high point of the Bolognese republic's greatness in 1276" and the beginning of papal hegemony. But Guidicini lists only five dates for the papal period, 1506 to 1796, and essentially nothing for the last 270 years.[11]

After the definitive establishment of papal control, the rare occasions when early modern Bologna was touched directly by international events chiefly arose from its ecclesiastical role, eclipsed only by that of Rome. One can come away from Dolfi, Guidicini, et al. with the impression that otherwise, after 1550, little happened in the second city of the papal realm. Leaving to others the epic military and political struggles from which early modern European histories are commonly constructed, the Bolognese concentrated instead upon mercantile, ecclesiastical, and academic enterprise. In Camillo Baldi's view, the Bolognese happily pursued wealth, comfortable living, and self-interest, relatively untroubled.

> Of course, I do not deny that this people, by natural inclination (caused by the lay of the land and the character of the air) now may not be rather soft and timid, and disaffected to work, fickled, contentious, and divided and very hostile to discomforts. This has all been increased by the fact that an extended tranquillity has set in in Italy and in this city. . . . Thus, a people disheartened in an extended peacetime, and grown enamoured of comforts, rarely and with great difficulty stirs itself to take offense and easily puts up with every discomfort, however great, in civic affairs.[12]

In sixteenth-century Bologna, the increasingly powerful papal legates supplanted the Bentivoglio clan as controllers of the oligarchy of leading families that constituted the Bolognese senate. Senatorial rank, which had become essentially hereditary in the reign of Pope Paul II (1464–71), left economic power chiefly in the hands of the forty to fifty most important Bolognese families, whose dependence upon and allegiance to the papacy were reinforced by substantial privileges and grants of regular city revenues. This administrative system remained in force until the arrival of Napoleon in 1796.

The economic life of the city, based on banking, the textile industry, and the university, continued to thrive during the first century of papal domination. In the Seicento, however, newly instituted Venetian protectionism in the hemp industry closed a primary Bolognese market. The resulting economic crises were further enhanced as the local silk and wool trades began to suffer from a lack of ready capital and the means to acquire raw materials. By 1650, Antonio di Paolo Masini was lamenting that "the poor artisan lived much better in 1590." Similar difficulties plagued the university, which for long stretches during the Seicento and early Settecento was largely abandoned by its population of foreign students.[13]

The Cinquecento and early Seicento were also a new era of expanding convent populations, most nearly approaching the previous boom of the late thirteenth century. The expansion was chiefly tied to forced monachization. Rather than squander their patrimony on the rising bridal dowries demanded by husbands of their own class, patrician families dispatched their daughters to convents in increasing numbers, with or without their consent.

Women religious thus played a discreetly prominent part in the increasingly constrained life of late sixteenth-, seventeenth-, and early-eighteenth-century Bologna, although because of post-Tridentine attempts to confine them within their cloisters, a much less visible one than in earlier times. Of Bologna's 59,000 inhabitants in 1595, 2,480 were nuns, more than twice the number of friars.[14] By the 1630s, the ratio of cloistered women to the total population of Bologna had increased by some 37 percent, compared to the same ratio in 1570. In 1631, 13.8 percent of the total female population of the city lived behind convent walls.[15] The ratio among daughters of Bolognese noble and upper-class families was considerably higher. As Bolognese monastic populations expanded, they came to control larger and larger sections of the city. It was only in 1705, when the number of women taking vows had begun to ebb, that city officials finally complained to Cardinal Archbishop Giacomo Boncompagni that, with one-sixth of the total area of the city already occupied by religious corporations, further expansion had to stop.[16]

MUSIC AT SANTA CRISTINA DELLA FONDAZZA

Against this somewhat troubled backdrop, the history of music at the convent of Santa Cristina della Fondazza unfolds. By the early Seicento, Santa Cristina had become Bologna's convent most renowned for music. For sixty-five years, it was also the home of the city's only publishing nun composer, Lucrezia Orsina Vizzana (1590–1662), who is virtually unknown to music historians. Vizzana's modest surviving corpus of music is of sufficient aesthetic interest to merit our attention as something more than a musico-historical artifact. There is no question that its potential interest is considerably enhanced by the cultural context that inspired it, which remains as little examined as the composer herself. It is quite probable that had Lucrezia Vizzana not entered Santa Cristina in childhood, she would never have studied music so extensively or have come to compose and publish her works. The daughters of upper-class Bolognese families dabbled in music as commonly as their counterparts in other cities. Such musical education rarely went beyond genteel amateurism, however, never extended to "public" performance, and hardly ever involved serious attempts at composition.

On the other hand, the abiding antipathy to convent music in the Bolognese diocesan hierarchy, especially during Lucrezia Vizzana's formative years, makes a thorough convent musical education seem equally improbable. I have tried to discover how Vizzana managed to learn, not only to compose, but to write in a sacred style as up-to-date as that of her Bolognese male contemporaries active in the world. The book provides a view that is quite different from the "reality" suggested by the church hierarchy's musical prohibitions and restrictions, until recently the primary source for a rather distorted view of early modern Italian convent musical traditions.[17]

Vizzana's motets also offer a window into her largely hidden world within the walls of Santa Cristina. This examination of her texts and music, viewed from within the cloister rather than from the more familiar world outside, suggests how much of her work relates directly to the religious and cultural life that immediately surrounded her. It also reflects in striking and intriguing ways much older traditions of female spirituality stretching back to the later Middle Ages, long before the emergence of new, post-Tridentine patterns of religious practice for women.

On the assumption that the material is likely to interest historians of culture, society, religion, and gender, whose musical knowledge may be rudimentary, I have tried to keep the musical discussion simple and untechnical in several of the earlier chapters, and for the same reason I have generally avoided the theoretical terminology of the late sixteenth and early seventeenth centuries. The analyses are very much phrase-oriented, as was Lucrezia Vizzana, who when composing worked from one phrase of text to the next in search of the most appropriate music. Indeed, modern listeners, accustomed to value "musical unity" and long-range planning, may occasionally be taken by surprise when they arrive unexpectedly at a motet's conclusion. They may wonder uneasily if Lucrezia Vizzana should have spent less time poring over her prayerbook and Church Fathers and more time stealing a look at her contemporaries' musical treatises on good counterpoint and modal practice. While one can be quite sure about her exposure to the Fathers, her familiarity with the latter remains less certain.

SANTA CRISTINA AND CONVENT WOMEN'S CULTURE

Betraying her limited interactions with the world at large, Lucrezia Vizzana's motets reflect her own, largely isolated female realm. If, throughout history, women musicians have generally been accorded a marginal place, which in turn governed their musical development, this is nowhere truer than in the nunneries. Vizzana's music, which offers a particularly apt representation of the familiar idea of a "women's sphere," suggests new applications of that concept, which I believe have considerable validity for discussions of early modern women's cloistered communities.

The notion of a "women's sphere," widespread in the nineteenth century, has provided a primary, much-debated metaphor in the second half of our own century. For historians in the 1960s and early 1970s, the concept of a "women's sphere" centered in the home and family was male-determined. Internalized by women in the course of their socialization, it both symbolized and implemented their victimization and subordination. In the mid 1970s, Carol Smith-Rosenberg and Nancy Cott reinterpreted these physical and psychic spaces where men found little place as partly developed by women themselves. This more clearly differentiated, women-centered view of women's activities, now commonly called "women's culture," recognizes some element of women's agency in history.[18]

In the late 1980s, historians broadened the applications of "women's sphere" / "women's culture" to include other eras and came to interpret them as more active elements in a wider society. Susan Porter Benson and Patricia Cooper usefully combine aspects of "women's culture" with concepts of work culture from American labor history. In their analyses of complicated power relations on the job, Benson and Cooper argue that women's culture became a resource through which women as informally organized working groups discovered some measure of autonomy and solidarity in their interactions with management. Equally important, these scholars recognize that women, lacking *authority* of their own, worked to effect change through *influence*—what Benson has aptly called "habits of persuasion instead of command."[19]

In a number of social situations involving issues of gender and relationships to male authority, the similarities to convent societies are notable. Both on the shop floor and in the store sales department, newcomers were initiated informally into the codes and unwritten rules of women's work culture, which involved similar subtle resistance and distancing of formal authority. Thus, factory workers and saleswomen informally set their own limits on their output or sales, or flouted the dress code imposed by superiors.

According to Benson, "saleswomen bent rules at every turn. . . . Rule-breaking was a way of life." The regularly published complaints and exhortations of store managers betray the reality of saleswomen's subversive activities on the job,[20] and the language of their complaints reveals factory and store management's interpretation of work culture as, not informal self-government, but evidence of irresponsibility, stubbornness, or stupidity. Saleswomen and women factory workers both found comparable informal ways to work to their advantage this authority system that "managed" them from above. For saleswomen, it was generally the buyer, and for factory workers, the foreman, who acted as primary buffers with upper management. Elusive bonds of loyalty and obligation could be worked to undermine supervision, as lower managers bent rules or turned a blind eye to minor infractions to protect those under them.

I have found the concepts of "women's sphere" and "women's (work) culture," with their various positive and negative connotations and their loosely metaphorical character,[21] useful for understanding the convents of the post-Tridentine Catholic world. It would be difficult to find a clearer example in which male domination devised a sexually segregated, constricted sphere for women, where they were locked away to preserve the family patrimony and protect family honor. Within the cloister, they interacted almost exclusively with one another, "protected" from men, and were kept subordinate.

Nuns' post-Tridentine rites of passage—their prostration before the altar beneath a black pall, symbolizing their death to the world, and the cropping of their hair, for example—emphatically articulated their entry into this separate sphere and their rejection of all others. Once within the separate women's sphere created and enforced by the church hierarchy, nuns behind impenetrable walls were to interact with men hardly at all, and then only under strictest control, through veiled windows protected by double grates. Any unauthorized contacts were almost invariably described in overtly or implicitly sexual language. Thus, *clausura* seems to embody the worst, most oppressive aspects of the "women's sphere."

Yet in Lucrezia Vizzana's time, when many—in some cities, most—young women of her class were destined for the cloister from an early age, this must have seemed the "natural" life option. Although the number of authentic religious vocations among early modern nuns may have been limited, many of the cloistered women must have found the life tolerable, or at least would never have thought to question whether such a system was "right" or "wrong." For the numerous widows and abused wives who sought places there later in life, the cloister came to represent the best choice, or at least the lesser evil, among life's meager options. For the artistically creative, the cloister provided a wider, if imperfect, space in which to exercise their talents than was readily available to them in the world. Such was almost certainly the case with Lucrezia Vizzana.

The women often forcibly enclosed within this imperfect, ambivalent, archetypical "women's sphere" also found means to manipulate their constricted sphere in ways resembling those of women's culture and work culture in the nineteenth and twentieth centuries. Although their indoctrination encouraged passive, unquestioning acceptance, many nuns developed a kind of agency, a little room for maneuver, by evolving informal rules and customs that interpreted, challenged, and subverted the formal prescriptions imposed upon them by the external patriarchal authority of the church.

The dynamic of such a convent women's culture parallels the flexible, accommodating methods developed by other groups lacking their own formal authority, whose strategies served to moderate or mediate formal structures of authority imposed from above. Social groups of women lacking in authority learned from one another how to rely on their powers of persuasion and on the exploitation of various sorts of influence to make their ways in their different worlds.

Within the convent, some aspects of acculturation were more formalized and intensified than in women's culture or work culture: a postulant's formal novice year, under the tutelage of the convent novice mistress, inculcated official rituals and rules. This period was often preceded by several years of informal convent socialization, frequently going back to the postulant's early childhood, during which she became familiar with most aspects of convent women's culture from a cloistered female relative, commonly her aunt.[22] Such a system was clearly ambivalent: aunts and novice mistresses in effect conspired with young women's families to encourage their passive acceptance of their lot, but also helped them find ways to work within and around the constraints of convent life.

Thus, nuns might choose to miss parts of the regular daily round of services in order to prepare musical or dramatic performances, or to make sweetmeats in the kitchen. Some modified their dress code by adorning their habits with jewels, ruffles, and other bits of finery. To achieve a little distance from the more austere realities of convent life, they found diversion in the public parlatorios as often as possible, even in the midst of services.

The constant stream of ecclesiastical superiors' prohibitions directed at these convent infractions reveal what the sisters must actually have been doing—not what they dutifully and obediently avoided. Church authorities' attempts to cover every contingency in their repeated prohibitions directed at nuns reveal that the sisters were past mistresses at discovering the sorts of loopholes also characteristic of women's work culture, even though for nuns, rule-breaking carried a much heavier psychic burden, laden with guilt, sin, and possible violation of their vow of obedience. In condemning nuns' perceived backsliding, church authorities persistently employed vocabularies similar to those of labor management, frequently harping on nuns' childishness and sinful disobedience. But effective enforcement was mediated by the complexities of the ecclesiastical bureaucracy, which provided nuns with ample and diverse opportunities to fragment authority. Above all, a malleable convent father confessor was perceived on both sides of the convent wall as the weak link in the diocesan curia's patriarchal chain of command.

The recent broadening in interpretation of "women's sphere" has also directed attention to the physical spaces in which women chose or were forced to live and work. Studies in American history have shown not only how separation was linked to subordination but also how, in some cases such as Quaker communities, women's physical separation served to enhance autonomy. Some have suggested that in the late nineteenth and early twentieth centuries, American women recognized the political utility of creating separate, but more public, spheres for themselves—the women's club movement, women's colleges, the women's community, Hull House in Chicago—within which they could create strategies for political change. Estelle Freedman has termed this approach "female institution building."[23]

The physical space of the post-Tridentine convent was an archetypical "women's sphere" in both its positive and negative aspects. At least to some degree, these cloistered spaces, clearly conceived to promote separation and subordination, could be shaped to the advantage of those enclosed within them. Nuns found numerous ways to render these female spaces somewhat less private; that is, to open windows in convent walls without demolishing them. Music was, I suggest, a powerful tool for partial deprivatization of architectural spaces—one deliberately employed by nuns to forge affective and, in the broad sense, political links with networks in the outside, public sphere.

In the nineteenth and early twentieth centuries, women's culture extended outward in intertwining social networks of work and community. Such networks in earlier centuries, I argue, constituted a particularly intense and vital aspect of convent women's culture: a complex and diverse web linking the convent with parish, neighborhood, and kin beyond the convent "workplace." For nuns, who had been set apart from the world and society in their "women's sphere," agency came to depend on their successful social interaction with and influence on such networks. These networks included not only men (members of their families, class, and religious orders) but also women: female members of their own families or of the Bolognese patriciate, nuns of the city or of their own religious order further afield, and even such female saints as Catherine Vigri of Bologna. That the nuns of Santa Cristina even invoked the influence of the mothers of cardinals in distant cities—with some success, apparently—suggests the existence of wide-ranging informal bonds of solidarity and shared expectations based on class and gender. Since they were not employed for thoroughgoing critiques of the patriarchal system and concrete plans for change, they cannot properly be termed "feminist." Nevertheless, they testify to the existence of a "female consciousness."

Work culture, women's culture, and "convent women's culture" as ana-
lyzed in the following chapters, generally focus on everyday social interactions rather than singular, dramatic events. The story of Lucrezia Vizzana
and her music conforms comfortably to this model until the publication of
her *Componimenti musicali* in 1623. Then, with another forty potentially
creative years ahead of her, Vizzana's modestly flourishing musical career
withered at its height, for the same milieu that had fostered her early creativity contributed to cutting it short. In the early 1620s, the nuns of Santa
Cristina moved from the everyday, ordinary world of women's culture into
a contrasting world of dramatic events, crises, and more direct action. The
struggles of the nuns of Santa Cristina, beginning internally and possibly
because of music in the earliest years of the Seicento, but chiefly precipi-
tated by Cardinal Archbishop Ludovico Ludovisi and the Bolognese diocesan hierarchy, expanded outward to involve confrontations with the diocesan curia, various Sacred Congregations of cardinals in Rome, and even
with the pope himself. Lucrezia Vizzana was caught up, swept along, and
lost in political events within and across the convent wall. The resulting
crises, which one sister claimed "began because of music," changed the
convent of Santa Cristina decisively, and seem quite literally to have overwhelmed its composing nun.

I originally intended to write a history of music at Santa Cristina and of
the composer Lucrezia Vizzana, but when I encountered the era of crisis
at the convent, I was compelled to redirect my narrative away from music,
which becomes a minor motif in the life of the convent during the turbulent 1620s, 1630s, and 1640s. Social and political considerations move to
the foreground, as they did for the nuns of Santa Cristina. As I examine
the sorts of strife that arose among ambitious, talented, and frequently
creative upper-class women, conscious of their abilities and their station,
Lucrezia Vizzana is eclipsed by others, who emerge as complex, strong, if
not always sympathetic, personalities. Yet, despite deep differences, the
nuns were able ultimately to unite when it became necessary to oppose
threats to what they valued in their way of life.

What started as the story of a "great woman" has become to a considerable degree a history of families that continue to reappear in successive
generations. In the hope of providing some sense of order in the confusing
tangle of Bombacci, Boncompagni, and Vizzani family relationships, I have
included a list of dramatis personae. To forestall some additional and, for
some readers, inordinate explanation in the text, a glossary of Latin, Italian,
religious, and musical terms follows the notes.

THE PRIMARY SOURCES

The challenge of rediscovering convent music and of recreating its place
in the life of Santa Cristina della Fondazza is compounded by the fact that

the post-Tridentine church hierarchy intended nunneries to be so private. One must rely on fleeting and often disconnected glimpses, drawn from widely scattered and fragmentary information, into a hidden world. Among the most important sources are the convent archives, transferred after the Napoleonic suppression to the Fondo Demaniale of the Archivio di Stato in Bologna. The Demaniale records, while much richer and more diverse in Bologna than in some other cities,[24] have been to some extent dispersed, pilfered, and misplaced.

Although the impersonal or formal nature of much convent archival material creates a barrier between modern observers and the nuns, some of the documents from the archive of Santa Cristina permit us to approach them more directly. The lengthy transcript of the pastoral visitation to the convent in 1622–23, in which a notary took down the nuns' comments largely verbatim, provides a wealth of information about convent life not directly relevant to the investigation. It permits us to hear some echo of the nuns' own voices, including Lucrezia Vizzana's. In dozens of private letters between the nuns and their advocates written during the struggles with the diocesan curia between 1696 and 1705, discussed in chapters 11 and 12, my protagonists speak much less guardedly.

Given the important control over convents exercised by the church hierarchy, the archives of the ecclesiastical bureaucracy have proved particularly useful. The Archivio Arcivescovile in Bologna contains a small but significant collection of documents related to post-Tridentine conventual reforms under archbishops Gabriele and Alfonso Paleotti, including important materials on music. It also includes fascicles of documents related to some individual convents, with a sampling of disparate materials from several centuries.

Of the congregations of the Roman curia established after the Council of Trent, the Sacred Congregation of Bishops and Regulars (Congregatio negotiis et consultationibus Episcoporum et Regularium praeposita), founded in 1572, was clearly most important for convent government, for it had the final voice on every aspect of discipline and conduct. Because music was suspect and frequently the subject of disagreement between nuns and their diocesan superiors, the archive of the Congregation of Bishops contains thousands of pages of nuns' petitions for dispensations and judgments related to music. These are interspersed among hundreds of thousands of documents related to all manner of other issues, great and small, from throughout the Catholic world, contained in some two thousand cartons in the Archivio Segreto Vaticano.[25] The records of the Congregation also proved particularly important in the reconstruction of details of the struggles between Santa Cristina and the diocesan hierarchy from 1620 to the early eighteenth century.

Because of the close relationship of music to liturgy, musical issues occasionally arise in the deliberations of the Congregation of Sacred Rites (Sacra Congregatio pro Sacris Ritibus et Caeremoniis), established in 1588. Although the Congregation of Sacred Rites is better known for its jurisdiction over proposals for beatification and canonization, it also saw to issues of liturgical discipline, in which it overlapped somewhat with other congregations. In the 1690s, the convent of Santa Cristina was embroiled for two years in a case before the Congregation of Sacred Rites. Because the decisions of the Congregation (including those relevant to Santa Cristina) have been published,[26] and because copies of records from the case in 1696–98 survive largely intact in the archive of Santa Cristina and/or the Archivio Arcivescovile in Bologna, it proved unnecessary to consult the archive of the Congregation of Sacred Rites directly.

The Sacred Congregation of the Council of Trent (Sacra Congregatio Concilii Tridentini), established by Pius IV in 1564 to interpret the decrees of the Council of Trent, has some relevance, because of monastic reforms passed at the twenty-fifth session of the council. The periodic episcopal reports from the dioceses (*ad limina*) used to evaluate the observance of Tridentine reforms outside Rome, preserved in the Congregation's archive at the Archivio Segreto Vaticano, occasionally refer to nuns, their music, and difficulties of convent government. The Congregation of the Council also ruled on individual cases related to Tridentine decrees, sometimes in ways that contradicted other congregations, as we shall see in chapters 10 and 11.

Some of the large gaps left by these various sources have been filled by consulting a wide range of documentary material preserved chiefly in the Archivio di Stato, the Biblioteca Comunale dell'Archiginasio, and the Biblioteca Universitaria in Bologna. These include many notarial acts from the Fondo Notarile at the Archivio di Stato and numerous jottings and records by various chroniclers and diarists. I have also relied on such formal and informal histories as Gasparo Bombacci's compendious notes on his own family (BUB, MS It. 3856) and various "official" and less formal manuscript convent histories. Although no formal history survives for Santa Cristina, the convent necrology, preserved in eighteenth-century copies, transmits details about individual nuns over several centuries. For Santa Cristina, the previously unknown "La caduta di Santa Cristina," by the Camaldolese monk Mauro Ruggeri, who served as convent confessor in the early 1620s, surviving in the archive of the monastery at Camaldoli (MSS 652 and 101), offers an extraordinary eyewitness account, rich in details from behind the scenes, of the turmoil of the 1620s, 1630s, and 1640s, which had barely concluded when Ruggeri put pen to paper.

All the translations from these various sources and any other unattributed translations are my own.

Struggles with diocesan superiors were hardly unique to the nuns of Santa Cristina. Similar scenarios were played out at other convents in Bologna and the rest of Italy. More unusual—at least given the present state of knowledge—is the indomitable persistence of generation after generation of nuns at Santa Cristina in refusing for most of the Seicento to submit to the will of the local archbishop, to relinquish their liberty, as represented by their links to the Camaldolese order. The attitudes and actions of the sisters of Santa Cristina contrast not only with Camillo Baldi's assessment of the tepid political commitment of the Bolognese upper classes in general, but also with modern views of the passivity of women religious in the early modern period. In the nuns' struggles, music and particular rituals emerge as central. Like many other tactical weapons that women with little direct power have utilized over the centuries, music and ritual provided an indirect, somewhat ambiguous, but potentially effective means of working toward their goals.

ONE

Donna Lucrezia Orsina Vizzana
of Santa Cristina della Fondazza

Of more than 150 women singers, organists, and composers once hidden behind convent walls in early modern Bologna and now forgotten, only one took the decidedly public step of venturing forth into print. Thanks to her *Componimenti musicali de motetti a una e più voci* (Musical Compositions in the Form of Motets for One or More Voices), published in Venice in 1623, Lucrezia Orsina Vizzana of the Camaldolese convent of Santa Cristina della Fondazza achieved a modest renown in her day. She has not quite been forgotten in our own, even if the standard modern dictionary of music managed to get her name wrong.[1]

Lucrezia Orsina Vizzana, like most nuns of her time, has remained little more than a name to us. As Elissa Weaver has put it, "Among the nuns only the saints have been remembered."[2] Not surprisingly, although the seventeenth-century Bolognese historian Gasparo Bombacci carefully set down the exemplary life of his and Lucrezia's aunt, madre donna Flaminia Bombacci of Santa Cristina, the only Benedictine nun in Bologna to have died in odor of sanctity before the mid seventeenth century, his family history makes no mention at all of his distinguished musical cousin.[3] By contrast, in an elegantly decorated necrology from Santa Cristina, which extolled not only the pious ends of those sisters who had achieved "good deaths," but also the artistic and intellectual accomplishments of others, the longest encomium honored Lucrezia Orsina Vizzana.[4]

Lucrezia Vizzana's life can only be pieced together from widely scattered scraps of information. Her father, Ludovico di Obizzo Vizzani, belonged to an old, distinguished family (see table 1), active in the city since the thirteenth century. Although some bellicose Vizzani distinguished themselves on the battlefield, others found comparable distinction in scholarship or the church. Indeed, Carlo Emanuele di Camillo Vizzani, Lucrezia's distant cousin, became rector of the Sapienza in Rome in the mid seventeenth century and inaugurated the Vatican Library in its modern form.

Since the late fourteenth century, the family had lived in via Santo Stefano, not far from the convent of Santa Cristina, at the site where in the 1550s and 1560s the imposing Palazzo Vizzani rose at what is now via Santo Stefano 43 (see fig. 1). Palazzo Vizzani became a place of some cultural distinction, the site of the weekly gatherings of the Accademia degli Oziosi, founded by three Vizzani brothers, Giasone, Pompeo, and Camillo di Camillo, in 1563. This branch of the Vizzani line was allied by marriage to the highest Bolognese elite, such as the Bentivogli, the Malvezzi, and the Ludovisi (through Ippolita Ludovisi, niece of the future Pope Gregory XV).[5]

The Palazzo Vizzani of today may be illuminated retrospectively by the modest reflected glory of Lucrezia Vizzana's artistic achievements in the field of music.[6] In the Cinquecento, however, her father Ludovico and his branch of the family could bask only in the reflected glory of their distant cousins at Palazzo Vizzani. For it had been Ludovico's great uncle, Giasone di Domenico Vizzani, who had continued that most illustrious Vizzani line. Ludovico Vizzani's own family lived much further downtown, near the corner of via d'Azeglio and via de' Carbonesi, south of the great city church of San Petronio. In 1607, Ludovico's brother, Vizzano di Obizzo, served a term among the *anziani,* who administered the city, as his father Obizzo di Pirro had in 1559 and, likewise, his grandfather Pirro di Domenico, in 1517. But Ludovico di Obizzo, who apparently achieved no such distinctions, goes unmentioned in Pompeo Dolfi's "who's who" of the Bolognese élite, *Cronologia delle famiglie nobili di Bologna.*[7]

Ludovico Vizzani could not expect to find a wife among the likes of the Malvezzi, Bentivogli, or Ludovisi. His future wife, Isabetta di Giovanni Bombacci, came to their marriage from an upwardly mobile family of long standing but of lower status than the Vizzani. In the marriage contract, Isabetta's father is described as *mercator,* the lowest of the three governing ranks of Bologna, below *cavalieri* and *gentilhuomini.* According to Camillo Baldi's early seventeenth-century description of the ins and outs of the Bolognese social hierarchy, *mercanti* were active in areas "involving little or no physical labor; but by diligent management they govern what must be done for the good of their business." Despite Gasparo Bombacci's special pleading in his family history that "in Bologna trading still remains highly honorable and has been practiced by nobles without losing their claim of nobility," we may safely assume that the Bombacci represented the sort of family to which a more illustrious Vizzani was unlikely to turn "if not for reasons of wealth or love," as Baldi put it.[8] Isabetta's father, Giovanni di Antonio Bombacci, had, in fact, achieved greater civic distinction than his future son-in-law would apparently ever manage, serving in 1570 as one of the sixteen *gonfalonieri del popolo* and three years later among the *anziani.*[9]

Just a few years before, in May 1568, Giovanni Bombacci moved his growing family to 35 Strada Maggiore (formerly 273), at the corner of via Borgonuovo. The Bombacci subsequently enlarged the ancient building, which had formerly belonged to the Fagnani, and which has been repeatedly modernized since then, so that today only the sixteenth-century capitals of the portico and a few feet of Romanesque terra-cotta arch testify to its venerable origins. It may have been far less imposing than Palazzo Vizzani, completed in those same years, but it still retains a certain luster, hallowed by Bolognese tradition as the birthplace of Pope Honorius II (reigned 1124–30).[10]

Isabetta Bombacci, born in June 1560, was the eldest survivor among Giovanni Bombacci and Camilla Luchini's twelve daughters. So impressive a brood was not extraordinary for upper-class Italian families of the period. Indeed, Isabetta's great-grandmother, Lodovica, had borne no fewer than twenty-four children, who (just as amazing) had all lived long enough to eat solid food. The fates of Isabetta and her eleven sisters were more typical. Half of them had died in infancy, within two days to three years. Another married rather late and rather modestly at age twenty-seven, but before long died in childbirth. Of the other five, only Isabetta Bombacci married, and after bearing at least three sons and two daughters, she expired before the age of forty. Isabetta's four remaining sisters all became nuns, three at the convent of Santa Cristina—where the trio outlived all their other siblings by ten to thirty years.[11]

On 12 May 1581, Ludovico Vizzani and Giovanni Bombacci had agreed to Isabetta's dowry of £10,000, of which £9,000 was to be invested in the thriving Bolognese silk trade. Although the Bombacci were associated with banking and financial exchanges, they made some of their money in the silk business, as their name suggests (*bombice* = silkworm grub). Ludovico's and Isabetta's marriage was recorded five months later, on 19 October 1581 in the Bombacci's parish church of San Tomaso, which once stood at the corner of Strada Maggiore and via Guerrazzi, just a block from Casa Bombacci.[12]

Their first child, Obizzo, named for his late paternal grandfather, arrived promptly, within a year of the marriage, on 25 September 1582, but must have died in infancy or early childhood. After a fourteen-month respite, Isabetta found herself pregnant again. Dionigio was born on 16 September 1584. A third son, Mario, followed much later, on 14 October 1593. In the meantime there had been two girls. Virginia arrived on 8 March 1587, and must have been given her rather uncommon name in memory of her mother's sister, suor Virginia of the convent of Corpus Domini, who had died on New Year's Day. Lucrezia Vizzana, the future composer, entered the world three years later, on 3 July 1590.[13]

It is not clear exactly when Ludovico Vizzani's daughters Verginia and Lucrezia entered the convent of Santa Cristina della Fondazza, although in 1607 they claimed to have been there since earliest childhood.[14] Santa Cristina was the obvious choice for these offspring of the Bombacci family. The convent on via Fondazza was only a five-minute walk from their maternal grandparents' home on Strada Maggiore and comparably close to the palace of their distinguished cousins, the Vizzani, on via Santo Stefano.[15] Of the forty-two professed nuns, or *professe*, at Santa Cristina in 1606, at least eighteen in fact came from families with palaces or family houses within a few minutes' walk of the convent, chiefly on Strada Maggiore and via Santo Stefano, or who had chapels in the nearby churches of Santa Caterina in Strada Maggiore (Bombacci), Santa Maria dei Servi (Glavarini, Gozzadini, Fuzzi), San Tomaso in Strada Maggiore (Leoni), San Biagio (Vizzani, Zani), Santo Stefano (Bianchi), and San Giovanni in Monte (Gozzadini, Vizzani, Bolognetti).[16] Hints of the relatively permeable boundaries between the nuns of Santa Cristina and their families common in the days of freer comings and goings before the Council of Trent were thus still evident at the convent when Lucrezia and Verginia Vizzani arrived there.[17]

By the late 1590s, the Bombacci had also already established strong family ties within the convent walls that made the Vizzani girls' arrival there almost inevitable. There were three Bombacci sisters in the convent already—one more than was deemed prudent and normally permitted in post-Tridentine Bologna, where the church hierarchy worried about any one family eclipsing the others in convent society. Flaminia Bombacci had been officially accepted in 1578, Ortensia (who as a nun had taken the name of her maternal aunt, Ortensia Luchini, who had died at Santa Cristina in 1576) in 1580, and Camilla (who had taken the name of her mother, Camilla Luchini) in 1588.[18]

The acceptance and socialization at the convent of Lucrezia and Verginia Vizzani were thus due primarily to matrilineal connections. Although their middle aunt, Ortensia Bombacci, seems to have become something of a recluse, the other two, Flaminia and Camilla, would become the convent's leading spiritual and political figures of the 1620s. Lucrezia and Verginia would be the only Vizzani at Santa Cristina for the first three decades of the Seicento.[19]

Lucrezia and Verginia Vizzani later claimed to have become nuns in 1598. Their mother Isabetta's death was recorded at San Giacomo de' Carbonesi on 19 April of that year. This probably prompted Ludovico Vizzani to dispatch his daughters, neither yet in her teens, to Santa Cristina. For six months later, on 7 November 1598, their father lent the convent £2,100. The following April 29, he increased the loan by another £3,800 for a term of four years. Lucrezia became a novice at eleven—a year short of the minimum age permitted after Trent—in 1601. Each of the two sisters

In the early 1630s, the Vizzanis' position at the convent would also be considerably enhanced by the acceptance of another Vizzani, Teresa Pompea, daughter of Senator Constanzo di Giasone Vizzani (d. 1622), knight of Savoy, from the other, most illustrious, side of the family at Palazzo Vizzani. Although Teresa Pompea Vizzana, like her distant cousin Lucrezia Orsina, also had musical gifts, Santa Cristina chiefly benefited from her musical and artistic patronage. On the early death of her brother, Senator Pompeo Vizzani, commander of Savoy, in 1640, Teresa Pompea and her sisters at the convents of Santissima Trinità and Sant'Agnese each inherited one-fourth of their brother's estate, once their more distant male relatives had also received their shares. Teresa Pompea Vizzana used her inheritance for convent adornments.[30]

Having entered Santa Cristina in earliest childhood, Lucrezia Vizzana scarcely knew the world beyond the convent walls. The world she had entered could, however, be called one of the best of all possible monastic worlds in Bologna. The convent's patron saint, Christina of Bolsena, seems ironically appropriate for these highly independent nuns, especially for singers among them. This early Christian virgin, who refused to worship idols, was locked up by her own father in a tower, where she was consoled with fruits and flowers brought her by angels. When subsequently thrown into a fiery furnace, like the Hebrew children, she passed the next five days singing with the angels. As if that were not enough, her father had her stripped and flogged until her flesh came off her bones, then tortured her on a Catherine wheel. She was later thrown into Lake Bolsena, but the millstone around her neck acted as a lifesaver until Christ could come down to offer a hand, and Saint Michael the Archangel could help her to the shore. She survived boiling in oil and imprisonment in a snake pit, where the serpents only licked her feet and clung affectionately to her neck. Even when her tongue was cut out, she could not be silenced, and still continued to speak; she used her severed tongue as a missile to blind the judge. Although most of the arrows later shot at her rebounded into the throats of her executioners, one finally managed to find its mark, hitting Christina between the eyes and releasing her to join the saints in glory. As portrayed in the convent altarpieces the young Lucrezia Vizzana would have known, the original indomitable twelve-year-old virgin may have filled out and matured, but she still smiles benignly beneath an arrow realistically protruding from her forehead (see fig. 2, left; fig. 9, right).[31]

By the early Seicento, Santa Cristina had become one of the wealthier, more exclusive, and most artistically distinguished of Bologna's monasteries for women. In 1574, it had tied with the convent of San Lorenzo for fourth place among twenty-eight diocesan convents in terms of yearly income (£6,000; by comparison, Santi Naborre e Felice had the highest income, £8,720); in 1614, it ranked sixth out of twenty-seven.[32] Catering to

Bolognese noble and patrician families such as the Bolognetti, Bottrigari, Pepoli, Malvezzi, and Bocchi, as well as to aspiring families of somewhat lower rank such as the Bombacci, Santa Cristina remained beyond the reach of what the nuns called "ordinary" women. Members of the convent tended to call each other *donna* ("lady") or *madre donna* for the most senior nuns, rather than *suora* ("sister"), a designation reserved at Santa Cristina for the servant nuns, and they referred to the convent as the *collegio* rather than the *monastero*. Some aspired as much, perhaps, to art or letters as to the religious life, or saw nothing incongruous about intermingling the arts and religion, as many male members of their order had done at various periods.[33]

The governing class of professed nuns, who were left free for chapel duties, was served by a separate class of servant nuns. These *converse,* usually simple, illiterate country girls, were accepted for much smaller dowries.[34] The *converse,* who were relieved of serious chapel responsibilities and had no voice in convent government, performed all the menial tasks of cleaning, cooking, gardening, and tending the animals; in addition, each saw to the personal needs of three or four of the *professe,* sometimes all members of a single family. During Lucrezia Vizzana's time, none of the *professe* seems to have maintained her own personal servant of the sort encountered in such other Bolognese patrician convents as San Guglielmo. And there were certainly no slaves, as in some convents elsewhere, particularly in Portugal and Spain.[35] Nevertheless, around 1620, when the thirty-eight *professe* at Santa Cristina were served by fourteen *converse,* the ratio struck ecclesiastical authorities as overly luxurious.[36]

By the time of Lucrezia Vizzana's arrival, the convent of Santa Cristina already had an illustrious history stretching back half a millennium; it survived for another two centuries after her entry, until the Napoleonic suppression of 1799. The original convent of that name may have been founded as early as 1097, by order of the Blessed Rudolph I, prior general of the Camaldolese order, a contemplative branch of the Benedictines that had grown out of the reforms of Saint Romuald (c. 952–1027) in the early eleventh century. The order, which flourished chiefly in Italy, but also in France, was associated particularly with an eremitical lifestyle, recalling the anchorites of the early church. Several Camaldolese houses, such as the mother house at Camaldoli, built c. 1015–1027 in the Tuscan Apennines, near Arezzo, and surviving to this day, included individual hermitages for those monks who had achieved greatest perfection and who devoted themselves entirely to contemplation. The less advanced followers of a cenobitic lifestyle continued to live in cells within a single, more conventional monastic building. Tensions between followers of the eremitic and cenobitic lifestyles continued through the centuries until 1616, when the hermits and cenobites became independent of one another. Female Camaldolese houses such as Santa Cristina della Fondazza adopted the cenobitic way of life and the more usual monastic architectural plan, with cells surrounding a central cloister.[37]

Santa Cristina, the second oldest Camaldolese foundation for women, was established with gifts from a Countess Cunizia, or Cunegonda, abbess of the convent of San Pietro di Luco, at Settefonti (or Stifonte), in inhospitable and eroded terrain, frequently threatened by landslides, about twelve miles from Bologna; Cunizia's daughter, Mathilda, became the first abbess. Papal recognition may only have come in 1125, a date frequently cited for the foundation of Santa Cristina di Settefonti.[38] Mathilda ruled until the mid twelfth century, when in 1149 she was succeeded by Lucia, who came to be known in the lore of Emilia as Blessed Lucia of Settefonti. Thanks to the pious legend of Blessed Lucia, the ancient convent of Santa Cristina di Settefonti found a modest place in public memory.

The noble Lucia, from the Clari family of Bologna, known both for her great beauty and her piety, had captured the heart of a young knight. He haunted the church of Santa Cristina di Settefonti during daily mass in hopes of catching a glimpse of her through her cell window, which opened into the sanctuary, so that she could adore the host daily, a practice among recluses going back to the ninth century.[39] Learning of his attentions, the modest and devout nun withdrew to the farthest corner of her cell, closed the cell window, and for the rest of her life never opened it again. Overcome by despair at the realization that Lucia would never be his, the amorous knight left for the Crusades, where he was captured and tortured by the Infidel. Amid his torments he cried out, "O Lucia, Christ's virgin, if you have found favor before God, help me and deliver me from this agony," then fainted into a deep sleep. He awoke at the sound of familiar church bells, to find himself a stone's throw from Santa Cristina di Settefonti, still in his chains. As he watched amazed, Lucia appeared to him, saying "Yes, I now live the true life. Go, bring to my tomb these chains, thanking God, who has delivered you out of such great peril." Ambrogio Traversari, who saw the fetters at the old church of Santa Cristina di Settefonti in 1433 and recorded the legend, was told that no force had ever managed to remove them. In the 1750s, the chains could still be seen at Lucia's tomb, which had been moved to the church of Sant'Andrea di Ozzano in 1572, long after the original convent was largely abandoned.[40]

Blessed Lucia of Settefonti's cult would continue to flourish among the nuns of Santa Cristina della Fondazza down through the eighteenth century. Indeed, Lucrezia Vizzana's pious aunt Flaminia Bombacci worked to have Lucia's relics removed to Santa Cristina in Bologna, but she died before the translation could be accomplished. It was only in the early 1640s that some of her bones and their wrappings found their way to Santa Cristina in a portable reliquary that survives to this day.[41] Beata Lucia appeared prominently in numerous convent frescoes and paintings, and she can still be seen, kneeling under the beneficent gaze of the Blessed Virgin, with her devoted knight's fetters beside her, across from Saint Romuald in Francesco Salviati's *The Blessed Virgin and Child with Saints* (1540) above the altar of Saint Romuald (fig. 2).

In 1245, the nuns of Santa Cristina di Settefonti received permission from the bishop of Bologna to move to safer, more hospitable quarters within the city, formerly occupied by Camaldolese monks. The site, east of downtown, stood on via Fondazza, halfway between Strada Maggiore, the main thoroughfare to Romagna and the city of Rimini, and via Santo Stefano, the route to Tuscany and Florence. The location was still then relatively remote, far outside the wall "dei Torresotti" enclosing the old city, which had gone up in the twelfth and thirteenth centuries. The convent was located on the very borders of the new city, in the shadow of the sections of wall running outward from Porta Maggiore, completed just a few years earlier in 1238. The wall segments adjoining the portal in Strada Maggiore would be incorporated into the second city wall built at the outskirts of Bologna before 1390. A stretch of the fourteenth-century wall behind Santa Cristina can still be seen today, incorporated into the back wall of Casa Carducci.[42]

In 1251, the abbess Scholastica III led her nuns in procession to occupy their new home, and they seem to have been flourishing on via Fondazza by the early 1300s, inasmuch as the church underwent significant remodeling in 1329.[43] By the end of the fifteenth century, portions of the monastery still recognizable today had begun to take shape. A memorial and two coats of arms dated 1494 on the south wall of the cloister commemorating Murzola (or Muzula) de' Salosmaij of Florence, who ruled as abbess from 1468 until 1498, mark the completion of the ground floor of the cloister.[44] The nuns' sanctuary may also have been remodeled in those years. About two-thirds of the so-called *chiesa vecchia,* cut off by the wall of the new church, to which it is connected by a grate above the side altar of Santa Cristina, still survives. The vault of the crumbling "old church" retains fine frescoes of Saint Romuald, Saint Christina, and Saint Benedict, attributed to Lorenzo Costa,[45] dating from 1501, now in very perilous condition.

In the late 1550s, as the city of Bologna expanded outward to meet the new city wall, the convent's own wall rose around it, not so much to keep the nuns inside as to keep undesirables out, to judge by a ban of June 1552 by the civil authorities of Bologna forbidding prostitutes to live anywhere along the entire length of via Fondazza, from Strada Maggiore to via Santo Stefano, or along via del Piombo, bounding the convent to the north. The nuns had in fact been complaining about the number of prostitutes residing in the neighborhood at least since 1529.[46] A notable process of expansion got under way after 1570 and continued for the rest of the century. It may have been long overdue, however, for in the dedication to the nuns of Santa Cristina of Serafino Razzi's *Vite de i santi e beati così huomini come donne del sacro ordine de predicatori, II* (Florence, 1577), his brother, Silvio Razzi, lamented the state of "the church, the refectory, the cells, and other small workshops, which appear almost completely in ruins and decayed by age and time."[47]

During Monsignor Ascanio Marchesini's apostolic visitation in November 1573, under the auspices of the newly founded Sacra Congregazione del Concilio di Trento, to implement the decrees of the Council of Trent, the visitor found the construction work on the new buildings in full swing, with the reception rooms, dormitories, sacristy, confessionals, and storage rooms already finished. That the rural landscape at the far reaches of the city was becoming more populated is suggested by Marchesini's insistence that the convent either acquire more of the surrounding property or increase the height of its wall to thwart the curious gaze of the public.[48]

Work on the convent continued into the 1580s, so that by the time of the Vizzani sisters' entry, shortly before the turn of the century, it had achieved the form commemorated rather tardily in J. Bleau's *Theatrum civitatum et admirandum Italiæ* (Amsterdam, 1663) (fig. 1), apparently modeled on the much earlier *Pianta scenografica di Bologna* (1581), attributed to Agostino Carracci. Through the convent gateway in the wall facing via Fondazza the sisters entered a small courtyard, offering entry to the external church, straight ahead. By way of an elaborate arch at the right (see fig. 3), they could enter the public parlatorios, where nuns conversed with visitors through grated windows (see fig. 4, M), and the external reception room (E1), with its elaborate stone portal. Leaving the world through the interior porter's lodge (E2), accessible via a door kept carefully locked and guarded by the nun porter, they found themselves in the northwest corner of a large cloister (L) with a wellhead at the center. Its deep and spacious arcades, dating from 1494, decorated on the front with finely detailed terracotta ornament, and rising from sandstone columns with simple, leafy capitals, would continue to protect the nuns from inclement weather in winter and from the oppressive heat of the Bolognese summers for two more centuries.

Lucrezia and Isabetta Vizzani entered this cloister through elaborate new terra-cotta or sandstone doorways, whose ornate decoration reflected Antonio Terribilia's work at the monastery of San Giovanni in Monte from thirty years before.[49] Above the arcades of the cloister rose a new second story, whose completion less than twenty years earlier, in 1581, was commemorated by a plaque on the west side honoring the reigning abbess, Benedetta Carlina, who had died during the third year of her term in April 1583.[50] The cloister survives to this day largely as the Vizzani sisters would have seen it, although the upper-story windows have been modernized.

Through doorways on the north side of the cloister, the nuns could enter the parlatorios (M), the remains of the so-called *chiesa vecchia* (F), and their own inner chapel (B), where they recited the Divine Office; there was yet another small chapel beside it (G). All these were certainly in disarray in the late 1590s as work on the new church continued behind them. By the time of the Vizzani sisters' arrival, the old campanile visible in Bleau's engraving had been pulled down to make way for the expanded new church; the elegant new campanile by a member of the Bibiena family (fig. 3), which still graces the eastern skyline of the city, would not rise until the 1690s. In the meantime a much more modest tower accommodated three bells, one of them so large that women could not ring it without help.[51]

The wings of the cloister incorporated broad galleries, furnished with various cupboards, where the nuns could exercise in inclement weather. Off the passage in the east wing were the laundry and common rooms (I), where the nuns did needlework together, and could sing or play without disturbing any sisters in the dormitories across the courtyard. In the southeast corner of the cloister stood another chapel (G) with an ornate altar depicting Saint Romuald, Saint Christina, Blessed Lucia of Settefonti, and another female saint identified only as "S.R.," whom in the eighteenth century the nuns took for Santa Rita.[52] The rest of the southern wing was completely taken up with a spacious, imposing refectory (H), described in the eighteenth century as "very large and magnificent, completely paneled in walnut, with its pulpit that protrudes from the wall," and displaying another notable painting of Beata Lucia, dated 1542, now lost.[53] An atrium to the west of the refectory was entirely decorated in fresco, including a Crucifixion with saints, attributed to the school of Francesco Francia,[54] now grown very dim with age and neglect.

Passing through another interior corridor to the west, adjoining three rooms intended to serve as the infirmary (J), the sisters arrived at the main staircase, just to the south of the porter's lodge where they had begun, by which they could ascend to the upper levels. The north side of the upper floor, abutting the church, was left as a single long gallery; the other sides also contained long, lofty central corridors, with various rooms opening off of them on both sides. This level of the cloister contained the nuns' individual cells (see fig. 5). Some of the more elaborate accommodations included a second, rather cramped chamber at mezzanine level, beneath the main cell, only accessible via a tiny staircase hidden within a floorless wall cabinet of walnut.[55]

How did the abandoned cell of figure 5 look in Lucrezia Vizzana's day? A list of the convent trousseau of her contemporary Colomba Glavarini (d. 1643) agrees very closely with another meticulous inventory from the early eighteenth century, outlining what a postulant should bring with her to Santa Cristina. Both also correspond in most details to surviving early seventeenth-century inventories from institutions comparable to Santa Cristina, such as the Benedictine convent of Santa Margherita, which catered to a similar clientele, and where music also flourished. Apart from clothing, linens, and various bits of crockery and similar utensils, the early eighteenth-century example from Santa Cristina enumerates:

> An altarpiece with four small paintings with gilded frames, a crucifix, and the certificate of profession. A bedstead with its furnishings, three chests, a casket, a portable altar, a small table, a Venetian shutter, the door, two little benches with backs, two highbacked chairs, a yarn winder, a footwarmer, an iron tripod stand . . . with a majolica basin. A poplar chest for unsightly woolens. A walnut inkstand furnished with a seal. Two copper vessels, one ordinary and one with a spout, a little kettle, a medium-sized kettle. A bedwarmer, a mixer, a small brass vessel for Holy Water, a cover of *zibata,* One of cotton, a blanket, a brass candlestick with a nightlight. Four wool cushions. . . . A fitted out sewing basket, three yarns of many sorts, a door curtain of leather, and a curtain with hooks and rings, and a curtain for the window and the window for the cell. A breviary, a missal, a psalter, a martyrology, a diurnal, an office of the Blessed Virgin, and two books in the vernacular.[56]

The most elaborate feature of the cell, frequently given pride of place in inventories from Santa Cristina and elsewhere, was the nun's private altar. Some were more modest than the one described above, such as Emilia Arali's "altarpiece with the crucifix and the angels and the altar table" at Santa Margherita in 1613. Others seem to have been more elaborate and lavish, such as Monica Felice Ariosti's "altar with altarpiece, with the cover for the altarpiece, a pair of angels, a pair of candlesticks, a crucifix, two altar frontals, one of silk and one of gilded leather, four white altar cloths," also at Santa Margherita in 1613. Colomba Glavarini's altar and its various furnishings for her cell at Santa Cristina, on the other hand, cost her family some £235. Glavarini's cell, and some at Santa Margherita, also included a relatively imposing armoire of walnut. The bedsteads of wood or iron were fitted out with straw mattresses, various linens, bed hangings, and different summer and winter covers, which could also be quite elaborate. Glavarini's were all fringed, and some were quilted. It is particularly interesting to find that the majority of the postulants' furnishings, particularly those involving sewing and decorative needlework, but also much of the furniture, were created in-house, then charged to the parents. The fitting out and provisioning of new members thus constituted a cottage industry for the convent.

The smaller room furnishings inventoried at Santa Margherita were also remarkably consistent with ones mentioned in the few surviving lists from Santa Cristina. What made the cells more personal were these decorative items omitted from the above inventory, such as Emilia Arali's "small painting with San Francesco di Paola," suor Angiola's "miniature altar with a Madonna," suor Giacinta Maria's "five little paintings of saints," or suor

Monica Felice Ariosti's "Annunciation with its frame," all from Santa Margherita. In addition to other common personal items such as bed-warmers, footwarmers, sewing baskets, and pincushions, the number of looking glasses listed would surprise any who take the church hierarchy's prohibitions of such "vanities" at face value.

The following list by Monica Felice Ariosti from Santa Margherita of her more precious possessions, including all the common ones encountered elsewhere, is longer than normal, but not especially unusual: "two thimbles, one of silver and one of ivory, a pick ornamented with silver and one with scissors, a compass and a pen of silver, a little silver box, four rings of gold, six pairs of silver buckles, a silver cup, two pairs of silver candlesticks, a silver fork and spoon, a silver reliquary cross, a golden inkwell with the stamper and seal of silver, six keys on a silver chain, a rosary and two *corone* decorated with silver." Among the most affecting of such personal items, perhaps, was Emilia Arali's inclusion of "a goldfinch in its cage." These inventories thus suggest that in affluent, unreformed convents such as Santa Margherita or Santa Cristina, the nuns still managed to surround themselves with many of the comforts of home.[57]

Even in the early Settecento, Santa Cristina continued to adjoin relatively open country. This was particularly true at the time of Lucrezia Vizzana's arrival, before the construction of the neighboring convent of the Discalced Carmelites of San Gabriele, founded in 1618, to the southeast of Santa Cristina, facing via Santo Stefano. At Santa Cristina, as elsewhere during the implementation of strict monastic enclosure after Trent, considerable effort was expended to balance the rising walls, grates, and obscured windows with pleasant, open spaces. As Carlo Borromeo's monastic architect, Pellegrino Pellegrini, called Tibaldi, put it in Milan:

> They should have pleasant places, such as gardens, fields, loggias, workrooms, windows that catch the light from without, but all placed inside, excluding other openings. They should not be kept like locked up slaves. . . . Enclosed in their convents and churches, it is appropriate to provide them with large and comfortable quarters and spacious cloisters and fair gardens and other things necessary for decent, human life.[58]

The nuns at Santa Cristina attempted to brighten the spacious interior courtyard of the cloister by balancing pots of flowers on window ledges, even going so far as to loosen the grills on outside windows to make room for them. The cloister proper was surrounded by sizable gardens and fields. At the convent's suppression in 1799, the area within the convent wall totaled six and a half acres.[59] In Lucrezia Vizzana's time, the gardens probably appeared much as they would when described toward the mid eighteenth century, with rosemary bushes, vines, rose gardens, small orchards of peaches, pears, and figs, the odd walnut tree or mulberry bush, and canebrakes. In Lucrezia Vizzana's day, a pergola also ran outward from the door in the east wing, and possibly another from the door in the south wing of the cloister, all the way to the convent's outer wall. The gardens also contained outlying holy sites and small chapels, including an area in the southeast corner of the fields, designated as the *campo santo,* or burial ground, and a chapel dedicated to Our Lady of the Snow, which the nuns visited in procession, carrying the image of the Madonna.[60]

More strictly utilitarian purposes were served by various farm outbuildings, including a chicken house, dovecote, and a stall for the horse, provided for the father procurator's use in visiting the convent's country properties; the convent icehouse survived into the early 1900s. Although the convent orchards and gardens were intended to be held in common, by the early Seicento, several nuns at Santa Cristina had expropriated portions for themselves. Lucrezia Vizzana's aunt, Flaminia Bombacci, was among those who kept a few chickens, sheep, and the odd cow or donkey for personal use, in spite of the church's rules to the contrary.[61]

The main staircase, near the northwest corner of the cloister, also gave access on the right to a large, lofty, airy choir, also known in the seventeenth century as the Cappella della Beata Vergine del Rosario.[62] The chapel was situated above the arcaded portico in front of the triple portals to the external church, to which the chapel of the Rosary was connected by three grated windows. At the time of the Vizzana sisters' arrival, this choir would probably still have been under construction.

When Lucrezia Vizzana entered the convent, the expansion and lavish decoration of the new church of Santa Cristina were already well along, under the direction of the architect, Giulio della Torre. The external church represented the primary nexus of the convent and the world. In this case the connection was particularly strong, for the church of Santa Cristina was one of seven convent churches in Bologna that also served as a parish church. The presence of parishioners as well as nuns' relatives among the convent clientele was another important aspect of the social network the nuns cultivated over the centuries, as we shall see. Ludovico Vizzani's loans to the convent in 1598 probably served to help underwrite the building costs. As early as 1575, a donna Caterina Vitali is supposed to have begun work on the new church, which continued for twenty-five years under the particular patronage of donna Margherita Glavarini (or Giovarini) and donna Ottavia Bolognetti, both members of families that played central roles in the remodeling and redecoration of the chapel.[63] At the time the Vizzani sisters entered the convent, the chapel must have been a busy work site, surrounded in scaffolding. Indeed, on 26 March 1598, twelve workmen had fallen from the building scaffold, five to their deaths.[64]

By the time the church was completed in 1602, the convent had already embarked upon a lavish program of decoration under the patronage of individual nuns. Significantly, Santa Cristina is the only convent for which Carlo Cesare Malvasia's *Le pitture di Bologna* (1686) provides the family names of the nun patrons of virtually every altarpiece in the external church.[65] Some altarpieces were transferred to the new sanctuary from the partially demolished *chiesa vecchia,* whose remains were now incorporated within the cloister. Francesco Salviati's *Virgin and Child with Saints* (fig. 2), donated by the convent father confessor around 1540 for the high altar of the old church, went to the chapel of Saint Romuald, to the left of the main entrance of the new church. Giacomo Francia's *Nativity* of 1551–52 (see fig. 6), was moved to the chapel of Saint Benedict immediately to the right of the doors, across from Salviati's altarpiece. According to Malvasia, this chapel had been commissioned by a nun from the Vizzani family. No Vizzani have come to light before the arrival of Verginia and Lucrezia in 1598. It seems probable, therefore, that one of their dowries paid for the chapel of Saint Benedict, and that one of the little girls thus unwittingly became the convent patron remembered by Malvasia.

Malvasia also claimed that Ludovico Carracci's *Ascension of Our Lord* had been commissioned by a nun from the Bottrigari family in 1597 for a location high on the wall in the *chiesa vecchia.* The nun can be identified as Maura Taddea Bottrigari (1581–1662), who is supposed to have paid 129 scudi for the painting. It is unlikely that Carracci's painting would have been ordered for the old church at a time when construction of the new church was already so far advanced, when much of the *chiesa vecchia* had been demolished. Interestingly, Francesco Cavazzoni made no mention of Ludovico's *Ascension* at Santa Cristina in his description of 1603, although Cavazzoni specifically refers to the transfer of Salviati's *Virgin and Child with Saints* from the high altar of the old church to the chapel of Saint Romuald in the new one and also mentions Francia's *Nativity.* This is probably explicable by the fact that Ludovico's painting was not yet installed in the new church. The work in fact seems only to have been installed on the high altar in 1608, when the metalworker Joseffo Bosi was paid for "nails and brackets for the altarpiece on the high altar" on 8 May.[66] It may be more likely that 1597 simply marks the time when the newly professed Maura Taddea Bottrigari provided the money that went toward Ludovico's *Ascension,* which may always have been intended for the new church, where it was only installed shortly before May 1608.[67]

Several other new altarpieces, also commissioned by various nuns, have imposing frames that clearly contrast with the style of the older altars flanking the doors. Lucio Massari's *Visitation,* dated 1607 (see fig. 7), for the second chapel on the right, was given by a Duglioli and a Bolognetti, who can be identified as Costanza Duglioli (d. 1614) and Ottavia Bolognetti (d. 1612). Passerotti's *Annunciation,* third on the right, was provided by a nun of the Zambeccari family, commemorated on the frame as "R.D.M.Z." and identifiable as donna Angela Maria (d. 1645), who had professed in 1601 and was remembered in the convent necrology for building the chapel. Interestingly, her religious name reflects the protagonists of the painting: the angel and Mary. The frame of the altar also commemorates an elusive "R.M.I.M.," possibly Isabella Malvasia, who had died in the 1590s. The three adjacent altars on the right thus commemorated three successive joyful mysteries of the Rosary: the Annunciation, the Visitation, and the Nativity.

The front chapel on the right, connected to the *chiesa vecchia* by a grate above its altar, and dedicated to Saint Christina, received a new altarpiece by Girolamo Bonini (or Bonigli) depicting the preliminaries to the saint's martyrdom. The painting disappeared after its replacement by Domenico Maria Canuti's *Martyrdom of Saint Christina* around 1680. Tiburzio Passerotti's *Christ's Fall beneath the Cross* (1603) for the front chapel on the left (see fig. 8) was commissioned by a Glavarini, donna Margherita (d. 1619), already singled out for her general patronage of the new church. For once the influence of the patron is clearly apparent, for her name saint, Saint Margaret, appears prominently in the painting at the lower right. Malvasia also mentions a nun from the Montecalvi family, a reference that is particularly puzzling and interesting. The only Montecalvi recorded at the convent during this period was suor Dorothea Montecalvi, who had entered Santa Cristina around 1565 as a *conversa*, a group that less frequently aspired to, or had significant means for, convent patronage.

Bernardino Baldi's *Coronation of the Virgin* (see fig. 9) for the third altar on the left, completed in the years shortly before the artist's death in 1615, was commissioned by a Grassi, who must have been donna Emilia Grassi, a dominant musical figure in the convent since before the turn of the century. According to inscriptions on the frame, another Glavarini, donna Columba (d. 1643) and her sister, Aura Felice (1582–1666), also commissioned Giovanni Battista Bertusio's *Resurrection* of 1603 for the second altar on the left.[68]

The artistic program of the altarpieces as a group, old and new, was quite consistent. It offered the outside world models of sanctity and spirituality that were predominantly female. Where the great expansion of female saints and mystics of the later Middle Ages had included a surprising percentage of laywomen, wives, and widows,[69] the holy women above the altars at Santa Cristina were overwhelmingly early Christian virgins or the female dignitaries of the Benedictine and Camaldolese orders.

Only Carracci's *Ascension* and Bertusio's *Resurrection* focus exclusively on Jesus. Passerotti's *Christ's Fall beneath the Cross* is paired across the nave with the only other scene of martyrdom: that of Christ's female namesake, Saint Christina. Passerotti's work focuses less on Christ than on the moment of female compassion when Saint Veronica wipes Christ's face with her veil, as an archetypical early Christian virgin, Saint Margaret, looks on. At the other end of the church, Francia's *Nativity* is as much a study of Mary as the Christ child, and it, too, includes another female onlooker. That the painting was also described as "Saint Benedict's Family" suggests that the woman in nunnish garb is Benedict's sister, Saint Scholastica, the first Benedictine nun, whose feast was celebrated at Santa Cristina with about thirty masses.[70]

The *Nativity* is nicely paired with the other common image of Mary and her infant son, Salviati's *Virgin and Child with Saints,* across from it. Salviati's work (fig. 2) was also made particularly apt by the inclusion, not only of Saint Christina and Saint Romuald, but also of Beata Lucia, whose charming legend exalts cloistered chastity. Saint Andrew, in back on the right, links the work to the country church of Sant'Andrea di Ozzano, governed by the nuns, and the site of Lucia's tomb. Most significant among the men is Nicola of Bari, who carries the three golden balls that traditionally symbolized the bridal dowry, whether for spiritual or earthly brides.[71]

The other altarpieces are all unequivocally female, chiefly glorifying Saint Christina, who figures not only in Salviati's *Virgin and Child* and Baldi's *Coronation of the Virgin,* but also in the *Martyrdom of Saint Christina* in her chapel. There the prominent large grate, incorporated into the altarpiece below the painting of the saint, connected the outer church to the closed-off world of *clausura,* and served as a ready reminder of the nuns' own sacrifice for their families and the city.

The second prominent female in the convent's artistic program is, of course, the Blessed Virgin. Passerotti's *Annunciation* and Baldi's *Coronation of the Virgin* form a pair across the nave from one another, providing one of the first and last images of the life of Mary, and traditional symbols for the ideal of virginity. Possibly the pair also reflected rites of passage in the nuns' own lives. The *Annunciation* could represent the nuns' espousal of the godhead. The *Coronation of the Virgin* was also a coronation or exaltation of virginity. At Santa Cristina, during the elaborate ritual consecration of the nuns' own virginity, they, like the Virgin Mary, also received elaborate jeweled crowns.

Lucio Massari's *Visitation* (fig. 7) includes the only prominent wife, mother, and presumably non-virgin in the art of Santa Cristina. But it is especially apt in the context of female monasticism, as presented in the external church, for it glorifies, not only Mary and her aunt Elizabeth, but also the important familial relationship of aunt and niece, long primary in convent social structures, in which the aunt takes in and cares for her younger niece.[72] The painting also commemorates the moment when Mary exclaimed, "My soul doth magnify the Lord," commonly sung by the nuns themselves at first and second vespers on their major feasts.

Between the altars, six monumental stucco statues, also provided by the nuns at their own expense, were installed in elaborate niches, whose sculpted decoration by Pietro Antonio Bonuzio was largely complete by 1597.[73] They also conform to a program. Nearest the doors of the church, two important female saints are given pride of place: Saint Christina, the convent's special protector, on the right; and, on the left, Saint Mary Magdalen, not only the first to testify to the Resurrection and a paradigm of the contemplative life, but also a female saint closely linked to music.[74] Both female saints were by the late-sixteenth-century artist Gabriele Fiorini. Ahead of them stood the chief saints of the Camaldolese order, Saint Benedict (right) and Saint Romuald (left), also by Fiorini. Nearest the high altar were the chief heroes of the early church, Saint Paul (right) and Saint Peter (left), both attributed to the young Guido Reni, who was rapidly becoming one of Bologna's most distinguished artists.[75]

The substantial transformation of the Cinquecento church into the imposing Seicento edifice is clearly apparent in the contrast between Bleau's engraving of 1663 and Filippo de' Gnudi's map of 1702, which, apart from its elegant campanile, built in the 1690s, most accurately reflects the church as Lucrezia Vizzana knew it (see fig. 10). Thus, during Lucrezia Vizzana's first decade as a nun, Santa Cristina was transformed from a relatively modest and unremarkable chapel into one of the three or four most elegant and lavish of Bologna's convent churches.[76] It achieved an artistic distinction that would be matched by a comparable musical renown, which also burgeoned during that same period, in part because of the developing talents of Lucrezia Vizzana herself.

TWO

Lucrezia Vizzana's
Musical Apprenticeship

How did young Lucrezia Vizzana, who entered Santa Cristina at the tender age of eight, not only learn music, but learn it so well that she also came to compose and even to publish her music? At first sight it might appear that the times were totally inauspicious for an illustrious monastic musical career. Bologna's musical nuns had to contend with a long string of decrees against their music, stretching back at least to Gabriele Paleotti's time as bishop of Bologna. On 30 January 1566, Pius V had promoted Gabriele Paleotti to the bishopric of the city, stressing in the announcement Paleotti's strong commitment to the implementation of the decrees of the reforming Council of Trent, concluded late in 1563. The convents of Bologna became an important object of Paleotti's reforming zeal.

Much earlier, as a student under the Bolognese composer Domenico Maria Ferrabosco, the young Paleotti had shown considerable aptitude for music, even composing and singing while he accompanied himself on the lute, an activity he also continued in adulthood. His own personal musical interests did not, however, make the reforming bishop any more sympathetic to those of the Bolognese nuns in his charge.[1] As early as March 1569, Paleotti forbade all vocal music except plainchant and banned any singing with organ accompaniment in the church of the nuns of Santi Vitale et Agricola,[2] a decree that probably applied to the other convents subject to the bishop as well. Paleotti's severe attitude toward convent music in fact largely corresponds to a preliminary proposal on convent government that had actually been judged too severe at the Council of Trent and rejected by the delegates in November 1563.[3]

During the 1570s, deliberations at the archbishop's palace continued to catalogue and address the issues of perceived monastic laxity—musical and otherwise—and how to combat it. In December 1576, one don Leone submitted a list of all the abuses commonly found in the nunneries of Bologna.

In addition to keeping dogs and birds, reading vain literature ("come furioso Petrarcha, Bochacio"), and playing cards and dice at Christmastime,

> They spend feast days in idle songs to the organ and in frivolous music.... [They have] conversations and friendships with [male] singers.... They spend too much time singing and playing[.] Some singers and organists have too much freedom, and sing and play vain things[.] Sometimes [male] singers sing with the nuns[.] They invite the magistrates for Holy Week and to Easter compline.[4]

Another report particularly emphasized imagined intimacies with male singers, either male religious or secular professionals, and confirms once again that on feast days, the outsiders joined forces with the singing nuns, who also lavished presents upon them.[5] The series of accounts continued with more detailed musical indictments that raise the familiar issues of time-wasting and the attracting of dangerous and distracting crowds. One such indictment also suggests music's potential, if undesirable, utility as a means of convent communication with the world, despite the walls rising, both literally and figuratively, around the nunneries:

> Experience demonstrates that the excessive study that the nuns devote these days to their songs not only fails to serve the end to which music was permitted them, [which is] to praise God and be aroused themselves to the contemplation of celestial harmony; but [rather] it impedes them from greater goods and encumbers their souls in perpetual distraction. It causes them vainly to expend precious time that they could use more fruitfully. And, while they stand with their bodies within the sacred cloisters, it causes them to wander outside in their hearts, nourishing within themselves an ambitious desire to please the world with their songs.[6]

Typically, behind the regular echoes of distraction and time-wasting, the paranoid fear of sexual contact also resonates.

All the interim measures finally came together in Cardinal Paleotti's "Ordine da servarsi dalle suore nel loro cantare e musica," seven succinct rules published in 1580 in a compendium of general decrees concerning all aspects of ecclesiastical government. This order set out the basic restrictions on music in a form that would set the standard in Bologna for at least the next century and a half, with periodic swings both in the liberal and more severe directions:

Orders to Be Observed by the Nuns in Their Singing and Music

1. The nuns' music should be performed down below in the choir where the other nuns stay. It is permitted, however, for a solo voice to sing to the organ at the times permitted—not vernacular pieces, but rather Latin, ecclesiastical ones having to do with religion.

2. The Divine Offices for Holy Week are to be recited as if spoken, that is in simple chant; and finally it is permitted to sing the Benedictus and Miserere in song, which should be *falsobordone,* or else, *giorgiana.*

3. On the Feast of the Resurrection it is not permitted to sing the psalms in polyphony [*canto figurato*], neither at vespers nor at compline, but only in plainchant; but it is permitted to play the organ between the psalms, with a solo voice that sings to the organ without any other concerto [i.e., musical interaction with instruments].

4. On the day of their feast, that is once a year, it is permitted to sing the psalms in polyphony [*canto figurato*] without any sort of concerto, and similarly the Mass.

5. During the rest of the year, on all solemn feasts, it is permitted to sing a motet once or twice when Mass is celebrated, and similarly at the end of vespers.

6. No type of musical instruments should be used except the viol for the bass where it is necessary, with the permission of their superiors, and in their cells, the harpsichord.

7. It is forbidden for any sort of music master to go to teach the said nuns, also to rehearse any of their music, whether on the organ or in song.[7]

Four years later, in November 1584, Paleotti undertook an even more severe campaign against convent music, which seems to have been regarded as a centerpiece of his monastic reform program.[8] With the sanction of a breve from Gregory XIII, Paleotti not only banned performances by secular musicians in the outer chapels of the convents, but also required the removal of convent organs to the nuns' inner chapels within a month, and the walling up of organ windows facing the outer churches.

A few years before Lucrezia Vizzana entered Santa Cristina, Cardinal Gabriele Paleotti had been succeeded as archbishop by his distant cousin and former coadjutor, Alfonso Paleotti. The new archbishop's particular antipathy to convent music is aptly summed up by a comment in 1607, from the last years of his reign: "Throughout the time that I have been coadjutor and archbishop, I have felt from my experience that the thing that removes the spirit, devotion, and peace within the nunneries is music, which they compete to present in the choirs of their convents."[9] In 1598, 1603, 1604, and 1605, Alfonso Paleotti reiterated earlier decrees forbidding outside musicians to perform or teach in the convents of the city, thereby provoking a stream of convent petitions to the Congregation of Bishops in Rome for exemptions to the rule. But between 1598 and 1610, the uniform response "Nihil" awaited repeated petitions for outside music teachers, however aged or godfearing, from convents such as San Lorenzo, Santa Margherita, San Giovanni Battista, and San Mattia, and from at least one music teacher himself, a "Geronimo del Trombone," who vainly pleaded for special dispensation because "my household is burdened with four female offspring."[10]

Eighteen months before the appearance of Lucrezia Vizzana's *Componimenti musicali* in 1623, Cardinal Archbishop Ludovico Ludovisi of Bologna renewed the campaign against convent music, forbidding all outside musicians to sing, play, or teach in the convents of the city. A few months later, at Ludovisi's behest, Suffragan Bishop Angelo Gozzadini banned all music but plainchant, all musical instruments but the organ or harpsichord, all performances by outside musicians, and music lessons by outside music teachers. This latest edict provoked an anonymous nun to lament:

> In all the cities of Italy, nuns sing and perform *concerti* in their churches, with the sole exception of the city of Bologna. . . . Music is at present quite destroyed, to the great detriment of the *virtuose,* and especially of the most eminent of them, who had spent their lives . . . acquiring such a noble talent to praise His Divine Majesty; and it is not right that . . . they should suffer such mortification, and, above all, those who entered the convents to practice their talent, given us [*sic*] by Divine Goodness for his praise.[11]

On paper, at least, all these various decrees by Gabriele and Alfonso Paleotti and their successors create the impression that in the late sixteenth and early seventeenth centuries, the convents of Bologna became pious musical wastelands. This clearly was not the case. It did not take long for the nuns to find ways to work within and around these restrictions imposed upon them from without. They would interpret such formal prescriptions, in which they had had no say, in informal ways that suited their own purposes and were justified in their eyes by the circumstances. As Gabriella Zarri has pointed out, much of what Paleotti and the church hierarchy came to see as "abuses" had represented the normal way of life at convents for a good century and a half before Trent.[12] By the imposition of a sweeping range of monastic reforms, the Council of Trent had abruptly overturned the basic assumptions under which many nuns had originally entered the convents. In 1601, a nun from Udine remarked quite matter-of-factly to her bishop:

> I was fifteen or sixteen when I became a nun . . . and I entered the convent willingly. For, because I had a lot of sisters, it seemed necessary to me that I come here. And when I took the veil I never thought that act obligated me to anything at all, if not to live with the freedom one had at that time to come and go, and that my family could come inside.[13]

In the midst of Paleotti's Bolognese reforms, on the other hand, the nuns of Santi Naborre e Felice in 1586 had cried out to the pope in words expressing more intensely and directly the reaction of others whose way of life had been doubly disrupted against their wills:

> The nuns of the Monastery of Santi Naborre e Felice in Bologna . . . express to Your Holiness with all humility their miseries and misfortunes that, not-

withstanding that most of them were shut up in this place by their relatives against their wills, for all that they have borne it with considerable patience, and during a time in which they have been so tormented with various statutes and orders that they no longer have the strength to endure it. . . . Now most recently, besides having removed the organ from here, the doctor has been denied them, so that nobody except their father and mother can see and speak to them. Their old servants who were accustomed to serve them in the convent cannot speak to any nun, and should they speak they incur excommunication reserved to the Apostolic See. . . . Wherefore we fear that, being deprived with such strictness and abandoned by everyone, we have only hell in this world and in the next.[14]

Such women's cloistered communities represent one of the most compelling examples of how male domination encouraged a "women's sphere" whose inhabitants worked to discover some measure of autonomy and solidarity. Their response was to develop their own informal rules and customs to interpret, challenge, and, in various ways, to subvert the formal prescriptions imposed upon them by external ecclesiastical authority, as outlined in the Introduction.

Within the convent, a socially constructed medium such as music, in which the same words could convey different meanings in different contexts, proved to be a notably valuable, persuasive tool of convent women's culture. Given music's normal place in liturgy, nuns' musical performance could be justified—and often was, by the nuns themselves and by their supporters—as a natural and regular part of the sanctified work of the professed nuns, which was the recitation of the Divine Office, prayer, and intercession. As I have suggested elsewhere,[15] the post-Tridentine restrictions, particularly the nuns' total banishment from the public gaze, made their "angelic voices," especially when resounding from behind grates placed high up in the walls, near the vaults, an even more powerful and affecting means of influence beyond the convent wall.

It is interesting how frequently outside ecclesiastical authorities afforded music pride of place in their lists of convent "abuses," and how their condemnations, such as those quoted above, occasionally help us to perceive music's usefulness in establishing patterns of socialization, clientage, and influence that remained important conventual strategies in a world dominated by male clerics. Nun musicians' methods of resistance to clerical prohibitions directed at their art, on which I shall primarily concentrate, reflect the same patterns of response apparent in other aspects of convent life and convent women's culture as well.

In December 1584, the nuns of Sant'Omobono were among the first to discover means to subvert Gabriele Paleotti's decree against convent organs, mentioned above, while still observing it to the letter. They did indeed remove the organ from their external church and wall up the opening as required, "to the entire satisfaction of our illustrious Archbishop Paleotti." But when they had the organ, enlarged and made more powerful, reinstalled in their own inner church six months later, it was positioned in such a way that "resounding excellently well, it still creates delightful harmony for those outside."[16]

The Sant'Omobono example illustrates a common strategy of taking episcopal decrees absolutely literally, observing them to the letter—but no further. Indeed, writers of episcopal pronouncements racked their brains to anticipate every possible loophole the nuns might uncover, as Archbishop Ludovisi's decree of 1621 demonstrates:

> We expressly command that in future every person, whether ecclesiastical or secular, regardless of their state, rank, or condition, neither dare nor presume to go near monasteries of nuns, both those of the city and those of the diocese; neither [should they visit] their parlors, grates, doorways, *ruote,* or their exterior churches, to sing or play, or to teach the same nuns or lay students who stay in the convents, even though they may be subject to regular orders; [nor should they] listen while they rehearse their musics, on any occasion, on the festivals of their churches, or for funerals in those churches annexed to them for the care of souls; nor [should they] perform there any sort of music, even though they may have been summoned by confessors, chaplains, or by any other sort of person, despite the fact that they may have had a license to do so.

Such a litany of prohibitions offers a tacit admission of failure, a response to subversion that was sustained and successful. Lest any convent try to claim unfamiliarity with such decrees, authorities sometimes required that they be read at least twice a year in the refectory or in chapter "so that their observance remains alive, so that no one may plead ignorance."[17] But pleas of ignorance would continue as significant strategies into the eighteenth century, as we shall see.

In the absence of much real authority of their own, the nuns also exercised various indirect means of influence upon the church hierarchy, chiefly by exploiting the conflicting and tangled lines of ecclesiastical authority, variously represented by the archbishop, the suffragan bishop, the vicar general, the nuns' vicar, the papal legate and vice-legate, the secular clergy, the regular clergy, convent confessors, and convent chaplains and curates, not to mention the civil authorities and the patriciate of the city. Monastic reforms represented only one area in which Gabriele Paleotti found his reform efforts thwarted by fragmented and inconsistent authority, or by opposition from elsewhere in the chain of command. And, as we shall see, a century and a half later, the same problems would still continue to plague Archbishop Giacomo Boncompagni of Bologna.[18] Such difficulties characterized attempts at convent reform within the post-Tridentine church generally. As A. D. Wright has observed: "The attempt to make of female convents less a particular part of lay society, and more a part of the hierarchical and professional Church, with clerical male control of funds and persons, was not a success: arguably the least successful campaign of the Counter-Reformation. . . . Female conventual life remained in Catholic Europe, in the seventeenth and eighteenth centuries, a notably relaxed part of the post-Tridentine Church."[19]

In the first wave of convent reform, the nuns and their families seem to have turned to the papal legate of Bologna for support. A series of letters from 1584–85 between Filippo Boncompagni, Cardinal San Sisto, in Rome and Giovanni Battista Castagna, Cardinal San Marcello, papal legate of Bologna, was clearly intended, for example, to firm up the legate's not exactly unwavering support of Paleotti's efforts, including the archbishop's removal of convent organs (which, according to the legate occurred "not without great lamentation"). Paleotti complained both to Rome and to his friend Carlo Borromeo on more than one occasion about conflicts with the legate in these matters. One of Cardinal Boncompagni's letters to the Bolognese legate also reveals that the nuns had been seeking sympathy among another of their most important sources of support, the citizenry of Bologna, "to [whom] . . . it seems harsh that there should be this penalty of excommunication [for infractions]."[20] The church authorities' normal reticence about exercising their authority in ways that could be perceived in the city as unreasonable or overly severe also encumbered their efforts and embroiled them in attempts at self-justification to the populace. Given that some members of the church hierarchy, civil government, and some segments of the intelligentsia saw nuns, enclosed within convent walls, as mediators for the city with a heavenly authority, and as sacrificial victims to the long-term financial security of their families, overly dictatorial actions by ecclesiastics could also tip the balance of public sympathy and support in the nuns' favor.[21]

In the early spring of 1585, the nuns inaugurated what would become a primary means of exploiting these conflicting lines of ecclesiastical authority: direct petitioning over the archbishop's head to a higher authority, the Roman curia. Although this could prove a useful strategy, it was also an unpredictable one, for the administrative congregations in Rome routinely requested the local bishop's opinion. The phrase *episcopo pro informatione et voto* ("to the bishop for information and his vote") was noted by the secretary of the congregation on the majority of such petitions. Nevertheless, the congregations of cardinals weighed other factors, such as tradition, local custom, and political lobbying from both sides, and often enough they offered their convent supplicants some measure of satisfaction.

In April 1585, for example, the Congregation of Bishops granted the nuns of San Pietro Martire of Bologna special license to use their organ "walled up as it is" on Easter and the feast of San Pietro Martire. The following year, the nuns of Santissima Trinità apparently got wind of their sisters' success via the convent grapevine and petitioned the Congregation of Bishops themselves, citing its earlier concession to San Pietro Martire and claiming that the inner chapel of their convent was simply too narrow to accommodate the organ entirely within it. The Congregation instructed Paleotti to satisfy "these poor little ones, who, closed up forever within these walls, deserve to be permitted some further relief." Some contemporaries recognized that nuns deserved a little compensation for their sacrifices, and the sisters were not above using such sympathy to their own advantage. A month later, a slightly defensive Cardinal Paleotti found himself reassuring the Congregation in Rome that he had never intended to deny the nuns the use of convent organs entirely and was willing to come to some accommodation with the nuns of Santissima Trinità. But in August, Paleotti was suggesting that after the appearance of initial agreement, "I see that they are going around looking for new avenues to achieve what is agreeable," and implying that Santissima Trinità should have been quicker to obey.[22]

This method of lobbying for small concessions or special licenses, which could then be parlayed into additional advantages when circumstances permitted, would remain a strategy of convent women's culture for centuries. When possible, in their petitions, nuns would cite cases in which similar license had already been granted elsewhere. As in the case of Santissima Trinità and San Pietro Martire cited above, convent gossip moving along family networks (it was not uncommon for a single family to have daughters in two or three different institutions) permitted one house to take advantage of concessions received elsewhere. The potential utility of such a strategy did not escape the archdiocesan curia in Bologna. One cleric put it rather extravagantly, around 1584, "One must be strong in not licensing music masters to teach [the nuns].... Otherwise, if the tiniest path is opened, it will be the ruin of these convents, which will never again be well governed."[23]

Generally, the hierarchy did stand firm when there was a possibility of setting a dangerous precedent. Thus, in 1601, once Cardinal Gabriele Paleotti had died, the nuns of Santa Margherita must have thought it was worth requesting permission to move the convent organs back to the outer church, where they had been before the ban of 1584. But the Congregation of Bishops denied the petition with the comment that "to concede this to these and not to the other nuns could provoke dissatisfaction among them, and also set a bad precedent."[24]

The nuns also worked the conflicting lines of authority to their own advantage by concentrating on intermediary authority figures. These ranged from powerful patrician or noble patrons to members of the senatorial government, or their own father confessors or curates, who could be made to serve as buffers between the nuns and the upper ecclesiastical hierarchy. To forge and strengthen such alliances, the nuns brought to bear diverse sorts of influence. These could be as simple as endearing, affectionate terms of quasi-kinship, such as *padrino*, used by the nuns of Santa Cristina for their confessor and ally Mauro Ruggeri in the 1620s. Like their female counterparts of later centuries, however, they also found demeaning or diminishing names for unsympathetic authority figures. The same diminutive employed for Ruggeri seems to take on a negative tone when appended to the name of the much despised and apparently corrupt nuns' vicar of Bologna, Giovanni Bondino, invariably called "don Gioa-nino," of whom much more must be said later. The nuns' strategies also included promises of their prayers, willingness to sing Masses on request, plates of toffee, and little gifts on feast days. The ecclesiastical hierarchy repeatedly decried these gifts as a useless squandering of convent resources; but the nuns regarded this important early modern medium of exchange as a sound and essential investment in public relations.

Noble intercession on nuns' behalf represented another time-honored practice, as is revealed by a letter from Isabella d'Este to the abbot of San Benedetto in Polirone, written in 1512, requesting that nuns of San Giovanni be permitted an outside music teacher, since their singing was presently so bad that "when we visit the said convent and hear such discord, our ears are deeply offended, and scarcely consoled."[25] As in this example, often the only surviving evidence for the nuns' behind-the-scenes treating with such advocates, who were frequently women allied to them by ties of class, family, or specially cultivated friendship, is the result it produced.

In the early 1620s, an unidentified exponent of nuns' music suggested that if the nuns hoped to overturn Archbishop Ludovisi's latest reinforcement of the old musical prohibitions, "it is necessary that some important prince demand the grace most efficaciously, because Monsignor Ingoli [Ludovisi's secretary] is very tough, and makes the excuse that this is the particular view of His Holiness and of Lord Cardinal Ludovisi."[26] This is exactly what the nuns of Corpus Domini did in similar circumstances forty years later, after their initial request for permission to accept a nun organist at half the regular dowry had been rejected by the Congregation of Bishops in March 1662. They turned to the Pepoli, one of Bologna's most illustrious and powerful banking families, who had supported them in musical matters for decades. At the end of May, Vittoria, daughter of Marquis Cesare Pepoli and second wife of Count Odoardo Michele Pepoli, wrote very politely but firmly to Cardinal Ginetti, secretary of the Congregation:

> I know that if you should wish to grant me this grace no one among the others will dispute it by saying the Sacred Congregation should be of a mind to remove all the organs from the nuns. I know that in Rome all convents sing and play, and I know of no scandal arising there. But, rather, devotion is

increased, as everything is done in God's honor. And for this reason I know
the fulfillment of such sophistical opinions will not follow. Forgive me, Your
Eminence, if I speak too freely.

She concluded with a personal note, in her own hand,

Lord Cardinal, my patron, I am so obligated to this Blessed Catherine [Vigri]
that I can do no less than be importunate to Your Eminence.

The mediations of both Vittoria Pepoli and Beata Caterina Vigri (d. 1463,
the founder of Corpus Domini, canonized in 1712) were apparently irresistible. The suit seems to have been granted, and the organist accepted,
within the month.[27]

Other Bolognese petitions permit us to observe the potential weaknesses
in the church's structure of authority. In 1657, for example, unnamed
"nuns of Bologna" complained to the Congregation of Bishops that while
the archbishop of Bologna was out of the diocese, and therefore out of
sight, his vicar general had begun to license "various teachers of languages,
singing, and playing, of an age inappropriate to these sorts of places."[28]

An agreement between the nuns of Sant'Orsola and their new father
confessor and curate, drawn up in 1684, on the other hand, not only reveals
exactly how the fragmented hierarchical system could be turned back upon
itself, but also how informal rules and customs, worked out by the nuns
themselves within their own sphere, subverted the prescriptions of both the
diocese and the Roman curia:

On the feast of Saint Catherine, when the curate sings the Mass . . . and the
nuns respond in plainchant, which is against the decrees of both the Congregation of the Council and the Congregation of Bishops and Regulars,
nevertheless, to please the nuns who wish it, with the consent of the Ordinary,
he [the confessor] shall permit it, with the approval of the Ordinary as appropriate. . . . And although the curate should not sing the solemnities with
the nuns, since abuses were introduced long ago without the confessor pro
tempore's objections to the curate's singing with the nuns who would go up
to the organ [cf. Paleotti's first rule of 1580!] to sing the Magnificat in plainchant, in order to please the nuns who wish it, . . . the confessor shall permit
it.[29]

This document illustrates plainly how nuns turned their confessors and
curates into accomplices to subvert higher authority. Powerful bonds
forged between father confessors and their charges in fact represented one
of the most important of the nuns' means of mediation. Such ties are manifest, not only in this sort of active complicity, but also in tangible and
intangible ways, such as the gift to the convent of Santa Cristina of Salviati's
altarpiece *Virgin and Child with Saints* (fig. 2) by their confessor, Giovan
Francesco da Bagno in 1539–41, or in the touching testimony of Girolamo

da Vigevano, confessor to the nuns of Sant'Agnese in Bologna, recorded in 1576 in an antiphonal he had given them, "I shall love them always, as mothers, sisters, and daughters, MOST DEAR, with no partiality."[30] In recognition of the fact that father confessors clearly could represent the weakest link in the ecclesiastical chain of command, the church hierarchy required that they rotate every three years and be subject to final approval by the local bishop, although these rules, too, were inevitably open to flexible interpretation. The issue of confessors would also become a key factor in later struggles between the nuns of Santa Cristina and their superiors, as we shall see.

Convents like Santa Cristina, under the jurisdiction of regular monastic orders—Dominicans, Benedictines, Franciscans, Lateran canons, or Camaldolese—and not subject directly to the authority of the local archbishop, found in this relationship another especially useful method of mediation. Given the traditional rivalries and antagonisms, especially in matters of jurisdiction, between regular orders and secular clergy bound by no monastic rule and affiliated with the diocesan curia, nuns in regular orders found naturally sympathetic ears among their male monastic superiors, to whom they could petition regarding diocesan decrees imposed by local bishops. The following letter from the general of the Lateran canons to his deputy, the abbot of San Giovanni in Monte, who governed the Lateran canonesses of San Lorenzo in Bologna, provides an excellent example of how the nuns could evade the letter of episcopal law and benefit from the flexibility the superiors of their own order were prepared to introduce:

> It is true that a few days ago donna Gentile as organist petitioned in great humility for permission to perform a concerto on the organ on their feast day. In light of the humility of her request . . . and [recognizing] her and her companions [as] good and obedient daughters, I was inclined to grant her that on the feast day she could have some motets sung with one or two voices at most, forbidding every sort of musical instrument, and not extending the license beyond the feast day of San Lorenzo. I gave this license because I could give it, expecting that, having made the laws, I can make exceptions; and I gave it because to me it seemed a reasonable favor. For I had a look in the decrees of the Illustrious Paleotti, printed in [15]79, in which the nuns are permitted to sing with one voice to the organ. If I was satisfied with two voices, it is not a sin in the Holy Spirit. I also deemed this grace reasonable, thinking thereby to relieve in part these embittered souls. . . . Nor does it seem to me a good idea to revoke it; nor do I believe further confirmation is required [i.e., from the diocesan curia]. As for anyone who may speak of this, Your Reverence may respond according to what I have written.[31]

This letter reveals how the nuns could play off the superiors within their order against each other. (The abbot of San Giovanni in Monte had evidently been irritated that the nuns had gone over his head, directly to the top.) The general's more liberal reinterpretation of Archbishop Paleotti's earlier decree (the seven rules quoted earlier) also illustrates why archbishops and the post-Tridentine ecclesiastical hierarchy perennially distrusted the rule of nunneries by regular clergy, which served to undermine their own authority, and the uniform implementation of curial policy. It also explains why the hierarchy waged frequent battles to wrest the nunneries from the control of regular orders. Indeed, as we shall see, Santa Cristina della Fondazza would soon play out such a battle in spectacular form.

In other cases, the nuns almost cavalierly disobeyed decrees they found unreasonable. Thus, the prohibition within convents of all instruments except the organ, harpsichord, or bass viol, instituted in 1580, was interpreted with considerable flexibility, or just ignored, to suit the nuns' own purposes. On 23 August 1602, for example, the nuns of Santi Vitale et Agricola drew up an official document commemorating their recent purchase of a matched set of five viols (a permissible bass, three illicit tenors, and an illicit treble), for the use of the *scola da cantare,* which were never to be sold or loaned out, on threat of severe reprisals, instituted by the nuns themselves. Similarly, the previously cited nuns' inventories of personal property from Santa Margherita reveal that in 1603, suor Monica Ariosti still owned a lute and its case. In 1613, suor Giacinta Maria Garzoni owned "an archlute," suor Emilia Arali owned "a spinet harpsichord, a guitar, and a lute," suor Angiola owned "1 clavichord, 1 lute, an archlute, 1 violin," and suor Olimpia Ghisilieri and another nun each owned a trombone. Additional evidence attests to the continued use of theoretically forbidden trombones at Santa Caterina, Santa Cristina, and San Giovanni Battista as well.[32]

To control such infractions required a degree of vigilance that a diocesan curia, with some two dozen convents in its charge, could scarcely hope to manage effectively. In the several convents subject to monastic orders, over which the archbishop had only limited sway, the difficulties were compounded. And the system of strict enclosure that represented the cornerstone of post-Tridentine reform exacerbated the problems with control. For the higher cloister walls not only kept the nuns in and discreetly hidden from view, but also kept their overseers to some extent out of their "women's sphere." It was certainly more difficult than before the Council of Trent to maintain a clear sense of what was going on inside without co-opting someone within the convent community to work on behalf of the hierarchy, as happened at Santa Cristina in the 1620s, as we shall see. On the other hand, the new management policy brought other unintended effects, for segregation bred solidarity as well as marginality. The nuns' internal community had traditionally socialized its members since childhood, first at the hands of their aunts and the novice mistress, but also informally by the community as a whole, to accept their group solidarity, particularly when the sphere bounded by the convent wall was threatened from without, when their own collective prerogatives were attacked. In such a situation, internal rivalries or minor disagreements might be put aside in the face of a perceived common enemy, as the nuns of Santa Cristina would likewise demonstrate in the course of the seventeenth century.

༄

Thus, for Lucrezia Vizzana, the musical reality was much less grim than ecclesiastical prohibitions suggest. She was also lucky to have entered one of the best of all possible worlds in Bologna for a budding female musician. The extent and nature of musical education in the upbringing of Bolognese laywomen has yet to be explored in any detail. One may be certain that the noble and patrician families of Bologna shared the view of their peers in other cities, an attitude reflected in, and shaped by, Castiglione's *Il corteggiano.* As Anthony Newcomb has observed,[33] Castiglione left room for respectable women to perform or possibly to teach in the private sphere of the court, but did not acknowledge the option of musical composition for them. Women's early musical training in the world concentrated on singing or playing, and it appears to have placed less emphasis on composition than did men's musical education.[34] A handful of late-sixteenth- and early-seventeenth-century women composers have come to light among the women who found increasing musical opportunities in the worldly realms of the court, the professional actress, or the courtesan—but one can be sure that no Bombacci or Vizzani would have wanted his daughters associated with the second or third of these options. Laywomen such as Maddalena Casulana and Barbara Strozzi, whose musical careers most closely reflected those of their male counterparts, and who may consciously have been trained for composing careers, are obvious exceptions to the general rule.[35]

As Jane Bowers has observed, girls' early musical education in the world was especially intense when they were being prepared for the religious life,[36] for reasons suggested in the Introduction above. Lucrezia Vizzana entered the convent of Santa Cristina at such a tender age that she is unlikely to have had much prior familiarity with music. Her musical education must have been entirely a product of her monastic environment. As far back as the fifteenth century, the nuns of Santa Cristina had developed something of a reputation for music. In 1433, for example, the Camaldolese prior general, Ambrogio Traversari, lauded the nuns for "a Divine Office [that] is nowhere celebrated more diligently in common; its psalmody is nowhere more expertly and more melodiously sung. As far as a monastery of virgins is concerned, nowhere was I so delightfully moved."[37]

Even if outside music teachers were banned from the convents at the time of Lucrezia Vizzana's arrival, there seems to have been no shortage of musical talent within Santa Cristina, on which the young Lucrezia Vizzana must have relied. As a rule, *educande* of the period received their first instruction from an aunt within the convent. Subsequent institutionalized training, including instruction in how to sing the chants of the Office and Mass, fell to the mistress of novices. Lucrezia's most probable mentor was one of her mother's three sisters, who looked after her upbringing. The youngest of her aunts, donna Camilla Bombacci, in fact, was a musician. At her death in 1640 at the age of seventy, donna Camilla was remembered in the convent necrology as "first organist, and three times mistress of the novices, and subsequently abbess." In 1623, the current abbess suggested Camilla Bombacci for *maestra del coro,* but donna Camilla ultimately became abbess instead.[38]

The early relationship between the young Lucrezia and donna Camilla Bombacci was probably much akin to another case described a century later in a petition to the Congregation of Bishops from the Monastery of Santa Caterina da Siena in Catanzaro: "The noble maiden Lucrezia Vigliarolo, eight years old, desires to remain under the care and direction of suor Margarita Almirante, her maternal aunt . . . in which she has made such progress that she now sings the Office with the nuns in the choir and reads at table." Similar musical precocity was not particularly unusual within the cloister. In 1668, for example, a ten-year-old singer being educated at the convent of Santi Gervasio e Protasio in Bologna was granted special permission by the Congregation of Bishops to sing a duet at Mass with an older nun (her aunt perhaps?) on the feast of the patron saints. And Lucrezia Vizzana was hardly the first musically precocious girl at Santa Cristina. In 1433, two other "nuns in miniature" had entranced Ambrogio Traversari: "It was most delightfully pleasing to admire a little girl about six years old in the choir, reciting chapters, verses, prayers, responsories from memory, so well that she made not one mistake, and likewise another girl, ten years old."[39]

Lucrezia Vizzana's own early studies must have resembled those described in the early 1620s by donna Paula Dorotea Vitali of Santa Cristina as consisting of reading and singing plainchant, and probably took place in the rooms of the novice mistress, which Vitali suggests were located "in the rooms up above, in the middle"—probably near the large storage area under the roof—"to be separated from the convent and not disturb the nuns."[40]

The probable student-teacher relationship of Lucrezia Vizzana and Camilla Bombacci partook of apprenticeship, paralleling within convent walls the apprenticeship training in womanhood and women's skills that went on outside. The musical aspect of this relationship also suggests the beginnings of a kind of modest musical dynasty within the walls on via Fondazza. Lucrezia Vizzana subsequently acted as overseer of the junior members of the convent at various times, as her memorial in the convent necrology indicates. Her relative Teresa Pompea Vizzana, who entered Santa Cristina in the 1630s and may have been trained by donna Lucrezia, would later also be remembered for her own musical abilities. It is therefore quite possible that this mentor relationship extended to a third generation of the family.

In writing the history of women and music, relatively unsuccessful recent attempts to establish the relationship of women musicians and composers to sixteenth- and seventeenth-century musical families active in the world have yielded only about half a dozen examples. These attempts have to some extent been wrongly directed toward the world outside the convent and to familiar patterns of father-son apprenticeship.[41] It is not surprising that in the early years of this century, Giovanni Livi apparently deemed all women, cloistered or otherwise, unworthy of attention in his researches on the Bolognese Ferrabosco dynasty: "In the family tree I have thought it well to add the names of the male children, as it is not impossible that in one or more of them a new musician may eventually be discovered."[42]

Livi's prediction of further musical Ferrabosco males has not been fulfilled. But a search within the cloisters of Italy has thus far turned up no fewer than four nun musicians to fill out the Ferrabosco family tree—who now balance the number of Italian musical males in the family. Leonora Florida (d. 1658) was at the convent of Sant'Agnese, Prudenza (d. 1603) was at Corpus Domini in Bologna, while farther afield we find the extraordinarily talented Elena, daughter of Amfione Ferrabosco, accepted at San Leonardo in Genoa in 1592, and her sister, Laura, accepted at San Bartolomeo in the same city the following year.

A similar search back in Bologna for other nun musicians has also yielded the organist stepdaughter of Ottavio Vernizzi of San Petronio, Samaritana Vernizzi (d. 1662) at the convent of Sant'Agostino, and the organist daughter of Ascanio Trombetti, Isabella Trombetta (d. 1614), who, like her father, also played the trombone, which she took with her when she entered the convent of Santi Gervasio e Protasio in 1577.[43] Thus the cloisters of early-seventeenth-century Bologna alone have yielded almost as many father-daughter or brother-sister musical relationships as have been uncovered in the secular world from the late sixteenth century until 1700.

The Bombacci-Vizzana-Vizzana musical relationship outlined above further suggests that we also should not ignore the common, if more elusive, strictly female lines of musical kinship within the cloister, where we find musical nieces instructed in the art by their musical aunts. Such intergenerational musical ties within convent walls turn out to have been reasonably common in Italy.[44] These generations of musical nuns may be commonly overlooked by the likes of Livi in worldly family trees, but they were carefully remembered for their artistic gifts in convent necrologies.

Lucrezia Vizzana's most probable music teacher, Camilla Bombacci, was only one of several nun musicians at Santa Cristina during her niece's formative years. Chief among the others was donna Emilia Grassi, clearly the dominant musical force at the convent in the early Seicento. In 1599 Emilia Grassi received the dedication of Adriano Banchieri's *Messa solenne a otto voci*, published in Venice and presumably underwritten by donna Emilia. The dedication by the garrulous composer and Olivetan monk warrants a closer look for what it tells us about both Emilia Grassi and music at Santa Cristina:

> On the day when the feast of the glorious Saint Christina was solemnized, finding myself in the church of your Reverence while first vespers was being sung, and hearing with great pleasure the harmonious concerti of voices, organs, and various musical instruments, directed with most exquisite sentiments of devotion, I endeavored to learn from a musician, my particular friend (who was present there), who was the head of these concerti; and from him I learned it was your Reverence. And justly he further added that in addition to your other most honorable qualities you are highly skilled both in singing and playing, using all [these talents] for the praise and glory of our Blessed Lord. . . . I desire no other reward, only that on occasions when you perform [these concerti], you and your dear sisters would remember to pray God for me in your devout and holy prayers.[45]

Emilia Grassi served as *maestra del coro* for most of the second decade of the century and into the 1620s. After her death in 1633, during her second term as abbess, she was remembered as one "who, above all, so excelled in playing all musical instruments that she was second to none"—except, presumably, Lucrezia Vizzana. Mauro Ruggeri, her former confessor, also singled out donna Emilia for her vocal abilities and for her talents on the organ, harp, and other instruments.[46]

Two years after the appearance of Banchieri's collection, another nun from Santa Cristina, donna Adeodata Leoni, received the dedication of the *Secondo libro de motetti* by the Camaldolese Gabriele Fattorini, organist of Faenza cathedral.[47] The dedication, written by the Camaldolese monk don Donato Beroaldo, who gathered the motets for publication, suggests that the collection had been put together at donna Adeodata's behest. Soon the singing nuns of Santa Cristina were the dedicatees of a third publication, the *Compieta con letanie* (1606) of Giovanni Battista Biondi, *alias* Cesena, which consisted, like the previous two collections, of works for eight voices. The dedicatory letter by the Venetian publisher Giacomo Vincenti marvels at the divine musical *concerti* at various Bolognese convents and singles out those at Santa Cristina in particular.[48] Finally, in 1613, Ercole Porta, organist of the collegiate church of San Giovanni in Persiceto, dedicated to donna Cleria Pepoli of Santa Cristina his *Vaga ghirlanda di soavi e odorati fiori musicali,* a more diverse collection of motets, psalms, and *falsobordone* settings for one to five voices.

It is surely significant that of some ten musical collections dedicated to convent women in Bologna and the immediate area between 1582 and 1675, no fewer than four were dedicated to nuns at Santa Cristina, all within the fourteen years of Lucrezia Vizzana's formative period. The testimony of these prints, as well as other evidence, suggests that the nuns' own music must have been quite elaborate—much more lavish than archiepiscopal prohibitions would suggest.

Architectural evidence points in the same direction. The new church of Santa Cristina included two raised organ rooms, one on each side of the high altar, only accessible from the nuns' inner chapel, and each containing an organ (fig. 11 shows one of the organ windows at the right). In 1607, the organ builder Paolo Cipri clearly indicated that the organs and choir lofts at Santa Cristina were arranged to permit double-choir singing by the nuns.[49] Although there were screens in front of the windows of these organ lofts, facing each other across the high altar, the screens could be removed during performances, enabling the singing nuns in the two choir lofts to see one another and to coordinate their performance as they responded to one another in song.

Such musical coordination would have been considerably easier in the nuns' other large chapel at the rear of the external church, above the church doors, whose three large grates could also easily have accommodated double choirs, invisible from the external church, but in full view of each other within the chapel itself (fig. 11 shows this choir at the far left). Mauro Ruggeri, father confessor at Santa Cristina in the early 1620s, claimed that this chapel was where the nuns performed "choirs of music" on feast days. Ruggeri further indicates that the nuns accompanied themselves, not only with the two organs, but also "with various instruments, violins, trombones, harps, and such like," presumably with the approval of their Camaldolese superiors, but not of the diocesan curia.[50] All this evidence suggests, not only that the various archiepiscopal decrees from 1580 onward had only limited effect at Santa Cristina, but also that the lavish descriptions of music at the convent by Adriano Banchieri and others were more than mere hyperbole.

The music from the collections dedicated to the nuns at Santa Cristina, which must have been conceived at least partly with the singing nuns in mind, must also offer some measure of their skills. Adriano Banchieri's *Messa solenne* of 1599, for example, includes a few pieces that meet Gabriele Paleotti's old rule permitting the nuns "to sing a motet once or twice when Mass is celebrated, and similarly at the end of vespers." Nothing in the collection, however, even approaches the limitation to a single voice with organ accompaniment. Both *Letamini et exultate quia surrexit Christus*, described as a "Four-Voice Fantasy to Sing and Play" clearly intended for Easter, and *Adoramus te dulcissime Jesu Christe*, a "Most Devout Sentiment for the Elevation of the Most Holy Sacrament," are scored only for four high voices, with the lowest part in the tenor rather than the bass range, which would have suited the nuns. The self-contained *Crucifixus* from the creed of Banchieri's Mass is likewise for four voices that descend no lower than the two motets. The motet *Decantabat populus Israel*, too, also only employs four higher voices, although the lowest part drops into the baritone range for half a dozen notes; these could easily have been transposed up an octave without marring the harmony.

The remaining items in Banchieri's collection largely feature eight voices: two contrasting four-voice choirs. One of the choirs, for higher voices, is juxtaposed with the second, lower choir. Indeed, in the so-called "Concerto at the Offertory," *Beata es tu Sancte N.* ("Blessed art thou, Saint X"—the appropriate saint's name could be inserted in this multipurpose piece), the upper choir stays higher than in any other work in Banchieri's collection and is featured particularly prominently on its own for the opening ten bars. This certainly suggests that Banchieri had the singing nuns of Santa Cristina in mind. The second choir, however, here and in the other double-choir pieces, tends to descend to the masculine depths where the nuns probably could not follow.

It is tempting to suggest that at least in the case of *Beata es tu*, the nuns, who seem successfully to have worked around other archiepiscopal musical prohibitions, might have been emboldened to sing together with a second choir of external musicians, just as earlier nuns had sung with outsiders before Paleotti's reform program got under way a few decades earlier. From their chapel above the portico adjoining the church doors, the nuns could have responded chastely through the grates to the second chorus situated in an adjoining choir loft, also above the church doors, but in the external, public church (fig. 11, left—choir loft within the church, directly adjacent to the nun's chapel, is not pictured). Such an arrangement, strictly speaking, would have involved no literal violation of *clausura*, since the church wall, pierced by three large grates, would have kept the extern musicians in the choir loft of the external church separate from the nuns in the chapel of the Rosary, above the portico, but technically within the cloister. As we shall see, over the next two decades, some of the same nuns involved in such singing devised other creative and unusual ways to interact with outsiders without actually violating the letter of the law on enclosure.

Such collaboration involved extreme bending of the rules. The fact that the ban on performances by outsiders in convent churches remained one of the most stringently enforced musical prohibitions at the time when Banchieri's collection appeared suggests that the nuns may have been left entirely to their own musical devices. They may therefore have relegated the lower voice parts from the second choir of Banchieri's double-choir pieces to the bass viol Paleotti had still permitted them, or to the trombone—forbidden, but apparently still occasionally in use. They may also have intabulated the pieces for the organ, a practice in Bolognese convents since the mid sixteenth century, which could have filled out the lower harmonies while the nuns sang what upper parts they could manage.[51]

The Fattorini and Cesena musical collections, on the other hand, are more uniform and traditional in their contents, making less obvious provisions for the special circumstances of convent singing. Both collections consist entirely of works for two four-voice choirs. Some of their contents seems difficult or impossible for the nuns to have performed.[52] Given the overall vocal ranges in the Fattorini and Cesena pieces, from the highest note of the top voice to the lowest note of the bottom voice, upward transposition, to bring the lowest parts up from the depths without at the same time driving the top parts to potentially excruciating heights, would probably have been at best a dangerous solution to this problem.

Some of Fattorini's motets, however, would have been especially effective if sung by hidden double choirs of nuns. *Audi coelum* employs especially striking and rather witty echo effects, with the second choir jumping in fleetingly to repeat a fragment of the first choir's last word, yet still making verbal sense (*et perfusa gaudio* [*Audio*], *et benedicam* [*dicam*], . . . *Porta orientalis* [*talis*], *pro culpis remedium* [*medium*], . . . *vitam aeternam consequamur* [*sequamur*], etc.). This wordplay would soon be imitated in soloistic settings of the same text, with the same echoes, by Ercole Porta and by Claudio Monteverdi in his well-known setting of *Audi coelum* from the popular *Vespers* of 1610. The question/response of Fattorini's *Himnum cantate nobis* may have been especially telling when sung by cloistered nuns, who occasionally used their incarceration as a means to arouse sympathy in the world. The first choir's fifteen-measure introduction, "Sing unto us a hymn," is answered by the second, "How shall we sing the Lord's song in a foreign land?" As the motet continues, it is the higher, "captive" second choir that pointedly introduces the rest of the text, "Those who led us captive into that place asked of us the words of our songs. Sing unto us a hymn. How shall we sing the Lord's song in a strange land?" An orthodox interpretation of the nuns' rendition of Psalm 136 would make it a symbol of their longing to escape the captivity of the *terra aliena* of earth in order to fly to heaven. But at least some of those hearing these words in the outer church at Santa Cristina, particularly as disembodied echoes from behind barred windows, would have recognised the analogy to the nuns' own real-life situation; they had been led into the captivity of the cloister by their own families.[53]

Resonating from within cloisters such as Santa Cristina in the years when Lucrezia Orsina Vizzana was growing up, such echoes, whether the clever single word fragments of *Audi coelum* or the calls and sorrowful responses of *Himnum cantate nobis,* represented an especially effective conceit. For, just as the sad mythological figure Echo, after her rejection by Narcissus, had gone to live in hidden, lonely caves, whence she tossed back sounds to the world, nuns had since the 1560s been compelled to withdraw into enforced seclusion behind the convent walls rising around them.[54] As Ann Rosalind Jones has observed, Echo had become a symbol commonly employed by women writers of the period for the silence imposed upon them. Indeed, male writers on female conduct even made Echo a paradigm for modern women. In 1552, Alessandro Piccolomini urged wives to be the echoes of their husbands; in 1588, Robert Cleaver affirmed "as the echo answereth but one word for many, which are spoken to her, so a Maid's answer should be a single word."[55]

The singing voice, echoing from behind the convent grate, plays upon this metaphor in a telling spiritual mode. Despite fifty years of control amounting to silencing by unsympathetic Bolognese churchmen, in Lucrezia Vizzana's time, the singing of the nuns of Bologna, like the voice of Echo, continued to call back mysteriously to the world beyond the walls.

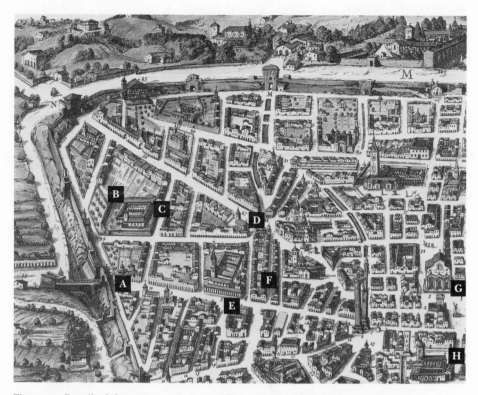

Figure 1. Detail of the eastern quarter of Bologna, showing Santa Cristina about 1590. After J. Bleau, *Theatrum civitatum et admirandum Italiæ* (Amsterdam, 1663). Reproduced with permission of the Biblioteca Comunale dell'Archiginnasio, Bologna. A: Porta and Strada Maggiore; B: Santa Cristina; C: Via Fondazza; D: Palazzo Vizzani; E: San Tomaso; F: Casa Bombacci (narrow building filling the intersection of Strada Maggiore and the two side streets); G: San Petronio; H: Cathedral of San Pietro.

Figure 2. Francesco Salviati, *The Blessed Virgin and Child with Saints* (c. 1540), outer church of Santa Cristina, chapel of Saint Romuald. Reproduced with permission of the Biblioteca Comunale dell'Archiginnasio, Bologna.

Figure 3. Gaetano Ferrattini, Santa Cristina, façade, campanile, and entrance to parlatorios (watercolor, after 1745). Reproduced with permission of the Biblioteca Comunale dell'Archiginnasio, Bologna.

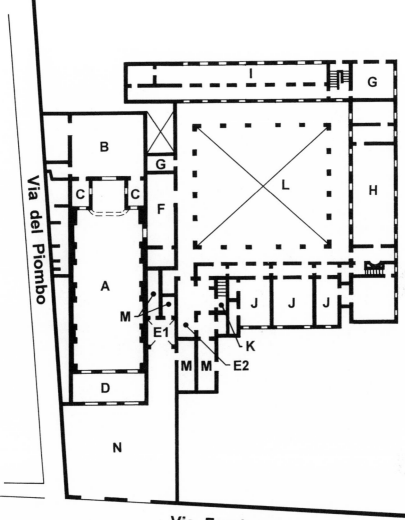

Figure 4. Plan, Santa Cristina della Fondazza. Based on Ugo Capriani, "Chiesa e convento di Santa Cristina della Fondazza: Ipotesi di ricerca e recupero" (Tesi di laurea, Università di Bologna, 1987–88), reproduced with permission.

Figure 5. Santa Cristina, a nun's cell on the upper floor, west wing of the cloister. Reproduced with permission of Ugo Capriani.

Figure 6. Giacomo Francia, *The Nativity* (c. 1552), outer church of Santa Cristina, chapel of Saint Benedict. Reproduced with permission of the Biblioteca Comunale dell'Archiginnasio, Bologna.

Figure 7. Lucio Massari, *The Visitation* (1607), outer church of Santa Cristina. Reproduced with permission of the Biblioteca Comunale dell'Archiginnasio, Bologna.

Figure 8. Tiburzio Passerotti, *Christ's Fall beneath the Cross* (1603), outer church of Santa Cristina. Reproduced with permission of the Biblioteca Comunale dell'Archiginnasio, Bologna.

Figure 9. Bernardino Baldi, *The Coronation of the Virgin* (before 1615), outer church of Santa Cristina. Reproduced with permission of the Biblioteca Comunale dell'Archiginnasio, Bologna.

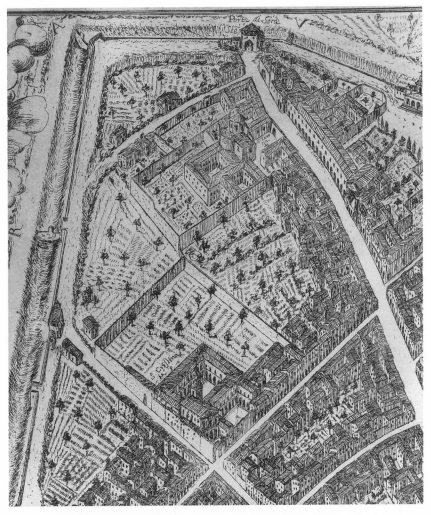

Figure 10. Detail of the eastern section of Bologna, showing Santa Cristina about
1700. After Filippo Gnudi, *Pianta iconografica* (1702). Reproduced with permission of the Biblioteca Comunale dell'Archiginnasio, Bologna.

Figure 11. Angelo Michele Cavazzoni, interior view of the external church of Santa Cristina (ink and watercolor, eighteenth century). An organ window facing the high altar is visible at the right. The chapel above the portal of the church is at the left. Reproduced with permission of the Soprintendenza delle Belle Arti and the Archivio Opera Pia Davia Bargellini, Bologna.

Figure 12. Pseudo-Jacopino, *The Dream of Saint Romuald* (c. 1340).
Reproduced with permission of the Pinacoteca Nazionale di Bologna.

Figure 13. Giovanni Battista Bertusio, *The Resurrection* (1603), outer
church of Santa Cristina. Reproduced with permission of the Biblioteca
Comunale dell'Archiginnasio, Bologna.

Figure 14. Domenico Maria Canuti, *Saint Christina* (c. 1680), outer church of Santa Cristina. Reproduced with permission of the Biblioteca Comunale dell'Archiginnasio, Bologna.

Figure 15. Commemoration of the investiture of Suor Maria Clotilde Lucia Benedetta Pannini (1706). Reproduced with permission of the Civico Museo Bibliografico Musicale, Bologna.

Figure 16. Santa Cristina, the Cappella del Santissimo Rosario, about 1987.
Reproduced with permission of Ugo Capriani.

Figure 17. Santa Cristina, west wing, the vault of the cloister staircase, about 1987. Reproduced with permission of Ugo Capriani.

THREE

Worldly Influences on Lucrezia Vizzana's
Componimenti musicali

Despite episcopal prohibitions, music in the convents of Bologna had continued to flourish. Clearly one of the most musical convents of the city, and especially well supplied with talented musicians of its own, Santa Cristina della Fondazza had long fostered a particularly lively musical tradition, from which the young Lucrezia Vizzana must have gained inspiration and learned many details of her art. There is an additional problem, however, in attempting to explain the nature of her own work. Vizzana's compositions belong to the novel *stile moderno*. This modern musical style, associated first with secular music, had also begun to find its way into Bolognese sacred music created in the world outside the convent, particularly in published collections such as Adriano Banchieri's *Nuovi pensieri ecclesiastici* (1613) and Ercole Porta's *Sacro convito musicale* (1620). Works in the *stile moderno*, whether secular or sacred, had been printed chiefly in the twenty years before the publication of Vizzana's *Componimenti musicali* in 1623. All but two of the twenty motets that make up her collection are for one or two soprano soloists, accompanied by the so-called *basso continuo* (simple, discrete chords improvised on the organ), the characteristic musical idiom of the *stile moderno*. The vocal-instrumental combination also happens to fall within Gabriele Paleotti's old musical restrictions. A number of Vizzana's solos seem especially self-conscious in their adoption of the new, highly expressive stylistic traits associated with the novel solo idiom of the early Seicento.

Her acutely affective *Usquequo oblivisceris me in finem?* (example 1) speaks that stylistic language with quiet intensity. It offers one or more examples of all her favorite musical gestures drawn from the *stile moderno,* always calculated to heighten details of the verbal language:

> How long wilt thou forget me? Forever? How long wilt thou hide thy face
> from me? How long shall I take counsel in my soul, having sorrow in my heart

56

daily? How long will mine enemy be exalted over me? Consider and hear me, O Lord, my God. Lighten mine eyes in death, lest mine enemy say, "I have prevailed against him."

The delicately virtuosic ornamentation is in no way a gratuitous show, but conveys, on the one hand, the restless unease of the opening line and, on the other, the broader, more languid resignation of the conclusion. The transposed repetition of phrases serves a rhetorical purpose, most notably at the opening, where the restatement of the first line up a step heightens the sense of questioning and the underlying anxiety. The disjunction between phrases caused by beginning a new line of text on the chord a whole-step below the cadence of the previous phrase seems to undercut the earlier moment of repose, clearly at bars 19 to 20, and probably also at bars 5 to 6.

Two other gestures are particularly arresting. The first involves the expressively jolting juxtaposition of two major chords a third apart, obviously at bars 25 to 26 (B♭ major versus G major, where the B♭ of the first chord lurches to B♮ in the second), and possibly also at bars 6 to 7, which can successfully be harmonized C major versus E major (contrasting the G♮ of the first chord with a G♯ in the second). Such immediate harmonic contrasts momentarily trick the ear in order to arouse at one point a feeling of confusion, at another a sense of quiet wonder or transformation. More unusual, and most striking of all, is the bold leap away from the vocal D, held over in the voice, clashing sharply against the bass E♭ for expressive effect at bar 14. Vizzana's unusual resolution of such dissonances represents a notable violation of the time-honored rules of sixteenth-century compositional practice, which normally required that the upper voice resolve the clash by descending quietly, smoothly, and logically to the next lower pitch. But for Vizzana that illicit leap aptly captures the mood of momentary despair. All these same features, including the boldest of them, carefully conceived to convey the moment-to-moment implications of the text directly, forcefully, and rhetorically, reappear in greater or less profusion throughout Vizzana's collection.

How could Lucrezia Vizzana have learned this particularly modern idiom? She and all of her potential nun music teachers at Santa Cristina had left the musical world outside the cloister at a crucial time when music was beset by significant changes. When Ludovico Viadana's immensely popular *Cento concerti ecclesiastici*, that temporal landmark of the new monodic texture in sacred music (although its musical style remained more traditional), first appeared in Venice in 1602, for example, Lucrezia had already been behind the convent wall for at least four years, while her probable nun music teachers, Camilla Bombacci or Emilia Grassi, had been cloistered for at least fifteen. One wonders when and how distinctly they first heard the echoes of the newer style also reflected in Lucrezia Vizzana's own motets.

Example 1. Vizzana, *Usquequo oblivisceris me in finem?*

The church hierarchy would have discouraged any open attempts to keep up with changing musical styles, at least to judge by the Congregation of Bishops' response to a petition dated 1606 from three modern-minded singing nuns at the convent of San Biagio in nearby Cesena:

> Sister Felicita Stellini, Sister Anna, and Sister Armellina Uberti, . . . all considerably versed in music, and desirous to study how to sing some spiritual motets *alla romana,* humbly request that you permit Canon Manzini to come once or at most twice to the public parlatorios to explain and teach to the above-mentioned nuns the way they are sung, . . . in the presence of the abbess and the appointed chaperones.[1]

Example 1 (*continued*)

This petition met with the almost inevitable response when it came to out-side music teachers: "Nihil."

Yet, despite the similarly severe restrictions in Bologna, outlined in the previous chapter, the evidence suggests that music from the outside world found its way inside the walls of the more musical convents such as Santa Cristina, chiefly thanks to the nuns' own reinterpretation of the rules im-posed upon them, and thanks to their indefatigable petitioning to Rome. In 1605, for example, over the strenuous and repeated objections of Arch-bishop Alfonso Paleotti, the Congregation of Bishops finally began to relax its previously emphatic prohibition of performances by outside musicians at convent festivities in Bologna.[2] After initial success by the nuns of Corpus Domini in 1605, aided by the illustrious Count Romeo Pepoli, who had taken up their cause, the convents of Santa Caterina, San Guglielmo, San Bernardino, Sant'Orsola, Santi Vitale et Agricola, and Sant'Omobono, one after the other, all requested and received permission to bring in musical outsiders for feast days and funerals in their own external churches. By 1607, secular musicians themselves, led by Camillo Coltellini, known as "il Violino" (a prolific composer, wind player at San Petronio, and eventual head of music for the Bolognese senate), were petitioning the Congregation of Bishops for permission to sing and play on feast days and at funerals in the nuns' external churches. Despite Alfonso Paleotti's charges about Coltellini's false claims to the Congregation and the archbishop's repeated predictions of "indecencies, scandal, and secret practices," recalling the sexual paranoia of post-Tridentine diocesan pronouncements, the Congregation overruled him in April 1607.

Evidence suggests that such outside musicians also came to perform at Santa Cristina, enabling the musical nuns to experience the newer musical styles of the early Seicento. The echoes of such new music should have reached their ears only faintly: through the grated window above the high altar of the external church, through the grate in the side chapel of Santa Cristina, or through those in the chapel of the Rosary, above the church doors. Evidence reveals, however, that musical nuns found better ways not only to hear but even to see outside performers. After a pastoral visitation of 1623, it was reported that the raised organ rooms on each side of the high altar had not only windows facing each other across the high altar (fig. 11, right) but also other windows facing directly outward toward the external church. These windows were equipped with screens that were moveable and perforated in such a way that the nuns could see into the nave. Furthermore, the large grated windows of the spacious choir at the opposite end of the public church, above the doors (fig. 11, left), also had movable screens and grills, through which the whole of the external church—including the choir loft, just beyond the grates, where outside musicians might presumably have performed—could be seen.[3]

Evidence also suggests that the nuns could not only hear, but also study the scores of new music. Although the dispersal of convent libraries at the Napoleonic suppression has made it impossible to determine the nature of their music collections, it is hard to imagine that the dedicatees of the musical prints of Banchieri, Fattorini, Cesena, and Porta never set eyes on the collections dedicated to them, which they or their families probably had paid for, although the music in those collections was largely more retrospective in style. Nuns from other Bolognese convents definitely owned volumes of music at exactly this time. Suor Emilia Arali's inventory from the convent of Santa Margherita, cited above, reveals that in 1613 she owned seven books "to sing and play," and the nuns of San Guglielmo were left a trunk full of vocal music by a benefactress in 1617.[4]

Furthermore, although musicians and music teachers may have been repeatedly forbidden to visit convent parlatorios, the nuns' own parents were not. There would therefore have been little to prevent the Bolognese composer, wind player, and esteemed music teacher Alfonso Ganassi[5] from visiting his daughter donna Alfonsina, who had entered Santa Cristina around 1591, and who at her death in 1619 was remembered as an outstanding novice mistress.[6] Perhaps he presented her with music or passed along musical information. At Santa Cristina the introduction of such musical information or music books may have become especially easy. Although Lucrezia Vizzana maintained in 1623 that it was still customary to request the abbess's permission to send or receive anything from outside, several other nuns admitted that the abbess no longer always bothered to examine all incoming and outgoing mail, and that there were no regular chaperones appointed to keep watch in the parlatorios.[7]

All this suggests that in the decade after Archbishop Alfonso Paleotti's death in 1610, episcopal vigilance around the convents probably relaxed, at least temporarily. In 1616, for example, Paleotti's successor licensed Ercole Porta to visit the convent of San Michele in San Giovanni in Persiceto two or three times to teach the nuns music for Rogationtide. From a musical point of view, the most telling witness of all to this new laxity at Santa Cristina was the fact that from around 1615, at the instigation of Emilia Grassi, the current abbess, Santa Cristina actually began quietly to employ a regularly salaried, unauthorized *maestro di musica*, Ottavio Vernizzi, the organist of San Petronio.[8] The prioress, donna Sulpizia Bocchi, explained in 1622 that a regular salary was necessary because there were three organists to be taught,[9] one of whom was certainly Lucrezia Vizzana. Church authorities would promptly put a stop to that practice when it finally came to their attention in 1623. Nonetheless, despite episcopal prohibitions, ways could be found to nurture Vizzana's musical talents, at least from her mid teens onward.

Having established that for Lucrezia Vizzana, *clausura* may have been rather less restricting than episcopal prohibitions might at first seem to indicate, can one go so far as to suggest what music may actually have reached her within the cloister walls? Carlo Ginzburg managed to recover many literary sources that shaped the cosmology of the sixteenth-century miller Menocchio on the basis of his own words,[10] but given music's natural elusiveness, one can scarcely hope to rediscover Vizzana's musical world from the musical language of her own works to the same extent. Nevertheless, the musical gestures of Vizzana's motets offer interesting clues, which I would like to explore.

Example 2. Chromatically contrasting chords in Banchieri and Vernizzi

Banchieri's *Messa solenne* of 1599, dedicated to Emilia Grassi, provides a plausible starting point, for, as we have seen, Banchieri himself seems to have assumed that the nuns of Santa Cristina would perform these works. Hence, it is intriguing to encounter in the opening bars of the motet for the elevation of the host from that collection—one of those works scored only for high voices, presumably with the nuns in mind—the expressive juxtaposition of two major chords a third apart (G major versus E major) on "dulcissime Jesu" (example 2). The same gesture can be seen in Vizzana's *Usquequo oblivisceris me* (example 1, mm. 6–7, 25–26). Vizzana particularly favored this harmonic contrast, sometimes to heighten the meaning of individual words, but as often to intensify the prevailing mood. Indeed, she introduces it in at least half of her own motets, sometimes several times in a single piece.[11]

By 1599, this musical device was common enough to have entered the general language of secular music, of course, particularly for expressive ends. One does not have to look far to find it in the later madrigal repertory, for example. It is safe to suggest, however, that the madrigal repertory is more readily available to us than it would have been to Lucrezia Vizzana. In the sacred repertory of the early Seicento, which Vizzana is more likely to have known, the gesture appears somewhat less commonly. Banchieri introduced it only three times in the whole of his 1599 *Messa solenne*, for example.[12] He came to use it a little more liberally in his more diversified collections containing new-style motets for one or two soloists and basso continuo, such as *Gemelli armonici* of 1609, *Vezzo di perle musicali* of 1610, and *Nuovi pensieri ecclesiastici* of 1613 (example 2).

Of these collections, *Nuovi pensieri* strikes the listener as most self-consciously modern, both by its title and by its contents, which employ many of the modern devices likewise common in Vizzana's works. This collection also happens to include a so-called *ghirlandetta* of motets by five local organists, whom Banchieri describes as "friends and loving companions of the author." Two of the names are already familiar to us. One, Ercole Porta, dedicated his own musical collection to donna Cleria Pepoli of Santa Cristina in 1613. The other is Ottavio Vernizzi, specifically singled out by Banchieri as "the most cordial friend of the author," who, as we have seen, also served as the unauthorized *maestro di musica* at Santa Cristina, and probable teacher of Lucrezia Vizzana, during the second decade of the Seicento. In roughly the same years when Banchieri was experimenting with the modern sacred style for one or two voices and continuo, Vernizzi published or republished three collections including several works for a few soloists and continuo: *Armonia ecclesiasticorum concertuum* (1604), *Angelici concentus* (1611), and *Caelestium applausus* (1612).

Thus, we find three musical friends, all with connections to Santa Cristina, who between 1604 and 1613 were all experimenting with the *stile moderno* and exchanging motets in that style, and who were also publishing one or more collections containing such works. Of these three composers, Vernizzi can most easily be placed on the musical scene at Santa Cristina over a period of years. Interestingly enough, of the three he seems to be the one to rival Lucrezia Vizzana in his preoccupation with the expressive juxtaposition of two triads a third apart, a device that appears in about 65 percent of his few-voice motets. In 1623, the abbess of Santa Cristina remarked that as part of Vernizzi's duties, the *maestro di musica* also composed "some pieces to play, that is *canzoni* and the like."[13] It is thus quite plausible that he might have been the one to extend this musical circle to include, indirectly, his probable pupil, the talented student composer from Santa Cristina, who was trying her hand at similar works in exactly those years.

The motets of Vernizzi and his friends could not have represented the farthest boundary of Lucrezia Vizzana's musical world, however. Although all the other elements of her musical language have precedents to a greater or less extent in the new-style solo and few-voice motets of Banchieri and Vernizzi, Vizzana's most striking expressive motif, the leap away from a dissonance held over in the vocal line, seems to find no place in the sacred works of this pair of Bolognese organist/composers. In the sacred repertory in general, this striking skipwise resolution of dissonances remained much less common than the juxtaposed major chords mentioned earlier. Even Vizzana's Venetian contemporary, the "avant-gardist" Giovanni Francesco Capello (whose harmonic idiom is generally much more adventurous than hers, particularly in its extensive use of chromaticism), introduces comparable leaps from suspended dissonances in only about 12 of the more than 110 motets from his five motet publications.[14] By comparison, the device appears in 6 of the 20 motets in Vizzana's collection.

Such expressive text setting inevitably calls to mind Claudio Monteverdi, the most familiar and distinguished composer known for the introduction of untoward dissonances in his works. In Monteverdi's *Vespers,* published in 1610, there was some precedent for Lucrezia Vizzana's attempts at expressivity in the solo vocal works. These include one identical use of her favorite leap from a dissonance in the opening monodic section of *Audi coelum* (the same echo-text set by Fattorini in his motets for Santa Cristina). Another example appears at the opening of Monteverdi's five-part *Christe, adoramus te,* published by Giulio Cesare Bianchi in 1620. But even in Monteverdi's sacred works, the most intense variety of skipwise resolution of dissonant suspensions turns up only rarely, usually in moments of special textual expressivity.[15]

The more common usages of this gesture occur, not in Monteverdi's sacred works from the early Seicento, but in his madrigals, particularly those of book 4 (1603) and book 5 (1605), and in the powerful and extremely influential *Lamento d'Arianna.*[16] From the two dozen or so similar passages in these works, only a few are illustrated in example 3.

In a study of Monteverdi's influence on colleagues and pupils, Denis Arnold has suggested that the introduction into Claudio Saracini's *Seconde musiche* (1620) of transposed repetitions of text fragments for rhetorical effect and the resolution of a suspended seventh by a leap (the same expressive gestures we have observed in Vizzana's motets) reveal "the sincerest form of flattery," so much a reflection of Monteverdi's influence that they "require no comment."[17] Obviously, the question of similar possible influence becomes considerably more problematic when the imitator in question is not a noble Sienese amateur, active in the world, but a woman immured within a Bolognese convent. Could the cloistered Lucrezia Vizzana have learned this expressive language and other features of her style from Claudio Monteverdi? Could the idiom of the madrigals from his books 4 and 5 somehow have served either directly or indirectly as a source for her own dissonant leaps?

Monteverdi's work was by no means unknown to Bolognese musicians. Indeed, the irregular dissonance treatment of madrigals from his books 4 and 5, including one of those cited in example 3, drew the fire of the old-fashioned Bolognese music theorist and canon regular of San Salvatore, Giovanni Maria Artusi.[18] The year after Artusi's second assault on the modern style that Monteverdi termed the *seconda prattica*, Adriano Banchieri in his *Conclusioni nel suono dell'organo* of 1609 commented that "when the words in compositions call for breaking the rules, this must be done in order to imitate the word," and then went on to single out "the most gentle composer of music, Claudio Monteverdi . . . with regard to modern composition. His artful sentiments in truth are worthy of complete commendation, uncovering every affective part of perfect speech, diligently explained and imitated by appropriate harmony."[19]

More significant for our purposes, when Banchieri founded his musical academy, the Accademia dei Floridi, in 1614, he stipulated that the motet or sacred madrigal by Lassus or Palestrina, whose performance was required at each of the weekly musical meetings, could be replaced by "one of those madrigals by that most gentle of composers, Claudio Monteverdi, at present the most worthy Director of Music at St. Mark's Venice, which have been changed into motets by Aquilino Coppini, by request of the Most Illustrious Cardinal Federico Borromeo."[20] Thanks to Coppini, many of Monteverdi's most renowned madrigals were sanctified by replacing their original and occasionally notoriously secular Italian texts with sacred Latin words. Something that began as a madrigal was thus not necessarily beyond a nun's ken. At least some of Coppini's pious contrafacta of Monteverdi originals had in fact been conceived with nuns in mind, for the 1608 collection bore a dedication to suor Bianca Lodovica Taverna at the convent of Santa Marta in Milan.[21] Virtually all of the Monteverdi madrigals-made-motets, including all of those cited in example 3, which were thus heard at the musical gatherings of Banchieri and his friends, certainly including the likes of Ercole Porta and Ottavio Vernizzi, came from Monteverdi's experimental books 4 and 5. Not only did these works have an honored place in Banchieri's weekly academies, but their composer himself was even feted at a meeting of the group on the feast of Saint Anthony of Padua in 1620, when Monteverdi was conducted to San Michele in Bosco by Banchieri and Girolamo Giacobbi, *maestro di cappella* and colleague of Vernizzi at San Petronio.[22]

Monteverdi seems to have had ongoing personal contacts with Bologna during these years. The year before he was honored by Banchieri's academy, he had visited the city to establish his musical son, Francesco, as a law

Example 3. Leaps from suspensions in Monteverdi madrigals

student there. For two weeks in late January and early February 1619, the composer stayed with his son, who was received at the monastery of Santa Maria dei Servi, next door to the Bombacci's old parish church and only about five minutes' walk, around the corner and up the street, from Santa Cristina della Fondazza. During that time, with Ottavio Vernizzi, the nuns might well have been preparing the music for the feast of the founder of their order, Saint Romuald, celebrated at the convent on 7 February.[23] It appears that later in the year, the young Francesco Monteverdi sang as a

Example 3 (*continued*)

Dorinda, ah diro (1605)

substitute at San Petronio, where he would surely have encountered Ottavio Vernizzi in his role as organist.[24]

One can thus establish clear links between Monteverdi, Bologna, and the Banchieri/Vernizzi musical circle and demonstrate that Monteverdi's experimental madrigals from books 4 and 5 were highly esteemed in that circle, at least in Aquilino Coppini's more decorous motet versions.[25] These would have provoked fewer blushes than the madrigalian originals if they also found their way into the convent of Santa Cristina. It is very tempting to suggest that Banchieri's or Vernizzi's greatest musical gift to Lucrezia

Vizzana, who obviously could not have joined them at the Accademia dei Floridi, was not some of their own attempts at the *stile moderno,* but an introduction to the music of Claudio Monteverdi.

At this point, a less illustrious figure reappears to offer a closing link in this putative chain of influence: that third and most elusive member of our trio of Bolognese composer-organists, Ercole Porta, off in the Bolognese suburb of San Giovanni in Persiceto. In 1620, Porta published a large and typically diverse compendium entitled *Sacro convito musicale.* The works in this later collection turn out to be more self-consciously modern than Banchieri's or Vernizzi's—or, indeed, than Porta's own earlier, more tentative *stile moderno* pieces, dating from before the founding of the Accademia dei Floridi. The solos and duets reveal a boldness of harmony and flights of ornamentation that must reflect Porta's own encounters with the works of Monteverdi in the intervening years. As illustrated in example 4, in half a dozen of these motets, we find Porta's own experiments with the boldest musical gesture employed by Vizzana, the leap from a suspended dissonance.

Confirming unequivocally his debt to Monteverdi, Porta actually borrows, reworks, and resets one of Coppini's contrafacta texts in his 1620 collection:

Monteverdi/Coppini	Ercole Porta
Ure me Domine amore tuo,	Ure me Domine amore tuo
quam [*sic*] fecit amor mori,	quem [*sic*] fecit amor mori
incende me, hoc igne	incende me, hoc igne
subiice cordi meo facem tuam	subiice cordi meo face tua [*sic*]
O IESU amore tuo,	O Iesu amore tuo
liquescere me velis,	
fugiat omnis amor mei a me,	
Iam fervent mihi propter te medullae	
O IESU amore tuo,	
anima mea languet	languet anima mea
iam rapior amore tuo dulci.	iam rapior amore tuo dulci.

No such musicological "smoking gun" emerges to demonstrate unequivocally whether it was the Monteverdi madrigals made into motets by Coppini or the Monteverdi style as filtered through Ercole Porta that most directly shaped Lucrezia Vizzana's musical style. Still, as I shall show in the next chapter, the fascinating motet *Sonet vox tua in auribus cordis mei,* a kind of exordium to her collection, in which Vizzana in effect presents her musical rhetoric, although not her face, to public gaze, reads remarkably like a response to one of Porta's motets from 1620, *Surge amica mea.*

Clearly, Bolognese experiments in the *stile moderno* were not limited to the better-known musical world around San Petronio, San Pietro, and San

Example 4. Leaps from suspensions in Porta's motets

Michele in Bosco, but were also pursued discreetly behind cloister walls on via Fondazza, where they have long been forgotten. Indeed, it is particularly intriguing to discover, as we shall in chapter 4, that some of the Bolognese attempts to adapt the boldest gestures of that style for sacred use were created within the aesthetically "marginal" environment of the convent by a woman who could have experienced that style only indirectly, illicitly, and at a distance. Vizzana's motets undoubtedly reflect a broadening in convent musical practice to include both the lavish, but not especially "modern," works characteristic of the Banchieri, Cesena, and Fattorini prints dedicated to nuns at Santa Cristina near the turn of the century and the more overtly modern musical idiom for solo voices and basso continuo that came to characterize the nuns' own performances for the rest of the Seicento.

The appearance of Lucrezia Vizzana's *Componimenti musicali* early in 1623, a decade after the flurry of modern publications by Banchieri, Porta, and Vernizzi and the last of the other four collections dedicated to the musical nuns of Santa Cristina, effectively marks the end of the most musically illustrious period in the history of the convent. After 1623, although she lived for another forty years, Bologna's only publishing musical nun never again ventured into print. Whether she continued to compose is impossible to say. Still, we are lucky to be able to glimpse as much as we can of her musical world, a world that its regulators intended to be so emphatically private. On 1 January 1623, Vizzana dedicated her *Componimenti musicali* to her fellow nuns at Santa Cristina, the fifth and final such dedication they would receive. It was a fitting choice, for it was the special nature of the hidden world they shared that helped her creativity to flower in ways that would have been largely impossible for her beyond the convent walls on via Fondazza.

FOUR

The Meeting of Music, Art, and Ritual in *Componimenti musicali*

In the previous chapters, I have attempted to suggest what composers and music from beyond the convent wall may have contributed to the making of Lucrezia Vizzana's own musical style, and how she actually managed to hear that music in what had to have been challenging times for nun musicians. In the following chapters, I move away from the world outside the wall, to center Vizzana's *Componimenti musicali* within the cloister at Santa Cristina. I shall examine the relationship of her own music to those artistically rich, but turbulent, times at the convent and suggest various ways her works and other aspects of convent music and ritual may have been intended to speak to the world beyond the walls on via Fondazza. I shall also explore how her motets reflect common themes of female spirituality, some of them surprisingly old, and speculate about what we might hear of the composer's own voice in her motets.

SPONSA VERBI

"In the beginning was the Word. . . . And the Word was made Flesh and dwelt among us." These opening words from John's Gospel, which close every Catholic Mass, amid a general rustling of coats and a habitual, nervous edging toward the door, remained at the heart both of Lucrezia Vizzana's approach to artistic creation and of her Christ-centered spirituality. Daily, weekly, and yearly repetitions of Scripture, liturgy, and the words of the Church Fathers—and, if the ecclesiastical hierarchy had its way, very little else—were the rhythms that marked a nun's life. The borrowings, echoes, and resonances between the words she had begun to recite at age eight would have been richer for Vizzana than they might have been for many nuns, given that her talents were nurtured within one of the more intellectual women's houses in Bologna. Even though she probably could not match the feat of John, abbot of Saint Albans, who in 1210 could recite all 150 psalms backward, verse by verse,[1] Vizzana must have found in these words her own living vocabulary, in a way other composers, such as Ottavio Vernizzi, active both in the church and in the world, would not have done. Nuns received only a restricted repertory of verbal and intellectual stimuli, which the church hierarchy kept as limited as possible. Although, as we have seen, Santa Cristina did not quite fit the pious ideals of either Saint Romuald or the post-Tridentine hierarchy, much of Vizzana's experience of art, music, and life must have been constructed around and filtered through the words of Scripture, liturgy, and the Fathers. This *sponsa Christi* ("bride of Christ") might also well, in the words of the eleventh-century Jean de Fécamp, addressed to another nun, be called *sponsa Verbi* ("bride of the Word").[2]

The language of the texts of Vizzana's *Componimenti,* with their reality heightened by details of her musical language, reveals their connection with traditions of female spirituality, with the monastic environment at Santa Cristina, and with the cultural flowering that occurred there during the early Seicento. Vizzana takes her texts seriously, and by her music suggests she accepted what they say. Her music thus opens the path she took to her hidden spiritual world, one that has practically vanished. If we are to follow that path, to discover something of her world, in many ways so different from our own, we must take her texts and the music that clothes them as seriously as she did. In an age when musical experience has dwindled to a largely passive, indeed impassive, one, she invites, she challenges us (as, in fact, do other composers of her age) to pay more than indolent attention to the wide resonance those words retained, and to the musical gestures that capture their affective spirit and give them life. If we do not share, at least for a moment, some measure of her commitment to the serious enterprise of how music is wed to words, if we cannot take the trouble to rediscover levels of musical meaning, and indeed, textual meaning, which she had first to discover herself, we may still indifferently hear the echoes of her voice like a vaguely exotic, arcane, and archaic Muzak, but we shall not hear her speak.

More than half the texts in *Componimenti musicali* have yet to come to light in settings by other composers, or redact older texts in ways that suggest the motets were intended to have specific relevance to Vizzana's life or the spiritual life at Santa Cristina (see table 2). Some of the more elusive texts may yet turn up in the rich spiritual writings of the Church Fathers. The text of Vizzana's *Praebe mihi, amantissime Domine,* for which no liturgical use is known, reappears, for example, in virtually identical form twenty years later as the second half of *O dulcis Jesu* by the nun composer Chiara Margherita Cozzolani, published in her *Concerti sacri,* opus 2 (Venice: Vincenti, 1642).[3] Although it is not impossible that Cozzolani might have borrowed the text from Vizzana, both composers are as likely to have discovered it independently in some unidentified work of devotional literature.

It is particularly surprising, given contemporary choices for motet texts in the world, that Vizzana shows so little interest in the Song of Songs, a favorite source for "free" motets in Bologna (where more than seventy settings from before 1630 survive) and elsewhere in the early Seicento.[4] At least half a dozen of her works probably relate directly either to Vizzana's own life or to the liturgical life of Santa Cristina. As many as eight seem specifically directed toward Jesus, an unusually high percentage by comparison with publications from the San Petronio/San Michele in Bosco circle mentioned in the previous chapter, but not surprising for a community of brides of Christ. Almost as many motets appear to relate to the precarious situation in which the convent found itself when *Componimenti musicali* appeared, and which may in part have motivated its publication.

That the great majority of the unique texts can be related to various aspects of the life of the institution suggests that they may reflect a tradition of biblical *imitatio* within its walls. Several of the unique texts share common details of language or rhetorical style that could indicate the hand of a single author, or at least affinity to a single tradition. Such rhetorical wordplay would not have been out of place at Santa Cristina, which may have been among the leading Bolognese convents in the cultivation of the Latin language. At that period the most distinguished convent rhetorician seems in fact to have been Lucrezia Vizzana's aunt, the venerable Flaminia Bombacci, praised by Gasparo Bombacci for "the fluency of her tongue and pen; for, having joined to the sincerity of her circumspect eloquence the knowledge of the Latin language, she spoke beyond the ordinary capacity of her sex, and composed most learned sermons and spiritual discourses."[5] Vizzana herself may even have rivaled her aunt and probable teacher in Latin composition. Her lengthy memorial in the convent necrology records that "she was likewise so gifted in Latin and Italian speech that she won the admiration of most eloquent and learned men."[6]

"CUIUS MIHI ORGANA MODULATIS VOCIBUS CANTANT"

In the field of music, Santa Cristina had few rivals among the convents of Bologna. There is something self-conscious about the attention called to music and the frequency with which the acts of singing and playing are invoked in the motets of Vizzana's collection. It is by no means uncommon, of course, for the subject to crop up in motet texts in general, especially in those based on popular psalms such as Psalms 33, 66, 81, or 105; indeed, Vizzana herself was one of close to fifty composers from before 1650 to set the musical verses from the beginning of Psalm 107, *Paratum cor meum* (". . . I will sing and play upon the psaltery in you, my glory"), although she

TABLE 2. *Componimenti musicali* (1623)

Title	Voices	Final	(ks)	Text	Theme
1. Exsurgat Deus	S	F	(♭)	Ps. 67:1–3	invocation in war
2. Sonet vox tua in auribus cordis mei	S	C	(♭)	Song of Songs 2:14	self-presentation
3. Ave stella matutina	S	g	(♭)	antiphon, BVM	invocation of BVM amid enemies
4. O si sciret stultus mundus	S	C	(♭)	?	Sacrament
5. Domine, ne in furore	S	g	(♭)	Ps. 6:1–4	penance
6. Praebe mihi	S	g	(♭)	?	Jesus
7. Usquequo oblivisceris me infinem?	S	g	(♭)	Ps. 12:1–4	abandonment amid enemies
8. O magnum mysterium	S	g	(♭)	?	the Passion
9. Confiteantur tibi	S	G		Ps. 144:10	praise
10. Veni dulcissime Domine	S	g	(♭)	?	Sacrament
11. Omnes gentes, cantate Domino	SS	G	(♭)	?	Sacrament
12. Amo Christum, in cuius thalamum introibo	SS	F	(♭)	S. Agnes	profession, consecration
13. Omnes gentes, plaudite manibus	SS	g	(♭)	Ps. 46:1–3	rejoicing at God's victory over enemies

14. Ornaverunt faciem templi coronis aureis	SS	F	(♭)	1 Mach. 4:57–58; 2 Mach. 10:38	altar dedication?
15. Domine, quid multiplicati sunt	SS	d		Ps. 3	abandonment, invocation amid enemies
16. Paratum cor meum	SS	F	(♭)	Ps. 107:1–3 Ps. 56:8–10	Resurrection
17. Filii Syon, exultate	SS	g	(♭)	?	dream of S. Romuald?
18. O invictissima Christi martyr	SS	d	(♭)	?	S. Cristina
19. Domine, Dominus noster, quam admirabile	SSA	d		Ps. 8	Ascension?
20. Protector noster	SATB	G		?	S. Benedict, S. Romuald?

may have had a special point in mind in this case, as we shall see. But this is the only one of Vizzana's six motet texts referring to music that is not rare and probably unique. Thus, when Vizzana causes the two sopranos to conclude *O invictissima Christi martir* with the words "Ut cantare possimus Alleluia" ("that we may sing 'Alleluia' "), when the soloist of *Confiteantur tibi Domine* exhorts "cantate et psallite" ("Sing and play the psaltery"), when the sopranos sing "cuius mihi organa modulatis vocibus cantant" ("whose instruments sing to me with harmonious voices") in *Amo Christum,* or when two sopranos open another duet with the more general "Omnes gentes cantate Domino" ("Sing unto the Lord all ye people"), the composer is highlighting one of the most widely recognized artistic distinctions of the house, one that particularly set it apart among the two dozen convents of Bologna.

Comparatively few of Vizzana's motets—all for two voices—employ generalized texts of praise and exaltation based on psalms set literally dozens of times by other composers:

(13) *Omnes gentes, plaudite manibus* (Psalm 46)
(16) *Paratum cor meum* (Psalm 107/Psalm 56)
(19) *Domine Dominus noster, quam admirabile* (Psalm 8)

These motets could have served on any number of liturgical occasions of rejoicing or communal enthusiasm, either at Santa Cristina or elsewhere. The frequently less individual character of their musical settings enhances their generalized or generic character. "Subiecit populos nobis et gentes sub pedibus nostris" ("He shall subdue the people under us, and the nations under our feet") from *Omnes gentes, plaudite manibus,* for example, could effectively have trumpeted the Catholic cause during the Bohemian phase that had recently opened the Thirty Years War. *Domine Dominus noster, quam admirabile,* on the other hand, happens to be prescribed in the Camaldolese Breviary for the vigil of the Ascension. This is the scene commemorated in Ludovico Carracci's large painting installed above the high altar of the new external church in 1608. Vizzana's more weighty musical setting for two sopranos, alto, and continuo, the second most elaborate motet in her collection, suggests that it was intended for an important context. Perhaps the feast of the Ascension, Carracci's painting, or its installation on the high altar could have prompted the motet's composition.[7]

A number of Vizzana's other motets also appear to be specially conceived for particular feasts in the liturgical life of the convent. These works link up most directly to the space where the convent met the world, the external church of Santa Cristina, which during these same years underwent dramatic expansion and artistic adornment, as outlined in chapter 1. The motets of this group can plausibly be related to particular feasts in the ritual life of Santa Cristina. The most obvious example, *O invictissima Christi mar-*

tyr, is addressed to Saint Christina, who was venerated in her own chapel in the external church, and whose great stucco statue must have been installed in the first niche on the right side of the nave during these years. Vizzana's motet obviously served for the matronal festival on 10 May, the most lavish feast of the church year for the convent and the parish.[8]

The more lavish scoring of *Protector noster*, Vizzana's only work for four voices, suggests that it was intended for a significant feast.[9] Vizzana could have intended the text to honor either of the two most important saints of the Camaldolese order, Saint Benedict or Saint Romuald. Both saints' feasts (on 21 March and 7 February, respectively) were also celebrated with music, and their large stucco statues, likewise attributed to Gabriele Fiorini,[10] were installed opposite each other in the external church.

Filii Syon exultate, which directly precedes these occasional pieces, first appears to be a more generalized exaltation of saints: " . . . for this day the earth is made heaven for us, not by stars falling from heaven to earth, but by saints ascending into heaven." It could perhaps have been used for any of the saints' days named above. But the central theme of Vizzana's text recalls one of the most striking images of the Camaldolese tradition: Saint Romuald's dream of the ladder to heaven. In 1080, the Blessed Rudolph, fourth prior of Camaldoli, described how Saint Romuald had come to found the Hermitage of Camaldoli high in the Apennines:

> When he came to the region in the countryside around Arezzo, desiring to discover a suitable site, he encountered a man by the name of Maldulus, who said he had a pleasant field, located up in the mountains, where once, as he slept, he saw a ladder like the one of the patriarch Jacob, raised up so that its top almost touched the heavens, on which a host of people, resplendent and robed in white, seemed to ascend. When he heard this, the man of God, as if enlightened by a divine oracle, thereupon sought out the field, saw the place, and built the cells on that site.[11]

Over the centuries, Maldulus's vision, transformed into the "Dream of Romuald," gained a firm place in Camaldolese tradition. That this revised legend was part of the Bolognese tradition of the order is revealed by an altarpiece fragment attributed variously to the Bolognese School, Jacopo da Bologna, Jacopino, and most recently to "Pseudo-Jacopino," and tentatively dated shortly before 1340[12] (see fig. 12): Romuald dozes before a cell in an alpine landscape, while over his shoulder a troop of Camaldolese monks in white ascend a ladder, with its feet firmly planted on the spot where the hermitage stands, that barely reaches a bit of the starry heavens, peeping through the gold-leaf background. Vizzana's *Filii Syon, exultate* may well commemorate this same important moment for her order, when "earth is made heaven for us."

Could Lucrezia Vizzana have known this painting? "Romuald's Dream" is one of six fragments assumed to derive from a single altarpiece. Given the Camaldolese connection, and the fact that another fragment represents the martyrdom of Saint Christina, it has been suggested that the altarpiece may have originated at Santa Cristina della Fondazza.[13] The fact that in 1755, Giovanni Benedetto Mittarelli described a Trecento "Romuald's Dream," part of an altarpiece preserved in Sant'Andrea di Ozzano, a church governed by the nuns of Santa Cristina, strengthens the possibility that the fragment derives from the convent.[14]

The nuns are known to have donated artwork to Sant'Andrea di Ozzano and to have sold off old artworks from Sant'Andrea to help cover expenses at the church.[15] It is not impossible that the altarpiece might also have been transferred from Santa Cristina della Fondazza to Sant'Andrea di Ozzano when the nuns in Bologna had no further need of it. And Lucrezia Vizzana's motet *Filii Syon*, which may well reflect the old Camaldolese legend of Saint Romuald's dream, might in fact have been influenced by this particular image.

Vizzana's *Ornaverunt faciem templi* sets a responsory text for October with the characteristic musical shape ABCB.[16] In spite of this, and despite the fact that the warlike character of the concluding verse of this commonly set text raises the possibility of another generic Thirty Years War piece similar to *Omnes gentes, plaudite manibus*, the opening verses suggest that the motet might have been prompted by the intense flurry of building and decoration in the external church of Santa Cristina during Lucrezia Vizzana's most musically creative years:

> Ornaverunt faciem templi coronis aureis et dedicaverunt altare Domino; et facta est lætitia magna in populo. In himnis et confessionibus benedicebant Dominum qui magna fecit in Israel et victoriam dedit illi Dominus et facta est lætitia magna in populo.

> They decorated the front of the temple with wreaths of gold and dedicated the altar to the Lord, and there was great rejoicing among the people. With hymns and confessions they blessed the Lord, who did great things in Israel, and the Lord gave the victory to her. And there was great rejoicing among the people.

Vizzana's *Ornaverunt faciem templi* could have been heard any number of times in the course of the twenty years before its publication, during which the church of Santa Cristina was transformed into one of Bologna's most artistically distinguished convent churches.

Amo Christum must be connected to the most lavish and rarest of all musical ceremonies at Santa Cristina, the ritual consecration of virgins. The opening segment of its text, borrowed from a responsory for the nativity of Saint Agnes, already suggests a nun's consecration:

> Amo Christum in cuius thalamum introibo, cuius Mater virgo est, cuius pater feminam nescit, cuius mihi organa modulatis vocibus cantant, quem cum

amavero casta sum, cum tetigero munda sum, eum accepero virgo sum; annulo suo subarrhavit me, et immensis monilibus ornavit me, et tanquam sponsam decoravit me corona. Alleluia.

I love Christ, whose bedchamber I shall enter, whose mother is a virgin, whose
father knows not woman, whose instruments sing to me with harmonious
voices, whom when I shall have loved I shall be chaste, when I shall have
touched I shall be clean, when I shall have received him I shall be a virgin;
with his ring he has betrothed me, and adorned me with countless gems, and
with a crown he has adorned me as a spouse. Alleluia.

This possibility is clearly confirmed by the additions to the end of this old
responsory text. "Et immensis monilibus ornavit me" concludes the antiphon sung by a consacree after receiving her crown, according to the Roman pontifical. "Annulo suo subarrhavit me" and "tanquam sponsam decoravit me corona" both appear in the antiphon she sings with her hand
raised high, to display the ring she has just received.

It is especially intriguing to discover, however, that the entire opening
segment of Vizzana's text, which had no official place in the Roman consecration rite of her time, had been sung by English nuns at their consecrations since the twelfth century and continued to find a place in the more
insular English consecration rite down to the Reformation.[17] Lucrezia Vizzana could, of course, simply have gathered all the phrases of her composite
motet text from the passion of Saint Agnes, from which they had also found
their way into nuns' consecration rites. It is possible, however, that her
motet still echoes a more ancient tradition, some of whose elements had
never been incorporated into the Roman pontifical first published in 1485,
and therefore had vanished from general continental use.

The lavish consecration rite at Santa Cristina, with music performed by
the nuns, who were not only heard but actually seen in the external church,
had no rivals in Bologna until well into the eighteenth century, when in
1739 the convent of Santa Margherita adopted the same practice.[18] In the
course of the Seicento, the consecration took on special political significance, as we shall see in chapters 10 and 11. This splendid rite of passage,
which had to have been completed before a nun at Santa Cristina became
eligible for high convent office, was celebrated only twice during the first
two decades of the seventeenth century, in years that can be established
thanks to the Vizzana sisters. As I mentioned in chapter 1, in March 1607,
Isabetta and Lucrezia Vizzana petitioned the Sacred Congregation of Bishops and Regulars in Rome for permission to participate in the first enactment of this lavish ceremony since 1599, despite the fact that neither had
reached the requisite age of twenty-five. Isabetta's request was granted, but
despite the padding of her age by two years (she claimed to be eighteen),
Lucrezia was still deemed too young. Following the customary procedure,
Lucrezia refused to take no for an answer and promptly petitioned again,

this time claiming that the consecration "is nothing else but a ceremony to confirm one's profession," which she had made previously. But the Sacred Congregation remained adamant, and Lucrezia was left to languish for a time as the only unconsecrated nun in the convent.

She had to wait six more years before another consecration was planned for late in 1613. Once again she had to petition the Congregation of Bishops for special permission to participate, however, since she was still twenty-two months short of twenty-five. Once again her request was initially denied. By now, however, Lucrezia was wiser in the ways of the ecclesiastical world. She repetitioned almost immediately, but with the intercession of Cardinal Antonio Zapata, archbishop of Burgos, a fact duly noted by the Sacred Congregation, which on 15 October 1613 finally agreed to grant her dispensation.[19] We can thus be almost certain that the motet *Amo Christum* was first heard at donna Lucrezia Orsina Vizzana's consecration in 1613, when she stepped for a few hours into the world outside the convent wall for the last time.

"QUASI CITHARE CITHARIZANTIUM" I

Even if she did not actually know that she was the first Bolognese nun to publish her works, Lucrezia Vizzana must have had an inkling of the singular nature of her musical talents and of her act of publication. Only ten other women in Italy, four or five of them nuns, are known to have ventured into print by 1623.[20] The second motet in Vizzana's collection, *Sonet vox tua in auribus cordis mei,* the first to mention music, centers not upon the convent choir but upon the composer herself as artist (see example 5). The placement of pieces of music in sixteenth- and seventeenth-century published collections could make a point, and it is difficult not to imagine that at some stage *Sonet vox tua* was conceived of as the opening number. For in this exordium the poet-singer self-consciously invokes the source and inspiration of her art:

> Sonet vox tua in auribus cordis mei, amabilissime Jesu, et abundantia plenitudinis gratiæ tuæ superet abundantiam peccatorum meorum. Tunc enim cantabo, exsultabo, iubilabo, et psalmum dicam iubilationis et laetitiæ. Et erit vox mea quasi cithare citharizantium et eloquium meum dulce super mel et favum.

> Let your voice sound in the ears of my heart, most beloved Jesus, and may the abundance of your grace overcome the abundance of my sins. Then truly I will sing, I will exult, I will rejoice, I will recite a psalm of jubilation and rejoicing. And my voice will be like the striking of the kithara and my speech sweeter than honey and the honeycomb.

It is as if Vizzana were answering the call of a versicle recited in late July, *Attende fili mi sapientiam meam, et ad eloquium meum inclina aurem tuam*

("Hearken my children to my wisdom, and turn your ear to my speech").[21] But various phrases from Vizzana's text would also have had a more familiar ring in Bologna around 1623, and might derive from a number of possible musical sources. Closest of all textually—intriguingly close—is a motet from Giacomo Finetti's *Corona Mariæ*, published in 1622: "Sonet vox tua in auribus meis Beate Pater Francisce, quia vox tua dulcis et eloquia tua super mel et favum" ("Let your voice sound in my ears, Blessed Father Francis, for your voice is sweet and your words sweeter than honey and the honeycomb").[22] But Finetti's print had appeared so shortly before Vizzana's own collection that it probably did not find its way inside Santa Cristina in time to influence her.[23]

The phrase "sonet vox tua in auribus meis" had appeared closer to home in the duet *Repleatur os tuum benedictum laude,* published in 1604 by Ottavio Vernizzi, who as we have seen was the unauthorized *maestro di musica* at Santa Cristina and a very likely influence on Vizzana's musical development. This version, sharing the tag "sonet vox tua," is directed to the Blessed Virgin:

> Repleatur os tuum benedictum laude alleluia. Suavi melodia decanta illi voce mea alleluia. Amorem tuum Virgo Virginum desidero. Ut sonet vox tua in auribus meis alleluia.
>
> Let your beloved mouth be filled with praise, alleluia. Sing unto her, my voice, in sweet melody, alleluia. Virgin of virgins, I desire your love, that your voice may sound in my ears, alleluia.

Vizzana's own text parallels Vernizzi's in its focus upon the active first-person singer. In Vizzana's case, the Blessed Virgin is displaced, however. Vizzana calls on neither the Virgin nor the conventional poet's lyre nor the figure of Orpheus, commonly invoked in the world, but on Jesus, who from the time of Clement of Alexandria down to her own day represented the new Orpheus, the singer of the "new song" of Christianity.[24] The speaker in Vizzana's text becomes the singer/poet as *sponsa Christi* ("bride of Christ"), who demands to hear the voice of her *own* beloved, Jesus. Then, inspired by the abundance of Christ's grace, her own voice will be heard.

Vizzana's concluding words, "Dulce super mel et favum," are found in Finetti's motet as well as in another by Adriano Banchieri, *Spiritus meus super mel et favum* (1610), arranged from Ecclesiasticus 24:27, "Spiritus enim meus super melle dulcis et hereditas mea super mel et favum" ("For my spirit is sweeter than honey and mine inheritance is sweeter than honey and the honeycomb"). More important, Vizzana surely knew the other most direct scriptural model for this phrase, Psalm 18:10–11, "iudicia Domini ... dulciora super mel et favum" ("the Lord's judgments are sweeter than honey and the honeycomb"), which she recited in chapel at least once a week.

Example 5. Vizzana, *Sonet vox tua in auribus cordis mei*

Example 5 (*continued*)

In the context of her motet and particularly of the view of herself she presents, the choice of words resonates most in sympathy with Psalm 118:103, "quam dulcia faucibus meis eloquia tua super mel ori meo" ("how sweet are thy words unto my taste! yea, sweeter than honey to my mouth"), or with the intensely rich language of a responsory from the common of a martyr for paschal time, which draws upon the same verse:

> De ore prudentis processit mel, alleluia; dulcedo mellis est in lingua eius, alleluia. Favus distillans labia eius, alleluia, alleluia. Quam dulcia faucibus meis eloquia tua super mel ori meo.

> Honey comes out of the mouth of the wise, alleluia; the sweetness of honey is on his tongue, alleluia; his lips like the dripping honeycomb, alleluia, alleluia. How sweet are thy words unto my taste, yea, sweeter than honey to my mouth.[25]

A musician such as Vizzana, literate in Latin, might have heard in such words the added play on *mellis* ("of honey") versus *melos* ("song"). And it is *melos,* of course, that will make Vizzana's own *eloquium* sweeter than honey and the honeycomb—and that makes it so singular.

In the emphasis upon *eloquium,* saved for the conclusion of her motet, Vizzana employs, not the plural, which might have been taken simply to mean "words," but the singular ("the word," "speech," "rhetorical eloquence"). Another motet by Vernizzi might have offered some inspiration:

> Jucundum sit Iesu eloquium meum. Ego vero in Domine Iesu delectabor alleluia. Bonus est Iesus animae quærenti illum alleluia. Filiae Hierusalem annuntiate Iesu dilecto meo quia amore langueo.

> May my word be pleasing unto Jesus. Truly, I shall delight in the Lord Jesus, alleluia. Jesus is good to the soul seeking after him, alleluia. Daughters of Jerusalem, proclaim it to my beloved Jesus that I am languishing with love.

Despite its opening, Vernizzi's text ultimately rings the changes on a much more common theme, borrowed from the Song of Songs. In this case, however, Vizzana did not need stimulus from other composers because she had plenty of in-house textual inspiration. She may simply have remembered the phrase from Song of Songs 4:3, "et eloquium tuum dulce."

With one or more of these texts possibly in her mind's ear, Vizzana's strategy at the conclusion to this motet becomes more intriguing. By saving *eloquium* for the end, Vizzana leaves her audience on a theme that would have continued to resonate with special meaning for a self-conscious, educated early modern woman—particularly a cloistered one. Rhetoric and the art of oratory had long been regarded as useless for women, if not actually dangerous. Francesco Barbaro in *De re uxoria* (1416) affirmed more than once that a woman's eloquence was evident in her silence:

Women should believe that they have achieved the glory of eloquence if they honor themselves with the outstanding ornament of silence. Neither the applause of a declamatory play nor the glory and adoration of an assembly is required of them, but all that is desired of them is eloquent, well-considered and dignified silence.

Nicolò Barbo expresses the reasons for this attitude clearly, succinctly, and in words that are particularly revealing and relevant: "An eloquent woman is never chaste."[26]

In Vizzana's own day, Thomas Coryat strikingly affirmed Barbo's blunt assessment, linking music and rhetoric as dangerous enticements of Venice's courtesans, in rhetoric heavily larded with innuendo of his own:

Moreover shee will endevour to enchaunt thee partly with her melodious notes that shee warbles out upon her lute, which shee fingers with as laudable a stroake as many men that are excellent professors in the noble science of Musicke; and partly with that heart-tempting harmony of her voice. Also thou wilt finde the Venetian Cortezan (if she be a selected woman indeede) a good Rhetorician, and a most elegant discourser, so that if shee cannot move thee with all these foresaid delights, shee will assay thy constancy with her Rhetorical tongue.[27]

These views were especially important for women religious. In the words of a mid-fifteenth-century English translation of Saint Ælred of Rievaulx's guide for anchoresses, *De institutione inclusarum* (1160–62), for example, chastity required the avoidance of "the conversacion of the world," which dilutes the relationship with God.[28] Such an equation of chastity with silence found emphatic reinforcement four centuries later in the post-Tridentine emphasis on the separation and silence of *clausura*.

In such a climate, at a time when the sense of hearing had only recently yielded to the sense of sight as the second most important provocation of lust in confessors' manuals (touch was first),[29] and only shortly after Archbishop Ludovico Ludovisi's resurrected bans on convent music, Lucrezia Vizzana's publication of her motets might have seemed an especially audacious act for a cloistered woman in Bologna. Vizzana's music not only breached the convent wall when it sounded from the choir lofts of Santa Cristina. Now, in printed form, her motets could scale the walls of Bologna itself.

As Vizzana would have recognized, the comparatively outspoken gestures of her musical language were rhetorical, reaching out, at times quite emphatically, to the forum of that outside world. She might have realized that some of her musical idioms, flying in the face of time-honored rules of counterpoint, belonged to a new musico-rhetorical style that her compatriot the canon regular of San Salvatore, Giovanni Maria Artusi, had previously called, in strongly gendered language, "a painted whore," whose modulations Artusi had described as "unnatural acts," and whose pieces he had implied were monstrous births.[30]

Like other religious women bold enough to make themselves heard, Vizzana adopts a time-honored ploy. She begins her motet text with a textual conceit partly of her own making, but also linked to older traditions of Christian spirituality. Like earlier writers, she draws upon the common biblical metaphor of the heart, both as the internal center of what is most defining and motivating (cf. Proverbs 23:7, "For as he thinketh in his heart so is he") and as the seat of vital forces that come specifically from within, rather than from without.[31] Vizzana's possible models, such as Saint Augustine, Saint Gregory, and Jean de Fécamp, had savored the words of Scripture with the *palatum cordis* ("the palate of the heart") or *in ore cordis* ("in the mouth of the heart"), and thirteenth-century Blessed Angela of Foligno had spoken of beholding the crucified Jesus "as much with the eyes of my heart as with those of my body."[32] Vizzana the musician appropriately calls upon her heavenly spouse to let his voice "sound in the ears of my heart." Vizzana implies that the source of her utterance is not from without—not from the world beyond the wall. Like female mystics of previous centuries, she also implies that her authorization to speak, and to speak rhetorically, thus derives from that divine inner voice, which sanctifies it.

Vizzana's trumpetlike musical setting of these opening words, in which the instrumental bass creates a fanfare of thirds, may be a relatively conventional musical metaphor for words such as *sonare*—although nothing very similar is adopted by Giacomo Finetti, Ottavio Vernizzi, Ercole Porta, or Francesco Barnaba Milleville in their settings of *Sonet vox tua*.[33] But for Vizzana it also recalls the time-honored view of prophets and mystics as trumpets or other wind instruments of God, a tradition stretching from Athenagoras ("the Spirit making use of them as a flautist might play upon his flute") to Hildegard of Bingen (the mystic is like a trumpet that "merely produces sounds but does not cause them; someone else blows into it, so that it will produce sound") to Mother Juana de la Cruz (God "spoke in an audible voice, as when the musician plays, it is not his own voice that sounds, but the voice of the flute or trumpet by means of the breath that he blows through it").[34] The fact that when the singer enters in bar 2 of Vizzana's motet, she is firmly grounded in the bass, which she dutifully—and rather obviously—follows in exact imitation two octaves higher for the whole of the fanfare, suggests that Vizzana, too, was responding to that tradition, making the poet/singer the passive instrument of the divine, embodied in the bass. It is significant, however, that the trumpet had also long represented a traditional symbol for preaching.[35] Vizzana's motets, particularly when performed in the ritualized context of the service, could have taken on the character of that other specifically male clerical occupation.

After this initial empowerment from within, Vizzana's response becomes both personal and affirmative: "Tunc enim cantabo, exsultabo, iubilabo, et psalmum dicam iubilationis et laetitiæ." Here, once again, the singer regularly follows the bass in even more blatant imitative entries. At the conclusion the words "Erit vox mea" echo the opening "Sonet vox tua," as donna Lucrezia's own voice makes audible that inner voice, and becomes "quasi cithare citharizantium" ("like the striking of the kithara").

This characterization, "quasi cithare citharizantium," offers a further clue to what may have been in the nun composer's mind and once again illuminates her striking relationship to an older tradition. The prophet or mystic as a stringed instrument was as venerable a concept as the trumpet metaphor that may lie behind the opening of Vizzana's motet. In his study of the sixteenth-century Spanish mystic Mother Juana de la Cruz, who had referred to herself in similar terms as the "guitar of God," Ronald Surtz cites examples of the metaphor from Hippolytus's *Treatise on Christ and Antichrist* (c. 200 A.D.) and onward to the sixteenth century. Clement of Alexandria had likewise taken up the image:

> Let the cithara be taken to mean the mouth, played by the Spirit as if by a plectrum. . . . "Praise him on strings and the instrument" refers to our body as an instrument and its sinews as strings from which it derives its harmonious tension, and when strummed by the Spirit it gives off human notes.

or

> The cithara, taken allegorically by the psalmist, would be according . . . to its second [meaning] those who continuously pluck . . . their souls under the musical direction of the Lord. And if the people who are saved are said to be the cithara, it is because they are heard to give honor musically through the inspiration of the Word and the knowledge of God, as they are played for faith by the Word.[36]

The latter remark is especially apt for Vizzana, empowered "through the inspiration of the Word and the knowledge of God." A comment by Hildegard of Bingen is particularly interesting, and not only because it nearly employs Vizzana's *citharizandium.* Comparing the "open" female body to the kithara, Hildegard plays upon the very permeability attributed to women and traditionally viewed as a danger: "ipsae apertae sunt ut lignum, in quo chordae ad citharizandum positae sunt, et quia etiam fenestrales et ventosae [sunt]"[37] ("they [women] are open like the wood, in which the strings are positioned for plucking, and also because they are also like windows and airy" [i.e., vain, light]). It is especially intriguing to find this old tradition apparently still alive and well in seventeenth-century Bologna.

It is also possible that Vizzana came to *cithare citharizantium* via a commentator of this same tradition, or that she found this particular word by

herself in scripture. The unusual *citharizantium* appears only once in the
Vulgate, in Apocalypse 14:2, where Saint John speaks of a voice:

> Audivi vocem de caelo tamquam vocem aquarum multarum et tamquam vo-
> cem tonitrui magni et vocem quam audivi sicut citharoedorium citharizan-
> tium in citharis suis.

> And I heard a voice from heaven, like the voice of rushing waters, and like
> the voice of great thunder; and the voice I heard was like the kithara playing
> of singers upon their kitharas.

The first dozen words—not, however, including *citharizantium*—might also
have been familiar to Vizzana as a responsory for the first few Sundays after
Easter.[38]

In this case, however, we can be almost certain where she heard the
word: in Giovanni Battista Cesena's *Compieta con letanie,* dedicated to the
nuns of Santa Cristina. The text of the motet *Cantabant sancti canticum
novum* from Cesena's collection is a cento based primarily on Revelation
14:2 and 3:

> Cantabant sancti canticum novum, alleluia; ante sedem Dei et Agni, alleluia;
> et resonabat terra in voces illorum, alleluia. Et audivi voces illorum sicut citha-
> redorum citharizantium in citharis suis. Alleluia.

> The saints were singing a new song, alleluia, before the throne of God and
> the Lamb, alleluia, and the earth resounded with their voices, alleluia. And I
> heard their voices like the kithara playing of singers upon their kitharas. Al-
> leluia.

Once again the composite text seems remarkably apt for the dedicatees of
Cesena's collection. His motet text begins with a responsory for matins on
the feast of Holy Innocents, whose liturgy is especially rich in texts from
Revelation. Holy Innocents nowhere prescribes the *citharedorum citharizantium* verse, however, which shifts the focus of Cesena's text to the acts of
singing and playing, for which the nuns were renowned. Lucrezia Vizzana
must have found especially sympathetic resonance in Cesena's motet. Not
only does her own inner voice parallel the voice Saint John heard from
heaven, but the nature of the music created through that voice, in the novel
stile moderno, also happens to resemble the accompanied solo singing implied by John's words.[39] The doubly creative act of composer's mind/heart
and singer's voice/body is sanctified.

If Vizzana borrowed *citharizantium* from verse 2, the implications of the
subsequent Apocalypse verses regarding the music John had heard, partly
quoted by Cesena, and all contained in the Holy Innocents liturgy, could
scarcely have escaped her:

3   *et cantabant quasi canticum novum* ante sedem et ante quattuor animalia et seniores et nemo poterat discere canticum nisi illa centum quadraginta quattuor milia qui empti sunt de terra
4   *hii sunt qui cum mulieribus non sunt coinquinati virgines enim sunt*
      hii qui sequuntur agnum quocumque abierit
      hii empti sunt ex hominibus primitiae Deo et agno
5   *et in ore ipsorum non est inventum mendacium sine macula sunt.*

3   *And they sang as it were a new song* before the throne, and before the four beasts and the elders; and no one could learn the song but the hundred forty-four thousand, who were ransomed from the earth.
4   *These are they who were not defiled with women; for they are virgins.* These are they who follow the Lamb wherever he goes. These were ransomed from among men, the firstfruits for God and for the Lamb.
5   *And in their mouth no falsehood was found; they are without stain.*

Although Vizzana's *Componimenti musicali* appeared some twenty years after Giulio Caccini's self-consciously titled secular collection in the modern style, *Le nuove musiche* (The New Musics), in the context of early Seicento Bolognese sacred music and the musical life in the convents of the city, her motets in the *stile moderno* could be heard as "quasi canticum novum" ("as it were, a new song").

This passage from Revelation, which Vizzana would have recited at least every 28 December, the feast of Holy Innocents, also offered further affirmation of Vizzana's musical eloquence and of the convent singers who sang her works, in the face of abiding suspicion of female eloquence and, within the Bolognese diocesan hierarchy, of convent music and convent singers. Her songs had been sung from within a "new Jerusalem," an image associated in her time, as Gabriella Zarri has demonstrated, with the convents of Bologna. Indeed, this connection was articulated quite emphatically at Santa Cristina as late as 1711, when, at the consecration of eight nuns, a rite traditionally known for the nuns' singing, the church was actually described, borrowing from Saint John, as the new Jerusalem:

> And it appeared as a new Jerusalem, as John saw in the Apocalypse at the moment when he wrote, "I saw the holy city, new Jerusalem, coming down from God out of heaven, prepared as a bride adorned for her husband."[40]

In comparison with the apocalyptic singers, those of this new Jerusalem, whether in 1623 or 1711, "were not defiled . . .; they are virgins . . . and in their mouth no falsehood is found, and they are without stain," words echoed toward the end of the consecration rite at Santa Cristina, which ritually reaffirmed the special status of the sacred virgins.

Finally, Vizzana's *Sonet vox tua* may take on special meaning as her response to Song of Songs 2:14. There would have been special reasons why the first and only musical nun in early seventeenth-century Bologna to venture into print would be drawn to the whole of the verse from the Song of Songs where the phrase "Sonet vox tua" appears:

Columba mea in foraminibus petræ in caverna maceriæ ostende mihi faciem tuam *sonet vox tua in auribus meis vox enim tua dulcis* et facies tua decora.

O my dove, in the clefts of the rock, in the hollow of the walls, show your face to me, *let your voice sound in my ears, for your voice is sweet* and your face is fair.

It is certainly reasonable to assume that she also knew the portion of the verse that appears before the phrase she actually quotes ("Sonet vox tua," etc.). Cantica 2:14 in its entirety seems not to have had a liturgical use in a context Vizzana is likely to have known. But its second half is prescribed as the collect for the feast of Saint Scholastica, sister of Saint Benedict and the first Benedictine nun, in the seventeenth-century Cassinese Benedictine breviary.[41] At Santa Cristina, the feast of Saint Scholastica ranked among the "other minor feasts," when "about thirty masses" were celebrated.[42]

But the whole of Cantica 2:14 had been set to music by Ercole Porta as a motet for two sopranos and basso continuo, *Surge amica mea speciosa mea,* in his *Sacro convito musicale.* This collection, which appeared just two years before Vizzana's, is among those most likely to have influenced Vizzana in matters of musical style, as I suggested in the previous chapter. Porta's text runs:

Surge, amica mea speciosa mea et veni, columba mea in foraminibus petræ, in caverna maceriæ. Ostende mihi faciem tuam, sonet vox tua in auribus meis. Vox enim tua dulcis et facies tua decora.

Arise, my beloved, my fair one, and come away. O my dove, in the clefts of the rocks, in the hollow of the wall, show your face to me, let your voice sound in my ears, for your voice is sweet and your face is fair.

Vizzana's motet offers a ringing response to the first half of verse 14, and perhaps to Porta's motet, which could even have been conceived with nuns in mind. Indeed, in 1610 the composer Giovanni Paolo Cima clearly felt the textual conceit of these verses from the Song of Songs appropriate for nuns, for he dedicated his own setting of *Surge propera amica mea* to the convent singer Paola Ortensia Serbellona of San Vicenzo in Milan.[43] Vizzana's own musical rhetoric reaches out to the world, as if in answer to Porta's call, while the singers of Santa Cristina present the words in an idiom, not merely sweet, but sweeter than honey and the honeycomb. But the nuns' faces will remain unseen, as they sing, like the dove of Cantica 2:14, hidden "in the clefts of the rock, within the hollow of the walls."

Since Saint Bernard of Clairvaux's sermons on the Song of Songs, the dove "in the clefts of the rock, within the hollow of the walls" had also become a symbol of the soul harbored within the wounds of Christ. As

Robert Kendrick has observed, the tradition not only remained alive in the early Seicento, but its relationship to music was articulated by Giovanbattista Marino in 1613:

> And as the voice is the instrument that reveals and makes public the inward conceit of the soul, so Christ is the means by which the Father's will is made known to us. . . . And finally, if Echo lives in the hollows of the rocks and within the depths of the grottos, behold the hollowed rock: *petra autem erat Christus* ["indeed, the rock was Christ"]; behold the deep caverns: *in foraminibus petrae et in caverna maceriae* ["in the clefts of the rock, in the hollow of the walls"].[44]

The words and music of several motets by Lucrezia Vizzana suggest that she, too, was touched by that tradition. The following chapter examines how Vizzana's music reveals her relationship to the Heavenly Bridegroom.

FIVE

Vizzana's Themes of Personal Piety
"O sweetness of the Godhead!"

The subject given pride of place in *Componimenti musicali,* especially in the opening section of solo motets, is Jesus, who figures in numbers 2, 4, 6, 8, and 10, as well as in the first two duets, 11–12, and possibly also in numbers 15 and 16. These also represent the motets in which the individual hand of the poet may be most readily apparent, for no direct models have come to light for the texts of numbers 4, 6, 8, 10, and 11, while numbers 2, 12, and 16 rework scriptural or liturgical phrases in significant ways. It should come as no surprise that Jesus as mediator/redeemer and spouse, present in the Sacrament or on the cross, should eclipse all other themes, given his special relationship to his chosen brides, a relationship reinforced from both sides of the convent wall.

Lucrezia Vizzana's musical preoccupation with Jesus in the Sacrament, featured particularly in *O si sciret stultus mundus, Veni dulcissime Domine,* and *Omnes gentes, cantate Domino,* resonates with a primary theme of post-Tridentine art: Christ's presence in the Sacrament, a theme particularly objectionable to Protestants, and a topic debated extensively at Trent. In this Vizzana is thus closely in touch with her time.[1] But Vizzana's preoccupation may also reflect the influence of her aunt, Flaminia Bombacci, who was especially devoted to the Sacrament. According to Gasparo Bombacci, donna Flaminia had written "a most beautiful discourse in honor of the most holy Sacrament," and as abbess she inspired among almost all the nuns a renewed and heightened devotion to the Eucharist. In 1622, donna Adeodata Leoni informed pastoral visitors that "at the present time they [the nuns] frequent the Sacraments more than they ever have done."[2]

Omnes gentes, cantate Domino (see example 6) is more ritualistic and less directly personal than the other Jesus motets, and its text does not articulate its eucharistic theme until a third of the way through the piece. It is thus strictly through her musical setting of the opening that the composer man-

Example 6. Vizzana, *Omnes gentes, cantate Domino*

ages to convey the heightened significance of the ritual act only revealed
later in the words. Any musically literate early-seventeenth-century listener
who took the trouble to listen carefully would have recognized immediately
from the music that enlivened the generic and rather neutral words *omnes
gentes* that Vizzana intended to convey the extraordinary. For her opening
she chooses an affective musical language that plays upon the strongly directed g-f♯-g of the bass versus the a-b♭-a pattern in both sopranos, all urgently working to resolve their half-steps either up or down. These strongly
directed melodic patterns point up from the outset the central sacramental
preoccupation of the work, although the piece otherwise remains more
coolly ceremonial in tone. From a noncommittal opening fragment of text
that belies the sacramental subject to come, Vizzana thus creates an affec-

Example 7. Vizzana, *Omnes gentes, plaudite manibus*

tive musical image that speaks to the listener on a level beyond its words. It usefully contrasts with the language of the musically more neutral motet *Omnes gentes, plaudite manibus* (example 7), whose opening words are largely identical, but which lacks the eucharistic theme. Instead, *Omnes gentes, cantate Domino* reflects the same spirit as the more overtly personal Jesus motet, *Praebe mihi, amantissime Domine.*

Both *Veni dulcissime Domine* and *O si sciret stultus mundus,* on the other hand, take up the considerably more individual expressions of the eucharistic theme, both in text and music, only hinted at in the opening music of *Omnes gentes, cantate.* The text of *Veni dulcissime Domine,* "Veni dulcissime Domine . . . Veni Hostia immaculata . . . Veni ieiuntium cibus . . ." ("Come, sweetest Lord, come immaculate sacrificial victim, come bread of fasting") suggests that it may have been conceived as an elevation motet, welcoming and commemorating the miracle of Christ become flesh, so odious to much of the Protestant north. *O si sciret* (no. 4), the first direct exposition of the eucharistic theme in the collection as a whole, and the most "artificial," expresses a longing for the world's illumination, but chiefly for Christ's flesh in the Sacrament of the altar. It also happens to be juxtaposed with the only other overtly poetic, rhymed text in the collection, *Ave stella matutina* (no. 3). Since *O si sciret* has come to light in none of the standard compendia of medieval hymn texts, it could be that Vizzana was encouraging comparison between Peter the Venerable's time-honored hymn to the Virgin *Ave stella matutina* and a hymn to the body of Christ she had actually written herself (see example 8).[3]

O si sciret stultus mundus
Cibus quantus sit iucundus
Carnes mei Domini
Fatigatus non sederet
Panem sanctum manducaret
Cum fervore fervido.
Quaeret panem. Vinum mixtum
Aqua, Jesum Christum,
Non videtur quaerere.
Quaerat ergo quidquid placet.
Meum cor solum delectet
Amor Jesu quaerere.

Oh, if the foolish world knew
What delightful nourishment
The flesh of my Lord is,
Though weary, it [the world] would not sit idle,
But it would eat the holy bread
With burning ardor.
It seeks [earthly] bread. The wine mixed
With water, Jesus Christ,
It seems not to seek.
Let it therefore seek whatever pleases.
Let my heart only delight
In seeking the love of Jesus.

Even if the words are not her own, from its opening notes, Vizzana's music illuminates the text in her most extraordinarily self-conscious rhetorical manner. The very first musical gesture is Vizzana's most extreme: an unorthodox skipwise leap from the voice's opening suspension; then the accompanying bass refuses to descend predictably down a step to C, as it should and as the listener expects, but instead immediately leaps upward to f♯, almost colliding with an f♮ that the soprano has barely abandoned just an eighth-note earlier. After launching itself upward through an octave run, the voice continues with a transposed repetition of its opening unorthodox

Example 8. Vizzana, *O si sciret stultus mundus*

Example 8 *(continued)*

leap from a suspended seventh. This double statement of a melodic gesture usually associated with anguish or languishing for the absent object of desire, combined with its unorthodox, unpredictable bass, makes explicit a longing beyond the bounds of meaning implicit in the opening words alone, "Oh, if the foolish world knew."

The object of such intense desire becomes immediately apparent at the beginning of the second line: Vizzana's favorite direct juxtaposition of two major chords (B♭ versus D, contrasting an f♮ and an f♯ in adjoining sonorities) shows at once that this *cibus* is no ordinary food. This harmonic transformation, which in Vizzana's other works underlines various sorts of physical or spiritual transformation, becomes a momentary symbol for the miracle of transubstantiation, Christ becoming fleshly food, in anticipation of the *Carnes mei Domini,* the next line. The plethora of urgently yearning half-steps in both voice and bass at "cibus quantus sit jucundus" likewise hinting at pleasures of great intensity, illustrate how this gesture associated with secular longing could be sanctified. As the musical setting continues its detailed, moment-to-moment commentary on the text, the words linked most intimately to Jesus as heavenly food and physical body stand out most emphatically. After busy scrambling in eighth-notes for "Fatigatus non sederet / Panem sanctum," the voice pauses abruptly for three beats near the top of the range at *manducaret,* a moment of profound stillness before launching into two and a half bars of ecstatic rapture, unparalleled in the piece up to this point. Vizzana's notable treatment of the word *manducaret,* meaning literally "would chew," thus reflects the centuries-old emphasis in female spirituality upon the very physicality of Christ's real presence, expressed earlier in terms such as "eating God" by Mechtild of Magdeburg, or experienced as tasting and feeling Christ's flesh in the mouth just by reciting *Verbum caro factum est* (John 1:14), as did Ida of Louvain, who went literally mad for the Sacrament and had to be chained up. The shift from one note per syllable to the ecstatic melisma on *manducaret* illustrates Vizzana's desire to convey the possibility of being caught up by the Eucharist into affectivity, as observed by Caroline Bynum in the lives and writings of these and other late medieval mystics. The gesture strikingly recaptures late medieval women's sense of release into mystical union with a human, literally "incarnate" Christ.[4]

The desperate search for earthly bread at "Quaeret panem"—ironically captured by the closest possible imitation, based on hectically leaping thirds and fourths, with the bass frantically chasing the voice, that barely manages to stay one note ahead of it—also calls to mind the emphatic rejection of such normal food by many earlier women religious particularly devoted to the Sacrament. Then, at "Vinum mixtum / Aqua, Jesum Christum," Vizzana takes her cue from the poetic line, which by dropping two syllables brakes the forward motion of the verse.[5] In the music, time virtually stops for the second element of the Eucharist. The voice delicately and rather languidly resolves another of Vizzana's favorite transposed phrygian cadences, with its affective held dissonance in the voice above the characteristic expressive descent by a half-step in the bass. After the short descending melisma on *aqua,* the voice pauses, at the bottom of its range, on the words "Jesus Christ" for two bars, on a chord warmed by the singer's sweetly raised third.

This affectionate treatment highlights most directly, of course, the commingling of water and wine at the altar in the Mass. The lingering reference focuses upon the traditional interpretation of the commingling as the absolute, inextricable union of Christ (the wine) and the faithful (the water), or of the divine (the wine) and the human (the water) natures of Christ.

But it also recalls the comparably ancient sacramental connection to the physical mixing of blood and water, flowing downward (like the musical gesture itself) from Christ's wounded side at the Crucifixion (John 19:34).[6] The musical emphasis on *aqua*, reinforcing an emphasis present in the text, therefore hints at another traditional focus of female devotions to Christ: his side wound.

The most common representation of this sacramental connection shows Christ's blood/wine caught into chalices by angels at the Crucifixion, or squirting into the chalice from the side wound, offered by Christ himself in a gesture Bynum has shown to recall the Virgin's offering of her breast.[7] The yearning musical gesture of Vizzana's "Vinum mixtum / Aqua, Jesum Christum" echoes the same intense preoccupation with Christ's blood and his side wound encountered in the visions of such earlier Italian mystics as Blessed Aldobrandesca of Siena:

> While she was feeding her soul again and again with the recollection of this vision [of Christ's Passion], she felt a great desire to taste the divine blood which she had seen welling up out of his right side. And while she kept her attention fixed on this and on the image of the crucified, begging for this grace from Jesus and Mary, she beheld one drop of blood burst forth from the side of his image; gathering it up with her tongue, she felt an indescribable sweetness and deliciousness in her mouth. In memory of this benefit, she had the Virgin Mary painted, holding in her arms the body of her son which had been taken down from the cross, and applying her mouth to that wound in his side.[8]

Angela of Foligno (1248–1309) not only drank from Christ's side herself, but also witnessed his placing the heads of the friars who were her "spiritual sons" in his side wound. Catherine of Siena's "nursing" from Christ's side was depicted a number of times in the early modern period.[9] Through musical gesture, Lucrezia Vizzana renews the many resonances of this old tradition of female devotion.

Praebe mihi, amantissime Domine and *O magnum misteryum,* Vizzana's two most overt love songs to the heavenly spouse, both in terms of their verbal and musical language, reveal once again her firm grounding in the common themes of Christ-centered female spirituality (see example 9).

> Praebe mihi amantissime Domine mihi indignæ ancillæ tuæ dulcissimum lumen. Infunde amantissime Jesu, suavissime Jesu, scintillam tuæ amabilissimæ lucis in animam meam, et illustra eam intus et foris. Ut sic illustrata et irradiata valeat te videre, videndo te amare, amando te frui, fruendo te possidere cum angelis et sanctis tuis in perpetuum.

> Most beloved Lord, show me, your unworthy handmaid, your sweetest light. Pour into my soul, most beloved Jesus, most delightful Jesus, the spark of your most lovely light, and enlighten it within and without. So that [my soul], thus enlightened and illuminated, may be able to behold you, beholding you, to

Example 9. Vizzana, *Praebe mihi, amantissime Domine*

love you, and loving you, to delight in you, and delighting in you, to possess you with your angels and saints forever.

Praebe mihi longs for mystical union in the time-honored language of light, rays, and brightness, common to women religious—and, of course, to their male counterparts as well—throughout the centuries. In Hildegard of Bingen's words:

It happened in the year 1141 of the Incarnation of the Son of God, Jesus Christ . . . that a fiery light of the greatest brilliancy coming from the opened heavens, poured into all my brain, and kindled in my heart and my breast a flame, that warms but does not burn, as the sun heats anything over which he casts his rays.[10]

Example 9 *(continued)*

Example 10. Vizzana, *O magnum mysterium* (mm. 20–42 are repeated in slightly varied form)

The musical language of *Praebe mihi* overflows with Vizzana's most explicit spiritually erotic vocabulary, to match the several superlatives of the text itself. The language includes the by now familiar urgent half-steps resolving upward in voice and bass, as well as strings of surging secondary dominants, to compel the harmony onward from one chord to the next. There are also the inevitable contrasts of chromatic chords a third apart and a single transposed phrygian cadence where the bass descends affectively by a half-step, implying intense, double suspended dissonances above it at *amabilissime lucis*. A clever canon, with the voice and bass chasing each other in interlocking triads, conveys *intus et foris*. The overflowing ecstatic

Example 10 *(continued)*

melismas at *vedere, possidere,* and *perpetuum,* are rivaled only by the melismas in the nuns' consecration motet, *Amo Christum,* as the singer is caught up in rapturous union.

O magnum mysterium grows out of a somewhat quieter, meditative spirit (see example 10).

> O magnum mysterium, O profundissima vulnera, O passio acerbissima, O dulcedo deitatis, adiuva me ad aeternam felicitatem consequendam. Alleluia.

> O great mystery, O deepest wounds, O most bitter passion, O sweetness of the Godhead, help me to reach eternal happiness. Alleluia.

The possible allusion to Christ's side wound at "Vinum mixtum / Aqua, Jesum Christum" from *O si sciret* becomes central in this meditation on one of the primary preoccupations of women religious, Christ's suffering and the wounds of the Passion.[11]

Christ and his Passion played surprisingly little role in the artistic program of the external church of Santa Cristina, which focuses primarily upon Mary and female saints, as mentioned earlier. This may seem surprising at first, given the fact that female spirituality tended to model itself on Christ, while Mary, as a model for women, was largely a male construct.[12]

Within the nuns' own private realm of the cloister at Santa Cristina, on the other hand, the opposite was true. The nuns need not have looked far for iconographical images to encourage meditation on the Passion, which had recently assumed new significance in their devotions. The chapter room of the cloister, for example, included a fresco of the Crucifixion with saints at the foot of the cross, attributed to the school of Francesco Francia. A large crucifix by a fifteenth-century Bolognese master (possibly Giovanni Martorelli) including Saint Christina in its iconography, now displayed in the Pinacoteca di Bologna, could well derive from the convent.[13] According to records of Cardinal Colonna's pastoral visitation in 1634, there was also "a fair image of Our Lord that the nuns visit every Saturday for their regular devotions" in the upper gallery of the cloister. The same visitation also mentions a depiction of the Deposition within these same arcades. One of these works must have been the *Crocifisso di pietà* that the nuns claimed had "miraculously" revealed itself on Good Friday in 1613 or 1614, during Emilia Grassi's term as abbess. Nothing further is known about the precise nature of this "miracle," however. Since then the nuns had gone every Friday in procession to say three Our Fathers and three Hail Marys before the crucifix in remembrance of Christ's three hours on the cross, thereby gaining an indulgence of a hundred days, granted them by Alessandro Ludovisi, archbishop of Bologna and the future Pope Gregory XV. At the insistence of Emilia Grassi, it had also become the custom after meals to offer thanks before this image, rather than in the nuns' choir.[14]

Vizzana's *O magnum mysterium,* which must grow out of this devotional tradition, may have been inspired by the mysterious revelation of the Crucifixion in the cloister in 1613–14. Every line of the brief text of *O magnum mysterium* is clothed in tropes from Vizzana's most spiritually ardent musical vocabulary. The triple invocation, "mysterium . . . vulnera . . . passio acerbissima" (possibly an allusion to Christ's three hours on the cross) is a study in cadential gestures involving affective stepwise descents in the bass, a series that begins and ends with the composer's favorite transposed phrygian gesture, in which the bass descent shrinks to a half-step. At the opening the pattern also encompasses the soprano, who, perhaps to convey the initial threefold *mysterium,* presents for ten bars a temporally free, ornamented canon with the bass.

The urgency of the subsequent petition that succeeds the contemplative stillness of the opening is conveyed by comparable transformations in the musical setting. The allusion to the "sweetness of the deity," which supplants the static opening with more forceful forward movement, once again recalls one of the strongest images from the vocabulary of female mysticism with reference to the Passion:

And then she was rapt in spirit before the Crucified, and looking on him, she immediately began to weep, sensing as a result of this sight extraordinary comfort and sweetness. ["Revelations and Miracles of Blessed Margarita of Faenza" (c. 1300)]

He came down with great sweetness and clearness of his divine goodness . . . and thus all united to me so very tightly, he took me with him onto the cross. . . . And feeling such pain from him, I felt myself totally aflame with the most sweet love of this most sweet Lord. [Suor Maria Domitilla Galuzzi, *Passione* (1622)]

This taste of sweetness in the mouth, which also resonates with Vizzana's own honeyed eloquence in *Sonet vox tua,* had become a standard motif of female spirituality, particularly connected with receiving Christ's body in the Eucharist. In the 1300s, Agnes Blannbekin assumed that all communicants tasted honeycomb.[15] Here the word provokes the almost inevitable "sweet" upwardly resolving leading tones in the bass, also a common musical trope for amorous or ardent urgency, intensified here by the singer's drooping leaps of affective tritones (precisely the interval used for a similar amorous longing in the opening upward leaps in "Maria" from *West Side Story* a few centuries later). The subsequent "adiuva me ad aeternam felicitatem consequendam" overwhelms us, not only with Vizzana's boldest supplicative leap from a dissonant suspension in the voice for *adiuva,* but also with juxtaposed chromatic chords at *felicitatem,* and the voice's accented sevenths above the bass at *consequendam,* all within the space of four bars, then dissolves and resolves into the ecstasy of *alleluia.* This final burst of Vizzana's full expressive vocabulary thus conveys the urgent desire to take on Christ's suffering on the cross, the central aspect of religious women's own *imitatio Christi.*[16]

The much less affecting *Paratum cor meum,* adopting Psalm 107:1–3 as a vehicle for more generalized musical rejoicing, at first glance might appear to have nothing to do with Jesus (see example 11).[17]

Paratum cor meum, Deus, paratum cor meum. Cantabo et psallam in gloria mea. Exsurge gloria mea, exsurge psalterium et cithara, exsurgam diluculo. Confitebor tibi in populis Domine et psallam tibi in nationibus. Alleluia.

My heart is ready, God, my heart is ready. I will sing and play upon the psaltery in my glory. Rise up, my glory, rise up psaltery and kithara. I will arise at the break of dawn. I will acknowledge you, O Lord, among the people, and praise you among the nations. Alleluia.

The text proves to be a cento combining words from different sources, largely based on Psalm 107, but also replacing verse 2 from Psalm 107 with verse 9 from the almost identical Psalm 56:8–10. This is, of course, the sort of free intermingling of biblical words that was quite characteristic of bib-

Example 11. Vizzana, *Paratum cor meum* (mm. 1–31)

lical *imitatio* among religious who constantly rehearsed the words of Scripture in their daily rituals.[18]

Given what we have seen of Lucrezia Vizzana's careful attention to words and their musical meaning, the interesting musical setting of this interpolated verse hints, however, that this textual switch was not a simple case of scriptural confusion. After an opening that has been uniformly major and upbeat, the musical setting of the inserted verse, "exsurge gloria mea," also opens optimistically with clear and simple major harmonies, leading to a sprightly and almost secular interchange *alla canzonetta*, with quick figures recalling the light madrigal, tossed between the sopranos at "exsurge psal-

Example 11 *(continued)*

terium." Then an abrupt contrast of B♭ major and D major chords at "et cithara," introducing Vizzana's favorite quick juxtaposition of f♯ in the first chord and f♮ in the second, signals an abrupt affective turn. The change is intensified by a subsequent rasping diminished fourth between the voices and by an enriched harmonic broadening out, complete with a chain of expressive suspended dissonances that brake the earlier forward movement before a cadence on g, the first prolonged minor emphasis in the piece.

It is possible, of course, that Lucrezia Vizzana's turn to the minor and to intensified harmonic color at this point was prompted simply by the recognition that by this point some sort of variety was in order. But her consistent preoccupation with matching verbal and musical meaning suggests that she was responding to some particular association inherent in *cithara,* which sparked the chromaticism in this context. A search backward into the older Christian tradition Vizzana probably knew provides the clue. In Pseudo-Origen's *Selecta in psalmos,* the psaltery symbolized the "pure mind," while the kithara, the instrument of Vizzana's motet, could represent the body:

> Figuratively the body can be called a cithara and the soul a psaltery, which are likened musically to the wise man who fittingly employs the limbs of the body and the powers of the soul as strings. Sweetly sings he who sings in the mind, uttering spiritual songs, singing in his heart to God. The ten strings stand for ten sinews, for a string is a sinew. And the body can also be said to be the psaltery of ten strings, as it has five senses and five powers of the soul, with each power arising from a respective sense.[19]

Since the time of Saint Augustine, the kithara, whose resonating cavity was placed lower than that of the psaltery, had also been associated particularly with Christ's earthly suffering. In his exegesis of Psalm 56:9, Augustine specifically links the kithara to Christ's earthly Passion:

> The flesh therefore working things divine, is the psaltery: the flesh suffering things human is the harp [i.e., kithara]. Let the psaltery sound, let the blind be enlightened, let the deaf hear, let the paralytics be braced to strength, the lame walk, the sick rise up, the dead rise again; this is the sound of the Psaltery. Let there sound also the harp [i.e., kithara], let Him hunger, thirst, sleep, be held, scourged, derided, crucified, buried.[20]

For centuries, Psalm 56 had also been associated with Christ's Resurrection. A twelfth-century *Psalterium glossatum* in the Vatican Library, drawing on Saint Augustine's *Enarrationes in Psalmos,* adds the title, "Christus in Passione dicit" to Psalm 56, for example.[21] In his discussion of Psalm 56 as the Easter psalm, F. P. Pickering has described how the opening two-thirds refer to Christ awaiting deliverance from the tomb. The beginning of 56:9, "exsurge gloria mea," the words Lucrezia Vizzana has added to the verse from Psalm 107 and sets as a solo for the lower soprano, represents God's command to Christ to arise from the tomb.

"Exsurge psalterium et cithara" thus had come to symbolize the rising of Christ as God (psalterium) and Man (kithara). According to Cassiodorus, in his commentary on Psalm 56:

> *Exsurge* (or *resurge*) *cithara.* "The harp [i.e., kithara] means the glorious Passion which with stretched sinews and counted bones . . . sounded forth his bitter suffering as in a spiritual song."[22]

That the same tradition continued down to Lucrezia Vizzana's time is revealed by Saint Bonaventure, who wrote in *The Mystical Vine,* "Your Spouse has become a Harp [i.e., kithara], the wood of the cross being the frame and His body, extended on the wood, representing the chords"; and by

Jacobus de Cassolis, who interprets Christ as Orpheus, with his cross as the lyre [i.e., kithara]:

> What is the melody of Orpheus's voice but the sermons that Christ delivered and His marvelous teachings? What is the harp [i.e., kithara] He played but the mysteries of the Passion He received on the cross, which was the true harp, whose strings were the sinews, bones, and flesh of Our Redeemer, stretched out like the strings on a guitar on the tree of the Cross?[23]

Vizzana's careful differentiation of "exsurge gloria mea, exsurge psalterium et cithara" may represent a continuation into the seventeenth century of this long exegetical tradition. *Paratum cor meum* could have been conceived as a commemoration of Christ's Resurrection. As such, it would also offer a remarkably apposite musical equivalent to Giovanni Battista Bertusio's *Resurrection,* newly commissioned by the Glavarini sisters for the external church at Santa Cristina during the extensive redecorations of the early Seicento. Bertusio's altarpiece strikingly depicts the allegorical interpretation of the second half of the psalm: Christ's rising out of the tomb (see fig. 13). Vizzana's highly individual interpretation of text and music in *Paratum cor meum* strikingly reaffirms once again the close interconnection of musical and artistic themes in the spiritual life at Santa Cristina.

"QUASI CITHARE CITHARIZANTIUM" II

The evocation of the kithara as a symbol for Christ's suffering in *Paratum cor meum* recalls, of course, the other appearance of the word in the exordial *Sonet vox tua,* discussed at the end of the previous chapter. In the light of *Paratum cor meum,* Vizzana's comparison of her voice to "the striking of the kithara" in the earlier motet raises the possibility that for Vizzana, the musician, "quasi cithare citharizantium," from *Sonet vox tua,* may also have represented an apt metaphor, not only for her mind/body as composer/ performer, played by the deity, but also for her own identification with Christ as kithara—with Christ's suffering humanity, which the singer had also aspired to assume in the final lines of *O magnum mysterium.* The body could displace the kithara as an instrument of spiritual melody, as Saint John Chrysostom had observed:

> Here there is no need of the cithara, nor taut strings, nor the plectrum and technique, nor any sort of instrument; but if you wish, make of yourself a cithara, by mortifying the limbs of the flesh and creating full harmony between body and soul. For when the flesh does not lust against the spirit, but yields to its commands, and perseveres along the path that is noble and admirable, you thus produce a spiritual melody.[24]

Lucrezia Vizzana need not have looked far for a model in the imitation of Christ's suffering. She grew up, not only under the guidance of her musical aunt, the convent organist Camilla Bombacci, but also in the shadow of her most obvious spiritual model, the learned and venerable Flaminia Bombacci, according to Antonio di Paolo Masini's *Bologna perlustrata,* the single Bolognese nun under the Rule of Saint Benedict to have died in odor of sanctity.[25] Holy women of the Cinquecento and Seicento continued the older tradition in which bodily suffering or a naturally infirm body remained essential means to their own *imitatio Christi.* Flaminia Bombacci apparently had not been granted the gift of illness. But, according to Gasparo Bombacci, she "subdued the rebellions of her body with sackcloth, with scourges, and with frequent fasting, so that its resistance to the number of such torments seemed marvelous."[26] The convent necrology claims that Lucrezia Vizzana's love of music was matched by an intense religious devotion, especially to the Mysteries of the Holy Rosary, in whose honor a chapel and company were established at Santa Cristina in November 1641. Vizzana was blessed with bodily sufferings that were not self-induced. In the year *Componimenti musicali* went to press, she claimed "on feast days everyone gets up for matins, but I do not get up because I am unwell."[27] The convent necrology also recorded that "she did not seek in vain from her immortal spouse the gift, the stone of purgatory in this mortal life. For afterward she endured infirmity and, in fact, the burden of greater misfortunes, with admirable patience and virile fortitude, as if it [the burden] had fallen straight from heaven, with a cheerful spirit," and "increasingly severe illnesses deprived her of highest monastic office."[28]

In this context the words of Caroline Bynum strike a remarkably responsive chord:

> Body is the instrument upon which the mystic rings changes of pain and of delight. It is from body—whether whipped into frenzy by the ascetic herself or gratified with an ecstacy given by God—that sweet melodies and aromas rise to the very throne of heaven.[29]

Perhaps, therefore, Vizzana sought to affirm, through the "cithare citharizantium" cited in the text of *Sonet vox tua,* not only her musical gifts and divine inspirations, but also the gift of lifelong earthly sufferings, her own *imitatio Christi.*

Lucrezia Vizzana's *Componimenti musicali* thus reflect many of the most illustrious moments in the liturgical, artistic, and devotional life at the convent of Santa Cristina. Another five motets, however, may allude to a darker side of convent life and offer some of the first hints of its decline. The illustrious musical tradition that had helped Vizzana's creativity to flower in ways that would have been largely impossible for her beyond the convent wall may also have been deeply implicated in internal political conflicts festering within the convent for years—strife that may have silenced her and would change Santa Cristina forever. To the history of these rifts, music's supposed place in them, and their relationship to *Componimenti musicali* we turn in the next chapter.

SIX

The Rhetoric of Conflict in
Componimenti musicali
"And it began because of music"

For the convent of Santa Cristina, things had taken a serious turn for the worse shortly after 28 August 1622, when an anonymous letter, supposedly from a group of devout and scandalized nuns of Santa Cristina, reached Cardinal Archbishop Ludovico Ludovisi in Rome. The letter alleged that many nuns did not bother to attend services, and that they ridiculed those who fasted and remained devoted to the Sacraments; that several kept animals for private gain; that others had expropriated the public rooms as their private quarters; that the novices lived in fear of their mistress, who knew nothing of strict observance; that the nuns in charge squandered communal funds and refused to open the books for inspection by outside administrators; and that many flouted the dress code by wearing added frills and bits of finery. Most troubling were the comments, "Chastity—I would not speak of it, out of respect" and "an investigation without the threat of papal excommunication will serve no purpose."[1]

After a false start in September, on the vigil of the feast of Saint Thomas the Apostle, 20 December 1622, just a week before Lucrezia Vizzana signed the dedication to *Componimenti musicali,* Suffragan Bishop Angelo Gozzadini, the Camaldolese visitor Don Desiderio Bardelloni da Monza, the nuns' vicar of Bologna Don Giovanni Bondini, and the episcopal notary Vittorio Barbadori entered Santa Cristina to begin their investigation of these charges. Although it was customary to start with the abbess and descend by seniority through the ranks to the novices and *converse,* the first to be called was the most junior *professa.* Mauro Ruggeri, then the convent's confessor, later suggested that this had been done to catch the nuns off guard. The pastoral visitors could well have chosen to begin, however, with those most likely to revere their authority—not an unreasonable decision, for the more senior nuns later showed less inclination to cooperate. The venerable madre donna Angela Cherubini's responses to some thirty questions, for example, yield barely ten lines: "Everybody behaves well toward the senior nuns and our superiors, and I know of no one who does what she shouldn't. Everything is fine and well done, and I don't have anything to say to you." Madre donna Verginia Fuzzi offered little more than "Because I am an old sister I attend only to my soul," while Lucrezia Vizzana's aunt, madre donna Ortensia Bombacci, justified her terse responses with the remark, "I live in seclusion, and I don't know anything." The less senior donna Paula Dorotea Vitali was even prepared to try a passive-aggressive counterattack: "So, should any reform be needed, let it be in the kitchen."[2]

Even the most junior nuns, whom Gozzadini called the first day, although more respectful, generally offered nothing that might really have piqued the interest of the visitors. Indeed, Giuliana Glavarini seems to have done her best to mislead: "I don't know of any dissension among them." At the end of the first day, Lucrezia Vizzana was the last of six to be questioned. By now, with close to twenty-five years of convent life behind her, she was no junior member. By their questions, the investigators could encourage a certain "spin" in the responses.[3] And, indeed, as the investigation progressed, they frequently departed from their prepared list of thirty questions. But Vizzana's shrewdly worded answers avoid both direct affirmations of leading questions and anything that could be cited as overtly misleading or outright perjury—in other words, the time-honored techniques for facing down inquisitors. "*I do not know* that there are abuses in the convent, nor wicked practices. . . . *I have not seen* profane paintings, not even dogs. . . . *Nor do I know* that there is any variety of dress among us, nor any vanities of precious stone or of other sorts." But she is also the first to recognize openly, but with characteristic understatement, the serious strife within the walls: "Nor do I know that there are any rifts. And it merely seems to me that between suor Emilia and suor Cecilia there may be some rivalry that causes some small disturbance within the convent."[4]

That donna Lucrezia was putting it mildly emerged promptly the second day, when six of the nine witnesses elaborated in detail upon the problem of Emilia Grassi and Cecilia Bianchi. Lucrezia's older sister, Isabetta Vizzana, put it bluntly:

> Between them there rages a rivalry, so that they put the convent in disorder. Donna Emilia observes the actions of donna Cecilia, and to be contrary, does something else, in such a way that even in reciting the Office in the chapel, they want to outdo one another with their voices; and each of them wants to get the better of the other.

This may not have been the most important problem, as far as the authorities were concerned, but it clearly preoccupied the nuns. At least a dozen of them raised the issue, and usually in terms of the choir. Several others who did not address the rift directly nonetheless complained about Cecilia

Bianchi's behavior in chapel. As Isabetta Vizzana had indicated, the choir had thus become the central arena in which the rivalry was played out more overtly:

> [Donna Cecilia] complains about everybody in the choir, saying that the Divine Office is not recited precisely and as it should be. . . . And it's not for her to correct. It's the job of the abbess. [Donna Olimpia Cattani]

> And especially in the chapel, donna Cecilia wants to direct the choir, and I believe she does it with good purpose, . . . so the Office will be said in an orderly way; and that's how she feels if it's not recited her way. [Donna Paola Dorotea Vitali]

> If one could see to it that donna Cecilia conforms to everyone else in the recitation of the Divine Office, that would remove many difficulties from the chapel. For she should recite the Office with a voice matched to the others, and not cause confusion by one time reciting high and another low. [Madre donna Silvia Bottrigari]

> Sometimes donna Cecilia has words in the choir because she wants us to follow how she recites, either fast or slow. . . . I don't know of other dissension except some rivalry between donna Emilia and suor Cecilia [note the difference implied by a change to the less respectful *suor*], each of whom claims to direct the choir according to her taste; the running of it pertains to donna Emilia as prefect. [Donna Anna Maria Righi][5]

It was Cecilia Bianchi who articulated the problem most explicitly. She began her second day of testimony with the statement,

> I have considered what you sought from me; and to expedite matters I offer you the present page on which is written everything that I can say regarding this investigation and its causes.

She handed them a document, which was dutifully recorded in the archbishop's copy of the proceedings but omitted from the copy intended for the eyes of the nuns themselves. Its first sentence reads, "It has been eighteen years that I have endured this persecution; and it began because of music."[6] She left little doubt about the nature of the difficulties and who had caused them:

> In [the recitation of the Office and the Mass], there is tremendous negligence, because in the summertime at that hour [the nuns] are always being called to the doorways and the nuns' grates by gentlemen and ladies, and thus the chapel is unattended. . . . Sometimes there are so few of us left that we cannot recite the Office. . . . As for the recitation of the Office, it is not said as it should be, following the calendar, because it was changed by donna Emilia Grassi when she became mistress of the choir, and this against the orders of our superiors. We have orders to recite the Office as if in song, but this is not done. . . . They bring dogs and cats into the chapel. There is madre

donna Emilia Grassi who has a little cat who comes looking for her in the chapel, and she doesn't send it away as she should. And there is also the prioress, donna Sulpizia Bocchi, who has a little dog, which she sometimes carries into the chapel; but at present she has sent it home. And donna Pantasilea Tovagli, while the Office is being recited, holds a little book, and doesn't pay attention to the service as she should. . . . The master of music has received his provisions, . . . and the mother abbess has complained about it, and it was madre donna Emilia who wanted him to receive them. We also have two organs, one of which could be sold. . . . Furthermore, you should establish the way and time to recite the Divine Offices and sing Masses, and so on, because, despite the fact that the mother abbess has ordered that they be performed in one way, suor Emilia [note the change to a less respectful title] does the opposite, which provokes disagreements and scandal.[7]

The testimony of the abbess, madre donna Lorenza Bonsignori, usefully balances Cecilia Bianchi's allegations, which were designed to reinforce the prelates' common view of independent-spirited nuns as disobedient, rebellious children. Bonsignori admitted that chapel could be better attended if nuns did not leave to answer summonses in the parlatorios or if they all attended services instead of sometimes making toffee in the kitchen—in fact typical and perennial complaints lodged by superiors at any number of convents. From the nuns' point of view, of course, meetings in the parlatorios and gifts of homemade sweets, a vestige of the much freer interchange between convent and city before Trent, served to maintain important ties to their own families and to reaffirm their place in the social structure of the community.

The abbess also acknowledged that dogs and cats, especially donna Emilia's cat, occasionally attended services in chapel, but denied that there was any indecorous gossiping or giggling, as donna Cecilia's ally, donna Maria Gentile Malvasia, had claimed. But restrictions on convent pets were perennially ambiguous, and pets' presence tended to be turned into a convent "abuse" when that could be used to someone's political advantage.[8] It further emerged that donna Emilia's alleged changes in the calendar had involved nothing more important than the insertion of further readings from the prophets, a practice that the Camaldolese father general had already put right. As for donna Cecilia, the abbess remarked,

> She should be advised to be more circumspect about talking too much and being insulting to the sisters; and sometimes in chapel she goes around imitating those poor old sisters who cannot contribute to the choir, and who utter certain words either too high or too low.[9]

Bonsignori did not, however, hide her resentment at Emilia Grassi's refusal to give up the position of choirmistress, which she had monopolized for more than six years, despite the fact that the mistress of the choir should have been an appointee of the abbess. Over Bonsignori's objections, Grassi also continued to insist upon a regular salary for the master of music, Ottavio Vernizzi, whom she had originally hired. The abbess made it clear that by 1623, the appointment of a new choirmistress was long overdue, and suggested Lucrezia Vizzana's aunt, the former organist Camilla Bombacci, for the position.[10]

By contrast, the shrewd Emilia Grassi, when her turn came, initially couched her own counterattacks against her rival much more evenhandedly:

> For the past six years I have been in charge of directing the choir. And in the chapel there doesn't seem to be anything else to disturb our common peace except that donna Cecilia sometimes either goes too fast or recites more slowly than the others, reproving some of the nuns heartily and often, primarily those on the side where she stands—although one wouldn't expect her to criticize, since I am in charge of the choir, as I said.[11]

She went on smoothly, and with extraordinary self-assurance, given that twenty-nine nuns, including donna Cecilia, had testified before her, to claim that there was no dissension within the convent. When the interrogators abandoned their script, hemming her in with accusations suggested by previous testimony against her, she held her ground, responding with dazzling audacity that eclipsed anyone else's feeble attempts at resistance:

> I don't know that the abbess should complain about what the organ tuner or music master get paid, and nobody's done any harm by having to go to the loggia for grace after meals before the crucifix. . . . And if anybody gives me something, they say it's from their own share, and not the convent's, and the convent has already had its share. . . . And, as for donna Cecilia, I don't know what to do about her, and I do her honor as I do any other nun and *conversa* in the convent. I'm not offended if the sisters study with suor Cecilia, and, sure, I've told the others in the absence of donna Cecilia—who's a hypocrite—not to be taken in by her. . . . And, as for my having told some nuns they needn't observe fasts and vigils strictly, it was when donna Giulia had a prolonged illness, and was with the doctor's consent. . . . Nor have I coached anybody on how they should answer in this visitation, and I didn't say I wanted to torment donna Cecilia. . . . I never insisted that the abbess do things my way, any more than I have added lessons at the expense of others while reading in the refectory. . . . As for wearing a hat, I admit I do it, for protection from the heat and the bad air. But it's the practice in the convent, and the mother abbess and the bursar wear hats too. And my shoulders are covered up by the scapular—and so is everything else.[12]

Clearly, then, by the 1620s, the nuns' choir had become an important battlefield, which helps explain donna Cecilia's cryptic line about music's role in her persecution, quoted above. The first hints of these musical rivalries can in fact be traced back to the turn of the century, which was around the time Cecilia Bianchi claimed her persecution had begun. In 1600, a petition had arrived at the Congregation of Bishops in Rome, suggesting that an overabundance of musical talent, praised by Adriano Banchieri in 1599 and by Giacomo Vincenti in 1606, was already beginning to divide the convent of Santa Cristina from within:

> Since time immemorial it has always been customary in the monastery of the nuns of Santa Cristina in Bologna, of the Camaldolese order, to elect an organist from among the nuns, and the election should always fall to the one who best knows how to play. And because ordinarily the number of those who knew how to play well was small, only once or twice was there strife in the election. Now that the said number who seek the office has grown considerably, there is such discord that it is impossible to arrive at the election of the most talented, the one who most deserves the position. Therefore, on behalf of the abbess and nuns of the convent, it is humbly requested of Your Most Illustrious Lordships, that you deign to command that now, and whenever the occasion for such an election should arise, the nun should be elected who best knows how to play, and is most adept, talented, and qualified for such an office, ahead of any other claim or respect.[13]

There may in fact have been as many as seven rivals for the organist's post. In addition to Emilia Grassi, who Banchieri in the dedication to his *Messa solenne* indicates was also leading the choir in those years, and who probably underwrote his musical collection, there would have been Camilla Bombacci, the former convent organist, and her talented niece, the young Lucrezia Vizzana, who had recently entered the convent but had yet to profess. In 1601, Adeodata Leoni commissioned Gabriele Fattorini's *Secondo libro de motetti,* which suggests her own strong commitment to the choir. Although the illustrious Cleria Pepoli apparently also took an interest in music, to judge by the dedication of Ercole Porta's *Vaga ghirlanda* of 1613, she is likely to have presented a threat only as a patron and not as a performer, since she seems to have long been a virtual invalid. Angelica Malvezzi, on the other hand, was a serious rival, not only because of her angelic voice, lauded at her death in 1615, but also because of her particularly illustrious lineage. Giuditta Nobili, Emilia Grassi's lifelong friend, was likewise remembered for her musical talents at her death. Alfonsina Ganassi, daughter of the prominent Bolognese musician Alfonso Ganassi, was very probably also a performer. And, of course, there was donna Cecilia.

The sort of musical contention revealed by the petition of 1600 probably came as no great surprise to church authorities, who had long cited such rivalries as a primary evil of convent music. A few years earlier, in 1593, for example, don Ercole Tonelli, father confessor to various Bolognese nuns, had complained to the Congregation of Bishops: "There are such wranglings and wars among [the nuns] because of musical rivalries that sometimes they would claw each others' flesh if they could." For don Ercole, as for many, it was convent music that provided the spark to set off what had long been seen as female fury, smouldering beneath the surface, women's imagined irrational propensity for jealousy, leading in turn to violence and the provocation of discord—an old, familiar theme.

Another anonymous, half-literate complaint from Bologna to the Sacred Congregation in March 1602 might well describe the continuing problem at Santa Cristina:

> For many years I have been a laywoman and in a convent, and I have seen many scandals [*scandagli*] especially about playing the organ and making music. These singers and players harass one another and take sides. One side says, "Our group does better," and the other side responds, "It isn't true. Our group sings and plays better." And this causes an uproar, the greatest hatred, and such infinite animosity that the convents are afire and aflame.[14]

Although it is impossible to establish any direct relationship to the festering musical rivalries within the walls on via Fondazza, in the year of the complaint from Santa Cristina, the Congregation of Bishops, on 21 November 1600, commanded the vice-legate of Bologna to undertake a "diligent and secret" investigation "regarding the government of the convent." The investigation is as likely to have resulted from a combination of complaints to the Congregation, including one a year and a half earlier, claiming that don Alessandro da Faenza, the convent procurator, came and went as if the cloister were his own home, and maintained an unseemly friendship with one of the nuns. Six weeks after the order, on 2 January 1601, the Congregation issued several follow-up decrees chiefly having to do with details of *clausura* (e.g., walling up of windows, modifications to grates and *ruote*), with no specific mention of music. Such disorders have a familiar ring, however, for they resemble the abuses Cecilia Bianchi would cite twenty years later, when her rivalry with Emilia Grassi reached its height.[15]

It is intriguing that Gabriele Fattorini's *Secondo libro dei motetti* saw the light in the immediate aftermath of the vice-legate's visitation. Donna Adeodata Leoni, the dedicatee and probable patroness of the collection, was singled out twenty years later as one of the nuns enlisted to reconcile donna Emilia and donna Cecilia.[16] The dedication of the *Secondo libro* by the Camaldolese don Donato Beroaldo, dated 28 May 1601, raises the possibility that Adeodata Leoni might have turned to music as a means of mediation as early as the beginning of the century. Beroaldo claims, for example, that "at your behest, gentle lady, as the person who can command me, I sought to try to arrange for you to have at such a time some of the sacred music of the reverend don Gabriele Fattorini."[17]

In this light, several texts in the *Secondo libro* seem especially intriguing. *Sacerdos et pontifex* and *Ecce sacerdos magnus,* for example, which appear side by side toward the end of Fattorini's collection, both appear in the common of a confessor bishop in the Camaldolese breviary, in exactly the form set by Fattorini.[18] They might have been used for Saint Romuald or Saint Benedict, the male saints whose feasts were celebrated with lavish music at Santa Cristina, who as abbots had episcopal authority. But these two motets also conform in their openings to the antiphon and responsory prescribed in the Roman pontifical for the solemn reception of a bishop or legate.[19] The conclusion to Fattorini's *Ecce sacerdos magnus,* "et in tempore iracundiæ factus est reconciliatio" ("and in the time of wrath he brought reconciliation"), following the Camaldolese breviary, may disagree with the conclusion to the text prescribed in the Roman pontifical for solemn receptions of bishops or legates, but it is remarkably apt for the situation of internal strife that may have partly provoked the vice-legate's investigation at Santa Cristina in 1600–1601. Furthermore, although neither of Fattorini's motet texts may quite have met the precise liturgical requirements for such a solemn reception, they were still entirely appropriate for introduction *after* the prescribed antiphon or responsory, when the Roman pontifical specifically permitted musical insertions.

Fattorini's *Sacerdos et pontifex* or *Ecce sacerdos magnus* could thus have served for a reception of the vice-legate at Santa Cristina in 1600–1601, if he visited the convent in fulfilling his mandate from the Sacred Congregation. The conclusion to *Ecce sacerdos* would have rung particularly true in the chapel at that time, and indeed, on several subsequent occasions over the next several years. Other motets chosen for Fattorini's *Secondo libro* could also have spoken to the present difficulties of internal strife and possible scandal. A fourth of the collection involves texts exhorting some sort of penitence or amendment of life, for example:

> *Impetum inimicorum:* "Do not be afraid of the attack of your enemies. You should remember how our Fathers were made safe; and now let us cry to heaven and our Lord will be merciful unto us." [responsory for October, Camaldolese breviary, fol. 153v]

> *Positis autem genibus:* "But kneeling, he cried in a loud voice, saying, 'Lord, reckon not this sin upon them.' And when he had said this he went to sleep in the Lord." [Feast of Saint Stephen]

> *Praeparate corda vestra:* "Prepare your hearts unto the Lord and serve him only, and he will deliver you out of the hands of your enemies. Return to him with all your hearts and he will deliver you out of the hands of your enemies." [responsory for the third Sunday after Pentecost]

Positis autem genibus has been redacted in ways that focus attention away from Saint Stephen, whose name is completely removed from the original liturgical versions, whose stoning likewise finds no place in the motet, and whose echoing of Christ's last words, "receive my spirit," is suppressed. What largely remains is the original phrase most appropriate to the wayward, wrangling nuns: "reckon not this sin upon them." Perhaps the peace-making and musical Adeodata Leoni may have tried to exploit this flexible, socially constructed medium, in which words could be infused with differ-ent meanings at different moments, in the hope that the singing of such motets by the warring nun musicians might help to reestablish tranquility among them.[20]

This brings us back to Lucrezia Vizzana's *Componimenti musicali*. Five motets, intriguingly positioned in the collection, reflect themes of peni-tence, abandonment, or vengeance:

1. *Exsurgat Deus et dissipentur inimici eius*
3. *Ave stella matutina*
5. *Domine, ne in furore tuo arguas me*
7. *Usquequo oblivisceris me in finem*
15. *Domine, quid multiplicati sunt qui tribulant me*

Four borrow directly from Psalms 67, 6, 12, and 3; *Domine, ne in furore tuo* and *Usquequo oblivisceris me* are drawn from the extremely popular peni-tential psalms, and *Domine, quid multiplicati sunt* was every bit as popular, to judge by the number of sixteenth-century polyphonic settings of the psalm. Vizzana's relatively brief texts recall similar redactions from medi-eval abbreviated psalters.[21] It is possible that she could have found her models in just such an abbreviated psalter, or her texts could be a seven-teenth-century continuation of that time-honored tradition of scriptural redaction.

Could these pieces have been in part a reflection of the conflicts and factionalism at Santa Cristina? One must be cautious about reading bio-graphical implications into settings of such extremely common biblical verses. Nevertheless, for those whose lives were regulated by the constant reading and recitation of Scripture, the language it speaks could come to be viewed as the language of their own lives. Vizzana's choice of these particular biblical texts and their redactions could also be to some extent biographical. The themes of alienation or abandonment apparent in some of these verses had, of course, been common ones in the writings of women religious for centuries,[22] and complaints about backbiters are equally fre-quent in the writings of religious who lived and described their lives in the language of the Bible and the psalter.

But a number of anomalous features about Vizzana's printed collection and its publication strengthen the possibility that this group of motets may be related to the current crisis within the cloister. Only two copies of *Com-ponimenti musicali* come down to us, one in the Civico Museo Bibliografico Musicale in Bologna, and the other in Wrocław, formerly in the Stadtbib-liothek and now housed in the University Library. One is immediately struck by the austerity of the title page, devoid of all ornamentation, in contrast to the usual practice in sixteenth- and seventeenth-century music prints. Most prominent after the title is the name of the convent, which eclipses even the name of the composer. More striking is the absence of any mention of a publisher, a feature very rarely absent from music title pages. "Nella Stamparia del Gardano IN VENETIA *Appresso Bartholomeo Magni* MDCXXIII." only appears in the colophon at the end of the volumes. Neither is there any mention of a *privilegio* (copyright). Such evidence suggests that Vizzana's *Componimenti musicali* was probably a privately contracted job, in which the Gardano printing firm had no financial interest, which had been specially commissioned and completely underwritten by the convent of Santa Cristina.[23]

What is most intriguing, however, is that the title page of the Wrocław copy, dated 1622, makes no mention of the nuns as dedicatees, by contrast with the Bologna copy, dated 1623. Furthermore, the less precise salutation to the Wrocław dedication, signed 1 December 1622, "Molto R[everen]de in Christo Giesu,"[24] has been expanded and made quite specific, "Alle M[olto] R[everende] Monache di S. Christina di Bologna," in the Bologna copy, signed exactly a month later, on 1 January 1623. The prefatory matter must thus have been recast during the printing process. Since title pages and dedications were often the last items to be printed, it is possible that the printing of the music itself had even been completed in December 1622. And these last-minute revisions that called attention to the convent more emphatically were apparently carried out right in the midst of the pastoral visit to Santa Cristina by episcopal authorities in December 1622 and January 1623.

This suggests that at least the final stages of the production were affected by that event. It is quite possible, however, that the entire enterprise may have been related to the struggle. The volume would have gone to press sometime not too long before December 1622, by which time the crisis at Santa Cristina had already been in the serious stage for at least six months. Cardinal Archbishop Ludovico Ludovisi's original order to Suffragan Bishop Angelo Gozzadini had demanded an investigation in September. For months—indeed, years—the Camaldolese hierarchy had already been trying in vain to defuse the crisis.[25]

An analogous contracted printing job in 1565 by monks of San Giorgio Maggiore in Venice offers a useful comparison with the Santa Cristina enterprise. The 1565 print had been issued only three months after the contract had been signed; its dedication had been dated midway through the process.[26] This suggests that the entire publication of Lucrezia Vizzana's more modest collection could easily have been carried out from start to finish within a few months, in the midst of the political maneuvering on both sides of the convent wall. The finished copies could have been delivered by February, before the matter had reached any sort of resolution.[27]

Componimenti musicali might thus have been conceived of as an instrument to influence the outcome of the crisis.

For the nuns of Santa Cristina, music had long been another means of clientage, of bridging the convent walls on via Fondazza, to influence those in the world. As suggested in earlier chapters, given the rigors of post-Tridentine *clausura,* nuns' patterns of clientage were largely indirect, reinforcing links to their own families and fostering others with potentially powerful advocates in the world. There can be no question that Lucrezia Vizzana's *Componimenti* were intended to enhance the luster of the convent that had paid for them. As in the case of the printing project from San Giorgio Maggiore, the convent may have received most, if not all, of the copies to distribute as it wished to families, friends, and allies. The contents and organization of the collection, and the last-minute revisions of the front matter, suggest that Vizzana's volume may have been intended not only to call attention to the house, its venerable history, and its distinguished artistic tradition, but also to arouse public sympathy and support for this honorable institution, currently under attack both from within and without.

That the "quasi-autobiographical" *Sonet vox tua,* discussed in an earlier chapter, is not printed first, but instead a motet beginning "Let God arise and let his enemies be scattered," in which a solo soprano invokes the Lord in rising trumpet calls, suggests there may have been a particular point behind the placement of this opening exhortation, the first of several motets in a similar vein:

> Exsurgat Deus et dissipentur inimici eius et fugiant qui oderunt eum a facie eius. Sicut deficit fumus, deficiant sicut fluit cera a facie ignis sic pereant peccatores a facie Dei. Et iusti epulentur, et exultent in conspectu Dei ⟨⟩ in laetitia. Alleluia.[28]

> Let God arise, and let his enemies be scattered, and let those who hate him flee before him. As smoke dies out, let them die out; as wax melts before a fire, let the sinners perish before the face of God. And let the righteous be joyful, and let them exult in the sight of God in joy. Alleluia.

Musical settings of these initial verses of Psalm 67 are hardly uncommon, of course; more than two dozen musical settings from this bellicose period could be named. Indeed, in 1571, the year of the battle of Lepanto, Bishop Gabriele Paleotti of Bologna had required the singing of Psalm 67, *Exsurgat Deus,* as a way to counter the Turkish threat.[29] But in Vizzana's case the careful positioning of the psalm suggests that we may not be dealing with generalized vindictive enthusiasm against Turk or Protestant. It is difficult to believe that Lucrezia Vizzana, her fellow nuns, and knowledgeable outsiders to whom the print was probably directed would not have read into such lines as "Let his enemies be scattered . . . let those who hate him flee before him. . . . Let them die out . . . let the sinners perish"—the last heard amid large and tricky leaps in the voice, accompanied by Vizzana's favorite chromatic chords a third apart (B♭ versus D and C versus A)—a special relevance to the political strife currently dividing Santa Cristina. Vizzana concludes her opening motet on a firmly positive note, "Let the righteous be joyful, and let them exult in the sight of God," dissolving into a string of jubilant alleluias. Within six years the troublemakers at Santa Cristina would have been scattered to other convents, and the prelates' beadles would have fled before a hail of bricks and stones, but, as we shall see, by then Vizzana's public show of optimism would have turned to sorrow.

As the collection unfolds, every other piece for most of the first half of the volume (nos. 1, 3, 5, and 7) insistently hammers home these themes. The same spirit also reappears in *Domine, quid multiplicati sunt qui tribulant me* (no. 15), which because of the customary organization of the volume by number of voices, could only find a place among the more uniformly optimistic duets.

Domine ne in furore (no. 5) also exists in innumerable musical settings by any number of other composers—at least nineteen from northern Italy before 1650.[30] Vizzana's motet, among her most emphatically rhetorical, includes one of her most plaintive leaps from a suspended dissonance in the voice at "have mercy upon me, O Lord," sliding chromatic moves in the voice, first from F to F♯, then immediately B♭ to B♮ at "for my bones are out of joint," and naggingly insistent repetitions of "heal me" in jerky figures rising more and more shrilly. In the context of *Exsurgat Deus* and the other "political" motets that surround it, Vizzana's particularly expressive setting of *Domine ne in furore* could once again reinforce a communal plea for redemption and restoration in the present time of trouble.

The psalm *Usquequo oblivisceris me* (no. 7), which we examined in some detail in an earlier chapter, was much less commonly set in the early Seicento. A Bolognese listener, aware of recent goings on, could have heard, even in its very first words, a communal cry of despair, leading to a final plea for deliverance:

> Usquequo ⟨⟩ oblivisceris me in finem? Usquequo avertis faciem tuam a me? Quamdiu ponam consilia in anima mea dolorem in corde meo per diem? Usquequo exaltabitur inimicus meus super me? Respice et exaudi me Domine Deus meus. Illumina oculos meos ⟨⟩ in morte, nequando dicat inimicus meus prevalui adversum eum.

> How long will you forget me, forever? How long will you hide your face from me? How long shall I take counsel in my soul, having sorrow in my heart daily? How long will my enemy be exalted over me? Have regard for me and hear me, O Lord my God. Lighten my eyes in death, lest my enemy say, "I have prevailed against him."

The subtle alterations of the original psalm text, which reappear in no other Cinquecento and early Seicento musical setting,[31] must represent conscious artistic decisions, since the composer unquestionably was all too familiar with the biblical original. Most surprising of these is the suppression of any mention of the Lord in the opening phrase, "Usquequo [*Domine*] oblivisceris me." The Lord is not overtly introduced at all until over halfway through the text, after the climax of the musical setting.

Although the addressee goes without saying, the opening omission creates an ambiguity about who is really being addressed. Indeed, for a convent audience, or anybody else who regularly ran through the psalter like clockwork every week, or regularly recited the penitential psalms, as the nuns of Santa Cristina did at least every Sunday,[32] the suppression of the opening "Domine" could signal that the Lord was specifically *not* being addressed, at least not until "Have regard for me and hear me, *O Lord my God*," after the most intense portion of the music—one of the most highly charged in any Vizzana motet—has run its course.

For quite some time now, the nuns of Santa Cristina had had reason to claim such oppression and abandonment. Since 1616, at least, when the Sacred Congregation of Bishops and Regulars in Rome had ordered diocesan ministers in Bologna to gather "accurate, secret, extrajudicial information" about alleged financial irregularities at the convent of Santa Cristina, the nuns' relationship to outside episcopal authorities had been steadily deteriorating. In 1618, the Congregation of Bishops had denied the nuns' petition to accept an additional *conversa*, claiming that the ratio of servant nuns to professing nuns was already overly luxurious. In 1620, the archbishop of Bologna had rejected two postulants, proposed by the convent as replacements for recently deceased members of the community.[33] There may well have been other petitions that had likewise fallen on deaf ears. There would certainly be sheafs of others that faced similarly hard hearts over the next decade, as the convent continued its inexorable decline, in the face of overwhelming, and ultimately irresistible, episcopal opposition. The altered opening of Vizzana's *Usquequo oblivisceris me* could thus have been intended to be heard as a plea, not only to the convent's ultimate superior, but also to the episcopal authorities, intended to arouse public sympathy at their hard-hearted rebuffs.

The text of Psalm 3, *Domine quid multiplicati sunt*, Vizzana's only duet of alienation, is commonly chanted at Easter matins, for the words were traditionally put in Christ's mouth, an interpretation based on Saint Augustine's *Enarrationes in psalmos.*

Domine, quid multiplicati sunt qui tribulant me! Multi insurgunt adversum me. Multi dicunt animae meae: non est salus ipsi in Deo eius. Tu autem, Domine, susceptor meus es ⟨⟩, et exaltans caput meum. Voce mea ad Dominum clamavi et exaudivit me ⟨⟩. Ego dormivi et soporatus sum; et exsurrexi, quia Dominus suscepit me. Non timebo millia populi circundantis me. Exsurge, Domine, salvum me fac, Deus meus.

Lord, how those who trouble me are increased! Many rise up against me. Many say to my soul, "There is no help for him in his God." But you, O Lord, are my protector, my glory and you raise up my head. I cried to the Lord with my voice and he heard me. I laid down and slept and he sustained me. I will not fear the thousands of people that surround me. Arise, O Lord, save me, my God.

It is therefore particularly interesting to find *Domine, quid multiplicati sunt* printed beside *Paratum cor meum,* which the composer, following Saint Augustine's interpretation, may have conceived as an Easter motet, as suggested earlier.

On the other hand, the text of this duet, which is clothed in the same heightened musical rhetoric as Vizzana's other "political" motets, with the inevitable chromatic juxtapositions, a startling leap from a vocal dissonance at "oppress me," and creeping chromatic lines in one voice after the other at "is not healthy," suggests another piece tailored to reflect the factionalism dividing the convent. Vizzana's suppression of the optimistic *gloria mea* from "tu autem susceptor meus es *gloria mea*" (key words in any Easter interpretation of Psalm 56) may make more sense in terms of the crisis at Santa Cristina. Similarly, verse 7, "for you have smitten all my enemies upon the cheekbone, you have broken the teeth of the ungodly," prescribed for Easter matins, may also have been suppressed in Vizzana's motet because it would have rung particularly false as a reflection of the struggles around 1620.

Ave stella matutina (no. 3) stands out clearly, not only from the other "political" motets, but also from the rest of the collection (see example 12). It represents Vizzana's only invocation of the Virgin Mary, a neglect that in fact accords with Caroline Bynum's observation that in female spirituality, Christ largely eclipsed Mary, who remained more a male preoccupation.[34] This hymn to the Blessed Virgin might first appear tenuously connected to the putative alternation of "crypto-political" solo motets. Once again, it is the tailoring of the text, especially as subtly highlighted by Vizzana's musical setting, that raises the possibility that the hymn was to be heard as the nuns' isolated plea to that other most common advocate of Roman Catholics.

Whether Lucrezia Vizzana concocted this version of the text herself or simply borrowed it from elsewhere, the present redaction fit this political agenda.

Ave stella matutina,
Mundi princeps et regina,

Virgo sola digna dici
Inter tela inimici,
Clipeum pone salutis
Tuæ titulum virtutis.
O Maria plena gratia,
O mater Dei electa,
Esto nobis via recta
Ad aeterna gaudia
Ubi pax et gloria.
Et nos semper aura [*recte:* aure] pia
Dulcis exaudi Maria.

Hail, morning star, ruler and queen of the world, only virgin worthy to be spoken of amid the weapons of the enemy. Place [before us] the shield of salvation, the insignia of your virtue. O Mary, full of grace, O chosen mother of God, be for us the upright path to eternal joys, where are peace and glory. And always hear us with affectionate ear, sweet Mary.

This antiphon of the Blessed Virgin Mary was already some five hundred years old by Vizzana's day; its fullest version has been attributed to Peter the Venerable, abbot of Cluny (d. 1156):[35]

1. *Ave stella matutina,*
   Peccatorum medicina,
   Mundi princeps et regina
   Esto nobis disciplina.
2. *Sola virgo digna dici,*   5
   Contra tela inimici
   Clipeum pone salutis
   Tuæ titulum virtutis.
3. Tu es enim virga Jesse   10
   In qua Deus fecit esse
   Aaron amygdalum,
   Mundi tollens scandalum.
4. Tu es area compluta,   15
   Caelesti rore imbuta,
   Sicco tamen vellere;
   Tu nos in hoc carcere
5. Consolare propitia,   20
   Dei plena gratia,
   O sponsa Dei electa,
   Esto nobis via recta
6. *Ad aeterna gaudia,*   25
   Ubi pax et gloria,
   Et nos semper aure pia
   Dulcis exaudi Maria.[36]

Example 12. Vizzana, *Ave stella matutina*

Example 12 (*continued*)

Earlier versions by Weerbecke and Brumel had appeared in Petrucci's *Motetti A* of 1502. A four-voice polyphonic setting of the long version, attributed to Maistre Jahn, had been published by Andrea Antico in *Motetti novi libro secondo* in 1520 and also survives in several manuscripts, one preserved in Bologna.[37]

Perhaps more familiar in the early Seicento was a plainchant antiphon for Benedictine use, with a much attenuated text,

Ave stella matutina,
Peccatorum medicina,
Mundi princeps et regina;
Sola virgo digna dici
Contra tela inimici,
Clypeum pone salutis
Tuæ titulum virtutis.
O sponsa Dei electa,
Esto nobis via recta
Ad aeterna gaudia.[38]

That this version remained familiar in Seicento Italy is revealed by its transmission in a polyphonic setting for double chorus by Agostino Agazzari, published in his *Sacrarum cantionum* of 1602.[39] The reappearance of lines from the opening section of the hymn in a composite text, *Salve Mater pia mundi*[40] from Ercole Porta's *Sacro convito musicale* (1620) indicates that the text was likewise familiar to the Banchieri/Vernizzi/Porta musical circle, which may well have influenced Lucrezia Vizzana.

Vizzana's text may omit the middle section (lines 10–20), but because her text retains lines absent from other shortened versions (lines 21, 26–28), it could not simply have been adopted from any of them. The largest omission—the richly erotic "The rod of Jesse is in you, in which God caused the almond of Aaron to be. . . . You are the open courtyard, wet with heavenly dew, while the fleece still remains dry," an exaltation of Mary's virginity startling to modern religious sensibilities in its language—makes most sense as an attempt to avoid distracting from the point of the revised text as a whole. Equally important, however, the excision also gets rid of that particularly loaded word at any convent, especially at Santa Cristina around 1620, given the serious rumors filtering out through the city, *scandalum.*

The omission of "Tu nos in hoc carcere / Consolare propitia" ("In this prison, console us"), on the other hand, may surprise any who have trouble conceiving of convents as anything but prisons for women forced into their monastic vocation. The arranger of this text is likely to have known the original prison lines and consciously to have omitted them, since Vizzana's version does include and modify the second line of the related couplet, "Consolare propitia / *Dei plena gratia*," even though this necessitates dropping a link in the chain of rhymes of the text as a whole. In their looming struggles with the episcopal authorities, the nuns of Santa Cristina pointedly claimed (rightly or wrongly) to have chosen the cloistered life freely. According to the Bolognese chronicler Antonio Francesco Ghiselli, in 1628 they told the prelates that "they were ladies that were not in that place by force, but voluntarily, and by choice."[41] By suppressing the prison reference, Vizzana's text tacitly affirms that same sentiment.

The emended and altered hymn text thus concentrates largely on the Virgin as protector from surrounding enemies, protection specifically through Mary's own virtue. And in the music, Vizzana makes virtue stand out as the most striking image, the musical high point of the first half of the piece, carefully and cleverly prepared. The motet opens in a rather musically schematic manner, with conscious solemnity, as the Virgin is invoked in a comparatively neutral tone, which extends onward into the second couplet. But at *inter tela inimici* that calm is disrupted from the first mention of "the enemy," as rhetorical repetition of textual fragments becomes more overt, while voice and bass struggle in constricted, extremely close imitations, based on trumpetlike calls to battle. It is also telling that Vizzana invokes the Virgin "*amid* the enemies" and not "*against* the enemies," which appears in several versions of the text. Vizzana's emphasis is thus upon the enemies in whose midst she stands, calling to mind, not only a direct biblical model, Psalm 109:2, "Virgam virtutis tuæ emittet Dominus ex Sion: Dominare in medio inimicorum tuorum" ("The Lord sends the rod of your virtue out of Sion: rule in the midst of your enemies"), but also the factionalism that had begun to divide Santa Cristina a good fifteen years before the appearance of *Componimenti musicali.*[42]

The continuing musical unfolding is structured to throw *virtutis* into special relief. Vizzana further intensifies the repetition of *clipeum* ("shield") in the voice by harmonizing it with her by now familiar favorite pair of chromatic chords (F-major vs. D-major) at bar 26. For the key line, *tuæ titulum virtutis* ("the insignia of your virtue"), she returns—certainly consciously—to the melodic and bass outlines of the opening invocation of the Virgin from the first couplet (from bars 10–12), but in a varied, more intensely animated form, to lull the listener into certain unconscious musical expectations. Then, for the last statement of *tuæ titulum virtutis,* having led us to anticipate the same cadence on B♭ (as heard back in the original version at bar 13), she lurches at the last moment unexpectedly into a transposed, sombre phrygian cadence, and then, in unorthodox fashion, leaps away from the suspended d in the voice for the last, anguished *virtutis.*

Such an unusual leap, so rare in Bolognese sacred music, is hardly the sort of musical setting that comes to mind, either for a modern or a seventeenth-century listener, in connection with the word *virtue,* and therefore can only have been worked in to make a particular rhetorical point. It begins to make sense if heard in the context of contemporary events within the convent. Honor and virtue represented the quintessential features of any convent's reputation, and therefore of any authority it might possess. This was a time when the collective virtue of Santa Cristina had been seriously called into question because of the secret defamatory letter sent to Rome, which provoked the pastoral visitation of 1622–23. The introduction of the unorthodox skipwise resolution of the vocal d—the boldest gesture of Vizzana's musical vocabulary, usually associated with despair, supplication, or languishing for lack of the object of desire—may therefore have been intended, not only to highlight "virtue," currently under attack, but also to convey the collective longing for its rightful restoration.

The second half of the motet lapses back into the more neutral tone of the opening, until the urgent petition of its last line compels a return to the earlier heightened musical rhetoric. At "Sweet Mary, hear us" the contrast of chromatic chords on *dulcis* ("sweet") reestablishes the spirit of the first half of the work. A second invocation, intensified both by its transposition upward to the top of the vocal range, and heightened at the last minute by a leap from the top e♭ to a momentary, bitter dissonance against the bass, reiterates one last time the central plea for the Virgin's protection in this time of trouble and threatened virtue.

It could well be that Vizzana saw in these motets a way to touch the hearts of those beyond the wall, in the midst of a crisis that Cecilia Bianchi claimed "began because of music." A search back through other archival documents, widening out from Bologna, to Camaldoli, and to Rome, reveals, however, that, although music had indeed been a significant element of discord, especially in the early days of the conflict, it was eclipsed by others more potent and elemental, likewise festering over two decades. These were the forces that would carry the convent to the brink of destruction.

SEVEN

The Social Dynamics of Division at Santa Cristina

"One provided the wood and kindling and the other piled them in the form whence followed the conflagration"

There was a certain donna Emilia of the Grassi family, but illegitimate, a full-blooded woman, and, as a result, cheerful, and free in her words and actions. . . . In her youth she was good-looking, eloquent, talented, a singer, a player of the organ, the harp, and other instruments—and well; splendid and open-handed, so that she won to her the hearts, not only of the nuns, but of others too, and therefore she wanted to have a hand in all the affairs and obligations of the nuns and the convent.

The other nun (. . . in her youth also a friend of donna Emilia's), was a donna Cecilia [Bianchi], who had only one ally, donna Gentile Malvasia, who, had she not been subverted, was as amiable as her name. But she consorted with the she-wolf and learned to howl. This donna Cecilia was melancholy and of swarthy complexion, dominated by irascibility and consequently spiteful, haughty, envious. She criticized the actions of others and retained a high opinion of herself. But above all she wanted to ape donna Emilia, but without her manner and grace.

This sketch of diametrically opposed rivals was drawn in the late 1640s by don Mauro Ruggeri, former prior general of the Camaldolese order (d. 1660).[1] Ruggeri could speak with some authority, for he had served as father confessor and titular abbot to the convent of Santa Cristina in Bologna during the crisis and the years that had led up to it. His rambling and discursive manuscript "Caduta di Santa Cristina di Bologna," surviving in the archive at Camaldoli, offers a detailed account of the crisis. When swept up in his own energetic verbal flights, Ruggeri may unwittingly have let drop the odd unsympathetic remark, unseemly, but common enough among nuns' superiors, when characterizing the nuns once in his care. But in matters of fact he is consistently confirmed by documents from the archives of the convent, city, diocese, and the Vatican, which enhance his credibility in the many instances where he remains our sole witness to what went on behind the walls on via Fondazza.[2]

Ruggeri's view proves more evenhanded than one might anticipate, for he apportions almost as much blame for the disaster that was to follow to Emilia Grassi as to the considerably less sympathetic Cecilia Bianchi. His chief villains lurk among the Bolognese episcopal hierarchy. Ruggeri does his best to hold himself and his fellow Camaldolese largely above reproach. Good-hearted, simple, and well-meaning, but at times a little foolish, the Camaldolese monks called upon to minister to the nuns appear at the mercy, on the one hand, of the infinitely more powerful Cardinal Archbishop Ludovico Ludovisi and his diocesan ministers, and, on the other, of the deluded aspirations and subtle persuasions of the likes of Emilia Grassi and Cecilia Bianchi.

Ruggeri's Polonian advice to don Giusto Bordino (or Bardino) of Santa Maria degli Angeli in Florence, who succeeded him as the nuns' confessor, was thus to keep his distance from Cecilia Bianchi, humoring her with kind words and glossing over her errors, and above all to elude Emilia Grassi, who, not about to be directed, "would have used every possible deceit to win him over." Ruggeri had barely left town, however, when the inexperienced Bordino, "an immature brain that presumes to know more than everyone else," promptly divulged everything to the forceful and fearless donna Emilia, who inevitably gained his confidence and easily won him to her cause with various gifts that the needy monk could not resist.[3]

The details of Mauro Ruggeri's story are woven into a kind of parable that illustrates how the absence from a few nuns' hearts of the seventeenth-century cardinal virtues of humility and obedience could undo the good work of many. To hear him tell it, his own beneficent ministrations did little to control these unreasonable and irrational enemies, for, as he puts it, in words that echo and reecho back at least as far as Ecclesiasticus, "the fury of a woman may well be covered up sometimes, but in fact it is never extinguished."[4] Ruggeri's gentle exhortations to patience and humility as a means to perfection had little effect on the implacable rivals, whose ways he contrasts with those of the likes of donna Laura Bocchi, known for her "sweet manner" and "patience," and, above all, with those of Lucrezia Vizzana's aunt, the venerable donna Flaminia Bombacci.

As a foil to donna Emilia and donna Cecilia, Ruggeri offers donna Flaminia's brief, pious biography, which would later help to earn her a place in *Annales Camaldulenses* and even in the Camaldolese menology down to the present day. It is interesting that Ruggeri leaves to others any mention of the "miraculous" side to donna Flaminia's history, reflecting his caution about violating Urban VIII's rules on the promotion of holy people, part of the turn in the post-Tridentine hierarchy from the marvelous as a symbol of sanctity toward morality and exemplary behavior, guided by the clergy. Less inclined, perhaps, to accept the current ecclesiastical view that miracles reflected misguided illusion rather than divine intervention, Gasparo

Bombacci carefully related that during a violent thunderstorm, donna Flaminia three times started for her cell and three times was distracted, and as she entered her sister's cell instead, her own was struck by lightning.[5]

Her father confessor concentrates instead upon virtually every paradigmatic saintly attribute fostered by the church in the post-Tridentine period. Indeed, the catalogue of donna Flaminia's virtues might almost have been culled from the official life of one of the newly minted post-Tridentine saints, Santa Francesca Romana, canonized in 1608:[6] asceticism; regular discipline; years of dedication to constant prayer; exemplary religiosity that provided an effective model to those around her. Donna Flaminia was filled with compassion—for a year she cheerfully tended to a dying nun's breast cancer, whose seven open wounds leaked pus black as ink (a detail recalling the ministrations of late medieval saintly women, particularly Saint Catherine of Siena, who had sucked the pus from the wound in a dying woman's breast). She was charitable—donna Flaminia dedicated what money she had to underwrite the sacramental life of the parish and loaned her clothing to poorer nuns, while she herself wore sackcloth (a contrast with the illicit bits of finery in dress decried during the visitation of 1622–23 and also noted by Ruggeri). Above all Flaminia Bombacci displayed perfect humility—even when verbally abused by other nuns, she patiently asked forgiveness for having offended. For Ruggeri, it was donna Flaminia's prayers that had held the devil and disaster at bay.[7]

"I CALLED HER MISBEGOTTEN"

It is one of the rivals herself, donna Cecilia, seconded by don Mauro Ruggeri, who reveals almost in passing a primary force, which not only provoked donna Cecilia's and donna Emilia's original falling out, but also set in motion the convent's slow decline. The key sentence from Cecilia Bianchi's memorial, offered to the visitors on her second day of testimony, had opened "And it began because of music." She then continued, "And because we had words, I called her misbegotten, and she responded to me most unvirtuously."[8] Ruggeri, on the other hand, had begun his description, "fù una certa d[onn]a Emilia de' Grassi, *ma naturale*" (emphasis added). Emilia Grassi may have come from one of Bologna's oldest and most illustrious families, active in the city since the twelfth century, and also one of the most prominent at the convent, to which the Grassi had sent more novices during the sixteenth century than virtually any other family. But she was also known to bear the taint of illegitimacy, a blot unlikely to have been overlooked by her aristocratic peers, and one she could not forget, as Cecilia Bianchi had learned all too well. In this light, the probable original scenario becomes clearer. Back in the early years of the century, Emilia Grassi, the already domineering *maestra del coro*, must have tried to impose her will on the singer Cecilia Bianchi, or to assert her superiority, once too often. Bianchi hit back with a word Grassi could not tolerate: *bastard.*

As Guido Ruggiero has suggested, during the early Renaissance, illegitimates—at least those fathered by sons of the family (but not any born to daughters)—were widely accepted in noble households, although they were commonly married off to families of somewhat lower rank. But they were also morally and legally ambiguous, and a potential threat to the family patrimony. As Thomas Kuehn puts it, "bastards were dishonorable creatures, scarcely better than beasts." By the sixteenth century, an increased Italian preoccupation with proper birth seems to have brought bastards a significant loss of status; they could be excluded from economic and political privileges and from family inheritance if not specifically singled out in wills or unless legitimized, as was the case in Bologna with Lucrezia Vizzana's illegitimate nephew, Angelo Michele, who became her father's sole heir in the absence of other male offspring.[9]

The taint to noble blood implied by illegitimacy might partly explain Emilia Grassi's presence at Santa Cristina in the first place. For, when Renaissance nobles looked for wives, they usually wanted unsullied bloodlines. As Francesco Barbaro had put it in *De re uxoria liber,* which was widely read and reprinted between 1513 and 1632:

> We know that many, and indeed most, superior species of vegetation and nuts will in no way grow if not in their characteristic and superior locality. But if they migrate to undistinguished territory, they put off their innate dispositions, and the defiled fruit deteriorates the better sap. Also, outstanding young shoots, if they are grafted to poorer branches, yield inferior fruit. Wherefore it is also reasonable that among actual human beings, they may hope for by far more illustrious children from distinguished women.[10]

The illegitimate Emilia Grassi may thus have been difficult to market. Rather than find her a husband of lower rank willing to take her, and perhaps have to compensate such a husband with a larger dowry than usual, her father chose a cheaper route: to send her off to Santa Cristina.

Such a defect of birth could also, however, affect a woman's chances outside the marriage market. In the 1580s, hints about the possible illegitimacy of the renowned convent-trained singer Laura Bovia, "niece" of Giacomo Bovio, *primociero* of San Petronio, had helped to derail the negotiations for her acceptance as a lady-in-waiting to the duchess of Mantua.[11] Nobles within the cloister were as sensitive to this issue as their sisters at court. A protest by the noble Benedictine nuns of the convent of San Zaccaria in Venice that a patriarch's proposed reform in 1521 would dishonor their convent by introducing "Greeks and common bastards" indicates that illegitimacy remained a political issue within patrician women's religious houses. That the Congregation of Bishops had to reassure the diocesan curia in "Cordea" and Spoleto in 1592 and 1594 that Sixtus V's bull *Contra illegitimos* did not apply to convents, where bastards could still be elected superiors, a point carefully noted in the documents of the archdiocesan curia in Bologna, reveals that the situation had not greatly changed by the end of the century.[12]

This aspersion must partly explain donna Emilia's extraordinary vengeful campaign against her former friend, "who she believed had undermined her reputation before our superiors and the laity, but I don't know the details," as the abbess put it. Emilia Grassi's preoccupations with her flawed origins also help to explain her obsessive attempts to attain and retain a dominant position within the cloister. Her natural musical talent seems initially to have helped her achieve a special artistic distinction on both sides of the convent wall. Furthermore, her lavish spending of her own private means, which amounted to £100 a year (a significant sum by convent standards[13]), supplemented by sizable amounts apparently drained off from the convent's own coffers during her reign as abbess, looks like a concerted effort to overcome the defect of her birth through musical and artistic adornments: on the musical side, Adriano Banchieri's *Messa solenne,* and on the artistic, Bernardino Baldi's altarpiece, *The Coronation of the Virgin,* for the external church.

The dedication to Banchieri's *Messa solenne,* whose title page lacks the coat of arms that appears on other publications dedicated to individual nuns, confirms this suspicion with remarkable clarity. Having lauded the musical performances at Santa Cristina under donna Emilia's direction, Banchieri continues,

> Recalling the affection that I have maintained since my earliest years for your most ancient and illustrious house, the Grassi, whence have come cardinals, prelates, senators, and other personages who always have, and still reflect great luster on this our city of Bologna, I responded to my friend that truly *from such a good tree nothing could issue but the most excellent fruit.*

The composer's proclamation of Emilia Grassi's good name and illustrious roots reads almost like a response to the remarks of Francesco Barbaro quoted above.[14]

To establish her political position, she also worked to win over the younger sisters with special favors. She was "cunning and shrewd in gaining followers," as don Mauro put it. She escorted the junior nuns to the gateway she controlled as porter so that they could visit with their relatives, and she provided little tea parties at the gate for those who had been accepted for future admission (a useful means to win them and, perhaps more important, their families, to her side before their entry). It came out during the investigation of 1622–23 that the most unusual of these parties had occurred just the summer before, when a long table had been arranged across the gateway, with half inside the convent for donna Emilia's cloistered allies and half outside for the laypeople—another fine example of how nuns observed the restrictions of enclosure imposed upon them to the letter, but no further. It turned out, however, that the guests had included Brandoligi Gozzadini, brother of donna Claudia Gozzadini of Santa Cristina—but also a relative of the chief interrogator in the investigation, Suffragan Bishop Angelo Gozzadini. In the copy of the testimony prepared for the archiepiscopal archive, the name of the bishop's relative has been discreetly scratched out and disguised with additional meaningless letters.[15]

To consolidate her power during her time as abbess, Emilia Grassi had shrewdly appointed as bursar one of her cronies, donna Pantasilea Tovagli, "who didn't know how to write anything but her name," as the abbess revealed.[16] Grassi had thus managed to concentrate both executive and financial control in her own hands, presumably to gain easier access to convent funds for her own pet projects. Donna Emilia's convent patronage and that of her allies aroused a proprietary spirit at odds with the monastic ideal of the *vita commune,* a textbook example of why convent superiors discouraged the control and dispersal of personal wealth by individual nuns within the cloister, where family ties and status, differences in wealth, and control of personal property could open rifts within the community. The investigation of 1622–23 confirmed the allegation in the earlier letter to Archbishop Ludovisi that Emilia Grassi and some of her immediate followers had even expropriated the spacious public rooms of the convent, intended for the novitiate and infirmary, as their informal personal quarters. For their part, Grassi and her followers offered the justifications that there was currently but one novice, and that in winter the infirm found it more comfortable and convenient to remain in their own cells. Grassi herself had even gone so far as to remove silver candelabra and other altar furniture from the sacristy to her rooms, although she later claimed that this was only for safekeeping. As abbess she had finally become so domineering that nobody was willing to reelect her to the office. But even after her demotion, she never lost her will to rule.

Donna Emilia's most damaging blow to Santa Cristina, again a product of her insecurities about the defect of her birth, had first been hinted at by donna Colomba Glavarina on the third day of testimony in 1622: "I believe that this dissension between these two sisters, that is suor Cecilia and donna Emilia"—note, again, the subtle distinction in title—"results from these *putte,*" young girls educated in convents in anticipation of their future profession. The abbess further clarifies Glavarina's meaning:

> Nor did she [Emilia Grassi] fail to cause an uproar at the time when attempts were made to introduce *educande,* as also in 1604, she wrote a truly infamous

petition against those who had kept lay students, and sent it to Rome to the Congregation of Most Illustrious Cardinals. And to support her opinion she provoked the greatest tumults, so that lay students no longer returned here for their education.[17]

Don Mauro's explanation of Emilia Grassi's action makes perfect sense:

She saw that the convent was filled with nuns from the leading families of Bologna: Pepoli, Malvezzi, Ariosti, Bolognetti, Gozzadini, [illegible], Malvasia, Zambeccari, Bocchi, and others like them, whose relatives were kept there to be educated, most of whom then received the veil. And as noblewomen, they consequently did not wish to be subjected to the beck and call of donna Emilia.[18]

In the years before 1604, Santa Cristina was graced by a Pepoli (a patron of music), a Malvezzi (a rival singer), two Bolognetti (patrons of art), a Gozzadini, two Malvasie, a Zambeccari (a patron of art), and two Bocchi, all families of senatorial rank, not to mention others from comparably distinguished families, two Bottrigari (patrons of art), a Leoni (a patron of music), and, of course, a Bianchi. In fact, of the forty-two *professe* in those years, no fewer than twenty-one hailed from the first families of the Bolognese elite, and another eleven from patrician families of the second rank, while the remaining ten included two Corbina sisters, related to Alessandro Ludovisi, the future Pope Gregory XV.[19]

In such illustrious company, donna Emilia had reason to feel eclipsed. Gentlemen from the second rank of the patriciate were hardly ever elevated to senatorial rank, because it would offend the *cavalieri* of the highest rank, and the socially compromised Emilia Grassi could not have expected better from the upper crust of convent society. Religious vows probably rendered cloistered sisters of the nobility no less likely than their brothers and sisters in the world to "adopt with their inferiors a less civil manner," to be "severe with their inferiors if they do not give way to them at once," as Camillo Baldi remarked in his acerbic critique of the Bolognese social hierarchy.[20] Shortly after the turn of the century, Emilia Grassi therefore had complained to the convent superiors that the *educande* of these noble families distracted the nuns from strict observance of their Rule, and that the lay students were kept in virtual imprisonment and treated like slaves or servants—claims ironically close to the ones repeated in the letter to Ludovisi in 1622. As a result, on 20 September 1604, the Sacred Congregation had forbidden the convent to accept *educande* in future.[21]

This meant, of course, that the natural flow of noble blood to Santa Cristina had been staunched, for girls almost invariably professed at the convents where they had been educated; once accepted, only in unusual circumstances did they go off to take their vows elsewhere. This left Emilia Grassi and her contingent in a better position to reject any undesirable prospects when their acceptance was voted on in chapter; the prospective postulant would not have been raised within the cloister, and she would thus not already have formed social alliances to support her election.

If this strategy failed, the Grassi faction could even scare the entrants off before their final admission. Don Mauro also hints at this practice, but unfortunately only the less reliable donna Cecilia offers details of how it worked. When the mother of a girl from the illustrious Orsi family was fed tales of what supposedly went on inside Santa Cristina, "she said she wanted to make her daughter a servant of the Lord and not of the world," and enrolled her instead among the Discalced Carmelites at that newly founded paradigm of piety, the convent of San Gabriele, just over the back wall from Santa Cristina. The case of the prospective postulant Anna Tovagli was even more extraordinary:

> When she asked who her [novice] mistress would be and she was told she would have donna Giuditta [Nobili], she decided not to come—she rejected her, and this happened in her presence. And donna Emilia, apart from other offensive comments that scandalized those in attendance, said that if she were in another's hands, she would always persecute her. And the girl's mother said she no longer wanted her to be a nun, and married her off instead.

Clearly, one cannot take donna Cecilia's testimony entirely at face value.[22] But, whether or not the tales she carried were completely true, the impact of the Grassi stratagem on the convent was disastrous. In the eighteen years between the Congregation of Bishops' ruling on *educande* and the investigation of 1622–23, a mere six girls seem to have joined the ranks of the *professe* at Santa Cristina. Of them, only Romea Ursina Bocchi hailed from one of the families identified by don Mauro as most illustrious. Of the four from the second rank of the patriciate—lower in the social hierarchy than the Grassi—only Giuliana Glavarini already had close relatives within the cloister who enjoyed a position strengthened by lavish convent patronage. The families of all the others were virtual newcomers to the convent. It is significant that when Lucrezia Vizzana's maternal uncle Antonio Bombacci sent his own daughter to the cloister, it was not to Santa Cristina, which had received his aunts, sisters, and nieces, but to San Giovanni Battista.[23]

Recognizing the seriousness of this trend, around 1620, the more astute sisters, led by madre donna Lorenza Bonsignori, conferred with Mauro Ruggeri, who composed a petition to the Congregation of Bishops to rescind the ban on *educande*. Suffragan Bishop Gozzadini was dispatched to Santa Cristina to poll the nuns on the issue. The abbess voted yes; the most senior nun, madre donna Vittoria Ghezzi, a friend of donna Emilia's for more than thirty years, next voted no; and thus it continued, back and forth. Many of the nuns had no opinion, or said Gozzadini should put them down with the majority. Ruggeri (who rarely had a good word to say about anyone in the diocesan curia) suggests that the suffragan bishop recorded those votes in the column that would most please the Congregation of Bishops: the nays. In the end, contrary to expectations, the measure was defeated, to the great consternation of the mother abbess and above all of Cecilia Bianchi, who had taken up the issue of *educande* as her own personal cause.

Various nuns' testimony during the investigation in 1622–23 also helps to clarify the political situation that had provoked the crisis concerning *educande*. In the interrogation of 1622–23, as in the vote a few years earlier, more than half the sisters ventured no opinion. Those who came out specifically in favor of *educande* included only Cecilia Bianchi, Maura Taddea Bottrigari, Lorenza Bonsignori (the abbess), and, interestingly enough, the venerable Flaminia Bombacci. Donna Flaminia's vote helps to explain the comment of the historian Gasparo Bombacci: "She [Flaminia] had different sentiments from her sister and from her nieces, desiring to concede part of the satisfaction demanded by the other nuns. But her own opinion had to follow the will of the majority."[24] This would not be the last manifestation of donna Flaminia's political savvy, as we shall see.

During the pastoral visitation of 1622–23, nine sisters lined up squarely behind Emilia Grassi, usually in words that echo her own so exactly that in this case, at least, there may well have been some advance coaching: "Educande non habbiamo et non ne voressimo havere" ("We do not have *educande* and we would not want to have them"). It is particularly interesting that the negatives included every single postulant from Olimpia Cattani and Lucrezia Vizzana (probably the last to enter before the ban of 1604) down to the two most recent (who did not commit themselves either way). Donna Emilia's faction thus encompassed just about all those junior members of slightly more humble origins, by Santa Cristina standards, whose entry she may have screened and whose favor she had presumably curried.

Lucrezia Vizzana's opposition to *educande* is particularly interesting, for it suggests that class distinctions could also touch even the more established, better-integrated sisters. Her vote may reveal that she had reason to share some of Grassi's sensitivity about her own status, in this case, because of the mercantile origins of her own mother's family, which, as it turns out, had also come in for caustic comment. Presumably because the Bombacci made their money in the silk trade, another nun had once called donna Lucrezia's aunt, madre donna Flaminia Bombacci, a "silkspinner, [one] of the worst affronts she knew, because she was a relative of merchants," as Mauro Ruggeri put it. Ruggeri was also careful to point out, of course, that the exemplary madre donna Flaminia reacted to this insult with patience and humility.[25] The incident reveals just how powerful and potentially divisive a force family status must have been in the social dynamic of the house.

The nuns' opinions, delivered to the visitors in 1622–23, offer striking testimony to the expertise with which donna Emilia had implemented her invidious stratagem. But although this scheme served to consolidate Grassi's own political position and that of her allies, the long-range effect would prove to be disastrous. A primary source of convent influence beyond the wall, its links to powerful patrician families at the highest level, had been severely weakened. It was a blow from which Santa Cristina never really recovered.

"A LOST SOUL"

The more immediate impact of this defeat concerning *educande*, which seems to have eclipsed any earlier musical rivalries, was to provoke donna Cecilia Bianchi's alleged epistolary campaign against the convent to Cardinal Archbishop Ludovisi, prompting the visitation in the winter of 1622–23. As don Mauro summed up donna Emilia's and donna Cecilia's handiwork, "one provided the wood and kindling, and the other, one might say, with her fiery rage, piled them in the form whence followed the conflagration."[26]

Cecilia Bianchi, who at this point moves from archrival to archvillain, had been a long time getting there. She remains a decidedly more elusive, enigmatic, and complicated figure than her implacable enemy. When she had arrived at Santa Cristina around 1590, Irenea Bianchi, the future donna Cecilia, already offered an interesting contrast to donna Emilia. The Bianchi were particularly ancient and distinguished among the hundred first families of Bologna, and especially prominent in the neighborhood of nearby via Santo Stefano. Curiously, however, Pompeo Dolfi's discussion of the Bianchi in his history of the Bolognese nobility entirely skips the years between 1576 and 1617 and includes no mention of donna Cecilia's father, Stefano di Giovanni Battista Bianchi.[27]

The family had had few connections, and apparently had developed no particular status, at Santa Cristina. A Maria de Blanchi had served as prioress in the 1330s and from 1343 through the 1350s, and two female members of her family had been benefactors in the same period, but after that the Bianchi do not reappear in the convent necrology. On 11 August 1590, in the terms of her entry into the convent, Irenea Bianchi, then about fourteen years old, resident in the parish of Santa Caterina in Strada Maggiore, not far from the convent of Santa Cristina, renounced any rights to paternal or maternal inheritance in favor of her father. Within three years, Stefano Bianchi was dead. When donna Cecilia's dowry was settled on 6 November 1593, apparently during her novitiate year, her brother, Luca

Bianchi, still a minor, was unable to come up with it in cash and instead transferred pieces of real estate to the convent, which in turn leased some of the property right back to him.[28]

Nevertheless, over the years, Cecilia Bianchi achieved considerable financial status—although, interestingly enough, no evidence of any convent patronage has come to light. In 1622, she claimed a private yearly income of no less than 27 scudi (approximately £135), one of the largest at Santa Cristina, and substantially more than Emilia Grassi's. That she had abandoned her secular name, Irenea, in favor of that of the patron saint of music, an uncommon choice at Santa Cristina, suggests a special enthusiasm for the art, one she managed to share, at least for a while, with her musical colleague Emilia Grassi up until the time when they "had words" (in Bianchi's extraordinary understatement).

By contrast with other nuns such as the Grassi, Bombacci, Glavarini, Bottrigari, Vitali, Bolognetti, Sarti, and Bocchi, who had strong historical and generational ties to the convent, even if they were not necessarily all outstandingly wealthy or noble, Cecilia Bianchi thus seems to have been something of an outsider from the start. Both the abbess and donna Cecilia testified that her rival frequently labeled her *un'anima persa*, a lost soul. Bianchi claimed also to have been called "a hypocrite, a sham, a fake." The abbess more than once brought up donna Emilia's epithet, "hypocrite," and Grassi invoked it herself in front of the clerical visitors.

In *hipocrita*, donna Emilia had found an especially loaded word. For hypocrisy had come down as a favorite characterization of feigned religiosity and false saintliness from Matthew 23:13ff, to Saint Ambrose, to Saint Thomas Aquinas, and flourished particularly in the late sixteenth and seventeenth centuries, especially in association with religious women. In Antonio Pagani's widely read *La Breve somma delli essercitii de' penitenti* of 1587, for example, hypocrisy is a sin associated with "diabolical vainglory" and acts as "a coverup for secret vices with deceits and simulations of virtue. . . . Hypocrites are called dissemblers. . . . Doing evil in secret, they make a show of doing good in public." By 1638, hypocrisy was classed as a diabolical art based on "the vanity and frivolousness of some petty women" in *Pratiche per discerner lo spirito buono dal malvagio*. For Jean-Joseph Surin, who in those years achieved notoriety as the exorcist of the even more notorious Seur Jeanne des Anges and the possessed Ursulines of Loudun, hypocrisy was "the detestable mask of those, corrupt to the core and leading a licentious life, who pretend to appear austere and modest, and seek to attain a reputation for sanctity."[29] The shrewd donna Emilia could hardly have chosen a more effective epithet in mounting her counterattack.

It is interesting that Mauro Ruggeri suggests a similar view in his initial description of donna Cecilia: "She wanted to ape donna Emilia." Gabriella Zarri has pointed out that, in addition to being one of the most common iconographical symbols of the devil, the monkey carried a second meaning, implying deception.[30] One could well imagine the Grassi faction reciting poems such as this later seventeenth-century example against "cursed and vain hypocrisy," within earshot of donna Cecilia:

> Scimmia de' Santi in pubblico ti fai,
> Ti scandolezzi, e contro il vizio esclami;
> Fingi quella bontà che in te non hai,
> Ed il Mondo fuggir, che segui ed ami.[31]

> Busily, publicly, Saints you are aping,
> Constantly scandalized, vice you abhor.
> Feigning that goodness that in you is lacking,
> To flee the world you pursue and adore.

"SHE CONSORTED WITH THE SHE-WOLF AND LEARNED TO HOWL"

Emilia's monkey was not the most startling characterization in don Mauro's original portrait of Cecilia Bianchi, cited at the opening of this chapter. To describe the transformation that donna Cecilia had worked on Maria Gentile Malvasia, donna Emilia's successor as Bianchi's closest friend, he wrote "praticò cola lupa, imparò ad urlare" ("She consorted with [played with, was on familiar terms with, dealt with, practiced with, had intercourse with] the she-wolf and learned to howl").

Ruggeri no doubt had in mind the proverb whose modern equivalent runs "Chi va col lupo impara ad ululare" ("Whoever runs with the wolf learns to howl"). He must also have been thinking of the biblical sheep/ wolves paradigm when he coined this phrase, particularly since clerical superiors often referred to their female charges as sheep. Indeed, don Mauro himself had just likened the diocesan curia's betrayal of Santa Cristina to "the parable of the ewe told to King David by the prophet Nathan"— another of his singular animal analogies, given the nature of the original parable. Later he would compare secular priests' actions to "putting the poor lambs in the mouth of the wolf."[32] Given Bianchi's and Malvasia's false claims to the pastoral visitors, in this case he probably had particularly in mind an antiphon for the eighth Sunday after Trinity: "Attendite a falsis prophetis, qui veniunt ad vos in vestimentis ovium, intrinsecus autem sunt lupi rapaces, a fructibus eorum cognosceris eos" ("Beware of false prophets, who come to you in sheep's clothing, but inwardly are ravenous wolves, and by their fruits you will know them").[33] It is even possible that Don Mauro was drawing upon the related traditional association of the wolf with hypocrisy. In Cesare Ripa's *Iconologia overo descrittione di diverse imagini cavate dall'antichità e di propria inventione* (Rome, 1603), "Hippocresia" is represented as a woman in religious garb, carrying a rosary and a prayerbook, but with the legs and feet of a wolf.[34]

But wolves and dogs had for centuries also commonly symbolized what the nuns saw as the primary aspect of Cecilia Bianchi's behavior: revenge and uncontrolled vengeance. Ruggeri's analogy resonates with a long and rich Renaissance tradition of dogs or wolves as symbols of treason, of quarrelsomeness and envy, of the fury of the vendetta. The wolf represented such a common symbol for vengeful madness at its most threatening that the truce ending a vendetta was known as *pace lupina* ("wolf's peace"). Similarly, those banished for wild acts of vengeance—as Cecilia and Maria Gentile had effectively been ostracized for what the nuns saw as their vendetta against the community—were symbolized by the wolf, and sometimes known as wolfmen. Ruggeri's words, "imparò ad urlare," likewise recall descriptions of rioting north Italian peasants as "barking dogs," or of vengeful Hecuba, who, after the death of her children, barked like a dog.[35]

According to biblical tradition, wolves were nocturnal animals, likely to get at the fold after dark, while dogs or she-wolves could also be symbols of promiscuity or wild sexuality.[36] Pastoral visitors' constant concerns with what the convent "sheep" in their care did at night suggests a negative significance, not only for Ruggeri's noun, but also for his verb: instead of the modern "*va* col *lupo*," we find "*praticò* cola *lupa*." *Praticare* could take on a pejorative implication, particularly in judicial contexts, as when the inquisitors at Santa Cristina asked "Se nel Monastero, ò pure alle grade *prattichino persone sospette*" ("If suspicious people frequent the convent or likewise the grates"), or when Lucrezia Vizzana responded "non conosco che vi siano abusi nel convento *ne cattive pratiche*" ("I do not know that there are abuses in the convent or evil practices"). And *praticare* or *pratica* could also take on sexual connotations.

In this light, it is possible that there might be some connection between Mauro Ruggeri's words to describe the relationship of donna Cecilia and donna Maria Gentile, and the words of several sisters in response to a question that inevitably came up during pastoral visitations. When asked if all the nuns slept alone at Santa Cristina, some nuns responded vaguely that sisters occasionally slept *accompagnate* of necessity, for reasons of health or in the depth of winter—although donna Claudia Gozzadini admitted candidly that "some nuns sleep in company out of fear, as I do when one of the nuns dies."[37] In those bitter winters, when the snow lay deep—so deep that in February 1615, the chapel roof at the convent of Sant'Agnese had collapsed under its weight[38]—when at Santa Cristina the primary heat may have come from the fire in a common room during the day, the nuns sensibly sought whatever warmth they could find, in spite of clerical misgivings about the practice.

But Romualda Ghirardelli, the most junior *professa,* called on to testify first, had also commented rather pointedly: "Every nun sleeps in her cell, and there are as many cells as nuns—and more. And two nuns sleep in the same cell, that is donna Cecilia and donna Gentile—and in the same bed."[39] Half a dozen other sisters remarked upon the fact that Bianchi and Malvasia slept together, although the abbess suggested that they slept in separate beds, while donna Romea Bocchi offered the justification that donna Maria Gentile was often sick. The most senior nun, madre donna Vittoria Ghezzi, on the other hand, rather emphatically seconded the claim of her most junior colleague, that the pair slept *in uno solo letto*—in contrast with the Vitali sisters ("but they have two beds").

It is significant that of the convent's two most assiduous critics, Maria Gentile Malvasia seems to have had nothing at all to say on this matter, although she could at least have pointed out that the Vitali sisters shared a cell, while Cecilia Bianchi's own testimony is notable for an uncharacteristic vagueness that for once rivals the other nuns' evasive responses—and garnered an "X" from the visitors in the margin of the original transcript:

> The nuns, every one, sleep in their own separate cells, and some sleep accompanied [—in the same cell or in the same bed?], on the pretext of illness; and in winter some nuns [—which ones?] sleep accompanied in some [—one? two?] beds; and in summer they sleep separately.[40]

What donna Cecilia's and donna Maria Gentile's sleeping arrangements actually were is impossible to say—but an on-site inspection did reveal two beds in Bianchi's cell, as well as no fewer than four in Emilia Grassi's.[41] And the reality is probably less important than what the various testimony suggests it was imagined to be, for that was the reality that directly affected the social dynamic within the convent walls.

The other nuns' testimony in this matter may also illuminate another of donna Cecilia's own singularly vague answers about her relationship to her earlier friend turned enemy, a response striking for its circumlocutory character, which makes clear translation difficult:

> La causa io no[n] lo so investigare, se no[n] ch[e] pare pretenda d'haverli io ad esserli sogetta particolarmente in più stretto modo di quello ch[e] sono co[n] l'altre, et io pretendo no[n] gl'esser' più obligata ch[e] sono co[n] l'altre, et essa si lamenta sempre di me ch[e] la perseguito.

> I do not know how to figure out the cause, if it isn't that it seems she would demand to have me be subject to her particularly, in a more intimate way than I am with the others; and I claim not to be more obligated to her than to the others. And she always complains that I torment her.

Cecilia Bianchi's description of the breakup contrasts with the abbess's more matter-of-fact account of the same event:

Il ch[e] anco procede p[er]ch[e] Dona Cecilia lavorava insieme con Dona Emilia et conoscendo essa Dona Cecilia ch[e] no[n] poteva soportare la sudetta Dona Emilia, ch[e] pretendeva fare la superiora adosso Dona Cecilia, per ciò separandosi da essa diede occasione d'acrescere sospetti et sdegni.

It also happens because donna Cecilia was working together with donna Emilia, and when donna Cecilia realized that she couldn't bear the said donna Emilia, who insisted on playing the superior to donna Cecilia, for that reason, in breaking away from her, she created an opportunity to increase suspicions and anger.[42]

The contorted syntax of donna Cecilia's own recounting of the rift, with its shifting, ambiguous pronouns, becomes a metaphor for their tortured, ambivalent relationship. Could Bianchi's language somehow be hinting that Emilia Grassi had attempted to create one of those "particular friendships" that nuns have been exhorted to avoid and that prelates have endeavored for centuries to suppress? Could the other nuns have hoped by their testimony as to Cecilia's sleeping habits to undermine her credibility, to suggest the inner corruption beneath her mask of hypocrisy by playing upon the imaginings behind their superiors' leading question?

The serious view among Bolognese clergy of this sort of transgression, real or imagined, had been demonstrated some twenty years earlier by Gabriele Paleotti's vicar general, Monsignor Domenico Ottolini, who after a pastoral visitation to Santa Margherita in June 1591 had threatened the nuns with six months' imprisonment, deprivation of the veil, and no access to the grates if they "should dare or presume in future to sleep together in the same bed or in the same room." Just how squeamish the diocesan curia remained about this issue is strikingly brought home by an incident during Cardinal Colonna's pastoral visitation to San Guglielmo in 1633: "He moved on to the cells of suor Diana Gabriela, and of suor Lesbia Ildebranda de' Grassi. And as for this last one, His Eminence changed her name, imposing upon her the name suor Maria Teresa, and ordering the prioress that henceforth she should be called thus."[43]

"Particular friendships" and their potential physical component had long been seen as a threat even to nuns' vow of chastity. Erasmus's colloquy of 1523, *Virgo* ΜΙΣΟΓΑΜΟΣ, later translated into French verse by Clément Marot as *Colloque de la vierge mesprisant mariage*, takes the form of a dialogue in which one Eubulus attempts to dissuade Catherine from the cloistered life by calling the nuns' chastity into question in just this way:

Eub. Nothing's virginal among those virgins in other respects either.
Cath. No? Why not, if you please?
Eub. Because there are more who copy Sappho's behavior than share her talent.
Cath. I don't quite understand what you mean.

Eub. And I say these things in order that the time may not come when you
do understand, my dear Catharine.

In the sequel, "The Repentant Girl," a sadder but wiser Catherine, having quickly abandoned the cloister, darkly hints at horrors, which she ada-
mantly refuses to reveal.[44]

This view must have retained a certain currency beyond pastoral visitors'
exhortations and prohibitions. In a sixteenth-century Italian songbook,
right beside a setting of a poem by Blessed Catherine Vigri, founder of the
convent of Corpus Domini in Bologna, on the austerities and strictures of
convent life, there also appears a satire on the joys of convent living, *Moni-
cella mi farei* ("I'd like to become a little nun"). One stanza seems coyly to
confirm what Erasmus, Marot, and other outsiders imagined went on there.
It also reconfirms the sexual paranoia that remained an abiding aspect of
clerics' views of convents:

Sopratutto vorria avere
'Na divota vaga e bella
Che mi dessi ogni piacere
Ed anch'io ne dessi ad ella.[45]

What would please me beyond measure
Is one pious, fair, and winsome,
Who would give me ev'ry pleasure,
As I'd give to her, and then some.

Although these various veiled hints directed back and forth by donna
Cecilia, by don Mauro, and by the other nuns at Santa Cristina said little
or nothing about "sexual identity," they were able to raise the specter of
"immodest acts," which might usefully call into question both the character
of the dominating donna Emilia and the vaunted sanctity of the "lost soul,"
the "hypocrite," the *riformatrice* Cecilia Bianchi. The possibility of some intensely emotional, psychosexual component to the original Bianchi-Grassi
relationship gone sour would also go a long way toward explaining the
extraordinary and especially bitter playing out of this implacable enmity
over two decades.[46]

But in this case, the ecclesiastical hierarchy showed little interest in
shared beds, or what some might have imagined went on in them. They
probably chalked it up to another commonly perceived failing of female
behavior, especially among nuns, articulated in a similar spirit by Cardinal
Desiderio Scaglia in the mid 1630s, in discussing imputations of sorcery:

Since among them, women's wars and rivalries easily arise, it is thus easily
credible that, should it happen that there be in their midst some less loving
person, and they make accusations about such things to their superiors, then
all the others get in a fuss and have nothing to do with the accused, and

whatever slight wrong they hear about, they attribute to her mischief, and claim it comes from her.[47]

Like their colleagues at various other times and places, whose choices of penalties for female intimacies were generally moderate, the visitors to Santa Cristina simply reiterated the oft-heard prohibition.[48] They were exclusively concerned with the impact of the personal relationships on the good order of the convent society as a whole.[49] As we shall see, their reaction to the slightest hint of suspicious familiarity with males was very different.

"ALL STIRRED UP AGAINST ME BECAUSE OF HER SUBORNATION"

Donna Emilia's campaign to isolate donna Cecilia had not been hindered by the fact that her rival had taken refuge in intense sanctimoniousness and punctilious piety. By her fault-finding, her inflexible calls for reform, and particularly by allegedly calling the honor of the convent into question, Bianchi had also alienated all but the one *professa,* donna Maria Gentile Malvasia, who had become her new, and perhaps particular, friend. Much more startling and, by the standards of her time, unbecoming, Bianchi was even reduced to an alliance with a *conversa,* suor Ludovica Fabbri, already judged "uppity for a *conversa*" by her betters, whose pejorative nickname for her, "the Theologian," also suggests that suor Ludovica displayed pretensions of religiosity similar to donna Cecilia's. The blue-blood society of *professe* at Santa Cristina in the seventeenth century would still have seconded the remark of Francesco Datini, a fifteenth-century merchant from Prato, that "no gentleman who wants honor ought to be advanced by a merchant."[50] Cecilia Bianchi's low-class alliance was even more dubious. Such an abandonment of her own class testifies to the extent of her alienation.

When they learned of the memorial donna Cecilia had handed to the pastoral visitors, in which she claimed the troubles had all begun because of music, and where she raised the issue of Emilia Grassi's illegitimacy, Ruggeri and the nuns imagined it was filled with further calumnies. But in fact the memorial turns out to contain nothing anyone really wanted to hear. Where almost everything else in the 110 pages of the trial transcript was intended to deflect attention away from the speakers, donna Cecilia's personal memorial turns obsessively inward. Because it thus witnessed eloquently to her own painful isolation, her sense of persecution, and the destructive effect of ostracization within an institution whose very nature was intended to be intensely communal, it is worth quoting at length:

> It has been eighteen years that I have endured this persecution, and it began because of music. And because we had words, I called her misbegotten, and

she responded to me most unvirtuously. And, thus, despite my conciliations and my other loving gestures, she has never wanted to believe me to be her true friend. And ever since then she has put me in disgrace before all our superiors and the confessors, and all the fathers of the Congregation, and achieved my disgrace before all the superiors, to such an extent that they won't risk speaking to me or availing themselves of my services. And also, at her command, I've felt the great repugnance of many. Then she accused me, always saying her every torment was my fault, that I was the one who made her unhappy. And she says and preaches constantly to the other sisters that I am a lost soul. And by this and other fabrications she tries to make me loathsome to the whole world and even among the layfolk. . . .

Well, if any may have gone to pay court to her—as many do—and because she sometimes may have said capriciously that what's white and black is black and white, so now those do the same thing who, to revenge themselves against me, claim that I have caused the convent to be reformed, pressing this matter so emphatically that they don't notice or don't care about committing perjury. . . . And if she is reprimanded [for such acts] by the superior, she says she commits no sin, but rather is justified, because there could be no counterclaims.

But I can't do that, because we're different in our inclinations and dispositions. My inclination is to be withdrawn, and mind my own business, and to live as quietly as possible. . . . I've said this little bit that I could remember, because I take no account of offenses, in order better to enjoy my soul's peace, for I take no notice of the rest.

I thought that we should be reformed in this, and that we need no reform but our own consciences. And there was no chance if not this one, so I wish to set free my will in that way permitted me, and for the honor of God, and for the service and benefit of the convent. And this is repugnant to her, and I'm sorry it's that way. But, truly, I can do no other.

And since sometimes the mother abbesses, present and past, have employed me to compose some letter or petition on behalf of the convent, for that reason one might imagine that the statements and petitions sent to our superiors in Rome might have been my work. And especially because of that, she and her other allies let it be known that they want me tormented, even unto death.[51]

Had Cecilia in fact written earlier to Rome, provoking the investigation, as virtually all the nuns and Ruggeri were convinced she had? The diocesan curia, right up to Archbishop Ludovico Ludovisi himself, would second her own denials emphatically. Don Mauro's case for the prosecution rests to some extent on convent gossip, although he makes the point that the conclusion to the August 1622 letter to Rome, "*supplico* di Rimedio" ("*I* petition for a remedy"), demonstrates it had been the work of a single author, rather than representing the sentiments of many.

It seems almost certain that the defamatory letter had indeed been Cecilia Bianchi's handiwork—just as it seems quite likely that Emilia Grassi coached various *professe* and *converse* before they testified at the resulting inquiry. For one thing, toward the end of a long second day of testimony, in responding to the twenty-eighth of thirty questions, donna Cecilia remarked, "I was moved to write the petition sent to the superiors so that they would see to the disturbance among the laypeople, who had been told of these, our imperfections." Clearly, then, she had written some letter to the clerical hierarchy. In recopying his original transcript of her testimony for the archiepiscopal archive, Vittorio Barbadori first wrote *mandato à Roma,* which he immediately crossed out and replaced with the original, vaguer *à superiori*—a natural slip if he had known the true destination.[52]

Phrases from Cecilia's testimony also echo bits of the accusations from the original defamatory letter: both specifically cite the wearing of illicit pleated veils (*velli stampati*), for example. Most striking, the lax nuns' alleged claim that "non è più il tempo de santi" ("it is no longer the age of saints") from the original letter of August 1622 becomes in Cecilia's actual testimony of four months later, "è quasi una voce comune ch[e] *no[n] è più il tempo di S. Benedetto*" ("They say as if with one voice that it is no longer the age of Saint Benedetto.")

The odd, highly irregular trio of donna Cecilia, donna Maria Gentile, and suor Ludovica had entirely convinced the rest of the community that they had brought the authorities down upon them. Again and again during the investigation, the other nuns, from the ranks of the *professe* down to the *converse,* accused them of bringing the honor of the house into disrepute. However factious the convent society may have been, in the face of such a threat, they rallied to their common interest. It also appears that donna Cecilia and her allies had made a practice of carrying tales for some time. The denunciation of an unnamed tertiary to the Inquisition seems to have been among their unsavory acts. Donna Cecilia's suggestion during the investigation in 1623 that they had been unjustly accused of this betrayal was rather undermined by suor Ludovica's own subsequent boast to the visitors that "donna Domitilla said to me lately that I did right in making an accusation to the Holy Office."[53] Thus it was that donna Cecilia earned for herself the title of *riformatrice.*

What Ruggeri saw as her envy, vanity, pride, and ambition, but which also emerges as her acute alienation and isolation, left Cecilia Bianchi particularly susceptible to the influence of Giovanni Bondini, the perennial nuns' vicar of Bologna. While suffragan bishops and vicars general of Bologna came and went, this archetypical ecclesiastical survivor, "don Gioanino," continued year after year to exercise various sorts of petty tyranny over the nuns in his charge. As the guardian of convent parlatorios, for example, he frequently made life difficult for those seeking permission to speak to the nuns. On one occasion he even refused to countersign an indult from the pope himself permitting the reunion of a brother and his cloistered sister at Santa Cristina, remarking that they would see each other in paradise.

One of the nuns revealed to don Mauro the way around this particular problem: "The remedy turned out to be to send him a plate of toffee or apples with the license under a big toffee, and then the license was signed without further difficulty."[54] This don Gioanino was, "like donna Cecilia, troubled and melancholy in temperament." He therefore knew just how to play upon her own weaknesses. His was not the run-of-the-mill seduction that has commonly fueled popular imaginings about priests and nuns, but an appeal to her lusts for revenge and power. As don Mauro put it, "Donna Cecilia was moved to do this wrong to her convent by her old hatred of donna Emilia . . . and by the hope that don Gioanino gave her . . . that she would become abbess or reformer."[55]

Another of Bianchi's supposed comments, "Nuns from San Maglorio would be needed here, who could reform [the convent], as was done eighty years ago," suggests how she may have hit upon the self-appointed role of *riformatrice.* Her sense of history proves very accurate, for ninety years earlier, after a visitation by the cardinals Lorenzo Campeggi and Antonio Pucci in 1533, Santa Cristina had indeed been reformed by the customary means of introducing a group of nuns of exemplary lifestyle from the Camaldolese convent of San Maglorio in Faenza after the reigning local abbess had been deposed and expelled.[56] Perhaps the yearly remembrance at Santa Cristina of the deaths of the reforming abbesses Cecilia de Rubeis and Scholastica de Panzatolis of Faenza[57] called the incident and its significance to Cecilia Bianchi's attention.

Despite Ruggeri's pious claim that "nothing was ever heard about the convent of Santa Cristina that might have offended the pious ears of the Bolognese," Bianchi probably knew that the convent had suffered from a somewhat tarnished reputation for even longer. In 1506, because of a scandal that seems to have been brewing since the late fifteenth century, the vicar general of Bologna, on bishop's orders, had found it necessary to transfer exemplary nuns from the convent of San Giovanni Battista in Bologna to Santa Cristina to reestablish regular observance.[58] And as long ago as 1433, during his visitation that May, Ambrogio Traversari, the Camaldolese prior general, had been appalled by the claim of his Bolognese friend Romeo Foscarari that "in the convent of Santa Cristina I had not uncovered even a morsel of truth, because they were all whores." Traversari refused to believe this imputation, however, because of the evidence to the contrary, "above all, their scruples and their uncommon knowledge of divine worship and of the sacred liturgy."[59] Looking back from the early eighteenth century, on the other hand, the anticlerical Antonio Francesco Ghiselli would also comment, "It is quite true, in fact, that they were never looked upon with favor. . . . But there is in them such a deep-rooted affection for friardom and monkery that it [the affection] survives even to this day."[60] Donna Cecilia need not have looked far for inspiration, and one can imagine why many in the outside world would have been inclined to believe her.

"CHASTITY—I WOULD NOT SPEAK OF IT OUT OF RESPECT"

More than twenty times the clerical party was seen to enter Santa Cristina between 20 December 1622 and 13 January 1623, first twice a day, then only once, because the light was so short-lived on those midwinter afternoons. The mortified speculations of the nuns' families and the prurient fantasies of the public at large in the meantime ranged free. They are unlikely to have strayed far from the inevitable theme that crops up whenever monks and nuns are the topic of conversation. If Ruggeri is to be believed, it was even rumored in the city that as many as eight nuns were pregnant.[61]

Donna Cecilia Bianchi entered the parlatorio for what promised to be the visitation's most significant, and presumably sensational, testimony late in the day on 22 December. It had been a comparatively uneventful and disappointing two and a half days. Apart from the many details of the Bianchi-Grassi feud, the previous twenty-one witnesses had revealed little beyond the sorts of accommodations to a convent lifestyle imposed from above that characterized convent women's culture and would have turned up had the visitors gone looking in other upper-class, unreformed convents such as Santa Margherita, San Guglielmo, or Santi Naborre e Felice.

Ruggeri's claim that Suffragan Bishop Gozzadini had actually upset the prescribed order and called donna Cecilia early, impatient to get to the real scandals he hoped to hear, simply is not borne out by the trial transcript. There is no question, however, that, once she began, Bianchi tried their patience, for her testimony dragged on for the rest of 22 December, for all of 23 December, and, after the holidays, for most of 28 December, when she only left time for one additional witness. She kept the episcopal notary, Vittorio Barbadori, scribbling for more than nineteen pages, compared to Emilia Grassi's eight and to sixteen for the mother abbess (who was also required to provide numerous details about various financial and administrative matters). There was hardly any aspect of convent life in which donna Cecilia failed to ferret out some fault, however minor. And they all seemed minor.

But the critical issue on both sides of the convent wall was embodied in the cryptic phrase from the defamatory letter sent to Rome, "Castità non ne parli p[er] riverenza" ("Chastity—I would not speak of it out of respect"). It had been shrewdly concocted, as Ruggeri recognized, since its ambiguity admitted either a positive or a negative interpretation. And, clearly, this was the issue that fired the wildest speculations among the populace, where no fewer than one nun in five was imagined to be with child.

Castità was critical to *onestà* (decency) and *onore* (honor), in which any claims the nuns might have to authority were grounded. Nuns' traditional role as perpetual intercessors for their cities derived its particular efficacy from the chastity of the consecrated virgins, a purity rarely matched beyond their cloisters. One abbess claimed her nuns' prayers were "more useful coming from persons of such great religion than are two thousand horses."[62] It was their perfection that guaranteed them a hearing in heaven, and also in the world.

Even if some no longer held this pious view by 1620, their belief in the relationship between a daughter's chastity and her family honor remained thoroughly intact. As Annibal Guasco warned his daughter in *Ragionamento . . . a D. Lavinia sua figliuola della maniera del governarsi ella in corte* (1586), "There is no cure for the loss of chastity; it besmirches a woman even after her death." And it was not only her own honor that remained at stake. Guido Ruggiero suggests "the sexual honor of a woman was not only hers, I would say not even primarily hers; it was tied to a calculus of honor more complex, which involved both the family and the men who dominated it. . . . The honor of an entire family and of the men responsible for it revolved about the conservation of a daughter's virginity."[63]

That situation certainly did not change when daughters entered the cloister. Indeed, the surrogates who supplanted their fathers as their new primary guardians—priests, secular or regular—now found their own honor also directly at stake in the maintenance of their spiritual daughters' virtue. And because of the nuns' special role in ritually affirming the continuity of public life by their prayers, any violation of their *onestà* constituted a violation of the honor, not only of the clergy and of their families, but also of the city as a whole.

The dramatic turns in Ruggeri's account of donna Cecilia's interrogation, in which the impatient Bishop Gozzadini puts aside her written statement unread the second morning, to "attack at the primary point, where the nail should be driven home," as don Mauro put it (in another of his more striking and dubious turns of phrase),[64] are scarcely evident in the original trial transcript. Sandwiched between an allegation that, contrary to their vow of poverty, the nuns grub for anything they can get, and an accusation that three nuns—including madre donna Flaminia Bombacci—had owned their own farm animals, the long-awaited response finally appeared, with nothing more remarkable to set it off than a full stop and the beginning of a new sentence: "And as for chastity, I deem everyone to be holy, as the sanctity of the place requires."[65] Judging by the trial transcript, the notary did not even look up from his furious scribbling as Cecilia Bianchi talked on for another full day. Ruggeri claims, however, that all were stunned at her crucial answer to the key question, that the timorous Camaldolese don Desiderio, who a moment before had been trembling with fear and dread, broke into a joyous grin.

Even if Ruggeri may have been making a good story even better, as one strongly suspects he was, his additional dramatic touches point up more clearly how crucial to the whole visitation this issue was seen to be. Thus, one can understand the timid don Desiderio da Monza's belief, in the moments after donna Cecilia's answer, that the worst was finally over. The investigation would drag on for another three weeks. But with the chastity issue settled, the diocesan representatives were chiefly going through the motions. Their most serious discovery turned out to be nothing more scandalous than donna Giuditta Nobili's hapless puppy, temporarily hidden out of sight in the bed of one of the *converse*. The suffragan bishop had descended upon the cell of the *conversa*, Ursolina de Sanctis, discovered the dog, and confronted donna Giuditta with the evidence. The nun claimed that the pup, which belonged to her sister-in-law, was to have been sent home three days before. Since dogs could not be excommunicated for violation of *clausura,* the visitors had to be content with its banishment from the cloister. High clerical drama, it seems, had dipped dangerously toward farce.[66]

Don Mauro, the appointed guardian of the nuns' *onestà,* had reason to exult:

> God Almighty, the Blessed Virgin, Saint Romuald, and Saint Christina, to whom the nuns constantly commended themselves, to sustain their innocence and defense, interceded so that donna Cecilia should answer truthfully and dauntlessly [lukewarmly?], with these solemn words: "In this I deem them holy."[67]

This was not to be the end of the affair however. Before another two years had passed, the efficacy of these heavenly intercessions would be much more severely tested.

EIGHT

The Struggle with
Cardinal Archbishop Ludovisi
"We cared for Babylon, and she is not healed"

After Cecilia Bianchi's anticlimactic revelations on the fifth day of testimony, the pastoral visitation was effectively over. But it dragged on for more than two weeks, as Bishop Gozzadini and don Desiderio dutifully worked their way through the ranks of the remaining *professe* and *converse*. These interrogations yielded only petty infractions of a sort that might have turned up in all but the most observant, reformed convents of Bologna. At the end, a few minor remedies were proposed. Mass and Office should occur when there would be no distractions. To remove the temptation for inappropriate socializing, services should be recited with the grates closed. Convent finances should be put in order and debts liquidated, investing a substantial portion of dowries and keeping orderly records. The chapel silver could no longer be borrowed from the sacristy; dogs were banned from the convent and cats from the chapel, where fans and alternative reading matter were also forbidden. There were to be no more picnics at the portals. Nuns, forbidden mirrors, were to limit themselves strictly to their regular habits, without jewelry, colored sleeves, pleated veils, or oversize collars. Even on the most sultry August days, they were never to go around with bare shoulders, with their bosoms exposed, or covered only with "indecent" see-through veils. As for Emilia Grassi and Cecilia Bianchi, the visitors declared prophetically, "One can anticipate the same—and worse—in future."[1]

At the publication of the decrees before the assembled nuns, Suffragan Bishop Gozzadini preached pointedly on the example of the harvest, when even the highest fruit is thrown to earth. As he had implied, donna Emilia was denied the post of bursar, while donna Cecilia was passed over for the position she had set her hopes on, that of novice mistress.[2]

The position of abbess fell to Lucrezia Vizzana's aunt, the venerable Flaminia Bombacci. Donna Flaminia must have mixed political acumen with her piety. Perhaps she questioned her own effectiveness, given the Bombacci's comparatively humble origins by the standards of Santa Cristina and in light of what she had witnessed in convent government over the past several years and during her previous term as abbess ten years earlier. Donna Flaminia attempted to decline in favor of the noble donna Cleria Pepoli, from one of Bologna's most powerful families. Since the convent's influence among the local patriciate had long been on the wane, donna Flaminia had hoped that donna Cleria's singularly illustrious and noble lineage and her ties by marriage to the powerful Riario family might serve to check Cardinal Ludovico Ludovisi and also provide important political allies close to the pope in Rome.[3] But donna Cleria was probably much too sickly to rule, a condition to which she had repeatedly referred in her testimony the previous December, when her shrillest complaint had been that convent toffee-making monopolized the communal fire and prevented her from keeping warm.[4] In the end, therefore, donna Flaminia could not decline to serve.

Flaminia Bombacci's reign was a time of comparative, albeit superficial, tranquility, welcome within the walls on via Fondazza. Mauro Ruggeri recounts that Cecilia Bianchi continued to conspire with archiepiscopal ministers, and with don Gioanino in particular, who fed her aspirations to become abbess and convent reformer. In the meantime, donna Cecilia also acquired another, more illustrious ally. Donna Lucidaria Bolognetti hailed from one of the most noble and well-connected families. Entering Santa Cristina, she had joined two of the distinguished and erudite Cardinal Alberto Bolognetti's sisters. Donna Lucidaria had also been an enemy of Emilia Grassi at least since Grassi's reign as abbess. In 1616, Bolognetti had complained to the Congregation of Bishops that donna Emilia and the convent father confessor had been thwarting her efforts to obtain a very substantial inheritance. A further lament from the end of the year, signed "the sisters of Santa Cristina," complaining about the financial mismanagement of Grassi and the father confessor, "her counselor [*consigliere*], secretary, and treasurer," had almost certainly been Bolognetti's work.[5]

Donna Lucidaria had also gradually been left friendless, first by the deaths of the Bolognetti sisters, and then by the passing in August 1621 of the placid donna Laura Bocchi, her only remaining comrade. According to Ruggeri, Lucidaria Bolognetti became so ill-tempered that even her more distant kin wanted nothing to do with her. So inevitably she was drawn into the faction of the bitterly alienated and disaffected: Cecilia Bianchi and Maria Gentile Malvasia.

Although the venerable madre donna Flaminia had reputedly prophesied the outcome of this alliance, she did not live to witness their handiwork. Worn out by decades of fasting, discipline, and twenty-two years of perpetual prayer in chapel with only brief periods of rest on bare boards, she survived her election as abbess by only a year and a half. Continually praising and glorifying God, donna Flaminia passed to a better life, assisted by Mauro Ruggeri at her bedside. On 28 September 1624, as first vespers sounded for the feast of Saint Michael, the archangel saw her safely on her way to paradise.

As madre donna Flaminia had also prophesied, her sister, the former convent organist madre donna Camilla Bombacci, was chosen to succeed her. Her elevation surprised Cardinal Ludovisi, who had insisted on coming from Rome to unseat Camaldolese overseers of the election; the outcome also dismayed Cecilia Bianchi, who had been deluded by the perpetually scheming don Gioanino into believing that the highest office would fall to her.[6] During 1625, the crisis once again escalated, as Archbishop Ludovisi worked to drive a wedge between Santa Cristina and the Camaldolese order. In February, the vicar general of Bologna declined to confirm the Lenten preacher elected by the nuns of Santa Cristina and approved by their Camaldolese superiors and instead appointed a preacher of his own choosing. When the Camaldolese abbot general protested to the Congregation of Bishops, Cardinal Ludovisi responded that the nuns should in no way be permitted such a choice, "because of the evil consequences that can result, since they can for various reasons and respects elect persons who, instead of edifying, might destroy them with public scandal." To settle the issue once and for all, Ludovisi further demanded that perpetual silence in the matter be imposed upon the Camaldolese.[7]

Ruggeri repeatedly claimed that such attempts increasingly to subjugate Santa Cristina to archiepiscopal control were motivated by diocesan ministers' desire to get their hands on beautiful and rich convent holdings. Don Mauro's fears were not without some foundation. As archbishop of Bologna, Ludovisi is known to have ordered the transfer to his private collection of Francesco Francia's altarpiece *Madonna and Child* from the church of San Lorenzo dei Guerrini detto alle Grotte in Bologna, and its replacement with a copy.[8]

Nevertheless, Ludovisi's stated objective was quite in line with the goals of the post-Tridentine Church, in whose eyes the governance of convents by regular clergy rather than by ordinaries had long constituted an impediment to a uniform and well-regulated ecclesiastical system. It was Ludovico Ludovisi's uncle, Gregory XV, who in 1623, in the bull *Inscrutabili*, established bishops' responsibilities for the discipline and financial administration of convents subject to regulars and gave diocesan authorities power to approve or remove convent confessors,[9] a situation that Cardinal Ludovisi saw as analogous to the issue of convent preachers, raised in 1625.

Hints of scandal within the cloister represented the standard means to justify changes in convent government. Such an opening appeared at Santa Cristina early in 1626, when new defamatory letters—presumably from Cecilia Bianchi, Maria Gentile Malvasia, and Lucidaria Bolognetti—provoked the Congregation of Bishops on 3 March to investigate improprieties allegedly committed by various Camaldolese monks and nuns at Santa Cristina during the previous Carnival. According to Ruggeri, the new suffragan bishop of Bologna, Carlo Bovio, was so completely in league with Cecilia Bianchi and her circle that he sent Lucidaria Bolognetti a festive olive branch, not as a symbol of peace, but as a sign of impending victory.

Common wisdom and received opinion dictated that, for the sake of charity and monastic reputations, any such investigations be carried out as circumspectly and prudently as possible. Public probes might create "suspicion among the laity that in such convents there might be some evil," as Cardinal Desiderio Scaglia observed to administrators of the Holy Office in the 1630s. "It follows that the ordinaries, who have frequent occasions [to intervene] in other matters, either regarding enclosure or good government, would not provoke any suspicion and might make provision, as required, with discretion."[10] Secrecy and discretion were not a consideration in this visitation. For almost a month, the Bolognese, who had scarcely had time to forget the events of 1623, were treated to a new spectacle. A contingent of constables was posted around the convent and in the public parlatorio during daily interrogations. Servants hung about outside gawking and loudly discussing the case, "provoking such great scandal, and fostering such loathsome opinions," according to Ruggeri, "that there was no place in the city, and throughout Italy—or one might say, throughout Europe—that the sacred virgins were not spoken of as women of the greatest ill repute imaginable, a thing to make one weep tears of blood." The crucial sources of the nuns' influence, their honor and reputation for virtue, already under a cloud, continued to slip away.

Bishop Bovio welcomed Bianchi, Malvasia, and Bolognetti ("the three furies," as Ruggeri calls them) to the parlatorio with smiles and encouragement. "Don't tell me trivialities, tell me major matters that I can use to help you," he said—at least according to other nuns who had hidden themselves close by to eavesdrop.[11] In Ruggeri's account, donna Lucidaria suborned Elena Cristina Peracini (d. 1670),[12] the most junior member and only seventeen at the time, to testify that the father confessor and the convent's Camaldolese procurator had illicitly attended an evening performance of a secular play in the parlatorio during Carnival. Donna Elena Cristina soon had second thoughts, however, and retracted her testimony. She continued to maintain her resolve even when imprisoned by Bovio.

True or false, her allegation did in fact find its way into the summary of the investigation forwarded to Rome, which mentions the performance after hours in the parlatorio of a secular play entitled *L'ore mascherate:*

> And all the nuns say it wasn't recited in the parlatorio, except a novice, who says that it was presented at night in the parlatorio, but she didn't observe

any other listener but the bursar; and she seemed to make out a [man's] white hat in the said parlatorio. And two other nuns [Bianchi and Malvasia?] say they heard from the said novice that it was performed in the said parlatorio, and they believe it to be true, because the nun performers from that night didn't turn up for matins.[13]

When he forwarded the summary of his investigation to the Congregation of Bishops on 18 April, Suffragan Bishop Bovio claimed that the nuns of Santa Cristina had rehearsed their responses together in advance—all, that is, but the two most junior nuns, whom he had taken by surprise:

> The first confesses that the play was recited in the parlatorio at night in her presence, and that the friars were there. The second doesn't dare to deny it at all, but says she can't remember it. The play was not only secular, but lascivious, and there was one role of a lady courtesan. As for the other charges, they have almost all been proven by the confessions of the monks themselves, and of the nuns. From such things the Sacred Congregation will see the inconveniences [*inconvenientà*], the dissolutions, and the laxity of these monks.[14]

Further allegations in the summary suggest that the three malcontents had accepted Bovio's challenge to concentrate on major offenses:

> The father confessor is almost always hanging around the *ruota* in the sacristy, and most of the time he is chatting with a niece of the abbess, and this according to three nuns [Bianchi, Malvasia, and Bolognetti?]; and another nun claimed that the said confessor told her that the first time he saw the abbess's niece, he went mad for her, saying that she was his little angel, and lamenting that he hadn't a lot of presents for her. And two nuns testified to having seen some of the same monks chatting with the nuns at the *ruota* with the door shut.[15]

Since madre donna Camilla Bombacci was the abbess, the only likely candidates for the niece who had won the heart of the father confessor were donna Isabetta Vizzana or the younger donna Lucrezia Orsina. At ages thirty-nine and thirty-six, respectively, they were a bit old for "little angel" status, however. Either the neophyte confessor, don Giusto Bordino, was every bit as young and foolish as Mauro Ruggeri had claimed elsewhere—not to say indiscriminate—or the convent malcontents' calumnies severely stretched the bounds of credibility.

Despite Ruggeri's protestations, there must have been at least a few grains of truth to these imputations, however, for in his rambling account, don Mauro describes activities that could well have been perceived as inappropriate. He may have been the monk observed in intimate conversation at the *ruota*, who, according to Bovio, had "confessed." Late in 1625, while passing through Bologna after an official Camaldolese visitation in Lombardy, Ruggeri had been summoned to Santa Cristina by Camilla Bombacci during the *carnevalino* customarily celebrated at the convent on the eight days before Advent. As Ruggeri conferred with madre donna Camilla at the grate of the confessional, Bishop Bovio arrived unexpectedly to obtain the required confirmation that a prospective postulant would take her vows freely and not because of family coercion. Bovio happened upon Ruggeri in the external church. The next day, the bishop summoned don Mauro and severely chastised him for having been observed with a nun at a secluded grate, rather than conversing with her in the public parlatorio. Ruggeri retorted that convent superiors were permitted access to such grates. Unfortunately for him, Cecilia Bianchi promptly informed the bishop, presumably by way of don Gioanino, that Ruggeri's authority as Camaldolese visitor no longer extended any farther south than Cremona. Ruggeri's departure for Venice the evening before Bianchi's denunciation was all that saved him from imprisonment by the bishop's chief constable, sent to arrest him.[16]

Such accusations, which may strike us as too trivial for serious attention, gained authority simply by bringing together the threats to nuns' virtue traditionally considered most grievous in the popular and ecclesiastical imagination: grates, parlatorios, seclusion, and confessors. These sites of potential worldly pollution remained the popular butt of anticlerical cynicism, as an excerpt from this eighteenth-century poem, *I costumi delle monache* demonstrates:

> Ad una grada un Cavalier in piede
> Finge con una di parlar segreto
> E mentre esser veduto non si crede
> Con allungar le man gli tocca il petto,
> Anch'ella tocca ciò che non possede,
> E va su e giu cercandogli diletto,
> Suonano, e in consonanza, e per appunto
> Del Vescovo al venir giungono al punto.

> Before the grating a gallant is standing,
> Feigning in private to speak with a sister,
> Thinking the chaperones sit unsuspecting,
> Straining his fingers on bosom to touch her.
> Faintly she fondles that thing she is lacking,
> Sliding up, slipping down, thrilling together.
> Fiddling in consort, to put it quite nicely,
> By bishop's arrival, they've finished precisely.

The public's worst, or favorite, imaginings, fed by pornographic works like Pietro Aretino's *Ragionamento della Nanna e della Antonia,* and periodically confirmed by complaints such as the following to the Congregation of Bishops in 1659, from the men of Bettona in the diocese of Assisi, turned even innuendos of impropriety into serious concerns to be dealt with severely:

> Don Giovanni Maria Penna, who serves the convent of Santa Catterina [as confessor], maintains an intimate relationship with suora Maria Fulvia, scandalizing nuns and layfolk alike. Shutting himself in the closet for communion, he was observed to put his member in her hands, and other actions. . . . These [confessors] want to send the brides of Christ to the Devil's domain.[17]

Ruggeri's account and the testimony from the visit of 1626 suggests maneuvering by the Bianchi faction and/or the diocesan curia against those who represented the new focus of convent authority. In the scenario they created, Camilla Bombacci, who had snatched the position of abbess from Cecilia Bianchi's grasp under the watchful eye of Cardinal Ludovisi himself, had been compromised by supposed improprieties involving a senior figure of the Camaldolese order. And one of her own nieces had apparently been implicated in unseemly practices with the Camaldolese monks, mandated to guard the nuns' collective *onestà*. The plotters had chosen their targets well, for Camilla Bombacci and Isabetta Vizzana dominate the paroxysms of the next three years.

Monsignor Prospero Fagnani, secretary of the Congregation of Bishops in Rome, and, according to Ruggeri, deep in Cardinal Ludovisi's pocket, found Bovio's latest accusations insufficiently damning, however. Later in 1626, Fagnani ordered Cardinal Uberto Ubaldini, papal legate in Bologna, to lay bare "the complete truth concerning the excesses in the enclosed transcript, allegedly committed in that convent of Santa Cristina, governed by Camaldolese monks." Ubaldini descended upon the convent, sequestered the nuns in the choir, confiscated all their keys, invaded the cloister with his men, and ransacked the convent from top to bottom. According to Ruggeri, "not content to have searched the chests, they even tore apart the beds; and even though they had done so without warning they found nothing to carry off."[18] This extraordinary act—almost unparalleled in the convents of Bologna during the Seicento[19]—designed, it seems, to leave only their chastity intact, represented a kind of ravishment, leaving nothing untouched and penetrating to the most private corners of the nuns' world.[20]

When this third visitation failed to turn up sufficiently damning evidence, Fagnani had no choice but to write the papal legate and the nuns on 30 April 1627, lauding "the good government and observance by which they live there under regular [Camaldolese] rule, and the good order of purity and goodness emanating from every corner of that holy place."[21] As in 1623, it appeared that Santa Cristina had been vindicated.

But Fagnani's letter was simply a sop to the nuns designed to divert their attention from the authorities' larger plan. A cancelled draft, dated a month earlier and never sent, concluded,

> Given this fine demonstration of the discipline in which they have lived up to now under the governance of these [Camaldolese monks], [the cardinals]

are led to believe that with each passing day they will profit in God's service under the salutary direction of the Illustrious Lord Cardinal Ludovisi, archbishop and ordinary of that city, to whose government they now find themselves subject.[22]

Some six weeks before that, the secretary of the Sacred Congregation had notified the Camaldolese prior general that Urban VIII had determined to transfer the convent of Santa Cristina from Camaldolese jurisdiction to Ludovisi's control:

It will therefore be expedient, for the sake of your order's reputation, Most Reverend Father, that within three days at most you make a voluntary renunciation into the hands of His Holiness, and give the appropriate orders for the release of control, and deliver them into my own hands, to be absolutely certain of their arrival.[23]

The nuns, who had got wind of what was afoot in Rome, implored Cardinal Barberini to intercede with his uncle, Urban VIII, "lest the reputation of the convent, and of such high nobility that reside therein, be tarnished." But it was a waste of time. On 2 June 1627, the pope acceded to Cardinal Ludovisi's wishes.[24] Suffragan Bishop Bovio dispatched his beadles to seize the church and the convent, "like an army of Turks, with screams, shouts, and clamour." Peering out his window at the approaching mob, don Vincenzo da Sant'Agata, the confessor extraordinary, was so terrified by the tumult that he fled out the back of his lodgings and across a garden to a neighboring house, where he begged layman's clothes and slipped away in disguise to take refuge downtown at the Camaldolese monastery of Santi Cosmo e Damiano.[25]

The nuns were well aware that in the eyes of their families and the city, the Sacred Congregation's recent assurances about unsullied virtue and honor meant nothing if at the same time their Camaldolese superiors were banished. In noble and patrician society, where reputation remained crucial, what *was* remained less important than what seemed to be. As Sherrill Cohen puts it, "*Onore* for a patrician woman or *onestà* (decency) for a plebeian woman was not so much a matter of actual behavior as one of what her community knew and said about her."[26]

Meekly to accept subjugation to the archbishop would imply the nuns' acknowledgement of their sullied *onestà,* and their families' disgrace. When secular priests were sent to Santa Cristina by the archbishop to administer the Sacraments, the nuns chased them away with threats and abuse. At the expiration of madre donna Camilla Bombacci's term as abbess at about the time of Urban VIII's decree, the nuns ignored Ludovisi's command to elect a successor. To preserve their reputation, under Bombacci's continued leadership, they took a solemn oath to reject the archbishop's authority and to recognize no superiors but the Camaldolese. All of them, that is, but Cecilia Bianchi and her two allies, who, as Cardinal Ludovisi later complained to the nuns, "for demonstrating their readiness to obey, or because of vain suspicion that they had made revelations against you, for the sake of their very lives, they had to be imprisoned within their own cells." Ludovisi further claimed that, having rejected confessors in secular orders, the nuns went so far as to convince a seriously ill younger nun, who eventually died, that it would suffice to make her confession before a crucifix, without a priest.[27]

In a periodic report on his diocese to the Sacra Congregazione del Concilio dated 31 May 1628, Cardinal Ludovisi testified to the nuns' continued obstinate refusal, after almost a year, to acknowledge his authority, and insisted that appropriate methods be found to curb their contumacy and disobedience. Within a month, the Congregation of Bishops cracked down hard, ordering the papal legate in Bologna, Cardinal Bernardino Spada, to apply any effective method to bring the nuns to heel: to imprison the most recalcitrant and rebellious nuns, if necessary; to deny the nuns access to their administrators and lawyers until they recognized Ludovisi and elected a new abbess; to break the will of the renegade madre donna Camilla Bombacci if she continued her refusal to abdicate; to remove the convent staff, especially those who had been publicizing the nuns' case in the outside world in letters and messages.

In August, Cardinal Spada reluctantly complied. After considerable difficulty even gaining admittance to Santa Cristina on 5 August, Spada was harangued for so long by Camilla Bombacci that he had to return to the convent another day, and then another, over the following two weeks. Even Spada's offer to oversee an election himself, in place of the deeply compromised Bishop Bovio, only aggravated what he called "the willful contempt of the nuns and the scandal of the city." Although Spada concurred with Bovio that the transfer to other monasteries of the five or six who resisted Ludovisi's rule most emphatically would quell further tumults more effectively than their imprisonment, he pointed out that their removal to another Camaldolese house outside the city would give them the victory. And he doubted that acceptable convents could be found locally without provoking further outcry and uproar.[28]

Within a month, the desperate nuns appealed again to Cardinal Borghese in Rome, as one of noble blood who could not fail to uphold the compromised reputation and honor of the many nobles among them.

> Our innocence is manifest from the investigations already carried out many times in repeated visitations. But as long as our honor is not restored, our families remain eternally defamed, and we, therefore, abandoned by them, so that we have come almost to damnation. . . . Prostrate, we implore your aid in the restitution of our honor and the welfare of our souls. . . . The cruel

threats are at hand, which like lions, hope to devour us. And, truly, if that comes to pass, the whole world will hear of us.

Within ten days, Francesco Ingoli, Ludovisi's ally on the recently founded Congregazione della Propaganda Fide, and his official auditor, responded on the cardinal archbishop's behalf that the nuns had no alternative but to obey.[29]

On 17 November 1628, the threatened reprisals became reality. To cut off further communications, the Sacred Congregation ordered Cardinal Ludovisi to close down the convent parlatorio, block all the convent gateways, and provide the nuns with only starvation rations. Twenty beadles and other workmen were dispatched under cover of darkness to wall up the doorway to the parlatorio. But, in the words of the Bolognese chronicler Antonio Francesco Ghiselli, this force "could not withstand the violence of the infuriated sisters," who by next morning had demolished the new masonry, leaving no trace of the offending bricks and mortar—much to the astonishment of the archbishop, who could not believe that high-born ladies were capable of such hard physical labor, and therefore imprisoned the convent servants for alleged complicity.[30]

For the next assault, the episcopal auditor returned in broad daylight with a full squadron of beadles and stonemasons to wall up the gateway to the cloister. The nuns, who had been praying before the Blessed Sacrament in their chapel, with one accord ascended to the upper reaches of the convent, whence they greeted the invaders with a dense shower of tiles and stones, provoking their retreat out of range to the main gateway on via Fondazza. As the alarm sounded from the belltower, crowds of parishioners, their loyalty sustained over the years by regular, illicit handouts from convent gardens, converged outside the wall. Donna Isabetta Vizzana appeared at a window of the loggia over the courtyard, her face veiled and with a crucifix in her hand. Her passionate four-hour harangue moved some to tears and others to indignant cries of "Long live the nuns of Santa Cristina!" All the while the neighborhood children were gathering up stones and tossing them into the convent through the small gateway, just in case the nuns might need additional ammunition. This proved unnecessary, for in the face of such overwhelming opposition from within and without, the members of the curia and their supporters beat a hasty retreat back downtown.[31]

Archbishop Ludovisi also tried sending his notary to the convent to persuade Camilla Bombacci and her nuns to listen to reason. Ghiselli offers the only description of this encounter:

> Finally, he was let into a certain courtyard inside the gate, . . . where he waited awhile until a nun came to a window not far from the roof and asked him what he wanted, to which he replied, "the mother abbess." And, having told

him to come closer, they let fall from the window a great piece of marble, with the words, "Here's the mother abbess." And if the poor man had not quickly jumped backward, he would have been overwhelmed and crushed by that blow.[32]

Although Ghiselli is not above improving upon history, his extraordinary tale hints at an attitude that naturally developed in the city, in the light of these violent developments. For the people of Bologna and Ghiselli, the infuriated attempt against the notary symbolized the potential havoc that could be loosed if irrational female energies ran wild and uncontrolled. The account confirms how the nuns' subjection to episcopal government would come to be seen as essential to the welfare of the city.

The episcopal hierarchy turned its efforts to less physically hazardous, but ultimately more effective, means to end the siege. They called upon the chief theologians of the city and the university, and even the Father Inquisitor to rule publicly on the nuns' common oath of disobedience. With that ruling in hand, the diocesan curia proclaimed:

> Be it known to all the nuns of Santa Cristina, that their oath, together to stand united, and not to obey the commandments of their superiors is false and void, and is against the vow and oath made by the nuns in their profession, when they took the vow of obedience to their superiors. . . . And therefore, whoever took that oath [of defiance], and whoever forced her to take it has committed mortal sin. . . . And this is the view of all the theologians of the city and of the University of Bologna. And because the oath should not be your chain to iniquity, for the greater peace of your consciences, we absolve you of the said oath, which we proclaim null and void, and of no value.[33]

Now the archbishop's agents could more easily influence the nuns' families and noble sympathizers, their chief remaining source of any potential support, already undermined by gossip. According to Ruggeri, our chief witness, the nuns' relatives finally persuaded them to petition Ludovisi in Rome for his forgiveness and for permission to be placed temporarily under Capuchin control. For his part, the absent archbishop could decry the earlier unruly violence of his own ministers. On his return to Bologna, Ludovisi visited Santa Cristina, said Mass, and implied that the convent might even return to Camaldolese rule eventually. Having thus deluded the nuns about his good intentions, the cardinal and his agents continued to thwart them at every turn.[34]

Ruggeri's further suggestion that Urban VIII had been temporarily persuaded by the nuns' own advocates in Rome to reconsider the matter and to place the nuns for the time being under Capuchin control, only to be dissuaded at the last minute by Ludovisi's allies, seems plausible. In a letter of 7 February 1629, the nuns gratefully acknowledged Cardinal Ludovisi's aid in securing the pope's authorization of Capuchin confessors, about which they had just learned from their agent in Rome. Ludovisi's mild-mannered response pointed out, however, that the very same day he had received contrary orders from the Sacred Congregation with "a decision very different from what you heard from your attorney." The Congregation's response, dated 1 February, which he enclosed with his letter, left no room for maneuver:

> In this matter one must not entertain in any way treaties and compromises so prejudicial to the authority of this Holy See, so injurious to the state and health of the nuns themselves, and offering such a pernicious example to anybody else to attempt to oppose the execution of apostolic orders. Obedience must be exact and complete, and not diminished. And it is no less scandalous than it is astonishing that nuns would dare to negotiate terms with the pope, their supreme lord. . . . [Authority] was granted by His Holiness so that you would be so kind as to exercise it, to crush once and for all such prolonged and obstinate impudence by these poor souls.[35]

Three weeks later the archbishop promulgated a decree bluntly rehearsing for the city's benefit the prolonged contumacy of the nuns of Santa Cristina and his own forbearance, and justifying his ultimate threat of excommunication unless the nuns capitulated.

> You, donna Camilla Bombacci, sometime abbess of the convent of Santa Cristina in this city of Bologna, of the Camaldolese order, and you, donna Lorenza Bonsignori, donna Ginevra Fuzzi, donna Sulpitia Bocchi, . . . professed nuns, and you, *converse* in the same convent, suor Girolama Lombardi, suor Ludovica Fabri, . . . and all other members, we pray you, by the Holy Spirit, the gift and power of reason and counsel, to see to the salvation of your souls. . . .
>
> Although in the school of religion, the opinion of Saint Jerome should suffice, that the true reputation of religious persons consists in prompt obedience, and in their right actions, and not in the praise or vain judgment of men, . . . you, happily ignoring the ear of your own hearts, have not heard the salutary voices of the cardinal legates, of your fathers and pastors, of your ministers, of such learned and virtuous religious, and of your own relatives, so that we may rightly exclaim, *curavimus Babylonem, et non est sanata* [We cared for Babylon, and she is not healed]. . . .Thus, this convent is become nothing else but a Babylon, where most grievous disorder rules and holds sway. . . . You put in manifest danger donna Serena Maria Celeste Teribili, to let her die without the Sacraments, rather than admit secular priests, to whom she might have confessed, wickedly claiming she could have done so before a crucifix, an intolerable folly, since there are plenty of confessors, and her soul was weighed down in mortal disobedience. . . .
>
> Lest the stink of such scandals spread, by order of the Sacred Congregation, your parlatorios were walled up. But you, with reckless audacity, had them torn open, throwing stones, and wounding not only the beadles, agents, and notaries, but even the auditor of the monsignor suffragan himself. . . . Your inconstancy and fickleness, first to accept, then to reject secular priests

as confessors, to promise then refuse to obey, your constantly increasing hardness and contumacy offer the most patent proof that the evil spirit, the author and father of discord and disobedience, has always been your counselor, companion, and master.

After everything that we have done to restore you to sanity, from your vile intercourse with most obvious ingratitude and ungratefulness, all must recognize that *curavimus Babylonem, et non est sanata*. If there be no emendment, we are left, in our infinite sorrow, *derelinquamus eam* [to cast her away].

To this we are constrained by our conscience, after such forbearance, by human and divine law, by our highly justified fear that disobedience breeds with impunity. . . .

Therefore, by our authority, . . . we do order and command you, donna Camilla Bombacci, former abbess, and you other nuns, in virtue of Holy Obedience, within the next fifteen days, . . . on pain of excommunication, to submit and subject yourselves to our authority. . . .

Finally, because the wicked are never lacking, who *dicunt malum bonum, et bonum malum* [say bad is good, and good is bad], we command everyone, on pain of excommunication, . . . that no one dare give counsel, aid, or protection that might impede or delay the execution of the apostolic breve and of our orders. And if in the prescribed time the said monastery does not submit in due obedience to the Supreme Pontiff and to Us, . . . from that hour we cast out the said Babylon, most justly abandoned for pertinacious disobedience by God and His Church, which the excommunicant has not for Mother, neither God for Father, but Satan in place of Father and Mother.[36]

Virtually cut off from the outside world by Cardinal Ludovisi's agents at the gates, rejected by their families because of their sullied reputations, which compromised the decency of family and city alike, provided with such meager rations that they may have been reduced to eating grass, having rejected the spiritual food of the Sacraments from the hands of secular priests for six months,[37] and finally faced with this ultimate threat of papal excommunication, which on 1 March 1629 was nailed to the cloister door, to the column in the chamber of the episcopal notary, and to the door of the cathedral of San Pietro, with two additional copies thrown over the wall into the convent, twenty-two months after Urban VIII had removed them from Camaldolese jurisdiction, the sisters of Santa Cristina finally submitted to the authority of the archbishop of Bologna.

But they did not do so meekly. On 4 March, the full community of nuns, ranging from the aged Lorenza Bonsignori and Junipera Fuzzi (who would both be dead before summer came) to the twenty-year-old Elena Cristina Peracini, gathered in the parlatorio before a public notary. They all affirmed the following official declaration, which, as was customary, they signed in order of seniority. Donna Lucrezia Orsina Vizzana, now thirty-nine years old, appeared twenty-sixth out of thirty-five on the list.

We protest and emphatically reject the subjection of ourselves and our convent by any act whatsoever, either public or private, that we may do. [This] will not be absolutely of our free will, but in fear of these censures, and so that our reputation will not suffer more than it has already suffered. And therefore we wish that whatever we might do to the contrary should not be taken as fact, and that this same protestation should always remain secure. Nor can it be said that we ever departed from it.[38]

Four months later, the three troublemakers Cecilia Bianchi, Maria Gentile Malvasia, and Lucidaria Bolognetti were removed from Santa Cristina, while Emilia Grassi and the other nuns transferred their dowries in the amount of £3,000 each to the three convents that had agreed to take them. Because of her own illustrious lineage, Lucidaria Bolognetti rode in the carriage of the marchioness Riaria, sister of donna Cleria Pepoli, to her new, humbler home, the Clarissan convent of San Bernardino, which had been subjugated to the archbishop of Bologna thirty years before, after a similar scandal, but one based on fact not innuendo. There she lived on inconspicuously for more than thirty years in the crowd of more than 130 other nuns, surviving just about everyone at Santa Cristina who had participated firsthand in the events of the 1620s that she had helped to provoke. According to Ruggeri, donna Lucidaria's repeated pleas over the years to return to Santa Cristina, sweetened with promises of lavish donations, were flatly refused. The other two had to settle for more common conveyance. Maria Gentile Malvasia found her way to the Augustinian convent of Sant'Agostino, among the poorest in the city, where she professed on 31 December 1629. Despite Ludovisi's insistence that she be granted the superiority due someone with thirty years of religion behind her, she renounced all rights to precedence in choir and in chapter, an act her new colleagues seem to have found entirely appropriate. Maria Gentile lived on at Sant'Agostino for almost twenty years, until 18 December 1647.

The chief troublemaker, Cecilia Bianchi, after years of ostracization within the walls on via Fondazza, was packed off as far as possible, all the way to the tiny Dominican convent of San Michele Arcangelo, with fewer than twenty *professe,* in the suburb of San Giovanni in Persiceto, twelve miles from Bologna. There she vanishes, virtually without a trace. And, as don Mauro put it, "thus ended their hopes of becoming abbesses [and] reformers."[39]

Ruggeri's account of the immediate aftermath of the nuns' defeat continues in a vein of deception, delusion, and demoralization. In a scene reminiscent of contemporary Venetian opera plots, the cardinal archbishop supposedly contrived to have a letter from him to the Roman curia, expressing sympathy with the nuns, dropped where it would be found and transmitted to Santa Cristina. Having thus convinced the nuns of his good offices, the cardinal and his agents continued to thwart them at every turn. When three carriages of Camaldolese, with Ruggeri among them, stopped in Bologna en route to their general chapter in Rome, the diocesan curia dispatched a squadron of beadles to stand guard at the convent, as if the monks might attempt to retake it by force.[40]

In reality the Camaldolese of Bologna appear to have abandoned the sisters. After Urban VIII's proclamation of a Universal Jubilee on 22 October 1629, the nuns requested as their customary confessor extraordinary the Camaldolese curate of San Damiano, don Bernardo da Venezia. To their consternation, the monk claimed that he was too busy with other parish matters, provoking the taunt from the archbishop's agents, "See how you are esteemed by your Camaldolese fathers, who decline to confess you during the Jubilee." On 5 January 1630, don Bernardo admitted in a letter to the general of his order that he had received two nocturnal visits from Ludovisi's emissaries warning him not to risk the cardinal's displeasure by agreeing to the nuns' request. Ruggeri's apologia on behalf of his order suggests that don Bernardo's explanation may have come too late to offer the nuns much solace. "If it be true that the nuns may call the Camaldolese fathers their betrayers (which is unbelievable), it is for no other reason than the evil notions that the agents and others of the archiepiscopate put or had put in their heads."[41]

Don Bernardo died shortly afterward, during the plague of 1630–31. Although Ruggeri passes no further comment on don Bernardo's demise, he leaves little doubt about the appropriateness of the fates of Ludovisi and his accomplices. Monsignor Fagnani, secretary to the Congregation of Bishops, and the archbishop's chief Roman ally in the takeover of Santa Cristina, was struck blind, Ruggeri tells us. (If true, this seems to have left Fagnani unhindered, for he later became an influential advisor to Alexander VII and survived until 1678, when he died at the ripe old age of eighty.)[42] The conniving nuns' vicar don Gioanino went on to enjoy a canonry at San Petronio, unmerited in Ruggeri's opinion, but he eventually received his comeuppance. During Carnival, Ruggeri says, Gioanino was accosted in the street by an unknown group of maskers, who forced him to dress up in costume, took him with them to one of the convents subject to diocesan control, and made the 60-year-old priest join them in dancing with the nuns across the grates of the parlatorio, with the nuns in the interior chamber and don Gioanino and his fellow maskers in the external chamber. Released with the warning to keep his mouth shut or regret it, don Gioanino never discovered the identity of his abusers. Although Ruggeri only had the story on hearsay—although from a very reliable source— he passed it on "so that it may be understood that nuns subject to [secular] priests are not better governed than those under regulars."

As for Cardinal Archbishop Ludovico Ludovisi, Ruggeri claimed he was disgraced for complicity with a faction of Spanish cardinals in a plan to depose the pro-French Urban VIII for alleged mental instability. "Ludovisi left Rome as fast as his feet would carry him, and returned to Bologna; full of anguish, he passed to another life."[43] Although Ludovisi's collusion in any putative Spanish plot, a suggestion attributed to the partisan Venetian envoy Alvise Contarini, appears improbable, the archbishop was definitely implicated with Cardinal Borgia, the leader of the Spanish cardinals, whose open defiance of Urban VIII in the secret consistory on 8 March 1632 stunned the curia and Rome. Shortly thereafter, the pope gave Ludovisi ten days to return to his diocese or risk being run out of the city. On the morning of 27 March, Ludovisi, "more a breathing corpse than a man," as Cardinal Domenico Cecchini put it, departed the *caput mundi*. On 18 November 1632, he died in Bologna, aged thirty-seven.[44]

NINE

The Confrontation with Cardinal Archbishop Albergati Ludovisi

"They have always been betrayed by secular priests"

Cardinal Archbishop Ludovico Ludovisi's corpse had scarcely cooled before the nuns of Santa Cristina once again turned their attention to Rome. In 1633, possibly at the instigation of madre donna Emilia Grassi, whom the nuns had finally reelected abbess after an interval of twenty years, they petitioned the pope for a rehearing of their case. After Ludovisi's disgrace, they may have hoped for a sympathetic ear from Urban VIII. Donna Emilia's death, barely two months after Ludovisi's, spared her further disappointment, for their letter seems to have been ignored.[1] Another petition to the Congregation of Bishops three years later paints a grim picture of the state to which the convent had been reduced:

> Abandoned by their own families, they have personally been kindly consoled by Your Eminences' many declarations of their decency and innocence. But the opposite impression nonetheless thrives throughout the city, to such an extent that, not only is their reputation still lacerated, but no one can be found, even of the ordinary sort, who wishes to be accepted and to profess in their convent, where formerly places were granted only to members of the nobility. And now, with as many as fifteen places vacant, the total destruction and annihilation of their convent may result.[2]

Their sense of defamation may have been acute, but the decimation of the convent population, more gradual than they suggest, owed much to Emilia Grassi's elimination of *educande* in the early years of the century. The ranks of the *professe,* which had stood at forty-nine in 1588, had slowly dwindled to forty-three in 1606, thirty-eight in 1623, and thirty-five at the time of Ludovisi's ultimatum in 1629. The number of deaths continued to outpace professions, so that by 1639, only thirty professed nuns remained.

It is also significant that the nuns' petition of 1636 abandoned hope of full reunion with the Camaldolese, assuring the Congregation of Bishops that they "did not intend ever to be withdrawn on any account from the jurisdiction and good government of His Eminence the lord cardinal archbishop" (now Girolamo Colonna). They simply requested a token Camaldolese confessor. The Congregation took a dim view of this symbolic gesture; the nuns continued to be confessed by the Celestine monks of Santo Stefano, who in 1638 were succeeded by Olivetans.[3]

But late in 1643, suor Francesca Malatendi, an aged *conversa* with more than forty years of service behind her, turned everything upside down. Faced with the imminent prospect of heavenly judgment, which she believed had already begun to afflict her (she died four weeks later), suor Francesca confessed that during the scandals of the 1620s, she had suggested to another *conversa,* suor Ludovica Fabbri, that a strange, intermittent indisposition affecting suor Cherubina Noci, presumably in the morning, might have been the unhappy result of suor Cherubina's friendly predisposition toward a certain convent gardener, Giacomo Sarti.

> Realizing . . . the immense damage that has befallen this convent and the nuns since 1626, . . . above all with respect to their reputation, because of which they were investigated . . . and later the Camaldolese monks, their spiritual directors, were removed, therefore suor Francesca . . . to unburden her conscience and in order not to damn her soul, . . . and to repair in the best way possible the reputation of the monastery and the nuns, and recognizing that Our Lord in His just wisdom has laid upon her the very same infirmity . . . that suor Cherubina once suffered, . . . she declares, confesses, and publicly recognizes that the said suspicions and words implied by her to suor Ludovica were and are false and vain, and having absolutely no basis in truth. . . . And in affirmation of the truth, not knowing how to write, she has made a cross in the presence of these witnesses.[4]

The summary of the investigation from 1626 makes no mention of such a scandal. A look further back to the complete transcript from the visitation of 1623 reveals that suor Francesca had at that time denied all knowledge of any convent improprieties. She had corroborated the view, promoted throughout the investigation, that almost every *professa* treated the *converse* with the indulgence and forbearance appropriate to women of their station, and almost every *conversa* knew her place and valued her good treatment. Ludovica Fabbri, the uppity, insolent, and disobedient *conversa* allied with Cecilia Bianchi, may have mentioned no specific sexual indiscretions among the *converse* in her indecorously detailed and protracted testimony, for someone of her position. But her description of recent goings on below stairs suggests that, right or wrong, suor Francesca's calumnies may have been spreading and taking their toll:

> Two or three months ago suor Geronima knocked suor Dorothea in the head, and blood flowed down to the ground; and she ripped suor Cherubina's

wimple [*bavaro*], and left her all roughed up. And this was because of this investigation, and I don't know why.

This suor Geronima, the other troublemaker among the servants, had claimed self-defense: "She [suor Cherubina] grabbed me by the throat, and I wanted to defend myself so I said I'd tear her veil and she didn't listen." Cherubina had proven singularly uncommunicative when it came time to testify; Barbadori, the notary, had recorded fewer than a hundred of her words, ending, "I don't know of any wranglings in the convent, nor anything unusual, and I'm very well treated by the nuns, and as to why I'm here, I've never been offended by anybody, and I don't have anything to say."[5]

Obviously some trouble had been brewing among the *converse* back in the 1620s. Suor Francesca Malatenda's imagined scandal, which came to weigh so heavily on her own conscience at the end, as visions of the maw of hell opened beneath her feet, may for a time have kept the servant nuns in turmoil, but probably remained beneath the notice of her betters, on earth and in heaven. Nevertheless, after the death of Urban VIII, even the professed nuns seized upon suor Francesca's confession as an excuse to press for a new hearing of their cause and for restoration to their pristine state. Led by the aging musician and peacemaker from earlier decades, Abbess Adeodata Leoni, and the bursar, Isabetta Vizzana, who had rallied the crowds during the nuns' last stand in 1628, the nuns began to bombard Cardinal Archbishop Niccolò Albergati Ludovisi, and the Congregation of Bishops in Rome with new petitions, requesting a return to Camaldolese rule:

> All Your Eminences' suppliants, unanimously desiring to see the redress of the damage that has resulted from [these calumnies], and that above all daily affects their honor and the reputation of the convent, which consists of the principal nobility of Bologna, and likewise to be freed after so long from their continual anxiety, humbly beseech Your Eminences benevolently to deign to grant that the justice of their cause be reconsidered.[6]

In its response of 31 August 1646, the Congregation of Bishops denied the nuns' request and imposed perpetual silence upon them in the matter. The moribund issue of Camaldolese reunion had been laid to rest once and for all. To make matters worse, the cardinals had discovered that ever since the 1620s, the nuns had still been permitted confessors in regular orders rather than the secular priests dictated by earlier decrees. The Congregation therefore insisted that the archbishop of Bologna now enforce the letter of the old law and replace the regular confessors with secular priests.

The issue of regular versus secular confessors now moved to center stage, displacing the lost cause of Camaldolese rule. But, for the nuns, it represented part of the same issue: their *libertà,* the maintenance of some measure of autonomy. In the decades after the Council of Trent and particularly in the seventeenth century, a certain flexibility and degree of freedom that had characterized pre-Tridentine affiliations between confessors and their cloistered charges shifted to a relationship of greater control from without and greater dependence within. The interactions of the nuns of Santa Cristina and Camaldolese confessors such as Mauro Ruggeri seem to have struck a balance between the pre-Tridentine confessor as spiritual counselor and the post-Tridentine confessor as spiritual governor. That balance may still have continued when the Camaldolese were supplanted at Santa Cristina in the late 1620s by other confessors from regular orders, and therefore still relatively independent of direct diocesan control.

The nuns' old enemy, the late Ludovico Ludovisi, remained a symbol in the issue of confessors, for it had been the archbishop's uncle, Gregory XV, who had given bishops the authority to approve and remove confessors in convents subject to regulars. For the nuns, confessors appointed by the archbishop represented an intrusion in convent government as well as an instrument of diocesan control. The potentially divided loyalties of such episcopal appointees, who represented the primary mediators between the cloister and the world, rendered them deeply suspect, especially in the matter of confidentiality. Such suspicions were not unfounded, for the inviolability of the seal of the confessional, much vaunted in the immediate aftermath of Trent, was compromised as the seventeenth century wore on, especially in relation to the investigative activities of the Holy Office.[7]

On 23 November, three months after their first letter in the matter of confessors, the Sacred Congregation reiterated its command even more emphatically to the dawdling archbishop of Bologna. This new and apparently rather reticent ordinary, Niccolò Albergati Ludovisi—in whose favor Archbishop Girolamo Colonna had renounced the archbishopric of Bologna on 2 February 1645, a month before Innocent X elevated Albergati Ludovisi to the cardinalate—was the cousin of the nuns' old adversary, Cardinal Archbishop Ludovico Ludovisi. Niccolò Albergati Ludovisi assumed the Ludovisi name after Prince Niccolò Ludovisi, duke of Fiano and prince of Venosa and Piombino, claimed him as a brother.[8] Ruggeri suggests that Niccolò Albergati Ludovisi's outward relations with the nuns of Santa Cristina were at first more than cordial and encouraging. "Such were the hopes that his Illustrious Eminence gave them that he seemed to them to touch heaven with his fingers." For Ruggeri, however, Niccolò Albergati Ludovisi was cut from the same cloth as his namesake. By the time the nuns' campaign began in earnest, their former confessor claims, even Albergati Ludovisi's public attitude had changed.[9]

A reading of the surviving documents suggests, however, that Niccolò Albergati Ludovisi was not the carbon copy of Ludovico Ludovisi that Ruggeri made him out to be. The relations between the latter-day Ludovisi and the nuns of Santa Cristina, markedly contrasting with the interaction of convent and archiepiscopal curia during the 1620s, illuminate the precarious political balance of nuns, priests, and patricians in the city. At the end of January 1647, the harried archbishop attempted to justify his five-month delay in implementing the Congregation's repeated orders. Niccolò Albergati Ludovisi appears to have had little faith in the draconian measures that had characterized the reign of his late cousin, but his own initial, gentler overtures proved as ineffective as Ludovico Ludovisi's harsher methods; the nuns flatly refused to accept secular confessors. He next tried a modicum of severity, firmly denying them permission to accept a novice, citing "the order of this supreme tribunal, which would no longer permit them to vest [postulants], to rip out for good the roots of such a foul rebellion."

The cardinal archbishop was soon visited by a leader of the Bolognese senate, indicating that the nuns had begun to exploit the conflicting and confused channels of authority that had mediated between them and episcopal authority in the past.[10] Alarmed at the sympathetic view of the nuns' plight circulating in the city, Albergati Ludovisi divulged what he called "the monstrous contumacy of the nuns, thus to arouse some shame in these disobedients" when his own version was spread around. He hoped to prepare the ground, so that if the sterner measures of the past were again required, they would not arouse further sympathy for the nuns, and additional disapprobation toward him, among the people.

Repeating the pattern of the 1620s, the nuns next enlisted the papal legate as negotiator. But, like his predecessor two decades earlier, the legate failed to find a solution. To combat an epistolary public relations campaign by the nuns, Cardinal Archbishop Albergati Ludovisi, in turn, summoned their relatives, to whom, as he put it, "the obstinacy of the nuns was expanded on." Taking a leaf from the earlier Ludovisi's book, the archbishop carefully pointed out how the unhappy affair could affect them and their families personally. "They left universally edified . . . and there was no shortage of people who heartily despised the good-for-nothing correspondence of the nuns"—or so he hoped.

It was only on 22 January 1647, after all these advance preparations, that the cautious Albergati Ludovisi finally got around to presenting the Congregation's decrees of 31 August and 23 November to Santa Cristina. He sweetened them, however, by the concession of confessors from the regular clergy during a two-month grace period, until 22 March. In the light of this concession, the nuns promptly dispatched another mediator, the distinguished Senator Barbazzi, their secular administrator, to the cardinal archbishop with a further request for regular confessors at Christmas and Easter and a Benedictine confessor to administer the last rites. Albergati Ludovisi's justification of his response to the Congregation of Bishops enumerates once again most of the informal sorts of influence that had long formed the basis of convent women's culture, suggesting that the sheep were still leading their pastor:

> The extravagance of their whims, so difficult to control, the ease with which the people sympathize and support the desires, right or wrong, of the weaker party, and the memory, still fresh, of their past rebellion, counseled me not to promise more than had been authorized by the Sacred Congregation. [But] the fragility of their sex, their condition as prisoners, and the quality of the women, deluded in their opinion, were accepted by a majority of the city, so that not to give in would have been interpreted as excessive rigidity. And their almost inevitable femininity of spirit, alas, proud to be insubordinate and rebellious, therefore reduced me to the point of assuring them, by virtue of my authority from this Sacred Congregation . . . that they would be entirely satisfied.[11]

Predictably, Albergati Ludovisi's concessions did not yield the happy outcome he had desired. When the two-month grace period expired, the nuns simply requested another extension for all of Lent. But even Ludovisi's leniency had its limits. After the cajolings of their confessor and the chief preacher of the duomo proved fruitless, on 22 March, the cardinal archbishop published a broadside throughout the city, reminiscent of his late cousin's ultimatum of eighteen years earlier, reproducing his own exhortation to immediate obedience and also including the Congregation's two most recent decrees, "so that their allies and their loved ones might see, from the very source, the paternal prudence so widely used by Your Eminences toward them for the space of twenty years."

By contrast with the stern commands and open threats of Ludovico Ludovisi's equivalent letter of March 1629, Niccolò Albergati Ludovisi's ultimatum reads like an attempt at self-justification: less a demand than a plea for obedience. There is no specific enumeration of the nuns' offenses, hardly a hint at possible excommunication, but chiefly a reiteration of the hierarchy's interpretation of what constituted nuns' true *imitatio Christi.*

> To the Nuns of Santa Cristina, most beloved in the Lord, true Peace and Health.
>
> The natural piety and religious discipline, clearly recognized and experienced by us in your persons, has never allowed us to doubt the readiness of your souls to obey the holy decisions of your superiors. Whence it has pleased the Congregation of the most eminent cardinals of the Council of Bishops and Regulars beneficently to hear these past months your entreaties to be restored to the care and government of Camaldolese monks. . . . They respond, in full agreement, that they cannot depart in any way from the most holy opinion of the supreme pontiff, whose decrees they do not arbitrate, but enforce. . . .
>
> Most beloved, by the bowels of Christ, and with all the power of our spirit, we pray you willingly to accept what God, by means of his supreme earthly

ministers, so expressly reveals to you as His will, in true certainty that you do not err so long as you follow, not your own spirit, but that of Jesus Christ, your spouse, who came down from the Throne of His Majesty only to obey, saying himself, *Veni non ut faciam voluntatem meam, sed eius, qui misit me Patris* [I came not to do my own will, but His, the Father who sent me. (John 6:38)]. Whilst he never ceased to obey, so long as he lived. *Factus,* as the Apostle writes, *obediens usque ad mortem* [He became obedient unto death. (Philippians 2:8)]. . . .

This is the true peace, the sole honor, and singular glory of religious persons: always to remain loyal and fixed in their desire for divine approval. . . . May it please the Spirit of Truth to assist you with his clearest light, as we hope, that you may not err in the recognition and election of the good.[12]

Albergati Ludovisi's letter also represented, of course, a carefully articulated defense to the public of episcopal policy. As a result, in his subsequent report to the Congregation of Bishops, the ever-optimistic cardinal archbishop claimed to have undercut a primary source of the convent's strength: "And, insofar as one can tell, this latest effort has succeeded most usefully among the people. And it seems that, not only the nobility, but also the citizenry and the common sort now betray their extreme distaste for such monstrous obstinacy."[13]

But Albergati Ludovisi continued to underestimate his strong-minded opponents. Two days before the publication of his broadside, the thirty-seven professed nuns of Santa Cristina, including Lucrezia Vizzana as the eleventh on the list, among nineteen survivors who had made a similar gesture eighteen years before, gathered once again to proclaim that

threatened with censures, excommunications, and other penalties if they choose not to obey, . . . they therefore protest and protest again that, should they agree to receive secular priests for their confessors and chaplains, it would not be of their own free will, but by force. For it seems to them that such a regular confessor to quiet their consciences should not be denied them, because they had entered this convent under the Rule and for the government of their souls by regulars. And otherwise they would not have entered. And therefore they once again protest and protest again that they would wish their rights always to remain safe and entirely unharmed, as they were before they were induced to agree to accept secular priests, . . . protesting that they do not do so voluntarily, but for fear of censure and penalties, . . . as a result of the main force of him who can command. And they do not act of their own will, but under compulsion . . . to escape the censure, punishments, and other charges with which they are threatened. And thus they protest, shall protest and declare, not only in the aforesaid manner and form, but by any other better means that is rightfully possible.[14]

This official, notarized declaration, echoing the words with which they had capitulated on 4 March 1629, but with the addition of a new breachof-contract argument, heralded the beginning of what at first appeared to be a replay of the 1620s. But perhaps in recognition that this was a less iron-fisted adversary, the nuns continued their new, less directly confrontational and more or less effective strategy. They agreed to obey the archbishop and the Congregation in all matters but the crucial issue of secular confessors, who were "prejudicial to their statutes," words that were to become another favorite theme for decades to come. They promptly made a token confession to secular priests in sign of obedience, but then immediately petitioned the pliant Ludovisi for another special regular confessor for Easter. This request was seconded, it seems, by many outside supporters, "less suppliant than importunate," as Ludovisi put it. "The demand struck me—and it really is—strange and astonishing," the archbishop remarked. "In any event, the torrent of prayers then grew to the point that finally I was prevailed upon to consent." The archbishop then had to find regulars willing to assume the task, "since the Olivetans don't want to enter the place on any account."[15]

Late in April, Albergati Ludovisi expressed such satisfaction with the spiritual progress produced in the nuns by his latest concession that he warmly entreated the Congregation to lift its ban on the acceptance of postulants, reassuring the cardinals in Rome that "one can find no more appropriate means to establish firmly every perfect consolation and quiet of the sisters in their new state." By the time the cardinal archbishop had written a second time to affirm the nuns' full compliance, they themselves had renewed their own barrage of petitions to Rome, even enlisting another intermediary, Christofano Pamfili, a member of the pope's own family, to back them. It is no wonder, therefore, that on 7 June, the skeptical Congregation of Bishops wrote asking Ludovisi for his absolute assurances of the nuns' full obedience.[16]

These he found he could not provide. In early July, Albergati Ludovisi had to admit that, after continuing to wheedle one extension after another out of him, the nuns had finally begun to ignore him altogether, apparently with the full complicity of the special Celestine confessor he had found for them the previous March, in the aftermath of his "ultimatum." This once again highlighted that traditional weakness in the church hierarchy's chain of command, a malleable and sympathetic confessor (and in this case, indeed, one from a regular order). At last Ludovisi had been pushed to the limit. When he cracked down, the nuns rebelled, as their sisters had done in the standoff of the 1620s, absolutely refusing to confess to or communicate from the hands of secular priests. They claimed, as Ludovisi put it, "that they can trust no secular priest, that they have always been betrayed by secular priests." The nuns' refusal of confession and communion stretched on from Ascension to Pentecost to the solemn feast of Corpus Christi, then dragged on through the summer and into the fall, as the nuns continued unflaggingly to petition for regular confessors, since they "could not entrust their consciences to the secular priests assigned them and totally ignorant of their statutes."[17]

"They not only persist more than ever in their disobedience, but what is more, with detestable pertinacity, they willingly deprive themselves of the use of the Sacraments, and of that celestial food that nourishes and maintains the religious in the spiritual life," the Congregation exclaimed in a letter of 27 September 1647 that was intended to stiffen Cardinal Archbishop Albergati Ludovisi's backbone once and for all. In a replay of their actions of 17 November 1628, the cardinals authorized the harshest measures, again including the walling up of all the grates and cutting off the nuns' access to the outside world completely. Ruggeri claims that they even threatened the nuns with the dissolution of their house and dispersal among the convents of the city.[18] Once again the convent of Santa Cristina seemed to be drifting toward destruction.

Had the nuns still been dealing with Ludovico Ludovisi, who had indeed made such a threat, Ruggeri's claim would appear to have been well founded. In the case of Niccolò Albergati Ludovisi, it seems less plausible. Even now, not about to act precipitously, the archbishop sent his emissary to Santa Cristina with a further warning of this latest, impending ultimatum. The nuns immediately responded with a request that he delay for fifteen more days while they petitioned the Congregation yet again to reconsider. As Ludovisi explained to the Sacred Congregation,

> Repulsed at their first try, they responded more fervently with a second—in the face of which, to avoid departing from my usual gentle principles in these latest experiences, I thought it good to be indulgent. And in fact I did yield to them. Not content, . . . the next day the nuns requested that if, within such a brief timespan, they had not obtained the desired result, I would be content to postpone [the implementation of the decree] until its arrival.

But even Niccolò Albergati Ludovisi had his limits. "In the face of such a request, I became totally inexorable, and that is where we stand."[19]

He did not, however, dispatch masons to Santa Cristina to wall up the grates, as dictated by Rome. Within the week, the nuns' other administrators, from one of Bologna's oldest and most illustrious families, the Malvezzi, appeared at the archbishop's residence with a new request. The nuns, they reported, had deeply repented their hardness of heart and in future would maintain due obedience, which even now they hastened to embrace. But their souls remained so ill disposed toward the secular priests they had been defying these past five months that they could only unburden themselves properly to a confessor in regular orders. By now, the "totally inexorable" archbishop's reaction should come as no great surprise. "As the loving father of the same nuns, I earnestly entreat that you deign to console them, for their convent (apart from this affair) is otherwise one of the most exemplary and most commendable in my jurisdiction."[20] With this recommendation, Niccolò Albergati Ludovisi forwarded the nuns' own latest petition to Rome—while his predecessor, Ludovico Ludovisi, no doubt turned over in his grave:

> Never would we have thought, Most Eminent and Reverend Lords, that poor religious women, shut in between walls and bars, merely requesting most humbly of you a confessor of their Rule, would so offend you that, not only would you decline to permit one, but would even order that we be walled in and severely punished according to canon law. ... Eminent Lords, we are innocent, we are discredited before this sacred tribunal, accused as disobedient and contumacious, that we would clash with our superiors. It is so false that we are horrified even to hear it! ... Prostrate before that Mother of Mercy, we humbly supplicate that you grant us the grace of a confessor of our Rule, that we may confidently purge our consciences. And remember, Fathers, that your sacred robes are dyed crimson in the blood of Jesus, that dripped down from Him to save souls, as it would be shed anew for a single soul. Pity us, imitating our Lord, whose ministers you are, before whom, humbly kneeling, we kiss your sacred mantles.[21]

Such eloquence, it seems, was able to soften even the hard hearts of cardinals in Rome. Within the week, on 15 November, the Congregation of Bishops granted "for one single time" a confessor extraordinary in regular orders, with the stipulation, however, that from then on, without further discussion, the nuns obey in full. Cardinal Archbishop Albergati Ludovisi, cautious to the last, informed the two Malvezzi that he was ready to console the nuns, once they had provided some visible pledge to assure him of their obedience. The next day, Cavalier Malvezzi returned with word that the nuns had deputized him, as their administrator, to make the pledge on their behalf. The circumspect, and by now a little wiser, archbishop sent him back to via Fondazza to point out that, after the events of last Easter, another secondhand verbal assurance would not satisfy without some clearer demonstration of obedience. Malvezzi retraced his steps, this time to express the nuns' "astonishment to hear that one had so little faith in their solemn word" and to test the cardinal archbishop's mettle again by insisting that their verbal pledge alone should suffice. "But in spite of that, I remained adamant in my first response"—words greeted, no doubt, with relief (and perhaps with astonishment) in Rome. Twenty-four hours later, Malvezzi reappeared finally to announce the nuns' capitulation, in confirmation of which they had begun at last to confess to secular priests.[22] The long process of their subjugation to archiepiscopal control, which had begun with the loss of their Camaldolese superiors and ended with the disappearance of a token regular confessor, was complete.

One cannot tell whether by then the nuns may have realized that the prelates saw the suspected blots on their reputation that had so preoccupied them and their families these twenty-five years, and had sparked their last crisis, as a useful means to an end. For the ecclesiastical hierarchy, "moral" reforms, provoked by convent "scandal," had long provided an effective excuse for political reforms within the cloister, often to right internal imbalances of dynastic power. Most likely, the nuns did grasp that when the issue was obedience to superiors, even with considerable outside sympathy and support within the city, and even if they could manage to hold their own against Cardinal Archbishop Niccolò Albergati Ludovisi, their diocesan superior (whom they seem to have learned to play almost as expertly as their musical instruments), women religious in particular, and few women of any kind, could realistically hope to prevail against the Roman curia.

On 22 December 1647, the Congregation of Bishops, commending Ludovisi's "paternal zeal," his "great prudence and pastoral solicitude," and his "gentle means in disposing the nuns to exact obedience," decreed that the convent of Santa Cristina could once again begin to accept novices and *educande.* By now, down in the crypts, Emilia Grassi, who had worked so hard to oppose them forty years before, was well beyond caring. It was twenty-five years, almost to the day, since the feast of Saint Thomas the Apostle in 1622, when Suffragan Bishop Angelo Gozzadini and the other visitors had begun their investigation of the strife at Santa Cristina that, as Cecilia Bianchi had claimed, "began because of music."

Donna Lucrezia Orsina Vizzana, whose *Componimenti musicali* had played a part in the earlier struggle, was the first nun singled out by Mauro Ruggeri at the opening of his long history of that turbulent quarter century for the luster her talents had brought Santa Cristina. She reappears a second time at the very end, as a living symbol of the toll those twenty-five years had taken:

> Such was the terror induced by this further blow [the convent's final defeat of 1647], that, as I have been assured, one donna Lucrezia Villani [*sic*], otherwise among the wisest, lost her reason. And whenever she heard the cloister bell ring, her imaginary fears were so great that she would lash out wildly.[23]

The clangor of the bells, which had rallied parishioners in the spectacular battle of 1628 and continued regularly to mark the daily rhythms of convent life, became the musical nun's undoing.

With don Mauro's last reference, donna Lucrezia Orsina Vizzana, who after her brief moment of renown in the early 1620s remained in the shadow of her activist aunt and older sister, disappears behind the wall into illness and the black hole of madness. This probably explains the cryptic reference in the convent necrology to "the weight of calamities, as if fallen straight from heaven" ("infortuniorum onus, tamquam e celo dilapsum"). Like her aunt, the venerable madre donna Flaminia Bombacci, Lucrezia Vizzana increasingly found comfort in her devotions, especially to the Mysteries of the Rosary. Living until 1662, she survived all the inhabitants of Santa Cristina who had endured the visitation of 1622–23 except two of the most junior *professe*. She outlived her sister Isabetta, who died in 1653, and Mauro Ruggeri, who died in 1660. After sixty-five years of religion, Lucrezia Vizzana passed to a better life on 7 May 1662, the eve of the Apparition of Saint Michael the Archangel, who had likewise seen Flaminia Bombacci to paradise. For the last forty years of her life, Vizzana never again ventured into print.

TEN

The Pontifical Consecration of Virgins
"Pomp indecent for religious observance and modesty"

At the end of the 1670s, the late Lucrezia Orsina Vizzana's cousin, madre donna Teresa Pompea Vizzana, commissioned a new altarpiece for the side altar of Saint Christina, located to the right of the high altar in the convent's external church. Domenico Maria Canuti's dramatic work (see fig. 14), completed between 1677 and 1680, which earned a special star in Malvasia's guide to the art of Bologna of 1686, presents none of the common episodes from the saint's highly eventful passion.[1] Instead, Christina's cruel father, Urbanus, dominates the scene, his right fist clenched, as he viciously grabs his daughter by the hair with his left, drives his knee into her side, and wrests her backward to the ground to bend her to his will, while astonished bystanders try to restrain him or look on in sympathy. The viewer comes away from the altar wondering uneasily whether Teresa Pompea Vizzana and the nuns of Santa Cristina intended to draw a specific, dark analogy between the classic artistic symbol of subjugation, grabbing the hair, and their own plight. Defeated in the 1620s by their policy of open confrontation in the matter of Camaldolese superiors, after a latter-day Urbanus, Pope Urban VIII, had subjected them to archiepiscopal control, then vanquished again in the 1640s in the matter of regular confessors, after decades of extraordinary resistance, they had finally been subjugated totally to the control of the diocesan hierarchy.

The nuns of Santa Cristina had lost the last of the obvious, direct links to the order that had governed them for five hundred years. But, just as the new Canuti altarpiece could be read as an artistic symbol of their own oppression at the hands of a paternalistic church hierarchy, there also remained a single, ritual act to symbolize their former independence under Camaldolese superiors. The ritual consecration of virgins, following the Roman pontifical—the Sacra, as they called it—was a third and final ceremony in a nun's rites of passage, only permitted when she reached the age of twenty-five, after the rites of investiture and profession. We have already encountered it earlier, in relation to Lucrezia Vizzana's life and her motet, *Amo Christum,* probably composed for the rite. In the periodic repetition until well into the eighteenth century of this particularly solemn ritual, which in Bologna was practiced only at Santa Cristina and invariably captured the attention and imagination of the city, the nuns of Santa Cristina may have come to recognize one of those "other better means" of protest cited in their official proclamation of 1647. Like Canuti's altarpiece, it represented an artistic, flexible, less direct means of public persuasion, which could reaffirm their *libertà,* their *onestà,* and their links to their old superiors. At the end of the Seicento, it also became a way to act out in some measure their independence from the usurping authority of the archbishop of Bologna.

NUNS' RITES OF PASSAGE

The power of that consecration of virgins at Santa Cristina is best understood against the background of nuns' more usual investiture and profession ceremonies, which were important in the social dynamic of convent, city, and curia. The rites focused symbolically upon the meeting—and the separation—of the cloister and the world, a symbolism intensified by the strict imposition of enclosure after Trent.[2] The lavish rituals of investiture, marking the girl's official acceptance, and profession, both traditionally underwritten by the nuns' parents, represented, in the ecclesiastical view, a violation of the monastic ideal of simplicity. But they also made manifest and reaffirmed the primary position of noble and patrician families as mediators in the relationship between the convent and the curia. Little wonder, then, that these ceremonies remained a source of tension between church authorities, the nuns, and their families, and were regularly under attack by ecclesiastical superiors, both in the diocesan curia and in Rome.

The nun's first rite of passage, her acceptance in chapter by the monastic community and her subsequent investiture, or clothing ceremony, came after an indeterminate period as an *educanda.* For some girls, such as Lucrezia Vizzana, this prenovitiate preparation extended from earliest childhood. Only at age fifteen, according to the Council of Trent, could a postulant officially enter the novitiate, an event marked by her acceptance into the convent and her reception of the habit in the clothing ceremony.

As the psalm *Laetatus sum* was sung, the postulant was led to the convent door, where the nuns awaited her. After the singing of the *Te Deum,* the parties returned to their respective churches (clergy and parents to the outer church, nuns and postulants to their inner church) for Mass. After Mass, the priest blessed the habit, veil, and crown, which were passed through the grate to the kneeling postulant, whose hair had been clipped in the meantime, sometimes to the accompaniment of sacred songs commenting upon the abandonment of earthly vanities. After the postulant's investiture, the exchange of the kiss of peace by nuns and novice, and the singing of the *Veni Creator*, the novice assumed her religious name.[3]

Benedictines such as the nuns of Santa Cristina had traditionally considered a year as the appropriate time for the novice's prayer, meditation, and study of the rules of monastic life and the constitutions of the order before profession. The Council of Trent made a full year's novitiate a general requirement. The nun's profession, when the novice was inscribed among the ranks of the religious, marked her second rite of passage. During the early modern period, the practice of an initial simple profession, followed in later years by a subsequent solemn profession, was also introduced.

This rite of passage began with the Mass, which was interrupted at the offertory, when the novice vowed perpetual poverty, chastity, and obedience before the altar. Bowing deeply, sometimes with arms extended, she sang *Suscipe me Domine secundum eloquium tuum*, and so on. After various prayers and the singing by the nuns of the *Veni Creator Spiritus*, the novice's new habit was blessed, and she received the kiss of peace from the abbess and her fellow nuns. While the nuns communicated, the novice lay prostrate until the priest called *Surge quae dormis*, to which she sang *Mel, et lac ex eius ore suscepi*, and so on. The ceremony concluded with the lengthy process of blessing and receiving the veil and crown.

The solemn consecration of the nun's virginity was a much rarer rite of passage, which could not occur before age twenty-five. After the mid sixteenth century, much of its liturgy was absorbed into the liturgy of solemn profession. As we shall see, the consecration largely fell into disuse after the Council of Trent.

When it came to all such rites of passage of the sacred virgins, post-Tridentine reformers attempted to restore monastic decorum and to enforce *clausura*. In practice these attempts resulted in disparity, with the ideal frequently at odds with the reality. On his arrival in Bologna early in 1566, the newly appointed Bishop Gabriele Paleotti had confronted a state of affairs that was common throughout much of Italy:

> On the days when nuns receive their habits, the convent fills up with laywomen, and they go around prattling everywhere, a largely useless activity. And in order to enjoy their relatives and friends at their own convenience, they hold these festivities after lunch. It seems it would be more suitable to perform [the ceremony] in the morning, and celebrate Mass and give Communion to the one, or to those, who receive the habit. The same can be said of the occasions when they profess.[4]

For the nuns and their families, of course, the festivities were hardly "useless." They not only reaffirmed the links between the nuns and their

lineages in the world, but also strengthened other informal social ties between convent and community, which remained primary forces in convent
women's culture. As we shall see, many of these social and festive aspects
of the nuns' acceptances, professions, and consecrations, almost exclusively
involving their female relatives, form interesting parallels to the informal
and, to some extent, clandestine reciprocal gifts and collations of Renaissance worldly marriages, worked out by custom rather than by law to balance the public dowry, which have been perceptively studied in recent years
by Christiane Klapisch-Zuber.[5]

"Abuses" in the rites of investiture, profession, and consecration became
one of the many objects of the bishop of Bologna's reforming zeal. Paleotti
imposed strict enclosure:

> When someone receives the monastic habit, or makes her profession, or the
> Sacrament of confirmation is administered to her, [neither] the bishop, nor
> any superior in regular or secular orders, nor the confessor or any other
> person, may enter the cloister; but all these rites should be carried out com-
> pletely at the window in the external church where the Sacrament of the
> Eucharist is administered, with the girl or nun standing (inside). Absolutely
> no window, door, or opening whatsoever that looks outside the cloister, in
> any convent whatsoever, may be opened without license of the bishop, who
> will not grant it without carefully considering the place and the necessity.

In his *Episcopale Bononiensis civitatis et diocesis,* published in 1580, Paleotti
addressed the issue of pomp and dynastic display by forbidding gatherings
of onlookers and relatives in the external church, and specifically banning
music during professions.[6]

It is unsurprising that although enclosure could be imposed rather easily
upon the ritual features of the investiture ceremonies and professions, it
was more difficult to moderate the festive aspects, including music, which
had commonly been observed by the nuns and their families for centuries.
At least since 1576, the newly established Congregation of Bishops had
attempted to reduce the indecorously lavish spending at clothing ceremonies and professions, which it claimed ranged from one hundred to two
hundred scudi, and to enforce greater uniformity among richer and poorer
houses in such rituals.[7] In March 1592, Cardinal Paleotti's coadjutor, Alfonso Paleotti, effectively acknowledged the inefficacy of earlier local attempts at reform by republishing a broadside, whose bleakly precise additional prohibitions provide, between the lines, a sense of what the common,
contrasting practice in the city must have really been like:

> On the day when the young girl is to enter the convent, she must go in the
> morning, without any sort of display, in simple dress, without ornament,
> fringework, or train, dressed in white, black, or buff or violet, lest as a vow or
> as a sign of devotion, she would wear no gray; [her hair should be] without

buns, twists, flowers, or other adornments on her head. And while she remains outside and otherwise at large in the city, she should not dare to go about in any other sort of dress but the above-named; and, briefly, [she should arrive] without the company of carriages, but bringing with her only two or three of her closest relatives, who should accompany her to the convent and then immediately withdraw. And the girl will be received at the door only by the superior and the doorkeepers. And then, on the day when she receives her habit, any gathering of people, music, and assembly should be excluded from the external church, while the church is kept closed; only those ministers necessary to give the habit to the girl, or to administer the profession to the novice, should be admitted, and no others.[8]

Alfonso Paleotti's drab prescriptions provide some sense of the nuptial displays for the brides of Christ that the families—and, indeed, the convents—were loath to give up. Despite twenty-five years of restrictions, the rites must still have retained some of the glitter and gaity of similar ceremonies in the days before Trent, as exemplified by the following description of the investiture of two noble Bolognese women, who at Epiphany 1475 had entered the convent of Corpus Domini:

[They entered] at the twentieth hour [c. 2:00 P.M.], completely clothed in white mantles, with sleeves of brocade, their tresses down over their shoulders, with worthy veils with gold brocade, accompanied by the Lady Ginevra Bentivoglio, with more than forty ladies, and the lords *anziani*. And almost all Bologna followed them to observe.[9]

A wide implementation of the new austerity remained a vain, if abiding, hope, even during the Paleottis' own lifetimes, for the patriciate was unwilling to embrace it. Antonio Francesco Ghiselli records, for example, that in 1607, three years before Alfonso Paleotti's death, when the illustrious Orsina Pepoli and Angela Boncompagni, from two of Bologna's loftiest noble families, took the veil at the convent of San Guglielmo, it required 250 men to carry their effects and the lavish banquet of special delicacies provided for the nuns and the attendants by Count Ercole Pepoli.[10] Ghiselli seems never averse to making a good story even better. But the convent records at San Guglielmo enthusiastically record the details of other similarly lavish *feste*. Twenty years later, in February 1628, for example, the marchioness Caterina Malaspina arrived at San Guglielmo from Genoa, and without further delay immediately received her habit as suor Maria Aloisa from the hands of Monsignor Antonio Albergati in the presence of the papal legate, Cardinal Bernardino Spada, and the vice-legate, Monsignor Malaspina. The ceremony was attended by a large number of marquises and marchionesses, counts, knights, and senators, who came to see "this lady who gave herself to God."

A week later, festivities continued when suor Maria Aloisa was paid a visit by her mother, the marchioness Aloisa Malaspina, and her aunts, the marchioness Maria Pepoli Malaspina and the lady Lelia Paleotti Malaspina, who, with special license (that could hardly have been denied the family of the vice-legate and a distant relative of the archbishop himself), entered the cloister and

> remained in the refectory with the sisters for lunch, and the whole of the day until two hours after dark, to our great consolation. And we did them every honor possible for us, and they visited every part of our convent; and they were always accompanied by Sister Maria Aloisa, daughter of the most illustrious lady Marchioness Aloisa, and the niece of those other ladies.[11]

Such family sendoffs, the sacred equivalents of the secular nuptials of the comparatively limited number of daughters who took earthly spouses, served as affirmations of the dignity and social status, not only of the families they left behind, but also of the convents they were entering.[12] A daughter's marriage to the Son of God rather than to the son of some noble or patrician family obviously complicates any comparisons with secular marriages. Yet, although some details may be different—much more of the overt gift-giving and provisioning comes from the bride's family than the convent, representing the groom, for example—the parallels help to explain why the festive and social aspects of these espousals to Christ were as hard to control by episcopal decree as their worldly equivalents in some cities were by secular law.

Ercole Pepoli's lavish and ostentatious provision for Orsina Pepoli at San Guglielmo in 1607 recalls, for example, the *donara,* or trousseau, delivered by a secular bride's family to her husband's home the day after her wedding, symbolizing her break with her old family. Similarly, the day-long reception and entertainment in 1628 of suor Maria Aloisa Malaspina's mother and aunts by the nun's new mothers and sisters within San Guglielmo, a week after she had entered the convent, certainly would have included modest gifts such as the nuns' much-sought-after *torte di frutta,* provided by the nuns on behalf of the heavenly bridegroom. These social gatherings and their attendant gifts parallel the gifts of foodstuffs and sweetmeats provided by worldly husbands' relatives for the marriage feast. Such convent receptions offer an interesting expansion of the common women's practice in secular marriage rituals where female relatives were drawn into kinship networks. Convent rites of passage incorporated not only the new bride of Christ but also her female relatives into the convent family, which extended the convent's circle in new and potentially useful ways. As in the world, these reciprocal exchanges were essential to round out such alliances. Klapisch-Zuber observes of similar worldly marriage rituals that "even more important than the material worth of these gifts, in fact, was the need people engaged in the process of alliance felt—on all levels of society—to make such offerings." The same appears to have been the case within the convent wall.[13]

The convent rites and festivities also renewed dynastic links, frequently extending back for centuries to a time before Trent, when greater freedom concerning enclosure had fostered more frequent and diverse reinforcements of family ties. With special license, or as best they could, the older convent brides of Christ, like equivalent matrons in the world, rehearsed the new alliance with the new bride who joined them, whose place in the convent "lineage" was thereby articulated. In the convent situation, the social network is also significantly expanded informally to embrace the novice's female lineage, for whom the gifts and honors created a sense of obligation, comparable to those in the world.

From the beginning, such displays also acted as a means of articulating and emphasizing an illustrious postulant's special place in the convent social structure. At the same time, prelates on the outside worked to moderate perceived differences in social status, to defuse potential dynastic rivalries within cloisters, and to minimize any conflict between the authority of the urban patriciate and that of the church with respect to these institutions.[14] For the first families of Bologna, these public rituals were almost as much an instrument of social promotion as their secular equivalents, a function they also served for the convents themselves, where the building of a strong network of family alliances was critical. For convent and family alike, it was important that these actions be performed publicly, not hidden away behind locked church doors, like some furtive clandestine marriage before an obliging friar. The ecclesiastical hierarchy therefore had great difficulty resisting the mediations of convent advocates in this matter. Indeed, the diocesan curia seems frequently to have capitulated quite happily, especially (as in the above example from San Guglielmo) when its own illustrious families were involved.

Secular wedding festivities were to some extent eclipsed by their sacred equivalents, inasmuch as the daughters of the patriciate entered, or were dispatched to, the cloister in increasing numbers during the Seicento. The sorts of expensive artistic display associated with secular marriages—not only music, but also lavish decorations, published commemorative poetry and engravings, pageants, plays, and fireworks—may actually have burgeoned as inevitable features of convent rites. Poetic effusions composed to commemorate taking the veil or profession, commissioned by parents and other relatives, but also as frequently by the cloistered aunts who received the girls, were the obvious sacred equivalent to their counterparts celebrating worldly marriages. No fewer than 105,000 commemorations of secular nuptials have been catalogued for the Settecento alone.[15] For the ex-Jesuit Saverio Bettinelli, these ephemeral works, printed in libretti on paper or white, red, blue, or yellow silk—"at times the most detestable sonnet totally embroidered 'round inside with greater nobility than was ever used on any ode of Horace and any psalm of David"—were one more manifestation of the ostentatious luxuries in the church and the ritual. As Bettinelli explained it, "they end up in the hands of the chambermaids and the footmen, they all perish before the day is out. And, while we smell the flowers and taste the sweets more or less, nobody reads the verses, neither more nor less."[16]

All that occasionally saved a poetic effort such as *Il trionfo dell'amor santo* (see fig. 15) was probably the lavish decorative scene that surrounds it. In this commemoration of the entry of Pannina Marta Pannini of Cento into the convent of Santa Caterina in Faenza as suor Maria Clotilde Lucia Benedetta in 1706, dott. Florio Maria Evangelista Novio's poetic excesses in twenty-four stanzas were aptly adorned with a comparable excess of musical art by Eville ("Evilmerodac") Milanta, who set the poem as a duet for soprano and bass. Milanta's closely imitative voices offer a strangely gendered musical rhetoric. Isidore of Seville had explained as early as the seventh century that "woman [*mullier*] gets her name from 'softness' [*mollitie*] or as it were 'softer', *mollier* with a letter taken away or changed."[17] Milanta's soprano sings in the key of G♭ major, with no fewer than six flats, just about the softest and most feminine key possible, given that *molle* (as in *hexachordum molle*) meant both "soft" and "flat." By contrast, the bass picks his way along in the contrastingly hard, masculine key of F♯ major (*hexachordum durum* = "hard" and "sharp"), with six sharps. Such musical offerings were less common than their strictly poetic equivalents. But the fact that several published musical collections dedicated to nuns appeared around the time of investitures, professions, or consecrations suggests that the music prints played a similar role.[18]

For the nuns, whose daily diet might be boring, unappetizing, or worse (there is an air of truth to the complaint of a nun in a seventeenth-century Florentine convent drama that the food, rotten or overcooked, was not fit for a dog),[19] the culinary arts provoked as much enthusiasm as the visual, musical, or literary. When Ginevra Fava took the veil at Santa Maria Nuova in 1653, for example, a convent chronicler described in loving detail the subsequent banquet of "first, liver soup [some sops of liver?], with so many plates per table; for antipasto, some melon, salami, and calf's liver; then some roast veal and half a roasted cockerel for each [of us]; some pieces of Parmesan cheese, and a beautiful pear for fruit; with exquisite wine at will."[20] Such post-acceptance or post-profession convent banquets, another reflection of the secular wedding collation, but in this case offered by the postulant's family rather than the "groom's," informally evolved into a requirement, necessitated by custom and itemized on expense lists for parents, as an expense in addition to the dowry. The nuns' meticulous recording of every course at such banquets, frequently eclipsing the description of the other festive splendors, offers another interesting parallel to the careful noting of the public and private details of marriage rituals in secular *recordanze,* where they served as a record of family obligations. Their enthusiasm speaks just as loudly about what life must have been like on more ordinary days for those within the convent wall, and thereby suggests why informal custom evolved into quasi-official law.[21]

The convents' presentation of plays was another favorite adornment of profession celebrations that in some measure helped to balance the families' offerings. Such performances, which spotlighted the talents of the nuns themselves, were particularly fascinating and attractive to outsiders— and therefore a constant source of archiepiscopal displeasure and vigilance. A decree issued by the nuns' vicar of Bologna in 1650 against such productions differs from others regularly promulgated over the decades only in offering slightly more specific detail than usual:

> It is the mind of the Sacred Congregation of Bishops and Regulars and of the most eminent and reverend lord cardinal archbishop that on the occasion when girls are accepted into the religious life, or receive their habits, or at their profession, a play should not be performed by the nuns either at the convent gateway or any place else where they can be seen or heard by laypeople . . . even when they are simple dialogues for two persons only, or soliloquies for one person.[22]

As near as one can tell, in Bologna such plays often seem not to have exceeded these stipulations by much. Examples from San Guglielmo, where convent drama flourished in the 1640s and 1650s, sound comparably modest:

> February 2, 1656. Note how suor Angiola Maria Caterina Grassi made her solemn profession, offering the customary honors to the convent and the gift of a luncheon, with a bar of soap for each [of us]. Sister Silvia Ortensia put on a most beautiful play in church, which was Christ's funeral, as she was prioress of Carnival.

By contrast with such comparatively simple dramas, there were also more lavish musical productions, such as the one in June 1706, when a daughter of the nobility received her habit at one of the most musical convents. This production seems to have received a second "command" performance:

> On the occasion of the vesting of Anna Margarita, daughter of Count Federico Berualdi, at the convent of Santa Margherita, an opera entitled *Attilio Regolo* was performed. And on the 27th the court of Modena, with twelve ladies, entered the monastery to see it.[23]

The fullest descriptions of such sumptuous superfluities tend to appear in the prohibitions intended to control them. One of the fullest for Bologna was published by Antonio Francesco Giovagnoni, nuns' vicar of the city, on 29 May 1677 (in response to a bull of Pope Alexander VII's from 1657 that Innocent XI had found it necessary to reconfirm in an edict of 1676) aimed at all sorts of superfluous display, but singling out investitures and professions in particular:

> It is further ordered in the said bull and edict that at times when novices receive their regular habits, or profess, on such occasions music, fireworks, shooting off firecrackers, playing of trumpets or drums, the handing out of flowers or things to eat in church or at doorways or in parlatorios is forbidden, either at the expense of the convent or of individuals, or of the relatives of the girls. It will therefore be the responsibility of the mother superior, immediately upon receipt of the present letter, to have it read publicly, so that it may be heard and observed by all. And may God bless you.[24]

Giovagnoni's decree was part of the curia's latest concerted attempt at sumptuary controls, for in January of that year, supposedly at the pope's insistence, the Congregation of Bishops, in a letter to the cardinal archbishop of Naples, had deplored the "displays inappropriate to religious observance and modesty," and had forbidden the invitation of outsiders and the continuation of such ceremonies past sundown. Six years later, the same decree was reiterated, largely word for word, in letters to Naples and Nola.[25]

From the church's point of view, sumptuary controls were theoretically directed at the sins of pride and gluttony. From a more practical viewpoint, the church hierarchy feared that the gifts, festivities, and especially the music that simply vanished into thin air squandered the dowry the convent had only just received and subverted its true function as an investment to ensure the convent's financial future.[26] For the nuns, on the other hand, these exchanges represented a different sort of investment in their political futures, nurturing their essential social networks. Clerical attacks on noble wealth and privilege did not sit well with the Bolognese patriciate, even in the midst of a long period of demographic and socioeconomic decline. The prohibition only fed the abiding noble-ecclesiastical tensions that characterized the Seicento in Bologna. These were further heightened by the fact that for eighty years, from the 1650s to the 1730s, the primary archbishops were from the Boncompagni family, who for decades had rented out Palazzo Boncompagni in Bologna to others. Their place in the senatorial ranks remained temporarily empty until the 1730s, and their primary allegiances thus now seemed to be to the curia and to Rome, where they had acquired the palace on via Veneto that now houses the American embassy.[27]

Control of these convent festivities was clearly something of a losing battle. A festival described in the records at San Guglielmo twenty-five years after Antonio Francesco Giovagnoni's order, which lasted more than a week and ignored most of the prohibitions outlined in the decrees of Alexander VII and Innocent XI, must have taken place by special license of the archbishop.

> Note how on December 19, 1703, the Chapter's acceptance of the illustrious lady Giuliana Maria Banzi took place, which was very beautiful. Then came the antevigil of Christmas, which was on Sunday, and at her entry into the church a most beautiful sinfonia was performed by players in the external church, with four trumpeters outside in the street, who played continuously until three hours after sundown. . . . She then received her habit on the feast of Saint John [27 December]. . . . She was invested to the accompaniment of music, with a general invitation [to the ceremony extended] to ladies; and it was Cardinal Giacomo Boncompagni who gave her the habit.[28]

Even the reformed monastic orders, traditionally the models of strict observance held up by the diocesan curia to their weaker sisters, could not resist the wishes of postulants' families. When Lucrezia Malvezzi took the veil at the austere Capuchin convent Natività di Maria Vergine in 1697, her father paid out £2:10 for two trumpeters, £22:10 for music at the ceremony, and £30 for three hundred firecrackers. In 1734–35, when suor Alba Rosa Malvezzi (*al secolo* Caterina) joined the Capuchins, her father paid no less than £150 for music (excluding firecrackers).[29] And in February 1720, at the acceptance of the daughter of Count Felicini, solemn music was even heard at the convent of Gesù e Maria, the paradigmatic reformed convent in Bologna, lauded shortly before its foundation a century earlier as a place where nuns would forgo "expenses for singing and playing, paid for by nuns [in other convents], only for ambition, for other ends besides the praise of God."[30] It is no wonder, perhaps, that in 1714, the lawyer Alessandro Macchiavelli, founder of the Accademia dei Filopatridi and chronicler of Bolognese daily life, exclaimed after an investiture at Sant'Agnese, "Every day people condemn the great sums spent to profess the nuns, but each one still wants to spend more than the next!" The following year, after a similar *festa* at San Trinità, he observed: "The expenses required for these functions are unspeakable, and yet nobody attempts a remedy."[31]

Occasionally, although rarely in Bologna, some within the wall voiced similar complaints. In 1664, Francesca Antonia Petrini of the convent of Santa Chiara in Acquaviva (Bari) requested that, in contrast with normal convent practice, she be allowed to receive her veil, not in the external church, "pompously, with music," but from the Ordinary at the grates, "to save on expenses and because such displays are excessive for religious humility." In 1697, the noblewomen Maddalena Liverolli and Anna Mucciarelli of the convent of Sant'Andrea in Ascoli, likewise hoping to avoid "rather unbecoming pomp and luxury," requested permission to receive their habits at the grate "in a more exemplary and decent manner."[32] Al-

though in the midst of riotous display, such extreme simplicity could likewise achieve distinction, any aristocratic audience present might speculate
whether such decorous piety masked an illustrious family with its fortunes
on the skids.

Voices of complaint, however, were seldom heard. For most families and
convents, the rites were well worth the expense and were probably even
regarded as their "duty," as a way to sustain family honor.[33] To balance the
perpetual complaints of bishops, the odd indignant Bolognese observer,
or the rare disgruntled nun, it is also useful to hear what little we can of
the voices from inside the wall. In the same years in which Alessandro
Macchiavelli voiced his complaints, the Dominican nuns of San Pietro Martire in Bologna instituted a more solemn rite of profession, described for
future reference in the convent records:

> August 15, 1713. The profession of Gentile Piana, now suor Maria Spera in
> Dio, was celebrated; and her profession, for the greater devotion of the laity,
> was carried out in the following way. After the customary homily by the father
> confessor, the organ was played briefly [until she] reached the Holy Com-
> munion grate, where the customary profession took place. Then, while she
> changed into her habit, but not the veil, the organ played. And thus vested,
> she prostrated herself before the Most Holy [Sacrament] and remained thus
> until the end of the singing of the psalm *Laudate Dominum de Caelis* [Psalm
> 148]. And when she had been helped to her feet, the two superiors led her
> to the altar of the Most Holy Virgin of the Rosary and then to the altar of
> Father Saint Dominic, while the choir sang *Maria Mater gr[ati]e* and the hymn
> of Father Saint [Dominic]. And so ended the ceremony. I have made note of
> it here so that there would be a record of it in case the other prioresses should
> wish to adopt this style, it being at their discretion to perform it as before—
> that is, the homily of the father confessor and the profession without other
> singing and playing, which provoked little devotion. [Added in another
> hand:] Instead of the said psalm, it is better to sing the hymn of Father Saint
> Dominic and of Saint Peter Martyr.[34]

Here there are no fireworks, trumpets, or drums to dazzle the world
outside the wall or to catch the particular attention of local chroniclers,
but simply some organ playing and a few psalms or hymns to capture the
sense of occasion, "for the greater devotion of"—significantly—"the laity,"
the nun's relatives, who presumably were loath to do without them. In such
rare instances when the voices within speak essentially to one another, with
no apparent assumption that their words will carry beyond the wall, one is
also left with a sense of how artistic adornment could be perceived as more
than the mere vanity prelates made it out to be. The San Pietro Martire
example may recognize the importance of a little modest splendor to appeal to the public. But there is no reason to question the nuns' own brief
reactions to other, more elaborate *feste,* recorded by the anonymous chron-

iclers at San Guglielmo over the years: "to the great contentment of all the sisters" (1644), "in sum, it was a thing of the greatest devotion" (1644), "to the spiritual pleasure of [us] all" (1656), "to our greatest consolation" (1692). For in these private and drabber worlds, cut off from the regular round of religious and secular festivals at San Pietro, San Petronio, Santa Maria dei Servi, and elsewhere in the city at large, such rare display need not represent the decadence or secularization suspect among the ecclesiastical hierarchy. Within the wall, even the most modest and unstaged adornment of rites of passage could seem miraculous:

> April 21, 1627. Remember how on this day madre suor Penelope Vizzana passed to a better life. And don Antonio Vanotti administered the Most Holy Sacraments to her. And as she died the birds came in great numbers to her window and sang their sweetest song, which inspired wonder and devotion in all those who were present.[35]

THE CONSECRATION OF VIRGINS

At Santa Cristina della Fondazza, nuns were accepted, took their habits, and professed with the customary, lavish festivities. Their Camaldolese superiors had likewise waged a losing battle to maintain some modicum of decorum. In 1433, when Ambrogio Traversari, the Camaldolese prior general, discovered that at Santa Cristina the investing of nuns was customarily followed by a banquet for families and friends within the convent itself, enlivened by music and song, he forbade such violations of enclosure in future, although he did not go so far as to touch the music.[36] The effect of Traversari's prohibition must have been short-lived, and post-Tridentine restrictions likewise made little difference. In June 1663, a daughter of dottore [Cesare?] Zoppi was still received at Santa Cristina "with the greatest display and pomp," including a dramatic performance that evening at the teatro di Zoppi, in the presence of the papal legate, vice-legate, and numerous other local worthies,[37] if not (obviously) of the girl herself. At Santa Cristina, as elsewhere, sumptuary restrictions were more the ideal than the reality.

What clearly set Santa Cristina apart from all the other convents of Bologna was its adherence for centuries to that additional rite, the consecration of virgins, following the Roman pontifical. This solemn group ritual, involving as many as a dozen professed nuns, was variously described in the Seicento as lasting from four to six hours. Limited specifically to certain days of the church year, it took place at Santa Cristina on an average of once every fourteen years. Affording special prominence to music, particularly performances by the nun consacrees themselves, the rite symbolized the nuns' perception of their singular status, their relationship to the Camaldolese order, and their relative autonomy vis-à-vis the archbishop of Bologna.

The venerable ritual, whose history has been traced by René Metz,[38] had attained more or less final form at the hands of Guillaume Durand, bishop of Mende, in 1292–95, after an evolution stretching back over the preceding millennium. Durand's version provided the model for Agostino Patrizzi Piccolomini's official Roman pontifical, prepared on the order of Innocent VIII and published in Rome in 1485. This compilation drew upon the *Passio* of Saint Agnes, the early Christian consecrated virgin and martyr par excellence, for many of the antiphons, traditionally sung in plainchant, that mark key moments of the consecration. It was constructed to reflect many details of the secular marriage ritual on the one hand and the ritual of ordination of male religious on the other. The ritual betrothal of the *sponsæ Christi,* or "brides of Christ," took from the secular marriage rite the giving of the brides by their parents (here, the consacrees' special, secular matron escorts, or *paranymphæ*), the joining of hands of bride and groom (here, the bishop as Christ's proxy), the giving of the ring, the imposition of the bridal crown, and the assistance throughout the rite by an older so-called *paranympha,* or matron, borrowed from her equivalent in antiquity, who enacted the ritual transfer of the bride to her heavenly spouse. From the ritual of ordination derived the dialogue of bishop and archpriest as to the worthiness of the consacrees, the virgins' promise of fidelity to Christ (represented by the bishop), and the singing of the ancient hymn *Veni Creator Spiritus* (Come Holy Ghost). Between 1485 and 1595, the consacrees were even permitted to drink from the chalice at the subsequent Communion.

As Metz makes clear,[39] the ritual unfolding of the ceremony grows out of the same spirit of theatricality that gave birth to liturgical drama, which emerged concurrently with it. Such theatricality also remained a primary aspect of seventeenth-century festivals and rituals.[40] Indeed, the consecration makes of the whole church a stage, which extends to the cloister gate. In the course of the drama, the brides of Christ, like their secular equivalents in the world, are displayed publicly in the wedding finery with which the bridegroom adorns them, marking their final, full integration into their new family.[41] The following summary offers some sense of the length, lavishness, and complexity of the ceremony:

> The beginning of the solemn mass, up to the alleluia, or the last verse of the tract or sequence, which is interrupted.
>
> The calling of the virgins by the archpriest from the back of the church, singing the antiphon *Prudentes virgines, aptate lampades* (inspired by the parable of the wise and foolish virgins). The consacrees enter the vestibule of the external church from the cloister door, with lighted candles, and follow the archpriest, two by two, up the nave to the front of the church, accompanied by their matron escorts, or *paranymphæ.*

The dialogue of bishop and archpriest at the altar concerning the worthiness of the consacrees.

The bishop's threefold sung invitatory to the consacrees, *Venite,* alternating with their threefold response, *Et nunc sequimur . . . ,* as they proceed in stages into the choir, where, kneeling deeply before the bishop at the altar, they sing *Suscipe me, Domine, secundum eloquium tuum. . . .*

The virgins' promises, and their joining of hands with the bishop, as Christ's proxy.

The chanting of the litany, with the consacrees prostrate before the bishop at the altar.

The singing of the hymn, *Veni Creator Spiritus.*

The bishop's blessing of the veils, rings, and crowns, while the consacrees retire, out of view.

The return of the virgins to public gaze in their newly blessed habits, but without veils, singing *Regnum mundi, et omnem ornatum saeculi contempsi. . . .*

The intonation by the bishop, and continuation by the choir, of *Veni, electa mea, et ponam in te thronum meum. . . .*

The virgins' reception of the veil, in pairs, singing *Ancilla Christi sum . . . ,* two by two; after receiving the veil, *Posuit signum in faciem meam . . .* is sung.

The bishop's invitation to the brides, singing *Desponsari, dilecta, veni. . . .*

The virgin's reception of the ring, two-by-two, followed by repetitions of the antiphon *Ipsi sum desponsata cui Angeli serviunt. . . .*

The display of the rings by the entire group of consacrees, with right hands raised, to the antiphon *Annulo suo subarrhavit me. . . .*

The bishop's invitation, *Veni sponsa Christi . . . ,* intoned by the bishop and completed by the choir.

The reception of the bridal crowns, two by two, followed by the antiphon *Induit me Dominum cyclade auro texta.*

The singing of *Ecce quod concupivi iam video . . .* by the consacrees.

The bishop's blessing.

The bishop's pronouncement of the anathema against any corruptors of brides of Christ.

The resumption of the mass from the alleluia or the last verse of the tract or sequence, and continuing to the offertory, when, one by one, the virgins offer their lighted candles.

The communion, after which the consacrees sing *Mel et lac ex eius ore suscepi. . . .*

The completion of the mass.

The ritual presentation of the breviary to the consacrees, and the charge to say the canonical hours.

The singing of the *Te Deum laudamus.*

> The return of the consacrees in procession to the cloister doorway, where, kneeling, they are returned by the bishop to the care of the abbess.

This rare and particularly lavish stylized liturgical drama was, strictly speaking, an extra ceremony, however. As Lucrezia Vizzana had pointed out, when it served her own interests, in a petition to the Congregation of Bishops in 1607, "It is nothing else but a ceremony to confirm one's profession."[42] Particularly in light of the post-Tridentine stipulations concerning *clausura* and the church's desire to moderate inappropriate pomp, for the curia the consecration of virgins was an increasingly inconvenient, expensive superfluity, and, for most convents of the Catholic world, one that may not usually have seemed worth fighting for. The fact that in editions of the Roman pontifical after 1595, the ritual consecration continued to be printed, but remained virtually unchanged until the end of the nineteenth century, suggests, as René Metz has pointed out, that the rite was rarely reenacted any longer. As early as 1634, Agostino Barbosa commented in *Jus ecclesiasticum*, "You may note that the custom of blessing virgins is no longer in use."[43]

The primary new post-Tridentine problem with the consecration rite involved, of course, the imposition of strict enclosure, which should have prevented the public display of the brides of Christ in the external church. This would remain the sticking point in the subsequent history of the increasingly obsolete ceremony, as it could be in investitures and professions. On 9 October 1584, for example, the Congregation of Bishops informed the bishop of Cefalù that to consecrate nuns "the bishop should enter the cloister with his assistants, and not have the nuns come outside," thereby obliterating a chief feature of the ceremony, the public presentation of the brides. But two years later the pope ruled that the lesser evil was for the consacrees to exit rather than have the bishop and all of his entourage enter the cloister.[44]

Divergent interpretations would continue throughout the Seicento. In 1647, for example, the Congregation of Bishops agreed to the wishes of some nuns of Santa Chiara in Sora to have their consecration in the external church, provided that this had long been the custom in the past—the force of tradition always remained a critical factor in the decisions of the Congregation. To meet the post-Tridentine requirements of strict enclosure, however, the cardinals added the further stipulation that the rite be performed at a window to be specially cut for the ceremony in the wall of the external church, then walled up immediately afterward.

In 1668, on the other hand, ten nuns from the Benedictine convent of Santa Caterina in Rieti petitioned, not only for a one-time relaxation of the local ban on elaborate music in the convent, but also for permission to perform their consecration rite according to the Roman pontifical, with the promise that their parents would happily bear all the extra expense, and that the consacrees themselves would "not take one step outside the cloister"; they presumably planned to get into their veils, crowns, and rings while huddled rather inelegantly around the cloister doorway.[45]

Such attempts to compensate for post-Tridentine reforms suggest that the pontifical consecration of virgins may have lingered on to a greater extent than Metz imagined, although in the form of exceptions to a pattern of general neglect. Fifty years after Barbosa's remark of 1634, his words were confirmed by Louis D'Eynac Thomassin: "It is astonishing that the consecration of virgins by bishops, formerly so solemn and so celebrated among all the monuments of ecclesiastical antiquity, could have vanished in such a way that hardly any trace of it remains."[46] Thomassin attributed this abandonment partly to the burgeoning numbers of seventeenth-century postulants—more than the poor overworked bishops could manage—and partly to proprietary abbesses' desire to veil their charges within the cloister themselves, but chiefly to the restrictions of post-Tridentine enclosure. René Metz managed to ferret out only a scant handful of late-seventeenth- and eighteenth-century consecrations, as exceptional events, and cited Joaquim Nabuco's claim that the nuns of the Chartreuse had been the only order to maintain the tradition unbroken.[47] Although the pontifical consecration of virgins may largely have faded into oblivion, however, another convent continued to maintain the tradition unbroken down to the Napoleonic suppression of the monasteries in 1799: Santa Cristina della Fondazza in Bologna.

ELEVEN

The Campaign for the Consecration of 1699

"They have won, to the honor and dignity of the entire Camaldolese order"

At the close of the Seicento, Bologna had not witnessed a pontifical consecration of virgins in almost twenty-five years. In 1696, the nuns of Santa Cristina approached Cardinal Giacomo Boncompagni, the reigning archbishop, to request the consecration of twelve nuns, the largest group of the century. Boncompagni opposed the rite in the external church, and would only agree to perform the ceremony in the privacy of the secluded communion chamber near the high altar, to avoid exposing the consacrees to the curious gaze of throngs inevitably drawn to the ceremony, as he imagined, by the chance to see them exit the cloister. It should come as no surprise that for the nuns of Santa Cristina such half measures would not do. They refused to take the archbishop's no for an answer.

Madre donna Luigia Orsina Orsi, the convent bursar, who would largely conduct the ensuing legal battle herself, turned for help to her brother, Ludovico Maria Orsi. Don Ludovico Maria also happened to represent a link to the convent's ancient allies, for he was prior of the Camaldolese hermitage of San Benedetto di Ceretola, five miles outside Bologna's Porta Saragozza. He called upon a former protégé, Giovanni Battista Sabbatini, "a learned and experienced fellow, . . . a great head and an ample brain, so that he knows well how to manage things," as Ludovico Orsi put it. Because Sabbatini had enjoyed particular favor with Cardinal Boncompagni, there was hope that his mediations on the nuns' behalf might meet with success.[1] When Sabbatini's pleas failed to move the cardinal, he cast his lot decisively with the Orsi and the nuns of Santa Cristina and went on to pursue the matter as the nuns' procurator before the curia in Rome.

The resulting campaign, a study in the ins and outs of curial diplomacy, offers an interesting contrast to the nuns' struggles and defeats over the preceding seventy years, which seem not to have been forgotten by either side. Profiting from some of their bitter lessons of the 1620s, 1630s, and

1640s, and heeding the advice of Ludovico Maria Orsi and Sabbatini, the nuns avoided the direct confrontations of the past and remained more discreetly, patiently, and, above all, obediently behind the scenes. With the help of Orsi and Sabbatini, they quietly worked the networks of influential friends in Bologna and Rome they had nurtured through the years, who might be able to wield power they lacked.

At the suggestion of don Agostino, the Camaldolese procurator general in Rome, who initially suggested that any other course would be a waste of time, Sabbatini turned directly to Pope Innocent XII, but first he also enlisted the aid of sons of the *patria*. Sabbatini's papal petition was partly prepared by Monsignor Alessandro Caprara, a member of another old Bolognese senatorial family, who promised to continue his surreptitious support of the nuns' cause. As early as August 1697, the petition was privately vetted by Monsignor Ulisses Joseph Gozzadini, the papal secretary of briefs and former professor of canon law in Bologna, who, like Sabbatini, insisted that his name be kept out of the affair as much as possible. At various stages in the proceedings, the Bolognese ambassador to Rome also took the nuns' part, as we shall see.

Sabbatini chose as his own intermediary Abbot Gargallante (or Gargalini), the agent of the protector of the Camaldolese order, Cardinal Ferdinando [Borromeo] d'Adda, and also an experienced papal lobbyist, who used his close personal friendship with Innocent XII to the advantage of many bishops. Gargallante declined to raise the matter during a number of papal meetings, when he found the pope's mood unpredictable. The abbot only judged that the time was right in late December 1697, after Innocent XII had been cheered by a gift from another of Gargallante's bishop clients. But the pope, refusing to rule on the nuns' petition, insisted that it follow the normal channels for such requests; he had Monsignor Gozzadini forward it to the Congregation of Sacred Rites.[2]

Sabbatini thus redirected his energies to the cardinals of the Congregation. To his surprise, he quickly learned that in July 1696, the nuns had already petitioned the Congregation of Sacred Rites about the Sacra. Once Cardinal Archbishop Boncompagni had requested that the Congregation insist that the consecration take place discreetly, at the communion window near the altar, the nuns had never been heard from again. The Congregation had therefore never come to a decision. At the limits of his patience after months of careful work and mediation, Sabbatini could not help lamenting, "Neither Your Reverence [Ludovico Maria Orsi] nor the nuns ever said anything to me about having appealed to the Congregation of Sacred Rites; for, had this been known, . . . so much trouble and so many labors need not have been expended, which now are useless."

Sabbatini further pointed out that in Cardinal Boncompagni's earlier response to the Congregation of Sacred Rites of 21 July 1696, the archbishop had rehearsed the notorious history of the convent's removal from Camaldolese control and its subjection to Cardinal Archbishop Ludovico Ludovisi in 1627. Boncompagni had even dug up an old letter from the Congregation of Bishops to Ludovisi authorizing the harshest reprisals against the disobedient nuns and had forwarded a copy to the Congregation of Sacred Rites. The exasperated Sabbatini once again exclaimed, "But what has that to do with our insistence that the consecration be performed in the external church in the form prescribed in the Roman pontifical?"[3]

Sabbatini's remarks suggest that he was less aware than either the archbishop or the nuns, both of what the Sacra might symbolize and of the convent's bitter lessons of the 1620s, 1630s, and 1640s. Sabbatini's letters reveal that Boncompagni himself had hinted at the significance of the consecration rite as a symbol of the convent's resistance to archiepiscopal control. The archbishop pointed out that the nuns' Camaldolese superiors had traditionally officiated at the Sacra until the 1620s, when the strife over diocesan jurisdiction had necessitated the abandonment of the practice. Boncompagni had also brought up the notorious visitation by Suffragan Bishop Angelo Gozzadini in 1622–23, which had resulted in the walling up of a large old grate between inner and outer church, through which, he claimed, the nuns had customarily received their habits. The visitation had, of course, also provided Ludovisi with an excuse to press for the ousting of the Camaldolese.

Sabbatini's apparent impatience with the nuns for a certain lack of candor in declining to mention their preliminary approach to the Congregation of Sacred Rites in 1696 suggests some unfamiliarity with the nuns' basic strategy. Over more than half a century of dealings with the curial authority, experience had taught them what has come to be seen as a characteristically female exercise of power, in the absence of real authority, by exerting influence indirectly, patiently, and evasively. On the other hand, Sabbatini's recognition that the nuns had overstepped their appropriate role by petitioning the Congregation directly in 1696 may only have exacerbated his annoyance.

The nuns must have known, as don Agostino, the Camaldolese procurator general, had also come to recognize, that any petition to the pope would normally find its way to one of the post-Tridentine congregations of the curia, which administered affairs in his name. In 1696, the nuns bypassed the pope and the Congregation of Bishops, with whom they had a long and notorious history of fruitless petitions, especially in the 1620s and 1640s. But when their appeal to the Congregation of Sacred Rites seemed destined to provoke a negative reaction, they quietly withdrew from the field to bide their time.

Some two years later, Sabbatini chose to approach the pope first, and the nuns were not about to contradict him, for there was always an outside chance that he might succeed. Nor would they remind him of their dealings with the Congregation of Sacred Rites two years earlier, which might prove prejudicial to the present effort. After all, they had benefited in the past from occasional memory lapses by the congregations of the Vatican bureaucracy. These tactical preferences are suggested in the nuns' praise for the campaign strategy of the abbess, madre donna Colomba Carrati, who, after all, had lived through the defeats of 1646 and 1647: "She knew how to manage it with clever and mature discretion, and to keep to herself everything that might have proved prejudicial to this cause."[4]

The full symbolic and historical implications of the Sacra, as viewed both from the archiepiscopal palace and from via Fondazza, become apparent when we look more closely at the relationship between the ritual, political events, and the nuns' struggles since 1620. In the very first stages of the dispute, in fact, the rite of consecration had become a symbol of the conflict between the convent of Santa Cristina and the archbishopric of Bologna, and had come to represent a public manifestation of the nuns' good name.

Mauro Ruggeri, the former father confessor to the nuns of Santa Cristina, reveals the connection. In the aftermath of the first visitation by Suffragan Bishop Angelo Gozzadini in 1623, which had marked the onset of the convent's decline, a consecration of seven nuns had been planned for 1624. This, which seems to have been the first consecration planned in over ten years, would have represented the most effective way to reaffirm the nuns' dignity and *onestà*, which had been compromised in the eyes of the city, and also to renew their links to Bolognese patrician families. Because the Camaldolese prior general would officiate, it would also most impressively point out the convent's place in the Camaldolese order.[5]

Ruggeri relates that Cecilia Bianchi contacted Cardinal Archbishop Ludovisi, who had returned to Bologna after the death of Gregory XV, suggesting that he come and see the huge amounts being squandered on luxury and ostentation. We have to take Ruggeri's word that Cardinal Ludovisi devised a way to humiliate the rival Camaldolese by sending don Gioanino, the scheming nuns' vicar of Bologna, to forbid the ceremony at the very last minute. But when don Gioanino arrived at Santa Cristina on the morning of the rite, he found the ceremony already well under way, with such crowds outside and such a traffic jam of carriages in the streets that even the papal legate, Cardinal Uberto Ubaldini, arriving fashionably late to observe the spectacle, had been forced to turn around and go home. When don Gioanino informed Ludovisi of his failure, the cardinal hurried to via Fondazza, still hoping to have his way. By the time the archbishop had managed to get inside the church, he found the consacrees already crowned and displaying their rings. In a fury, he returned to his carriage, where he was reported to have exclaimed, "Friars! Friars! Even if I should lose the red hat, never again will you consecrate nuns in Bologna."[6] His words, of course, turned out to be prophetic.

Seventy years later, Cardinal Boncompagni more explicitly articulated the connection between the consecration rite, the Camaldolese, and the nuns' perceived disobedience to archiepiscopal authority in one of his memoranda to the Congregation of Sacred Rites. Having claimed that the immense crowds drawn to the rite had provoked notable disturbances, and had prompted previous archbishops to postpone the consecrations time after time, Boncompagni concluded:

> I firmly want to believe that my predecessors as archbishop would have per-
> severed [in outlawing the rite] if they had not been mindful of the survival
> of all or a faction of those nuns (none of whom is still living), who were bitterly
> tried by their removal from their regulars, and by their subjection to the
> bishop. I suspect they [the diocesan curia] considered it expedient not to
> object, lest the continued extravagances get out of hand. . . . But since by now
> all the old ones have died off, as I said, one can only hope for the fulfillment
> of the good work, so strongly commended by the authorities cited above,
> seconded by the decision, admitting no appeal, by the Sacred Congregation.[7]

Giacomo Boncompagni and some of his archiepiscopal predecessors may have come to recognize that the timely staging of the ritual consecration back in 1624, close on the heels of the humiliating first visitation by church officials the previous year, played an important role as a kind of reunification of convent and the patrician community that served to mediate between the nuns and the world. It is surely significant that several other enactments of the rite, before 1624 and particularly later in the Seicento, seem to have been timed to coincide with critical moments in Santa Cristina's history.

The behind-the-scenes negotiations surrounding the performances of this invariably controversial ceremony as early as the 1590s illuminate the nuns' basic strategy, which so exasperated Giovanni Battista Sabbatini in the 1690s. They provide a particularly apt illustration of what we have seen from the beginning: how nuns worked within and around the restrictions created to control them. Like many women before and after them, they exercised influence by employing tactics of evasion and delay, the discovery of loopholes, the use of intermediaries, and patience.

Early in 1599, for example, the convent had written the Congregation of Bishops on behalf of six or eight nuns "who for awhile have wished to receive the veil with that same solemnity with which all others have always been veiled until now," and requesting dispensations for any consacrees still short of the requisite age of twenty-five.[8] It is significant that this Sacra was timed to coincide with the long and expensive expansion and rebuilding of church and cloister. The nuns' petition made no mention of the planned location of the consecration, and the Congregation's abbreviated response noted down on the back of their letter also ignored the matter. The convent may also have benefited from the slowness in Roman bureaucratic operations, for the ceremony must have taken place before the arrival of another critical ruling by the Congregation on 2 January 1601, which included the following stipulation:

> It is prohibited in future for the general or other [Camaldolese] superiors to celebrate solemn or low mass within the cloister at the times when nuns are invested or admitted to their professions, or for any other cause, despite any customs or usages whatever to the contrary. And, finally, the ceremony of the black veil as they required in their consecration must be performed within the cloister, at the grates, without permitting the nuns under any circumstances to enter the external church.[9]

It would appear that the nuns, seconded by their Camaldolese superiors, chose simply to ignore this new stipulation at the next Sacra in 1607, which was staged when the decoration of the new external church with nine altars and six monumental stucco statues was largely complete. Just as important, this consecration took place three years after the Congregation of Bishops' 1604 ban on the acceptance of *educande*, at a time when Santa Cristina had begun to feel an increasing neglect by the daughters of the highest nobility.

Mauro Ruggeri's description of the lavish 1624 Sacra in the external church indicates that the convent clearly continued to ignore the Roman curia's ruling of 1601; the nuns' petition to the Congregation of Bishops early in 1624 had avoided any mention of the location of the rite. It would have been quite characteristic for the nuns and their superiors to choose which of the contradictory rulings by the various Roman curial powers they would observe. The Camaldolese claimed, for example, to have been granted the privilege of performing the rite according to the Roman pontifical by an earlier unnamed pope. The Congregation of the Council was also supposed to have issued a similar comprehensive ruling to the general of the Camaldolese order, insisting that consecrations occur "in the EXTERNAL church, on condition that only the virgins to receive the veil leave the cloister, and no other nuns exit, considering that the laywomen relatives could help the virgins put on the veil."[10]

Repetitions of the consecration rite after 1624, as the convent's decline continued, largely coincided with the nuns' later campaigns against local archiepiscopal control. Problems in the staging generally arose only if the archbishop of Bologna raised objections. The nuns knew better than to repeat the consecration while Cardinal Ludovisi was still alive; the series of crises at the convent during the later 1620s, followed by the plague of 1630, which struck Santa Cristina first of all the parishes in Bologna,[11] would clearly have precluded it. After Ludovico Ludovisi's death, citing the continued damage to their reputations because of the events of the 1620s, the nuns unsuccessfully petitioned, first for reunion with the Camaldolese order, then at least for the concession of a Camaldolese confessor. The next Sacra, in 1636, was staged in the aftermath of those defeats, with the participation of Cardinal Archbishop Girolamo Colonna, who seems to have been prepared to go along with the nuns' desires in the matter of the Sacra. According to Ruggeri, Colonna was "charmed by the beautiful consecration of nuns he performed."[12]

In 1643, following the *conversa* Francesca Malatendi's deathbed admission of her calumnies during the investigations of the 1620s, the nuns mounted a new campaign for a rehearing of the case from the 1620s. Later that year, the nuns staged the next Sacra, at which Cardinal Antonio Barberini, the influential cardinal nephew, officiated, at a total cost of more than £6,000, six times the normal amount. Expenses included a costly silver collar with a statue of Saint Romuald for Barberini, which took his breath away. The 1643 Sacra thus seems to have laid the groundwork for this next attempt at reunion with the Camaldolese order, which may have been disrupted by the death of Urban VIII in July 1644. The campaign eventually ended, of course, in the confrontations of 1647, which rivaled those of the 1620s, resulting in the nuns' absolute subjugation to diocesan control.[13]

It is unsurprising that the first talk of the next consecration began within a few months of the accession of the next pope, Alexander VII, in April 1655. In their petition to the convent's old adversary, the Congregation of Bishops, requesting age dispensations for some of the nine potential consacrees, the nuns made the mistake of mentioning the proposed location for the rite. The Congregation granted dispensations for the six oldest consacrees, but, predictably stipulated that the ceremony must take place at the grates, not in the external church. The nuns reacted by postponing the ceremony for another two years. Re-petitioning in the spring of 1657, they quietly added an extra eleven months to the age of the youngest nun rejected in 1655 and also made no mention of the external church. The Congregation of Bishops still excluded the junior nun from the rite, but neglected to specify where the ceremony should occur.[14] Hence, when the nuns finally staged the Sacra in 1658, after a postponement caused by a disastrous fire that gutted the nuns' inner church late the previous year,[15] they presumably considered themselves free to perform the ritual, as always, in the external church. The new archbishop of Bologna, Girolamo Boncompagni, apparently raised no objections.

In the 1620s, 1630s, and 1640s, then, the timing of the Sacra appears to have played a part in a larger scheme of political action—a connection that Santa Cristina's chronicler Mauro Ruggeri did not fully understand. From his point of view, the consecrations of 1636 and 1643 were part of a tragedy featuring helpless nuns deluded into spending vast sums on these and other vain schemes to win the favor of such powerful potential allies as Colonna and Barberini. But these prelates repaid their lavish gifts only with sweet words and empty promises. Ruggeri likens the nuns' treatment to the parable of "the fox with the lion": another animal analogy that reveals the father confessor's attitude toward the caged creatures whom he had once helped to guard.

In their twenty-five-year campaign in Bologna and Rome, the nuns had indeed shown an extraordinary unwillingness to give up hope of reestablishing their reputation for *onestà*, which was critical to any influence they hoped to exert on the urban patriciate. The nuns assumed that the lavish financial investment in Sacra gifts and festivities would promote the sorts of obligations that such genteel bribery was traditionally expected to create. In March 1697, Ludovico Maria Orsi commented to his sister at Santa Cristina regarding the case, "I'm starting to discern the usages of Rome: you have to work with your purse." Eighty years earlier, the observer of Bolognese society and government Camillo Baldi had also noted: "Every year [the Bolognese nobility] offer gifts [to Roman prelates], believing that by this means they may prime their protector to make them exempt from liability to the laws, and different from other citizens who are subject to them."[16]

The nuns' resolve to take financial risks and to use whatever means they had to regain what they had lost seems largely unparalleled in female monastic communities in Italy, insofar as their history is currently known. It also calls into question the common view of the passivity of women religious in the early modern period. What Ruggeri may have seen as delusion, what the church hierarchy saw as obdurate contumacy, may well have appeared from inside the wall, and in the language of Seicento sanctity, as a kind of heroic virtue.[17]

The methods employed by the nuns of the 1690s had, then, developed over a century. While Sabbatini guided their latest case in Rome, the nuns continued to pursue it, working hard, but discreetly, behind the scenes to reinforce old lines of influence and establish new ones that might be to their advantage. Once the cause had been forwarded to the Congregation of Sacred Rites, Sabbatini urged that Cardinal Leonardo Colloredo be appointed *ponente* to oversee the case in the Congregation, since the prelate had married off one of his female relatives to a member of donna Luigia Orsina Orsi's family. Sabbatini also advised the abbess, donna Colomba Carrati, to make an ally of Cardinal Ferdinando [Borromeo] d'Adda, papal legate in Bologna, who could mediate on the convent's behalf with cardinals in the Congregation. As official protector of the Camaldolese order, d'Adda was a more promising advocate than his predecessor, Cardinal Barberini, the legate of fifty years earlier. The Camaldolese procurator general, don Agostino, also became intimately connected with the enterprise, as his numerous letters in the archive of Santa Cristina reveal. In late May, Sabbatini suggested that the nuns enlist other supporters to testify that previous consecrations had taken place without scandal. The nuns were well ahead of Sabbatini in this matter, for by December 1696, they had already secured testimonials from the distinguished Francesco Agucchi, Giacomo Malvezzi, Senator Andrea Bovio, and Francesco Gherardi, doctor of theology and canon of San Petronio, that the consecrations of 1658 and 1675 had been models of modesty and decorum. And Sabbatini urged them to appeal to their ultimate advocates in heaven: "even with all our good justifications, when dealing with an archbishop who is also a cardinal, one can lose, because in these cases it isn't enough to be in the right."[18] That they did so is almost certain, although this kind of effort leaves no traces in the records.

As lobbying intensified on both sides, Sabbatini encouraged madre donna Maria Caterina Allè, convent mother superior, to enlist a secular ally, Count Paolo Bolognetti, who had witnessed the Sacra of 1675. "Because of the considerable esteem the count enjoys with many cardinals," he was in an excellent position to advance the nuns' cause. By May, the count, whose illustrious noble line had been linked to Santa Cristina for generations— indeed, it had furnished one of the troublemakers of the 1620s, the ill-tempered Lucidaria Bolognetti—had become a key figure in the enterprise. His intercessions played a primary role in subsequent political maneuvers.[19]

Even more intriguing are the subtler sources of influence among whom the nuns found sympathetic ears: networks of female relatives and friends, and other women of their class active in the world. The nuns apparently had already approached the princess Pallavicina, to whom Sabbatini suggested the abbess write a second time in January 1698, because of the princess's influence in the Congregation of Sacred Rites. In March, Sabbatini also advised that "it would not prove fruitless for the mother superior to write a letter to the princess Ottoboni in Venice, requesting that she recommend the cause to her son, Cardinal Ottoboni, and to some other cardinals in the Congregation." Pietro Ottoboni, who had served his namesake, the late Pope Alexander VIII, as cardinal nephew (or principal aide), was a shrewd choice. In the subsequent papal reign of Innocent XII, he continued to serve as papal vice-chancellor; moreover, he was a lifelong enthusiast about music and patron of Arcangelo Corelli, and he had already interceded successfully for the nuns of Santa Radegonda in Milan about musical matters at the beginning of the decade. He also served as vice-protector of the Camaldolese order, and by the later stages of the lobbying, he had begun to work on behalf of the nuns of Santa Cristina.[20]

The Orsi letters also testify to personal visits to Santa Cristina, discussions of private family matters, and other written exchanges between donna Luigia Orsina Orsi and at least one female member of the nobility, a "Contessa Isabetta," possibly Lisabetta Bargellini-Bolognetti, wife of Count Camillo

Bolognetti. All these actions testify in a particularly intriguing way that the sorts of social alliances with highly placed women within the Bolognese nobility nurtured and reaffirmed at convent festivities could also be established with women much farther afield. The nuns of Santa Cristina had learned to manipulate networks, especially of influential women, in ways comparable to those their counterparts in other cities and other centuries also developed, with considerable success. In a later letter of May 1698, for example, Sabbatini commented: "We found almost all the cardinals disposed to oblige the nuns, and Cardinal Grimani should also be well warmed up, especially to please the countess" (who remains unnamed). This all begins to reveal how ties of sisterhood, family, and class, powerful, if elusive, were at work long before the emergence of more familiar examples from the nineteenth and twentieth centuries.[21]

Boncompagni's own strategy likewise followed the time-honored methods of his predecessors. On 18 May 1698, Sabbatini informed the nuns that their archbishop had proposed to Cardinal Colloredo, *ponente* for the suit in the Congregation of Sacred Rites, that the consecration be performed discreetly near the high altar, at the communion window or through a larger hole cut specially in the wall at that spot. Boncompagni justified this request with the comment that "this was not a pique that he might have with the nuns, . . . but a pure motive of his conscience." Colloredo's auditor had secretly passed along to Sabbatini the nature of the archbishop's complaint: "In his letter . . . he again writes little good about the nuns, and about certain ones in particular, but I don't know which ones; and his justification of his conscience must rest upon this." The implications of these familiar old veiled hints about the nuns' *onestà* were not lost upon the nuns' lawyer Zanelli and on their secret Roman supporter, Monsignor Caprara, who had both crossed themselves in astonishment when they learned of Boncompagni's claims. For, as Sabbatini put it,

> by claiming he could not perform the ceremony in any other way but the one described above, for reasons of conscience, he is going to defame the whole convent, as much before the city as before all the other convents of the order. For if they saw the ceremony performed differently than on other occasions, they might rightly fear some great defect among the nuns, that among the consacrees there might be someone who might have amorous links outside the convent.[22]

The nuns' public consecration could thus be seen as more than just a symbol of independence; once again it had become an affirmation of their honor and good name, which were under attack in the usual ways.

It seems that Boncompagni had miscalculated. That very same week, madre donna Allè received a letter, probably from Count Paolo Bolognetti, likewise reporting the archbishop's "accustomed slanders against the convent and the nuns, . . . that he acted not out of spite but according to the dictates of his conscience." To the letter writer, Boncompagni's veiled hints redounded against him, inasmuch as the archbishop's remarks reaffirmed other rumors about his perceived lack of charity. Boncompagni had "contrived to write to the Congregations in similar ways, and especially against the nuns or sisters of San Mattia and San Luca, discrediting them and slandering them as much as he could to achieve his objective, instead of concealing deficiencies, if such there may have been, as a charitable pastor should."[23]

Unfortunately for Boncompagni, the Bolognetti family had two close relatives among the slandered nuns at San Mattia. In reaction to this latest affront to their honor, Count Paolo Bolognetti was to become an especially vigorous advocate on behalf of the nuns of Santa Cristina. Ludovico Maria Orsi subsequently remarked to his sister that Bolognetti's letter was "nothing if not blessed." Before his return to Bologna in early June, the count personally lobbied almost all the cardinals in the Congregation of Sacred Rites, extolling the nuns' good name and the decorum of the consecration rite. As Sabbatini observed, "almost always [the cardinals] have resolved against him [Boncompagni], and therefore this, his disgrace, can only be good luck for the nuns." There is particular irony that the potent force of family honor, which had been a critical issue in the crises of the 1620s and had so preoccupied the nuns during those years, should have come back to haunt Ludovico Ludovisi's successor seventy years later.[24]

By pleading his conscience and by his latest imputations about the nuns, Boncompagni had restored the old rhetoric and hints of scandal from the 1620s and 1630s. The implications were lost neither on the nuns nor on Count Bolognetti, who strongly urged the nuns to inform the curia that their archbishop's rejection of a public consecration would result in such defamation and discredit to the convent that Santa Cristina would no longer be able to attract girls to be educated and to profess there—precisely what the nuns themselves had lamented to the Congregation of Bishops half a century before, when their removal from Camaldolese jurisdiction had provoked similar gossip. The mother abbess, madre donna Colomba Carrati, prudently responded to the count that perhaps it would be better to hold off until it became clear that such a strong petition was absolutely necessary. Nevertheless, privately she could not help remarking, "If we are all so wicked and scandalous, where are the scandals? . . . In such a short time are we become such demons?"[25]

When, a few days later, on 28 May 1698, Zanelli, the nuns' lawyer, hinted tentatively at the possibility of compromise, the nuns of Santa Cristina responded emphatically and publicly in words that echo the proclamations of their earlier sisters. Once again their rhetorical eloquence, matching the elegant calligraphy of their documents, further testifies to the high cultural level within the convent walls:

> Let it therefore please your lordship [Sabbatini] to believe, and to make Signor Zanelli clearly understand, that we would rather risk a negative verdict in the Sacred Congregation regarding the justice we desire than to stop short of the most just and justifiable . . . plea set forth in our petition to the supreme pontiff. This monastery of ours is a holy receptacle of brides of Christ, where the veil is granted only to those from the ranks of ladies and gentlewomen. Here we live with sentiments both of nobility and religiosity, which is to say, of absolute honor and esteem. We have always lived with this respect, and at present our utmost esteem is more than ever at its height, as much within as without, by the grace of God. And whoever presumes to claim or to make people believe otherwise had better produce, not airy imaginings, but particular, distinct examples. We tell your lordship this so you may realize that here we suppose that, to thwart our objective, someone there might have presumed certain opinions against our esteem and reputation. But whoever has a clear conscience need fear nothing.
>
> Then onward. We are resolved, either to lose everything and preserve that esteem which has always been proper to this convent, or to obtain from the Sacred Congregation what those most eminent lords in so many years past and present have considered to be in agreement with the Roman pontifical.[26]

On 5 July, Zanelli's brief was discussed by the cardinals in the Congregation of Sacred Rites in Rome. Since precedents and established custom weighed at least as heavily as political influence for legally trained members of the congregations of the curia, the lawyer's meticulously researched case marshaled numerous precedents for the nuns' claims. Zanelli cited, for example, the efforts by that paradigmatic post-Tridentine reformer and subsequent saint Carlo Borromeo to restore the consecration of nuns in Milan to the pristine form used earlier. No doubt deliberately, Zanelli refrained from mentioning that Borromeo's decree of 1582 had also continued with the words *dummodo intra monasterium id fiat* ("provided that it be within the convent").[27]

Particularly telling was another example of female networks: the notarized testimonial from fellow sisters at the convent of San Maglorio in Faenza, the Camaldolese house linked to Santa Cristina since 1533, when several of its nuns had been sent from Faenza to reform Santa Cristina. The abbess and prioress of San Maglorio affirmed that in 1686, a consecration had been celebrated in their external church, conducted by Bishop Antonio Pignatelli, who, as the nuns carefully underlined, in 1691 had become Pope Innocent XII.

In addition to rulings by the Congregation of the Council of Trent of 1587 and 1632 and another of 1591 by the Congregation of Bishops (including the future Gregory XIV, as Zanelli was careful to point out) stipulating that consecrations occur in external churches, the lawyer also cited an undated general decree by the Congregation of the Council, directed specifically to the prior general of the Camaldolese order, the nuns' old superiors, requiring that consecrations occur in external churches. The Camaldolese had not officiated at any Sacra at Santa Cristina in over seventy years, but in the case Zanelli was building, the ancient links between Santa Cristina and its old superiors, and centuries of tradition, had more weight than the whims of the current archbishop.[28]

Meanwhile, Sabbatini had continued his own effective work behind the scenes, finally winning over the inimical Cardinal Barberini at the last moment, for example, with the witty remark that Boncompagni's own dangerous suggestion that the nuns be consecrated through a hole cut specially in the ancient church wall near the high altar ran the risk "di fare una frittata spirituale, e religiosa" ("of making a spiritual and religious omelette [mess]").[29] After weighing evidence and influence, the cardinals ruled that the consecration should be performed in the accustomed manner.[30] But the battle still was not over, for the Congregation left it to Boncompagni to provide for the consacree's modest and discreet egress from the cloister, saying "the means of egress [from the cloister] into the outer church [is left to] the judgment of the most eminent archbishop" (*quoad modum Egressus in Eccl[es]iam exteriorem arbitrio Em[inentissim]i Archep[iscop]i*).

Obviously, nuns and their representatives were not the only ones adept at ferreting out possible loopholes in previous decrees. Still loath to abandon the fight, the archbishop chose not to recognize the intended implication of the ruling, taking it to mean that he could choose the actual point of entry into the external church. He was encouraged in this by his partisans in the cardinalate, who claimed that "if he wanted to have them [the nuns] exit even from the rooftops, he could do so." Boncompagni therefore returned to his original proposal that a special doorway be cut between the internal and external church of Santa Cristina, near the high altar, adjoining the presbytery—a solution remarkably similar to one stipulated by the Congregation of Bishops to the nuns of Santa Chiara in Sora back in 1647, mentioned earlier.[31]

Through their advocates in Bologna and Rome, the nuns of Santa Cristina continued the struggle. After Boncompagni refused to receive further overtures from the convent's patrician emissaries, provoking Count Bolognetti to remark that "the lord cardinal can garner no praise by his chosen form, to decline to hear men of honor," the nuns insisted on the total observance of the rubrics of the Roman pontifical. They also forwarded drawings to illustrate the hopelessly constricted location proposed by Boncompagni, as opposed to the decorous traditional route from the parlatorio through the courtyard to the vestibule into the external church. Faced with this evidence, even Cardinals Negroni, Colloredo, and del Giudice, who

wished to support Boncompagni, acknowledged that his alternative proposal was impossible.[32]

On 27 September 1698, the cardinals of the Congregation of Sacred
Rites took the decision out of Boncompagni's hands, rather pointedly informing him:

> It was the wish that Your Eminence be informed that the Tribunal of Sacred
> Rites declared that the pontifical should be observed without any change
> whatsoever concerning their exit and return to the convent, in the precise
> manner prescribed by the pontifical: that the consacrees may leave through
> the regular door to the convent, and at the end of the ceremony, reenter by
> the same door.[33]

Thus defeated, Boncompagni resigned himself to officiating at the consecration, as a stand-in, not only for Christ, but ironically also for the Camaldolese, who Ludovico Ludovisi had vowed would never consecrate another nun at Santa Cristina. A delighted Count Bolognetti, after gently
teasing Mother Superior Caterina Allè, whom he dubbed "a doubting
Thomas" for her earlier pessimism about the case, went on to exult, "It
now remains to behold the peculiarities of the cardinal and [nuns' vicar]
Pini performing the ritual with all the constipation their feigned zeal will
bring down upon them."[34]

Still unwilling to give in entirely, being just as obdurate as the nuns
themselves, Archbishop Boncompagni declined to sing the pontifical Mass,
which was also an essential part of the ceremony, to the consternation of
the twelve consacrees. In her usual way, tugging on the tangled ties of
authority and influence within the ecclesiastical hierarchy, the convent bursar, madre donna Luigia Orsina Orsi, went quietly back to work to change
his mind. After her first emissary, Giovanni Marcigoni, master of ceremonies at the cathedral of San Pietro, got nowhere with the prelate, the bursar
sought out a "more suitable" mediator. She called upon Domenico Villani,
chief chaplain to the papal legate and Camaldolese protector, to persuade
Cardinal Ferdinando d'Adda to act as intermediary. In the face of this
latest, more powerful advocate, even Cardinal Boncompagni finally came
to realise that it would be impolitic to resist further. Villani hurried to Santa
Cristina, arriving shortly after dark to find the unsuccessful Marcigoni already ahead of him at the gates with the welcome news. Following the rules
of the game to the end, Luigia Orsi amply rewarded both for their good
and discreet offices, although Villani rightly received the greater gift, as
the nuns carefully recorded.[35]

On 11 January 1699, the long fought-for consecration of twelve nuns
finally occurred, with Cardinal Archbishop Giacomo Boncompagni officiating "in the amplest and most dignified form ever employed," or so it
seemed to the nuns.[36] The celebration of the rite was largely consistent with

former (and future) practice, although it undoubtedly seemed particularly significant in 1699. The clearest sense of the ritual and its meaning can be reconstructed from surviving descriptions and commemorations of the rite through the centuries.

Like other celebrations of the rite, the Sacra of 1699 was commemorated by the inevitable collection of laudatory verses, *La verginità consacrata*,[37] presumably commissioned by the nuns themselves, who are named as the patrons. In this case, at least, the modest offering (on ordinary paper, not silk, and with little decoration), aptly matches the modest talents of some eighteen poetasters, four of whom chose anonymity as "signor NN" or "the unlucky one among the Arcadians." Although their poetic effusions are from the literary point of view as mediocre as most other works in this poetic tradition, the images to which the authors regularly return suggest what must have been expected by the public and the patrons.[38]

In his dedication, for example, Giovanni Pellegrino Nobili seems to allude elliptically to the convent's recent episcopal confrontations: "Your most eminent pastor now acknowledges you wholly as that flock whose spirit embodies fidelity to its Lord." Dott. Francesco Ferrari's learned Latin couplets at the back of the collection, on the other hand, which compare the nuns' veils to the helmet of "The highminded warrior, about to endure the arduous battle, / Managing to carry back the palm from his vanquished foe," hint discreetly at the nuns' own recent victory over a vanquished archbishop in the same sort of language that crops up in less public communications. In the uncertain days before the final victory in Rome, on 4 August, Ludovico Maria Orsi had consoled his sister: "Even if everything turned out worse and you didn't at least obtain the favorable decree, you will always be esteemed as such Amazons, for taking up the sword in defense of your arguments in such an improper and difficult nuisance." After the final victory, on 11 October, another admirer wrote Luigia Orsi to compare recent events to Alexander the Great's victory over Rome (!) and to suggest that, although the bursar might not be an Amazon in war, she had had the stout heart to sustain the entire enterprise.[39]

As in earlier times, the spectacular aspects of the consecration at Santa Cristina ignored sumptuary laws about nuns' rites of passage from Gabriele and Alfonso Paleotti's in the decades after Trent to Innocent XI's of 1676. They seem consciously to have set out to eclipse in splendor the monastic professions at every other convent in the city, none of which practiced this additional rite. Particulars from the 1675, 1699, and later consecrations, and Mauro Ruggeri's more general comments regarding the ceremonies of 1624 and 1643, suggest practices consistent with the most detailed account from the Sacra of 1711, on which we must rely most heavily. This effusive description by don Antonio Morazzi, dedicated to the nuns of Santa

Cristina, ignores little about the ritual, although much is obscured by hyperbole and the author's abundant enthusiasm.[40]

The rite at Santa Cristina created many additional ritual features not specifically articulated in the Roman pontifical that were designed to enhance its drama, splendor, and political utility. During the chanting of the litany at Santa Cristina, for example, the consacrees, prostrate before the high altar, presumably to symbolize their transformation into fit occupants of high monastic office, were all covered by a single, large black pall, starkly representing, not only their death to the world, but also in effect their symbolic sacrifice on behalf of the city.[41] The same traditional theme of oblation is reconfirmed repeatedly in *La verginità consacrata*. Giovanni Pelligrino Nobili's dedication speaks, for example, of "heroic confirmation of such a Sacrifice. By such a generous act you reveal a heart worthy of God." One anonymous sonnet opens with an image of virginal tribute to God ("Behold us, O God, little virgins united at Thy feet, to offer up to Thee our heart, together with our soul"). Another is more explicit: "A holy Zeal destines you as sacrificial victims to God."[42] Nevertheless, it was still less likely to have been pious zeal than insistent fathers at home that brought the consacrees to the altar.

The singular moment that Archbishop Boncompagni found so troubling, the consacrees' stepping forth into public gaze, did not escape the poets either. Dott. Eustachio Manfredi begins, for example,

> Thee now the World, amidst his own, observeth
> (Foes of this World, and unto God espousèd),
> Beholds thee come (whence his foot rarely passeth,
> Or ne'er), on whom a veil once was imposèd.[43]

To heighten the solemnity of that moment when the consacrees emerged through the doors of the public church into view, each consacree in 1675 and 1699 was provided with a seminarian as well as a *paranympha* to assist her at her entrance and throughout the rite. In 1711, although the number of consacrees had dropped from twelve to eight, their eight seminarian escorts were joined by another twenty-five alumni of the seminary, making a total of thirty-three, one for every year in the life of the nuns' heavenly spouse. Such an "intrusion" of seminarians probably fits into the post-Tridentine agenda of stressing seminaries, which were not fully operational in many dioceses until the late seventeenth century. In Bologna, on the other hand, the assiduous Gabriele Paleotti had founded the seminary as early as 1567.[44]

The singularity of the ritual space created especially for the consecration emerges most clearly in the account of the 1711 Sacra, although many of its general details are reaffirmed in other earlier and later descriptions. Both sides of the spacious nave of the external church were fitted out with bleachers for the patrician audience of lords, ladies, and clergy. These seats extended from just inside the portals of the church to the front side altars of the Martyrdom of Saint Christina and the Road to Calvary. The genteel spectators thus had an excellent view of the consacrees, who were venturing forth from the cloister into public view for the first—and last—time in years. Rich festoons, gathered in clusters, hung down from near the ceiling, decorated with red banderoles ornamented with arabesques. Large medallions bearing gilded Latin inscriptions also were affixed near the vault. Below the windows, colored bunting garnished with white taffeta was arranged on the wide cornice molding to form a loggia containing twelve large statues representing the fairest virtues, discreetly draped for the occasion. These virtues of false marble, highlighted with gold, rented for the occasion from the sculptor il Rodellone (Sebastiano Sarti),[45] matched the scale of the eight monumental stucco saints by Reni, Fiorini, and Mazza in niches below them. Between the sculptures stood eighteen vases filled with laurel and cypress, symbolizing respectively the consacrees' honor and victory and their death to the world. The pseudo-loggia was also embellished with red and yellow streamers, below which hung damask in similar colors. All the columns and pilasters of the church and the high altar were hung from floor to ceiling with the customary draperies of crimson damask.

The high altar was ablaze with silver. In addition to permanent furnishings, silver vessels and seven candlesticks, symbolizing the seven gifts of the Holy Spirit, two stepped credenzas flanked the altar, to display over a hundred pieces of silver and silver gilt, most of them on loan from the flower of the nobility. These included the customary large salvers containing the habits of each consacree to be blessed by the archbishop. The richly furnished altar offers a direct parallel to the ostentatious displays of plate on similar credenzas at secular *feste* to celebrate the induction of *anziani* or *gonfalonieri* into Bolognese public office.[46] Also on display were the renowned bridal crowns, the rings, and other regalia. This was a long way, indeed, from Alfonso Paleotti's prescription in the late Cinquecento of a simple, unornamented dress of white, black, buff, or violet for the would-be nun, and a ceremony conducted in an empty church, with the doors closed.

As in previous centuries, the music of the ritual seems to have captured as much or even more attention than the visual spectacle. As early as 1433, when Ambrogio Traversari, as general of the Camaldolese order, officiated at the vesting of a novice at Santa Cristina, a ceremony conducted with pomp comparable to later consecrations, he simplified the rite and excluded the laity, provoking comments from the nuns that they had never taken part in a more austere ceremony. It is significant, however, that Traversari had agreed not to simplify the music, "in order not to appear in total disagreement with custom." Two centuries later, Mauro Ruggeri's remark that the entire consecration ran five to six hours, "depending on whether the music took more or less time," suggests music's abiding central role.[47] Virtually every subsequent commentator continued to make some reference to the music.

Here again, the most extensive comments regarding music at the Sacra come from 1699 and later. The theme of music also regularly runs through the nuns' commemorative verses. In his dedication for *La verginità consacrata,* the ever-effusive and flattering Giovanni Pellegrino Nobili suggests that the nuns compel even the rival celestial choirs to join the applause. One of the anonymous sonneteers exclaims,

Fulfill that great Desire! Those teardrops wringing
From inmost heart no more signify sorrow.
But subtle breezes sweeten at thy singing.[48]

Music regularly caught the attention of diarists and chroniclers, too, although some commented on it in only the most general terms. One anonymous account from 1699 merely remarks that at the consecration in January of that year, the Mass began "with the greatest constant rumbling of fireworks, drums, and trumpets." Such imprecision might indicate that the writer never got inside the church, except for his concluding remark that the rite finally ended four hours later, "by the grace of God." The nuns' own account books confirm payments for no fewer than eight trumpeters and six drummers, plus twelve hundred fireworks, seven hundred rockets, and four lights.[49] Antonio Francesco Ghiselli, who adds another hour to the ceremony (still another chronicler claimed it lasted as long as six hours), lauded the "innumerable and most exquisite voices," including, apart from trumpets and drums, a choir of extern musicians brought in specially for the occasion, who sang terce, the Mass Ordinary, the *Veni Creator,* and the *Te Deum,* under the direction of the illustrious Giacomo Perti, *maestro di capella* of San Petronio.[50]

But the real focus was upon the consacrees themselves, who, according to Ghiselli, accompanied virtually every ritual action with song. On receiving the veil, the consacrees "sang certain motets with great applause from the people and cardinals present." They received the rings "with various songs." They donned the crowns "with other songs, always accompanied by their instruments." After the communion, "two of the said nuns sang the most beautiful motet possible, accompanied by the organ and instruments."[51] Some of the music must have been the traditional plainchant, whose stark purity would have set off the real musical highpoints, apparently involving polyphony.

The musical descriptions from 1711 are even more effusive. One diarist recorded only the inevitable "resounding of trumpets, drums, timpani, and the shooting off of a sizable quantity of fireworks." The nuns did indeed

pay some £116 for four trumpeters to play before and after the consecration, as well as for the archbishop's two trumpeters, and for six drummers
and timpanists; expenses also included a payment for a hundred rockets
and a thousand firecrackers the evening before the ceremony, plus another
hundred pyrotechnic mortars immediately following the ritual. Expendi-
tures for fireworks surpassed what the nuns paid the extern musicians in
1711, again led by Giacomo Perti as *maestro di cappella,* who provided music
for triple choirs. In his effusive description of the rite, dedicated to the
nuns of Santa Cristina, don Antonio Morazzi suggests that Perti's musicians
in the choir loft above the portals of the church were arranged in separate,
balanced choruses, with a full range of instruments, including "warlike"
oboes. As in 1699, Perti's musicians performed terce, the *Veni Creator,* the
Creed, and the *Te Deum,* in addition to "a most harmonious and noble
sinfonia" and a motet at the offertory.[52]

In the minds of the chroniclers, however, the extern musicians were
eclipsed by the singing nuns themselves. One writer in 1711 attested that
"each of the eight nuns sang a motet." Alessandro Macchiavelli enthusiastically recorded that "during the ceremony they also sang one motet each,
with voices as if of angels."[53] He may not have been the most impartial
judge, however, since on this occasion there was a Macchiavelli among the
consacrees.

Unfortunately, when it came to the nuns' singing, the most meticulous
witness to the 1711 consecration, don Antonio Morazzi, expended more
of his creative energies on ecstatic rapture than on precise description of
their music. His indication that *Suscipe Domine secundum eloquium tuum* was
sung by an alto and a soprano on behalf of their fellow consacrees, who
were lying prostrate before the archbishop, suggests a polyphonic setting.
He specifies that the basso continuo for the singing nuns was played by
don Angelo Laurenti on the organ, with a cello on the bassline, discreetly
placed in the chamber to the right of the high altar that served as the
confessional. But then he lapses into another of his typical effusions:
"Rightly might the spectators exclaim with the great Seraph of Assisi, '*satis
est,* no more, no more,' as every one remained as if in ecstasy of love for
the great God of most excellent mercies because of the sweetness of the
melodious voices."[54]

The singing consacrees, who thus took center stage, most effectively convey the immediate and broader resonances of the ritual. To be sure, the
trumpeters and drummers, the double or triple choirs of extern musicians
who performed the imposing, impersonal elements of the Ordinary such
as the Creed, and the *Veni Creator* and festive *Te Deum,* amid volleys of
pyrotechnics, may have enhanced the splendor and solemnity of the rite.
But the ritual words of the consacrees themselves, whether in the ancient
plainchant accompanied by the organ, or in polyphony, articulated the

more direct and particular meanings of the rite by affirming their own specialness, singularity, and their virtue, recently called into question yet again by the archbishop himself:

> The kingdom of this world and every trapping of the age have I despised, for the love of Our Lord, Jesus Christ. . . . To Him I am betrothed whom the angels serve, whose beauty sun and moon do wonder at. . . . With His ring has My Lord Jesus Christ betrothed me, and with a crown, adorned me as a bride. . . . The Lord has wrapped me round with cloth of gold, and with countless gems He has adorned me. . . . Behold, that which I have desired, now I behold, that in which I hoped, I now hold fast. To Him am I joined in heaven, whom yet on earth I have, with all devotion, loved.[55]

Of the large cast of characters in this sacred drama, therefore, those in the starring role most persuasively encouraged the audience to unite in affirming their virtue and esteem. The same had been the case 250 years earlier, when Ambrogio Traversari officiated at the reception of a novice in 1433. It was "above all, [the nuns'] scruples and their uncommon knowledge of divine worship and of the sacred liturgy" that had persuaded the Camaldolese prior general to reject emphatically current rumors about the *onestà* of the nuns of Santa Cristina.[56] The congregation and the city could join with the archbishop—in the words of Revelation, which also inspired many of the sonnets of *La verginità consacrata*—to pray God's grace upon

> Your handmaids, who have vowed to serve you with a pure mind and spotless heart; that you may think them worthy to be numbered among the hundred and forty-four thousand who have remained virgins, and have not debased themselves with women, in whose mouth no guile is found; so likewise you cause these your handmaids to remain spotless to the end [cf. Rev. 14:4–5].[57]

Other sorts of ritual stagecraft, once again frequently elaborating upon the original prescriptions of the Roman pontifical, also served the political goals of acknowledging and reinforcing affiliations to the urban patriciate, reestablishing and nourishing old social patterns of clientage and creating new ones, winning support where it was likely to matter. It had become part of the lore of the Sacra at Santa Cristina that no "ordinary" people could hope to get into the ceremony, which, according to Ruggeri in 1624, was limited to "lords, ladies, and the clergy," words echoed by virtually every later chronicler. In 1624, twelve halberdiers stationed at the gate to keep back "the common people," did their job so well that the papal legate could not get in. In 1675, "the whole Swiss guard" fulfilled a similar function. In 1699, one chronicler also wrote of "people filling all the streets, trying to witness the ceremony; but the gates were closed from outside with the help of the Swiss guards of His Eminence the Legate."[58]

The flower of the nobility who did manage to get in were there to see, be seen, or, indeed, even *not* be seen—but as ostentatiously as possible. In

1699, no chronicler or diarist failed to mention that the papal legate and protector of the Camaldolese religion, Cardinal Ferdinando d'Adda, Monsignor Grimani, the vice-legate, and the visiting Cardinal de' Medici all watched "incognito" from a prominent spot near the high altar, but behind gilded screens. Surely some must have recognized how deliciously appropriate it was that the papal legate and protector of the Camaldolese order, whose aid behind the scenes had been enlisted early in the struggle by the mother abbess and who, at the behest of the mother superior, had later secured Cardinal Boncompagni's grudging participation in the rite, should also witness the fruits of his influence, "behind the scenes," but known to be present.

The luster of the local nobility in fuller view was enhanced, as the nuns carefully recorded, by the flower of the nobility from other parts. In January 1699, Cardinal de' Medici and other dignitaries made a special detour to Bologna en route to Modena to pay court to Amalia of Brunswick, then proceeding to Vienna to wed Joseph of Hapsburg, king of Hungary. In 1711, from behind similar gilded screens, members of the illustrious Borghese family, up from Rome, likewise added a special discreet brilliance to that consecration.[59]

The nuns of Santa Cristina also devised a variety of ways for the best of local society to be drawn into a more active participation than simply as viewers. The Roman pontifical was noncommital about the ritual crowns and rings that played a central role in the rite. At Santa Cristina they became a dazzling focus of attention. The poems of *La verginità consacrata* draw liberally on jewels, crowns, and garlands to represent literally the bridal accoutrements, and, metaphorically, the consacrees themselves. For Girolamo Azzoguidi, the heavenly and earthly treasures were inseparable:

> Go, plaite ye
> Thy Crowns of innocence, lilies and roses.
> You, diamonds most select, make haste! Fly quickly
> To throat, to breast of divas here espousèd.
> Hasten, gems refulgent, entangle tightly
> These iv'ry hands 'midst golden bands concealèd.[60]

These jewels represented, literally and figuratively, the wealth of Bologna, embodied in its illustrious citizens. In Marquis Francesco Bendini Monti's sonnet, for example, Bologna, with its own twelve portals, and Santa Cristina, with its twelve virgins, become Jerusalem, the heavenly city of Saint John's apocalyptic vision:

> A city I beheld. Gold walls surround it,
> With portals twelve, open throughout the ages.
> The portals were of gold, with pearls resplendent.
> On what foundation was that wall erected?
> Upon a dozen gems it was dependent.[61]

Such poetic preoccupation with gems and jewelry was understandable, for the crowns, first prominently displayed beside the banks of borrowed silver and silver gilt about the altar, then worn by the brides during the ceremony at Santa Cristina, were hardly simple coronets. In 1711, they were described as "interlaced with gems, quantities of the finest pearls and diamonds and with as many necklaces." In 1699, the nuns recorded that the crowns "were set with the most beautiful and rich jewels of all the nobility of Bologna"; Ruggeri had also carefully made clear that at the Sacra back in 1624, the jewels were all borrowed.[62] Thus, the convent enlisted the help of the wealthiest ladies of the city by borrowing from their jewel boxes, then permitting them to bask in the reflected splendor of their own generosity.

Convent usage, furthermore, plays effectively in a spiritual mode upon secular marriage practice. To bedeck their brides, husbands borrowed wedding finery and jewelry from relatives and friends. But much of the wedding ornament was then returned to its owners.[63] In the case of Santa Cristina, the Bolognese nobility, by their loans of jewelry and silver, not only symbolically joined the family of the heavenly bridegroom, clothing these brides of Christ; they were also assumed into the convent family, initiating or reviving systems of mutual obligation to be tended carefully in future. This incorporation is implicit in Fernando Ghedini's sonnet from *La verginità consacrata,* which opens by playing upon the crowns and the enactment of the Sacra within the octave of the Epiphany:

> Golden diadems this earthly sovereignty,
> Prostrate before an infant God, now proffers.
> These tributary crowns, in turn, He offers,
> Gifts unto his brides, signs of love's certainty.[64]

Furthermore, following the time-honored method of choosing godparents, the nuns sought out the cream of Bolognese society to participate actively in the consecration rite as *paranymphæ,* the female escorts of the consacrees, prescribed by the Roman pontifical. These matrons, it will be remembered, served partly to effect the ritual transfer of the brides from their families to their heavenly spouse. In 1598, Alfonso Paleotti had stipulated that a postulant be attended by "only two or three of her closest relatives" at her reception at the convent door. The glittering lists of matrons for the 1699 and 1711 consecrations at Santa Cristina, however, read like a Bolognese Who's Who. Names in small capitals represent local nobility of the first rank; those italicized are of the second rank; asterisks indicate senatorial families:[65]

1699

Matrons

Countess Elena PEPOLI* ALDROVANDI*
Countess Laura *Conti* BONFIGLIOLI*

Maria Angiola MARESCALCHI* *Zanchini*
Marchioness Costanza SCAPPI* SAMPIERI*
Marchioness Camilla CAPRARA* BENTIVOGLI*
Ginevra FAVA SAMPIERI*
Countess Flavia Fasoli BOLOGNETTI*
Marchioness Isotta ERCOLANI* BUOI*
Countess Anna BOLOGNETTI* LEGNANI* (daughter of Count Paolo Bolo-
    gnetti and Veronica Allamandini; wife of Count Giovanni Legnani Ferri)
Francesca BOVA *Ferri* BANZI
Countess Anna BOLOGNETTI* *Bombacci* (wife of Count Antonio Maria Bom-
    bacci; daughter of Carlo Bolognetti and Silvia Canobbi Tizzinali)
Countess Bulgarini ROSSI*

Consacrees

Maria Teresa Diamante Brighenti
Maria Marsibilia Vittoria BOLOGNINI*
Maria Romualda Teresa Diamante Lucchini
Maria Diletta Vittoria *Muzzi*
Florida Rosaura *Garzaria*
Teresa Madalena Liberata MORANDI
Maria Angelica Teresa Geltruda Gaetana Riguzzi
Maria Christina Teresa Prudenza Deodata Cavazzi
Maria Emilia Chiara Antonia Vittoria *Vittorii*
Maria Giuditta Carla Carrati
Maria Giuditta Ginevra BOLOGNINI*
Barbara Teresa BOLOGNINI*

1711

Matrons

Countess Maria Teresa TANARA*
Countess ZANI
Marchioness Anna ALBERGATI*
Marchioness Gonzaga PEPOLI*
Marchioness Teresa Segni BARBAZZI*
Countess BERO
Francesca BOVIJ*
Countess ORSI in ORSI*

Consacrees

Diana *Andalò Branchetti*
Paola ZANI
Maria Eleonora Lemmi
Anna Maria *Mantachetti*
Maria Colomba Castelbarchi
Maria Amata *Giovanetti*

Maria Adelaide Guglielmini
Isabella *Macchiavelli*

There is no one on either list of matrons who had not been born or married into one of the hundred best families of Bologna, judging by Pompeo Dolfi's *Cronologia delle famiglie nobili di Bologna* (1670). Only four of the twenty were not countesses or marchionesses. More significant, only one of the matrons on either list was directly related to a consacree in an immediately obvious way.

The consacrees themselves are rather less distinguished. The 1699 list included only four from first families (three of them from a single senatorial family), three others mentioned by Dolfi, but also five whom he does not mention at all, even though some of the families (e.g., Cavazza, Carrati) achieved distinction in Bologna. Of those on the 1711 list, only one ranked among the old first families (although the Zani never achieved senatorial status), while four other consacrees' families had been mentioned by Dolfi. But half the families on the 1711 list of consacrees seem to have been comparative social unknowns.

The unimpressive pedigrees of many nuns consecrated in 1699 and 1711 may in part reflect the declining demographic fortunes of the old families, many of whom became extinct in the early years of the Settecento. It likewise may reflect an eclipse of the patriciate by the middle classes in convents generally.[66] Whatever the explanation, these cohorts of consacrees stand in marked contrast to their predecessors. Of the four identifiable consacrees from the modest group of five in 1675, all had come from the first families; of nine in the 1650s, five were of the first rank, one of the second rank, two from the old Carrati family, long connected with the convent, and only one was a social nonentity. And, of course, the social profile of Santa Cristina at the turn of the seventeenth century bears little resemblance to that of a century earlier, before Emilia Grassi's campaign against *educande,* when at least half the *professe* had hailed from the highest echelons of the Bolognese élite.[67]

Thus, at the end of the Seicento, by their careful invitations to *paranymphæ,* the nuns of Santa Cristina managed to retain an illusion of venerable nobility, which had been real before the crises of the early 1600s. To compensate for social decline, they managed to forge or reestablish ritual family ties between the consacrees and their *paranymphæ* godparents, recruited from the highest level of Bolognese society, with an eye toward future financial and political utility. The choice of matrons in 1699 also betrays sweet, but subtle, revenge, for at least three families active behind the scenes in the suit against Cardinal Boncompagni are represented. Monsignor Alessandro Caprara had served as an intermediary in Rome, Senator Andrea Bovio had testified to the decorum of earlier consecrations, while

Count Paolo Bolognetti had played an especially critical role in the later stages of the campaign. It seems especially fitting that the matrons of 1699 also included Countess Anna Bolognetti Bombacci, a last link to the family central to the spiritual, political, and musical life of Santa Cristina a century earlier.

The end of the consecration did not mark the end of the drama. "As a sign of gratitude for the service he had performed majestically with the true zeal of a loving pastor," the nuns sent Cardinal Boncompagni a huge bouquet of silk flowers, several large candles of white wax, and a beautiful and costly crucifix of silver, with a pair of statues at its base—recalling the lavish gift to Cardinal Barberini after the Sacra fifty years earlier. But when the offering was brought into his presence, the archbishop sent it back, saying he would accept nothing: his parting shot at the victorious nuns, with pique masquerading behind an unusually punctilious sense of ecclesiastical propriety.[68]

After seventy years, the nuns of Santa Cristina must finally have felt vindicated. Archbishop Boncompagni had been right in his claim to the Congregation of Sacred Rites in 1696 that the Vizzani, the Bombacci, and the others from the 1620s were long dead. The last of the Bombacci-Vizzani clan, Lucrezia Vizzana's niece, madre donna Maria Clorinda Vizzana, had died just the previous year. Boncompagni had also been largely correct in observing that the leading troublemakers who had fomented the protests of the 1640s had exited the stage. But witnesses to past troubles were not quite all gone. Madre donna Maria Caterina Allè, who as mother superior had courted Count Paolo Bolognetti and the princess Ottoboni in the campaign of 1698, and the prioress, madre donna Geltruda Malvezzi, had been present in the parlatorio of Santa Cristina on 20 March 1647 to be counted in the nuns' last official protest. The abbess, madre donna Maria Colomba Carrati, who managed the campaign of 1698 "with clever and mature discretion," had, at age eighteen, been the most junior signatory to that protest of half-a-century earlier.[69]

Among the male protagonists of this story, don Mauro Ruggeri had fought the battles of the 1620s and 1640s chiefly on paper after they were over and the damage was done. Seventy years before, the nuns' Camaldolese superiors stood rather helplessly by, leaving the nuns to fight their own battles alone—or so the surviving documents largely seem to indicate. But in the 1690s, Cardinal Ferdinando d'Adda, protector of the Camaldolese religion, atoned to some extent for the earlier inactivity of Cardinal Domenico Rivarola, his predecessor of the 1620s. Don Ludovico Maria Orsi, prior of the Camaldolese hermitage of San Benedetto, worked closely on the convent's behalf with his sister, madre donna Luigia Orsina, throughout the campaign of 1698. More important, he recruited his protégé, Giovanni Battista Sabbatini, who, in the words of Monsignor Caprara, has had fourteen months of agitation for the suit of the Camaldolese nuns, . . . has lost the favor of the cardinal archbishop, and, much more, has incurred the wrath of His Eminence. . . . He thus merits substantial recognition, . . . and therefore should receive no less than ten doubloons, . . . which is very restrained, as the recognition is very modest. And that is what I have to say to you.[70]

From our point of view, Sabbatini's commitment symbolically balanced the diffidence of don Bernardo da Venezia, the Camaldolese curate of San Damiano, who, when faced with threats of his archbishop's displeasure, had ignored the nuns during the Universal Jubilee of 1629. At the time, however, it was primarily the old and potent ties of family loyalty and *onore* that had compelled Orsi, Sabbatini, and Count Paolo Bolognetti to action. Ironically, it seems to have been largely among the nuns of Santa Cristina, not their male superiors, that Camaldolese loyalties burned most brightly. It had been the nuns' own *onore* and *onestà*, after all, that were chiefly at stake.

The symbolic implications of the decision by the Congregation of Sacred Rites in 1698 were not lost on this later generation of nuns, who subsequently collected all the documents from their latest battle, carefully bound all Sabbatini's and the Orsi's letters, and stored everything in a box beside the memorials from the crises of the 1620s. This volume of documents concludes with the affirmation that "finally, all the nuns of our convent of Santa Cristina have worked in support of this consecration," a fitting complement to its opening inscription commemorating

> our superior, the most reverend mother abbess donna Colomba Carrati, the prioress, the most reverend donna Geltruda Marsibilia Malvezzi, the bursar, the most reverend donna Luigia Orsina Orsi, who, working together with skillful and mature wisdom, had the victory, to the glory of His Divine Majesty, and the honor and dignity of the entire Camaldolese order, as commemorated in the archive of our convent, in perpetual memory of those who had a part in it.[71]

This was madre donna Colomba Carrati's last battle; she died on 11 March 1702, at the age of seventy-three. The Settecento was barely under way, however, before the survivors, Geltruda Marsibilia Malvezzi, Maria Caterina Allè, and Luigia Orsina Orsi, would wage one more battle with the archiepiscopal curia. Like the earliest struggles near the dawn of the Seicento, this one would begin because of music.

TWELVE

A Last Musical Battle with the Bishop
"In the midst of a tempest of calamities"

In January 1684, as my usual and habitual bad luck would have it, it fell to me to go to Bologna by stagecoach, with much inconvenience and exorbitant expense, because of the illness of my uncle the cardinal, who at that time died of it. And for me it turned out to be a most unfortunate business, as everybody knows. Spring brought me back from there to Rome that same year. . . . And I arrived at the beginning of Holy Week[.]

Yet do I shun the memory of Bologna's every horror.[1]

Such was Giacomo Boncompagni's inauspicious recollection of the see of which he was named archbishop on 29 April 1690. He returned to a see that had remained effectively vacant since the death of his uncle, Girolamo Boncompagni, on 24 January 1684. Girolamo's successor, Cardinal Angelo Maria Ranuzzi, named archbishop of Bologna only in May 1688, had never set foot in the archdiocese. Ranuzzi instead spent several eventful years in Paris as papal nuncio extraordinary, some of them under arrest by order of Louis XIV.[2]

It had been a long time since the city had seen such a committed and reform-minded archbishop as Giacomo Boncompagni. In a manner reminiscent of his sixteenth-century predecessor, Gabriele Paleotti, he promptly fulfilled the post-Tridentine requirement of episcopal residency that his immediate predecessor had neglected. Indeed, according to Umberto Mazzone, Giacomo Boncompagni placed as the cornerstones of his ministry the decrees of the Council of Trent, the model of Milanese diocesan reform under Carlo Borromeo, and the treatise on episcopal government *Episcopalis sollicitudinis enchiridion* (Paris, 1668), which had held up the first archbishop of Bologna, Gabriele Paleotti, as the paradigmatic *bonus pastor*.[3] "Musical abuses," as we have seen, were a primary target of Paleotti's monastic reforms. Convent music for all the same reasons would preoccupy Boncompagni's attention as well.

"Ever watchful, ever sleepless, everywhere present . . . visiting with rest-less feet, he climbed the lofty and precipitous heights of mountains, and descended into the deepest valleys, where waters inundated open fields."[4] There is only slight hyperbole in this anonymous characterization of the earnest new archbishop's determination to carry out the first systematic pastoral visitation of the archdiocese of Bologna in decades, which began within five months of his election, on 25 September 1690. Boncompagni's suspicion of nuns' music emerges clearly during his visits to the twenty-nine convents of the diocese, which began in November 1690 and continued until September of the following year. In some of them he reiterated the old decrees that the view through organ windows be obscured. At Santis-sima Concezione, Sant'Elena, Sant'Orsola, and Santi Naborre e Felice he also inquired whether nuns or *educande* were receiving music lessons from outside teachers—this at a time when the Congregation of Bishops in Rome seems temporarily to have been liberalizing its own attitude toward the admission of such music masters.[5]

Not surprisingly, Boncompagni's archdiocesan synod of June 1698 (the first in Bologna in more than forty years) reconfirmed older decrees from the most recent synods under Girolamo Colonna in 1634 and Girolamo Boncompagni in 1654, which had denied the nuns all song except plain-chant and all musical instruments but the organ and harpsichord, except by special license from the diocesan curia. As the lavish Sacra at Santa Cristina in January 1699, with Giacomo Boncompagni himself reluctantly presiding, clearly indicates, initially the revived decrees were not observed to the letter, any more than those of the earlier synods had been. Indeed, before the same year was out, at least half a dozen special solemn masses with multiple choirs, trumpets, drums, and firecrackers were performed at the convent of Corpus Domini alone.[6]

Boncompagni seemed particularly obsessed by the prospect of elaborate music attracting crowds to convent ceremonies. As he reported to the Con-gregation of Bishops in 1704,

> The irreverences committed in nuns' churches when they celebrate their fes-tivals were constantly increasing, to the great dishonor of the house of God. All the same, not only the edicts and admonitions of confessors and preachers regarding the appropriate respect for the church proved useless, but, what is more, the order in the last edict of His Holiness as well. . . . I thus saw as inevitable the scandals if music were to continue there. The resulting assembly of the people is so abundant, with men and women irreparably intermingling together in the continuous crush, that great improprieties and tumults re-sulted, with less respect than if it took place in a public square or open market, with the most licentious types gathering there to avail themselves of the op-portunity that the confusion of such throngs usually lends to their evil ends.[7]

Not since the days of Archbishop Alfonso Paleotti a century earlier had the rhetoric against convent festivals sounded quite so shrill.

The archbishop's worries had some foundation. Crowds presented serious problems other than the sexual improprieties that preoccupied Boncompagni, as they had so many of his clerical predecessors. Not long after Boncompagni's arrival, during the titular festival at the convent of San Pietro Martire on 29 April 1691, Girolamo Zanchetti, having challenged Carlo Marescalchi for insults to his family honor, took a sword blow to the head and was run through before he could even unsheath his own sword. The wounded Zanchetti managed to hold off Marescalchi and his supporters at gunpoint long enough to flee the sacred ground of San Pietro Martire, pursued by a screaming crowd into via Santo Stefano and on to the convent of Sant'Omobono, where he escaped into the house of the nuns' confessor. The crowds drawn to the convent of Santa Maria Maddalena on 22 July 1700 to hear the music at a particularly lavish titular festival were so large that, at the height of the ceremony, a sepulchre in the floor of the nave collapsed, swallowing up a child and burying Senator Count Ercole Bonfiglioli up to his shoulders.[8]

In late January 1703, the throngs literally went too far. According to the archbishop:

> In the church of the nuns of Sant'Agnese, subject to the government of the Dominican Fathers, not only did they pursue the usual immodesties there, but also second vespers could not be completed because the crowds reached all the way up to the high altar. During the singing of the Magnificat, it was impossible for the priest, attired in his cope, and for the other two assistants to proceed to cense the altar, and they had to retreat to the sacristy; the [extern] musicians also [started] leaving, unable to perform their music because of all the noise that prevented their hearing the voices.[9]

Such commotion provided Cardinal Boncompagni with the excuse once again to prohibit the use of music in all the convents of Bologna. Three weeks later, on 12 February, the feast of Saint Matthias, the nuns of San Mattia were the first to pay the price for the tumults at Sant'Agnese. On 9 March, even Blessed Catherine Vigri of Bologna had no immunity to the ban. The remarks of the chronicler Antonio Francesco Ghiselli could well reflect general disapproval of the archbishop's policy:

> But the festival was not celebrated with all that pomp commonly practiced in tender devotion by her affectionate devotees, since they are prohibited from providing the music; and the same prohibition likewise extends to all the other nuns' churches on their feast days, and that by order of the archbishop, an order that, apart from the displeasure it causes these poor religious, reduces musicians, one might say, to beggary, since we see them everywhere denied the opportunity to support themselves by their virtuous profession;

and it removes the crowds at the same churches, and jeopardizes not a little the services and attendance at the same.

Another chronicler, recording the visit the previous day to Corpus Domini of the duchesses of Modena and Hanover, with twelve court ladies, to kiss the feet of Blessed Catherine, likewise remarked upon the archbishop's musical ban. Licenses for special music for the feasts of saints Vitale and Agricola and the Nativity of the Blessed Virgin during the first two decades of the Settecento, carefully preserved in the archive of the convent of Santi Vitale et Agricola, also break off abruptly after 1702, testifying to the enforcement of Boncompagni's ban.[10]

Boncompagni's crackdown was thus widely known and widely observed. But when the time came for the feast of their patron saint in May 1703, the highly independent nuns of Santa Cristina chose to ignore it. The ever-observant Ghiselli, remarking upon their disobedience, points out that they celebrated lavishly with music but declined to invite any of their superiors to the festival, "with the comment that they had been forbidden to make merry, and all the other convents should have done likewise, saving themselves the lavish gifts they give their superiors."[11] It seems that the "gift economy" characteristic of convents and long decried by their clerical governors also continued to flourish.

Three weeks later, at the investing of the novice Silvia Maldachetti on 28 May 1703, the nuns even sang the Mass in the presence of the nuns' vicar of Bologna, Bernardo Pini, who officiated ("simply to do him honor," the nuns would later claim; "to his astonishment," according to Boncompagni). What actually transpired the following day, when Francesco Luigi Barelli, *penitenziero* of the duomo was sent to Santa Cristina to convey the archbishop's displeasure to the abbess, is unclear; it would remain a bone of contention in subsequent litigation. This time, however, Boncompagni chose to let them off with a warning.

But on the feast of Santa Cristina the following year, the nuns tried to ignore the archbishop once too often. On 21 May 1704, both first and second vespers and Mass were sung in polyphony by donna Maria Giuditta Ginevra Bolognini, donna Maria Christina Teresa Prudenza Deodata Cavazza, and donna Maria Diletta Vittoria Muzzi, three of the nun consacrees from 1699, accompanied by organ and cello. "Anyone who attended this feast could attest that not the slightest murmuring was heard, and that we all stood back from the grates and doorways, as is the custom at our monastery," the singing nuns were careful to point out.[12] "When the nuns [were] singing first vespers, few attended because people were unaware of it, the prohibition to the contrary being well known in the city; but on the following day, the concourse was great and tumultuous, because there are some fine voices in this monastery," the archbishop noted, however.[13]

Three days later Cardinal Boncompagni promulgated a fresh general ban on convent music, to be hung in the choir of every nunnery in the city, although it seems he may only have officially presented it at Santa Cristina. He further decreed that, for permitting the singing on 21 May, the abbess of Santa Cristina, madre donna Maria Elisabetta Azzolini, should be suspended from office for three days, while the three vocalists were condemned to silence and denied all access to the grates, their families, and to the outside world at the archbishop's pleasure. In an extraordinary scene on 27 May, when the aging prioress of Santa Cristina refused to accept the archbishop's decrees against the abbess and the three singing nuns from the public messenger sent to deliver them at the gate, the archbishop's deputies "threw them [the decrees] into the tube or trumpet through which one speaks to the prioress, who had injured her hearing many years ago."[14]

After eighty years and more than fifty petitions to the Congregation of Bishops, the nuns had learned something about the realities of ecclesiastical politics. The abbess and the three singing nuns, in sign of obedience, promptly accepted the penance meted out by Boncompagni. But then, employing a tactic reminiscent of those used with the more tractable Archbishop Niccolò Albergati Ludovisi in 1647, they sent the noble governors of the convent to plead their case before the archbishop. As the nuns put it in a letter to the Congregation of Bishops, which they wisely chose not to send, presumably recognizing that it was indecorously blunt, "given over to frenzy, [Boncompagni] refused to hear them, responding that if the nuns were aggrieved, they could have recourse to the Sacred Congregation in accordance with their usual practice." They took him at his word. And thus it was that for the second time in barely five years, the nuns of Santa Cristina once again found themselves "in the midst of a tempest of calamities," as the abbess put it. They were led into the fray by their abbess, madre donna Maria Elisabetta Azzolini, "an honest person and a lady of advanced age, timid and of feeble constitution," and by their prioress—perhaps flourishing her ear trumpet.[15]

In July 1704, letters, memorials, affidavits, claims, and counterclaims once again began to circulate, officially and unofficially, between Bologna and Rome. The nuns' first, and rather thin, defense emphasized that neither the abbess nor the singing nuns could have violated the archbishop's command, because a formal, written legal document announcing the prohibition of polyphony in convents had never been handed to the abbess; it had only been delivered verbally as a "suggestion" (*insinuazione*)—Boncompagni's very word in his own response to the Congregation, as the nuns were careful to point out. To support their claim that there had been no formal ban, the nuns submitted the abbess's sworn affidavit that she had never received such a document. Exploiting the old, informal cooperative network among the convents of the city, they also offered notarized testimony from witnesses to performances of polyphony at the convents of Santi Naborre e Felice and Sant'Omobono during the period of the alleged ban. Most impertinent of all, they presented sworn confirmation that they themselves had sung no fewer than ten times in 1703 and 1704. Had they known of a ban, they claimed, they would not have sung, and if such a ban had existed and had it applied to music in their internal church, they would not have gone unpunished.

Both sides spent substantial effort confronting this point. The archbishop's repeated, if imprecisely worded, attempts to discredit the nuns' claims suggest that he recognized that they had found his weak spot. Those with a little more distance saw through these legalistic sophistries. As the nuns' lawyer, Giovanni Battista Narici, conceded on 6 September, "even if there were no concrete decree or order, there is at least a certain sure knowledge that they should not have been singing." The comments of Ghiselli and other chroniclers cited above, as well as the actions of the nuns of San Mattia, Corpus Domini, and elsewhere confirm the accuracy of Narici's assessment. The lawyer was seconded by Cardinal Leonardo Colloredo, who in the weeks after his appointment as *ponente,* or overseer of the case, in early September, advised the nuns to eschew this line of argument: "especially, do not get yourself overly entangled in the issue of your unfamiliarity with the known order of the lord cardinal archbishop."[16]

Behind such niggling and evasions, which the nuns of Santa Cristina, like their cloistered sisters elsewhere, had learned over the years in order to work around the regulations imposed upon them from without, and behind the diocesan curia's attempts to plug the loopholes the nuns had discovered, remained the familiar old issues of independence and obedience. The nuns repeatedly emphasized that any episcopal prohibitions should refer only to music performed by outsiders in the exterior churches, and not to the nuns' own music in the inner chapel of Santa Cristina. Strictly speaking, they were right: Boncompagni's synod of 1698 had reconfirmed the musical ban from the synod of 1654, which in turn had cited the Congregation of Bishops' rulings to Gabriele and Alfonso Paleotti in 1584 and 1593. These earlier decrees, aimed at extern musicians, had quite specifically declined to touch the music of the nuns themselves. More important than this latest legalistic nicety (which, in any event, the nuns may well not have known), polyphony had long been permitted to the nuns of Santa Cristina by their own Camaldolese Benedictine constitutions, which, they claimed, the bishop himself had no authority to override. Such music was a convent tradition, going back for centuries, with the force of law.

Thus music, which had originally helped to provoke the crises of the 1620s and had played a role in the legal battles of 1698 over the Sacra that had whetted the archbishop's appetite for revenge in 1704, emerges once more as the clearest remaining symbol of the nuns' Camaldolese heritage and of their independence from the long-contested control of the archbishop. The nuns' frequent outraged references to the public manner in which Boncompagni's latest decree had been presented, defaming them in the eyes of the city, recall the impugning of their *onestà* and their families' *onore* in the notoriously public visitations of the 1620s. Their repeated suggestions, openly to the Sacred Congregation and privately to Cardinal Colloredo, that their confessor might have been suborned by the archbishop recall the nuns' demands of the 1640s for Camaldolese confessors, premised on their stated contention that they could not have complete faith in any appointed by the diocesan curia. The statement in their first petition to the Congregation of Bishops in 1704 that "if it is asserted that our confessor acts as accuser for the archbishopric against our convent, our trust will at once be wounded and the secret of our consciences put in doubt" implies the fulfillment of their own prophecies of sixty years earlier, as related by Archbishop Niccolò Albergati Ludovisi in July 1647: "they can trust no secular [priest], for they have always been betrayed by secular priests."[17] And their closing plea in that same petition of 1704, not for permission to sing but for "the continuance of what our Holy Founder permitted us in his deeply considered statutes," focuses upon their original superior, Saint Benedict, whose authority in their view superseded that of any local archbishop. Indeed, every time they had sung in their inner chapel, they had continued to act out their allegiance to that superior and their perceived independence from episcopal control.[18]

Particularly interesting are further remarks that articulate an awareness, never before voiced so clearly, of their marginal place as women in the Catholic order of things. The exorbitant penance Boncompagni had imposed—stripping madre donna Maria Elisabetta Azzolini of her office, a penalty appropriate only for mortal sin—was magnified, they argued, by the fact that "the removal from executive power is one of the greatest penalties that can be meted out to heads of religion, and above all when one considers the dignity of the office of abbess, which is the highest of all in the ecclesiastical hierarchy that pertains to the female sex." Their several comments about scandalous crowds raise the objection that convent churches should not be treated differently than others, suggesting a rejection of the isolation imposed upon nunneries ever since Trent:

> His Excellency's motive, to remove the scandals that hide in the crowds in the churches, does not undermine our arguments, because these scandals lurk in all the other churches too. But music is not forbidden there, even though they may be churches subject to the archbishop. And there are a hundred other more universally applicable, and therefore better, means to remove these abuses without penalizing cloistered religious women for the misdeeds committed by laymen, of which the nuns are completely innocent,

above all those in this most holy house. Or if one must remove all the causes, even laudable ones, that produce evil effects, it would be necessary henceforth to change the entire system, not only ecclesiastical but temporal as well.[19]

Archbishop Boncompagni may have been smarting particularly from the slap at his authority implicit in the Sacra affair of 1698, referred to several times in the surviving documents of 1704. But evidently he, too, recognizing the connection between singing at Santa Cristina and earlier history, interpreted the nuns' latest challenge as just another example of the same disobedience that the diocesan curia had faced since the 1620s. Lest the link escape the Congregation of Bishops, Boncompagni apparently searched out and sent along to Rome a fresh copy of Cardinal Archbishop Ludovico Ludovisi's final threat of excommunication against the earlier generation of recalcitrant nuns back in March 1629, for the twelve-page letter survives complete in the fascicle of Vatican documents from the dispute of 1704.

In the weeks before the case was first scheduled to come up in the Congregation of Bishops, machinations on both sides intensified. As early as 7 September, the nuns' lawyer in Rome, Giovanni Battista Narici, passed on suggestions from the newly appointed *ponente*, Cardinal Leonardo Colloredo, who had played a similar role in the nuns' suit over the Sacra six years before. Colloredo urged them to compose a letter of compromise to Cardinal Boncompagni, the possible contents of which he outlined in detail. Narici tactfully indicated certain weaknesses in their case, and pragmatically pointed out that "the Congregation that takes the side of bishops will very likely support more readily still even what the lord cardinal has done." In addition, he warned that in the critical vote in Congregation, the cardinals whose opening votes would set the pattern for those to follow included the especially scrupulous (*delicatissimi*) cardinals Acciaioli, Carpegna, and Ferrari, who easily could and probably would carry the day. In a letter written just the day before, Camillo Bolognetti, who seems to have assumed the role Count Paolo Bolognetti had played as the nuns' particular advocate in the struggles of 1698, commenting that Boncompagni was "harsh, and inimical to song in nuns' churches," reiterated Colloredo's suggestion about compromise, which he went on to second himself, pointing out the precariousness of the political realities.[20]

Willingness to compromise had rarely, however, been the nuns' way. In the same spirit as their predecessors in earlier generations at Santa Cristina, they responded to Colloredo with a long and detailed list of their grievances and the legal bases for their defense. The case was repeatedly postponed during the rest of the summer and through the fall, as Colloredo and Narici continued to urge compromise. Buoyed, perhaps, by the happy outcome of 1698, the nuns attempted a replay of the strategy that had worked for them then. They prepared a meticulously documented defense, probably modeled on Zanelli's of six years earlier. Indeed, the legal citations from the nuns' petition seem to have been cribbed by Narici for several details of his own Latin brief of 1704.

They failed, however, to recognize the particular social and political dynamic of the case in 1704. The Sacra at issue in 1698–99 not only had an unbroken history, backed by tradition, which weighed heavily in decisions of the Sacred Congregations: as a ritual, it opened out to incorporate the powerful families of the city, who could therefore be drawn into the convent's defense. In contrast, legal niceties aside, Bolognese nuns' singing—often touched by hints of impropriety, real or imagined—had had an ambivalent history at least since Trent. The clear hints of disobedience at Santa Cristina in 1703 and 1704, which, as we have seen, had not escaped notice in the city, exacerbated a somewhat embarrassing situation in which the nuns were unlikely to find much support, even from politically dispassionate cardinals or patricians who otherwise might have been able to help them.

What finally happened in the Sacred Congregation is not entirely clear. At the end of November, the nuns doggedly continued to refuse to settle. "Your lawyer Narici prepared very beautiful briefs. Our most illustrious ambassador spoke to more than one cardinal on their behalf, and especially to your cardinal *ponente*," noted a last-minute letter to the nuns from an apparent supporter in Rome, Paolo Zambeccari, which reveals that some local *potenti* had attempted to help. However, "this case had been placed on the docket for the meeting on 5 December 1704, and then was settled amicably by His Eminence [Cardinal Colloredo]," according to a scribbled note on the cover of the sheaf of documents in the Sacred Congregation.[21] On the day the suit was to be discussed, Cardinal Colloredo acted on his own initiative. Rather than risk a vote that could only embarrass either the archbishop of Bologna or the nuns and their families, he took it upon himself to suspend the case.

Informing the nuns of his decision on 6 December 1704, Colloredo commented, "I would malign, not only your daughterly discretion, but also that good and prudent wisdom God has granted you were I to doubt that you all would approve my judgment, and recognize how it serves your advantage."[22] The cardinal also sent along a carefully composed petition for the singing nuns to transcribe and sign, with his assurances that Archbishop Boncompagni would then readily reconcile them to "his paternal esteem and affection." It took two weeks for the nuns to swallow this bitter pill. On 13 December, the anxious Colloredo wrote from Rome again, expressing the hope that the nuns would "embrace my counsel, to get out of such a quandary with their reputation [intact]." Finally, on 22 December 1704, the abbess and the three singing nuns signed the petition largely ghost-written by Colloredo, affirming

> that although they are unaware of the same, to have ever disobeyed the most reverend commands of Your Excellency, just as they would be incapable of such an error, nevertheless having heard that it was variously represented to Your Excellency on occasion that this past May the solemnities of Santa Cristina were celebrated by the nuns with polyphony, they do not try thereby consciously to displease, and much less to see themselves deprived for that reason of the honor of your most prized grace. In order to merit that grace they have fulfilled with due promptness the penance which it pleased you to impose. They thus submit themselves forever as daughters and most obsequious subjects in obedience to Your Eminence.[23]

The archbishop received the letter "with sentiments of paternal love," as the nuns later acknowledged. Boncompagni must have deemed it prudent to accept this carefully composed declaration, which admitted to no wrongdoing save having provoked his displeasure. Two days later, he therefore responded:

> Considering that the nuns have punctually observed, as they declare, the penance imposed by us, we kindly grant them the grace they requested [in fact, they had asked none]. But the prohibition of the synod, expressed in our manifest order, which they must observe inviolably, remains in force, not to sing in polyphony [canto figurato], [song] mixed [with organ], or any other concerted music. They are permitted only ecclesiastical song, which they call plainchant, and likewise not to have music performed by others in their external church.[24]

This was not quite what the nuns of Santa Cristina had been led to expect. In their report of the outcome to Colloredo, the disappointed nuns expressed themselves in an icy flow of polite negatives, passives, and subjunctives:

> But one cannot help protesting, with the requisite reverence for Your Eminence, that in general this did not quite appear to have corresponded to the graces that were hoped for through the beneficent intercession of Your Eminence.

The door they tried to leave open for still further recourse to the Congregation of Bishops was politely closed by Colloredo in his own response of 7 January. Attempting to present Boncompagni's ruling in the best possible light, he closed the matter with the inevitable exhortation that the nuns

> resign themselves with good cheer to God's ordering of things, as made manifest through their superiors, and be convinced that the true glory and reputation of good religious women consists in always making their obedience shine forth amid all their other Christian virtues.[25]

For women, and women religious in particular, obedience outweighed all other concerns.

Cardinal Colloredo may not have had the final word, however. The nuns, it seems, turned once again to other discreet channels of influence beyond the convent walls, which had also served them in 1698. A letter to donna Marsibiglia Bolognini, the convent bursar, on New Year's Day 1707 reveals the gentle intercessions of Countess Orsi, who with members of her family had played a central role in the suit of 1698 over the Sacra and would march among the *paranymphæ* at the next Sacra in 1711. Particularly intriguing, the letter is signed by Ippolita Ludovisi Boncompagni. Wife of Gregorio Boncompagni, duke of Sora, and sister-in-law to Archbishop Giacomo Boncompagni, she was the last survivor of the Ludovisi line that had produced the nuns' original adversary of the 1620s, Cardinal Archbishop Ludovico Ludovisi of Bologna.[26] This suggests in a particularly intriguing way that once again the ties of sisterhood among women of similar social strata, embodying flexible, reciprocal patron-client relationships, assiduously cultivated by the nuns, transcended the cloister to balance even the powerful ties of family.

The initial results were less than the nuns desired, however. The lady Ludovisi Boncompagni reported with regret:

> As regards the matter it pleased you to communicate to me there, I attempted to mediate most zealously with the lord cardinal archbishop, but I did not meet with all that [positive] inclination that I had hoped for in serving your illustrious ladyship; and I left the response to the lady Countess Orsi, because he has communicated [the response] to her. I therefore pray you to reward my mortification with the favor of your further commands.

But it appears that the "zealous mediations" of Countess Orsi and Duchess Ludovisi-Boncompagni bore at least some fruit. On an unsigned, undated slip of paper enclosed with the other documents from the case in the convent archive, we read:

> We concede to the nuns of the monastery of Santa Cristina in Bologna license that in future they can practice the use of mixed or altered song, only in ecclesiastical ceremonies, after the method and manner that the other monasteries of this city use, notwithstanding the order they have to the contrary.[27]

Thus it was that Cardinal Archbishop Giacomo Boncompagni apparently saved face. The nuns had to be satisfied with a kind of private, partial, somewhat ambiguous, but thoroughly characteristic, sort of vindication. After more than eighty years of periodic petitioning and protest, the voluminous waves of documents from "those nuns of Santa Cristina," as the cardinals in the Congregation of Bishops had come to call them, seem largely to recede. After 1704, Santa Cristina della Fondazza rarely turned to the Congregation, and then generally about mundane matters. The long struggle testifies to the independent spirit passed from one generation to another within a female institution striving to preserve traditions that provided its identity and seemed to offer some measure of self-direction. They had doggedly and—in the eyes of the church hierarchy—exasperatingly persisted in taking their case to Rome. They had exploited indirect means of influence, extending beyond their own families in the urban patriciate to informal links of one woman to another. Such actions reveal the continuation into the eighteenth century of methods of maneuvering extending back beyond the Council of Trent and well into the Middle Ages.

Citing a revealing remark by the Spanish noblewoman Doña Leonor López de Córdoba (c. 1362–c. 1412), "You already know how rights depend on one's petition being granted," Katherine Gill has pointed out that recourse to Rome was a primary means to guard some measure of autonomy for fourteenth- and fifteenth-century religious women. As Gill puts it, "[medieval] women's communities had no reason to believe they should apply to themselves the ideas of every bishop, ordinary, or monastic superior who set himself up in their diocese." Such a view may have become considerably less realistic after Trent, but it was one that the nuns of Santa Cristina continued to hold throughout the Seicento. The case of Santa Cristina indicates that within the more highly regulated post-Tridentine church, supported by various Sacred Congregations in Rome, persistence, patience, and political maneuvering might still bring some small measure of success in a world where the rights of religious women *still* "did 'depend on [their] petition being granted.' "[28]

Maria Elisabetta Azzolini, the frail mother abbess at Santa Cristina, did not long survive the struggles of 1704. She died of cancer in 1708. One of the singing nuns, Maria Giuditta Ginevra Amorini Bolognini, lived on into her eighties. A "pillar of the choir," she also served three years as bursar, six as mistress of novices, fifteen as prioress, and nine as abbess before her death in 1762, having earned through her piety and a particularly good death a place, alongside the Venerable Flaminia Bombacci, in the Camaldolese menology, where she is remembered to this day every 16 January.[29] Donna Maria Diletta Vittoria Muzzi went on to hold high office and to become an artistic patron of the convent, as we shall see. Donna Maria Cristina Cavazza's subsequent career proved less illustrious. In July 1708, disguised as an abbot, she was caught sneaking out of the convent once too often with the help of a priest to attend the opera. Sentenced to a decade of imprisonment at Santa Cristina for violations of *clausura*, she repeatedly petitioned for transfer until 1719, when she was moved to the convent of Lateran canonesses, Sant'Agostino at Lugo. Instead of making her repeat the novice year as the Congregation of Bishops had stipulated, the nuns of Sant'Agostino elected her abbess. Cristina Cavazza proceeded to mismanage convent finances so badly, however, that she finally had to flee the irate nuns of Lugo, in violation of *clausura,* back to Santa Cristina in Bologna, where in 1735 she was reluctantly received. When she died of apoplexy in 1751, the convent necrologist chose to remember only her musical talents.[30]

Archbishop Boncompagni, too, lived on into the 1730s, possibly wondering whether his efforts had done any good. On 21 January 1705, within a month of the settlement with Santa Cristina, another Bolognese chronicler recorded the performance of elaborate music, "in spite of the archbishop's prohibition," at the convent of Sant'Agnese where all the trouble had started two years earlier.[31] In February 1706, the nuns' vicar of Bologna, Bernardo Pini, began once again to sign annual licenses continuing in a largely unbroken stream into the 1720s for lavish music at Santi Vitale et Agricola. This did not prevent Pini's self-satisfied, disingenuous response to a universal letter from the Congregation of Bishops in February 1708, that

> One may reflect upon the fact that here in Bologna music making in nuns' churches has in fact already been forbidden. . . . Here they do not sing to the organ, nor at the grates in any way whatsoever, as they do elsewhere. . . . In this city we do not have that practice of [laypeople] associating with nuns, as in Ferrara and in all the other surrounding territories.[32]

Just three weeks later, Pini's pious picture of strict observance was contradicted during Carnival. Francesco Galliani recorded that

> When a spiritual play was being performed by the nuns of San Guglielmo in their internal church, their father confessor removed the Blessed Sacrament and the tabernacle from the altar in the external church and installed a bench, which was filled with outside spectators, who enjoyed the recitation through the grated window [above the altar]. When word of this reached their superiors, it led to the suspension of the priest, pending further orders from Rome.[33]

And that summer Cristina Cavazza began her series of nocturnal excursions from Santa Cristina to the opera. The following year, a new stream of at least ten musical *feste* at the convents was recorded by chroniclers. The number of lavish convent celebrations rose to as many as thirty in 1712, when Catherine Vigri finally achieved sainthood. From then on, despite Pini's claims or prohibitions to the contrary, the nuns' churches in the city were rarely silent for long. Finally, sometime around midcentury, with little apparent fuss, the nuns of Santa Cristina were restored to communion with the Camaldolese order.[34]

On 11 September 1729, toward the end of his life and exactly a century after the nuns' bitter resignation to episcopal control, Cardinal Archbishop

Giacomo Boncompagni found himself at Santa Cristina one last time, for the consecration of ten nuns. The bursar's accounts record that the seventy-seven-year-old archbishop was played into and out of the church by four trumpets, hunting horns, and the resounding reports of the obligatory five hundred firecrackers. He was accompanied during the ceremony by no fewer than forty-eight extern musicians, led yet again by Giacomo Perti as *maestro di capella*. Rivaling the angelic voices of the singing nuns, a singer to His Majesty of Sardinia sang a special motet.[35]

One can but wonder whether, as the musicians washed down 112 pastries with wine at the lavish reception after the ceremony, His Eminence, nearing the end of his forty-year reign, but probably still "harsh and inimical to song in nuns' churches," ate crow in silence.

THIRTEEN

Codetta

"An ancient church, gone wrong
and waiting to fall down"

In the spring of 1796, the armies of Napoleon broke into Italy. The Piedmont and the Po fell in April; by mid May, Napoleon himself had reached Milan. In the evening on 18 June, after the defeat of General Augerau, an advance guard of forty French soldiers passed through Porta San Felice in Bologna. A few days later, Napoleon entered the city and laid down the terms for a new order. With the Peace of Tolentino in February 1797, Pope Pius VI formally gave up Bologna and the church's northern holdings. Within the month, the first of Napoleon's new states, the Cispadane Republic, had been created, with Bologna as its capital. The following year, the province was added to the Cisalpine Republic. Nuns would find little place in the new regime.

As the armies of the French Republic continued southward, Santa Cristina and the other religious houses of Bologna began to confront a program of abolishing monastic enclosure. The mammoth task of inventorying convent property dragged on through 1798. In October, the great table from the refectory at Santa Cristina was hauled off for the use of the occupying forces. Four months later, at the beginning of February 1799, some thirty-one male monasteries and thirty-eight convents in Bologna were officially suppressed. As for the nuns of the city, a final entry in a convent chronicle from Santa Maria Maddalena records, "all the poor religious women were constrained to put off their sacred habit and withdraw to God knows where."[1]

At Santa Cristina, the last of the nuns had scarcely ventured back into the world, pensioned off with a stipend matching her original dowry, before the sale of convent furnishings got under way. The volume of material was so vast that the auction stretched on for the rest of February, through March, and on into April. A month later the orchards, icehouse, and part of the convent were bartered by the nascent state for rice to feed the occupation forces. The following year, the troops themselves moved into the unsold wings of the cloister. On and off for most of the next two hundred years, the convent of Santa Cristina would serve chiefly to house military personnel. It was a slightly more dignified fate than awaited some religious houses in Italy, such as the Bolognese male monastery of San Giovanni in Monte, which became the city prison. In March 1805, Napoleon was crowned king of Italy. The following year, the old parish of Santa Cristina was officially incorporated into the adjoining parish of San Giuliano; two years later, the external church of Santa Cristina reopened for services.[2]

In 1815, after Napoleon's fall, the Congress of Vienna restored the city to papal control. Shortly thereafter, a few of the former sisters began to find their way back to via Fondazza, joining a trickle of nuns from other orders with nowhere else to go. Cardinal Oppizzoni, archbishop of Bologna, who had spent part of the intervening years imprisoned at Vincennes, reacquired portions of the convent from the family that had bought them in 1799, as a refuge for some twenty-two nuns, unprepared for a more modern world, who wished to return to their old way of life. Over ten years, their numbers grew to thirty, not so many fewer than in former times, although they represented an array of monastic traditions: Augustinians, Dominicans, Lateran canonesses, Franciscans, Benedictines, and Camaldolese, now united under the Rule of St. Augustine. In 1827, there were but two Camaldolese among them: Maria Claudia Dotti, who had entered Santa Cristina half a century before, around 1776, and another who had scarcely entered the convent before the Napoleonic suppression—Countess Barbara Malvasia, a final link to a family that had helped create the crises at Santa Cristina exactly two centuries earlier. The members of the community lived quietly and inconspicuously on via Fondazza for another forty-five years. But in May 1862, the church and the convent were closed once again, and the buildings were taken over entirely by the military. The church would reopen only in 1896, still as part of the parish of San Giuliano. But, as a convent, Santa Cristina had closed for good.[3]

For another hundred and twenty years, the cloister continued to serve as a military barracks, the Caserma Pietramellara. Outbuildings became stables and haylofts, while the venerable *chiesa vecchia* was turned into a warehouse. By World War I, Costa's Saint Benedict, Saint Romuald, and Saint Christina looked down from the vaults on tangles of bicycles, which would remain there for decades. In the final stages of World War II, part of the convent became a refuge for evacuees and their livestock, driven from the surrounding countryside and into the city by the fighting, as generation after generation of countryfolk before them had been during similarly hard times. After the war, the youth of Italy, still called to obligatory military service, continued to live and exercise within the convent walls. The troops were followed by sharpshooters (*bersaglieri*), replaced in turn by the fire brigade, and other sorts of military personnel. Only in 1982 did the military begin its final retreat. The last antiquated army vehicle was finally towed away in 1985, and the convent was abandoned.[4]

Today church and convent alike remain closed. With the demolition of the wall at the corner of via del Piombo and via Fondazza in 1913–14, the old convent courtyard, where in 1628 the nuns had held the diocesan ministers and beadles at bay with bricks and stones, was transformed into the unprepossessing Piazzetta Morandi. The throngs of onlookers, once kept out of the courtyard by the papal legate's Swiss guard during the periodic reenactments of the Sacra, have given way to the few cars and motorbikes that can crowd into every inch and angle of the piazzetta, creeping up onto the curb before the church, and kept from the portico only by the spiked iron gates, which never open. Up above, the Capella del Rosario, where on feast days choirs of nuns sang through grated windows into the public church, now stands empty, the grates walled up long ago, with only scars in the plaster to mark the site of the high altar. The west windows, through which in 1628 an eloquently defiant donna Isabetta Vizzana rallied the parishioners and neighborhood children to the convent's defense, are filled halfway down with masonry, like drooping eyelids, but otherwise stare darkly onto the piazza, open to the elements and to flocks of pigeons, who for more than a decade have transformed the chapel into an increasingly squalid dovecote.

Within the incongruously stunted and far less imposing old wall along via Fondazza and via del Piombo, the remains of the convent gardens, nibbled away around the edges little by little until 1958 to make way for Piazza Carducci to the east and for blocks of housing built in the 1920s and 1930s, now open every morning as a happy and pleasantly kept public park. Beneath tall trees planted long after the nuns' departure, the very young exhaust themselves under the watchful eyes of the old. On the grass, teenage couples, constrained by circumstances to live at home, find in the shadow of the wall a kind of public privacy for experiments with earthly delights that earlier occupants, monastic and military, may have experienced within these walls only in their imaginations.

Surrounded by makeshift wire fencing, posted with warnings of falling masonry to keep back the curious, the monastery buildings continue their unobtrusive decline. The resident caretaker and his family, who have moved into the nuns' old laundry and the common rooms of the east wing, keep ordinary intruders, vandals, graffiti artists, and drug addicts at bay, but cannot hope on their own to stay the natural forces of decay and dilapidation. On a sweltering July day, the cloister's central courtyard, dominated by Bibiena's elegant campanile, remains almost as whitely bright and open to the sky as when the nuns passed along the cooler, darker stillness of its deeply shaded arcades. But the kitchen garden that has taken over—a weedy tangle of squash vines, peppers, stick tents for runner beans, and a jungle of clotheslines, fig trees that overtop the second story, and a fir tree beginning little by little to challenge the belltower—calls to mind less a *hortus conclusus* from the Song of Songs than God's Little Acre.

The *Crocifisso di pietà* that miraculously appeared in 1613–14 in the cloister, where Lucrezia Vizzana and the other nuns commemorated Christ's Passion every Friday and grudgingly said grace after meals at the insistence of Emilia Grassi is long gone. Perhaps it was felled by the lightning bolt that in July 1745 blasted the weathervane depicting Saint Christina off the top of the belltower and brought part of the campanile tumbling onto the roof and down into the cloister. Most other, subsequent depredations have been acts of men, however, not of God. Only in 1978 was the artistic and historical importance of the site officially recognized by the state.

The refined detail in terra-cotta and sandstone on the fifteenth- and sixteenth-century corbels, capitals, and doorways to the nuns' inner chapel, the *chiesa vecchia*, and the infirmary has largely disappeared beneath layers of battleship gray. Signora Giovanna, the caretaker's wife, pointing to the lintel above the most elaborate doorway, likewise submerged in gray, explains that this was a replacement by the sixteenth-century nuns themselves, after the discovery of the previous donor's pregnancy and her banishment from the cloister. Favorite old themes die hard.

Of the extensive frescoes that entirely covered some rooms off the cloister, next to nothing remains. The *Crucifixion with Saints* attributed to Francesco Francia, high on the wall of the chapter house, is still visible, its figures but ghostly shadows in an imaginary landscape, hazed by latter-day pollution and neglect. In a niche on the upper floor, less distinguished images of Saint Romuald and Beata Lucia di Settefonti can still be made out in the upper gallery. But the other art work, including the decoration of another chapel described in the 1930s as "completely covered in fresco,"[5] has vanished. Perhaps some remains hidden, "protected," as the caretaker optimistically puts it, under layers of whitewash.

The nuns' *chiesa interiore*—where the quarrels of Cecilia Bianchi and Emilia Grassi regularly erupted in the 1620s, where Pantasilea Tovagli kept one eye on inappropriate reading matter hidden in her prayerbook, and where worshippers were distracted by the nuns' feline and canine companions wandering in and out—is by now scarcely recognizable, although its original architecture seems to remain largely intact beneath a heavy weight of accretions. By 1920, the chapel had been transformed into a parish theater for activities of the Associazione Leone XIII, which periodically closed and reopened, depending on good or hard times. After the war, it became the Cinema Leone XIII, which lasted only a few seasons before closing its doors for good by 1970.[6]

In the still, fetid dimness, chilly even at midsummer, feeble light filtering through gaps in the sagging and mouldering black drapes that effectively shut out the sun from the four great windows reveals no trace of the Colonaesque frescoes of the Madonna and saints that could still be seen there as late as the 1930s. An abandoned proscenium cramps the once lofty space. Its yards of gold-fringed and musty red curtain, hanging at half mast, have supplanted the fragment of the True Cross, the head of one of Saint Ursula's martyred companions, the bodies of Saints Felice and Lucio,[7] and other relics as the dominant focus. Like the spirits of those departed, any ghosts of the comfortable, neighborhood intimacy depicted in Salvatore Tornatore's *Cinema Paradiso,* or of the amiable chaos of variety theater such as that of Fellini's *Roma,* which may also briefly have flourished here in the days of the Associazione Leone XIII, now resist conjuration. Herded in disarray into a corner opposite a jumble of upturned, rickety, and fractured straight chairs, broken ranks of the wooden theater seats that replaced the nuns' choirstalls await some victory bonfire.

But high above all this, some of the ancient vaults rise free and unaltered. And below them the old catwalk still hugs the wall, linking the original organ rooms, up near the ceiling, from which the choirs of disembodied voices once sang through grated windows. Only a basketball goal mounted just below, its orange, netless hoop mysteriously slam dunked flat against the wall, mars the image.

To pass from the oppressive, perpetual dusk of the interior church into the bright expanse of the external church is to enter quite a different world. Thanks to one or two faithful caretakers, recalling their fifteenth- and sixteenth-century predecessors who devotedly tended Santa Cristina di Settefonti long after it too had effectively been abandoned, the annual feast of Saint Christina might have been celebrated here only yesterday. Rich and festive crimson damask, showing its years as it fades and begins to split here and there under its own weight, still adorns every doorway and the impressive length of every pilaster. Streaming shafts of light from north and south windows high in the vaults flood the lofty, airy space, striking upon the imposing, gilded side altars, whose startling brilliance belies the passage of some four centuries.

Eight monumental stucco statues still stare just as intently down from their niches, but to an empty floor, some gesturing to one another, and to no one else, across the open spaces. Up in the vault above the high altar, the paired doves of the old Camaldolese coat of arms may now be hidden beneath the Augustinian equivalent, a memento of the convent's second monastic incarnation in the nineteenth century. The eagles, boars, and wild goats from the coats of arms of illustrious nun benefactors have been obliterated from the altars they donated. But otherwise the church might well persuade that little has changed.

After the Napoleonic depredations and decades of abandonment, of course, there may be an anachronistic and appealingly modern austerity about the place. The relics of Saint Christina and others, languishing behind a grill above the side altar of Saint Romuald, but miraculously still here, have spawned no silver encrustations of ex-votos of the sort that continue to multiply and creep up the walls of a living parish such as Santa Maria dei Servi, a few blocks west. At Santa Cristina the few surviving altar furnishings bespeak an ascetic sparseness and hermetic simplicity of which Saint Romuald, surveying the church from his niche in the north wall, would approve.

Amid the general anonymity, six silver candlesticks still standing on the high altar, their tall candles listing like the Torre Garisenda downtown, offer one last link to earlier, more vital times. For if one looks closely, it is possible to find the date 1730 and the name of the donor, Diletta Vittoria Muzzi.[8] Donna Maria Diletta Vittoria Muzzi (1670–1748), one of the last of the many convent benefactors to have left her mark in the church of Santa Cristina, marched down its nave three centuries ago among the twelve consacrees at the victorious Sacra of 1699. She went on to perform with two other nun musicians, in defiance of Cardinal Archbishop Giacomo Boncompagni, on the Feast of Santa Cristina in 1704, provoking the last struggle of the singing nuns of Santa Cristina.

Here for a moment one can imagine how it must once have been and overlook the telltale signs of darkening damp creeping across the vaults above and spreading a haze up the marbling of the altars below. Disregarding the incursions of pigeons, looking to extend their empire beyond the adjoining Capella del Rosario above the portico, one can almost forget the rising crusty tide of their droppings that already carpets the floor of that derelict chapel (see fig. 16), where in the emotional disorder of her final years Lucrezia Vizzana must have knelt and lost herself in special devotions to the Mysteries of the Rosary. One can forget for a while the collapsing roof above the cloister staircase (see fig. 17) ascending to the nuns' cells. But such an imaginative leap will not be possible much longer. For once the roof begins to go, the building's back will break.

Most of Bologna's more renowned convents and convent churches have disappeared by now, or been remade to fit a more modern world. Santi Gervasio e Protasio was supplanted by the covered market between via Ugo Bassi and via San Gervasio. Santa Maria Nuova became a tobacco factory, then was largely reduced to rubble by the Allied bombings of World War II. San Giovanni Battista was turned into a psychiatric hospital in 1869. Santa Maria Maddalena, its inner and outer churches combined into a barn for hay in 1798, had its other buildings partly knocked down in 1810 to make way for the Arena del Sole. The church of Sant'Agnese was demolished after 1819 and its cloister refurbished as the Caserma Minghetti.

Corpus Domini survived a devastating direct hit by an Allied bomb that dropped through the dome and into the nave on 5 October 1943. It has managed to rise again, thanks perhaps to the abiding influence, spiritual or otherwise, of Bologna's *santa cittadina,* Saint Catherine Vigri, who still keeps company there with a handful of her Clarissan disciples, continuing their cloistered life within its walls.

Across town, at Santa Cristina, a few fragments of Blessed Lucia of Settefonti long lay forgotten, as they had been once before in another older Santa Cristina—"an ancient church gone wrong and waiting to fall down," as Bedinus Marzochi put it back in 1571,[9] shortly before most of Santa Cristina *vecchia* in the hills outside of town was pulled down, and Lucia's remains began their peregrination from Settefonti to Sant'Andrea di Ozzano and in the 1640s partly to Bologna. Now, with every grate bricked over, and the doors locked, barred, or walled up, a stricter *clausura* than even the most reform-minded prelate ever envisioned has descended upon church and convent alike at the new Santa Cristina on via Fondazza, where some of Lucia rested for 350 years. *Clausura,* which once held the corruptions of the world at bay, now shields the world outside from the quiet decay that works slowly and largely unnoticed within.

Santa Cristina della Fondazza, among the last largely intact memorials to the bounded world in which thousands of Bolognese women over the centuries made lives for themselves as best they could, now faces a threat more serious than those posed by Cardinal Archbishop Ludovico Ludovisi in the 1620s or by Napoleon and the Directory in the 1790s. The convent's fate depends, as it always has, upon the mediation of outsiders. But the old patterns of clientage and the influential links to families and community vanished long ago with the forgotten nuns who once nurtured them. Only a few of the old names can still be heard in the neighborhood: Albertazzi, Cavazza, Malvezzi, Panzacchi.

Over the past fifty years, the communal, provincial, and regional administrations in Bologna and Emilia Romagna, aided by various banks, have confronted the daunting task of preserving their artistic and architectural patrimony more vigorously and successfully than most other administrations in Italy. But, as one inhabitant of the city remarked in 1993, "They can't save everything."[10]

In crises of former centuries, it was the echo of disembodied voices that bridged the walls of *clausura* to catch the ear of a concerned community. Perhaps today Lucrezia Orsina Vizzana, who four centuries ago turned her back on the world and passed within the walls on via Fondazza, may speak once again to a wider world through the music she left behind. The eloquence of her voice, "sweeter than honey and the honeycomb," which once touched Seicento Bologna from "within the hollow of the walls," may yet reach out to move a new generation to reaffirm the value of its fragile, hidden past.

> *Ornaverunt faciem templi coronis aureis, et dedicaverunt altare Domino; et facta est lætitia magna in populo. . . . Et victoriam dedit illi Dominus. Et facta est lætitia magna in populo.*

> They adorned the front of the temple with wreaths of gold and dedicated the altar unto the Lord. And there was great rejoicing among the people. . . . And the Lord granted unto her the victory. And there was great rejoicing among the people.
>
> —Lucrezia Orsina Vizzana, 1623

NOTES

INTRODUCTION

1. James McKinnon, *Music in Early Christian Literature* (Cambridge: Cambridge University Press, 1987), 133. My thanks to Pamela Starr for first bringing these words to my attention.

2. Jane Bowers, "The Emergence of Women Composers in Italy, 1566–1700," in *Women Making Music: The Western Art Tradition, 1150–1950,* ed. Jane Bowers and Judith Tick (Urbana and Chicago: University of Illinois Press, 1986), 135.

3. A number of other poor or orphaned girls were helped to respectable marriages by various charitable organizations and confraternities, which provided them with dowries. On such organizations in Rome, see Marina D'Amelia, "La conquista di una dote: Regole del gioco e scambi femminili alla Confraternità dell'Annunziata (sec. xvii–xviii)," in *Ragnatele di rapporti: Patronage e reti di relazione nella storia delle donne,* ed. Lucia Ferrante, Maura Palazzi, and Gianna Pomata (Turin: Rosenberg & Sellier, 1988), 305–43. I thank Anne Jacobson Schutte for bringing this collection to my attention.

4. The nuns of San Vito in Ferrara are known today chiefly from the comments of Ercole Bottrigari in *Il desiderio: Overo de' concerti di varii strumenti musicali* (Venice: Amadino, 1594). Relevant excerpts in translation appear in Carol Neuls-Bates, ed., *Women in Music: An Anthology of Source Readings from the Middle Ages to the Present* (New York: Harper & Row, 1982), 43–49. See also Giovanni Maria Artusi's related remarks in *L'Artusi: Overo delle imperfettioni della moderna musica* (Venice: Giacomo Vincenti, 1600), fols. 1v–2v. On the nuns of Milan, see Robert Kendrick, "Genres, Generations and Gender: Nuns' Music in Early Modern Milan, c. 1550–1706" (Ph.D. diss., New York University, 1993), and id., "The Traditions of Milanese Convent Music and the Sacred Dialogues of Chiara Margarita Cozzolani," in *The Crannied Wall: Women, Religion, and the Arts in Early Modern Europe,* ed. Craig Monson (Ann Arbor: University of Michigan Press, 1992), 211–33.

5. See Kendrick, "Genres, Generations and Gender."

6. Ludovico Frati, *La vita privata in Bologna del secolo XIII al XVII,* 2d ed. (Bologna: Nicola Zanichelli, 1928; repr., Rome: Bardi editore, 1968), 184–85. Camillo Baldi

also confirmed that the city's prime revenues derived from the export of hemp and silk; see Mario Fanti, "Le classi sociali e il governo di Bologna all'inizio del secolo xvii in un'opera inedita di Camillo Baldi," *Strenna storica bolognese* 11 (1961): 141. For further details on the Bolognese trade in hemp and silk, see Giampiero Cuppini, *I palazzi senatorii a Bologna: Architettura come immagine del potere* (Bologna: Nicola Zanichelli, 1974), 16–17. For an especially detailed discussion of the Bolognese silk industry, see Carlo Poni, "Sviluppo, declino e morte dell'antico distretto industriale urbano (secoli xvi–xix)," in *Storia illustrata di Bologna,* ed. Walter Tega (Milan: Nuova editoriale AIEP, 1989), 3: 321–80.

7. Frati, *La vita privata in Bologna,* 4. Frati points out that similar porticoes are common in the ancient university town of Padua as well. Their presence in many other northern cities suggests the weather as an equally probable cause.

8. For a summary of religious life in Bologna, see Gabriella Zarri, "Istituzioni ecclesiastiche e vita religiosa a Bologna (1450–1700)," in *Storia illustrata di Bologna,* 2: 161–200. On Bolognese women religious, see id., "I monasteri femminili a Bologna tra il xiii e il xvii secolo," *Deputazione di storia patria per le province di Romagna: Atti e memorie,* n.s., 24 (1973): 133–224.

9. Baldi quoted in Fanti, "Le classi sociali," 148. Giancarlo Angelozzi takes some exception to Baldi's view, however. See "Nobili, mercanti, dottori, cavalieri, artigiani: Stratificazione sociale e ideologia a Bologna nei secoli xvi e xviii," in *Storia illustrata di Bologna,* 2: 46.

10. Some (not including Baldi) are listed and briefly discussed in Peter Burke, "Conspicuous Consumption in Seventeenth-Century Italy," in *The Historical Anthropology of Early Modern Italy: Essays on Perception and Communication* (Cambridge: Cambridge University Press, 1987), 145–47.

11. Pompeo Dolfi, *Cronologia delle famiglie nobili di Bologna* (Bologna: Giovanni Battista Ferroni, 1670; repr., Bologna: Forni editore, n.d.), 1–27. Giuseppe Guidicini, *Cose notabili della città di Bologna,* vol. 2 (Bologna: Monti, 1869), 415–20.

12. Fanti, "Le classi sociali," 144.

13. Masini's remark is quoted in *Guido Reni, 1575–1642: Pinacoteca Nazionale, Bologna; Los Angeles County Museum of Art; Kimbell Art Museum, Fort Worth* (Bologna: Nuova Alfa editoriale, 1988), 6. Details of the economic crises from Cuppini, *I palazzi senatorii a Bologna,* p. 14–18.

14. Population figures recording 2,480 nuns and 1,127 friars are from BCB, MS B3567, entry for 30 Sept. 1595. According to BCB, MS B81 (appendix, 42), there were 2,600 nuns, compared to 831 friars, in 1624, and 2,302 nuns, compared to 1,004 friars, in 1632.

15. See Zarri, "I monasteri femminili a Bologna," esp. 144–45. For further details on monastic expansion in Bologna in the later Cinquecento and forced monachization, see Zarri, "Monasteri femminili e città (secoli xv–xviii)," in *Storia d'Italia: Annali,* 9: *La chiesa e il potere politico dal Medioevo all'età contemporanea,* ed. Giorgio Chittolini and Giovanni Miccoli (Turin: Giulio Einaudi, 1986), 415, 420–21.

16. M. Giovanna Cambria, *Il monastero domenicano di S. Agnese in Bologna: Storia e documenti* (Bologna: Tipografia SAB, 1973), 20–22. The total figure involved both male and female religious houses. About one-eleventh of the area within the city walls was occupied by female monasteries. See Zarri, "I monasteri femminili a Bologna," 145.

17. See, e.g., Bowers, "The Emergence of Women Composers," esp. 141–46. "On the other hand, Bowers also recognizes that in convents "an atmosphere conducive to women's musical creativity existed that was found in few other places" (128).

18. The most influential discussions of nineteenth-century American "women's spheres" and "women's culture" are Carroll Smith-Rosenberg, "The Female World of Love and Ritual: Relations between Women in Nineteenth-Century America," *Signs* 1 (1975): 1–29, and Nancy F. Cott, *The Bonds of Womanhood: "Women's Sphere" in New England, 1780–1835* (New Haven: Yale University Press, 1977). Ellen DuBois, Mari Jo Buhle, Temma Kaplan, Gerda Lerner, and Carroll Smith-Rosenberg, "Politics and Culture in Women's History: A Symposium," *Feminist Studies* 6 (1980): 26–64, offers a useful overview of earlier debates surrounding the issues of "women's sphere" and "women's culture" and their relationship to feminist politics, including Ellen DuBois's sharp criticisms of the two terms, which she tends to regard as more or less synonymous (ibid., 28–36). My own summary of the debates has greatly benefited from Linda K. Kerber's very useful "Separate Spheres, Female Worlds, Woman's Place: The Rhetoric of Women's History," *Journal of American History* 75 (1988): 9–39.

19. Susan Porter Benson, *Counter Cultures: Saleswomen, Managers, and Customers in American Department Stores, 1890–1940* (Urbana and Chicago: University of Illinois Press, 1988); the quotation appears on p. 5. Also Patricia A. Cooper, *Once a Cigar Maker: Men, Women, and Work Culture in American Cigar Factories, 1900–1919* (Urbana and Chicago: University of Illinois Press, 1987), esp. the chapter " 'Independent as a Hog on Ice': Women's Work Culture," esp. 218–24. See also Barbara Melosh, *"The Physician's Hand": Work Culture and Conflict in American Nursing* (Philadelphia: Temple University Press, 1982). For a summary of research directions in work relations, see Jeremy Brecher, "Uncovering the Hidden History of the American Workplace," *Review of Radical Political Economy* 10 (1978): 1–23, esp. "IV. Worker Action."

20. Benson, *Counter Cultures,* 256 for the quotation; 229–30 for managers' complaints.

21. Linda K. Kerber aptly points out that "when they used the metaphor of separate spheres, historians referred, often interchangeably, to an ideology *imposed on* women, a culture *created by* women, a set of boundaries *expected to be observed by* women." See "Separate Spheres," 17.

22. Nuns' nurturing of the female children of their relatives in the world offers an interesting, if divergent, parallel to a characteristic shared activity of nineteenth-century American women's culture. Where nineteenth-century women often counted on their sisters to protect their children from future stepmothers, as Kerber has summarized in "Separate Spheres," (23), nuns frequently and actively sought custody of their dead *brothers'* daughters to protect them from future step*fathers*.

23. Quaker women are discussed in Kerber's "Separate Spheres," 31, which cites Mary Maples Dunn, "Saints and Sisters: Congregational and Quaker Women in the Early Colonial Period," in *Women in American Religion,* ed. Janet Wilson James (Philadelphia, 1980). On "female institution building," see Estelle Freedman, "Separatism as Strategy: Female Institution Building and American Feminism, 1870–1930," *Feminist Studies* 5 (1979): 512–29; on Hull House, Kerber, "Separate Spheres," 33–

37. Although not obviously affected by the work of social and political women's historians, chiefly centered in nineteenth- and twentieth-century America, some recent work has examined artistic and cultural aspects of late medieval women's monastic buildings as buildings, without addressing their political implications. A few other recent studies in the arts have begun to touch upon various ways in which late medieval and early modern women regarded or confronted the literal boundaries of the religious spheres in which they found themselves, how they resisted, escaped, or worked around the literal and metaphorical boundaries that separated them from society, how they made them havens or a means of subversion. See Jeffrey Hamburger, "Art, Enclosure and the *Cura monialium:* Prolegomena in the Guise of a Postscript," *Gesta* 31 (1992): 108–34; Caroline A. Bruzelius, "Hearing Is Believing: Clarissan Architecture, ca. 1213–1340," *Gesta* 31 (1992): 83–92; Katherine Gill, "Open Monasteries for Women in Late Medieval and Early Modern Italy: Two Roman Examples," in *The Crannied Wall: Women, Religion, and the Arts in Early Modern Europe,* ed. Craig Monson (Ann Arbor: University of Michigan Press, 1992), 15–47; Carolyn Valone, "Roman Matrons as Patrons: Various Views of the Cloister Wall," ibid., 49–72; Elissa B. Weaver, "The Convent Wall in Tuscan Convent Drama," ibid., 73–86.

24. In Venice, for example, their equivalents for most convents consist only of financial records (Anne Jacobson Schutte, personal communication).

25. For an overview of the archive of this and other congregations, see Leonard E. Boyle, O.P., *A Survey of the Vatican Archives and of Its Mediaeval Holdings* (Toronto: Pontifical Institute of Mediaeval Studies, 1972).

26. *Decreta authentica Congregationis Sacrorum Rituum ex actis eiusdem collecta eiusque auctoritate promulgata sub auspiciis SS. Domini Nostri Leonis Papae XIII* (Rome: Typographia polyglotta S. C. de Propaganda Fide, 1898). Aloisi Gardellini, *Decreta authentica Congregationis Sacrorum Rituum,* 3d ed. (Rome: S. C. de Propaganda Fide, 1856). See also P. Ferdinando Antonelli, OFM, "L'archivio della S. Congregazione dei Riti," in *Il libro e le biblioteche: Atti del primo congresso bibliologico francescano internazionale, 20–27 febbraio 1949,* sez. 2: *Conferenze di carattere particolare* (Rome: Pontificium Athenaeum Antonianum, 1950), 61–76.

1. DONNA LUCREZIA ORSINA VIZZANA

1. A complete copy is preserved in the Civico Museo Bibliografico Musicale, Bologna. A second copy, missing the canto secondo, survives in the Biblioteka Uniwersitecka, Wrocław. Jerome Roche's entry on the composer in *The New Grove Dictionary of Music and Musicians,* ed. Stanley Sadie (London: Macmillan, 1980), 13: 874, appears under "Orsina, Lucretia." Her name appears more accurately in *The New Grove Dictionary of Women Composers,* ed. Julie Anne Sadie and Rhian Samuel (London: Macmillan, 1994), 479–80.

2. Elissa Weaver, "Spiritual Fun: A Study of Sixteenth-Century Tuscan Convent Theater," in *Women in the Middle Ages and the Renaissance,* ed. Mary Beth Rose (Syracuse, N.Y.: Syracuse University Press, 1986), 173.

3. BUB, MS It. 3856: 133–36. Donna Flaminia's sanctity is singled out in Antonio di Paolo Masini, *Bologna perlustrata,* third printing (Bologna: Erede di Vittorio Benacci, 1666). See Gabriella Zarri, "I monasteri femminili benedettini nella diocesi

di Bologna (secoli xiii–xvii)," in *Ravennatensia ix: Atti del convegno di Bologna nel xv centenario della nascita di S. Benedetto (15–16–17 settembre 1980)* (Cesena: Badia di Santa Maria del Monte, 1981), 347. To this day Flaminia Bombacci is remembered in the menology of the Camaldolese order on 28 September. See Anselmo Giabbani, *Menologia camaldolese* (Tivoli: De Rossi, 1950), 59. See also Alberigo Pagnani, O.S.B., *Storia dei Benedettini camaldolesi: Cenobiti, eremiti, monache ed oblati* (Sassoferrato: Prem. tipografia Garofoli, 1949), 229.

4. Biblioteca Arcivescovile, Libreria Breventani, Bologna, MS 64; the manuscript seems to have disappeared from the Biblioteca Arcivescovile early in this century. An eighteenth-century transcription by Baldassare Antonio Maria Carrati appears in BCB, MS B921. See also Archivio del monastero, Camaldoli, MS 1087.

5. On the most distinguished branch of the Vizzani family, see Alessandro Longhi, *Il Palazzo Vizani (ora Sanguinetti) e le famiglie illustri che lo possedettero* (Bologna: Zamorini & Albertazzi, 1902). See also Giancarlo Roversi, *Palazzi e case nobili del '500 a Bologna: La storia, le famiglie, le opere d'arte* (Bologna: Grafis edizioni, 1986), 196–213. For a description of some of the early artistic furnishings, paintings, and the library of Palazzo Vizzani, see Ludovico Frati, *La vita privata in Bologna dal secolo xiii al xvii*, 2d ed. (Bologna: Nicola Zanichelli, 1928; repr., Rome: Bardi editore, 1968), 20–21.

6. See Longhi, *Il Palazzo Vizani*, 87–88, where she is presented among the worthies from the main branch of the family.

7. For details of the Vizzani family, see Pompeo Dolfi, *Cronologia delle famiglie nobili di Bologna* (Bologna: G. B. Ferrari, 1670; repr., Bologna: Forni editore, n.d.), 710–11; ASB, Giuseppe Guidicini Alberi genealogici, 123; BCB, MS B700, no. 150. On the Palazzo Vizzani, see Longhi, *Il Palazzo Vizani;* see also Corrado Ricci and Guido Zucchini, *Guida di Bologna: Nuova edizione illustrata* (Bologna: Edizioni Alfa, 1968; repr., 1976), 50; Giampiero Cuppini, *I palazzi senatorii a Bologna: Archittetura come immagine del potere* (Bologna: Nicola Zanichelli, 1974), 14–18, 320; Roversi, *Palazzi e case nobili del '500*, 196–213. Ludovico Vizzani's father, Obizzo di Pirro, was also a distinguished member of the College of Notaries. At his death in November 1581, he held the office of corrector, and he was interred in the large mausoleum with a pyramidal baldachino, supported by columns, in Piazza San Domenico, reserved for those who had died in office. See Giuseppe Guidicini, *Cose notabili della città di Bologna*, vol. 1 (Bologna: Giuseppe Vitali, 1868), 472. See also Ricci and Zucchini, *Guida di Bologna*, 27.

8. Baldi is quoted in Mario Fanti, "Le classi sociali e il governo di Bologna all'inizio del secolo xvii in un'opera di Camillo Baldi," *Strenna storica bolognese* 11 (1961): 152. Bombacci: "In Bologna è stata ancora in grande honore la mercanzia, et è stata essercitata da nobili senza perdere il nome di nobiltà." BUB, MS It. 3856: 144.

9. BUB, MS It. 3856: 98, 103, 122.

10. On Giovanni Bombacci's house in Strada Maggiore, see Guidicini, *Cose notabili*, vol. 3 (1870), 54–56. For other details on the property on Strada Maggiore, including its earlier architectural details, see Umberto Baseghi, *Palazzi di Bologna*, 4th ed. (Bologna: Tamari editori, 1964), 181–82. Gasparo Bombacci also called attention to the papal heritage of Casa Bombacci in Strada Maggiore. See BUB, MS It. 3856: 122.

11. Bombacci family details from BUB, MS It. 3856: 75–76, 122, 133. For Margaret King's comments on wealthy women's tendency to bear unusually large num-

bers of offspring, see *Women of the Renaissance* (Chicago: University of Chicago Press, 1991), 2–4. In Bologna and elsewhere, one positive effect of the enforcement of enclosure was to shield nuns from the hazards of contagion and random violence, not to mention childbirth. A comparatively high percentage lived extraordinarily long lives. Judith Brown's recent demographic study of the convents of San Jacopo a Ripoli and Santa Maria Annunziata delle Murate in Florence suggests that cloistered women consistently enjoyed longer lives than their counterparts in the world, both because of protections from biological and physiological risks that convents afforded and because of the social and psychological support cloistered communities could provide. See "Monache a Firenze all'inizio dell'età moderna: Un'analisi demografica," *Quaderni storici* 85 (1994): 117–52. I thank Elissa Weaver for bringing Brown's article to my attention.

12. The dowry contract survives in ASB, Demaniale 9/2870 (Santa Cristina), no. 47/I "1581. Die 17 Octobris Dos D[omi]nae Isabettae di Bo[m]basijs Uxoris D[omi]ni Ludovici de Vigianis £10000." The record of their marriage appears in BCB, MS B901: 373. Giovanni Bombacci's in-laws, the Luchini, were known particularly for silk trading, as well as banking. On the Luchini and Bombacci, see Guidicini, *Cose notabili*, vol. 1 (1868), 163; ibid., vol. 3 (1870), 55–56. The church of San Tomaso has long since been pulled down to make way for the beautiful arcade of the church of Santa Maria dei Servi.

13. For the sons' births, see BCB, MS B860: 76, 132, and B861: 198. For suor Verginia, see BUB, MS It. 3856: 75. Verginia Vizzana's birth is recorded in AAB, Reg. Batt. 1587–88, fol. 10v. The name Verginia rarely appears in Bolognese baptismal records of those years. Lucrezia's name appears ibid., 1590–92, fol. 74v.

14. These details are gleaned from petitions in ASV, VR, posiz. 1607, A–B.

15. The Bombacci family sepulchre was in front of the high altar in San Giacomo Maggiore, in via Zamboni (Dolfi, *Cronologia*, 731). The Palazzo Vizzani was just across the street from their parish church of San Biaggio, formerly at the corner of via Guerrazzi and via Santo Stefano, and was comparably close to Santa Cristina.

16. Strada Maggiore 46 (Bolognetti), 40 (Gozzadini until 1519, then Glavarini), 38 (Gozzadini), 35 (Bombacci), 15 and 17 (Malvasia); via Fondazza at via Santo Stefano (Sarti); via Santo Stefano 75 (Agucchi), 71 (Bianchi), 56 (Zani), 43 (Vizzani), 36 (Gozzadini), 13–14 (Bianchi). Based on identifications of family houses and palaces in Ricci and Zucchini, *Guida di Bologna;* Roversi, *Palazzi e case nobili del '500;* Cuppini, *I palazzi senatorii a Bologna;* Baseghi, *Palazzi di Bologna;* Guidicini, *Cose notabili.* The altars are listed in Carlo Cesare Malvasia, *Le pitture di Bologna (1686),* ed. Andrea Emiliani (Bologna: Edizioni Alfa, 1969), passim. It is not clear, however, that all the nuns in question came directly from branches of the families resident at these addresses.

17. In the 1430s, for example, the nuns had regularly visited their families, and strongly resisted the attempts of Ambrogio Traversari, the Camaldolese prior general, to restore strict enclosure. Traversari ultimately agreed that they could visit their families once every two years, in cases of urgent necessity. See Ambrogio Traversari, *Hodoeporicon,* ed. Vittorio Tamburini (Florence: Felice le Monnier, 1985), 165. A highly useful and informative comparison to the relationship between the convent of Santa Cristina, the surrounding neighborhoods, and their patrician fam-

ilies appears in Jodi Bilinkoff, *The Avila of Saint Teresa: Religious Reform in a Sixteenth-Century City* (Ithaca, N.Y.: Cornell University Press, 1989), esp. 35–52, 56–59, 111–16, 159–66. My thanks to Robert Kendrick for bringing this work to my attention.

18. This was not a "remaking" of her mother's name, however. Camilla Luchini Bombacci survived until 30 Dec. 1612. She was buried in the Bombacci vault in San Giacomo Maggiore. See BCB, MS B912: 384.

19. The Vizzani sisters' dowry agreement survives in ASB, Notarile, Belvisi Giulio, Prot. 8, fol. 379r. On Francia's altarpiece, *Il Presepio,* see Malvasia, *Le pitture di Bologna,* 266 [181].

20. *Editto de li ordini, et decreti del Sacro Concilio Tridentino sopra li monasteri di monache della città, & diocesi di Bologna* (Bologna: Alessandro Benacci, 1565), fols. Aiijr–Aiijv. In a list of nuns dated 10 Dec. 1603, the sixteen-year-old Donna Isabetta Vizzana is the most recent *professa;* Lucrezia's name does not yet appear. See ASB, Demaniale 7/2868 (Santa Cristina), no. 30/G.

21. Isabetta Vizzana's death is recorded in BCB, MS B911: 374. She was buried in the Vizzani tomb in the church of San Francesco. On the "remaking" of names, see Christiane Klapisch-Zuber, "The Name 'Remade': The Transmission of Given Names in Florence in the Fourteenth and Fifteenth Centuries," in *Women, Family, and Ritual in Renaissance Italy,* trans. Lydia Cochrane (Chicago: University of Chicago Press, 1985), 283–309.

22. Details on the Vizzani sisters' earliest years at Santa Cristina derive from ASV, VR, posiz. 1607, A–B, and from the document cited in n. 20 above.

23. Borromeo's prohibition of convent loans is quoted in Enrico Cattaneo, "Le monacazioni forzate fra Cinque e Seicento," in *Vita e processo di suor Virginia Maria de Leyva, monaca di Monza,* ed. Giancarlo Vigorelli (Milan: Garzanti, 1985; 3d ed., 1986), 165. A similar, if less precise, prohibition appears in *Editto de li ordini, et decreti del Sacro Concilio Tridentino,* fols. Aiijr–Aiijv. Giovanni Boccadiferro, BCB, MS B778: 175: "Seguita dunque esser neccessario il monacato Feminile, acciò non restino le Giovani nelle Paterne Case al pericolo di gittar l'honore non solo con li estranei, ma anchor con li Domestici di Casa, e che è peggio sin con li proprii Fratelli, et forse anchor con li istessi Padri." Portions of Boccadiferro's "Discorso sopra il governo delle monache" are quoted in Mario Fanti, *Abiti e lavori delle monache di Bologna* (Bologna: Tamari, 1972), 12–28 (not including the present quotation). In his foreword to the Rule of the Ursuline sisters of 1587, Bishop Giovanni Leoni addresses the common view that it was impossible for girls to remain chaste amid the moral dangers of paternal houses. See Gabriella Zarri, "Orsola and Catherine: The Marriage of Virgins in the Sixteenth Century," in *Creative Women in Medieval and Early Modern Italy: A Religious and Artistic Renaissance,* ed. E. Ann Matter and John Coakley (Philadelphia: University of Pennsylvania Press, 1994), 237–78.

24. For the dowry arrangements, see ASB, Demaniale 51/5009 (Santa Cristina), fols. 1v and 2v, and ASB, Notarile, Belvisi Giulio, Prot. 8, fols. 378r and 379r. For their requests regarding the nuns' consecration, see ASV, VR, posiz. 1607, A–B, posiz. 1613, B–F, Reg. regular. 8 (1607–8), fol. 55v, and 14 (1613), fol. 132r.

25. On the *exclusio propter dotem* and its fifteenth-century interpretation, see Thomas Kuehn, "Some Ambiguities of Female Inheritance Ideology in the Renaissance," *Continuity and Change* 2 (1987): 11–36; reprinted in *Law, Family, and Women:*

Toward a Legal Anthropology of Renaissance Italy (Chicago: University of Chicago Press, 1991), 238–57.

26. The Zani family was also part of the network around Santa Cristina. The Palazzo Zani was just down the street from Palazzo Vizzani, at via Santo Stefano 56 (now Palazzo Rossi). The Zani also had strong family ties at Santa Cristina, where several family members were *professe.*

27. Proof of Ludovico Vizzani's remarriage appears in BCB, MS B700, no. 150, and ASB, Notarile, Sturoli Ventura, Prot. 1, fol. 2r, dated 21 Oct. 1610, where "Elena d[e] zanis" is named as Ludovico Vizzani's wife. Elena lived on until Aug. 1636 (see BCB, MS B913: 255.3). For the records of the deaths of Ludovico and Dioniggio Vizzani, see ibid.: 254.2. For the legitimation of Angelo Michele, son of Dioniggio di Ludovico Vizzani, by Ludovico Vizzani and the subsequent litigation with Lucrezia and Isabetta Vizzani, see ASB, Famiglia Banzi, busta 8, nos. 104–8. Angelo Michele at least came from the highest class of illegitimates, the *naturales,* born in a long-term relationship of marriageable parents. See Thomas Kuehn, "Reading between the Patrilines: Leon Battista Alberti's *Della famiglia* in Light of His Illegitimacy," in *Law, Family, and Women,* 160. See also id., " 'As if Conceived within a Legitimate Marriage': A Dispute Concerning Legitimation in Quattrocento Florence," ibid., 181.

28. Gabriella Zarri claims that by the early Seicento, such relationships of aunts and nieces became rare and the continuity of convent family groups began to weaken. See "Monasteri femminili e città (secoli xv–xviii)," in *Storia d'Italia: Annali,* 9: *La chiesa ed il potere politico dal Medioevo all'età contemporanea,* ed. Giorgio Chittolini and Giovanni Miccoli (Turin: Giulio Einaudi, 1986), 415.

29. Maria Clorinda Vizzana's dowry contract, in the amount of £6,000, survives in ASB, Demaniale 20/2881 (Santa Cristina), no. 15/V. Other copies survive ibid., 2/2863 (Santa Cristina), B/no. 25, and 12/2873 (Santa Cristina), no. 2/L. The convent's attempts to obtain back support, many years in arrears, are described ibid., 35/2896 (Santa Cristina), no. 4/H.H.

30. At the time of Cardinal Colonna's pastoral visit to Santa Cristina in November 1634, donna Teresa Pompea is mentioned, using her secular name, Elena, as one of two probationers (BUB, MS It. 206/2, no. 12, fol. 94r). For the dowry agreement of Teresa Pompea Vizzana, see ASB, Demaniale 51/5009 (Santa Cristina), fol. 9r. After her death on 13 June 1684, she was remembered as *in cantu peritia* (BCB, MS B921: 256); in 1666, she compiled a 552-page book of plainchant antiphons, hymns, and masses for the use of the choir. Formerly in the Biblioteca Ambrosini, it is now lost. Teresa Pompea Vizzana also commissioned Domenico Maria Canuti's *Martirio di Santa Cristina* for the chapel of the same name. See Malvasia, *Le pitture di Bologna,* 267/[181]. See also ASB, Giuseppe Guidicini Alberi genealogici, 123. For the details of the division of Pompeo Vizzani's estate, see ASB, Demaniale 18/2879 (Santa Cristina) nos. 3/5 and 7/5; see also ibid. 10/2871 (Santa Cristina) no. 24/K. Innumerable other related documents survive ibid. 2/2863 (Santa Cristina).

31. On the trials of Saint Christina, see Louis Réau, *Iconographie de l'art Chrétien,* 3: 1 (Paris: Presses universitaires de France, 1958), 302–4; also Marcello Moscini, *Cristina di Bolsena: Culto e iconografia* (Viterbo: Agnesotti, 1986). Imprisonment in a tower became a symbol for nuns' own imprisonment. On the symbolism of the

tower, see Beatrice del Sera, *Amor di virtù*, ed. Elissa B. Weaver (Ravenna: Longo editore, 1990), esp. 46–50.

32. For the listings of 1574, see ASV, VR, posiz. 1588, A–B. In the listing for 1588 in the same document, no income is given for Santa Cristina, although the copy of the document in AAB, Misc. vecchie 808 indicates an income of £4,400. See Roberta Zucchini, "Santa Cristina della Fondazza: Storia architettonica e storico artistica" (Tesi di laurea, Università di Bologna, 1987–88), 134. For the convent incomes of 1614, see ASV, Sacra Congregazione del Concilio, Visite ad Limina 136A, fol. 55r. The income of the convent of Santa Cristina, £15,400, lagged substantially behind the leader, in this case Sant'Agnese, with an income of £22,168. On the history of the convent of Santa Cristina, its architecture, and art, see Zucchini, "Santa Cristina della Fondazza," and Ugo Capriani, "Chiesa e convento di Santa Cristina della Fondazza in Bologna: Ipotesi di ricerca e recupero" (Tesi di laurea, Università di Bologna, 1987–88). I thank dottoressa Zucchini and dottore Capriani for providing me with copies of their theses, and for many other kindnesses over several years.

33. In 1622, the Congregation of Bishops, in a ruling to Cardinal Federico Borromeo of Milan, declared that nuns at the convent of Santa Maria Regina could be called *donna* instead of *suora* (ASV, VR, Reg. regular. 28 [1622], fol. 53r, dated 4 Mar. 1622). In Benedictine institutions, it was customary for professed nuns to be addressed as *donna,* whereas *converse* were called *suora.* See Robert Kendrick, "Genres, Generations and Gender: Nuns' Music in Early Modern Milan c. 1550–1706" (Ph.D. diss., New York University, 1993), 818, 820. On the early Camaldolese love of learning, see M. Elena Maghieri Cataluccio and A. Ugo Fossa, *Biblioteca e cultura a Camaldoli: Dal medioevo all'umanesimo* (Rome: Editrice anselmiana, 1979). See also Pagnani, *Storia dei Benedettini camaldolesi.* On the Camaldolese in later centuries, see Giuseppe M. Croce, "I Camaldolesi nel Settecento: Tra la 'rusticitas' degli eremiti e l'erudizione dei cenobiti," in *Settecento monastico italiano,* ed. Giustino Farnedi and Giovanni Spinelli (Cesena: Badia S. Maria Del Monte, 1990), 203–70.

34. In 1623, the *converse* Benedetta Pagani and Felice Tamarra claimed to have paid a total of £2,000; earlier *converse* had paid as little as £200. See ASB, Demaniale 48/2909 (Santa Cristina), no. 3/L (processo 1622–23), fols. 47v–48r, 50v, 52v. In 1623, the normal dowry of a *professa* was £5,550, of which £2,550 constituted the dowry, and the rest gifts and furnishings. See AAB, Misc. vecchie 820, no. 2 (processo 1622–23), fol. 18r.

35. Numerous cases of private servants accepted at San Guglielmo are recorded in ASB, Demaniale 80/814 (San Guglielmo). Convent slaves were most common on the Iberian peninsula. In 1607, for example, a convent in Cordoba was licensed to acquire three slaves, in accordance with past practice (BAV, MS Borg. Lat. 71, fol. 154v). In 1614, two ailing sisters at the convent of Santa Chiara in Amarente (Braga, Portugal) requested that their brother be permitted to buy them a Moorish slave, who would remain convent property after their deaths (ASV, VR, posiz. 1614, B–C). Convent slaves were also not unknown in the Veneto. In 1431 a woman at the convent of San Lorenzo in Venice stipulated in her will that her personal slave should be freed at age twenty-two. The woman seems to have been a secular living at San Lorenzo, not a *professa,* however. See Silvio Tramontin, *Storia della cultura*

veneta (Vicenza: Neri Pozza, 1976–85), 3/1: 453. I thank Elissa Weaver for this reference.

36. In 1618, the Congregation of Bishops had refused to permit the nuns of Santa Cristina to admit another servant nun, because the ratio was already 43 to 13. ASV, VR, Reg. regular. 21 (1618), fol. 242v.

37. The standard history of the Camaldolese order through the mid eighteenth century is Giovanni Benedetto Mittarelli and Anselmo Costadoni, *Annales Camaldulenses ordinis Sancti Benedicti* (Venice: Aere Monasterii Sancti Michaelis de Muriano, 1755–73). See also Pagnani, *Storia dei Benedettini camaldolesi;* also Croce, "I Camaldolesi nel Settecento."

38. Zucchini, "Santa Cristina della Fondazza," 12–13.

39. Caroline Walker Bynum, *Holy Feast and Holy Fast: The Religious Significance of Food to Medieval Women* (Berkeley and Los Angeles: University of California Press, 1987), 54.

40. Traversari, *Hodoeporicon,* 150–51. See also *Annales Camaldulenses,* vol. 3 (Venice, 1758), where Lucia is discussed on 345–48, and Enzo Lodi, *I santi della chiesa bolognese nella liturgia e pietà popolare* (n.p., 1987), 67–73.

41. The convent acquired the fragments at the time when the nuns effected the translation of Lucia's body from the high altar to a side chapel at Sant'Andrea di Ozzano in 1642. See ASB, Demaniale 44/2905 (Santa Cristina), "Per le sacre reliquie del corpo della Beata Lucia di Stifonte dell'ordine camaldolese."

42. The license by the bishop of Bologna, dated 9 Mar. 1245, to erect the convent in Bologna appears in ASB, Demaniale 12/2873 (Santa Cristina), no. 25/M. See also Ricci and Zucchini, *Guida di Bologna,* 59 and 221–22; Zucchini, "Santa Cristina della Fondazza," 53.

43. The indulgence for a new altar of Saint Catherine, dated 16 July 1529, survives in ASB, Demaniale 11/2872 (Santa Cristina), no. 33/L.

44. On the early fourteenth-century remodeling, see *Annales Camaldulenses,* vol. 5 (Venice, 1760), 340, and appendix, cols. 476–77. On Salosmaij, see Zucchini, "Santa Cristina della Fondazza," 167 n. 49, a list of the abbesses of the convent through the early sixteenth century, which indicates that she ruled until 1502. The convent necrology indicates her death in 1498, however, after she had ruled for thirty years (BCB, MS B921:35); her confirmation as abbess appears in ASB, Demaniale 6/2867 (Santa Cristina), no. 10/E. On the dating of the lower level of the cloister, see Capriani, "Chiesa e convento," 13.

45. Ricci and Zucchini, *Guida di Bologna,* 60.

46. ASB, Demaniale 51/5009 (Santa Cristina), fol. 11. On the nuns' complaint of 1529, see Guidicini, *Cose notabili,* vol. 5 (1873), 32.

47. Quoted in Zarri, "Monasteri femminili benedettini," 354–55.

48. Capriani, "Chiesa e convento," 81.

49. Ricci and Zucchini, *Guida di Bologna,* 48 and 60.

50. BCB, MS B921: 14.

51. Camaldoli MS 652, fol. 12r.

52. Details of the layout and use of rooms from Camaldoli MS 652, fols. 11r–v; for the chapel altar, see Capriani, "Chiesa e convento," 142.

53. Capriani, "Chiesa e convento," 76 and, for the painting of Beata Lucia, 141.

54. Ricci and Zucchini, *Guida di Bologna*, 60.

55. The two-story cells are described in Camaldoli MS 652, fol. 11v. Emilia Grassi seems to have had one of these, for in 1623 she remarked to pastoral visitors "I freely confess to having a lower closet, with the blessing of the mother abbess" ("Confesso bene haver' uno sotto Camerino con la Benedittione della Madre Abbadessa"). See AAB, Misc. vecchie 820, no. 2 (processo 1622–23), fol. 11r.

56. Zucchini, "Santa Cristina della Fondazza," 103–5: "Un' ancona con 4 quadretti di pittura, con cornici dorate, un crocifisso e la cartella della professione. Una lettiera fornita, 3 casse, un cassanino, un altarolo, un tavolino, una gelosia, l'Uscio, due Banzole dalla poggia, due scranne, un depanatore, uno scaldapiedi, un trepiedi in ferro ... col catino di maiolica. Una cassa di pioppa per li panni brutti. Un calamaro di noce fornito col sigillo. Duoi calcedri di rame, uno ordinario, et uno col spinello, una caldarina, un caldaroncino d'ottone per l'acqua Santa, una coperta zibata. Una di dobletto, et un panno, un candelieri di ottone col lumino. Quattro cossini di lana. ... Una paniera per cucire fornita, refe di più sorti n[umer]o 3, una portiera di corame, et una cortina di tela col ferro et anella, et una cortina per la fenestra, e la fenestra per la cella. Un Breviario, un Messale, un Salterio, un Martirologio, un Diurno, un Officio della B.V. e due libri volgari." Corrected against the original in BCB, MS B450, no. 7. For several copies of a similar list for Paola Zani, dated 1701, see ASB, Demaniale 43/2904 (Santa Cristina). Colomba Glavarini's furnishings are listed ibid., 18/2879 (Santa Cristina), no. 19/S, "Scritture delle RR.DD. Colomba et Aura Felice Giavarini."

57. Monica Felice Ariosti listed "due didali, un d'argento, e un d'avolio, un stuzo fornito d'argento e un con le cesure, Un sesto, e una penna d'argento, Un statolino [sic] d'argento, quatro Anele d'oro, Sei para di fiubbe d'argento, Una tazza d'argento, due para di Candelieri d'argento, un chochiare, e una forzina d'argento, Una Croce da Reliquie d'argento Un Calamare messo a Oro con il tinbrarino, e il sigillo d'argento, Sei Chiave con la Catena d'argento, Un Rosario e due corone fornite d'argento." Emilia Arali's inventory included "un Cardelino in Chabia." The inventories from Santa Margherita survive in ASB, Demaniale 51/3918 (Santa Margherita). That similar artwork decorated the cells at Santa Cristina is revealed by a list of some twenty sixteenth- and seventeenth-century paintings belonging to individual nuns, displayed for a festival in 1777. See Capriani, "Chiesa e convento," 146–47. The specific prohibition of mirrors and jewelry at Santa Cristina after the visitation of 1622–23 confirms the presence of similar "vanities" there. See AAB, Misc. vecchie 820, no. 2, "Ordini che si devono dare p[er] rimediare alle cose ritrovate nella Visita."

58. Quoted in Gabriella Zarri, "Recinti sacri: Sito e forma dei monasteri femminili a Bologna tra '400 e '600," in *Luoghi sacri e spazi della santità*, ed. Sofia Boesch Gajano and Lucetta Scaraffia (Turin: Rosenberg & Sellier, 1990), 386, 393 n. 28.

59. Capriani, "Chiesa e convento," 73.

60. These features are mentioned in Cardinal Colonna's visit of 1634. See ibid., 81–82.

61. On the gardens, see ibid., 83–85, 121–22; on processions to the chapels, see Camaldoli MS 652, fol. 11r; on Flaminia Bombacci's menagerie, see AAB, Misc. vecchie 820, no. 2 (processo 1622–23), fol. 6v.

62. Capriani ("Chiesa e convento," 77, 116) suggests that this may have been the cappella della Madonna della Vita. In 1688, however, don Giovanni Battista Reggiani, father confessor at Santa Cristina, testified that it was the chapel of the Rosary (ASB, Demaniale 30/2891 [Santa Cristina], FF no. 1). According to her memorial in the convent necrology, Lucrezia Vizzana was intensely devoted to the mysteries of the Rosary.

63. Guidicini, *Cose notabili*, vol. 2 (1869), 145. The only Caterina Vitali recorded in the convent necrology was only born in 1583, however, and only entered the convent in 1593 (BCB, MS B921: 49). Donna Ottavia Bolognetti survived until 1612, and donna Margarita Glavarini until 1619 (ibid.: 18 and 8).

64. Giuseppe Guidicini, *Miscellanea storico-patria bolognese*, ed. Ferdinando Guidicini (Bologna: Monti, 1872; repr., Bologna: Forni editore, 1972), 74.

65. Malvasia, *Le pitture di Bologna*, 266–68 [181–83].

66. Capriani, "Chiesa e convento," 23, 131.

67. These details appear chiefly in Malvasia, *Le pitture di Bologna*, 266–68 [181–83], and in Capriani, "Chiesa e convento," 125–39. For biographical details regarding Maura Taddea Bottrigari, who is named as donor of Carracci's painting in an inscription, see BCB, MS B921: 13. Details of Bottrigari's donation, following Malvasia and his dating of 1597, appear in Andrea Emiliani, "Ludovico Carracci," and Gail Feigenbaum, "Catalogo dei Depinti," in *Ludovico Carracci*, ed. A. Emiliani (Bologna: Nuova Alfa editoriale, 1993), lix, 96. The painting in its recently cleaned state is reproduced as plate 44.

68. Donna Ottavia Bolognetti died aged sixty-four in 1612. See BCB, MS B921: 4. Costanza Duglioli died in her sixties on 18 Aug. 1614. Ibid.: 28. The only description of Girolamo Bonigli's *Saint Christina* appears in Antonio Masini, *Bologna perlustrata*, 1: 629. Malvasia simply mentions the old altarpiece by Girolamo Bonigli, in speaking of its replacement (*Le pitture di Bologna*, 267/[181]). The sometime abbess, Margherita "de Javerinis," died on 20 Feb. 1619 (BCB, MS B921: 8); Columba "Clavarina" died on 20 Aug. 1643 (ibid.: 29); Aura Felix "de Clavarinis" lived until 14 July 1666, when she died aged eighty-four, after seventy years in the convent (ibid.: 26); a donna Giuliana Glavarini, who died in Dec. 1659 aged seventy-one (ibid.: 45), may have entered Santa Cristina too late to contribute to the commissions. Donna Angela Maria Zambeccara died in 1645 aged sixty-six; her memorial also recognizes her lavish donations of "gold, silver, and silk" (ibid.: 50). Isabella Malvasia is the only nun recorded in the convent necrology during this period who had the initials "I.M." and who was also a *reverenda madre*. In ASB, Demaniale 48/2909 (Santa Cristina), no. 3/L (processo 1622–23), fol. 52v, Dorothea Montecalvi claimed to have been at the convent for fifty-eight years. In a list of nuns who had entered Santa Cristina between 1553 and 1570, she is listed under 25 May 1567. No other Montecalvi appears in the list. See ibid., 43/2904 (Santa Cristina), "Qui all'incontro se metterà la memoria delle sore che sono venute in casa."

69. See Lucia Ferrante, Maura Palazzi, and Gianna Pomata, eds., "Introduzione," in *Regnatele di rapporti: Patronage e reti di relazione nella storia delle donne* (Turin: Rosenberg & Sellier, 1988), 26–27; see also Anna Benvenuti Papi, "Il 'patronage' nell'agiografia femminile," ibid., 201–16.

70. The connections of the altar with Saint Benedict appear in ASB, Misc. delle corporazioni religiosi soppresse 129, no. 69. The inclusion of the feast of Saint

Scholastica among the minor feasts at Santa Cristina appears in AAB, Misc. vecchie 262 I/615/11e.

71. Malvasia not only misidentified Lucia as Santa Monica, but also San Nicola of Bari as Sant'Agostino.

72. See Luke 1:40–56. The convent was granted a special indulgence for this altar on 2 October 1613. See ASB, Demaniale 11/2873 (Santa Cristina), no. 36/L.

73. Capriani, "Chiesa e convento," 50–51.

74. See H. Colin Slim, "Music and Dancing with Mary Magdalen in a Laura Vestalis," in *The Crannied Wall: Women, Religion, and the Arts in Early Modern Europe,* ed. Craig Monson (Ann Arbor: University of Michigan Press, 1992), 139–60.

75. Two additional statues by Giuseppe Mazza were only added in niches cut in the east wall, flanking the high altar, in 1688 (Capriani, "Chiesa e convento," 27): Saint Joseph (right) and Saint John the Baptist (left). It is not clear when the six-teenth-century terra-cotta half-figures of Saint Christina (right) and Saint Claire (left) were added; their presence in the church is only documented in this century (ibid., 37–38).

76. Zarri points out that the seven convent churches that, like Santa Cristina, also served as parish churches tended to be more elaborate. Four of these had more than five altars ("Recinti sacri," 394 n. 32). Santa Cristina had a total of nine altars in the external church.

2. LUCREZIA VIZZANA'S MUSICAL APPRENTICESHIP

1. Paolo Prodi, *Il cardinale Gabriele Paleotti (1522–1597)* (Rome: Edizioni di storia e letteratura, 1959–67), 1: 44–45, 230. In his lengthy and detailed study, Prodi does not concern himself to any extent with Paleotti's reform of the nunneries.

2. Craig Monson, "Molti concerti, poca concordia: Monache, parrocchiani, e musica nella chiesa e convento dei SS. Vitale e Agricola, 1550–1730." In *Vitale e agricola: Il culto dei protomartiri di Bologna attraverso i secoli nel xvi centenario della tras-lazione,* ed. Gina Fasoli (Bologna: EDB, 1993), 195.

3. See Stephen Ehses, ed., *Concilii Tridentini actorum pars sexta complectens acta post sessionem sextam (xxii) usque ad finem concilii (17. Sept. 1562–4. Dec. 1563)* (Freiburg: Herder, 1965), 1043, lines 33–37. In the discussion of the proposed decree, a few prelates rose to speak against it. A subsequent *summa censurarum* included the note "non prohibeantur cantus musici" (ibid., 1068, l. 43).

4. AAB, Misc. vecchie 804, fasc. 23, 3: "Li giorni delle feste si spendono in otio canto nel organo et musiche vane[.] . . . Conversationi et amicitie de Cantori[.] . . . Troppo tempo spendono in canti et suoni[.] Alcune cantatrici et organiste hano troppo liberta, et cantano et sonano cose vane[.] Cantano alle volte li cantori et le suore[.] Invitano li Magistrati la set[tima]na santa et alle compite paschali." Some comments in this document are cited in Gabriella Zarri, "Monasteri femminili e città (secoli xv–xviii)," in *Storia d'Italia: Annali, 9: La chiesa e il potere politico dal Me-dioevo all'età contemporanea,* ed. Giorgio Chittolini and Giovanni Miccoli (Turin: Giu-lio Einaudi, 1986), 391.

5. AAB, Misc. vecchie 804, fasc. 13, 1: "Alchuni Mon[aste]ri consumano molto tempo in cantar' et sonar' tenendo troppo stretta pratica de cantori, oltra che gli

dano grossi presenti et questi in alchuni Mon[aste]ri li giorni delle feste delle loro chiese entrano in Mon[aste]ro et cantano con l'istesse Monache." ("Some convents spend too much time in singing and playing, maintaining relationships that are too intimate with [male] singers, apart from the fact that they give them lavish gifts; and in some nunneries these [male] singers enter the nunneries on the feast days of their churches and sing with the nuns themselves.")

6. AAB, Misc. vecchie 808, fasc. 6, "Ordine da servarsi dalle suore nel loro cantare et musica": "L'esperienza dimostra che'l soverchio studio, del quale hoggidi le suore usano ne suoi canti, non solo non serve al fine, per lo quale la musica gli è stata permessa, di lodare Dio et eccitare se medesime alla contemplatione dell'armonia celeste; ma le impedisce da maggiori beni, et ingombra gli animi loro d'una perpetua distrattione: fagli spendere vanamente quel precioso tempo, del quale elle potriano più fruttuosamente valersi, et vagare col cuore fuori, mentre stanno col corpo ne sacri chiostri, nuderndo in se una ambitiosa voglia di piacere co suoi canti al secolo."

7. Original Italian cited in Craig Monson, "La prattica della musica nei monasteri femminili bolognesi," in *La cappella musicale nell'Italia della Controriforma,* ed. Oscar Mischiati and Paolo Russo (Cento: Centro studi G. Baruffaldi, 1993), 145–46. The meaning of *giorgiana* is unclear, but appears not to be a mistake for *gregoriano.* According to David Bryant (personal communication), the same word turns up in Venice as well, and does not appear to imply chant.

8. In the discussion of convent government in a manuscript entitled "Governo archiepiscopale di Bologna," prepared for the curia as a guide to diocesan administration, the recent reform of music is particularly singled out. See AAB, MS H537, fol. 25v. See also Paolo Prodi, "Lineamenti dell'organizzazione diocesana in Bologna durante l'episcopato del card. G. Paleotti (1566–1597)," in *Problemi di vita religiosa in Italia nel Cinquecento,* ed. M. Maccarrone, G. G. Meersseman, E. Passerin d'Etrèves, and P. Sambrin (Padua: Editrice Antenore, 1960), 354–55.

9. ASV, VR, posiz. 1607, A–B, letter dated 31 Jan. 1607: "Dal tempo, che son stato Coadiut[o]re et Arciv[escov]o hò p[er] esperienza provato che quello, che leva il spirito, la devotione, e pace nelli Monast[e]ri delle Monache è la Musica che contendono à garra di fare nel Choro de loro Monast[e]ri."

10. For a discussion of the abiding attempts by Gabriele and Alfonso Paleotti to control convent music, see Craig Monson, "Disembodied Voices: Music in the Nunneries of Bologna in the Midst of the Counter-Reformation," in *The Crannied Wall: Women, Religion, and the Arts in Early Modern Europe,* ed. Craig Monson (Ann Arbor: University of Michigan Press, 1992), 191–209. The remark of Geronimo del Trombone, "sua casa gravata particolarm[en]te di quattro figlie femine," appears in ASV, VR, posiz. 1609, A–M. This Geronimo del Trombone is almost certainly the well-known wind player and composer Girolamo Trombetti. My thanks to Carlo Vitali for pointing out this connection to me. See also Gian Lodovico Masetti Zannini, "Espressioni musicali in monasteri femminili del primo Seicento a Bologna," *Strenna storica bolognese* 35 (1985): 193–205.

11. BUB, MS It. 206/2, no. 5, a memorial commenting on Gozzadini's ban, a copy of which is included with it: "In tutte le città d'Italia si canta et fan[n]o concerti dalle monache nelle loro chiese eccettuate solamente la Citta di Bologna, . . . è di

p[rese]nte affatto distruta la Musica con tanto p[re]giuditio delle Virtuose, et Massime delle piu eminenti, le quali hanno impiegata la loro età et havere per acquistare Virtù tanto nobile per lodare S[ua] D[ivina] M[aestà] non essendo beni [*sic*] che . . . patischino cotanta mortificatione, Et Massime di quelle, che sono intrate ne i Monasterij per essercitare il talento loro donatoci [*sic*] dalla D[ivina] Bontà per lode sua." Other copies of Gozzadini's decree survive in ASB, Demaniale 48/ 4891 (Sant'Agostino), no. 23/1622; ibid., 104/3472 (San Lorenzo); ibid. 84/3233 (Santi Vitale et Agricola). Ludovisi's printed broadside survives ibid., 84/3233 (Santi Vitale et Agricola) and ibid., 48/4891 (Sant'Agostino), no. 22/1621. Neither prohibition escaped the notice of Bolognese observers of notable events in the city. The earlier ban is recorded in BCB, MS Gozz. 185, fol. 318, which assigns it to 1620; the latter ban is mentioned in BCB, MS B80: 21 and ibid., MS B3595: 109. Ludovico Ludovisi's biographer Lucantonio Giunti described the archbishop's ban on convent music as a chief aspect of the cardinal's conventual reforms. See BAV, Cod. Boncompagni-Ludovisi B8, fol. 15r.

12. Zarri, "Monasteri femminili e città," 386–87.

13. Quoted ibid., 386.

14. Quoted in Craig Monson, "Introduction," in *The Crannied Wall,* 2–3.

15. Monson, "Disembodied Voices," 191–92.

16. Quoted ibid., 194.

17. In 1621, Archbishop Ludovisi decreed that "espressamente comandiamo ad ogni persona tanto Ecclesiastico, come secolare, di che stato, grado, & conditione si sia, che per l'avvenire non ardisca, nè presuma di accostarsi à i Monasteri di Monache, tanto della Città, quanto della Diocese, nè à loro parlatorij, grade, porte, ruote, ò alle Chiese loro esteriori per cantare, sonare, o insegnare alle stesse Monache, ò secolari, che stanno in detti Monasteri, se bene siano soggetti à i Regolari, ò ascoltarle mentre provassero le loro Musiche in qualsi voglia occasione, anche delle Feste delle loro Chiese, ò di Funerali ancora in quelle Chiese, c'hanno annessa la Cura delle anime; nè farvi alcuna sorte di Musica, se bene fosse chiamata da' Confessori, Cappellani, ò da qual si voglia altra persona, ancorche ne havesse licenza." ASB, Demaniale 48/4891 (Sant'Agostino), no. 22/1621. "Acciò resti viva l'osservanza, ne alcuna possa allegare ignoranza." Ibid., 84/3233 (Santi Vitale et Agricola), order of 27 June 1686 (illegible—46?); cf. "accio non possa alcuna monica part[icola]re scusarsi di non haver havuto notitia di questa nostra monitione, et ordine" (ibid., order of 24 Dec. 1642).

18. This is clearly apparent from Prodi, *Il cardinale Gabriele Paleotti.* On analogies between reform attempts by Paleotti and Boncompagni, see Umberto Mazzone, "La visita e l'azione pastorali di Giacomo Boncompagni, arcivescovo di Bologna (1690– 1731)," *Cristianesimo nella storia* 4 (1983): 343–66.

19. Anthony David Wright, *The Counter-Reformation: Catholic Europe and the Non-Christian World* (New York: St. Martin's Press, 1982), 48. My thanks to Robert Kendrick for calling Wright's book to my attention.

20. Castagna, ASV, Legazione di Bologna, vol. 3, fol. 19v: "non senza molte lamentationi"; Boncompagni, ibid., fol. 51v: "à questo Publico par dura che vi sia quella pena di scommunica." See also ibid., vol. 182, fols. 128r, 293r, 363r.

21. Giovanni Boccadiferro's *Discorso sopra il governo delle monache* (c. 1550) emphasizes the number of girls forced into convents to preserve the family patrimony.

See Mario Fanti, *Abiti e lavori delle monache di Bologna* (Bologna: Tamari editore, 1972). For a detailed discussion of nuns as sacrificial victims to their families and the city, and their perceived public role, see Zarri, "Monasteri femminili e città." Virginity also had a long association with martyrdom, and the virgin with the sacrificial victim, reinforced in the case of nuns by their reception of a crown, another symbol of martyrdom, at their consecration. See Gabriella Zarri, "Orsola and Catherine: The Marriage of Virgins in the Sixteenth Century," in *Creative Women in Medieval and Early Modern Italy: A Religious and Artistic Renaissance*, ed. E. Ann Matter and John Coakley (Philadelphia: University of Pennsylvania Press, 1994), 237–78. For late-seventeenth-century expressions of nuns' "sacrifice," published in *La verginità consacrata* (1699), commemorating the consecration of nuns at Santa Cristina, see chapter 11. Daughters married off in order to fulfill their families' long-term social ambitions were also seen as sacrificial victims, of course, as Marina D'Amelia points out in "La conquista di una dote: Regole del gioco e scambi femminili alla Confraternità dell'Annunziata (secc. xvii–xviii)," in *Ragnatele di rapporti: Patronage e reti di relazione nella storia delle donne*, ed. Lucia Ferrante, Maura Palazzi, and Gianna Pomata (Turin: Rosenberg & Sellier, 1988), 305–306. I thank Anne Schutte for bringing this book to my attention.

22. For San Pietro Martire, see ASV, VR, posiz. 1585, A–B. For the reference to the nuns of Santissima Trinità, "quelle poverelle, che rinchiuse perpetuam[en]te dentro à quei muri meritano che le p[er]messo qualche solleva ancora," see ibid., posiz. 1586, A–C; Reg. episcop. 12 (1586/III), dated 2 May; Paleotti's comment, "et hora vedo ⟨⟩ vanno investigando nuove stra⟨⟩ fare q[ue]llo che si conviene," appears in Bologna, Archivio Isolani-Lupari, Fondo Paleotti, cartone 62, F32/5, lettere VIII (1586), fols. 135r–v. See also ibid., fol. 106r, for another relevant letter. Both letters are badly burned and incomplete.

23. AAB, Misc. vecchie 808, fasc. 2: "Prima, che si stia forte in non dar' licenza alli Maestri di Musica p[er] insegnar', . . . altrimente se si apre niente di strada, sarà la ruina di quelli Monasterij, che mai più si indiricciaranno bene."

24. ASV, VR, Reg. regular. 3 (1600–1601), fol. 93v, dated 2 May 1601: "Il conceder ciò a queste et no[n] all'altre monache le potesse essere di mala sodisfattione et anco di poco buon essempio."

25. Isabella d'Este: "quando andamo in lo ditto monestero et sentimo tanta discordantia, restamo molto offese nelle orechie et pocho consolate." I thank William Prizer for providing me with a copy of Isabella d'Este's letter, which survives in Mantua, Archivio di Stato, Archivio Gonzaga, Busta 2996, libro 30, fol. 15r (copialettere); the full text will appear in his forthcoming book on music in Mantua.

26. For the remarks regarding Ludovisi's prohibitions, "fà mestieri che un qualche gran Prencipe addimandi la gratia con efficatia molto grande perche il d[ett]o Monsig[no]re Ingoli è molto duro, con scusarsi che questa sia mente particolare di S[ua] B[eatitudine] et del Sig[no]r Cardinale Lodovisi," see BUB, MS It. 206/2, no. 5. For a useful discussion of how Florentine nuns exploited such patterns of clientage, see K. J. P. Lowe, "Female Strategies for Success in a Male-Ordered World: The Benedictine Convent of Le Murate in Florence in the Fifteenth and Early Sixteenth Centuries," *Studies in Church History* 27 (1990): 209–21.

27. Vittoria Pepoli, ASV, VR, sez. monache, 1662 (aprile–giugno): "Sò che s'ella mi voria far q[ues]ta gra[zia], nessuno de gl'altri impugnarà contro Il dir poi che

la Sac[ra] Cong[regazione] habbia pensiere di levar tutti gl'Organi alle Monache; so che à Roma tutti i Monasterij sonano e Cantano e non saprei che scandalo ne naschi, anzi s'accresce la divot[io]ne mentre tutto si fà à honor di Dio, e p[er] q[ues]to sò non seguirà l'adempim[en]to di si sofistiche oppinioni; mi scusi V[ostra] Em[inen]za s'io parlo con troppo libertà . . . Sig[no]r Cardinal patrone, son tanto obligata à questa beata Caterina, ch'io non posso di meno, di non essere importuna à V[ostra] E[minen]za." First read 3 Feb., rejected 16 Mar., then left to the vicar general to decide in a packet dated 23 June. The identification of Vittoria Pepoli is based on Pompeo Dolfi, *Cronologia delle famiglie nobili di Bologna* (Bologna: G. B. Ferroni, 1670; repr., Bologna: Forni editore, n.d.), 604.

28. The nuns spoke of "diversi maestri di lingue, cantare, è sonare, anche di età non conveniente in simili luoghi." ASV, VR, sez. monache, 1657 (settembre–dicembre), packet of 28 Sept. The vicar general responded that in the twenty-eight convents of the diocese, licenses had been granted to only two houses, for daughters of the illustrious Fantuzzi, Gessi, and Malvezzi families, who were surely capable of finding teachers of impeccable reputation. Ibid., letter of 19 Nov., in packet of 7 Dec.

29. Quoted in Monson, "Disembodied Voices," 202–3.

30. On Giovan Francesco da Bagno's donation, see Capriani, "Chiesa e convento di Santa Cristina della Fondazza in Bologna: Ipotesi di ricerca e recupero" (Tesi di laurea, Università di Bologna, 1987–88), 127. The remark of the confessor to the nuns of Sant'Agnese is recorded in M. Giovanna Cambria, *Il monastero domenicano di S. Agnese in Bologna: Storia e documenti* (Bologna: Tipografia SAB, 1973), 117.

31. ASB, Demaniale 120/1460 (San Giovanni in Monte), letter dated 3 Aug. 1583 from don Theodosio di Piacenza to don Arcangelo, abbot of San Giovanni in Monte: "E vero ch[e] ai giorni passati Dona Gentile come organista co[n] molta humilita si add[imand]o per gratia di poter' il giorno della lor festa far' un concerto sull'organo Io vedendo l'humilta co[n] ch[e] le addimandava . . . e lei e le compagne buone figliole et ubedienti m'inchinai à concederle ch[e] il giorno della festa potesse far' cantar' qualch[e] motetto co[n] una ò due voci humane al piu, prohibendole ogni sorte d'instr[ume]nto musicale, e no[n] estendendo la licenza piu oltra, ch[e] il giorno della festa di S[an]to lorenzo[.] Questa licenza l'ho datto perch[e] l'ho potuto dar', ateso ch[e] havendo io fatto le leggi le posso dispensar' e l'ho datta p[er]ch[e] mi è parso gratia ragionevole, p[er]ch[e] mi sono spechiato nell'ordini dell'Ill[ustrissi]mo paleoti, stampati l'anno 79 nei quali permette alle sue monache, ch[e] possano cantar' nell'organo co[n] una voce, s'io mi fossi contentato di due voci, no[n] è peccato in Spirito S[an]to. Ho giudicato anche ragionevolle questa gratia pensandomi co[n] questa mia di ne adolcir' in parte quelli animi exacerbati . . . ne mi par bene a rivocarla ne credo ch[e] habbi bisogno d'altra confirma[tio]ne V[ostra] r[everen]zia p[er]o potra [?—illegible] responder'a chi ce ne parlarà conforme à quanto io le scrivo."

32. The viol document survives in ASB, Demaniale 83/3232 (Santi Vitale et Agricola); the copy of Paleotti's rules and the inventories at Santa Margherita survive ibid., 51/3918 (Santa Margherita); a suor Angela Maria Rugieri brought a trombone and a bass viol with her to Santa Caterina in 1618 (ibid., 95/4021 [Santa Caterina]); Isabella Trombetta also brought her trombone with her to Santi Ger-

vasio e Protasio in 1576 (ibid., 32/6061 [Santi Gervasio e Protasio], record book, opening 48 and coverless record book, fol. 60). In 1600, in requesting license for outside trombone lessons from the Congregation of Bishops, the nuns of San Giovanni Battista claimed that they had customarily used various instruments and recently had introduced the trombone in their ensembles (ASV, VR, posiz. 1600, A–B). For trombones at Santa Cristina, see n. 50 below.

33. "Courtesans, Muses, or Musicians? Professional Women Musicians in Sixteenth-Century Italy," in *Women Making Music: The Western Art Tradition, 1150–1950,* ed. Jane Bowers and Judith Tick (Urbana and Chicago: University of Illinois Press, 1986), 108.

34. Jane Bowers offers comparative examples in support of this view in "The Emergence of Women Composers in Italy, 1566–1700," ibid., 124, 151 n. 49.

35. For discussions of various early modern women musicians who composed, see Newcomb, "Courtesans, Muses, or Musicians?" and Bowers, "The Emergence of Women Composers." On Barbara Strozzi, see Ellen Rosand, "Barbara Strozzi, *virtuosissima cantatrice:* The Composer's Voice," *JAMS* 31 (1978): 241–81, and id., "The Voice of Barbara Strozzi," in *Women Making Music,* ed. Bowers and Tick, 168–90. For an exemplary study of the Venetian courtesan with a few references to music, see Margaret F. Rosenthal, *The Honest Courtesan: Veronica Franco, Citizen and Writer in Sixteenth-Century Venice* (Chicago: University of Chicago Press, 1992).

36. Bowers, "The Emergence of Women Composers," 130.

37. Ambrogio Traversari: "Officium divinum nusquam studiosius in commune celebratur; nusquam peritius, & modulatius psallitur; nusquam, quantum ad Monasterium Virginum adtinet, suavis adfectus sum." Letter no. 73 to his brother Gironimo, 1433, in *Ambrosii Traversarii generalis Camaldulensium aliorumque ad ipsum, et ad alios de eodem Ambrosio latinae epistolae,* ed. Pietro Cannetti and Laurence Mehus, 2 (Florence: Typographico Caesareo, 1759; repr., Bologna: Forni editore, 1968), col. 555.

38. BCB, MS B921: 50: "*1640* 6 xbre D[onn]a Camilla Bombaci d'anni 70 organista prima e tre volte M[aest]ra delle Novizie indi Abbadessa." For her nomination as *maestra del choro,* see AAB, Misc. vecchie 820, fasc. 2 (processo, 1622–23), fol. 14r.

39. Petition from Catanzaro: "La Nobile Zitella Lucretia Vigliarolo in età di anni otto . . . desidera star sotto la Cura e direzzione di suor Margarita Almirante sua Zia materna, . . . nella q[ua]le ha fatto tanto profitto che canta l'Officio con le monache in Choro e legge in Tavola." ASV, VR, sez. monache, 1710 (gennaro–febraro), dated 21 Feb. 1710. For the ten-year-old at Santi Gervasio e Protasio, see ibid., 1668 (giugno–luglio), packet dated 8 June 1668. Ambrogio Traversari: "Puellam infantem sex ferme annorum in choro capitula, versus, orationes, responsoria memoriter dicere, ita ut in nullo offenderet, & aliam itidem decennem suavissime libuit admirari." *Ambrosii Traversarii . . . latinae epistolae* 2, col. 561. Gabriella Zarri coined the phrase *monache in miniatura* ("Monasteri femminili e città," 396).

40. Paula Dorothea Vitali, ASB, Demaniale 48/2909 (Santa Cristina), no. 3/L (processo 1622–23), fol. 19v: "nelle stantie à meggio di sopra vi sta la Maestra co[n] la Novitia à leggere et ca[n]tare di Canto fermo p[er] esser' separata dal Monasterio et no[n] impedire le Monache."

41. Jane Bowers managed to uncover only five women from musical families in "The Emergence of Women Composers," 312.

42. Giovanni Livi, "The Ferrabosco Family," *Musical Antiquary* 4 (1912–13): 139.

43. For Leonora Florida Ferrabosco, see BCB, MS B921: 141; for Prudenza Ferrabosco, see AAB, Archivio della Beata Caterina, 37/7: 255; Amfione Ferrabosco's cloistered daughters are mentioned in Maria Rosa Moretti, *Musica e costume a Genova tra Cinquecento e Seicento* (Genoa: Francesco Pirella editore, 1992), 131–33. My thanks to Robert Kendrick for bringing the reference to my attention. For Samaritana Vernizzi, see BCB, MS B922: unnumb. page; for Isabella Trombetti, see BCB, MS B919: 148, and ASB, Demaniale 32/6061 (Santi Gervasio e Protrasio), record book, opening 48. The cases of musical nuns from non-Bolognese musical families are too numerous to mention.

44. In Bologna, Anna Maria Cavalazzi, who joined Santi Bernardo ed Orsola as organist in 1644, had been taught by her aunt, the current organist, whom she succeeded in that post (ASV, VR, sez. monache, l'anno 1644 [gennaio–maggio], packet of 18 Mar.). A similar relationship may have existed between Marsibiglia Maria Vittoria Bolognini, musician and organist, who professed at Santa Cristina in 1683, and Maria Giuditta Ginevra Bolognini, a singer and future mainstay of the choir, who professed there in 1699. Examples from outside Bologna include an Anna, educated in singing and organ playing by her aunt, and accepted at the convent of Sant'Anna in Senigaglia in 1685 (ibid., 1685 [gennaio–marzo]), and several from Milanese convents, such as the musical Cozzolani at Santa Radegonda. On Milanese musical dynasties both within and across convent walls, see Robert Kendrick, "Genres, Generations and Gender: Nuns' Music in Early Modern Milan, c. 1550–1706" (Ph.D. diss., New York University, 1993).

45. "Ritrouandomi il giorno nel quale si solennizaua la festa della Gloriosa Santa Cristina nella Chiesa di V[ostra] Reuerentia, mentre si cantaua il primo Vespro, & sentendo con mio molto gusto, gli armonici Concerti di voci, Organi, & varij strumenti Musicali, guidati con soauissimi affetti di deuotione, procurai sapere da un Musico mio particolar amico (che iui era presente) chi era capo di detti Concerti, & dal detto fui raguagliato esserne V[ostra] Reuer[enza] & meritamente (disse) soggiungendomi, che oltre le altre sue honoratissime qualitadi, esser lei si nel cantare come al sonare molto intelligente tutto servendosene a laude, & gloria d'Iddio Benedetto; ... altro in ricompensa non desidero, solo che concertandogli all'occasioni, lei insieme con le sue care sorelle habbino in pensieri pregare Iddio per me nelle sue deuote & sante orationi." Adriano Banchieri, *Messa solenne a otto voci* (Venice: Ricciardo Amadino, 1599), fol. A1v.

46. For Emilia Grassi's tenure as *maestra del coro*, see AAB, Misc. vecchie 820, fasc. 2 (processo 1622–23), fol. 14r. BCB, MS B921: 5: "In primo Anno secundi trienii obiit maximo casu dolore Soror Nobiliss[i]ma huius Mon[aste]rii Abbadissa D. Emilia ex Ill[ustrissi]ma Familia de Grassis integritate maximo profund.e Virtutum ornatissima quæ præcipue in Instrumentorum omnium Musicalium pulsatione ita excelluit ut nulli secunda fuerit." Ruggeri's comments appear in Camaldoli MS 652, fol. 12v.

47. Gabriele Fattorini, *Secondo libro de motetti* (Venice: Ricciardo Amadino, 1601). A copy, missing the canto primo part, survives at the Archivio del duomo in Vercelli;

another copy of the canto secundo survives in the Biblioteka Jagiellónska in Kraków. I thank Robert Kendrick for first bringing this collection to my attention.

48. Giovanni Battista Biondi (*alias* Cesena), *Compieta con letanie che si cantano nella casa di Loreto, et motetti a otto voci, di s. Gio: Battista Cesena* (Venice: Giacomo Vincenti, 1606).

49. ASV, VR, posiz. 1607, A–B.

50. The movable screens in the organ lofts are mentioned in AAB, Misc. vecchie 820, fasc. 2, document dated 27 Apr. 1623. Ruggeri, Camaldoli MS 652, fol. 11v: "Sopra la loggia vi è un salone, qual risponde in Chiesa, ove le Monache fanno orazioni particolari, e in tempo di Feste, Cori di Musicha. . . . con due orghani in faccia, sonati di dentro dalle Monache, quali sempre si sono ingegnate con varij istromenti, di violini, tromboni, Arpe, e cosi simili."

51. On the presence of such keyboard intabulations of vocal pieces at the Bolognese convent of Sant'Agnese, and their possible use for accompaniment, see Craig Monson, "Elena Malvezzi's Keyboard Manuscript: A New Sixteenth-Century Source," *Early Music* 9 (1989): 73–128. For a detailed discussion of performance problems in all-female monastic choirs, and their possible solutions, see Kendrick, "Genres, Generations and Gender."

52. In Fattorini's case, the two choirs exploit comparable ranges (both choirs employ either soprano-alto-tenor-bass clefs, or treble-mezzosoprano-alto plus tenor or baritone clefs); Cesena contrasts a higher choir (soprano-alto-tenor-bass clefs) and a lower choir (most commonly alto-tenor-tenor-bass clefs; in one case mezzosoprano-tenor-tenor-bass; in another soprano-alto-tenor-bass).

53. When Archbishop Federico Borromeo sent a musical setting of Psalm 136 to suor Angela Flaminia Confaloniera at Santa Caterina in Brera in Milan, he suggested the text was suitable for anyone who longed to escape to heaven (Robert Kendrick, personal communication). The text is also a responsory for the fourth Sunday after Easter in *Breviarium monasticum secundum ordinem Camaldulensem* (Venice: Johannes Variscum, 1580), fol. 123v.

54. Robert Kendrick makes this point with reference to an echo piece by Giovanni Paolo Cima dedicated to Paola Ortensia Serbellona, a Milanese nun from the convent of San Vicenzo. See "Genres, Generations and Gender," 444. An alternative explanation was that Echo had been torn to pieces by shepherds driven mad by Pan, who had loved her in vain. Earth hid the pieces of Echo's body, which still reflect other sounds.

55. Ann Rosalind Jones, *The Currency of Eros: Women's Love Lyric in Europe, 1540–1620* (Bloomington: Indiana University Press, 1990), 28, 205 n. 41. Piccolomini's comments, cited in Jones, appear in *Della institutione di tutta la vita dell'uomo nato nobile e in città libera* (Venice, 1552).

3. INFLUENCES ON *COMPONIMENTI MUSICALI*

1. ASV, VR, posiz. 1606, A–C: "D. Felicita Stellini, D. Anna, et D. Armellina Uberti . . . tutte alquanto versate in musica, desiderose d'imparare à alcuni mottetti Spirituali alla Romana supp[lica]no humilmente le S[igno]rie V[ostre] Ill[ustrissi]me; che voglino conceder licentia al Can[on]ico Manzini di detta Città,

che possa andare una volta sola, ò due al più alli publici parlatorij per discorrere, et insegnare alle sud[et]te monache il modo, come vanno cantati, . . . con l'intervento della M[ad]re Badessa et delle deputate Ascoltatrici."

2. See Craig Monson, "Disembodied Voices: Music in the Nunneries of Bologna in the Midst of the Counter-Reformation," in *The Crannied Wall: Women, Religion, and the Arts in Early Modern Europe*, ed. Craig Monson (Ann Arbor: University of Michigan Press, 1992), 191–209.

3. AAB, Misc. vecchie 820, fasc. 2, "Visitatio localis Ecclesie et Monasterij Monialiu[m]. S. Christine. Bonon." The remedies demanded after the visitation of 1623 were only partially successful, for after Archbishop Girolamo Boncompagni's pastoral visitation of 1654, he decreed "Alle finestre delli Organi si levino li Cartoni, e vi si ponghino tavole permanenti." BUB, MS It. 231/1, fols. 8r–v; see also AAB, Misc. vecchie 262, for another copy of Boncompagni's decree.

4. For the inventories from Santa Margherita, see ASB, Demaniale 51/3918 (Santa Margherita); for the musical bequest at San Guglielmo, see ibid. 80/814 (San Guglielmo), entry no. 21.

5. See Gaetano Gaspari, *Musica e musicisti a Bologna* (Bologna: Forni editore, n.d.), 170–75.

6. ASB, Demaniale 31/2892 (Santa Cristina), fol. 128r. See also BCB, MS B921: 46.

7. ASB, Demaniale 48/2909 (Santa Cristina), no. 3/L (processo 1622–23), esp. fol. 11r.

8. For Porta's license, see ASB, Demaniale 26/7756 (San Michele in San Giovanni in Persiceto). For the abbess's testimony, see AAB, Misc. vecchie 820, fasc. 2 (processo 1622–23), fol. 15r.

9. ASB, Demaniale 48/2909 (Santa Cristina), no. 3/L (processo 1622–23), fol. 39r: "si da la p[ro]visione all'organista p[er]ch[e] vi sono tre organiste alla q[u]ale da l'Intavolatura." Bocchi's vague wording might also imply that Vernizzi gave them musical scores.

10. Carlo Ginzburg, *The Cheese and the Worms: The Cosmos of a Sixteenth-Century Miller*, trans. John Tedeschi and Anne Tedeschi (Baltimore: Johns Hopkins University Press, 1980).

11. It is interesting that the juxtaposition of third-related chromatic chords represents the most striking feature of her style singled out by Jerome Roche, "Orsina, Lucretia," in *The New Grove Dictionary of Music and Musicians*, ed. Stanley Sadie (London: Macmillan, 1980), 13: 874.

12. Banchieri also introduces the device, again for expressive effect, in the Creed at "ex Maria Virgine." It appears for coloristic effect in the *Te Deum* at "tibi coeli et universae terrae."

13. AAB, Misc. vecchie 820, fasc. 2 (processo 1622–23), fol. 15r: "V'è anco Ottavio Vernitio Mastro della Musica ch[e] scrive delle cose da sonare cioè, Canzoni et simili."

14. On Capello, see Jeffrey Kurtzman, "Giovanni Francesco Capello: An Avant-gardist of the Early Seventeenth Century," *Musica disciplina* 31 (1977): 155–82. Leaps from dissonances turn up in three motets from the *Sacrorum concentum* (1610), in five from *Motetti opera quarta* (c. 1612–13), and in four from *Motetti in*

dialogo (1613). I thank Professor Kurtzman for kindly allowing me to examine his transcriptions of Capello's complete works. There is nothing to connect Capello with Bologna. One cannot rule out the possibility that Vizzana might have had a chance to examine copies of these publications. The rhetorical transposed repetition of a leap from the seventh at the opening of her *O si sciret stultus mundus* offers an interesting parallel to the opening of Capello's *Tristis est anima mea.*

15. Isolated examples appear as early as the *Sacrae cantiunculae* and the six-voice mass, however. See Hellmut Federhofer, "Die Dissonanzbehandlung in Monteverdis Kirchenmusikalischen Werken und die Figurenlehre Christoph Bernhard," in *Claudio Monteverdi e il suo tempo: Relazioni e comunicazioni,* ed. Raffaello Monterosso (Verona: Valdonega, 1968), 464–66.

16. For Gary Tomlinson's exploration of Monteverdi's own experiments with the leap from a suspended seventh, and his increasing sophistication in its use, see *Monteverdi and the End of the Renaissance* (Berkeley and Los Angeles: University of California Press, 1987), 121.

17. Denis Arnold, "Monteverdi: Some Colleagues and Pupils," in *The New Monteverdi Companion,* ed. Denis Arnold and Nigel Fortune (London: Faber & Faber, 1985), 115–16. Saracini's collection was dedicated to Monteverdi.

18. Of the substantial literature on the Monteverdi-Artusi controversy, particularly useful is Claude V. Palisca, "The Artusi-Monteverdi Controversy," in *The New Monteverdi Companion,* 127–58. See also Gary Tomlinson, *Monteverdi and the End of the Renaissance,* 21–30, 106–9. See also Suzanne Cusick's fascinating interpretation of the gendered rhetoric of Artusi and Monteverdi, "Gendering Modern Music: Thoughts on the Monteverdi-Artusi controversy," *JAMS* 46 (1993): 1–25.

19. *Adriano Banchieri: Conclusions for Playing the Organ (1609),* trans. Lee R. Garrett, Colorado College Music Press Translations, vol. 13 (Colorado Springs: Colorado College Music Press, 1982), 50–51.

20. Quoted in Denis Stevens, *The Letters of Claudio Monteverdi* (Cambridge: Cambridge University Press, 1980), 211, which also summarizes the Monteverdi-Banchieri contacts. Banchieri printed the statutes for his academy in his *Cartella musicale* (Venice: Giacomo Vincenti, 1614). For a full translation of them, see Clifford A. Cranna, Jr., "Adriano Banchieri's *Cartella musicale* (1614): Translation and Commentary" (Ph.D. diss., Stanford University, 1981), 25–36. Amid the contrafacta by Monteverdi, Coppini had also included one by Banchieri, who thanked him effusively for doing so in his *Lettere armoniche* (Bologna: Girolamo Mascheroni, 1628; repr., Bologna: Forni editore, n.d.), 121.

21. See Margaret Ann Rorke, "Sacred Contrafacta of Monteverdi Madrigals and Cardinal Borromeo's Milan," *ML* 65 (1984): 175. I thank Professor Rorke for lending me her copies of the Coppini prints, and Robert Kendrick for originally calling my attention to the link between Coppini's collection and Milanese nuns.

22. See Giuseppe Vecchi, *Le accademie musicali del primo seicento, e Monteverdi a Bologna* (Bologna: A.M.I.S., 1969), 73–92, for a discussion of Banchieri's academy and Monteverdi's contacts with it. See also Stevens, *The Letters of Claudio Monteverdi,* 211–12. The primary information regarding Monteverdi's contact with Banchieri and his academy derives from Banchieri's two letters to Monteverdi included in *Lettere armoniche,* 141, with the second letter added in the appendix to the new edition of 1630.

23. February 7 was the anniversary of the translation of Saint Romuald's body to Fabriano. A "Libro, nel quale vengono notate diverse memorie attinenti al Camerlingato," dated 1728, which records the customary chapel expenses, includes the note, "A di 7 Febraro. Festa del nostro P.S. Romualdo Il Monas[te]r[o] fà Cantare la Messa Aparata" (ASB, Demaniale 26/2887 [Santa Cristina]). The same expense book also includes the feast of Saint Romuald on June 19. In 1640 and 1666, Antonio di Paolo Masini had also indicated that it was customary to celebrate the feast on February 7 (*Guida spirituale che serve ogni giorno in perpetuo per visitare tutte le chiese di Bologna* [Bologna: per Giacomo Monti & Carlo Zenero, 1640], 35, and *Bologna perlustrata,* third printing [Bologna: Erede di Vittorio Benacci, 1666], 225, respectively).

24. Monteverdi's younger son, Massimiliano, also studied in Bologna during the 1620s, taking his degree in medicine in 1626. The details of the Monteverdi sons' stays in Bologna appear in Vecchi, *Le accademie,* 80–82, 91 n. 88; see also Stevens, *The Letters of Claudio Monteverdi,* 142–44, 211–14, 240–43.

25. Aquilino Coppini had also been in contact with Bologna in the years immediately after the Monteverdi-Artusi controversy. In 1609, he had written to Vincenzo Cavalli of Bologna, inquiring after Artusi, "who lashed out at the divine Claudio Monteverdi's music, and published something from the Cavaliere Butrigarius [Bottrigari] aimed against him." Quoted in Claudio Sartori, "Monteverdiana," *MQ* 38 (1952): 406.

4. MUSIC, ART, AND RITUAL IN *COMPONIMENTI MUSICALI*

1. Thomas J. Heffernan, *Sacred Biography: Saints and Their Biographers in the Middle Ages* (Oxford: Oxford University Press, 1988), 80.

2. "Sicut lilium inter spinas, sic vera sponsa inter filias. Tu quoque imitare vestigia eius, si sponsa Verbi esse desideras." Jean Leclercq and Jean-Paul Bonnes, "Lettre a une moniale," in *Un Maître de la vie spirituelle aux xie siècle: Jean de Fécamp* (Paris: Librairie philosophique J. Vrin, 1946), 206.

3. I thank Robert Kendrick for recognizing the concordance in Cozzolani's motet and calling it to my attention. On Cozzolani's work, see Robert Kendrick, "Genres, Generations and Gender: Nuns' Music in Early Modern Milan, c. 1550–1706" (Ph.D. diss., New York University, 1993).

4. Adriano Banchieri's *Vezzo di perle* (1610) contains as many as eighteen Song of Songs settings. There were at least 129 settings in the Milanese repertory of the period. See Robert Kendrick, " 'Sonet vox tua in auribus meis': Song of Songs Exegesis and the Seventeenth-Century Motet," *Schütz Jahrbuch* 16 (1994): 99–118.

5. Gasparo Bombacci, BUB, MS It. 3856: 134: "facondia di lingua, e di penna, perche havendo congiunta alla naturalezza della sua circospetta eloquenza la cognitione dell'idioma latino, parlò sopra l'ordinaria capacità del sesso, e compose dottissimi sermoni, e Discorsi spirituali." On donna Flaminia's talents, see also Camaldoli MS 652, fols. 19r–20r.

6. BCB, MS B921: 50–51: "Latino pariter, ac Etrusco sermone sic prædita ut eloquentissimos, doctissimosque viros in sui admirationem traheret."

7. See *Breviarium monasticum secundum ordinem Camaldulensem* (Venice: Johannes Variscum, 1580), fol. 126v. The opening words also appear as an antiphon in the common of confessors, not bishops, in the Camaldolese breviary. See ibid., Sanctuarium per totum annum, fol. 183r.

8. The festival was celebrated in May, not on 24 July, as in the modern calendar.

9. A motet with the same title appears in Gabriello Puliti's *Sacræ Modulationes* (Parma: Erasmus Viothus, 1600); otherwise the text is completely different. My thanks to Robert Kendrick for calling it to my attention.

10. Ugo Capriani, "Chiesa e convento di Santa Cristina della Fondazza in Bologna: Ipotesi di ricerca e recupero" (Tesi di laurea, Università di Bologna, 1987–88), 137.

11. "Nam cum pervenisset ad partes Arretini territorii locum idoneum huic proposito cupiens invenire, occurrit ei quidam vir nomine Maldulus dicens se campum habere amoenum in alpibus positum. Ubi cum aliquando dormiret, instar Jacob patriarchæ scalam vidit excelsam, coelum quasi suo vertice tangentem, per quam splendentium atque albescentium videbatur ascendere multitudo. Quo audito, vir Dei, tamquam divino illustratus oraculo, mox campum petiit, locum vidit, cellas ibidem construxit." Giovanni Benedetto Mittarelli & Anselmo Costadoni, *Annales Camaldulenses*, vol. 3 (Venice, 1758), appendix, col. 518, from "Beati Rodulphi constitutiones."

12. Anacleto Guadagnini, *R. Pinacoteca di Bologna* (Bologna: Stab. tip. Zamorani e Albertazzi, 1906), 80; Enrico Mauceri, *La Regia Pinacoteca di Bologna* (Rome: Libreria dello stato, 1935), 36; Rosalba D'Amico and Marzia Faietti, *Le pubbliche virtù: Donazioni e legati d'arte alla Pinacoteca Nazionale di Bologna (1803–1982)* (Bologna: Edizioni Alfa, 1983), 86; Carla Bernardini et al., *La Pinacoteca Nazionale di Bologna* (Bologna: Nuova Alfa editoriale, 1987), 6.

13. On the current attribution and provenance, see Bernardini, *La Pinacoteca Nazionale*, 5–8; for Mittarelli's and Costadini's description, see *Annales Camaldulenses*, 1: 346–52. For details on Savorgnan's collection, see d'Amico and Faietti, eds., *Le pubbliche virtù*, 28 and 86. On the translation of Beata Lucia, see *Annales Camaldulenses*, vol. 3 (Venice, 1758), 347. The breve of Gregory XIII for the translation of Lucia's relics appears in ASB, Demaniale 2/2863 (Santa Cristina), no. 11/B.

14. "Pariter in paroecia sancti Andreæ Ozzani, unita asceterio monialium sanctæ Christinæ Bononiæ, servatur vetus tabula altaris coloribus expressa seculo XIV. in cujus angulo conspicitur sanctus Romualdus alba cuculla indutus dormiens prope scalam, summitate sua coelo innixam, quam scandunt monachi aliquot alba veste contecti. Forte pertinuit ipsa tabula ad veterem ecclesiam sanctæ Christinæ non longe a castro Septem-fontium, quæ duobus milliaribus distabat ab ecclesia paroeciali sancti Andreæ, & ubi olim degebant nostræ moniales sanctæ Christinæ Bononiam translatæ." *Annales Camaldulenses*, vol. 1 (Venice, 1755), 348. G. F. Rambelli, "Sant'Andrea di Ozzano di Sopra," in *Le chiese parrocchiali della diocesi di Bologna: Ritratte e descritte*, vol. 2 (Bologna: Litografia di Enrico Corty, tipografia di San Tommaso d'Aquino, 1847; repr., Bologna: Forni editore, 1976), no. 76. Savorgnan's presence in Bologna can be traced back to at least 1737, when he is mentioned in a document in ASB, Demaniale 6027 (Santa Maria in Galliera), Som. I, no. 3, fol. 411. Savorgnan's will was drafted 30 May 1776, with a codicil drafted 27 November. My thanks to dott. Giampiero Cammarota for this information.

15. The nuns donated an eighteenth-century gilded "Holy Image of Our Lady of Sorrows," which was later brought back to Bologna for restoration of the gilding by Antonio Lama and subsequently returned to Sant'Andrea, where G. F. Rambelli noted its presence and attribution to Scandellari in 1847. See Capriani, "Chiesa e convento," 188–89, which quotes from ASB, Demaniale 44/2905 (Santa Cristina). For the presence of the statue in the church, see Rambelli, "Sant'Andrea di Ozzano." A record of "Entrata e spesa generale" for 1770–71 includes the note, "Spese del riattamento della nostra chiesa di S. Andrea d'Ozano £27:18- Qual somma levato £30- ricevuto da un'ornato vecchio che era in detta chiesa." AAB, Misc. vecchie 262, I/615/11e.

16. See *Breviarium monasticum secundum ordinem Camaldulensem*, fol. 153v. Interestingly enough, Vizzana's choice of responsory text comes right after *Impetum inimicorum*, the text of the first motet in Gabriele Fattorini's *Secondo libro de motetti*, dedicated to Adeodata Leoni of Santa Cristina.

17. Anne Bagnall Yardley, "The Marriage of Heaven and Earth: A Late Medieval Source of the *Consecratio virginum*," *Current Musicology* 45–47 (1990): 305–24, esp. 311–12.

18. BCB, MS B1163: 180.

19. For the Vizzana sisters' requests regarding the Sacra, see ASV, VR, posiz. 1607, A–B, posiz. 1613, B–F, Reg. regular. 8 (1607–8), 55v, and Reg. regular. 14 (1613) fol. 132r.

20. See Jane Bowers, appendix to "The Emergence of Women Composers in Italy, 1566–1700," in *Women Making Music: The Western Art Tradition, 1150–1950*, ed. Jane Bowers and Judith Tick (Urbana and Chicago: University of Illinois Press, 1986), 162–64: Vittoria (= Raffaella?) Aleotti (1591, 1593), Caterina Assandra (1609, 1616), Claudia Sessa (1613), Sulpitia Cesis (1619).

21. See *Breviarium monasticum secundum ordinem Camaldulensem*, fol. 147v.

22. I am indebted to the late Jerome Roche for kindly finding this concordance, and the Milleville mentioned below, for me in his computer data base.

23. In 1616, on the other hand, Francesco Barnaba Milleville had published a cento combining these and other Song of Songs verses with the Magnificat, *Sonet vox tua & Magnificat insieme a 8 in concerto*, in his *Una messa in concerto*, op. 5. There is nothing that connects this work with Vizzana's motet, however.

24. On Clement's interpretation, see Robert A. Skeris, CHROMA THEOU: *On the Origins and Theological Interpretation of the Musical Imagery Used by the Ecclesiastical Writers of the First Three Centuries, with Special Reference to the Image of Orpheus* (Altötting: Verlag Alfred Coppenrath, 1976), esp. 54–65. Also cited in Ronald E. Surtz, *The Guitar of God: Gender, Power, and Authority in the Visionary World of Mother Juana de la Cruz (1481–1534)* (Philadelphia: University of Pennsylvania Press, 1990), 73.

25. See *Breviarium monasticum secundum ordinem Camaldulensem* (1580), Sanctuarium per totum annum, fol. 174v. Cf., in much the same spirit, Proverbs 16:24, "Favus mellis verba composita dulcedo animae et sanitas ossum" ("Ordered words are as the honeycomb, sweetness to the soul and health to the bones"). The same words had also been used by the fourteenth-century anonymous monk of Farne in an image Vizzana would also have found compelling, given her devotion to Christ's body and blood: "[He] opens his side to give us suck; and though it is blood he

offers us to suck we believe that it is health-giving and *sweeter than honey and the honey-comb.*" Quoted in Carolyn Walker Bynum, " . . . And Woman His Humanity: Female Imagery in the Religious Writing of the Later Middle Ages," in *Fragmentation and Redemption: Essays on Gender and the Human Body in Medieval Religion* (New York: Zone Books, 1991), 159.

26. Barbaro is quoted in Ann Rosalind Jones, *The Currency of Eros: Women's Love Lyric in Europe, 1540–1620* (Bloomington: Indiana University Press, 1990), 21. Barbo is quoted in Margaret L. King, "Thwarted Ambitions: Six Learned Women of the Renaissance," *Soundings* 59 (1976): 284.

27. Quoted in Margaret F. Rosenthal, *The Honest Courtesan: Veronica Franco, Citizen and Writer in Sixteenth-Century Venice* (Chicago: University of Chicago Press, 1992) . ¬ɔ.

28. Karma Lochrie, *Margery Kempe and Translations of the Flesh* (Philadelphia: University of Pennsylvania Press, c. 1991), 25.

29. Carlo Ginzburg, "Titian, Ovid, and Sixteenth-Century Codes for Erotic Illustration," in *Clues, Myths, and the Historical Method,* trans. John and Anne C. Tedeschi (Baltimore: Johns Hopkins University Press, 1989), 93. According to Bartolomeo Caimi's *Interrogatorium sive confessionale* (1474), it was even a mortal sin to compose "cantiones vel sonetos . . . lascivia turpia et inhonesta ad provocandum."

30. See Suzanne Cusick, "Gendering Modern Music: Thoughts on the Monteverdi-Artusi Controversy," *JAMS* 46 (1993): 6–7.

31. This is especially clear in Mark 7:18–23.

32. Augustine: "Doctrina sapientiæ . . . ori cordis non carnis est dulcis" ("The doctrine of wisdom is sweet to the mouth of the heart, not of the flesh"); Gregory: "Librum vitæ ex palato cordis tangite, ut probantes eius dulcedinem amare valeatis" ("Touch the book of life from the palate of your heart, that, experiencing its sweetness, you may be able to love it"). Quoted in Leclercq and Bonnes, *Un Maître de la vie spirituelle,* 99 n. 3. Jean de Fécamp uses the expression specifically with reference to women religious: "Quando autem ista leguntur cum lacrimis et devotione nimis, tunc mitis lector ipso cordis palato sapit quid dulcedinis intus lateat" ("But when those are read with tears and devotion beyond measure, then the gentle reader knows from the palate of the heart what sweetness lies within it"). Angela of Foligno is quoted in Elizabeth Alvilda Petroff, *Consolation of the Blessed* (New York: Alta Gaia Society, 1979), 58. Angela of Foligno's choice of words is also strikingly similar to Saint Bonaventure's, near the beginning of the chapter on the remembrance of Christ's Passion from *De perfectione vitae ad sorores:* "We must picture to the eyes of our heart Christ dying on the Cross if we would prevent the fires of devotion within us burning themselves out." See *Holiness of Life: Being St. Bonaventure's Treatise "De perfectione vitae ad sorores",* trans. Laurence Costello, ed. Fr. Wilfrid, O.F.M., 2d ed. (St. Louis: B. Herder, 1928), 62. Compare also Hugo of Folieto's commentary on Revelation 10:11, "the word of God may begin by being sweet in the mouth of our heart" and Thomas of Celano on Thomas Aquinas, "whenever he read in the Sacred Books, and something was once tossed into his mind, he indelibly wrote it in his heart." Both quoted in Mary J. Carruthers, *The Book of Memory: A Study of Memory in Medieval Culture* (Cambridge: Cambridge University Press, 1990), 169, 174.

33. Porta's use of the words in his motet, *Surge amica mea speciosa mea,* is introduced later in this chapter.

34. All cited in Surtz, *The Guitar of God*, 63–64. According to Pseudo-Origen, "The trumpet is the contemplative mind, the mind which has accepted spiritual teaching" (see James McKinnon, *Music in Early Christian Literature* [Cambridge: Cambridge University Press, 1987], 39), likewise appropriate for Vizzana's reception in the "ears of my heart."

35. Various examples are presented in Surtz, *The Guitar of God*, 66.

36. McKinnon, *Music in Early Christian Literature*, 32, 35.

37. Surtz, *The Guitar of God*, 62–85; Hildegard is quoted in n. 3. For a discussion of the dangerously "open" female body, see Lochrie, *Margery Kempe and Translations of the Flesh*, esp. 19–27.

38. "Audivi voces in caelo, tanquam tonitrui magni . . . " See *Breviarium monasticum secundum ordinem Camaldulensem*, fol. 118v.

39. "Citharoedorum" refers to those who play the kithara as accompaniment to their voices, as opposed to "citharista," a simple player. See Charlton T. Lewis, *A Latin Dictionary Founded on Andrews' Edition of Freund's Latin Dictionary* (Oxford: Clarendon Press, 1980), 345.

40. Gabriella Zarri, "Recinti sacri: Sito e forma dei monasteri femminili a Bologna tra '500 e '600," in *Luoghi sacri e spazi della santità*, ed. Sofia Boesch Gajano and Lucetta Scaraffa (Turin: Rosenberg & Sellier, 1990), 389.

41. My thanks to Robert Kendrick for pointing out to me the relationship of the verse to the liturgy of Saint Scholastica. Songs of Songs 2:14 is not cited, however, in *Breviarium monasticum secundum ordinem Camaldulensem* (1580). The reference to the dove is particularly apt in that context, since Scholastica's soul was observed ascending into heaven in the form of a dove. See Gregory the Great, *Dialogues*, vol. 2, trans. Paul Antin, ed. Adalbert de Vogüé (Paris: Editions du Cerf, 1979), 234–35.

42. AAB, Misc. vecchie 262, I/615/11e: "Per le altre Feste minori, cioe di S. Placido, S. Mauro, S. Scolastica, e S. Geltrude, fà parimente celebrare dà 30 Messe in circa."

43. Cima's setting is discussed in Kendrick, "Genres, Generations and Gender," 441–45. Kendrick points out that Cima reinforces the conceit by making his setting an echo piece. See also Kendrick's " 'Sonet vox tua in auribus meis': Song of Songs Exegesis and the Seventeenth-Century Motet."

44. From Giovanbattista Marino, *La musica: Diceria seconda sopra le sette parole dette da Cristo in croce*, in *Dicerie sacre e la strage de gl'innocenti*, ed. G. Pozzi (Turin: Einaudi, 1960), at 330–31, quoted in Kendrick, "Genres, Generations and Gender," 441–45.

5. VIZZANA'S THEMES OF PERSONAL PIETY

1. Peter Burke, citing Emile Mâle, has commented on the extent to which seventeenth-century Catholic art reiterated themes that had provoked Protestant protest. See "Sacred Rulers, Royal Priests: Rituals of the Early Modern Popes," in *The Historical Anthropology of Early Modern Italy* (Cambridge: Cambridge University Press, 1987), 181.

2. Gasparo Bombacci's remark, "Ho letto in suo bellissimo sermone in honore del santissimo sacramento, alla frequenza del quale essendo superiora dispose la divotione di quasi tutte le monache," appears in BUB, MS It. 3856: 134; for the

testimony of donna Flaminia's father confessor, see also Camaldoli MS 652, fol. 19r. For Adeodata Leoni's testimony, see ASB, Demaniale 48/2909 (Santa Cristina), no. 3/L (processo 1622–23), fol. 20r, "li S[antissi]mi Sacrame[n]ti si freque[n]tano al prese[n]te più ch[e] si sia mai fatto."

3. Some of the modest word play (*fervore fervido* and *Quaeret . . . quaerere* versus *Quaerat . . . quaerere*) reflects the sort of thing apparent in other texts apparently unique to the collection.

4. See Caroline Walker Bynum, "Women Mystics and Eucharistic Devotion in the Thirteenth Century," in *Fragmentation and Redemption: Essays on Gender and the Human Body in Medieval Religion* (New York: Zone Books, 1991), esp. 129–34; also "The Female Body and Religious Practice in the Later Middle Ages," ibid., 192. I have appropriated Bynum's words, "profound stillness," used in another context, because they seem so aptly to characterize the beginning of Vizzana's affective moment.

5. On this sort of relationship between time and meter, see Emma Mellard Kafalenos, "Possibilities of Isochrony: A Study of Rhythm in Modern Poetry" (Ph.D. diss., Washington University in St. Louis, 1974).

6. The symbolism is discussed in Joseph A. Jungmann, S.J., *The Mass of the Roman Rite: Its Origins and Development*, trans. Francis A. Brunner (Westminster, Md.: Christian Classics, 1986), 2: 38–40, 62–65. Jungman traces the crucifixion analogy back at least to Saint Ambrose.

7. Caroline Walker Bynum, "The Body of Christ in the Later Middle Ages: A Reply to Leo Steinberg," in *Fragmentation and Redemption*, esp. figs. 3.10–3.11, 110–111; and id., "The Female Body," esp. figs. 6.5–6.7. Another visual interpretation particularly apt for the convent some two centuries before Vizzana's time appears in "La Sainte Abbaye" (British Library MS 39843), fol. 29r, in which a nun kneels before an altar on which a chalice collects the water and blood from the wounds of Christ, who swoops down toward her from the clouds. The miniature is illustrated in Jeffrey F. Hamburger, *The Rothschild Canticles: Art and Mysticism in Flanders and the Rhineland circa 1300* (New Haven: Yale University Press, 1990), fig. 187.

8. Elizabeth Alvilda Petroff, *Consolation of the Blessed* (New York: Alta Gaia Society, 1979), 172.

9. Bynum, "Women Mystics," 129, and "The Female Body," 206 and fig. 6.8, 211.

10. Elizabeth Alvilda Petroff, *Medieval Women's Visionary Literature* (New York: Oxford University Press, 1986), 151. The Hildegard quotation is from *Scivias*. Compare Umiltà of Faenza's exclamation from her *Sixth Sermon in Honor of Jesus Christ*, "O my sweetest Christ, who are my only hope, come to me, and do not delay. Visit my heart that has such need of divine love. Fill it with divine grace, and cause my mind and my soul to be joined and burn always in you who are flame without smoke, wholly resplendent . . . O sweet resplendent Jesus, flame of charity, enflame me with your love and make me luminous like a torch that can cast brightness into any kind of darkness." Ibid., 251.

11. An interesting local affirmation of the appropriateness of that theme for women is provided by Ottavio Vernizzi's *Jesu dulcissime fili David* (1612), which combines phrases from the Song of Songs with images from the Passion, and is made unequivocally feminine at its conclusion: "Jesu dulcissime fili David, quam suavia

sunt vulnera tua, quam fulget aspectus oris tui. Amore langueo dum te sanguine perfusum in crucem pendentem conspicio. *Miserere mei in tua misericordia confidens peccatricis indigne.*" ("O Sweetest Jesus, son of David, how sweet are your wounds, how the appearance of your face gleams. I languish with love, while I contemplate you hanging upon the Cross, bathed in blood. *Have mercy upon me, an unworthy [female] sinner, trusting in your mercy.*") Emphasis added.

12. Caroline Walker Bynum, " . . . And Woman His Humanity: Female Imagery in the Religious Writings of the Later Middle Ages," in *Fragmentation and Redemption,* 152–53.

13. Illustrated in Carla Bernardini et al., eds., *La Pinacoteca Nazionale di Bologna: Catalogo generale delle opere esposte* (Bologna: Nuova Alfa editoriale, 1987), 51.

14. Ugo Capriani, "Chiesa e convento di Santa Cristina della Fondazza: Ipotesi di ricerca e recupero" (Tesi di laurea, Università di Bologna, 1987–88), 142, 145, "una bella immagine di N[ostro] S[ignore] a Che le monache visitano ogni sabato per gli ordinari." On the miraculous image, see AAB, Misc. vecchie 820, fasc. 2 (processo 1622–23), fol. 10, the testimony of Emilia Grassi, who dates the miracle to 1613. The abbess gives the date as 1614 (ibid., fol. 19v). Both the abbess and Cecilia Bianchi complained that during prayers after meals before the crucifix, the nuns suffered from the heat in summer and the cold in winter (ibid., fols. 2v and 19v).

15. For Margaret of Faenza, see Petroff, *Medieval Women's Visionary Literature,* 12; for Domitilla Galluzzi, see E. Ann Matter, "The Personal and the Paradigm: The Book of Maria Domitilla Galluzzi," in *The Crannied Wall: Women, Religion and the Arts in Early Modern Europe,* ed. Craig Monson (Ann Arbor: University of Michigan Press, 1992), 92. On sweetness in the mouth and Agnes Blannbekin, see Bynum, "Women Mystics," esp. 126, 129.

16. Bynum, "Women Mystics," 130–31.

17. The opening two-thirds of the text appear more or less literally as the responsory and verse for matins on feria 4. See *Breviarium monasticum secundum usum Camaldulensem,* fol. 65v.

18. On biblical *imitatio,* see Jean Leclercq, *The Love of Learning and the Desire for God,* trans. Catharine Misrahi, 3d ed. (New York: Fordham University Press, 1982), esp. 71–77, and id., "La 'Lecture Divine,' " *La Maison-Dieu* 5 (1946): 21–33. See also John A. Alford, "Biblical *imitatio* in the Writings of Richard Rolle," *English Literary History* 40 (1973): 1–23, and Jeffrey F. Hamburger, *The Rothschild Canticles.*

19. McKinnon, *Music in Early Christian Literature,* 38.

20. Surtz, *The Guitar of God,* 72. Augustine's organological distinctions between psaltery and kithara and their theological interpretation are discussed in Henri Rondet, "Notes d'exégèse augustinienne: Psalterium et cithara," *Recherches de science réligieuse* 46 (1958): 408–15.

21. Pierre Salmon, *Analecta liturgica: Estraits des manuscrits liturgiques de la Bibliothèque vaticane,* Studi e testi, vol. 273 (Vatican City: Biblioteca Apostolica Vaticana, 1974), 18. The MS in question is BAV, Vat. Lat. 98.

22. F. P. Pickering, *Literature and Art in the Middle Ages* (Coral Gables, Fla.: University of Miami Press, 1970), 292.

23. Both quoted in Surtz, *The Guitar of God,* 72–73.

24. McKinnon, *Music in Early Christian Literature,* 81. Compare also Eusebius of Caesarea, "It is upon a living psaltery and an animate cithara and in spiritual songs that we render the hymn." Ibid., 98.

25. Gabriella Zarri, "I monasteri femminili benedettini nella diocesi di Bologna (secoli xiii–xvii)," in *Ravennatensia ix: Atti del convegno di Bologna nel xv centenario della nascità di S. Benedetto* (Cesena: Badia di Santa Maria del Monte, 1981), 347.

26. BUB, MS It. 3856: 133: "Coi celici, coi flagelli, e coi frequenti digiuni, domò le ribellioni del corpo si che pareva maravigliosa la resistenza al numero di tanti patimenti." The text is also paraphrased in Antonio Masini, *Bologna perlustrata*, third printing (Bologna: Erede di Vittorio Benacci, 1660), 1: 468.

27. The official establishment of the company of the Rosary on 5 Nov. 1641 is commemorated in ASB, Demaniale 11/2871 (Santa Cristina), no. 1/J. Ibid., 48/2909 (Santa Cristina), No. 3/L (processo 1622–23), fol. 9v: "Le feste si levano tutte à matuttina ma io no[n] mi levo, p[er]ch[e] son Indisposta."

28. BCB, MS B921: 51: "Suo immortali sponso in hac mortali vita Purgatorii pætras donu[m] non innane petiit; nam postea admirabili patientia et virili fortitudine infirmitatem nec non infortuniorum onus, tamquam e cælo dilapsum illari animo pertulit. . . . Ingravescentibus enim morbis, qui supremum Monasterii Imperium ei interceperunt."

29. Bynum, "The Female Body," 194.

6. THE RHETORIC OF CONFLICT

1. Camaldoli MS 652, fol. 15v, contains a summary of the letter, including the statements "Castità non ne parli p[er] riverenza" and "Esaminare senza scomunica papale non servirà niente."

2. Angela Cherubini, ASB, Demaniale 48/2909 (Santa Cristina), no. 3/L (processo 1622–23), fols. 38r–v: "Ogn'uno si porta bene a le Madre e li Nostri Superiori, et no[n] so ch[e] alcuna faccia cosa ch[e] no[n] sia da fare. . . . Tutte le cose stano bene et si fanno bene, et no[n] hò cosa ch[e] dirvi." Verginia Fuzzi, ibid., fol. 37r: "essendo io sor Vecchia atte[n]do solo alla anima mia." Ortensia Bombacci, ibid., fol. 33r: "sto ritirata et [illeg.] no[n] so niente." Paula Dorotea Vitali, ibid., fol. 19r: "in som[m]a quando vi fosse bisogno di riforma la fare nella Cucina."

3. Giuliana Glavarini, ibid., fol. 9r: "No[n] so ch[e] vi sia alcuna disse[n]zione fra di loro." Citing S. L. Payne, *The Art of Asking Questions* (Princeton, 1951), Peter Burke has commented on sociologists' and social historians' increased awareness of the relationship between how questions are phrased and the answers they provoke ("The Bishop's Questions and the People's Religion," in *The Historical Anthropology of Early Modern Italy* [Cambridge: Cambridge University Press, 1987], 40).

4. Lucrezia Vizzana, ASB, Demaniale 48/2909 (Santa Cristina), no. 3/L (processo 1622–23, fols. 10r–11r): "No[n] conosco ch[e] vi siano abusi nel co[n]ve[n]to ne cative pratiche. . . . No[n] ho veduto pitture p[ro]fane, ne meno cani. . . . Ne so ch[e] fra noi ci sia varietà di vestire, ne vanità alcuna di litio ò d'altro." Ibid., fol. 10r: "Ne so ch[e] vi siano alcune disse[n]zioni, et solo à me pare ch[e] trà Sor Emilia et Sor Cecilia vi sia qualch[e] emulatione ch[e] causa qualch[e] poco disturbo nel monastero."

5. Isabetta Vizzana, ibid., fol. 14r: "Tra le quali regna garra ch[e] mettono in scombilio il Conve[n]to. Don[n]a Emilia osserva l'attioni di Don[n]a Cecilia, et p[er] il contrario, l'altra fa, in modo tale ch[e] in sino nel recitar l'uff[iz]io in

Choro si vogliono superare l'una l'altra co[n] la voce, et ciascuna d'esse voria più superare l'altra." Donna Olimpia Cattani, ibid., fol. 12r: "Quale si querella tutte in Choro con dire ch[e] no[n] si recita puntualme[n]te et come si dovria l'uff[iz]io divino. . . .et no[n] tocca à lei à Coreggiere è parte dell'Abbadessa." Donna Paola Dorothea Vitali, ibid., fol. 19r: "et particulare in Choro Dona Cecilia vole guidar lei il Choro et credo lo faccia p[er] bene, con tutto ch[e] si dica l'uff[iz]io ordinatamente, et è p[er] ch[e] pare cosi a lei qua[n]do no[n] si dice à suo modo." Silvia Bottrigari, ibid., fol. 32r: "Se si potesse provedere ch[e] Dona Cecilia si co[n]fermasse co[n] l'altre nel recitare il Divino uff[iz]io si levarebbono molti sca[n]doli dal Choro, dove[n]do lei co[n] voce uniforme all'altre recitar l'uff[iz]io, et no[n] mettere co[n]fusione co[n] dire una volta alto et l'altra basso." Anna Maria Righi, ibid, fol. 47r: "alle volte Don[n]a Cecilia in Choro dice q[u]alch[e] cosetta vole[n]do ch[e] la seguiviamo secondo dice essa, ò presto ò adaggio. . . . No[n] so vi sia altra disse[n]zione se no[n] q[u]alch[e] competenza fra Don[n]a Emilia et Sor Cecilia ch[e] ogn'una di esse prete[n]de far caminar il Choro à suo gusto; il governo del quale come prefetta tocca a Donna Emilia."

6. Cecilia Bianchi, AAB, Misc. vecchie 820, fasc. 2 (processo 1622–23), fol. 4r: "Ho co[n]siderato à quanto mi ricercaste et per più espedittione vi presento il presente foglio dove, è, scritto tutto quello ch[e] ne posso dire in questo esamine et le cause, et presentavit foliu[m] . . . cuius pridem Folii tenori talis est qui sequitur, Dicciotto an[n]i sono ch[e] patisco questa persecutione et cominciò per causa di Musica."

7. Ibid., fols. 1r–v, 8r; ASB, Demaniale 48/2909 (Santa Cristina), no. 3/L (processo 1622–23), fols. 23v–24r: "In questo v'è negligenza grandissima, perche l'estate à quell'hora sempre vengono addimandate alle porte et grade delle suore dalli Gentilhuomini e gentildon[n]e, et cosi il Choro no[n] , è, frequentato . . . alle volte restiamo tante poche ch[e] no[n] potiamo recitar l'uffitio. . . . Habbiamo ordine di dire l'uffitio quasi in canto, ma questo no[n] si serve . . . et conducono Cani et gatti in Choro, vi, è la Madre Dona Emilia Grassi quale ha una Gattina che la viene à ritrovare in Choro, et lei no[n] la manda via come dovrebbe, vi è ancor la Madre Priora cioè Don[n]a Sulpitia Bocchi, quale ha una cagna che porta alle volte quella in Choro ma al presente l'ha mandata à casa, et Don[n]a Pantasilea Tovagli quando si dice l'uffitio tiene un libretto davanti et no[n] sta attenta all'uffitio come doverebbe[.] . . . Il Mastro della Musicha hà havuta la sua provisione . . . et La Madre Abbadessa s'è lame[n]tata di questo, et è stata la Madre Don[n]a Emilia ch[e] hà voluto ch[e] se le dia. Habbiamo anco duoi organi che se ne potrebbe vender' uno. . . . Di più si deve determinare il modo e tempo di recitar li divini uffitij, Cantare messe et altri perch[e] no[n] ostante ch[e] la Madre Abbadessa ordini in uno modo Dona Emilia fà il contrario dal che ne nasce dissentione et scandolo."

8. In 1635, for example, the nuns of Santa Maria della Regina in Naples had informed the Congregation of Bishops that bans on dogs only applied to males (ASV, VR, sez. monache, 1635 [marzo–dicembre], packet of 17 Aug.), which apparently had been confirmed in 1638 (see BAV, MS Borg. Lat. 77, fol. 23v, "Cagnolina femina permessa à monaca in Clausura"), although it would be overturned at other times and places (e.g., at Genoa in 1683; see ASV, VR, Reg. monial. 30 [1683], fol. 197v, dated 27 Aug. 1683). Male dogs—indeed, male animals of any

description—were frowned upon particularly for sexual reasons, as in 1678, when an anonymous supplicant from Assisi complained that a majority of the nuns kept little male dogs, which caused "not a little sensuality among these same nuns, who also take them into their own beds" ("non poca sensualità nelle medeme Monache, che li tengono anco ne proprij letti" [ibid., 1678 (agosto), packet of 5 Aug.]), or as in 1703, when the nuns of Santa Chiara in Acquapendente complained that the abbess's bitch had not only dropped a litter in the chapel during divine services, but had recently been visited daily by a male dog, "who, to the greatest scandal of the nuns, uses the said bitch carnally, a thing that has never been heard of for time immemorial" ("che con sommo scandalo delle Monache usa carnalmente con detta Cagnolina; cosa, che è ab immemorabile inaudita" [ibid., sez. monache, 1703 (novembre–dicembre), packet of 7 Dec.]).

9. Lorenza Bonsignori, AAB, Misc. vecchie 820, fasc. 2, (processo 1622–23), fol. 16v: "Deve esser' avertita detta Don[n]a Cecilia à esser più circo[n]spetta in parlare troppo et dir' villania alle suore et alle volte in Choro va contrafaccendo quelle povere sore Vecchie ch[e] no[n] possono fornire co[n] il Choro et ch[e] proferiscono certe silabe, ò più alte ò più basse." Bonsignori's testimony is on fols. 13r–20v, as well as in ASB, Demaniale 48/2909 (Santa Cristina), no. 3/L (processo 1622–23), fols. 39v–47r.

10. AAB, Misc. vecchie 820, fasc. 2 (processo 1622–23), fol. 14v.

11. Emilia Grassi, ibid., fol. 9v; ASB, Demaniale 48/2909 (Santa Cristina), no. 3/L (processo 1622–23), fol. 33v: "Io ho Carico di regulare il Choro da sei an[n]i in qua et in Choro no[n] pare ch[e] vi sia altro ch[e] conturbi la quiete comune se no[n] ch[e] Don[n]a Cecilia alle volte ò core in fretta, ò dice più addaggio delle altre, riprende[n]do bene et spesso delle Monache massime dalla parte dove sta lei, co[n] tutto ch[e] no[n] s'aspetti ad essa di far queste repre[n]sioni havendo io il Caricho del Choro come hò detto."

12. Emilia Grassi, AAB, Misc. vecchie 820, fasc. 2 (processo 1622–23), fols. 12v–13r: "No[n] so che la Madre si sia lamentata di quello ch[e] si da all'organista o Mastro della Musica, è no[n] si patisse anda[n]do sotto la loggia à render le gratie doppo magnare [sic] davanti il Crucifisso; . . . et se alcuno mi da qualch[e] cosa, dicè ch[e] sono del suo proprio et non della parte del Convento et ch[e] il Convento hà havuto la parte sua; . . . et quanto à Don[n]a Cecilia no[n] so ch[e] fare con essa et la honoro come ogn'altra Don[n]a et suora del Convento. . . . No[n] hò per male che le suore Imparano da suor Cecilia et facilmente in absentia di Don[n]a Cecilia, che, è, una Hippocrita, et hò detto ad altre ch[e] no[n] si lasciano persuadere da lei, . . . et quanto ad haver'avertito qualche don[n]a di non volere fare rigorosi digiuni et vigilie, è stato co[n] occasione di Don[n]a Giuglia che hebbe una longha infirmità, et con participatione del medico, . . . ne io hò instrutta alcuna come dovesse rispondere nella visita et no[n] hò detto di voler perseguitare Don[n]a Cecilia. . . . Io no[n] hò persuaso mai alcuna ch[e] à mio modo faccia l'Abbadessa, ne meno nel leggere in Reffettorio hò aggiunto lettura che fosse in pregiuditio d'altri, Quanto al portare Cappello co[n]fesso portarlo per diffendermi dal Caldo et dalla mala aria, ma è usanza del convento et lo portano la Madre Abbadessa et la Camerlenga coperte però le spalle dalla patienza et tutta." (The final remark is presumably a response to the allegation that she went around with her bosom uncovered.)

13. ASV, VR, posiz. 1600, A–B: "E' sempre stato solito da tempo immemorabile che nel Mon[aste]rio delle monache di S[ant]ta Christina di Bologna del Ordine di Camaldoli s'elegga dalle Monache una organista, et la elettione sempre si suuol far' di q[u]ella, che sà meglio sonare, et p[er]che ordinariam[en]te il nummero di q[ue]lle che sapevano sonar bene era in poche, d'una ò doi poche volte c'è stata discordia in detta elettione. Hora che il detto nummero è ridotto à più, che pretendano quest'off[ici]o c'è tal discordia che non si può venire ad elettione della più Idonea, et di q[ue]lla che merita più, percio p[er] parte della Badessa, et monache d'esso monasterio humilm[ent]e si supplica alle S[ignorie] V[ostre] Ill[ustrissi]me che si degnino commandare, che adesso, et sempre venendo il caso di tale elettione si debba eleger q[ue]lla monaca, che sappia sonar meglio, et sia più atta, Idonea et sufficiente a tal off[izi]o postponghi ogn'altro p[re]testo e rispetto."

14. Ercole Tonelli, ASV, VR, posiz. 1593, B–C, letter of 3 Nov. 1593: "Sono in discordie, et guerre tali fra di loro p[er] emulationi di queste Musiche, che alle volte sono p[er] straciarsi le carni fra di loro se potessero." Ibid., posiz. 1602, A–C, anonymous letter of 6 Mar. 1602: "Sono stata molti anni seculara e nelli monasterio e ho veduti molti scandagli particolar sopra il sonar organo e far musica queste sonatrice e cantatrici si perseguitono luna e laltra e fano le parte una parte dice la nostra fa meglio e laltra parte dice no[n] e vero la nostra sona e canta meglior e da queste si fa rumor grandissimo odio e nemicicie infinite a tal ch[e] i monasterio stano in foco e fiama."

15. The complaint against the convent procurator, dated 26 May 1599, survives in ASV, VR, posiz. 1599, A–C. The Congregation of Bishops' order for an investigation, which was unusually slow in coming, appears in ASV, VR, Reg. regular. 3 (1600–1601), fol. 43 (21 Nov. 1600). In July 1600, there had also been difficulties and misunderstandings between Archbishop Alfonso Paleotti and the convent regarding the admission of an unauthorized barber, in his capacity as surgeon, at a time of urgent necessity. See ASV, VR, posiz. 1600, A–D, letters registered 10 and 24 July. The Congregation's follow-up orders of Jan. 1601 appear in ASV, VR, Reg. regular. 3 (1600–1601), fols. 6or–v (2 Jan. 1601).

16. In the visitation of 1622–23, the abbess confirmed that Adeodata Leoni, as well as Flaminia Bombacci, had been called on to reconcile the rivals as recently as Lent of 1622. AAB, Misc. vecchie 820, fasc. 2 (processo 1622–23), fol. 10r.

17. "Per parte di Vossignoria da persona, che mi può commandare ricercato, à volerle fare havere tal'hora qualch'una dell'opere Ecclesiastiche di Musica del R. Don Gabriel Fattorini." *Il secondo libro de mottetti a otto voci di Gabrielle Fattorini da Faenza* (Venice: Ricciardo Amadino, 1601).

18. *Breviarium monasticum secundum ordinem Camaldulensem* (Venice: Johannes Variscum, 1580), fols. 176r, 179r.

19. "Tum, si intrans est Episcopus, vel maior, aut Presbyter vel Episcopus Cardinalis, Cantores incipiunt & prosequuntur antiphonam Sacerdos Pontifex. . . . Vel dicatur Responsorium Ecce Sacerdos magnus." *Pontificale Romanum Clementis VIII. Pont. Max. iussu restitutum atque editum* (Antwerp: Officina Plantiniana apud Balthasarem Moretum, 1627), 476–77.

20. The various antiphons, responsories, and verses employing these words for the Feast of Saint Stephen appear in the *Breviarium monasticum secundum ordinem*

Camaldulensem, fols. 33r–35r and fol. 46r (octave). *Praeparate corda vestra* was quite commonly set in the Cinquecento. Eleven settings published between 1529 and 1591 are listed in Harry B. Lincoln, *The Latin Motet: Indices to Printed Collections, 1500–1600* (Ottawa: Institute of Mediaeval Music, 1993), 494. Lincoln lists five settings of *Impetum inimicorum* between 1528 and 1559 (ibid., 474), and three versions of *Positis autem genibus* between 1550 and 1599 (ibid., 493). For the text of *Praeparate corda vestra,* see *Breviarium monasticum secundum ordinem Camaldulensem,* fol. 141v. An alternative and more pragmatic solution to the problem of rival organists was to divide the responsibilities among the various rivals. Indeed, the presence of two organs and organ lofts in the expanded and remodeled external church of Santa Cristina made at least two organists a necessity. The practice was adopted, and must have become normal, because in 1623, madre donna Sulpizia Bocchi testified that there were three nun organists at that time, a policy that can be traced at least down to the end of the Seicento. See ASB, Demaniale 48/2909 (Santa Cristina), no. 3/L (processo 1622–23), fol. 39r. The *camerlenga's* records in 1698 indicate that three organists received a *cortesia* of £5 a year. See ibid., 43/2904 (Santa Cristina), "Uscita de denari Spese e pagati dalla Madre Camerlenga il p[re]sente Mese [Mar. 1698]."

21. Lincoln's *The Latin Motet* (451, 510, and 462 respectively) lists ten settings of *Domine ne in furore,* fourteen of *Usquequo Domine,* and sixteen of *Domine, quid multiplicati sunt.* Vizzana's two penitential psalms, for example, offer interesting comparisons with their equivalents in the popular ninth-century *Flores Psalmorum* of Prudence, bishop of Troyes. See Pierre Salmon, *Analecta liturgica: Extraits des manuscrits liturgiques de la Bibliothèque vaticane,* Studi e testi, vol. 273 (Vatican City: Biblioteca Apostolica Vaticana, 1974), 94–95. The tenor of Vizzana's *Exsurgat Deus* and *Domine, quid multiplicati sunt,* on the other hand, is quite different from the redactions in *Flores Psalmorum.* Coincidentally, a version of Psalm 6 virtually identical to Vizzana's appears in another abbreviated psalter, Trinity College, Dublin MS E4.2. See Salmon, *Analecta liturgica,* 71.

22. For brief comments on this theme, see Elizabeth Alvilda Petroff, *Medieval Women's Visionary Literature* (New York: Oxford University Press, 1986), 35–36.

23. The absence of a printer's name and *privilegio* leads Margaret F. Rosenthal to suggest similar origins for the *Lettere familiari a diversi* of Veronica Franco. See *The Honest Courtesan: Veronica Franco, Citizen and Writer in Sixteenth-Century Venice* (Chicago: University of Chicago Press, 1992), 118.

24. Robert Eitner was in fact misled by the salutation to claim that Vizzana's collection had been dedicated to Jesus Christ. See *Biographisch-Bibliographisches Quellen-Lexikon,* 2d ed. (Graz: Akademische Druck- und Verlagsanstalt, 1959), 9: 116.

25. Camaldoli MS 652, fols. 15r–v. For the postponement of the visit, see ASB, Demaniale 48/2909 (Santa Cristina), no. 3/L (processo 1622–23), fol. 1r.

26. Richard J. Agee, "A Venetian Music Printing Contract in the Sixteenth Century," *Studi musicali* 15 (1986): 59–65. The contract was signed on 8 March, the dedication on 1 May, and the five hundred finished copies were delivered to the monastery on 10 June.

27. The resulting reform decree was dated 27 Apr. 1623. See AAB, Misc. vecchie 820, fasc. 2.

28. The symbols ⟨⟩ indicate an omission from the original psalm.

29. *Episcopale Bononiensis civitatis et diocesis—Raccolta di varie cose, che in diversi tempi sono state ordinate da monsig. illustriss. & reverendiss. Cardinale Paleotti Vescovo di Bologna* (Bologna: Alessandro Benacci, 1580), 97. It is interesting that *Exsurgat Deus* was less commonly set in the Cinquecento, to judge by Harry B. Lincoln's *The Latin Motet*, 469, which lists only one setting.

30. Information on settings of *Domine ne in furore* kindly supplied by the late Jerome Roche from his database of early seventeenth-century motets.

31. All fourteen settings in Lincoln's *The Latin Motet*, 510, also include "Domine." Early Seicento settings of Psalm 6 beginning "Usquequo *Domine*" appear in Felice Anerio, *Sacri hymni lib. 2* (Rome: Zanetti, 1602), Giovanni Martino Cesare, *Concerti ecclesiastici* (Venice: Magni, 1614), and Ignazio Donati, *Sacri concentus* (Venice: Vincenti, 1612). The late Jerome Roche was kind enough to search these out from his computer database.

32. ASB, Demaniale 48/2909 (Santa Cristina), no. 3/L (processo 1622–23), fol. 20v. Adeodata Leoni: "et si dicono ogni Domenica li sette salmi d'obligo."

33. ASV, VR, posiz. 1616, A–C, documents registered 10 Aug., 8 Oct., and 8 Nov. 1616; ibid., Reg. regular. 19 (1616), fol. 162r; ibid., posiz. 1619, A–C, documents dated 13 July 1618, 12 Mar., and 20 Dec. 1619; ibid., Reg. regular. 21 (1618), fol. 242v; ibid., posiz. 1620, A–C, undated petition.

34. Caroline Walker Bynum, " . . . And Woman His Humanity: Female Imagery in the Religious Writings of the Later Middle Ages," in *Fragmentation and Redemption: Essays on Gender and the Human Body in Medieval Religion* (New York: Zone Books, 1992), 153.

35. The attribution is based largely on the presence of the text in a source rich in Peter's works, and on stylistic grounds. See Guido Maria Dreves, *Analecta hymnica*, vol. 48 (Leipzig: O. R. Reisland, 1905), 243, which transmits a slightly different version.

36. Version from Guido Maria Dreves, *Analecta hymnica*, vol. 32 (Leipzig: O. R. Reisland, 1899), 47. Lines in italic reappear in Vizzana's setting.

37. Lincoln, *The Latin Motet*, 449. Martin Picker, ed., *The Motet Books of Andrea Antico*, Monuments of Renaissance Music, vol. 8 (Chicago: University of Chicago Press, 1987), 30–31.

38. *Processionale monasticum ad usum congregationis Gallicae ordinis Sancti Benedicti* (Solesme, 1893), 277.

39. Only the basso continuo part survives from an additional setting of *Ave stella matutina* for soprano and continuo by Arcangelo Bussoni, published in 1614. Although Bussoni's text therefore cannot be recovered, the fact that his motet was comparable in length to Vizzana's motet suggests that it also involved a similarly attenuated version of the hymn.

40. "Salve *stella matutina* lux aurora lux divina, finus pudicitiæ, *peccatorum medicina* spes es vera veniæ."

41. BUB, MS It. 770/26: 293: "Ma esse vi protestarono, ch'erano Dame, che non siano in quel luogo per forza, ma volontariamente, e per elezione."

42. My thanks to Carlo Vitali for pointing out the connection with Psalm 109.

7. THE SOCIAL DYNAMICS OF DIVISION

1. Mauro Ruggeri, Camaldoli MS 652, fols. 12v–13r: "fù una certa D[onn]a Emilia de Grassi, ma naturale, Donna sanguigna, e p[er] conseguenza, allegra, et libera nel parlare, et procedere. . . . La d[et]ta D[onna] Emilia, nel tempo della sua Gioventù era bella d'aspetto, eloquente, virtuosa, cantatrice, sonadora d'organo, d'arpa, et altri instromenti, et bene; splendida et liberale, di dove tirata à sè non solo gli animi delle monache, mà d'altri ancora, de qui ne nacque voleva poi interesarsi in tutti i fatti, e obbedienze delle Monache, e Monast[er]o. . . . L'altra Monache (. . . in gioventù anco amica di D[onna] Emil[i]a) Era una Donna Cecilia Bianchi quale aveva una sola adderente D[onna] Gentile Malvasia, quale, quando non fosse stata conversa era proprion[ament]e Gentile; praticò cola lupa imparò ad urlare. Questa D[onna] Cecilia era Melenconica, e di color fosco dominata dall'arabile conseguent[ement]e dispetosa arogante, invidiosa, censurava l'actioni dell'altri si reputava di vaglia molto, mà sopra il tutto voleva essere la simia di D[onna] Em[ili]a, ma senza modo e grazia." On Ruggeri, see Giovanni Benedetto Mittarelli and Anselmo Costadoni, *Annales Camaldulenses*, vol. 8 (Venice, 1764), 322, 372.

2. Ruggeri's account is preserved in Camaldoli MS 101 and MS 652, "D. Mauro Ruggeri: storia della caduta di iv. Mon[aste]ri Cam[aldolesi]. Notizie particolari sopra alcuni generali." I have relied on the latter, slightly more legible copy.

3. Details from Camaldoli MS 652, fols. 18r–v, quotations from fol. 21v: "quale avrebbe usata ogni più finzione p[er] tirarlo à se"; "il Bardino cervello giovennino, che supponè saper più d'Ogni altro."

4. See Ecclesiasticus 25:23, "And there is no anger above the anger of a woman." Some ancient authorities change "a woman" to "an enemy." See *The Apocryphal/ Deuterocanonical Books of the Old Testament: New Revised Standard Version* (New York: Oxford University Press, 1989), 100 n. z. The verse continued to be paraphrased down through the centuries. E.g., "Anyone seeking to restrain an angry woman wearies himself with wasted effort. . . . Moreover, the anger of any woman is aroused at the slightest, most unsubstantiated remark" (Andreas Capellanus, *De amore*, c. 1185); "But it is also true, without fail, that a woman is easily inflamed with wrath. . . . And thus she remains a very irritable animal. Solomon says that there was never a head more cruel than the head of a serpent and nothing more wrathful than a woman" (Jean de Meun, *Le Roman de la rose*, c. 1275). Both quoted in Alcuin Blamires, ed., *Woman Defamed and Woman Defended: An Anthology of Medieval Texts* (Oxford: Clarendon Press; New York: Oxford University Press, 1992), 121, 163.

5. BUB, MS It. 3856: 134. Gasparo Bombacci's account of madre donna Flaminia was evidently based on a letter from Mauro Ruggeri. See *Annales Camaldulenses*, 8: 271. In the decree, "On the Invocation, Veneration, and Relics of Saints, and on Sacred Images" from Session 25 at the Council of Trent, the prelates had ruled that no miracles should be accepted without prior episcopal approval. See Judith Brown, *Immodest Acts: The Life of a Lesbian Nun in Renaissance Italy* (New York: Oxford University Press, 1986), 184 n. 17. This attitude was reinforced in the early seventeenth century, particularly by Urban VIII in various decrees to the Holy Office and in his *Caelestis Hierusalem* of 5 July 1634. See Albano Biondi, "L'inordinata devozione' nella *prattica* del Cardinale Scaglia (ca. 1635)," in *Finzione e santità tra Medioevo ed età moderna*, ed. Gabriella Zarri (Turin: Rosenberg & Sellier, 1991), 310–11. On the

eclipse of the miraculous by morality and good behavior, see Adriano Prosperi, "L'elemento storico nelle polemiche sulla santità," ibid., esp. 112–14.

6. See Giulia Barone, "La canonizzazione di Francesca Romana (1608): La riproposta di un modello agiografico medievale," in *Finzione e santità*, ed. Zarri (cited in n. 5 above), 264–79. For additional discussion of appropriate post-Tridentine female saintly virtues, see Andrea Tilatti, "Riscritture agiografiche: Santi medioevali nella cultura friulana dei secoli xvii e xviii," ibid., 280–305.

7. Camaldoli MS 652, fols. 18r, 19r–20r.

8. AAB, Misc. vecchie 820, fasc. 2 (processo 1622–23), fol. 4r: "Et perch[e] venessimo à parole io gli diedi della male nata in risposta ch[e] lei disse à me piena di vitij."

9. Guido Ruggiero, *The Boundaries of Eros* (New York: Oxford University Press, 1985), 40, 55; Ruggiero concentrates his discussion on Venetian practice. For Thomas Kuehn's very useful observations on bastards and legitimation, see *Law, Family, and Women: Toward a Legal Anthropology of Renaissance Italy* (Chicago: University of Chicago Press, 1991), esp. "Reading between the Patrilines: Leon Battista Alberti's *Della famiglia* in Light of His Illegitimacy," 157–75, and " 'As if Conceived within a Legitimate Marriage': A Dispute Concerning Legitimation in Quattrocento Florence," 176–93. The quotation appears on 160. For the sixteenth century, see Linda L. Carroll, *Angelo Beolco (Il Ruzante)* (Boston: Twayne, 1990), 2–4. Donna Emilia seems to have had financial difficulties with her own family, perhaps related to the circumstances of her birth. Between Nov. 1610 and Aug. 1612, the convent carried on a suit with a Geronimo Grassi and his mother and guardian, Margherita Grassi, who finally agreed to pay the convent £200 on Emilia's behalf. See ASB, Demaniale 51/5009 (Santa Cristina), no. 1/L, fol. 3v.

10. Attilio Gnesotto, "Francisci Barbari De re uxoria liber," *Accademia patavina: Atti e memorie della r. accademia di SLA in Padova* 32 (1916): 41.

11. Richard Sherr, "Mecenatismo musicale a Mantova: Le nozze di Vincenzo Gonzaga e Margherita Farnese," *Rivista italiana di musicologia* 19 (1984): 3–20.

12. For the complaint from San Zaccaria, see Gabriela Zarri, "Monasteri femminili e città (secoli xv–xviii)," in *Storia d'Italia: Annali*, 9: *La chiesa e il potere politico dal Medioevo all'età contemporanea*, ed. Giorgio Chittolini and Giovanni Miccoli (Turin: Giulio Einaudi, 1986), 368 n. 33. For the Congregation of Bishops' rulings, see BAV, MS Ferrajoli 612, fols. 41r, 54r. The reference to "Cordea," or possibly "Condea," on fol. 41r might perhaps indicate Cordes or Condé (France) or Cordoba (Spain). The 1592 ruling, marked "Cordua," is copied in AAB, Misc. vecchie 807, fasc. 27.

13. Emilia cites her income in AAB, Misc. vecchie 820, fasc. 2 (processo 1622–23), fol. 12, and indicates that the highest yearly income of any nun was £200 a year; only about half a dozen nuns mentioned their yearly earnings in the investigation of 1622–23.

14. Adriano Banchieri: "sovenendomi a memoria l'affettione, che fin da i miei primi anni tenni verso la sua antichissima et Illustrissima casata de i Grassi, dalla quale ne sono riusciti Cardinali, Prelati, Senatori, & altri personaggi, che hanno sempre reso, & rendono gran splendore a questa nostra Città di Bologna, risposi all'amico, *veramente da si buon albero non può riuscire se non eccellentissimi frutti*" (emphasis added). *Messa solenne a otto voci* (Venice: Amadino, 1599).

15. AAB, Misc. vecchie 820, fasc. 2 (processo 1622–23), fol. 3. Such a way around the restrictions of *clausura* was hardly limited to Santa Cristina. On Holy Thursday 1617, the nuns at the convent of Santa Maria Maddalena in Bologna were discovered in the middle of a meal for various friars, whose table was set up in the external parlatorio, while the nuns ate at their own table, across the open grates, in the internal parlatorio. See ASV, VR, Reg. regular. 20 (1617), fol. 174r, dated 30 June 1617.

16. AAB, Misc. vecchie 820, fasc. 2 (processo 1622–23), fol. 14v.

17. ASB, Demaniale 48/2909 (Santa Cristina), no. 3/L (processo 1622–23), fol. 22v (where the sentence has been underlined): "Credo che questa disse[n]zione di queste due suore cioè Sor Cecilia and Dona Emilia p[ro]cede da queste putte." AAB, Misc. vecchie 820, fasc. 2 (processo 1622–23), fol. 14v: "Nè manchò co[n] occasione di procurare d'havere le educande di far gran rumori, come anco fecce del *1604* uno memoriale nefandissimo contro quelle ch[e] havevano tenute le se-colari [sic] et lo mandò a Roma alla Cong[regazio]ne dell'Ill[ustrissi]mi Car[dina]li et p[er] mantenere la sua oppinione hà fatto gra[n]dissimo rumore, perch[e] no[n] tornino più le secolari [sic], per educatione."

18. Camaldoli MS 652, fols. 13r–v: "Vide che il Convento era pieno di monache delle prime famiglie di Bologna, Pepoli, Malvezzi, Ariosti, Bolognetti, [others added superlinea:] Gozzadini, [illeg.], Malvasia, Zambeccari, Bocchi, et altre simili delle quali, erano tenute le parenti in educazione de quali molte poi riceverano l'habito, e conseguentem[en]te come sig[no]re nobili non volevano soggetarsi à ceni, et commandi di D[onn]a Emilia."

19. According to seniority, those of first rank were Zani, Bolognetti (2), Mal-vezzi, Bocchi (2), Grassi, Bottrigari (2), Vitali (3), Nobili (2), Bianchi, Pepoli, Leoni, Zambeccari, Gozzadini, Malvasia, and Vizzani (2); of second rank were Glavarini (3), Duglioli, Bombacci (3), Agucci, Sarti (2), and Cattani; the less distinguished included Fuzzi (2), Ghezzi, Zibetti, Tovagli (2), Corbini (2), Bonsignori, and Ga-nassi. Based on Pompeo Dolfi, *Cronologia delle famiglie nobili di Bologna* (Bologna: Giovanni Battista Ferroni, 1670; repr., Bologna: Forni editore, n.d.).

20. Mario Fanti, "Le classi sociali e il governo di Bologna all'inizio del secolo xvii in un'opera inedita di Camillo Baldi," *Strenna storica bolognese* 11 (1961): 154. Giancarlo Angelozzi suggests, on the other hand, that the attitudes of the Bolognese nobility may have been somewhat more moderate. See "Nobili, mercanti, dottori, cavalieri, artigiani: Stratificazione sociale e ideologia a Bologna nei secoli xvi e xviii," in *Storia illustrata di Bologna*, ed. Walter Tega (Milan: Nuova editoriale AIEP, 1989), 2: 45–51.

21. ASV, VR, Reg. regular. 5 (1604), fol. 149v.

22. AAB, Misc. vecchie 820, fasc. 2 (processo 1622–23), fol. 7r: "Voleva fare una serva del Sig[no]re sua figliuola et no[n] del Mondo." The sister of marchese Mario Orsi received the veil at San Gabriele in Feb. 1622 as suor Maria Valeria della Croce and professed on 3 Feb. 1623. She died on 5 Mar. 1668, after a life of particular piety and ecstatic devotions. See BCB, MS B922: 56–57. "Adimando ch[e] Maestra dovesse havere et le fu detto ch[e] havria Don[n]a Judith, et lei fecce rissolutione di no[n] venire et fu in sua presenza et la rifiuttò, et Don[n]a Emilia oltre l'altre parole impertinenti co[n] le quali scandelizò li circo[n]stanti ch[e] erano presente,

disse ch[e] in altre mani la voleva sempre perseguitar et la Madre della Giovane disse ch[e] non la voleva monachare et la maritò poi." Although she also claimed that the only novice, La Terribila (Maria Serena Celestis Terribila) had been so mistreated by Donna Giuditta and Donna Emilia that she had lost her health, the novice made no complaints about her treatment to Archbishop Gozzadini (although it is possible, of course, that she dared not), and went on to make her profession. AAB, Misc. vecchie 820, fasc. 2 (processo 1622–23), fols. 7r–v; on "La Terribila" see also ibid., fol. 8v. She must indeed have been sickly, however, for she died in 1628. BCB, MS B921: 5.

23. See BCB, MS B922: 259. Livia Maria Bombacci died at the convent of San Giovanni Battista on 31 Dec. 1621.

24. Gasparo Bombacci, BUB, MS It. 3856: 135: "Hebbe anche senso diverso dalla sorella, e dalle nipoti, desiderando di concedere parta delle soddisfattioni pretese ad alcune monache, ma il suo parere devea seguire la risolutione del maggior numero de voti."

25. Mauro Ruggeri, Camaldoli MS 652, fol. 19v: "le disse di quelle maggiori ingiurie che seppe il dirle filandara [sic?—orthography ambiguous] p[er] esser parente di Mercanti." The dowry agreement of Lucrezia Vizzana's parents had described her maternal grandfather as *mercator* and stipulated that Giovanni Bombacci should invest £9,000 of his daughter's dowry in a silk manufacturing company. See ASB, Demaniale 9/2870 (Santa Cristina), no. 47/I.

26. Mauro Ruggeri, Camaldoli MS 652, fol. 12v: "Una preparò la legna, e materia, e l'altra si può dire con un stizzo di fuoco le desse la forma di donde ne segui l'incendio."

27. Dolfi, *Cronologia delle famiglie nobili di Bologna*, 159. The identification of Cecilia's father's father appears in ASB, Notarile, Mazzolini, Carl'Antonio, Prot. Q (1590), fols. 6v and 92r.

28. Maria de' Blanchi appears in a list of abbesses from Camaldoli MS 1087, reproduced in Roberta Zucchini, "Santa Cristina della Fondazza: Storia architettonica e storico artistica" (Tesi di laurea, Università di Bologna, 1987–88), 166, where the date of her election appears as 1339. The official confirmation of her election appears in ASB, Demaniale 10/2871 (Santa Cristina), no. 27/K. Cecilia Bianchi's renunciation appears in ASB, Notarile, Mazzolini, Carl'Antonio, Prot. Q (1590), fols. 192v–93r. For a summary of the settlement of Cecilia Bianchi's dowry, including Cecilia's name *al secolo*, see Demaniale 51/5009 (Santa Cristina), fol. 8v. Copies of the actual document appear in ASB, Demaniale 31/2892 (Santa Cristina), fols. 130v–31r, no. 54, and in Demaniale 1/2862 (Santa Cristina), no. 65/A. For the Bianchi donors at Santa Cristina, see BCB, MS B921: 31 and 46. Donna Cecilia's brother Luca may have come to an ignominious end. On 17 Nov. 1621, a Luca Bianchi was killed with more than thirty sword blows in the church of San Martino by the dancer, tumbler, and fencing master Alesandro de Negri. See Ferdinando Guidicini, *Miscellanea storico-patria bolognese tratta dai manoscritti di Giuseppe Guidicini* (Bologna: Giacomo Monti, 1872), 284–85.

29. The treatises of 1587 and 1638, including the quotation "vanità e leggierezza d'alcune femminuccie" are discussed in Gabriella Zarri, " 'Vera' santità, 'simulata' santità: Ipotesi e riscontri," in *Finzione e santità*, 20–21. Surin's characterization of

hypocrisy is quoted in Giuseppe Orlandi, "Vera e falsa santità in alcuni predicatori populari e direttori di spirito del Sei e Settecento," ibid., 437.

30. Zarri, " 'Verra' santità, 'simulata' santità," 11.

31. This and other excerpts are cited in Orlandi, "Verra e falsa santità in alcuni predicatori," 442–43.

32. My thanks to Carlo Vitali for bringing the modern proverb to my attention. Mauro Ruggeri, Camaldoli MS 652, fol. 11r: "Il fatto della Peccora narato dal Prof[e]ta Natan al Rè David," a reference to II Samuel 12:1–13, the story of the rich man who took a poor man's only little ewe, "that did eat of his own meat, and drank of his own cup, and lay in his bosom, and was unto him as a daughter." Ibid., fol. 23r: "Fù un mettere le povere Peccore in bocca al Luppo."

33. *Breviarium monasticum secundum ordinem Camaldulensem*, fol. 166v. The antiphon is based on Matthew 7:15.

34. Zarri, " 'Vera' santità, 'simulata' santità," 11. The image is illustrated on the cover of *Finzione e santità*.

35. For an illuminating discussion of the dog, wolf, and vendetta, see Edward Muir, *Mad Blood Stirring: Vendetta and Factions in Friuli during the Renaissance* (Baltimore: Johns Hopkins University Press, 1993), esp. 222–31, on which the preceding paragraph is largely based. Hecuba took revenge by killing the children of Polymester, who prophesied that she would turn into a bitch before her death.

36. Cf. Jeremiah 5:6 ("Wherefore a lion out of the forest shall slay them, and *a wolf of the evening shall spoil them*") or Zephaniah 3:3 ("Her princes within her are roaring lions; *her judges are evening wolves;* they gnaw not the bones till the morrow") (emphasis added). For dogs and promiscuity, see Muir, *Mad Blood,* 224. Cf. Jehan LeFèvre, "And just like the she-wolf on heat, that always takes the worst male as her mate, so the widow always chooses badly." Quoted in Blamires, ed., *Woman Defamed and Woman Defended,* 187–88.

37. Claudia Gozzadini, ASB, Demaniale 48/2909 (Santa Cristina), no. 3/L (processo 1622–23), fol. 17v: "Alcune suore dormono in Compagnia p[er] paura come faccio io qua[n]do more q[u]alch[e] suora."

38. BCB, MS B3595: 26.

39. Romualda Ghirardelli, ASB, Demaniale 48/2909 (Santa Cristina), no. 3/L (processo 1622–23), fol. 4v: "Ciascuna monacha dorme nelle [sic] sua cella et vi sono tante celle qualle Monache, et di piu, et Dormono in una medema stantia Due Monache cioè Don[n]a Cecilia et Dona Ge[n]tile et in uno medemo letto."

40. Cecilia Bianchi, AAB, Misc. vecchie 820, fasc. 2 (processo 1622–23), fol. 6r; ASB, Demaniale 48/2909 (Santa Cristina), no. 3/L (processo 1622–23), fol. 27r: "Le Monache ogn'una dorme nelle loro proprie celle separate et qualch[e] d'una dorme accompagnata sotto pretesto d'infirmità, et l'inverno dormono accompagnate q[u]alch[e] duna in qualche letto, et l'estate dormono separate."

41. AAB, Misc. vecchie 820, fasc. 2, "Visitatio localis Ecclesie et Monasterij Monialiu[m] S. Christine. Bonon."

42. AAB, Misc. vecchie 820, fasc. 2 (processo 1622–23), fols. 16r–v.

43. ASB, Demaniale 51/3918 (Santa Margherita). See BUB, MS It. 206/12, fol. 77r, for the description from Colonna's pastoral visitation: "Passò alle Celle di Suor Diana Gabriela, e di Suor Lesbia Ildebranda de Grassi, et à q[u]esta ult[im]a S[ua]

Em[inenz]a mutò il nome, imponendoli il nome di Suor Maria Teresa, et ordinando alla M[ad]re Priora, che cosi la fecesse nominare da suo inanzi." The erotic relationship of the Theatine abbess Benedetta Carlini with a younger nun who shared her cell at night has, of course, become particularly well known through Judith Brown's *Immodest Acts*.

44. [Desiderius Erasmus,] *The Colloquies of Erasmus*, trans. Craig R. Thompson (Chicago: University of Chicago Press, 1965), 108. For the Latin original, see *Opera omnia Desiderii Erasmi Roterodami*, 1: 3, ed. L.-E. Halkin, F. Bierlaire, and R. Hoven (Amsterdam: North-Holland Publishing, 1972), pp. 289–97, esp. 294. For Marot's verse translations, see Clément Marot, *Oeuvres complètes*, vol. 6: *Les Traductions*, ed. C. A. Mayer (Geneva: Slatkine, 1980), 269–308, esp. 286. I thank Edward Duval for pointing out to me Erasmus's colloquies as the basis of Marot's works.

45. Carol MacClintock, ed., *The Bottegari Lutebook* (Wellesley, Mass.: Wellesley College, 1965), 37.

46. It is significant that in the *Giornata prima* (devoted to a nun's life) of Pietro Aretino's *Ragionamento della Nanna e della Antonia . . . composto . . . a correzione dei tre stati delle donne*, the exceedingly meager examples of what might be construed as female-female sexual activity (which are totally swamped there by diverse nun-monk and novice-monk couplings) are clearly conceived of as only temporary, and decidedly poor, substitutes for "the real thing," male-female sex. See Pietro Aretino, *Ragionamento dialogo*, ed. Nino Borsellino (Milan: Garzanti editore, 1984), 63–64. Although nuns' superiors did not think in modern terms of "sexual identity" of the sort implied, at least in the title, by Judith Brown's *Immodest Acts: The Life of a Lesbian Nun in Renaissance Italy*, any more than Aretino apparently did, it was not unknown for them to confront cases involving somewhat similar sexual ambiguity among nuns. In 1722, for example, the Congregation of Bishops had to deal with the case of a nun from Turin who "claimed to have become a hermaphrodite" and had described her anatomical transformation to her bishop meticulously. The Sacred Congregation ruled that if the male—*fe* had been written first, then crossed out— sex was found to be dominant, the nun should be removed from the convent, where she "daily jeopardized the decency of the other nuns." See ASV, VR, Reg. monial. 66 (1722), dated 24 Apr. 1722, and ibid. sez. monache, 1722 (aprile) in packet of 24 Apr. For a valuable reinterpretation of female relationships, written in response to Judith Brown, see E. Ann Matter, "Discourses of Desire: Sexuality and Christian Women's Visionary Literature," in *Homosexuality and Religion*, ed. Richard Hasbany (New York: Hawthorne Press, 1989), 119–31.

47. Quoted in Biondi, "L''inordinata devozione' nella *prattica* del Cardinale Scaglia," 317.

48. According to Robert Kendrick, incidents of actual female-female sexual activity in the convents of Milan were usually punished no more severely than petty thievery, even during the reign of Carlo Borromeo (personal communication). See P. Renée Baernstein, "The Birth of the Counter-Reformation Convent: The Convent of San Paolo in Milan, 1530–1630" (Ph.D. diss., Harvard University, 1993).

49. Saint Teresa of Avila devoted special attention to such "particular friendships" for exactly the same reason: less from any preoccupation with any potentially sexual aspect than because of their tendency to promote factionalism. See Jodi

Bilinkoff, *The Avila of Saint Teresa: Religious Reform in a Sixteenth-Century City* (Ithaca, N.Y.: Cornell University Press, 1989), 131.

50. Richard C. Trexler, *Public Life in Renaissance Florence* (Ithaca, N.Y.: Cornell University Press, 1991), 139.

51. Cecilia Bianchi, AAB, Misc. vecchie 820, fasc. 2 (processo 1622–23), fols. 4r–5r: "Dicciotto an[n]i sono ch[e] patisco questa persecutione et cominciò per causa di Musica et perch[e] venessimo à parole io gli diedi della male nata in risposta ch[e] lei disse à me piena di vitij et così mai più ne per racconciliationi ne p[er] altro mio atto amorevole no[n] hà voluto credere ch[e] gli sia amica vera, et sempre dall'hora in qua mi hà messo in disgratia à tutte le superiori, et alli confessori et padri tutti della Conggregatione [sic] et procurata la disgratia di tutte le superiori talmente ch[e] no[n] si arischiano parlarmi ne di servirsi di me, et anco à sua requisitione hò havuto da alcune molti disgusti; mi ha poi imputato dice lei sempre ch[e] ogni suo travaglio gli venghi sempre da me, sia chi si voglia ch[e] gli faccia dispiacere, et ch[e] sono una anima persa dice et predica del co[n]tinuo alle altre sorelle et con queste et altre inventioni cerca di rendermi odiosa à tutto il Mondo, sino co[n] secolari. . . . Horsù se andassi à cortegiarla come molte fano et ch[e] dicessi all'occasione di suo capritio il Bianco nero, è nero bianco come fan[n]o adesso quelle ch[e] per vendicarsi contro di me che mi imputano ch[e] habbia procurato sia riformato il Monasterio premendoli tanto questa cosa ch[e] no[n] guardano ne stimano à fare uno spergiuro et gli pare d'haver merito. . . . Et che è ripresa dalla superiora dice no[n] fa peccato ma si bene hà merito, No[n] havria contro pretensione alcuna, ma questo no[n] lo posso fare perche siamo dissimili d'inclinatione et humore; et il mio gusto l'hò in star rittirata et attendo à fatti miei, et in vivere più quieta che posso. . . . Hò detto questo pocco ch[e] mi son raccordato, perch[e] io no[n] tengo conto d'offese per godere la pace dell'animo al meglio, ch[e] del resto posso mi curo. Tenevo ch[e] in questo fossimo riformate et ch[e] altro no[n] occoresse p[er] riformare ch[e] la conscienza propria; et non era niente di occasione, se no[n] questa ch[e] io voglio libera la mia volontà in quello ch[e] mi è concesso et per honor di Dio et per utille et beneffitio del Monasterio, et questo gli, è, di disgusto et à me, mi spiace ch[e] così sia, ma giustamente no[n] posso far'altro. Et perch[e] alle volte la Madre Abbadessa presenta et passata si sono valse di me informare qualch[e] scrittura ò memoriale per servitio del convento per ciò persuppongo ch[e] le scriture et memoriali à superiori di Roma mandati siano state mie compositioni, et per ciò maggiormente essa et altre sue seguacci si lasciano intendere volermi perseguitare sino alla morte."

52. Ruggeri's observation regarding the wording "supplico di Rimedio" appears in Camaldoli MS 652, fol. 15v. Cecilia Bianchi, ASB, Demaniale 48/2909 (Santa Cristina), no. 3/L (processo 1622/23), fol. 28r: "Io mi son mossa a fare ["questo" crossed out and replaced with:] il memoriale mandato à superiori p[er] provedere al scandalo del secolo quale era informato d[i] queste n[os]tre Imperfettioni." The version with the copying slip survives in AAB, Misc. vecchie 820, fasc. 2 (processo 1622–23), fol. 7r.

53. Ludovica Fabri, ASB, Demaniale 48/2909 (Santa Cristina), no. 3/L (processo 1622–23), fol. 48v: "à giorni Dona Domitilla mi disse ch[e] havevo buona pratica di querellere al S. Uffitio."

54. Camaldoli MS 652, fol. 31r, and fol. 14v: "Si fù trovato rimedio col mandargli un piato di zucherini, o mele con sotto un zuccarone la licenza era segnata senza altra difficoltà." According to Ruggeri, similar bribes also proved useful in securing permission to vest postulants.

55. Mauro Ruggeri, Camaldoli MS 652, fol. 16r: "Si mosse D. Cecilia far questo torto al suo Monastero p[er] l'odio antico contro D. Emilia, . . . e dalla speranza, che le dava D. Gionino . . . che sarebbe Badessa, o Riformatrice."

56. Gabriella Zarri, "I monasteri femminili benedettini nella diocesi di Bologna (secoli xiii–xvii)," in *Ravennatensia ix: Atti del convegno di Bologna nel xv centenario della nascità di S. Benedetto* (Cesena: Badia di Santa Maria Del Monte, 1981), 353. Clement VII's breve is preserved in AAB, Misc. vecchie 820, fasc. 2.

57. See BCB, MS B921: 1 and 34; see also *Annales Camaldulenses*, vol. 7 (Venice, 1762), appendix, cols. 402, 422. The nuns had died in 1552 and 1543 respectively.

58. Mauro Ruggeri, Camaldoli MS 652, fol. 12v: "del Mon[aste]ro di S[ant]a Christina mai s'è udito cosa, che abbi offeso le pie orrecchie de Bolognesi." See BCB, MS Gozzadini 132, entry under 1506. The reform, which also involved the convents of Santi Gervasio e Protasio and San Guglielmo, is described in exhaustive detail in the history of San Giovanni Battista, ASB, Demaniale 171/5131 (San Giovanni Battista); for the rough copy of the history, see ibid., 166/4650 (San Giovanni Battista). A document in the Archivio Arcivescovile seems to describe the same reformation by seven nuns from San Giovanni Battista, but is dated Jan. 6, 1499. See AAB, Misc. vecchie 820, fasc. 2, "Ristretto di ciò, che si contiene nell'Instromento della Riforma del monastero delle Monache Camaldolensi di S. Cristina della fondazza."

59. Ambrogio Traversari, *Hodoeporicon*, ed. Vittorio Tamburini (Florence: Felice le Monnier, 1985), 116.

60. Antonio Francesco Ghiselli, BUB, MS It. 770/26: 295: "E ben vero che non videro mai di buon occhio . . . restò sempre in loro radicata una tale affettione al fratismo o Monachismo, che anche in hoggi dura."

61. Mauro Ruggeri, Camaldoli MS 652, fols. 16r–v: "P[er] la città si dicevano le più esorbitanti cose si potessero mai dire sino, che v'erano otto gravide."

62. Trexler, *Public Life in Renaissance Florence*, 35.

63. Guasco is quoted in Ann Rosalind Jones, *The Currency of Eros: Women's Love Lyric in Europe, 1540–1620* (Bloomington: Indiana University Press, 1990), 16. Ruggiero's comment appears in Margaret L. King, *Women of the Renaissance* (Chicago: University of Chicago Press, 1991), 29.

64. Mauro Ruggeri, Camaldoli MS 652, fol. 16v: "Si attacorno al punto principale, ove si doveva battere il choido." Cf. one of Nanna's many descriptions of the goings on between monks and nuns in the *Giornata prima* of Aretino's *Ragionamenti*: "E perchè il chiodo stesse più fermo nel forame, accennò dietrovia al suo erba-da-buoi."

65. C. Bianchi, AAB, Misc. vecchie 820, fasc. 2 (processo 1622–23), fol. 6v: "Et quanto alla Castità tengo ogni una per santa, come vole la riverenza del luogo."

66. The incident is described in ASB, Demaniale 48/2909 (Santa Cristina), no. 3/L (processo 1622–23), fols. 50r–v.

67. Mauro Ruggeri, Camaldoli MS 652, fol. 16v: "Dio Benedetto la B[eat]a Vergine S[an] Romualdo S[ant]a Christina, a quali le Monache del continuo si rac-

commandarono, che fossero second[at]o la loro inocenza, e sua difesa, op[er]arono, che D. Cecilia rispondesse conforme al vero, et intrepidam[en]te [unclear—intepidam[en]te?], queste formali parole (in questo le tengo p[er] sante)."

8. THE STRUGGLE WITH LUDOVISI

1. AAB, Misc. vecchie 820, fasc. 2, "Ordini che si devono dare p[er] rimediare alle cose ritrovate nella Visita di Santa Xpina": "Si può sperare l'istesso, et peggio per l'avvenire." Mauro Ruggeri provides a less detailed summary in Camaldoli MS 652, fols. 17r–v.

2. Camaldoli MS 652, fol. 17v.

3. On the election, see ibid., fol. 18r, and BUB, MS It. 3856: 135. Donna Flaminia's first term as abbess must have preceded Emilia Grassi's. She is listed as abbess in ASB, Demaniale 16/2877 (Santa Cristina), no. 28/Q, dated 28 Jan. 1614. Senatore Raffaele di Giulio Riario, ambassador to the papal court in the 1590s, had married Ottavia del conte Fabio Pepoli, with an astonishing dowry of 10,000 scudi; his son, marchese Francesco Riario, the grand duke of Tuscany's ambassador to the imperial court, married Laura Pepoli. See Pompeo Dolfi, *Cronologia delle famiglie nobili di Bologna* (Bologna: Giovanni Battista Ferroni, 1670; repr., Bologna: Forni editore, n.d.), 652–53.

4. ASB, Demaniale 48/2909 (Santa Cristina), no. 3/L (processo 1622–23), fols. 23r–v.

5. The petitions appear in ASV, VR, posiz. 1616, A–C, letters dated 30 July and 26 Nov. 1616.

6. Camaldoli MS 652, fol. 20r.

7. ASV, VR, posiz. 1625, A–C, documents dated 16 Feb., 7 Mar., and 18 Mar.: "Per le male consequenze, che possono nascere, potendo quelle per diverse cause, e rispetti eleger persone, che in vece d'edificar, distrughino con scandalo publico." Other copies appear ibid., sez. monache, 1627 (gennaio–novembre).

8. Klara Garas, "The Ludovisi Collection of Pictures," *Burlington Magazine* 109 (1976): 287 n. 6, 347 n. 274. Francia's altarpiece is now at the Hermitage, Saint Petersburg. A *Nativity* by Veronese may also have been removed from the convent of San Nazaro as a gift to the cardinal. These are the only known cases of such expropriation, according to Carolyn Wood (personal communication, May 1993).

9. Gabriella Zarri, "Monasteri femminili e città (secoli xv–xviii)," in *Storia d'Italia: Annali,* 9: *La chiesa e il potere politico dal Medioevo all'età contemporanea,* ed. Giorgio Chittolini and Giovanni Miccoli (Turin: Giulio Einaudi, 1986), 410.

10. The sections, "Delle monache" and "Della santità affettata" from Cardinal Scaglia's treatise are published in Albano Biondi, "L'`inordinata devozione' nella *prattica* del Cardinale Scaglia (c. 1635)," in *Finzione e santità tra Medioevo ed età moderna,* ed. Gabriella Zarri (Turin: Rosenberg & Sellier, 1992), 316–23; the quotation appears on 320.

11. The Sacred Congregation's commission to Bishop Bovio survives in ASV, VR, Reg. regular. 35 (1626), fol. 53, dated 3 Mar. For Ruggeri's account, see Camaldoli MS 652, fol. 23r: "dando occasione si grande di scandalo, e de' giudicij esecrandi, che non v'era luogo nella Città, et fuori p[er] tutto italia, ove che si può

dire p[er] tutt'europa, che non si parlasse de vergine [sic] sacre, come di Don[n]e infami, delle maggiori che si potessero imaginare, cosa da piangere con lagrime di sangue[.] . . . non ditte Bagatelle, ditte della robba grossa che io vi servirò di aiutto."

12. BCB, MS B921: 10.

13. AAB, Misc. vecchie 820, fasc. 2, "somario del p[ro]cesso delle Monache di s[an]ta Christina": "è tutte le monache dicono non esser stata recitata nel parlatorio eccetto una Novizza la qual dice, che fù recitata di notte nel parlatorio; ma non vidde altro ascoltante, se non la madre Camerlenga, e ch[e] le parve vedere un capello bianco nel d[ett]o parlatorio; et altre due monache dicono della detta novicia haver inteso, che si recitò nel detto parlatorio, e credono ciò esser vero perche le monache recitanti quella sera non si trovorono al matutino."

14. Carlo Bovio, ASV, VR, sez. regolari, 1626 (febraio–settembre), letter dated 18 Apr. in packet of 30 May: "La prima confessa la Comedia essere stata recitata in Parlatorio di notte presente lei, e che v'erano li frati; la seconda non ardisce negarlo affatto, mà dice no[n] raccordarselo: la Comedia no[n] solo era profana, mà lasciva, e v'era una parte di donna Cortigiana; Al'altri capi sono quasi tutti provati per co[n]fessioni delli Monaci istessi, e delle Monache: dalle quali cose vedrà la sacra Congreg[azio]ne gl'inco[n]venie[n]tà, le dissolutioni, e inosservanze di questi Monaci."

15. Camaldoli MS 652, fol. 23r. The summary of the investigation is preserved in AAB, Misc. vecchie 820, fasc. 2, "somario del p[ro]cesso delle Monache di s[an]ta Christina": "Che il P[ad]re confessore si tratiene quasi sempre alla Rota della sacristia, e la maggior parte del tempo ragiona con una nepote dell'Abbadessa, e ciò costa per dette di tre monache; et un'altra Monacha dice, che il d[ett]o confessore gl'hà detto che quando vidde la p[rim]a volta la detta nepote dell'Abbadessa, perse il cervello, e che è la sua Angioletta, rincrescendogli non haver assai cose da regalarla[.] E due monache depongono haver veduto delli monaci sud[ett]i ragionar con le monache alla Ruota à porta serata."

16. Camaldoli MS 652, fols. 22r–v.

17. For the poem, see Venice, Biblioteca Correr, MS Cicogna 1863. ASV, VR, sez. monache, 1659 (novembre–dicembre), in packet dated 10 Nov. 1659: "S[ignor] Gio[vanni] M[ari]a Penna che serve il Monast[er]o di S[anta] Cat[erin]a tiene stretta amicitia con suor M[ari]a fulvia con scandolo delle Monache, e secolari[;] se riserra nel Camerino dove si comunicano, et è stato veduto . . . dare membro nelle mani e altre attioni. . . . Vogliono mandare in Casa del diavolo le spose di Christo."

18. Prospero Fagnani, ASV, VR, Reg. regular. 35 (1626), an unnumbered folio in an unbound fascicle inserted before the fascicle dated 5 June: "l'Intiera verità degl'eccessi, che nell'alligato processo si pretendono commessi in cot[est]o monast[er]o di S[an]ta Christina governato da monaci Camaldolensi." Mauro Ruggeri, Camaldoli MS 652, fol. 23v: "non contenti di aver vedutto nelle Casse disfecero anco letti, e benche fosse d'improviso non trovorno cosa da potersi estracare."

19. In the middle of the night in Dec. 1649, the nuns of SS. Lodovico e Alessio in Bologna were subjected to a similar invasion, provoking a vitriolic letter to the Congregation of Bishops rivaling some from Santa Cristina. See ASV, VR, sez. monache, 1650 (gennaio–febbraio), packet for Jan. 7. The letter is dated 15 Dec. 1649.

20. This "violation" of the cloister may well have conjured up a sense of physical violation of the nuns themselves. There is an interesting parallel in the language used to describe circumstances surrounding the sexual violation of Elena, daughter of Zuan Cumano of Feltre, by Gian Battista Facena, who had actually climbed a ladder to enter her father's house, in effect, "violating" the walls: "Gian Battista . . . violating the security of my house, villainously to betray and deflower Elena, my daughter." The Cumano house and household were thus violated by the deflowering of Zuan Cumano's daughter. See Guido Ruggiero, " 'Più che la vita caro': Onore, matrimonio e reputazione femminile nel Tardo Rinascimento," *Quaderni storici* 66 (1987): 761.

21. Prospero Fagnani, ASV, VR, Reg. regular. 36 (1627), fol. 195v–196r, dated 30 Apr. 1627: "Il buon governo, et osservanza in che ivi si vive della disciplina regolare et il buon'ordine che da tutte le parte spire p[er] quel Sacro luogo di purità e di buontà."

22. Ibid. 38 (1627), minute dated 26 Mar. 1627: "Havendo havuto questo buon saggio dell'osserv[anz]a in che han vissuto sin'hora sotto il governo di quelli, si danno à credere, che ogni giorno piu siano per approfittarsi nel serv[iti]o di Dio sotto la buona direttione di Mons[ignor] [illeg.] Ill[ustrissi]mo Ludovisio Arciv[escov]o et Ordinario di cot[est]a Città, al cui governo si ritrovano hora soggettate."

23. Ibid. 36 (1627), fols. 52r–v, "Ex Audientia Sanct[issi]mi habita die 13.a dicti Mensis februarij": "Sarà però espediente che V.P.R.ma per riputat[ion]e della sua Cong[regation]e ne faccia in mano della S[anti]tà S[ua] una spontanea renuntia in termine di tre giorni al più, et dia gli ordini opportuni per la rilassatione di detto governo con farmeli havere in mano prop[ri]a per più sicuro ricapito."

24. Santa Cristina nuns, ASV, VR, sez. monache, 1627 (gennaio–novembre), letter dated 30 Apr.: "Non resti macchiata la riputat[io]ne del Monast[e]rio, e di tanta nobiltà, che vi si ritrova." The pope's breve is printed in *Annales Camaldulenses*, vol. 9 (Venice, 1773), appendix, cols. 311–13.

25. Mauro Ruggeri: "à guisa de Turchi, con gridi, urli e rumori." This and other details from Camaldoli MS 652, fol. 25r.

26. Sherrill Cohen, *The Evolution of Women's Asylums since 1500: From Refuges for Ex-Prostitutes to Shelters for Battered Women* (New York: Oxford University Press, 1992), 121. At Santa Cristina, *onestà* was as much a part of the patrician vocabulary as *onore*.

27. The nun's petition survives in ASV, VR, sez. monache, 1628 (febbraio–maggio), letter registered 19 May 1628. Ludovisi's accusation, "Per essersi mostrate pronte ad'ubbidire, ò per vano sospetto che habbino rivelata alcuna cosa contro di voi, per sicurezza della propria vita sono state necessitate incarcerarsi nelle proprie Camere," and his claim concerning the nuns' refusal to confess appears in ASV, VR, sez. monache, 1704 (agosto); other copies in AAB, Misc. vecchie 820, fasc. 2, and 808, fasc. 1; BUB, MS It. 770/26: 297–316; Camaldoli MS 652, fols. 26r–29v. Ruggeri claims the imprisonment of the three malcontents took place on the order of Cardinal Ubaldini, and that the other nuns also hoped thereby to control the three malcontents' machinations with outsiders.

28. Cardinal Archbishop Ludovico Ludovisi, ASV, Sacra Congregazione del Concilio, Visite ad limina 136A, fols. 67r–v; another copy in BUB, MS It. 206/2: "Qua

propter de remedijs opportunis cogitandum esset, ut aliquae ex istis contumacibus, et inobedientibus refrenentur." The orders to the papal legate appear in ASV, VR, Reg. regular. 39 (1628 minute), unnumbered folio dated 23 June. Cardinal Bernardino Spada's letters expressing his reluctance to accept the commission and repeated doubts about the efficacy of his participation survive in ASV, Legazione di Bologna, vol. 4A, fols. 239–41. Spada, ibid., fol. 240r: "Ogni mio ingerimento in quest'affare non solam[ent]e sarebbe inutile, ò non apporterebbe momento a la prudenza sollecitud[in]e di Mon[signo]r Suffrag[ane]o, ma servirebbe à gravare la contumacia dele Monache, e lo scandalo di q[ue]sta Città."

29. Santa Cristina nuns, ASV, VR, segretario di stato, lettere di particolari, vol. 11, fol. 108r: "La n[ost]ra innocenza appare dalli processi già fatti più volte p[er] replicate visite, e mentre non ci viene solevato l'honore, le n[ost]re Case eternamente restano infamate, e noi p[er] ciò da q[u]elli abbandonate, quasi alle dan[n]atione sciamo gionte[.] . . . Prostratte la supplicano del presto suo soccorso, e potentiss[i]mo agiuto, alla reintegratione del n[ost]ro honore, e salute dell'anime[.] . . . Im[m]inenti sono le minacie crudeli, che come Leoni ci vogliono divorare, e senza dubio occorrendo, si sentira p[er] il mondo di noi." The inventory of the volume indicates that the letter was addressed to Cardinal Borghese. Ingoli's letter appears ibid., fol. 110r; the inventory of the volume indicates that it was addressed to a D. Fonseca domenicano.

30. The orders of the Sacred Congregation survive ibid., VR, Reg. regular. 39 (1628 minute), unnumbered folio dated 17 Nov. Various accounts of the walling up of the doorway, each offering different details, appear in Camaldoli MS 652, fol. 25v; BUB, MS It. 3856: 137–38; BCB, MS Gozz. 185, fol. 142v (a copy of the previous); BUB, MS 770/26: 292–93: "Ma questo [?] però non poté resistere alla violenza delle infuriate Monache." Ghiselli seems to embroider the story as he goes along (e.g., in his account every opening, from the smallest to the principal gate, had been walled up).

31. Details from BUB, MS It. 3856: 138, and Camaldoli MS 652, fol. 25. Ludovisi's final ultimatum also confirms some of the details, including donna Isabetta's oration from the convent window, although she is not singled out by name. The length of the oration is mentioned in Lucantonio Giunti's biography of Ludovico Ludovisi, which likewise records many of the same details. See BAV, Fondo Boncompagni-Ludovisi, Codex B8, fol. 99r.

32. Antonio Francesco Ghiselli, BUB, MS It. 770/26: 294: "Finalmente fu introdotto in certa corte dentro la porta sudetta, . . . e qui stato altro pezzo aspetando affaciatasi ad una finestra puoco lontana dal tetto una Monaca e domandatoli che voleva, rispose, che la Madre Abbadessa, e dettoli che a facesse innansi lasciarono da detta finestra precipitare à basso un grosso marmoro, dicendo ecco la Madre Abbadessa, e se il povero huomo non fosse stato presto à ritirarsi sarebbe rimasto oppresso, et infranto da quel colpo."

33. See the undated, unsigned letter in ASB, Demaniale 48/2909 (Santa Cristina), beginning "Se bene si maravigliaranno." Ibid., another letter, also unsigned and undated: "Si notifica à tutte le Monache di S[an]ta Christina, che il giuramento fatto da loro di stare unite insieme a no[n] obedire alli commandamenti delli suoi superiori, è irrito, e nullo, et è contro il voto, e giuramento fatto dalle Monache

nella loro professione, quando fecero il Voto di Obedienza alli suoi superiori. . . .
E per tanto chi ha fatto d[ett]o giuramento, e chi l'ha fatto fare hanno peccato
Mortal[men]te. . . . E q[ues]to è il parere di tutti li Theologi della Città, et Università
di Bologna. E perche poi il giuramento non deve essere vincolo d'iniquità Noi per
maggior quiete delle conscienze Vostre vi assolviamo da d[ett]o giuramento, che
dichiariamo irrito, e nullo, e di niun valore."

34. Camaldoli MS 652, fol. 26; see also BUB, MS It. 3856: 138, which might
possibly be indebted to Ruggeri, however.

35. The nuns' letter of 7 Feb. and Ludovisi's reply survive in ASV, Demaniale
48/2909 (Santa Cristina); the Sacred Congregation's decision appears in ASV, VR,
Reg. regular. 40 (1629 minute), unnumbered folio dated 1 Feb.: "Non si debba in
modo alcuno dar'orecchio à trattati, e temperamenti così pregiuditiali all'autorità
di questa santa sede, così dannosi allo stato, e salute delle Monache istesse, e di si
pernitioso esse[m]pio à chiunque altro tentasse d'opporsi all'essec[utio]ne de gli
ordini Apostolici l'obedienza deve esser [crossed out: "totale"] essatta, e totale, e
no[n] diminuta; et è non meno di scandalo, che di maraviglia, che Religiose Monache [crossed out: "tentino"] ardischino di venir à patti col sommo Pontefice lor
supremo Sig[no]re . . . l'è stata data da S[ua] B[eatitudi]ne perche si compiaccia
di porla in op[e]ra p[er] franger'una volta cosi lunga, et ostinata protervia di queste
poverelle."

36. Cardinal Archbishop Ludovico Ludovisi, ASV, VR, sez. monache, 1704
(agosto): "Voi D. Camilla Bombacci altre volte Abb[adess]a del Monas[te]ro di S.
Cristina di questa Città di Bol[ogn]a dell'ord[in]e Camaldolese, et à Voi D. Lorenza
Bonsignori, D. Ginevra Fuzzi, D. Sulpitia Bucchi, [list of all the *professe*] . . . Monache
Professe, et à Voi Converse nell'istesso Monas[te]ro Suor Girol[am]a Lombardi, S.
Ludovica fabri, [list of all the *converse*] . . . et à tutti gl'altri, à quali s'appartiene,
preghiamo dallo Spirito Santo Dono, e Virtù d'inteletto, e di consiglio per provedere alla salute dell'Anime vostre. . . . Benche nella scuola della religione vi doveva
bastare il considerare con S. Girolamo, che la vera riputazione di Persone Religiose
consiste nella pronta ubbedienza, e nelle loro Rette operazioni, e non nella lode,
ò vano giudiz[i]o degl'huomini, . . . Voi volontariam[ent]e privandovi dell'udito
del Cuore non havete ascoltato le voci salutiferi de' predetti S[igno]ri Card[ina]li
Legati, del V[ost]ro Padre, Pastore, de' suoi Min[ist]ri, di tanti dotti, e virtuosi
Religiosi, e de' proprij Parenti: di modo, che possiamo ragionevolm[ent]e dire,
curavimus Babylonem, et non est sanata. . . . cosi cotesto Monas[te]ro hora non è altro,
che una Babilonia dominando, e regnando in esso una graviss[im]a confusione. . . .
Havete posto in evidente pericolo di lasciar morire senza Sacram[en]ti D. Serena
M[ari]a Celeste Teribili Monaca Professa, piùtosto, che am[m]ettere sacerdote secolare, con il quale si confessasse, empiam[ent]e asserendo, che ciò havrebbe fatto
avanti un Crocifisso, errore intolerabile, poiche ove è copia di Confessore, e l'animo
è aggravata di disubbidienza mortale. . . . Acciò non si diffondesse al mal'odore di
tanti scandali, d'ord[in]e della S[acra] Cong[regazion]e furono murati li vostri
Parlatorij, e Voi con temerario ardire li havete fatti smurare, tirando sassi, et ingiu-
rando non solo li sbirri, esecutori, e Notari, mà anco l'istesso Audit[o]re di
Mon[signo]r Suffraganeo. . . . L'incostanza, e leggerezza d'accettare, e ricusare un
sacerdote secolare per Confessore, di promettere, e dispromettere, d'obbedire, la

sempre aumentata durezza, e contumacia sono argum[en]ti evidentissimi, che lo spirito maligno autore, e P[ad]re della disubbedienza, e discordia vi è stato sempre guida, compagno, e Maestro. Dà quel molto, che Noi habbiamo fatto per ridurvi à sana mente della pessima corrispondenza di manifestis[sim]a ingratitud[in]e, e sconoscenza, ogn'uno deduca che *curavimus Babylonem, et non est sanata,* Resta dunque con N[ost]ro infinito cordoglio, che se non si corregge *derelinquamus eam.* A questo ci sforza la Nostra conscienza dopo tanta longanimità, la legge Humana, e la Divina, lo scandalo publico, gl'espressi command[amen]ti di N[ostro] S[igno]re, e della S[acra] Cong[regazion]e sop[r]a Vescovi, e Reg[ola]ri, il giustiss[im]o timore, che con l'impunità si propaghi la disubbidienza. . . . Noi dunque, per l'autorità . . . com[m]andiamo, et ordiniamo in virtù di S[anta] Obbedienza à Voi D. Camilla Bombaci già Abb[adess]a, et à Voi altre Monache . . . che frà il termine di quindeci giorni prossimi . . . sotto pena della scommunica . . . sottoporvi, e sottomettervi all'autorità Nostra. . . . Finalm[ent]e perche non sono mancati, ne mancano empij, qui *dicunt malum bonum, et bonum malum,* com[m]andiamo à tutti sotto pena di scommunica . . . che niuno ardisca dar conseglio, aiuto, ò favore, col quale s'impedisca ò ritardi l'esecuz[ion]e del Breve Apost[oli]co, e de' sud[ett]i Ordini Nostri, e se nel termine prefisso cotesto Monas[te]ro non si sottoponga all'obbedienza dovuta al Sommo Pontefice, et a Noi . . . adesso per all'hora abbandoniamo cotesta Babilonia, abbandonata per la pertinace disobbedienza giustissimam[ent]e dà Dio, e dalla sua Chiesa, la quale lo scommunicato non hà per Madre, ne Dio per Padre, mà Satanasso in luogo di Padre, e di M[ad]re." Other copies in Camaldoli MS 652, fols. 26r–29r, BUB, MS It. 770/26: 297–316, and AAB, Misc. vecchie 820, fasc. 2, and 808, fasc. 1.

37. The details of the nuns' plight, including the eating of grass and their families' urging them to give in to Ludovisi, appear in Camaldoli MS 652, fols. 25r–v. The nuns claimed to have been abandoned by their families in the letter to Cardinal Borghese quoted above and in a letter to the Congregation of Bishops registered 2 May 1636 (ASV, VR, sez. monache, 1636 [gennaio–maggio]), quoted at the beginning of the next chapter.

38. Santa Cristina nuns, ASB, Notarile, Belvisi, Giulio, Prot. 18 (1628–1630), fols. 133v–135r: "Ci protestiamo et reproboliamo che ogni soggettione di Noi e del Monasterio per qual si voglia atto, tanto publico, quanto privato, che sia per farsi da noi, ò in qual si voglia tempo, e stato, e sarà non assolutamente spontaneo, ma per timore di dette Censure, et acciò che la nostra reput[azion]e non patisca più di quello che sin hora habbiamo sopportato, et perciò vogliamo che quanto si farà da noi in contrario sia per non fatto, et che salva sempre rimanga la detta protestatione ne si possa dire che da quella ci siamo mai partite." Rough copy in ASB, Demaniale 43/2904 (Santa Cristina).

39. Mauro Ruggeri: "e cosi furono finite le speranze dell'esser Badesse Riformatrici"; details from Camaldoli MS 652, fol. 29v. Bianchi's presence at San Michele Arcangelo by 30 June 1629 is confirmed by ASV, Misc. delle corporazioni religiose soppresse 43: 59, and by ASV, Demaniale 3/7733 (San Michele Arcangelo di San Giovanni in Persiceto), no. 159. For details of Malvasia's career at Sant'Agostino, see BCB, MS B922: 158–59, 175, and ASB, Demaniale 7/2868 (Santa Cristina), no. 38/G, which includes transcriptions of documents from Sant'Agostino regarding

Malvasia's profession and death there. In December 1629, Malvasia and Bolognetti were exempted by the Sacred Congregation from repeating their novice year at their new homes and granted positions in choir and chapter appropriate to nuns with thirty years of religion. ASV, VR, sez. monache, 1629 (settembre–dicembre). By Jan. 1630, Malvasia had been assigned a place at Sant'Agostino a mere four places above the bottom of the list of *professe.* ASB, Demaniale 11/4854 (Sant'Agostino), L. no. 354, dated 24 Jan. 1630. Lucidaria Bolognetti last appears in the list of nuns at San Bernardino in a notarial document of 30 Jan. 1662. Her name disappears from the next such list of 28 July 1663. See ibid., 14/2925 (San Bernardino), nos. O/12 and O/22. In the lists of nuns at San Michele in San Giovanni in Persiceto, Cecilia Bianchi's name is absent from documents of the 1630s and 1640s. See ibid., 4/7734 and 5/7735 (San Michele in San Giovanni in Persiceto).

40. Camaldoli MS 652, fol. 31r.

41. Ibid., fol. 30r: "Vedete che conto fan[n]o li vostri Padri Camald[ole]si di Voi, che non vogliono venire a confessarvi in questo Giubileo." Don Bernardo's letter is transcribed on fol. 30v. Mauro Ruggeri, ibid., fol. 34v: "Quando sia vero, che le Monache chiamino i Padri Camal[dole]si loro traditori (il che non è da credere) non è p[er] altro, che p[er] le mali impressioni, quali le mettono e fanno mettere in capo i ministri et altri dell'Arcivescovato."

42. Ludwig Pastor, *The History of the Popes,* trans. Ernest Graf (St. Louis: B. Herder, 1952), 31: 127 and n. 2.

43. Mauro Ruggeri, Camaldoli MS 652, fol. 31r: "Acciò s'intendi che le Monache sotto Preti non sono meglio governate, che da Regolari." Ibid.: "Ludoisio [*sic*] parti di Roma più presto, che di passo e ritornato à Bologna pieno di afflizione passò all'altra vita."

44. Cardinal Domenico Cecchini, BAV, MS Vat. Lat. 12174, "Vita del Card[ina]l Cecchino Scritta da lui Med[esi]mo," fol. 78r: "Più tosto Cadavere spirante, che Huomo." Ludovisi's biographer, Lucantonio Giunti, cites the cardinal's struggle with Santa Cristina as primary among the four most notable events of his reign. See BAV, Fondo Boncompagni-Ludovisi, Codex B8, fols. 98v–100r. On Ludovisi's fall, see Ludwig Pastor, *History of the Popes,* 28: 290–93.

9. THE CONFRONTATION WITH ALBERGATI LUDOVISI

1. The petition of 1633 is printed in *Annales Camaldulenses,* vol. 9 (Venice, 1773), appendix, col. 324.

2. Nuns of Santa Cristina, ASV, VR, sez. monache, 1636 (gennaio–maggio), dated 2 May 1636: "Oltre l'esser state perciò abbandonate da proprij parenti, benche siano state benignam[en]te consolate dall'Em[inen]ze V[ostre] di molte dichirationi della loro honestà et innocenza, riesce però tale l'impressione contraria in tutta la Città, che non solo restando esse ancora lacerate nella riputatione: Mà perche dopo l'essecutione dell'ordine sudetto, non s'è ritrovata, ne trova persona, ben che ordinaria, che voglia esser accettata & vestita per professa nel loro Monastero, dove che à per prima erà concesso à persone Nobili solam[en]te, et essendovi da 15. luochi vacanti, ne risulta la totale annihillatione, e destruttione di d[ett]o Monastero."

3. Nuns of Santa Cristina, ibid.: "Non intendendo perciò di sottratersi mai in conto alcuno dalla giurisd[izio]ne et retto governo dell'Em[inentissi]mo Sig[no]r Card[ina]le Arcivescovo." The petitions of 1642 survive ibid., 1642 (gennaio–luglio).

4. Francesca Malatendi, ibid., 1646 (gennaio–marzo): "Sapendo essa Suor Francesca il danno grandiss[i]mo venuto sino dell'anno 1626 . . . al sud[ett]o Monasterio, et Monache, et massime nella loro reputacione essendogli stato sopra cio . . . formato Processo, et dopoi levatogli li Monachi Camandulesi [sic], che governano le loro Anime. Percio essa Suor Francesca con la presente per sgravamento della sua conscienza, et per non danare l'anima sua, . . . et per ressiucire [= risarcire] nel meglior modo che può la reputacione al d[ett]o Mon[aste]ro, et conoscendo che N[ostro] S[ignore] per suo giusto Giudicio gl'ha mandata l'istessa Infirmita . . . che pativa l'istessa Suor Cherubina, . . . Dichiara confessa et publicamente riconosce le dette opposicione sospeti, et parole per lei inferita a d[ett]a suor lodovica esser state, et esser falsi, false, et vane; et non haver havuto sopra cio fondamento alcuno di verità; . . . Et in Fede della verità per non saper scrivere hà Fatto una croce alla presenza dell'In[fra]s[crit]ti Testimonij." Malatendi confessed on September 10. Her death on October 8 is recorded in the convent necrology, BCB, MS B921: 37.

5. Suor Ludovica, ASB, Demaniale 48/2909 (Santa Cristina), no. 3/L (processo 1622–23), fol. 48v: "Sor Gironima circa due o tre mesi sono ruppe la testa à Sor Dorotea et il sangue andò in terra et à Sor Cherubina strazzò il bavaro et la lasciò scapigliata et questo è stato daperch[e] si fa questa visita et la causa no[n] lo sò." Suor Geronima, ibid., fol. 49v: "Lei mi prese nella golla et mi volsè deffe[n]dere et lei dissè ch[e] li strazai il vello et no[n] mi audi di questo." Suor Cherubina, ibid., fol. 52r: "No[n] so disse[n]zione alcuna nel monasterio, ne cosa di rilievo, et benissimo son trattata dalle monache et daperch[e] son qui no[n] ho mai ricevuto disgusto da alcuna, et no[n] ho ch[e] dirvi." The nuns' reactions to Suor Ludovica appear ibid., fol. 20v, and AAB, Misc. vecchie 820, fasc. 2 (processo 1622–23), fol. 12r.

6. Nuns of Santa Cristina, ASV, VR, sez. monache 1646 (gennaio–marzo): "Desiderando unitam[en]te tutte le Oratrici dell'Em[inen]ze V[ost]re di veder riparato al pregiud[izi]o, che n'è risultato, et ne risulta giornalm[en]te maggiore all'honor loro, et alla riputacione del Monastero, che consiste della principal Nobilità di Bologna, come anche di liberarsi doppo cosi longo tempo da una continua loro inquietudine supplicano humilmente l'Em[inen]ze V[ost]re al volerli benignam[en]te concedere che sia riveduta la Giustitia della lor Causa."

7. For valuable recent discussions of women, confessors, and the Holy Office, see Giovanna Paolini, "Confessione e confessori al femminile: Monache e direttori spirituali in ambito veneto tra '600 e '700," in *Finzione e santità tra Medioevo ed età moderna,* ed. Gabriella Zarri (Turin: Rosenberg & Sellier, 1991), 366–88, and Ottavia Niccoli, "Il confessore e l'inquisitore: A proposito di un manoscritto bolognese del Seicento," ibid., 412–34.

8. Pompeo Dolfi, *Cronologia delle famiglie nobili di Bologna* (Bologna: Giovanni Battista Ferroni, 1670; repr., Bologna: Forni editore, n.d.), 35.

9. Mauro Ruggeri, Camaldoli MS 652, 31v–32r: "Tant'erano le speranze quali le dava sua Em[inen]za Ill[ustrissi]ma che le pareva di toccare il Cielo co[n] le dita." On Prince Ludovisi, see Ludwig Pastor, *History of the Popes,* trans. Ernest Graf (St. Louis: B. Herder, 1952), 30: 33.

10. An undated letter "Agl'Ill[ustrissi]mi S[igno]ri li S[igno]ri di Regimento" survives with the documents in the convent archive regarding their removal from Camaldolese jurisdiction. Although its content suggests the tumults of the 1620s, it reveals that the nuns had appealed to the senate in the past in combating the incursions of the diocesan curia. See ASB, Demaniale 48/2909 (Santa Cristina).

11. Ludovisi's remarks quoted in the preceding paragraphs all come from the same letter, ASV, VR, sez. monache, 1647 (gennaio–marzo), letter dated 30 Jan.: "Affermai esser ordine di cotesto supremo tribunale, che non si permettesse loro di più vestirne, per estirpar in tal modo le radici di si brutta rebellione . . . fù essaggerata l'ostinazione delle Moniche. . . . Partirono costoro edificati universalmente . . . e non mancarono di q[ue]lli, che fortemente detestassero la poca buona corrispondenza delle Madri. . . . La stravaganza degli humori difficili à maneggiarsi, la facilità di questo popolo à compatire, e secondare le voglie giuste, ò ingiuste della parte più debole, e la memoria fresca del sollevam[en]to passato, mi consigliavano à non impegnar più oltre l'auttorità della sac[ra] Cong[regazio]ne. La fragilità del sesso, la condizione di gente imprigionata, e la qualità di donne ingannate nella loro opinione erano apprese in maniera dalla maggior parte della città, che il non condescendere si stimava un'eccesso di rigidezza, et un quasi necessitare femine di spirito pur troppo altiero ad esser contumaci, e ribellate laonde in virtù dell'auttorità, che tengo dalla sac[ra] cong[regazio]ne mi ridussi ad assicurarle . . . che sarebbono intieram[en]te consolate."

12. Cardinal Archbishop Niccolò Albergati Ludovisi, ibid. (aprile–maggio), packet of 5 Apr. 1647: "Alle dilettissime nel Signore le Moniche di Santa CHRISTINA vera Pace, e Salute. La natural Pietà, e la religiosa Disciplina chiaramente conosciuta, & esperimentata da noi nelle persone vostre non ci hanno permesso il metter' in dubbio giamai la prontezza de gli Animi vostri in ubbidire alle sante determinationi de' Superiori. Laonde essendosi compiaciuta la sacra Congregatione de gli Eminentissimi Cardinali sopra le consulte de Vescovi, e Regolari di ascoltar' benignamente a' mesi passati le supplichevoli instanze, che faceste di essere restituite alla cura, e governo de Monaci Camaldolesi. . . . Risposero concordemente non potersi discostar punto dalla me[n]te santissima del prefato sommo Pontefice, delle cui ordinationi erano essi non Arbitri, mà essecutori. . . . Dilettissime, nelle viscere del Signore, e con tutta la virtù dello spirito nostro vi preghiamo à concorrere di buona voglia in cosa, che tanto espressamente Iddio per mezo de' supremi suoi Ministri in terra vi palesa essere di sua volontà, sicurissime di non errare mentre seguirete, non lo spirito proprio, mà quello di Christo Giesù vostro Sposo, il quale discese dal Trono della Maestà sua per solmente ubbidire, dicendo egli stesso: *Veni non ut faciam voluntatem meam, sed eius, qui misit me Patris:* intanto che non prima cessò di ubbidire, che di vivere: *Factus,* come scrive l'Apostolo, *obediens usque ad mortem.* . . . Questa è la vera Pace, l'Honor' unico, e la Gloria singolare delle persone religiose; l'esser sempre leali, et uniformi di Volontà al beneplacito divino. . . . Piaccia allo Spirito di Verità di assistervi col suo chiarissimo lume, si come speriamo, acciò non erriate nella cognitione, & elettione del meglio." A transcription also appears in Camaldoli MS 652, fols. 32r–34r.

13. Cardinal Archbishop Niccolò Albergati Ludovisi, ASV, VR, sez. monache, 1647 (aprile–maggio), packet of 5 Apr. 1647: "Questa, qual si sia, ultima diligenza

è riuscita, per quanto si congettura, di grand'utile appresso il popolo, e parmi, che tanto i nobili, quanto i cittadini, e la plebe istessa mostrino di sentir malissi-mam[en]te un'ostinazione simile per ogni capo mostruosa."

14. Nuns of Santa Cristina, ASB, Notarile, Belvisi, Giulio, Prot. 23 (1646–52), fols. 105r–6r: "Minacciate censure, scommuniche, et altre pene in caso, che non vogliono obedire, . . . protestano, e reprotestano caso, che aderissero à pigliar per lor Confessore, et Capellani Preti secolari, far ciò per paura delle censure, et pene, et non altrim[en]te volontariam[en]te, mà p[er] forza, parendogli non se gli do-vesse negare tal Confessore Regolare per quiete delle loro conscienze, essendo en-trate nel d[ett]o Monasterio sotto la Regola, et governo delle loro anime mediante Regolari, che in altro modo . . . non si sariano entrate, et perciò di nuovo protestano, et reprotestano voler che le lor ragioni li siano sempre salve, et illese in tutto, e p[er] tutto, come erano avanti s'inducessero à consentire di pigliar Preti secolari, . . . protestando come sopra non farlo volontariam[en]te, mà sforzatam[en]te e per paura delle Censure, e pene, . . . mà il tutto procederà dalla viva forza di chi può commandare, et non che lo faccino volontariam[en]te, mà sforzatam[en]te come sopra, e per sfuggire le Censure, pene, et altri aggravij minacciatoli, et cosi protes-tano, reprotestano, e dicchiarano, et no[n] solo nel modo, e forma predetti, mà in ogni altro miglior modo, che di raggione si può." Another copy in ASV, VR, sez. monache, 1647 (aprile–maggio), notarial document dated 13 Apr. 1647.

15. Cardinal Archbishop Niccolò Albergati Ludovisi, ASV, VR, sez. monache, 1647 (aprile–maggio), letter dated 20 Mar., in packet for 3 May 1647: "La domanda mi parve com'è realmente, strana, e maravigliosa: ad ogni modo il torrente delle preghiere è poi cresciuto à segno, che n'hà finalmente spuntato il mio consenso; . . . non volendo gl'Olivetani entrarvi in conto alcuno."

16. Cardinal Archbishop Niccolò Albergati Ludovisi, ibid., letter of 24 Apr., in packet of 3 May 1647: "Mezzo più opportuno di questo non possa ritrovarsi per saldamente stabilire ogni perfetta consolazione, e quiete delle Monache nel nuovo stato." Cristofano Pamfili's petition appears ibid. (giugno–agosto) in the packet for 14 June. The Congregation's request for assurances appears ibid., Reg. monial. 2 (1647), fol. 328r, dated 7 June 1647.

17. Cardinal Archbishop Niccolò Albergati Ludovisi, ibid., sez. monache, 1647 (giugno–agosto), letter of 3 July, in packet of 19 July: "In niun secolare possono haver confidenza, che da' secolari furono sempre tradite." Ibid. (settembre), packet of 13 Sept.: "Ne potendo . . . assicurare le sue Conscienze ne Preti secolari Depu-tatoli non informati in conto alcuno del suo Instituto."

18. Cardinal Archbishop Niccolò Albergati Ludovisi, ibid., Reg. monial. 2 (1647), fols. 521r–v, dated 27 Sept. 1647: "Non solo continovino più che mai nella loro disubbidienze, mà di più con detestabil p[er]tinacia si privino volontaria-m[en]te dell'uso de' Sacram[en]ti, e di quel cibo celeste, che nodrisce, e mantiene in vita spirituale il Religioso." For Ruggeri's remark, see Camaldoli MS 652, fol. 34r.

19. Cardinal Archbishop Niccolò Albergati Ludovisi, ASV, VR, sez. monache, 1647 (novembre–dicembre), letter of 30 Oct. 1647, in packet of 15 Nov.: "Repulsata la prima, ne replicarono, e con maggior fervore, la 2.a istanza, alla quale, per non discostarmi in queste ultime esperienze da' soliti principij di morbidezza, hebbi per bene di condescendere, e di fatto vi condescesi. Non contente le Madri . . . man-

darono il giorno appresso à ripregarmi, che quando dentro si breve spazio no[n] havessero ottenuta la sperata risposta, io mi fossi contentato di soprassedere fin'all'arrivo dell medesima. . . . A tal richiesta io mi resi affatto inesorabile, et in questi termini ci troviamo."

20. Cardinal Archbishop Niccolò Albergati Ludovisi, ibid. letter of 6 Nov. 1647, in packet of 15 Nov.: "Come Padre amorevole dell'istesse Monache, supplico vivam[en]te à degnarsi di consolarle, essendo per altro il lor Monastero (toltone quest'accidente) una de più esemplari, e più commendabili, ch'io m'habbia nella propria giurisdittione."

21. Nuns of Santa Cristina, ibid., undated, included with previous document in packet of 15 Nov.: "Non mai havressimo pensato Em[inentissi]mi è R[everendissi]mi Sig[no]ri che povere Religiose serrate trà ferri è murri, solo humiliss[imamen]te chiedendoli un Confessore di n[ost]ra Regola restassero tanto offesi, che non solo non lo volessero concedere, mà ancora ordinar restassero fossimo murate è conforme à sacri canoni severam[en]te castigate. . . . Em[inentissi]mi Sig[no]ri siamo innocenti, siamo state screditate app[ress]o q[ues]to Sacro Tribunale accusate per disubidenti, contumaci è vogliamo cozzar con superiori ciò è tanto falso che in solo udirlo habbiamo orrore. . . . avanti questa M[ad]re di Misericordia humilm[en]te supplicando ne facii gratia d'un Confessore di n[ost]ra Regola acciò con confidenza possiamo espurgare le nostre conscientie, e si raccordino Padri che i loro sacri Manti sono fatti vermigli nel sangue di Giesù da' esso per Salvar l'Anime sparso [illeg.] di novo spargeria per un Anima sola habbiano pietà di noi imitando il nostro Dio di cui sono Ministri che humilm[en]te inchinandoci le bacciamo le sacre Porpore."

22. Cardinal Archbishop Niccolò Albergati Ludovisi, ibid., letter dated 27 Nov. 1647, in packet dated 11 Dec.: "La meraviglia concepita dalle Monache in sentendo, che alla lor ferma parola non si desse più che tanto di fede; mà ciò non ostante io rimasi immobile nella prima risposta." The Congregation's letter of 15 Nov. appears ibid., Reg. monial. 2 (1647), fol. 555r, dated 15 Nov. 1647.

23. For the Congregation's final letter, see ibid., fol. 576v–77r, dated 11 Dec. 1647. Mauro Ruggeri, Camaldoli MS 652, fol. 34r: "Fu tanto il spavento, che ricevettero da quest altro colpo, che come son stato accertato Una D. Lucrezia Villani [*sic*] p[er] altro prudentissima fù offesa nel cervello, et quando sentiva sonare la campanella della Clausura dal timore grande, ch'aveva conciputo faceva motti di conquassione."

10. THE PONTIFICAL CONSECRATION OF VIRGINS

1. On the dating of Canuti's painting, see Francesco Arcangeli et al., *Maestri della pittura del Seicento emiliano* (Bologna: Edizioni Alfa, 1959), 159. For a listing of the common representations of Saint Christina, see Louis Réau, *Iconographie de l'art Chrétien*, 3: 1 (Paris: Presses universitaires de France, 1958), 303–4. Marcello Moscini points out the unusual subject matter of the altarpiece at Santa Cristina in *Cristina di Bolsena: Culto e iconografia* (Viterbo: Agnesotti, 1986), 196. My thanks to Robert Kendrick for bringing Moscini's book to my attention.

2. Gabriella Zarri suggests how certain aspects of the ritual in the seventeenth and eighteenth centuries were specifically intended to emphasize this separation. See "Recinti sacri: Sito e forma dei monasteri femminili a Bologna tra '500 e '600," in *Luoghi sacri e spazi della santità*, ed. Sofia Boesch Gajano and Lucetta Scaraffia (Turin: Rosenberg & Sellier, 1990), 385–86.

3. This generalized description is based on Gian Lodovico Masetti Zannini, " 'Suavità di canto' e 'purità di cuore': Aspetti della musica nei monasteri femminili romani," in *La cappella musicale nell'Italia della Controriforma*, ed. Oscar Mischiati and Paolo Russo (Cento: Centro studi G. Baruffaldi, 1993), 123–41, which includes examples of texts for the *tonsura* on 136–37; also *Ordo admittendi virgines ad monasterii ingressum . . . secundum morem congregationis Cassinensis* (Milan: Heirs of Pacifico Pontio and Giovanni Battista Piccaleum, 1607), which includes the rite of profession as well. My thanks to Robert Kendrick for providing me with a copy of the *Ordo*. The rites for use in Bologna appear in *Ritus recipiendi virgines ad religionis habitum nec non ad professionem novitias in civitate & diocesi Bononiæ* (Bologna: Vittorio Benacci, 1626).

4. AAB, Misc. vecchie 808, fasc. 13, "Informatione sopra Mon[aste]ri alla cura ep[iscop]ale sottoposti": "Li giorni che vestono le suor' s'empie il Mon[aste]ro di donne secolari et vano discorsendo da per tutto cosa che porta poco utile. Et per haver' piu commodità di goder' le parenti et amiche fanno queste feste il doppo pranzo. Pare saria piu convenevole farlo la matina et celebrar' la messa, et communicare quella, o, quelle che si vestono. L'istesso si dice quando fanno la professione."

5. See Christiane Klapisch-Zuber, "The Griselda Complex: Dowry and Marriage Gifts in the Quattrocento," in *Women, Family, and Ritual in Renaissance Italy*, trans. Lydia Cochrane (Chicago: University of Chicago Press, 1985), 213–46. For a description of various noble Bolognese weddings from the fifteenth to the seventeenth centuries, see Ludovico Frati, *La vita privata in Bologna dal secolo xiii al xvii*, 2d ed. (Bologna: Nicola Zanichelli, 1928; repr., Rome: Bardi editore, 1968), 41–49.

6. "Costitutioni generali da osservarsi dalle monache le quali viveranno in congregatione, et clausura" ("General Constitutions to be observed by the nuns who live in community and within the cloister"), Bologna, Archivio Isolani-Lupari, Fondo Paleotti, cartone 33: 40: "Quando s'havrà da dare l'habito monacale à qualch⟨⟩ ò accettarla alla professione, overo ministrarle il sacra ⟨⟩ della confirmatione, il Vescovo, ne qualsivoglia superior⟨⟩ Regolare come secolare, ne il Confessore, ò altra persona ent⟨⟩ dentro la clausura, ma à tutte queste fontioni sia da comp⟨⟩ alla finestrella della chiesa di fuori, dove si ministra il san⟨⟩ sacramento dell'eucharestia, stando le gioveni, ò Monache d[?⟨⟩] Nissuna finestra, uscio, ò buco alcuno, che guardi fuora dell ⟨⟩sura di qualsivoglia Monasterio non s'apra mai senza lic⟨⟩ vescovo, il quale non la concedera se non considerato dilige⟨⟩ il luogo, et la necessità." Some of the beginning pages of Paleotti's "Costitutioni generali" survive in cartone 25. The margins are damaged by fire, with some loss of text, as indicated above. *Episcopale Bononiensis civitatis et diocesis* (Bologna: Alessandro Benacci, 1580), fol. 188, "Modo da Osservarsi nel Fare la Professione."

7. ASV, VR, Reg. episc. 1 (1573–76), 847–48, dated c. 16 May 1576.

8. Archivio Isolani-Lupari, Fondo Paleotti, cartone 25, E68/4: "Quel giorno, nel quale la giovane haverà da entrare nel Monasterio, debba andare la mattina per

tempo senza sorte alcuna di pompa, con habito semplice, senza ornamento, frappatura & coda, vestita di bianco, ò nero, ò leonato, over pavonazzo: eccetto, che se per voto, ò devotione non portasse il berettino, senza rizzi ritorti, fiori, ò altri abbigliamenti in capo. Come anco per la Città, mentre sarà fuori, non ardira andare in altro habito, che nel sopradetto, & in somma senza compagnia di carrozze: ma havendo solamente seco due, ò tre delle più prossime parenti, che l'accompagnino al Monasterio: le quali subito se ne ritornaranno in dietro. & la giovane sia ricevuta alla porta solamente dalla superiora, con le portinare, & nel giorno, poi che haverà da pigliar l'habito santo, si escluda dalla Chiesa di fuori ogni concorso di persone, & di musiche, & di adunanze, & si tenghi serrata la Chiesa, dovendo solo intrare li Ministri necessarij, per vestire la secolare, ò far professione la Novitia, & non altri." An earlier, largely identical *Ordini da servarsi nell'admettere dentro li monasterii di monache le putte . . . & darli l'habito di novizza & della professione* (Bologna: Alessandro Benacci, 1577) survives in AAB, Misc. vecchie 808, fasc. 21.

9. Quoted in Zarri, "Recinti sacri," 385.

10. BUB, MS It. 770/21: 588.

11. ASB, Demaniale 80/814 (San Guglielmo), entries 199 (2 Feb. 1628) and 200 (8 Feb. 1628): "Stetero in refettorio con le moniche à pra[n]so, e tutto il giorno sino alle due hore di notte co[n] nostra gran consolatione, et se gli fece tutto quel'honore à noi possible, et andorono p[er] tutto il nostro monasterio, e furono se[m]pre accompagnate da Sor Maria Aloisa figlia della Ill[ustrissi]ma Sig[no]ra Marchesa Aloisa, et nepote di quelle altre Sig[no]re." Caterina Malaspina had been accepted on 25 Apr. 1627 (ibid., entry 158). On 18 Jan. 1628, she had undertaken her final brief visit to her family (ibid., entry 197).

12. In this respect investitures, professions, and consecrations had much in common with other aspects of early modern conspicuous consumption described by Peter Burke in "Conspicuous Consumption in Seventeenth-Century Italy," in *The Historical Anthropology of Early Modern Italy: Essays in Perception and Communication* (Cambridge: Cambridge University Press, 1987), 132–49.

13. "The Griselda Complex," 223. On *torte di frutta* at San Guglielmo, see Mario Fanti, *Abiti e lavori delle monache di Bologna* (Bologna: Tamari, 1972), 90–91.

14. In 1609, for example, the Sacred Congregation decreed that only saints' portraits could be hung in choir, and not cardinals' portraits, even if their sisters lived in the convent. BAV, MS Borg. Lat. 71, fol. 32v. Nuns were also forbidden to display their coats of arms above cell doorways or to embroider them on door coverings. See Gabriella Zarri, "Monasteri femminili e città (secoli xv–xvii)," in *Storia d'Italia: Annali,* 9: *La chiesa e il potere politico dal Medioevo all'età contemporanea,* ed. Giorgio Chittolini and Giovanni Miccoli (Turin: Giulio Einaudi, 1986), 391. At least at Santa Cristina they continued to do so, however.

15. Gian Lodovico Masetti Zannini, "Composizioni poetiche e trattatelli spirituali per monacazioni benedettine del Settecento," in *Settecento monastico italiano,* ed. Giustino Farnedi and Giovanni Spinelli (Cesena: Badia di Santa Maria del Monte, 1990), 582, which cites Olga Pinto, *Nuptialia: Saggio di bibliografia di scritti italiani pubblicati dal 1484 al 1799* (Florence, 1971). I thank Robert Kendrick for calling Masetti Zannini's article to my attention. For a bibliography of Venetian examples, see Gabriele Mazzucco, "Discorsi e poesie per monache stampati a Venezia nel secolo xviii," *Benedectina* 32 (1985): 161–200.

16. Masetti Zannini, "Composizioni poetiche," 583.

17. Quoted in Alcuin Blamires, *Woman Defamed and Woman Defended: An Anthology of Medieval Texts* (Oxford: Clarendon Press; New York: Oxford University Press, 1992), 43.

18. In Bologna, see, for example, Giulio Cesare Arresti's Masses, op. 2 (1663), commissioned by Giulia Maria Vittoria Malvezzi of Santa Maria Nuova, who made her solemn profession in October 1663 at age eighteen. Three collections dedicated to nuns at Santa Cristina appeared around the time of consecrations there: Banchieri's *Messa Solenne* (1599), which refers to its dedicatee Emilia Grassi rather pointedly as "madre donna," as if she had recently been consecrated, Cesena's *Compieta con letanie* (1606), and Porta's *Vaga ghirlanda* (1613). For collections intended to fill similar purposes in Milan, see Robert Kendrick, "Genres, Generations and Gender: Nuns' Music in Early Modern Milan, c. 1550–1706" (Ph.D. diss., New York University, 1993).

19. Elissa Weaver, "The Convent Wall in Tuscan Convent Drama," in *The Crannied Wall: Women, Religion, and the Arts in Early Modern Europe*, ed. Craig Monson (Ann Arbor: University of Michigan Press, 1992), 83.

20. ASB, Demaniale 167/734 (Santa Maria Nuova), "Raccordi delle monache," unnumbered folio: "P[rim]a delle suppe di fegadelli in tanti Piatti per Tavola; Per antipasto del Melone, salame, et un figadelo di vitello; di poi del Vitello allesso e mezo Polastro per ciascuna arrosto; del formaggio di forma, et una bella Pera per frutta. Con del Vino a tutto Pasto esquisitiss[im]o." Descriptions of sermons tend to eclipse banquet menus in these "Raccordi delle monache," however.

21. On the notations in secular *recordanze,* see Klapisch-Zuber, "The Griselda Complex," 218. By the late Seicento, nuns at Santa Cristina were customarily charged a flat fee of £80 for each of the banquets at their acceptance, profession, and consecration. BCB, MS B450/7, "Nota della dote, et mobili, che si danno alle giovani, che vogliono accettarsi, vestirsi, professarsi, e consecrarsi nel monastero di Santa Christina."

22. ASB, Demaniale 48/4891 (Sant'Agostino): "Essendo mente della Sagra Congreg[azion]e de Vescovi, e Regolari, e dell'Em[inentissi]mo e R[everendissi]mo Sig[no]r Card[ina]le Arcivesc[ov]o che in occasione d'accettare zitelle alla Religione, ò ammetterle all'habito, ò alla Professione, no[n] si facci dalle Monache Rapresentatione, ò sula Porta de Monisteri ò in altro luogo, che possano esser vedute o udite da p[er]sone secolari . . . quant'anco fossero semplici dialoghi di due p[er]sone solame[n]te; ò soliloqui d'una sol p[er]sona." For a similar prohibition from 1608, see ibid., 51/3918 (Santa Margherita).

23. ASB, Demaniale 80/814 (San Gugliemo), entry no. 1019: "Adi 28 febraro 1656. Raccordo Come Sor A[n]giola Maria Catterina Grassi fece la santa proffessione facendo le Honoranze Consuette del Monastero et Regalo di Una Colatione co[n] una forma di sapone p[er] ciascheduna.—Sor Silvia Ortensia fece una Beliss[i]ma festa in chiesa ch[e] fù il detto Mortorio di xpo [i.e., Christo] Essendo Essa priora del carnevale." On the play tradition at San Gugliemo, see Gian Lodovico Masetti Zannini, "Lavori, 'fioretti' e rappresentazioni nel monastero di San Gugliemo (1624–1659)," *Strenna storica bolognese* 33 (1983): 162–73. BCB, MS B83: 399: "In occasione della vestizione d'An[n]a Margarita del Co[nte] Federico Be-

rualdi nel monast[er]o di S. Margarita si cantò un'Opera intitol[at]a Attilio Regolo, et il di d[ett]o del 27 p[er] vederla entrò nel Monast[er]o la corte di Modona con dodici Dame." The Santa Margherita *Attilio Regolo* may have been a revival of Pietro Paolo Laurenti's *Attilio Regolo in Affrica*, performed in Bologna by the Accademia degli Instabili during Carnival in 1701, for which the printed libretto survives in the Civico Museo Bibliografico Musicale in Bologna (no. 2628 [in the printed catalogue, no. 2648]).

24. Antonio Francesco Giovagnoni, ASB, Demaniale 48/1817 (Sant'Elena): "Il che vien'ancor ordinato in d[ett]a Bolla, et Editto in occasione d'ammettere le Novizze all'habito regolare, ò Professione non permettendosi con tal'occasione musiche, fuochi, spari di mortaletti, suono di Trombe, o Tamburi dispensamento in Chiesa, ò Porte, ò Parlatorij di fiori, e robbe comestibili, ne a spese de Monasteri, ne di particolari, ò Parenti delle Citelle, sarà dunque parte della M[ad]re Superiora subito ricevuta la presente lettera farla leggere in publico, acciò da tutte sia udita, et osservata, e Dio le benedichi." Other copies ibid., 17/4798 (Santissima Concezione) and 84/3233 (Santi Vitale et Agricola).

25. ASV, VR, Reg. monial. 24 (1677), fols. 15r–v, dated 22 Jan. 1677; ibid., 30 (1683), fols. 234v–35r, dated 24 Sept. 1683, and fols. 310r–v, dated 17 Dec. 1683.

26. Both worries regarding conspicuous consumption were commonly voiced throughout the early modern period. See Burke, "Conspicuous Consumption," 143–44.

27. Alfeo Giacomelli, "La dinamica della nobiltà bolognese nel xviii secolo," in *Famiglie senatorie e istituzioni cittadine a Bologna nel Settecento: Atti del colloquio, Bologna, 2–3 febbraio 1980* (Bologna: Istituto per la storia bolognese, 1980), 55–112, esp. 66–71. See also Giancarlo Roversi, *Palazzi e case nobili del '500 a Bologna* (Bologna: Grafis edizioni, 1986), 70–81, 363.

28. ASB, Demaniale 80/814 (S. Guglielmo), unnumbered entry: "Ricordo come alli 19. Decembre 1703 si Misse il Capitolo della Accetatione dell'Ill[ustriss]ma Sig[no]ra Giugliana Maria Banzi, quale fu Belissima venne puoi L'Antivigilia di Natale che fu in Domenica, e nell'entrare in Chiesa si fece una sinfonia Belissima da Sona[to]ri in Chiesa fuori, con quatro Trombetti in strada che sonorono sempre sino alle tre hore di notte ... si vesti puoi il giorno di S. Giovanni ... si vesti con Musica, con invito generale di Dame e fu il Cardinale Giacomo Boncompagni che li diede l'habito."

29. ASB, Archivio Malvezzi de' Medici, filza 308.

30. BUB, MS It. 225/2, fol. 42; ASB, Demaniale 82/3088 (Gesù e Maria), letter of 13 Oct. 1621 from Monsignor Buratti in Rome to suor Agostina Tomacelli: "spese che fanno le [altre] monache ... per sola ambitione, delle musiche et suoni con altro fine che per lodi d'Iddio."

31. Alessandro Macchiavelli, BCB, MS Gozz. 358: 12: "Tutto giorno publicam[en]te si declama contro le grandi spese vi vogliono p[er] far delle Suore, ma pure ognuno vuol fare piu dell'altro." Ibid., 359: 9: "Sono indicibile le spese vi vogliono p[er] queste funzioni, e pure niuno vi cerca riparo."

32. Francesca Antonia Petrini, ASV, VR, sez. monache, 1664 (gennaio–febbraio), letter of 2 Jan. 1664: "Pomposam[en]te con Musiche ... p[er] evitare le spese, e perche tali pompe sono eccessive per humiltà Religiosa." Maddalena Liverolli and

Anna Mucciarelli, ibid., 1697 (luglio–agosto), letter of 5 July 1697: "Pompa è lusso più tosto inconveniente . . . con modo più essemplare è decente."

33. See Burke, "Conspicuous Consumption," 134.

34. Nuns of San Pietro Martire, ASB, Demaniale 53/2027 (San Pietro Martire), opening 6: "Adi 15 Agosto 1713. Se fece fare la Professione alla Gentile Piana, hora Suor Maria Spera in Dio, e nella Professione p[er] piu devotione de secolari, si pratico il seguente stile cioè, Doppo il discorso solito fattoli dal P[ad]re Confessore, si sona brevem[en]te L'Organo, arivata al Fenestrino della S[an]ta Comunione fece la solita Professione, poi mutandoli L'Abito, ma non il Velo, sono L'Organo, e vestita, si prostro avanti al S[antissi]m[o Sacramento] vi stata sino che fu finito di cantare in coro il salmo Laudate Dominum de Celis; e fatta alzare Le due superiore la condusero avanti al Altare della S[antissi]ma del Rosario, da indi al Altare del P[ad]re S[an] Dom[enic]o; cantando il coro Maria Mater gr[ati]e, e L'Inno del S[an]to P[ad]re e cosi terminò la funtione; che ho qui notato, p[er]che ne ne sia Memoria se le altre Priore vorano seguitare questo stile, essendo in loro arbitrio il fare come p[rim]a, cioè il discorso del P[ad]re Confess[o]re, e la Professione senza altro canto ne suono che rendeva poca devotione. [In different ink:] Invece del salmo sud[et]to e meglio cantare L'Inno del P[adre] S[an] Dom[eni]co e di S[an] Pietro M[arti]re."

35. ASB, Demaniale 80/814 (San Guglielmo), entry no. 156: "Ri[cor]do come in questo giorno passò à Miglior Vita la Madre sor penelopea Viggiani et gli ministro i santissimi sacramenti Il Sig[no]r Do[n] Antonio Vanotti et Nell spirare che fece li augelli venero in gra[n] numero alla sua fenestra è fecero un' suavissimo canto qual rende stupore et devotione à tutte quelle che herano prese[n]te."

36. Costanzo Somigli and Tommaso Bargellini, *Ambrogio Traversari monaco camaldolese* (Bologna: Edizioni Dehoniane, 1986), 156.

37. BCB, MS Gozz. 328, entry for "11 Giugno [1663]." The discussion of the Zoppi family in Pompeo Dolfi, *Cronologia delle famiglie nobili di Bologna* (Bologna: Giovanni Battista Ferroni, 1670; repr., Bologna: Forni editore, n.d.), 290, suggests the distinguished Cesare Zoppi, doctor of philosophy, medicine, and law as the probable father. Compare also BUB, MS It. 225/2, fol. 49: "Adi 20 [giugno 1720] si fece monaca una figlia dell' Sig[no]re Senatore Beccadelli nelle R[everende] M[adri] di S. Christina con invito di tutta la nobiltà, con musica solenne." BCB, MS B3667: 107: "Adi 29 [novembre 1726] La mattina prese l'Abito nel Monastero di S. Christina la Sig[no]ra Marchesa Margherita Bolognini Amorini con grande concorso di Nobiltà, e v'intervenne il Re [i.e., the Stuart Pretender] col Figlio Maggiore."

38. René Metz, *La Consécration des vierges dans l'église romaine: Etude d'histoire de la liturgie* (Paris: Presses universitaires de France, 1954). For a brief study of consecrations among English nuns, with an edition of the relevant chants, see Ann Bagnal Yardley, "The Marriage of Heaven and Earth: A Late Medieval Source of the *Consecratio virginum*," *Current Musicology* 45–47 (1990): 305–24.

39. Metz, *La Consécration*, 281, 354, 361.

40. Burke, "Conspicuous Consumption," 140–41.

41. For the secular equivalent, see Klapisch-Zuber, "The Griselda Complex," esp. 224–28.

42. Lucrezia Vizzana, ASV, VR, posiz. 1607, A–B: "la quale non è altro, che una cerimonia che conferma la professione."

43. Metz, *La Consécration,* 340–41.

44. BAV, MS Ferr. 612, fol. 12r: "Per consacrare le Monache il Vescovo deve entrare nella clausura con i assistenti, et no[n] far'uscir fuori le Monache." The pope's contradictory ruling, to the bishop of Ascoli, is recorded in ASV, Reg. episc. 12 (1586/III), fol. 92.

45. ASV, VR, Reg. monial. 2 (1647), fol. 245v, dated 12 Apr. 1647; ibid., sez. monache, 1668 (giugno–luglio), letter of 7 July 1668.

46. Metz, *La Consécration,* 341.

47. Ibid., 343, citing Joaquim Nabuco, *Pontificalis romani expositio juridico-practica* (Petrópolis, Brazil, 1945).

11. THE CAMPAIGN FOR THE CONSECRATION

1. Ludovico Maria Orsi's assessment, "homo dotto e pratico, . . . gran testa e cervelone che lui sa bene menare le saccole," appears in a letter of 15 Mar. 1696 to donna Luigia Orsina Orsi in ASB, Demaniale 49/2910 (Santa Cristina), "Lettere del Molto Rev[eren]do Padre Lodovico Maria Orsi."

2. ASB, Demaniale 49/2910 (Santa Cristina), volume of letters, primarily from Sabbatini, regarding the Sacra of 1699; don Agostino's original view that recourse to anyone but the pope *saria tempo perso* appears in a letter from Ludovico Orsi to his sister dated 16 Feb. 1697. Barely two weeks later, don Agostino had reversed his view, correctly predicting the pope's response to the petition, in a letter, probably to Ludovico Orsi, of 2 Mar. 1697. For other relevant details, see also letters from Sabbatini dated 20 Aug. 1697 and 1 Jan. 1698.

3. Ibid., letter from Sabbatini to Ludovico Maria Orsi, dated 11 Jan. 1698, and another from Sabbatini to Orsi of 18 Jan. 1698, containing the two quotations, "Ne V.R. ne le Monache mi hanno mai detto che havessero fatto questo ricorso alla d[ett]a Cong[regazio]ne dei Riti perche se l'havesse saputo . . . non si sariano fatto tante fatiche ne tante diligenze che hoggi non servano à niente. . . . Mà che hà che fare questo con l'instanza, che si fà che la Consecratione si faccia nella Chiesa esteriore nella forma che prescrisse il Pontificale Romano?"

4. Ibid., "Piena e distinta Informatione del fatto occorso in Occasione della Lite . . . ": "quale con Destra, e Matura Prudenza hà saputo regolare, et in se ritte-nere tutto ciò ch'havrebbe potuto riuscire pregiudiciale à questa Causa."

5. A petition requesting age dispensations for the four youngest consacrees, Anna Maria Righi, Giulia Caterina Belvisi, Domitilla Felice Gandolfi, and Romualda Angellica Ghirardelli, survives in ASV, VR, posiz. 1624, B–F.

6. Ludovico Ludovisi, quoted in Camaldoli MS 652, fols. 20v–21r: "Frati Frati, se io dovessi p[er]dere la Beretta più non farette sagrare in Bologna."

7. Giacomo Boncompagni, BUB, MS It. 3897/39 ("MSS—LXVIII v. 2"): "Im-mobilm[en]te, voglio credere, dagli Arcivescovi antecessori si saria perseverato, se [illegible—fossero?] considerando essi la sovravivenza di tutte, o parte di quelle stesse che amaram[en]te provasono d'esser levate da loro regolari, e sottomesse all'ordin[ari]o (delle quali più alcuna ora non vive) cred'io giudicassero ispediente

non dissentire, a fine non si eccitassero continue stravaganze, . . . Ma di presente che tutte le antiche sono morte come ho detto, altro non è da sperarsi se non quel compimento di bene tanto com[m]endato dagli Autori sudetti appoggiati alla inappellabile risoluzione del Cot[est]a Sagra Cong[regazio]ne." The document is unsigned and undated, and contains no overt links to Boncompagni, but clearly refers to the suit involving the archbishop and nuns of Santa Cristina in the 1690s.

8. ASV, VR, posiz. 1599, A–C, letter dated 30 Mar. 1599: "Le quali è già un pezzo che desiderano esser' velate con quella medesima solenità con la quale sono sempre fin' qui state velate tutte l'altre."

9. ASV, VR, Reg. regular. 3 (1601), fol. 6ov, dated 2 Jan. 1601: "Si prohibisca che nell'avvenire il G[e]n[er]ale, ne altri superiori possano in modo alcuno in occasione di vestir monache o di ammetterle alla professione o per qualsivoglia altra causa celebrare messa solenne, ne bassa dentro il monas[ter]o no[n] p[er] tanta qualsivoglia consuetudine, o uso in contrario. Et che finalmente si facia la cerimonia del velo negro che dimandano della Sacra dentro la clausura, et alle grate senza lasciar più uscire in modo alcuno le monache nella chiesa esteriore."

10. The nuns' petition appears in ASV, VR, posiz. 1624, B–F. According to Mauro Ruggeri, the old papal privilege could not be found when Ludovico Ludovisi and his ministers demanded that it be produced; it subsequently turned up in the Camaldolese archive at Sant'Ipolito di Faenza, in the general's study. See Camaldoli MS 652, fol. 21r. The ruling by the Congregation of the Council, "nella Chiesa ESTERIORE, purche solam[ent]e le Vergine da velarsi usisca dal Monastero, e niun'altra uscisca delle Monache, attesoche le Donne Secolari Parenti potevano esse assistere alla Vergine da Velarsi," was cited in the case before the Congregation of Sacred Rites in 1698, but is singularly vague, citing neither year, volume, nor folio. ASB, Demaniale 49/2910 (Santa Cristina), quoted in "Scrittura in Jure fatta dal Sigr. Scipione Zanelli . . . nella Causa delle RR Madri di S. Christina." A transcription of Zanelli's Latin original, including the full text of the ruling by the Congregation of the Council, appears in BUB, MS It. 770/61, fols. 28ar–iv. For another copy, see AAB, Misc. vecchie 262.

11. Ugo Capriani, "Chiesa e convento di Santa Cristina della Fondazza in Bologna: Ipotesi di ricerca e recupero" (Tesi di laurea, Università di Bologna, 1987–88), 147.

12. The petition to Urban VIII of 1633 is printed in *Annales Camaldulenses*, vol. 9 (Venice, 1773), appendix, col. 324. For the petition to the Congregation of Bishops, see ASV, VR, sez. monache, 1642 (gennaio–luglio), letter registered 18 July 1642. Ruggeri's comment, "invaghito dalla bella Sagra che fece delle Monache," appears in Camaldoli MS 652, fol. 31v.

13. Ruggeri quotes the £6,000 figure in Camaldoli MS 652, fol. 31v. His claim that it was six times normal is confirmed by convent expense records from much later, when in 1658 the total was £720 (AAB, Misc. vecchie 262, "RR MM S. Xpna cum D. Butrigario Haer.e," fols. 34v–35v); in 1699, £939:16:2; in 1711, £923:9:-; in 1729, £1,027:19:4 (see ASB, Demaniale 49/2910 [Santa Cristina]); in 1771, £1041:6:- (see AAB, Misc. vecchie 262, "Entrata, E Spesa Generale dalli 15. Marzo 1770 a tutto li 31 Marzo 1771").

14. ASV, VR, sez. monache, 1655 (settembre–dicembre), letters dated 17 Sept. 1655. The response appears ibid., Reg. monial. 7 (1655): 306–7, dated 17 Sept.

1655. Ibid., sez. monache, 1657 (gennaio–aprile), letter dated 20 Apr. 1657, with response, "Concedatur quoad 2a et 3a quoad p.a Nihil."

15. The fire destroyed all the choir stalls, the altars, and some paintings, and required £8,000 in repairs. See ibid., sez. monache, 1658 (gennaio–marzo), letter registered 12 Mar. 1658; ibid., 1659 (maggio), letter registered 23 May 1659.

16. Orsi's comment, "scorgo all'usanza di Roma, bisogna lavorare di bursa," appears in a letter dated 11 Mar. 1697 in ASB, Demaniale 49/2910 (Santa Cristina). Baldi's remark appears in Mario Fanti, "Le classi sociali e il governo di Bologna all'inizio del secolo xvii in un'opera inedita di Camillo Baldi," *Strenna storica bolognese* 11 (1961): 153.

17. Ruggeri, for example, speaks of the nuns' "heroic defense" of their liberty against the forces of Ludovico Ludovisi (Camaldoli MS 652, fol. 25r). References to their "heroic" sacrifice and valiant defense of their liberties in 1698 are discussed subsequently. On the nature of the heroic ideal, see Romeo De Maio's classic study, "L'ideale eroico nei processi di canonizzazione della Controriforma," in *Riforme e miti nella chiesa del Cinquecento* (Naples: Guida editori, 1973), 257–78, which includes a substantial bibliography of other writings on heroicism and sanctity. On the special emphasis upon heroic virtue as an increasingly essential saintly attribute in the first half of the Seicento, see Ottavia Niccoli, "Il confessore e l'inquisitore: A proposito di un manoscritto bolognese del Seicento," in *Finzione e santità tra Medioevo ed età moderna,* ed. Gabriella Zarri (Turin: Rosenberg & Sellier, 1991), 417–18, and Gabriella Zarri, " 'Vera' santità, 'Simulata' santità: Ipotesi e riscontri," ibid., 19.

18. ASB, Demaniale 49/2910 (Santa Cristina); Colloredo's relationship to the Orsi is mentioned in a letter from don Agostino dated 11 Jan. 1698. See Sabbatini's letters of 1 Jan. and 18 Jan.: "Perche con tutte le nostre ragioni trattandosi d'un Arcivescovo, che è Card[ina]le si può perdere per che non basta in questi Casi d'haver ragione"; "Coppia d'Attestati di Cavaglieri Bolognesi in Occasione di Sacra" (dated 1 Dec. 1696). In a letter of 21 Aug. 1697, Sabbatini had already requested a copy of the testimonials of Agucchi, Malvezzi et al.

19. ASB, Demaniale 49/2910 (Santa Cristina), letters of 18 March and 14 May. Several of Bolognetti's own letters survive among the documents from the case.

20. On the princess Pallavicina's intercessions, see Sabbatini's letter to Ludovico Maria Orsi of 11 Jan. 1698 ibid. The remark regarding the princess Ottoboni, "non stimare infruttuosa che la Madre Superiora scrivessi una lettera alla S[igno]ra P[ri]n[ci]pessa Ottoboni à Venezia e la supplicasse di raccomandar la Causa al Sig[no]r Card[inal]e Ottoboni suo figliuolo et à qualche altro Cardinale della Cong[regazio]ne," appears in a letter to the bursar dated 18 Mar. 1698. On Ottoboni's active musical patronage, see Hans-Joachim Marx, "Die Musik am Hofe Pietro Kardinal Ottobonis unter Arcangelo Corelli," *Analecta musicologica* 5 (1968): 104–77. On his intercession on behalf of Santa Radegonda, see Robert Kendrick, "Genres, Generations and Gender: Nuns' Music in Early Modern Milan, c. 1550–1706" (Ph.D. diss., New York University, 1993), 201 and n. 59, 871–73. Ottoboni was also an intimate of Boncompagni's, and it had first been hoped that he might be able to influence the Bolognese archbishop in the nuns' favor. On Ottoboni's relationship to Boncompagni, see Sabbatini's letters of 12 and 15 Oct. 1697. Sabbatini's letter of 28 June 1698 indicates that although Ottoboni would not be present in

congregation at the critical meeting, he had promised to try to influence other cardinals in the nuns' favor.

21. ASB, Demaniale 49/2910 (Santa Cristina), letters of 1 Jan. and 18 Mar. On exchanges with the contessa Isabetta, see letters of 20 Dec. 1697 and 23 Mar. 1698. Sabbatini's remark, "trovassimo quasi tutti li Card[ina]li inclinati a favorire le Monache, e il S[ignor] Card[inal]e Grimani si farebbe anche riscaldato maggiorm[en]te per favorir la S[ignora] Contessa," appears in a letter dated May 1698. The development of similar networks by the nuns of Le Murate in Florence, stretching as far afield as Portugal, are stressed in K. J. P. Lowe, "Female Strategies for Success in a Male-Ordered World: The Benedictine Convent of Le Murate in Florence in the Fifteenth and Early Sixteenth Centuries," *Studies in Church History* 27 (1990): 209– 21. On various aspects of such networks in Italy, see Lucia Ferrante, Maura Palazzi, and Gianna Pomata, eds., *Ragnatele di rapporti: Patronage e reti di relazione nella storia delle donne* (Turin: Rosenberg & Sellier, 1988). Paola di Cori's "Unite e divise: Appunti su alcuni problemi di storia della solidarietà fra donne" from that collection offers a useful analysis of the divergent approaches to this theme in American and Italian feminist historiography of the 1970s and caveats about the dangers of anachronistic projection in analysis of the evidence.

22. Giovanni Battista Sabbatini, ASB, Demaniale 49/2910 (Santa Cristina), letter dated 14 May 1698: "questa non è una picca ch'habbia con le monache, . . . ma un puro motivo della sua Coscienza. . . . Nella detta lettera . . . scrive ancora poco bene delle Monache, et in particolare di alcune mà non sò di quali, e sopra di questo deve appoggiare il motivo della Coscienza. . . . Col dire di non poter far la funzione in altra forma che nella sud[ett]a p[er] motivo di Coscienza, vien ad infamar' in questa forma tutto il Monastero tanto appresso la Città com'appresso tutti gl'altri Monasteri della Religione che col veder far la funzione diversamente dall'altre volte potrebbe giustam[ent]e dubitar di qualche gran demerito delle Monache che fra le Consecrande ve ne sia qualche d'una ch'habbia corrispondenza d'affetto fuori del Monastero."

23. ASB, Demaniale 49/2910 (Santa Cristina), unsigned letter to Madre Allè dated 14 May 1698 whose contents and handwriting suggest Paolo Bolognetti: "Suo solito maledicenze contro cotesto monas[te]rio, ò Monache, . . . ch[e] ciò nol faceva p[er] picca mà p[er] impulso di Conscienza. . . . Simil modo di scrivere alle Cong[regazio]ni hà praticato altre volte, e massimo contro le Monach[e], ò Suore di S. Mattia, e S. luca, screditandole e diffamandole quanto poteva p[er] haver il suo intento i[n]vece di coprire i mancam[en]ti quando ve ne fosse stato, come Pastore pio." Bolognetti's view that for an archbishop, protection of his subject-clients was an obligation and point of honor was characteristic of his age, as is evident in the remarks of Mauro Ruggeri and Cardinal Desiderio Scalia quoted in chapter 8 above. See also "Introduzione," in Ferrante, Palazzi, and Pomata, eds., *Ragnatele di rapporti,* esp. 9–11, for a discussion of the complexities of honor and obligation that characterized such superior-subject relationships.

24. Ludovico Maria's comment, "q[ue]lla [lettera] del Sig[no]r Quar[ant]a Bolognetti no[n] è lettera se non benedetta," appears in an undated letter in ASB, Demaniale 49/2910 (Santa Cristina), which also speaks of "le sue figlie in S. Matheo." *Quaranta* was a common Bolognese term for any of the city's forty senators.

The unsigned letter from Rome dated 14 May 1698, apparently from a Bolognetti, remarks "vi [a San Mattia] havevo due sorelle." The two nuns from San Mattia were suor Maria Ippolita Bolognetti and suor Maria Gesualda Bolognetti, active at the convent from around 1680 until shortly after the turn of the century. See ASB, Demaniale 37/5798 (San Mattia), and BCB, MS B921: 212–13. Sabbatini's comments on Bolognetti's lobbying and the remark "e quasi sempre gli sono risolti contro, onde questa sua disgrazia non è, ch'una buona fortuna p[er] le Monache" appear in a letter of 12 June 1698 in ASB, Demaniale 49/2910 (Santa Cristina).

25. Bolognetti's suggestion appears in the unsigned letter of 14 May 1698 in ASB, Demaniale 49/2910 (Santa Cristina). For the earlier nuns' lament, see chapter 8 above. Colomba Carrati's remarks to Paolo Bolognetti, "Se tutte siam cattive, scandalose; dove sono gli scandali? . . . In cusi puoco tempo siam diventate tutte tanti Demonij?" appear in a letter of 23 May 1698.

26. Nuns of Santa Cristina, ASB, Demaniale 49/2910 (Santa Cristina), letter to Giovanni Benedetto Sabbatini, 28 May 1698: "Piaccia dunque a Vossignoria di credere, e di far ben concepire al S[igno]r Zanelli, che piu tosto vogliamo arrischiarci alla Negativa della sperata Giustitia presso la Sac[ra] Congreg[azion]e che arrestarci dalla giustissima, e . . . giustificata dimanda, espressa nel nostro Memoriale al Sommo Pontefice. Questo nostro Monastero è un Sacro Ricettacolo di spose di Xpro [i.e., Christo], dove per il Velo non s'accettano Persone d'altra condizione, che di Dame, ò Gentildonne. Qui si vive con sentimenti e di Nobiltà e di Religiosità: voglio dire, di tutta honorevolezza, e di tutta stima. Sempre s'è vissuto con questi rispetti se presentemente è piu che mai in colmo questa nostra Massima, tanto, per grazia del Signore, interiormente quanto esteriormente; e chi presume dire, ò far credere in contrario, bisogna mettere in campo, non cose in aria, ma casi particolari, e distinti—Questo sia detto a Vossignoria acciò sappia, che ci viene qui supposto, che, per impossibilitarci il nostro intento, sia stato supposto cola qualche sentimento contrario alla nostra stima, e reputatione. E che hà netta la conscienza, non teme di nulla. . . . Orsu Noi siamo risolute, ò perder tutto, e conservare quella stima, ch[e] fà sempre propria di q[ues]to Monastero; ò conseguire dalla Sag[ra] Congreg[azione] ciò, che hanno stimato cotesti Em[inentissi]mi Signori in tanti anni scorsi, e ne presenti, essere conforme al Pontificale Romano." The nuns even entertained the possibility of snubbing Boncompagni by replacing him in the ceremony with Cardinal D'Adda, the Camaldolese protector. Sabbatini, seconded by Monsignor Caprara, cooled their ardor with the remark, "first we win the case, as we hope, and at that time we shall discuss how to perform the ceremony" ("vinciamo prima la Causa come speriamo è all hora la discorremmo circa al far la funtione"; see Sabbatini's letter of 18 June 1698 ibid).

27. BUB, MS It. 770/61, fol. 28br; the additional text of Borromeo's decree is cited in André Metz, *La Consécration des vierges dans l'église romaine: Etude d'histoire de la liturgie* (Paris: Presses universitaires de France, 1954), 342.

28. BUB, MS It. 770/61, fols. 28gr–hv.

29. ASB, Demaniale 49/2910 (Santa Cristina), letter of 6 July 1698.

30. The ruling is published in *Decreta authentica Congregationis Sacrorum Rituum ex actis eiusdem collecta . . . sub auspiciis SS. Domini Nostri Leonis Papae XIII*, vol. 1 (Rome: Typographia polyglotta, 1898), 437, no. 2001. See also Aloisi Gardellini,

Decreta authentica Congregationis Sacrorum Rituum, 3d ed., vol. 2 (Rome: S. C. de Propaganda Fide, 1856), 168.

31. Sabbatini's remark, "che volesse per cosi dire farle fino uscire per i tetti possa farlo," appears in ASB, Demaniale 49/2910 (Santa Cristina), letter to Donna Luigia Orsina Orsi of 26 July 1698. The roof exit is also mentioned in his next letter, dated 2 Aug.

32. Ibid., undated letter from Count Bolognetti to the bursar: "Il S[ignor]e Card[inal]e non può acquistar loda dalla forma tenuta di non voler udire [illeg.] galanti huomini." Boncompagni's particular advocates are listed in Sabbatini's letter of 3 Aug. 1698 to Donna Luigia Orsina Orsi.

33. *Decreta authentica . . . Leonis Papae XIII*, 440–41, no. 2012; see also Gardellini, *Decreta*, 172–73.

34. ASB, Demaniale 49/2910 (Santa Cristina), Paolo Bolognetti, letter dated 2 Oct. 1698: "Resta hora il vedere le straniere del Card[inal]e e del Pini in fare la funtione con tutte le stitichezze ch[e] loro Jettarà il finto Zelo."

35. Ibid.: "Piena e distinta Informatione del fatto occorso in Occasione della Lite."

36. Ibid.: "Nella più ampla, e più decorosa forma, che sia mai stata fatta."

37. A copy of Giovanni Pellegrino Nobili, *La verginità consacrata* (Bologna: Eredi del Sarti, 1699) survives in BUB, MS It. 770/61, between fols. 28iv and 29r.

38. Peter Burke comments on the use of such printed ephemera to reinforce and explain seventeenth-century ritual messages in "Sacred Rulers, Royal Priests: Rituals of the Early Modern Popes," in *The Historical Anthropology of Early Modern Italy* (Cambridge: Cambridge University Press, 1987), 179–80.

39. Giovanni Pellegrino Nobili: "Il vostro Eminentissimo Pastore adesso intieramente vi riconosce per quella Greggia, che hà per Anima la Fedeltà al suo Signore" (*La verginità consacrata*, 3–4). Francesco Ferrari: "Ardua magnanimus subiturus praelia Miles, / Ut palmam victo ex Hoste referre queat" (ibid., 21, misbound after 4). ASB, Demaniale 49/2910 (Santa Cristina), letter dated 4 Aug. 1698 from Ludovico Maria Orsi to his sister: "Dato il caso, che tutte le cose andassero alla peggio e non havessero ottenuto ne meno il decreto favorevole saranno sempre stimate tante Amazone, in havere conpugnata la spada per difesa delle sue raggioni, in una molestia cosi impropria o dificile." The signature of the other letter, dated 11 Oct. 1698, is illegible ("Ant.o Santeni"?).

40. Parts of Morazzi's description are transcribed in Roberta Zucchini, "Santa Cristina della Fondazza: Storia architettonica e storico artistica" (Tesi di laurea, Università di Bologna, 1987–88), 43–44, based on BCB, MS Gozz. 184. For another copy, see also BUB, MS It. 4/22, which I have also consulted for the full text.

41. On the association of prostration with popes' purification and transformation into fit occupants of their new ecclesiastical office, see Burke, "Sacred Rulers, Royal Priests," 172. According to the *Ordo admittendi virgines ad monasterii ingressum*, published in 1607 for use in Milan, during the profession rite, novices were also required to lie "decently" (*honestè*, as the rubric put it) under a black pall after receiving the habit. Cited in Kendrick, "Genres, Generations and Gender," 253. No such pall is mentioned in *Ritus recipiendi virgines ad religionis habitum nec non ad professionem novitias in civitate & diocesi Bononiæ* (Bologna: Vittorio Benacci, 1626).

42. Giovanni Pelligrino Nobili: "l'Eroica conferma tal Sagrificio. Voi con tal atto magnanimo vi fate conoscer d'un Cuore degno di Dio" (*La verginità consacrata,* 3); "Per tributarti, o Dio, con l'Alma il Cuore / Ecco unite a tuoi piè noi Verginelle" (ibid., 13); "Ostie a Dio vi destina un santo Zelo" (ibid., 19).

43. Eustachio Manfredi: "Hor, che il Mondo fra suoi pur vi rivede / (O del Mondo nemiche, e a Dio già Spose) / E uscir vi mira di là d'onde il Piede / Raro trasse, o non mai chi un dì vel pose" (ibid., 8).

44. The presence of seminarians in 1675 is mentioned in BCB, MS Gozz. 329, entry for 27 Jan. 1675; for 1699, see BUB, MS It. 770/61: 21. For the analogy to Christ's thirty-three years on earth, see Morazzi's description in BUB, MS It. 4/22, fols. 204v–205r. On the foundation of the Bolognese seminary, see Paolo Prodi, *Il cardinale Gabriele Paleotti* (Rome: Edizioni di storia e letterature, 1959–67), 2: 138–45.

45. Capriani, "Chiesa e convento," 139.

46. Contemporary illustrations from secular *feste* in 1704 and 1711 are reproduced in Giampiero Cuppini, *I palazzi senatorii a Bologna: Architettura come immagine del potere* (Bologna: Nicola Zanichelli, 1974), plates V and VIII. For examples from Palazzo Vizzani in 1693, see Giancarlo Roversi, *Palazzi e case nobili del '500 a Bologna: La storia, le famiglie, le opere d'arte* (Bologna: Grafis edizioni, 1986), 209, 211.

47. Traversari's remark appears in *Hodoeporicon,* ed. Vittorio Tamburini (Florence: Felice Le Monnier, 1985), 115. For Ruggeri's comment, "e secondo dura più or meno la musica," see Camaldoli MS 652, fol. 20v.

48. Giovanni Pellegrino Nobili: "sforzate i Cori Celesti a gli applausi" (*La verginità consacrata,* 4); "S'adempia il gran Desio. Stille di pianti / Dal core interno duol non più vi sprema; / Mà s'indolciscan l'aure a i vostri Canti" (ibid., 19).

49. BCB, MS Gozz. 184, fol. 65v: "con grandissimo Mormorio di Sparate, Tamburi, e Trombe . . . e termino la Fonzione alle hore 22 1/2 per Grazia di Dio." Records of expenses are preserved in ASB, Demaniale 49/2910 (Santa Cristina).

50. BUB, MS It. 770/61: 17–27. Giacomo Perti, as *maestro di cappella,* received £90 for the outside music. ASB, Demaniale 49/2910 (Santa Cristina).

51. BUB, MS It. 770/61: 23: "Cantorono certi moteti con grande applauso di tutto il Popolo, e Cardinali presenti." Ibid.: "con diversi canti"; "con altri canti accompagnati sempre da suoi Instrumenti." Ibid., 24–25: "Due di dette Monache cantorono un bellissimo Mottetto accompagnato da suo organo e strumenti." It is not entirely clear who played the instruments.

52. BUB, MS 225/1, fol. 58: "Coll rimbombo di Trombe, e Tamburi, e Timpali e sbaro d'una ben grande quantità di mortaletti." Another similar brief entry appears in BCB, MS B83: 473. The Sacra expenses appear in ASB, Demaniale 49/2910 (Santa Cristina). Morazzi's remarks are in BCB, MS Gozz. 184 and BUB, MS It. 4/22, fol. 204r.

53. BUB, MS It. 225/1, fol. 58; cf. BCB, MS B83: 473. BCB, MS B3666: 369: "E ciascheduna di dette otto Monache cantarono un Motetto." BCB, MS Gozz. 355: 25: "Nella funzione cantarono anche un motetto p[er] cadauna con voci quasi d'Angelli."

54. BUB, MS It. 4/22, fol. 203r: "à ragione potean li spettatori esclamare con il gran' Serafico d'Assisi *satis est non più, non più* restand'ogn'Uno per la dolcezza delle cannore Voci come in Estasi d'amore verso il Gran Dio delle più fine misericordie."

The nuns' accounts include a payment of 12 soldi for moving the organ. ASB, Demaniale 49/2910 (Santa Cristina).

55. The complete text appears in Metz, *La Consécration,* 430, 440–43, 445.

56. Traversari, *Hodoeporicon,* 116.

57. Metz, *La Consécration,* 444.

58. Ruggeri's remarks in Camaldoli MS 652, fol. 20v; "tutta dalle Guardia Svizzere" (BCB, MS Gozz. 329, entry for 27 Giorno Domenica [gennaio 1675]); "Gente per tutte le strade a fine di vedere la Fonzione, ma Essendo chiuse le Porte di fuori coll'Assistenza de Svizzeri dell'Em[inentissi]mo Legato" (BCB, MS Gozz. 184, fol. 65v).

59. For 1699, see BCB, MS Gozz. 184, fol. 65v; ibid., MS Gozz. 331, entry for 11 Jan. 1699; BUB, MS It. 616/7: 21; ibid., MS It. 770/61: 19; ASB, Demaniale 49/ 2910 (Santa Cristina). For 1711, see BUB, MS It. 4/22, fol. 202r.

60. Girolamo Azzoguidi: ". . . Ite, intrecciate / Innocenti Corone e Gigli, e Rose. / Voi Diamanti più eletti ite, volate / Al Collo, al Seno de le Dive Spose: / E voi Gemme lucenti ite, annodate / Le bianche man trà fila d'oro ascose." *La verginità consacrata,* 16.

61. Francesco Bendini Monti: "Con mura d'oro una Città mirai / Porte dodici aprir di là da gli Anni. / Le Porte erano d'Or Perle lucenti; / Mà su quai basi era il gran muro eretto? / Eran dodici Gemme i Fondamenti." Ibid., 11.

62. BUB, MS It. 4/22, fol. 203r: "Corone intrecciate di Gemme e quantità di finissime Perle e Diamanti." ASB, Demaniale 49/2910 (Santa Cristina), "Piena e Distinta Informatione": "Erano tutte tempestate delle più belle, e riche gioie di tutta la nobiltà di Bologna." Camaldoli MS 652, fol. 20v.

63. See Christiane Klapisch-Zuber, "The Griselda Complex: Dowry and Marriage Gifts in the Quattrocento," in *Women, Family, and Ritual in Renaissance Italy,* trans. Lydia Cochrane (Chicago: University of Chicago Press, 1985), esp. 225–31.

64. Fernando Ghedini: "Le sue Corone d'Or la Monarchia / Prostrata ai piè d'un Dio Bambin depone: / Ei gradisce l'Omaggio; e le Corone / Offerte, in dono alle sue Spose invia." *La verginità consacrata,* 20.

65. The 1699 list derives from BUB MS It. 770/61: 20–21; the 1711 lists appear in BUB, MS It. 4/22, fols. 201v–2r.

66. Alfeo Giacomelli, "La dinamica della nobiltà bolognese," in *Famiglie senatorie e istituzioni cittadine a Bologna nel Settecento: Atti del colloquio, Bologna, 2–3 febbraio 1980* (Bologna: Istituto per la storia bolognese, 1980), 71. Gabriella Zarri suggests the possibility that the number of noble *professe* was on the wane. See "Monasteri femminili e città (secoli xv–xviii)," in *Storia d'Italia: Annali,* 9: *La chiesa e il potere politico dal Medioevo all'età contemporanea,* ed. Giorgio Chittolini and Giovanni Miccoli (Turin: Giulio Einaudi, 1990), 423.

67. BCB, MS Gozz. 329, entry for 27 Jan. 1675: GRATI, BOLOGNINI, ZANI, and SECCADENARI; ASV, VR, sez. monache, 1655 [settembre–dicembre], letter registered 17 Dec. 1655: PALEOTTI, MALVEZZI, ORSI, BOTTRIGARI, AZZOLINI, *Mogli,* and one without surname.

68. The quotation "in contrasegno di gratitudine de tale funtione fatta da esso Maestosamente con vero Zelo d'Amoroso Pastore" is from the nuns' description of the whole affair in ASB, Demaniale 49/2910 (Santa Cristina), added at the end of

"Piena e distinta Information" by a different hand. The details of the gifts appear in BUB, MS It. 770/61: 27. This sort of lavish gift-giving to convent superiors was another aspect of convent professions, consecrations, and general festivities commonly condemned by the church hierarchy.

69. The few details of the nuns' individual histories have been retrieved from Carrati's transcript of the convent necrologies in BCB, MS 921.

70. Alessandro Caprara, ASB, Demaniale 49/2910 (Santa Cristina), inclusion at end of book of Sabbatini letters: "Hà havuto da quatordici mesi d'aggitatione p[er]la Lite delle Monache Camaldolesi, . . . hà perduta la Gracia del Card[ina]le Arcivescovo, anzi è incorso nell'indignatione di S[ua] E[minenza] . . . Onde merita grossa reccognitione, . . . non seli puo dare meno di dieci doppie, . . . che è moderata assai, e assai moderata la Recognitione, e questo è quello le devo dire."

71. ASB, Demaniale 49/2910 (Santa Cristina): "Superiora la Rev[erendissi]ma Madre Abbadessa Donna Colomba Carati Priora la Molto Rev[erendissi]ma Donna Geltruda Marsibilia Malvezzi Camerlenga la Molto Rev[eren]da D. Luigia Orsina Orsi Quali tutte con destra, e matura Prudenza operando Hanno Vinto a Gloria di S[ua] D[ivina] M[aest]à honore, e decoro di tutto l'ordine Camald[ole]se come nel Archivio del n[ost]ro Monastero si depongono a p[er]petua Memoria di chi hà in ciò Operato."

12. A LAST MUSICAL BATTLE

1. Undated, unsigned memorial marked "Jacobus Boncompagni Card. Archiepiscopus Bononiæ," BUB MS It. 79/3:

"Di Gennaro del 1684 p[er] mia poco buona sorte, solita però, e consueta mi convenne andar à Bologna sù le Poste co[n] molto incomodo, ed esorbitante spesa, p[er] la malatia del Card[ina]le mio Zio il q[ua]le nell'istesso tempo se ne morì, e p[er] me riusciò una infelicis[si]ma condotta, sicome e nota à tutti, e dell'istesso anno me ne ritornai à Roma . . . la Primavera e vi giunsi nel principio della Settimana S[an]ta[.]

"Quanqua[m] omnius meminisse horror bononie refugio."

2. After being freed by Louis XIV in early summer, Ranuzzi had died on 27 Sept. 1689 on his way to the papal conclave in Rome. See Ludwig Pastor, *The History of the Popes*, trans. Ernest Graf, vol. 32 (St. Louis: B. Herder, 1952), esp. 387–92, 405, 525 n. 2.

3. Umberto Mazzone, "La visita e l'azione pastorali di Giacomo Boncompagni, arcivescovo di Bologna (1690–1731)," *Cristianesimo nella storia* 4 (1983): esp. 343–45.

4. Anon., quoted ibid., 352 n. 38.

5. For Boncompagni's *visita pastorale,* see AAB, MS 70.H.562, esp. fols. 110v, 123v, 211v, 224v. The Sacred Congregation granted licenses to music teachers at Brescia and Mazzara (Apr. 1697), Ferrara and Novara (Aug. 1697), Ancona and Fossombrone (Jan. 1698), and Ferrara (Aug. 1698), for example. See ASV, VR, sez. monache, 1697 (aprile–maggio and luglio–agosto) and 1698 (gennaio–marzo and agosto–settembre).

6. BCB, MS B3666: 188–89; ibid., MS B3641, entries 2 June and 8 Dec. 1699; BUB, MS It. 616/7: 95; ibid., MS It. 3851, fol. 14v; ibid., MS It. 770/61: 709, 712.

7. Giacomo Boncompagni: "l'Irriverenze quali Commetevansi nelle Chiese delle Monache in occasione di celebrarvisi le feste loro, andavano sempre più crescendo con grande disonore della Casa di Dio, sperimentandosi tuttavia inutili non solo gl'Editti sopra il dovuto rispetto delle Chiese, l'am[m]onizioni de Confessori, e de Predicatori, mà anche il di più prescritto nell'Ultimo Editto stato publicato d'ordine di n[ost]ro Sig[no]re, ... onde considerando io essere inevitabili gli scandali quando vi si continuasse la Musica, per la quale essendo copioso il concorso del Popolo, e Stando Irreparabilmente framischiati insieme huomini, e donne nella continua Confluenza, erano grandi l'immodestie, e li strepiti che nè seguivano, con meno rispetto, che se si fosse stato in publica Piazza, ò in mercato aperto, concorrendovi li più licenziosi ad' oggetto di valersi del commodo, che al loro mal fine presta p[er] l'ordinario la confusione di tali concorsi." Two copies in ASV, VR, sez. monache, 1704 (agosto); another in ASB, Demaniale 48/2909 (Santa Cristina).

8. BUB, MS It. 616/4: 66–67 (1691); ibid., 616/7: 296 (1701).

9. Giacomo Boncompagni, ASB, Demaniale 48/2909 (Santa Cristina), "Risposta dell' Em. Arcivescovo Alla Sacra Congregatione": "Nella Chiesa delle Monache di S[ant']Agnese soggette al governo de P.P. Domenicani no[n] solo vi seguirono le solite Immodestie, mà altresi nel Secondo Vespro non puotè terminarsi, poiche occupato sino lo stesso Altar Maggiore dalla gente, nell'Atto di cantarsi il Magnificat, non fù possibile al sacerdote parato col Piviale, et alli due Assistenti andar ad' Incensare l'Altare, e gli convenne portarsene in Sagrestia, partendo li Musici Ancora, che no[n] puotero proseguire la Musica à cagione del gran rumore, che impediva loro di Sentire le voci."

10. Initial enforcement of the ban is mentioned in BCB, MS B3666: 213–14. Antonio Francesco Ghiselli's comments on the feast at Corpus Domini appear in BUB, MS It. 770/65: 22: "Ma questa solennità non fù celebrata con tutta quella pompa solita à pratticarsi dalla tenera devotione de' gli affettionati Devoti, mentre le venne prohibito il farvi la Musica, come ancora si estende la medesima prohibitione à tutte le altre Chiese di Monache nelle loro feste, e ciò d'ordine dell'Arcivescovo, ordine, ch'oltre il disgusto ch'apporta a queste povere Religiose, riduce li Musici ad andare, quasi dissi, elemosinando, mentre si vedono da tutte le parti levata l'occasione di sostenarsi con la loro virtuosa professione, et anco leva alle medesime Chiese il Concorso, e non pregiudica puoco al culto, e frequenza delle medesime." The duchesses' visit to Corpus Domini is described ibid., MS It. 616/8: 628. For the licenses at San Vitale, see ASB, Demaniale 84/3233 (Santi Vitale et Agricola), no. 22, "Licenze Diverse per le Funzioni della Chiesa."

11. Antonio Francesco Ghiselli, BUB, MS It. 770/65: 40: "Dicendo che gl'era stato prohibito di far festa, e cosi havrebbero dovuto fare tutti gl'altri Monasteri sparagnando i Regalli sontuosi che praticano con i superiori."

12. ASB, Demaniale 48/2909 (Santa Cristina), "Primo ricorso dalle M.M. alla Sacra Congregatione": "Ogn'uno che intervenne a q[ues]ta festa potra attestare che in chiesa non si senti minimo sussurro e che noi tutte stavimo retirate dalle grate e Porte come e costume del n[ost]ro Mon[aste]ro per tutto l'anno."

13. Ibid., "Risposta dell' Em. Arcivescovo alla sacra congregatione": "Cantando le monache nel primo Vespro, v'intervenne poca gente, perche non si sapeva, essendo all'incontro nota nella città la proibit[io]ne, mà nel giorno seguente il con-

corso fù grande, e strepitoso, p[er] esservi in questo monastero alcune ottime voci."

14. Ibid., "Primo ricorso": "Ma q[ue]sti li gettarono dentro un Tubo ò Tromba con la quale si parla à detta Priora pregiudicata nell'udito da molti Anni Addietro."

15. Ibid., "Lettera o Memorial da presentare alla Sacra Cong. che poi non vi si mandò": "Ma egli datto nelle smanie non volle udirle, replicando, che se le monache erano aggravate ricorressero a cotesta S. Congregat[io]ne conforme il solito loro." The nuns' self-censored version read, "that to qualify for his grace there was no other route but to obey, or to have recourse to the [sacred] congregation if they thought themselves overburdened" (ibid., "Primo ricorso": "che per abilitarsi alle sue gratie n[on] v'era altra via che l'Ubbidire, o riccorrere alla Congreg[atio]ne se si stimavano aggravate"). Ibid.: "Persona innocente, e dama avanzata nell'età, apprensiva, e di debolissima complessione."

16. Ibid., "Lettera dell' n[ostr]o Avocato Narici": "Quando non vi sia ordine o precetto positivo, almeno vi è una tale certa notitia, che non dovessero cantare." Ibid., letter of 19 November: "Specialm[en]te a non impegnarsi davantaggio circa il non esserle stato noto il consaputo precetto del Sig[no]r Card[ina]le Arciv[escovo]."

17. Ibid., "Primo ricorso": "Se si pretende che il n[ost]ro Confess[o]re serva all'Arcivescovado d'Accusattore del n[ost]ro medemo Monas[te]ro sarà ben presto vulnerata la Confidenza e posto in dubbio il Secreto delle n[ost]re Conscienze." ASV, VR, sez. monache, 1647 (giugno–agosto), packet of 19 July 1647: "In niun secolare posson haver confidenza, che da' secolari furono sempre tradite."

18. ASB, Demaniale 48/2909 (Santa Cristina), "Primo ricorso": "La manutentione di quanto ci permetta il n[ost]ro Santo Institutore nelle sue ponderate constitutioni [crossed out in first draft: "nel modo di solenizare le funtioni della Sacra e le Feste Correnti"]."

19. Ibid., "Raggioni sopra il fondamento della nostra causa": "Essendo la privacione di governo una delle maggiori [pene] che possi darsi a capi de Religiosi, e massime se si considera la dignità d'Abbad[ess]a, che è la maggiori di tutti nella Linea Ecclesiastica, che possi competere al sesso feminino. . . . Ne pregiudica alle raggioni dette il motivo di S[ua] E[minenza] che è il levare li scandali che nascono ne concorsi delle Chiese, poiche q[ue]sti nascono ancora in tutte l'altre chiese, ne p[er] q[ue]ste si proibisce la musica, benche siino chiese soggette all'Arcives[cov]o, e vi sono cento altri modi più universali e perciò Migliori che ponno levare q[ue]sti abusi senza mettere in pena le Religiose claustrali, de delitti fatti da secolari, de quali esse ne sono innocentissime massime quelle di q[ue]sto Religiosiss[i]mo Monas[ter]o [crossed out in draft: "che non à grate scoperte nella chiesa"] e se si dovess[e]ro levare tutte le cause ancorche buone che producono efetti cattivi, bisogneria mutar hormai tutto il sistema n[on] solo ecclesiastico ma anche secolare." Boncompagni's penance was actually not entirely out of line. Alexander VII's *pro comissio* of 27 Sept. 1667, which the nuns had in fact quoted in their own defense because it allowed music in the inner chapels of the convents of Rome, had also stipulated deprivation of office for any convent superior, and of active and passive voice to any nuns (i.e., the right to speak and be spoken to), who permitted performances by extern musicians. See Fiorenza Romita, *Ius musicae liturgicae* (Taurini: Officina libraria Marii e Marietti, 1936), 63 n. 3.

20. ASB, Demaniale 48/2909 (Santa Cristina), "Lettera dell' n[ostr]o Avocato Narici," dated 6 Sept. 1704: "La Congreg[atio]ne sostenendo in questa parte li vescovi molto più sosterrà quel tanto, che hà fatto il Sig[nor] Card[ina]le." Ibid., letter from "Camillo Bologneti Sen[ator]e de Bologna," dated Rome, 6 Sept. 1704: "[Boncompagni] e severo et e inemica del canto nelle chiese de monache." Niccolò Acciaioli and Gaspare Carpegna, both with more than thirty years in the college of cardinals behind them, were among the *zelanti,* known for voting along strict ecclesiastical rather than political guidelines. See Pastor, *The History of the Popes,* 32: 413, 525, 583; 33: 3.

21. ASB, Demaniale 48/2909 (Santa Cristina), letter of 9 Dec. 1704: "il V[ostro] Avocato Narici habbi fatto belissime scritture. Mo[?nsignore?] Ambasciatore Nostro hà parlato à più d'un Cardinale i[n] loro favore particularmente al V[ostro] Cardinal Ponente." ASV, VR, sez. monache, 1704 (agosto): "Questa Causa fù posta in foglio per la Cong.ne delli 5. xmbre 1704; e poi aggiustata amicabilmente dall'Em[inentissi]mo Ponente."

22. ASB, Demaniale 48/2909 (Santa Cristina), letter of 6 Dec. 1704: "Io farei torto no[n] solam[en]te alla loro filiale discretezza, ma ancora alla buona, e saggia cognizione, di cui le hà dotate il Sig[no]re Dio, se no[n] mi assicurassi, ch'elle giudicheranno buono il mio arbitrio ed in esso riscontreranno servate le loro convenienze."

23. Ibid., petition dated 22 Dec. 1704: "Che sebene non sono consapevoli à se stesse d'avere già mai disobedito à riveritiss[im]i commandi della E[minenza] V[ostra], come quelle che non sarebbero capaci d'un tanto errore, nondimeno avendo sentito che sia stato diversamente rappresentato all'E[minenza] V[ostra] in occasione che nel prossimo passato Mese di Maggio si celebrava dalle Or[atri]ci la solennità di S[anta] Cristina con canto figurato, ne sperimentano perciò sensibilissimo dispiac[iut]e, e molto più dal vedersi prive p[er] tal causa dell'onore della sua pregiatissima grazia, per meritar la quale sicome hanno adempita con la prontezza dovuta la penitenza, che l'è piaciuto di loro imporre, così per sempre si rassegnano come figlie e suddite ossequiosissime all'obedienza dell'E[minenza] V[ostra]."

24. Giacomo Boncompagni, ASB, Demaniale 48/2909 (Santa Cristina), "Atteso, che l'Oratrici habbiano pontualm[ent]e osservata come espongono, la penitenza da Noi ingiontale benignam[ent]e gli facciamo la grazia dà esse domandata, ferma però rimanendo la proibiz[io]ne ne' sinodi, e nel nostro precetto espresso, quale dovranno inviolabilm[ent]e osservare, di non cantare in Canto figurato, misto, ò qualsisia altro Musico concerto, permettendosegli solam[ent]e il Canto Eccles[iasti]co, che chiaman Fermo, come anco di non far far Musica da altri nelle loro Chiesa esteriore."

25. ASB, Demaniale 48/2909 (Santa Cristina), copy of undated, unsigned letter: "Mà non si può di meno di non protestare con la dovuta venerazione all'E[minenza] V[ostra], che nell'universale non è parso sia stato corrisposto alle gr[azi]e che si speravano dalla benigna interpositione di V[ostra] E[minenza]." Ibid., letter of 7 Jan. 1705: "Si rassegnino di buon'animo alle disposit[io]ni di Dio, manifestate, per mezzo de' superiori, e persuadersi, che la vera gloria, e reputat[io]ne delle buone religiose consiste in far sempre risplendere, tra le altre loro christiane virtù l'Obbedienza."

26. See U. Coldagelli, "Boncompagni, Gregorio," in *Dizionario biografico degli italiani,* vol. 11 (Rome: Istituto della Enciclopedia italiana, 1969), 693–94; id., "Boncompagni, Antonio," ibid., 679–81.

27. ASB, Demaniale 48/2909 (Santa Cristina), letter dated "Roma p[ri]mo del 707 [*sic*]": "Rispetto all'Affare, che le piacque communicarmi costì, Io ne passai col Sig[no]r Cardinal Arciv[escov]o i miei più premurosi Ufizzj, mà non incontrai in S[ua] Em[inen]za tutta quella propensione, che Io mi era bramata per servire a Vossignoria Ill[ustrissi]ma, e ne lasciai la Risposta alla Sig[no]ra Contessa Orsi, perche ad ella la partecipasse. La prego dunque a compensarmi la mortificazione col favore d'altri suoi comandam[ent]i." Ibid., unsigned, undated slip of paper: "Concediamo Licenza alle Monache del Monastero di S[ant]a Cristina di Bologna di potere in avenire praticare l'uso del Canto Misto, o alterato [sic], solo nelle fonzioni Eclesiastiche, nel modo, e maniera, che usano gl'altri monasterij di questa Città, non ostante il Precetto che hanno in contrario."

28. Katherine Gill, "Scandala: Controversies Concerning Clausura and Women's Religious Communities in Late Medieval Italy," in *Christendom and Its Discontents: Exclusion, Persecution and Rebellion, 1000–1500,* ed. Scott Waugh (Cambridge: Cambridge University Press, forthcoming). Leonora López de Córdoba's comment appears in her autobiographical *Las Memorias,* which is translated in Elizabeth Alvilda Petroff, *Medieval Women's Visionary Literature* (New York: Oxford University Press, 1986), 329–34.

29. Biographical details from BCB, MS B921: 266. Anselmo Giabbani, *Menologia Camaldolese* (Rome: S. Gregorio al Celio, 1950), 5. Giuditta Bolognini's kinswoman from Santa Cristina, Barbara Teresa Bolognini (d. 1762) is also commemorated in the Camaldolese menology on June 5 (ibid., 37).

30. BCB, MS Gozz. 184, fol. 67r. A somewhat different account, ascribing the visit to the opera to the year 1710, appears in BCB, MS Gozz. 185, fol. 251v, while BCB MS B3666: 565 claims that the event occurred on 7 May 1719. See also Carlo Vitali, "I viaggi di Faramondo (Venezia, 1699–Bologna, 1710)," in *Drammaturgia musicali veneta,* 9: *Il Faramondo* (Milan: Ricordi, 1987), xxvi–xxvii. Ample documentation has recently come to light to clear up the confusion surrounding the various stages in Cavazza's eventful career, which I hope to discuss elsewhere.

31. BCB, MS B3666: 243: "Non ostante la proibizzione dell' Arcivescovo."

32. AAB, Misc. vecchie 820, fasc. 17: "Si potrà riflettere che quivi in Bologna si sono già proibito affatto le Musiche nelle Chiese di Monache, . . . quivi non si canta sù gl'organi, ne alle Grade in nissun modo, come si prattica fuori di qui. . . . in q[ues]ta Città non v'è quest'uso di frequentare Monache, come in Ferrara, et in ogn'altro circonvicino Paese." Pini's rather mean-spirited remarks in defense of his acceptance of convent gifts suggest that he may have been cut from the same cloth as his predecessor of the 1620s, the nuns' vicar don Gioanino, who, it will be remembered, was susceptible to convent bribes: "Quanto alli Regali qui, come sà V[ostra] E[minenza] non si pratticano Regali di sorte alcuna, se non dalli Monas[te]ri per occasione della Festa mandano invitare con quatro cose dolce malfatte, e di niun' valore oltre in: scattole di Cottognate, e se sì và alla Festa, à celebrare Messa dano una Rama di Fiori piccola."

33. Quoted in Craig Monson, "Introduction," in *The Crannied Wall: Women, Religion, and the Arts in Early Modern Europe* (Ann Arbor: University of Michigan Press, 1992), 4.

34. *Annales Camaldulenses,* vol. 8 (Venice, 1764), 343: "quae demum recentioribus annis est ipsis restituta."

35. ASB, Demaniale 49/2910 (Santa Cristina): "Conto Generale di tutte le spese fatte per la funzione della Consecrazione di numero dieci Monache Seguita li 11 Settembre 1729."

13. CODETTA

1. For a recent summary of the Napoleonic era in Bologna, see Angelo Varni, "Il periodo napoleonico," in *Storia illustrata di Bologna,* ed. Walter Tega (Milan: Nuova editoriale AIEP, 1989), 2: 341–60. On the requisitioning of the refectory table, see Roberta Zucchini, "Santa Cristina della Fondazza: Storia architettonica e storico artistica" (Tesi di laurea, Università di Bologna, 1987–88), 22. BCB, MS B3283, final entry: "Onde tutte le povere Religiose furono costrette a dimettere il loro S. Abito, e ritirarsi Dio sa dove." The number of suppressed convents appears in Corrado Ricci and Guido Zucchini, *Guida di Bologna: Nuova edizione illustrata* (Bologna: Edizioni Alfa, 1968; repr. 1976), 231.

2. On the length of the auction, see Ugo Capriani, "Chiesa e convento di Santa Cristina della Fondazza in Bologna: Ipotesi di ricerca e recupero" (Tesi di laurea, Università di Bologna, 1987–88), 196–97. On the sale of property for rice and the reopening of the church, see Zucchini, "Santa Cristina della Fondazza," 22–23.

3. Nuns' pensions are mentioned in Zucchini, "Santa Cristina della Fondazza," 110. For the reacquisition of convent property, see Capriani, "Chiesa e convento," 41–42. The surviving pair of Camaldolese nuns appear in a listing of nuns with their various orders in AAB, Misc. vecchie 262. For their original entries into Santa Cristina, see ASB, Demaniale 21/2882 (Santa Cristina), nos. Y/23, Y/43, and Y/44.

4. On the conversion of the *chiesa vecchia* into a bicycle warehouse, see Zucchini, "Santa Cristina della Fondazza," 78, and Capriani, "Chiesa e convento," 43; on the uses of the convent during World War II, see Zucchini, "Santa Cristina della Fondazza," 24, and Capriani, "Chiesa e convento," 44; on the abandonment of the convent, see ibid. My thanks to Signora Giovanna, wife of the current custodian, for the details of the convent's last occupants and their final departure.

5. Ricci and Zucchini, *Guida di Bologna,* 60.

6. I am grateful to Signor Luciano Malossi, secretary of the surviving members of the Associazione Leone XIII, for details of the uses to which the *chiesa interiore* was put in the twentieth century.

7. Capriani, "Chiesa e convento," 246.

8. Ibid., 198.

9. "Una chiesa vecchia, mal'andata, e che stà per cascare." The complete document appears in *Annales Camaldulenses,* vol. 9 (Venice, 1773), appendix, col. 161. The portable reliquaries were removed from the church for safekeeping several years ago.

10. At Christmas 1992, a proposal for the restoration of the inner and outer churches and the Capella del Rosario was presented to the city administration by Monsignor Niso Albertazzi, *abbate parroco* of the parish of San Giuliano, and by the architects Glauco, Giuliano, and Roberto Gresleri. It presently remains under consideration.

GLOSSARY

al secolo:	("in the world") term used with reference to a nun's time before entering the convent, particularly associated with her secular name.
antiphonal:	a book of plainchant consisting of chants of the Divine Office; also a style of musical performance in which different groups answer one another.
anziani:	eight officials elected from the upper classes by the Bolognese senate for two-month terms; by the Seicento, the *anziani* retained little real authority beyond rendering judgments in minor civil and criminal cases.
assonti (sometimes *operai*):	laymen, generally from wealthy and powerful families, nominally in charge of a convent, who served as advisors and mediators in the world, and frequently supported the institution with substantial donations; cf. trustees of modern private universities.
basso continuo:	the underlying harmonic accompaniment, consisting of chords played chiefly on organ or harpsichord, almost invariably present in musical works of the seventeenth and eighteenth centuries.
canto figurato:	as opposed to plainchant (*canto fermo*); used to refer to more elaborate music such as polyphony.
cardinal nephew:	a papal relative, usually a nephew, who served as chief advisor and collaborator; common from the time of Paul III (1534) to Alexander VIII (1691).
cenobite:	a member of a religious order whose members live within a single monastic building.
cento:	a composite text assembled of quotations from various sources.

choir (*coro*):	a term applied to a group of singers, to the place where they sing, and frequently to the place where religious recite the Divine Office ("nuns' choir," "internal church").
church—internal/external:	the double church of a female monastery or convent, consisting of an internal sanctuary, inside *clausura*, for the nuns, and an external church accessible to the public and outside *clausura;* the two are generally separated by a wall, most commonly behind the high altar, frequently pierced by a grate.
clausura (enclosure):	the physical separation of nuns from the world, legislated by the Council of Trent and enforced in 1566 by Pope Pius V; violation of *clausura*, either by nuns setting foot outside the convent or by laypeople setting foot inside, resulted in excommunication.
communion window:	a secluded window covered with a grate, generally near the high altar of a convent church, through which Holy Communion was passed to the nuns by the priest during Mass.
compline:	the last of the eight canonical hours of the Divine Office, originally celebrated after dinner.
concerto:	term widely used to describe various combinations, alternations, or interactions of voices and instruments in music of the seventeenth and eighteenth centuries.
confessor extraordinary:	confessors specially appointed at times such as Lent or during Jubilees to confess the nuns.
contrafactum:	a reworking of a preexistent piece of music into an alternative form, as, for example, in providing a secular piece with a sacred or Latin text.
conversa:	a servant nun, admitted for a much smaller dowry, who did not profess final vows and was not required to recite the Divine Office.
corista:	an alternative term for *professa,* a nun who has professed her final vows, with the obligation to recite the Divine Office in choir.
Divine Office:	the eight canonical hours, consisting of prayers, readings, and psalms, that must be recited daily by those who have professed in most major religious orders.
donna:	the title adopted for a *professa* in Benedictine religious houses such as Santa Cristina della Fondazza.
educanda:	a girl permitted to reside in a convent to be educated (*in educazione*), on the assumption that she will go on to become a novice.

elevation motet:	a motet whose text adores Christ, present in the consecrated bread and wine of Holy Communion, through the miracle of transubstantiation; performed during the elevation of the host.
eremite:	a religious who does not live under the same roof with other religious, but in isolation.
falsobordone:	a simple sort of polyphony in which a text is chanted in hymnlike chordal harmony, frequently based on Gregorian chant.
gonfaloniero del popolo:	governmental representative of the lower ranks of Bolognese society; the original four (one from each quarter of the city) were increased to sixteen in 1376; *gonfalonieri*, who served four-month terms, ruled in civil and criminal matters concerning the common people.
grate (*ferrata, grata*):	the iron grill that covered the windows facing the world in convents. They were found chiefly in the *parlatorio*, on the communion window, and on the window above the high altar of the external church, through which the nuns adored the consecrated host at the elevation during Mass. After the Council of Trent, grates were to be double and locked, with the inner key entrusted to the abbess and the outer key to a male religious superior such as the convent confessor.
investiture (clothing ceremony):	the rite of passage in which a postulant is accepted into the convent, receives her habit, takes her religious name, and becomes a novice.
Jubilee:	a year in which remission of sins is granted on confession, repentance, and the carrying out of prescribed religious acts. Although in the seventeenth and eighteenth centuries, Jubilees customarily fell every twenty-five years (1600, 1625, etc.) the pope could declare additional Jubilees at critical times (e.g., 1629).
license (*licenza*):	special permission granting exemption, in a single instance or for a prescribed period, from some ecclesiastical law. A license was necessary for laypeople to visit their cloistered relatives, for doctors or barbers to enter *clausura*, or for organ tuners, music teachers, or outside musicians to work in convents.
madrigal:	a work of polyphony, setting a secular text, often of a very worldly, at times lascivious, character.
magnificat:	the canticle of the Blessed Virgin Mary, recited at vespers, frequently sung in polyphony, even in convents.
matins:	the first of the eight canonical hours of the Divine Office, customarily performed at midnight or dawn.

melisma:	a type of musical word setting involving several musical notes to a single syllable of text.
menology:	a listing of saints and religious of particular merit, arranged according to the calendar.
mistress of novices:	the *professa* who teaches novices the rules of the order, how to recite the Office, and, at convents such as Santa Cristina della Fondazza, the elements of reading and music.
monody:	a type of music involving a single singing voice; the term is used even if the single voice is accompanied by the *basso continuo*.
motet:	a musical setting in polyphony of a Latin text, in the seventeenth and eighteenth centuries, normally of sacred character.
novice:	a woman who has gone through the rite of acceptance and investiture at a convent and is undergoing a period (normally one year) of prayer, meditation, and instruction in the rules of the order.
ordinary:	a bishop, archbishop or his deputy serving as an authority.
paranympha:	a secular matron who assists a nun at the consecration of virgins.
parlatorio:	the parlor in which nuns could meet outsiders, consisting of an interior chamber for the nuns, separated by a double grate from an exterior chamber for visitors; a convent frequently had several *parlatori*.
phrygian cadence:	a musical cadence, or momentary point of rest, in which the lowest musical line descends to the stopping point by a half-step (e.g., from F to E); concurrently an upper part frequently includes a suspension. Phrygian cadences are traditionally associated with sadness, somberness, or moments of particular affectivity.
plainchant:	the traditional single-line melodies to which texts of the Catholic liturgy were sung; during the seventeenth and eighteenth centuries, they were frequently accompanied by the organ.
polyphony:	music involving several independent musical voices or parts of varying complexity performed simultaneously.
ponente:	a prelate appointed to supervise the presentation of a suit before a curial body; a cardinal was appointed *ponente* to shepherd a petition through the Congregation of Bishops or the Congregation of Sacred Rites in Rome, for example.

pontifical:	a book containing liturgies performed specifically by bishops.
primociero:	("first candle") the head of the chapter of a collegiate church such as San Petronio in Bologna.
professa, or *corista:*	a nun who has professed final vows, is required to recite the Divine Office, and normally has a voice in convent government. The *professa* normally paid a full dowry, unless granted a special reduction by the Congregation of Bishops for special reasons (e.g., because she would assume the position of convent organist).
profession:	the rite in which a novice professes her final vows of poverty, chastity, and obedience, and is admitted to full rights in her religious order.
regulars:	religious subject to a religious rule or monastic order (e.g., Benedictine, Augustinian, Franciscan), by contrast with seculars.
r(u)ota:	a device shaped like a barrel with a section cut out, fixed in a cloister wall, through which items could be introduced into the convent without the necessity of direct contact with the nuns inside.
Sacra:	consecration of virgins; the final, particularly solemn rite of passage of a nun, only to be performed after age twenty-five; at convents such as Santa Cristina della Fondazza it enabled her to serve in the highest monastic offices.
secular clergy:	clergy not belonging to a religious order (cf. regulars), subject to the authority of a local bishop or archbishop.
serbanza:	("service") term used to describe the activity of an *educanda,* who could be said to be *in serbanza.*
stile moderno:	the musical style(s) introduced around 1600, involving freer use of solo voices, instruments, more unusual or irregular harmonies, and a generally more variegated, overtly dramatic character.
suffragan:	an auxiliary bishop appointed to assist an archbishop, who is his superior.
s(u)or(a) ("sister"):	the customary title for *professe* and *converse* in most religious orders (Franciscans, Augustinians, etc.). In Benedictine or Camaldolese houses, the term was generally reserved for *converse.*
suspension:	a musical device in a piece of polyphony in which one or more voices or parts hold a note over from one sonority to the next; in the second sonority, the suspension commonly clashes with the other voices of the new sonority, which usually pause while the suspension resolves to a consonant note.

vespers:

the penultimate of the eight canonical hours of the Divine Office, customarily recited in the late afternoon or evening.

vicar general (*vicario generale*):

a high official of the diocesan curia who oversees the functions and discipline of the diocese.

vicar of nuns (*vicario delle monache*):

the diocesan official appointed to oversee the convents of the diocese, sign licenses, grant most exemptions, and so on.

visitation:

periodic or special investigations of convents by the bishop of a diocese or his deputy, by regular superiors, or in cities under papal control, sometimes by the papal legate or vice-legate, to monitor their good order or look into possible improprieties.

viol (*viola*):

a bowed stringed instrument particularly common in the sixteenth and seventeenth centuries, usually with six strings and frets on its fingerboard (similar to the frets on a lute or guitar), held between the legs when played. Although viols came in various sizes, like members of the violin family, the bass viol was most common, and frequently used in convents to support the bassline in a piece of polyphony.

SELECTED BIBLIOGRAPHY

Agee, Richard. "A Venetian Music Printing Contract in the Sixteenth Century." *Studi musicali* 15 (1986): 59–65.

Alford, John A. "Biblical *imitatio* in the Writings of Richard Rolle." *English Literary History* 40 (1973): 1–23.

Angelozzi, Giancarlo. "Nobili, mercanti, dottori, cavalieri, artigiani: Stratificazioni sociali e ideologia a Bologna nei secoli xvi e xviii." In *Storia illustrata di Bologna*, ed. Walter Tega, 2: 41–60. Milan: Nuova editoriale AIEP, 1989.

Amico, Rosalba d', and Marzia Faietti, eds. *Le pubbliche virtù: Donazioni e legati d'arte alla pinacoteca nazionale di Bologna (1803–1982)*. Bologna: Edizioni Alfa, 1983.

Antonelli, P. Ferdinando, O.F.M. "L'archivio della S. Congregazione dei Riti." In *Il libro e le biblioteche: Atti del primo congresso bibliologico francescano internazionale, 20–27 febbraio 1949*, sez. 2: *Conferenze di carattere particolare*, 61–76. Rome: Pontificium Athenaeum Antonianum, 1950.

The Apocryphal/Deuterocanonical Books of the Old Testament: New Revised Standard Version. New York: Oxford University Press, 1989.

Arcangeli, Francesco, Maurizio Calvesi, Gian Carlo Cavalli, Andrea Emiliani, and Carlo Volpe. *Maestri della pittura del seicento emiliano*. Bologna: Edizioni Alfa, 1959.

Aretino, Pietro. *Ragionamento dialogo*. Edited by Nino Borsellino. Milan: Garzanti editore, 1984.

Arfelli, Adriana, ed. *Carlo Cesare Malvasia: Vite di pittori bolognesi (Appunti inediti)*. Bologna: Commissione per i testi di lingua, 1961.

Armstrong, Nancy, and Leonard Tennenhouse. *The Ideology of Conduct: Essays in Literature and the History of Sexuality*. New York: Methuen, 1987.

Arnold, Denis. "Monteverdi: Some Colleagues and Pupils." In *The New Monteverdi Companion*, ed. Denis Arnold and Nigel Fortune, 107–24. London: Faber & Faber, 1985.

Artusi, Giovanni Maria. *L'Artusi: Overo delle imperfettioni della moderna musica*. Venice: Giacomo Vincenti, 1600.

Baernstein, P. Renée. "The Birth of the Counter-Reformation Convent: The Convent of San Paolo in Milan, 1530–1630." Ph.D. diss., Harvard University, 1993.

[Banchieri, Adriano]. *Adriano Banchieri: Conclusions for Playing the Organ (1609).* Translated by Lee R. Garrett. Colorado College Music Press Translations, vol. 13. Colorado Springs: Colorado College Music Press, 1982.

―――. *Lettere armoniche.* Bologna: Girolamo Mascheroni, 1628. Repr., Bologna: Forni editore, n.d.

―――. *Messa solenne a otto voci.* Venice: Ricciardo Amadino, 1599.

―――. *Il principiante fanciullo.* Venice: Magni, 1625.

[Barbaro, Francesco]. "Francesci Barbari De Re Uxoria Liber." Edited by Attilio Gnesotto. *Accademia patavina: Atti e memorie della R. Accademia di SLA in Padova* 32 (1916): 7–103.

Barone, Giulia. "La canonizzazione di Francesca Romana (1608): La riproposta di un modello agiografico medioevale." In *Finzione e santità tra Medioevo ed età moderna,* ed. Gabriella Zarri, 264–79. Turin: Rosenberg & Sellier, 1991.

Baseghi, Umberto. *Palazzi di Bologna.* 4th ed. Bologna: Tamari editori, 1964.

Battistella, Antonio. *Il S. Officio e la riforma religiosa in Bologna.* Bologna: Nicola Zanichelli, 1905.

Benson, Susan Porter. *Counter Cultures: Saleswomen, Managers, and Customers in American Department Stores, 1890–1940.* Urbana and Chicago: University of Illinois Press, 1988.

Benzoni, Gino. *Gli affanni della cultura intellettuali e potere nell'Italia della Controriforma e barocca.* Milan: Feltrinelli editore, 1978.

Bernardini, Carla, Rosalba D'Amico, Giovanna Degli Esposti, Angelo Mazza, Massimo Medica, and Carla Pirani. *La Pinacoteca Nazionale di Bologna: Catalogo generale delle opere esposte.* Bologna: Nuova Alfa editoriale, 1987.

Bilinkoff, Jodi. *The Avila of Saint Teresa: Religious Reform in a Sixteenth-Century City.* Ithaca, N.Y.: Cornell University Press, 1989.

Biondi, Albano. "Aspetti della cultura cattolica post-tridentina: Religione e controllo sociale." In *Storia d'Italia: Annali,* 4: *Intellettuali e potere,* ed. Corrado Vivanti, 253–302. Turin: Giulio Einaudi, 1981.

―――. "L''inordinata devozione' nella *Prattica* del Cardinale Scaglia (ca. 1635)." In *Finzione e santità tra Medioevo ed età moderna,* ed. Gabriella Zarri, 306–25. Turin: Rosenberg & Sellier, 1991.

Biondi, Giovanni Battista (*alias* Cesena). *Compieta con letanie che si cantano nella casa di Loretto, et motetti a otto voci, di s. Gio: Battista Cesena.* Venice: Giacomo Vincenti, 1606.

Blamires, Alcuin, ed. *Woman Defamed and Woman Defended: An Anthology of Medieval Texts.* Oxford: Clarendon Press; New York: Oxford University Press, 1992.

[Bonaventure, Saint]. *Holiness of Life: Being St. Bonaventure's Treatise "De perfectione vitae ad sorores".* Translated by Laurence Costello. Edited by Fr. Wilfrid, O.F.M. 2d ed. St. Louis: B. Herder, 1928.

Bottrigari, Ercole. *Il desiderio: Overo de' concerti di varii strumenti musicali.* Venice: Amadino, 1594.

Bowers, Jane. "The Emergence of Women Composers in Italy, 1566–1700." In *Women Making Music: The Western Art Tradition, 1150–1950,* ed. Jane Bowers and Judith Tick, 116–67. Urbana and Chicago: University of Illinois Press, 1986.

Boyle, Leonard E., O.P. *A Survey of the Vatican Archives and of Its Mediaeval Holdings.* Toronto: Pontifical Institute of Mediaeval Studies, 1972.

Bradshaw, Murray E. *Gabriel(e) Fattorini: "I concerti a due voci" (1600).* American Institute of Musicology Miscellanea, 5, Early Sacred Monody, vol. 2. Neuhausen-Stuttgart: Hänssler-Verlag, 1986.

Brecher, Jeremy. "Uncovering the Hidden History of the American Workplace." *Review of Radical Political Economy* 10 (1978): 1–23.

Breventani, Luigi. *Supplemento alle cose notabili di Bologna e alla miscellanea storico-patria di Giuseppe Guidicini.* Bologna: Garagnani, 1908.

Breviarium monasticum secundum ordinem camaldulensem: nunc recens reformatum, summaque diligentia emendatum et excusum. Venice: Johannes Variscum, 1580.

Brown, Judith. *Immodest Acts: The Life of a Lesbian Nun in Renaissance Italy.* New York: Oxford University Press, 1986.

———. "Monache a Firenze all'inizio dell'eta moderna: Un'analisi demografica," *Quaderni storici* 85 (1994): 117–152.

Brucker, Gene. *Giovanni and Lusanna: Love and Marriage in Renaissance Florence.* Berkeley and Los Angeles: University of California Press, 1986.

Bruzelius, Caroline A. "Hearing is Believing: Clarissan Architecture, ca. 1213–1340." *Gesta* 31 (1992): 83–92.

Bugge, John. *Virginitas: An Essay in the History of a Medieval Ideal.* International Archives of the History of Ideas, Series Minor, 17. The Hague: Martinus Nijhoff, 1975.

Burke, Peter. *The Historical Anthropology of Early Modern Italy: Essays on Perception and Communication.* Cambridge: Cambridge University Press, 1987.

Bynum, Caroline Walker. *Fragmentation and Redemption: Essays on Gender and the Human Body in Medieval Religion.* New York: Zone Books, 1991.

———. *Holy Feast and Holy Fast: The Religious Significance of Food to Medieval Women.* Berkeley and Los Angeles: University of California Press, 1987.

———. *Jesus as Mother: Studies in the Spirituality of the High Middle Ages.* Berkeley and Los Angeles: University of California Press, 1982.

Cambria, M. Giovanna. *Il monastero domenicano di S. Agnese in Bologna: Storia e documenti.* Bologna: Tipografia SAB, 1973.

Capriani, Ugo. "Chiesa e convento di Santa Cristina della Fondazza in Bologna: Ipotesi di ricerca e recupero." Tesi di laurea, Università di Bologna, 1987–88.

Carroll, Linda L. *Angelo Beolco (Il Ruzante).* Boston: Twayne, 1990.

Carruthers, Mary J. *The Book of Memory: A Study of Memory in Medieval Culture.* Cambridge: Cambridge University Press, 1990.

Cataluccio, M. Elena Maghieri, and A. Ugo Fossa. *Biblioteca e cultura a Camaldoli: Dal Medioevo all'umanesimo.* Rome: Editrice anselmiana, 1979.

Cattaneo, Enrico. "Le monacazioni forzate fra cinque e seicento." In *Vita e processo di Suor Virginia Maria de Leyva Monaca di Monza,* ed. Giancarlo Vigorelli, 145–95. Milan: Garzanti, 1985. 3d. ed., 1986.

Chiappafreddo, Franco. "L'Archivio della Sacra Congregazione del Concilio." In *La Sacra Congregazione del Concilio: Quarto centenario della fondazione (1564–1964): Studi e ricerche,* 395–406. Vatican City, 1964.

Chojnacki, Stanley. "Patrician Women in Early Renaissance Venice." *Studies in the Renaissance* 21 (1974): 176–203.

Ciammitti, Luisa. "Fanciulle monache madri: Povertà femminile e previdenza a Bologna nei secoli xvi–xviii." In *Arte e Pietà: I patrimoni culturali delle opere pie.* Catalogo della mostra. Bologna: Cooperativa libraria universitaria editrice Bologna, 1980.

Ciampelli, D. Parisio, O.S.B. *Vita di S. Romualdo Abate fondatore dei Camaldolesi.* Ravenna: Arti grafiche, 1927.

Cohen, Elizabeth. "La verginità perduta: Autorappresentazione di giovani donne nella Roma barocca." *Quaderni storici* 67 (1988): 169–91.

Cohen, Sherrill. *The Evolution of Women's Asylums since 1500: From Refuges for Ex-Prostitutes to Shelters for Battered Women.* New York: Oxford University Press, 1992.

Coldagelli, U. "Boncompagni, Antonio." In *Dizionario biografico degli Italiani,* 11: 679–81. Rome: Istituto della Enciclopedia italiana, 1969.

———. "Boncompagni, Gregorio." In *Dizionario biografico degli Italiani,* 11:, 693–94. Rome: Istituto della Enciclopedia italiana, 1969.

Cooper, Patricia A. *Once a Cigar Maker: Men, Women, and Work Culture in American Cigar Factories, 1900–1919.* Urbana and Chicago: University of Illinois Press, 1987.

Cori, Paola di. "Unite e divise: Appunti su alcuni problemi di storia della Solidarietà fra donne." In *Ragnatele di rapporti: Patronage e reti di relazione nella storia delle donne,* ed. Lucia Ferrante, Maura Palazzi, and Gianna Pomata, 481–94. Turin: Rosenberg & Sellier, 1988.

Cott, Nancy. *The Bonds of Womanhood: "Women's Sphere" in New England, 1780–1835.* New Haven: Yale University Press, 1977.

Cranna, Clifford A., Jr. "Adriano Banchieri's *Cartella musicale* (1614): Translation and Commentary." Ph.D. diss., Stanford University, 1981.

Creytens, Raymond. "La giurisprudenza della Sacra Congregazione del Concilio nella questione della clausura della monache (1564–1576)." In *La Sacra Congregazione del Concilio: Quarto centenario della fondazione (1564–1964): Studie e ricerche,* 563–97. Vatican City, 1964.

Croce, Giuseppe M. "I Camaldolesi nel Settecento: Tra la 'rusticitas' degli eremiti e l'erudizione dei cenobiti." In *Settecento monastico italiano,* ed. Giustino Farnedi and Giovanni Spinelli, 203–70. Cesena: Badia di S. Maria del Monte, 1990.

Cuppini, Giampiero. *I palazzi senatorii a Bologna: Architettura come immagine del potere.* Bologna: Nicola Zanichelli, 1974.

Cusick, Suzanne. "Gendering Modern Music: Thoughts on the Monteverdi-Artusi Controversy." *JAMS* 46 (1993): 1–25.

D'Amelia, Marina. "La Conquista di una dote: Regole del gioco e scambi femminili alla Confraternità dell'Annunziata (secc. xvii–xviii)." In *Ragnatele di rapporti: Patronage e reti di relazione nella storia delle donne,* ed. Lucia Ferrante, Maura Palazzi, and Gianna Pomata, 305–43. Turin: Rosenberg & Sellier, 1988.

Damian, Peter. *Vita Beati Romualdi.* Edited by Giovanni Tabacco. Fonti per la storia d'Italia, 94. Rome: Istituto storico italiano per il Medio Evo, 1957.

Decreta authentica Congregationis Sacrorum Rituum ex actis eiusdem collecta eiusque auctoritate promulgata sub auspiciis SS. Domini Nostri Leonis Papae XIII. 2 vols. Rome: Typographia polyglotta S.C. de Propaganda Fide, 1898.

De Maio, Romeo. "L'Ideale eroico nei processi di canonizzazione della Controriforma." In *Riforme e miti nella chiesa del Cinquecento,* 257–78. Naples: Guida editori, 1973.

Dolfi, Pompeo. *Cronologia delle famiglie nobili di Bologna.* Bologna: Giovanni Battista Ferroni, 1670. Repr., Bologna: Forni editore, n.d.

Dreves, Guido Maria. *Analecta hymnica*, 32. Leipzig: O. R. Reisland, 1899.

―――. *Analecta hymnica*, 48. Leipzig: O. R. Reisland, 1905.

Dubois, Ellen, Mari Jo Buhle, Temma Kaplan, Gerda Lerner, and Carroll Smith-Rosenberg. "Politics and Culture in Women's History: A Symposium." *Feminist Studies* 6 (1980): 26–64.

Editto de li ordini, et decreti del Sacro Concilio Tridentino sopra li monasteri di monache della città, & diocesi di Bologna. Bologna: Alessandro Benacci, 1565.

Ehses, Stephen, ed. *Concilii Tridentini actorum pars sexta complectens acta post sessionem sextam (xxii) usque ad finem concilii (17. Sept. 1562–4. Dec. 1563).* Freiburg: Herder, 1965.

Emiliani, Andrea, ed. *Ludovico Carracci: Bologna, Museo Civico Archeologico–Pinacoteca Nazionale, Fort Worth Texas, Kimbell Art Museum.* Bologna: Nuova Alfa editoriale, 1993.

Episcopale Bononiensis Civitatis et Diocesis: Raccolta di varie cose, che in diversi tempi sono state ordinate da Monsig. Illustriss. & Reverendiss. Cardinale Paleotti Vescovo di Bologna. Bologna: Alessandro Benacci, 1580.

[Erasmus, Desiderius]. *Opera omnia Desiderii Erasmi Roterodami recognita et adnotatione critica instructa notisque illustrata ordinis primi tomus tertius colloquia.* Edited by L.-E. Halkin, F. Bierlaire, and R. Hoven. Amsterdam: North-Holland Publishing, 1972.

Fanti, Mario. *Abiti e lavori delle monache di Bologna.* Bologna: Tamari, 1972.

―――. "Bologna nell'età moderna (1506–1796)." In *Storia di Bologna*, ed. Antonio Ferri and Giancarlo Roversi, 197–282. Bologna: Nuova edizione Alfa, 1978. 2d ed., 1984.

―――. "Le classi sociali e il governo di Bologna all'inizio del secolo xvii in un'opera di Camillo Baldi." *Strenna storica bolognese* 11 (1961): 133–79.

Fattorini, Gabriele. *Il secondo libro de mottetti a otto voci di Gabrielle Fattorini da Faenza.* Venice: Ricciardo Amadino, 1601.

Federhoffer, Hellmut. "Die Dissonanzbehandlung in Monteverdis Kirchenmusikalischen Werken und die Figurenlehre Christoph Bernhard." In *Claudio Monteverdi e il suo tempo: Relazioni e comunicazioni*, ed. Raffaello Monterosso, 435–78. Verona: Valdonega, 1969.

Ferrante, Lucia, Maura Palazzi, and Gianna Pomata, eds. *Regnatele di rapporti: Patronage e reti di relazione nella storia delle donne.* Turin: Rosenberg & Sellier, 1988.

Ferri, Antonio, and Giancarlo Roversi, eds. *Storia di Bologna.* Bologna: Nuova edizione Alfa, 1978. 2d ed., 1984.

Franklin, Harriet Apperson. "Musical Activity in Ferrara, 1598–1618." Ph.D. diss., Brown University, 1976.

Frati, Lodovico. *La vita privata in Bologna dal secolo xiii al xvii.* 2d ed. Bologna: Nicola Zanichelli, 1928. Repr., Rome: Bardi editore, 1968.

Freedman, Estelle. "Separatism as Strategy: Female Institution Building and American Feminism, 1870–1930." *Feminist Studies* 5 (1979): 512–29.

Garas, Klara. "The Ludovisi Collection of Pictures in 1633." *Burlington Magazine* 109 (1976): 287–89, 339–48.

Gardellini, Aloisi. *Decreta authentica Congregationis Sacrorum Rituum.* 3d ed. 2 vols. Rome: S. C. de Propaganda Fide, 1856.

Gaspari, Gaetano. *Musica e musicisti a Bologna.* Bologna: Forni editore, n.d.

Giabbani, Anselmo. *Menologia camaldolese.* Tivoli: De Rossi, 1950.

Giacomelli, Alfeo. "La dinamica della nobiltà bolognese nel xviii secolo." In *Famiglie senatorie e istituzioni cittadine a Bologna nel Settecento: Atti del colloquio, Bologna, 2–3 febbraio 1980,* 55–112. Bologna: Istituto per la storia di Bologna, 1980.

Gill, Katherine. "Scandala: Controversies Concerning *clausura* and Women's Religious Communities in Late Medieval Italy." In *Christendom and Its Discontents: Exclusion, Persecution and Rebellion, 1000–1500,* ed. Scott Waugh. Cambridge: Cambridge University Press. Forthcoming.

Ginzburg, Carlo. *The Cheese and the Worms: The Cosmos of a Sixteenth-Century Miller.* Translated by John Tedeschi and Anne Tedeschi. Baltimore: Johns Hopkins University Press, 1980.

―――. *Clues, Myths, and the Historical Method.* Translated by John Tedeschi and Anne Tedeschi. Baltimore: Johns Hopkins University Press, 1989.

Goffart, W. "Le Mans, St. Scholastica, and the Literary Tradition of the Translation of St. Benedict." *Revue bénédictine* 77 (1967): 107–41.

[Gregory the Great, Saint]. *Dialogues.* Translated by Paul Antin. Edited by Adalbert de Vogüé. 3 vols. Paris: Editions du Cerf, 1978–80.

Guadagnini, Anacleto. *R. Pinacoteca di Bologna.* Bologna: Stab. tip. Zamorani e Albertazzi, 1906.

Guidicini, Giuseppe. *Cose notabili della città di Bologna.* 5 vols. Bologna: Giuseppe Vitali, 1868–73. Repr., Bologna: Forni editore, 1972.

―――. *Miscellanea storico-patria bolognese.* Edited by Ferdinando Guidicini. Bologna: Monti, 1872. Repr., Bologna: Forni editore, 1972.

Guido Reni, 1585–1642: Pinacoteca Nazionale, Bologna; Los Angeles County Museum of Art; Kimbell Art Museum, Fort Worth. Bologna: Nuova Alfa editoriale, 1988.

Gutman, Herbert A. *Work, Culture, and Society in Industrializing America: Essays in American Working-Class and Social History.* New York: Knopf, 1976.

Hamburger, Jeffrey F. "Art, Enclosure and the *Cura monialium:* Prolegomena in the Guise of a Postscript." *Gesta* 31 (1992): 108–34.

―――. *The Rothschild Canticles: Art and Mysticism in Flanders and the Rhineland circa 1300.* New Haven: Yale University Press, 1990.

Haskell, Francis. *Patrons and Painters: A Study in the Relations Between Italian Art and Society in the Age of the Baroque.* London: Chatto & Windus, 1963.

Heffernan, Thomas J. *Sacred Biography: Saints and their Biographers in the Middle Ages.* Oxford: Oxford University Press, 1988.

Hughes, Diane Owen. "Sumptuary Law and Social Relations in Renaissance Italy." In *Disputes and Settlements: Law and Human Relations in the West,* ed. John Bossy, 69–99. Cambridge: Cambridge University Press, 1983.

Ignesti, Bernardo. "Il canto sacro nel S. Eremo di Camaldoli prima della venuta di Paolo Giustiniani." *Rivista camaldolese* 2, no. 8 (August 1927): 434–38.

Jones, Ann Rosalind. *The Currency of Eros: Women's Love Lyric in Europe, 1540–1620.* Bloomington: Indiana University Press, 1990.

―――. "Surprising Fame: Renaissance Gender Ideologies and Women's Lyrics." In *The Poetics of Gender,* ed. Nancy K. Miller, 74–95. New York: Columbia University Press, 1986.

Jungmann, Joseph A., S.J. *The Mass of the Roman Rite: Its Origins and Development.* Translated by Francis A. Brunner. Westminster, Md.: Christian Classics, 1986.

Kafalenos, Emma Mellard. "Possibilities of Isochrony: A Study of Rhythm in Modern Poetry." Ph.D. diss., Washington University in St. Louis, 1974.

Kendrick, Robert. "Genres, Generations and Gender: Nuns' Music in Early Modern Milan, c. 1550–1706." Ph.D. diss., New York University, 1993.

———. " 'Sonet vox tua in auribus meis': Song of Songs Exegesis and the Seventeenth-Century Motet." *Schütz Jahrbuch* 16 (1994): 99–118.

———. "The Traditions of Milanese Convent Music and the Sacred Dialogues of Chiara Margarita Cozzolani." In *The Crannied Wall: Women, Religion, and the Arts in Early Modern Europe,* ed. Craig Monson, 211–33. Ann Arbor: University of Michigan Press, 1992.

Kerber, Linda I. "Separate Spheres, Female Worlds, Woman's Place: The Rhetoric of Women's History." *Journal of American History* 75 (1988): 9–39.

Kertzer, David I., and Richard P. Saller, eds. *The Family in Italy from Antiquity to the Present.* New Haven: Yale University Press, 1991.

King, Margaret. "Thwarted Ambitions: Six Learned Women of the Italian Renaissance." *Soundings* 59 (1976): 280–304.

———. *Women of the Renaissance.* Chicago: University of Chicago Press, 1991.

Klapisch-Zuber, Christiane. *Women, Family, and Ritual in Renaissance Italy.* Translated by Lydia Cochrane. Chicago: University of Chicago Press, 1985.

Kuehn, Thomas. *Law, Family, and Women: Toward a Legal Anthropology of Renaissance Women.* Chicago: University of Chicago Press, 1991.

———. "Some Ambiguities of Female Inheritance Ideology in the Renaissance." *Continuity and Change* 2 (1987): 11–36.

Kurtzman, Jeffrey. "Giovanni Francesco Capello: An Avant-Gardist of the Early Seventeenth Century." *Musica disciplina* 13 (1977), 155–82.

Leclercq, Jean. "La 'Lecture Divine.' " *La Maison-Dieu* 5 (1946): 21–33.

———. *The Love of Learning and the Desire for God.* Translated by Catharine Misrahi. New York: Fordham University Press, 1982.

Lewis, Charlton T. *A Latin Dictionary Founded on Andres' Edition of Freund's Latin Dictionary.* Oxford: Clarendon Press, 1980.

Livi, Giovanni. "The Ferrabosco Family." *Musical Antiquary* 4 (1912–13): 121–42.

Lochrie, Karma. *Margery Kempe and Translations of the Flesh.* Philadelphia: University of Pennsylvania Press, [1991?].

Lodi, Enzo. *I santi della chiesa bolognese nella liturgia e pietà popolare.* N.p., 1987.

Longhi, Alessandro. *Il Palazzo Vizani e le famiglie illustri che lo possedettero.* Bologna: Zamorini & Albertazzi, 1902.

Lowe, K. J. P. "Female Strategies for Success in a Male-Ordered World: The Benedictine Convent of Le Murate in Florence in the Fifteenth and Early Sixteenth Centuries." *Studies in Church History* 27 (1990): 209–21.

Lunardi, Giovanni. "Le monache benedettine nel Settecento." In *Settecento monastico italiano,* ed. Giustino Farnedi and Giovanni Spinelli, 523–44. Cesena: Badia S. Maria del Monte, 1990.

MacClintock, Carol, ed. *The Bottegari Lutebook.* The Wellesley Edition, vol. 8. Wellesley, Mass.: Wellesley College, 1965.

Malvasia, Carlo Cesare. *Le pitture di Bologna 1686.* Edited by Andrea Emiliani. Bologna: Edizioni Alfa, 1969.

Marot, Clément. *Oeuvres complètes*, vol. 6: *Les Traductions*. Edited by C. A. Mayer. Geneva: Slatkine, 1980.

Martinelli, Serena Spanò. "La canonizzazione di Caterina Vigri: Un problema cittadino nella Bologna del Seicento." In *Culto dei santi: Istituzioni e classi sociali in età pre-industriale*, ed. Sofia Boesch Gajano and Lucia Sebastiani, 721–33. L'Aquila and Rome: L. U. Japadre, 1984.

Marx, Hans Joachim. "Die Musik am Hofe Pietro Kardinal Ottobonis unter Arcangelo Corelli." *Analecta musicologica* 5 (1968): 104–77.

Masetti Zannini, Gian Lodovico. "Composizioni poetiche e trattatelli spirituali per monacazioni benedettine del Settecento." In *Settecento monastico italiano*, ed. Giustino Farnedi and Giovanni Spinelli, 581–97. Cesena: Badia S. Maria del Monte, 1990.

———. "Espressioni musicali in monasteri femminili del primo Seicento a Bologna." *Strenna storica bolognese* 35 (1985): 193–205.

———. "Il cardinale Baronio e la musica nei monasteri femminili." In *Baronio e l'arte: Atti del convegno internazionale di studi, Sora, 10–13 ottobre 1984*, 787–98. Sora: Centro studi sorani "Vincenzo Patriarca," 1985.

———. "Lavori, 'fioretti' e rappresentazioni nel monastero di San Guglielmo (1624–1659)." *Strenna storica bolognese* 33 (1983): 161–73.

———. *Motivi storici dell'educazione femminile (1500–1650)*, vol. 1. Bari: Editorialebari, 1980.

———. " 'Suavità di canto' e 'purità di cuore': Aspetti della musica nei monasteri femminili romani." In *La cappella musicale nell'Italia della Controriforma*, ed. Oscar Mischiati and Paolo Russo, 123–41. Cento: Centro studi G. Baruffaldi, 1993.

Masini, Antonio di Paolo. *Bologna perlustrata*, 3d printing. Bologna: Erede di Vittorio Benacci, 1666.

———. *Guida spirituale che serve ogni giorno in perpetuo per visitare tutte le chiese di Bologna*. Bologna: per Giacomo Monti & Carlo Zenero, 1640.

Matter, E. Ann. "Discourses of Desire: Sexuality and Christian Women's Visionary Literature." In *Homosexuality and Religion*, ed. Richard Hasbany, 119–31. New York: Hawthorne Press, 1989.

———. "The Personal and the Paradigm: The Book of Maria Domitilla Galluzzi." In *The Crannied Wall: Women, Religion, and the Arts in Early Modern Europe*, ed. Craig Monson, 87–103. Ann Arbor: University of Michigan Press, 1992.

———. *The Voice of My Beloved: The Song of Songs in Western Medieval Christianity*. Philadelphia: University of Pennsylvania Press, 1990.

Mauceri, Enrico. *La Regia Pinacoteca di Bologna*. Rome: Libreria dello stato, 1935.

Mazzone, Umberto. "La visita e l'azione pastorali di Giacomo Boncompagni, arcivescovo di Bologna (1690–1731)." *Cristianesimo nella storia* 4 (1983): 343–66.

Mazzucchelli, Mario. *The Nun of Monza*. Translated by Evelyn Gendel. New York: Simon & Schuster, 1963.

Mazzucco, Gabriele. "Discorsi e poesie per monache stampati a Venezia nel secolo xviii." *Benedectina* 32 (1985): 161–200.

McKinnon, James. *Music in Early Christian Literature*. Cambridge: Cambridge University Press, 1987.

Melosh, Barbara. *"The Physician's Hand": Work Culture and Conflict in American Nursing*. Philadelphia: Temple University Press, 1982.

Meluzzi, Luciano. *I vescovi e gli arcivescovi di Bologna.* Bologna: Collana storico-ecclesiastica, 1975.

Mercati, Giovanni. *Ultimi contributi alla storia degli umanisti, fascicolo I: Traversariana.* Studi e testi, 90. Vatican City: Biblioteca Apostolica Vaticana, 1939.

Metz, René. *La Consécration des vierges dans l'église romaine: Etude d'histoire de la liturgie.* Paris: Presses universitaires de France, 1954.

Mittarelli, Giovanni Benedetto, and Anselmo Costadoni. *Annales Camaldulenses ordinis Sancti Benedicti.* 9 vols. Venice: Aere Monasterii Sancti Michaelis de Muriano, 1755–73.

Mone, Franz Joseph. *Lateinische Hymnen des Mittelalters,* vol. 2. Freiburg, 1854. Repr., Scientia Verlag Aalen, 1964.

Monson, Craig. "Disembodied Voices: Music in the Nunneries of Bologna in the Midst of the Counter-Reformation." In *The Crannied Wall: Women, Religion and the Arts in Early Modern Europe,* ed. Craig Monson, 191–209. Ann Arbor: University of Michigan Press, 1992.

———. "Elena Malvezzi's Keyboard Manuscript: A New Sixteenth-Century Source." *Early Music History* 9 (1989): 73–128.

———. "The Making of Lucrezia Orsina Vizzana's *Componimenti musicali* (1623)." In *Creative Women in Medieval and Early Modern Italy: A Religious and Artistic Renaissance,* ed. E. Ann Matter and John Coakley, 297–323. Philadelphia: University of Pennsylvania Press, 1994.

———. "Molti concerti, poca concordia: Monache, parrocchiani, e musica nella chiesa e convento dei Ss. Vitale e Agricola, 1550–1730." In *Vitale e Agricola: Il culto dei protomartiri di Bologna attraverso i secoli nel xvi centenario della traslazione,* ed. Gina Fasoli, 195–200. Bologna: EDB, 1993.

———. "Organi ed Organiste nei monasteri femminili a Bologna." *L'Organo: Rivista di cultura organaria e organistica.* Forthcoming.

———. "La prattica della musica nei monasteri femminili bolognesi." In *La cappella musicale nell'Italia della Controriforma,* ed. Oscar Mischiati and Paolo Russo, 143–60. Cento: Centro studi G. Baruffaldi, 1993.

Moretti, Maria Rosa. *Musica e costume a Genova tra Cinquecento e Seicento.* Genova: Francesco Pirella editore, 1992.

Moscini, Marcello. *Cristina di Bolsena: Culto e iconografia.* Viterbo: Agnesotti, 1986.

Muir, Edward. *Civic Ritual in Renaissance Venice.* Princeton: Princeton University Press, 1981.

———. *Mad Blood Stirring: Vendetta and Factions in Friuli during the Renaissance.* Baltimore: Johns Hopkins University Press, 1993.

Neuls-Bates, Carol, ed. *Women in Music: An Anthology of Source Readings from the Middle Ages to the Present.* New York: Harper & Row, 1982.

Newcomb, Anthony. "Courtesans, Muses, or Musicians? Professional Women Musicians in Sixteenth-Century Italy." In *Women Making Music: The Western Art Tradition, 1150–1950,* ed. Jane Bowers and Judith Tick, 90–115. Urbana and Chicago: University of Illinois Press, 1986.

———. *The Madrigal at Ferrara, 1579–1597.* 2 vols. Princeton: Princeton University Press, 1979.

Niccoli, Ottavia. "Il confessore e l'inquisitore: A proposito di un manoscritto bolognese del Seicento." In *Finzione e santità tra Medioevo ed età moderna,* ed. Gabriella Zarri, 412–34. Turin: Rosenberg & Sellier, 1991.

Nobili, Giovanni Pellegrino. *La verginità consacrata: Poesie consecrandosi nel nobilissimo monistero di S. Cristina . . . le molto reverende monache.* Bologna: Eredi del Sarti, 1699.

Odorisio, Ginevra Conti. *Donna e società nel Seicento: Lucrezia Marinelli e Arcangela Tarabotti.* Rome: Bulzoni editore, 1979.

Ordini da servarsi nell'admettere dentro li monasterii di monache le putte . . . & darli l'habito di novizza & della professione. Bologna: Alessandro Benacci, 1577.

Ordo admittendi virgines ad monasterii ingressum, habitumq[ue]; regularem suscipiendi, ritus item servandus ad professionis emissionem. Secundum morem Congregationis Cassinensis. Milan: Heirs of Pacificus Pontij & Giovanni Battista Piccaleum, 1607.

Orlandi, Giuseppe. "Vera e falsa santità in alcuni predicatori popolari e direttori di spirito del Sei e Settecento." In *Finzione e santità tra Medioevo ed età moderna,* ed. Gabriella Zarri, 435–63. Turin: Rosenberg & Sellier, 1991.

Pagnani, Alberigo, O.S.B. *Storia dei Benedettini camaldolesi: Cenobiti, eremiti, monache ed oblati.* Sassoferrato: Prem. tipografia Garofoli, 1949.

Palisca, Claude V. "The Artusi-Monteverdi Controversy." In *The New Monteverdi Companion,* ed. Denis Arnold and Nigel Fortune, 127–58. London: Faber & Faber, 1985.

Paolin, Giovanna. "Confessione e confessori al femminile: Monache e direttori spirituali in ambito veneto tra '600 e '700." In *Finzione e santità tra Medioevo ed età moderna,* ed. Gabriella Zarri, 366–88. Turin: Rosenberg & Sellier, 1991.

Paschini, Pio. "I monasteri femminili in Italia nel '500." In *Problemi di vita religiosa in Italia nel Cinquecento: Atti del convegno di storia della chiesa in Italia,* ed. M. Maccarrone, G. G. Meersseman, E. Passerin d'Entrèves, and P. Sambin, 31–60. Padua: Editrice Antenore, 1960.

Pastor, Ludwig. *The History of the Popes.* Translated by Ernest Graf. 34 vols. St. Louis: B. Herder, 1952.

Petroff, Elizabeth Alvilda. *Body and Soul: Essays on Medieval Women and Mysticism.* New York: Oxford University Press, 1994.

———. *Consolation of the Blessed.* New York: Alta Gaia Society, 1979.

———. *Medieval Women's Visionary Literature.* New York: Oxford University Press, 1986.

Picker, Martin, ed. *The Motet Books of Andrea Antico.* Monuments of Renaissance Music, vol. 8. Chicago: University of Chicago Press, 1987.

Pickering, Frederick P. "Das gotische Christusbild: Zu den Quellen mittelalterlicher Passionsdarstellungen." *Euphorion* 47 (1953): 16–37.

———. *Literature and Art in the Middle Ages.* Coral Gables, Fla.: University of Miami Press, 1970.

Poni, Carlo. "Svillupo, declino e morte dell'antico distretto industriale urbano (secoli xvi–xix)." In *Storia illustrata di Bologna,* ed. Walter Tega, 3: 321–80. Milan: Nuova editoriale AIEP, 1989.

Pontificale romanum Clementis VIII. Pont. Max. iussu restitutum atque editum (Antwerp: Ex Officina Plantiniana Apud Balthasarem Moretum, 1627).

Processionale Monasticum ad usum Congregationis Gallicae Ordinis Sancti Benedicti. Solesme, 1893.

Prodi, Paolo. *Il cardinale Gabriele Paleotti (1522–1597).* 2 vols. Rome: Edizioni di storia e letterature, 1959–67.

———. "Lineamenti dell'organizzazione diocesana in Bologna durante l'episcopato del card. G. Paleotti (1566–1597)." In *Problemi di vita religiosa in Italia nel Cinquecento,* ed. M. Maccarrone, G. G. Meersseman, E. Passerin d'Entrèves, and P. Sambin, 323–94. Padua: Editrice Antenore, 1960.

Prosperi, Adriano. "L'elemento storico nelle polemiche sulla santità." In *Finzione e santità tra Medioevo ed età moderna,* ed. Gabriella Zarri, 88–118. Turin: Rosenberg & Sellier, 1991.

———. "Intellettuali e chiesa all'inizio dell'età moderna." In *Storia d'Italia: Annali,* 4: *Intellettuali e potere,* ed. Corrado Vivanti, 159–252. Turin: Giulio Einaudi, 1981.

Rambelli, G. F. "Sant'Andrea di Ozzano di Sopra." *Le chiese parrocchiali della diocesi di Bologna ritratte e descritte,* vol. 2. Bologna: Litografia di Enrico Corty, tipografia di San Tommaso d'Aquino, 1847. Repr., Bologna: Forni editore, 1976.

Réau, Louis. *Iconographie de l'art Chrétien.* Paris: Presses universitaires de France, 1958.

Ricci, Corrado, and Guido Zucchini. *Guida di Bologna: Nuova edizione illustrata.* Bologna: Edizioni Alfa, 1968; repr., 1976.

Ricci, Giovanni. *Bologna.* Bari: Laterza, 1980.

Ripa, Cesare. *Iconologia.* Edited by Piero Buscaroli. 2 vols. Turin: Fogola editore, 1986. 2d ed., 1987.

Ritus recipiendi virgines ad religionis habitum nec non ad professionem novitias in civitate & diocesi Bononiæ. Bologna: Vittorio Benacci, 1626.

Roche, Jerome. "Musica diversa di compietà: Compline and Its Music in Seventeenth-Century Italy." *Proceedings of the Royal Musical Association* 109 (1982–83): 60–79.

———. *North Italian Church Music in the Age of Monteverdi.* Oxford: Oxford University Press, 1984.

———. "Orsina, Lucretia." In *The New Grove Dictionary of Music and Musicians,* ed. Stanley Sadie, 13: 874. London: Macmillan, 1980.

Romita, Fiorenza. *Ius musicae liturgicae.* Taurini: Officina libraria Marii e Marietti, 1936.

Rondet, Henri. "Notes d'exégèse augustinienne: Psalterium et Cithara." *Recherches de science réligieuse* 46 (1958): 408–15.

Rorke, Margaret Ann. "Sacred Contrafacta of Monteverdi Madrigals and Cardinal Borromeo's Milan." *ML* 65 (1984): 168–75.

Rosand, Ellen. "Barbara Strozzi, *virtuosissima cantatrice:* The Composer's Voice." *JAMS* 31 (1978): 241–81.

———. "The Voice of Barbara Strozzi." In *Women Making Music: The Western Art Tradition, 1150–1950,* ed. Jane Bowers and Judith Tick, 168–90. Urbana and Chicago: University of Illinois Press, 1986.

Rose, Mary Beth, ed. *Women in the Middle Ages and the Renaissance.* Syracuse, N.Y.: Syracuse University Press, 1986.

Rosenberg, Margaret F. *The Honest Courtesan: Veronica Franco, Citizen and Writer in Sixteenth-Century Venice.* Chicago: University of Chicago Press, 1992.

Roversi, Giancarlo. *Palazzi e case nobili del '500 a Bologna: La storia, le famiglie, le opere d'arte.* Bologna: Grafis edizioni, 1986.

Ruggiero, Guido. *The Boundaries of Eros: Sex Crime and Sexuality in Renaissance Venice.* New York: Oxford University Press, 1985.

————. " 'Più che la vita caro': Onore, matrimonia e reputazione femminile nel tardo Rinascimento." *Quaderni storici* 66 (1987): 753–75.

Salmon, Pierre. *Analecta liturgica: Estraits des manuscrits liturgiques de la Bibliothèque vaticane.* Studi e testi, 273. Vatican City: Biblioteca Apostolica Vaticana, 1974.

Sartori, Claudio. "Monteverdiana." *MQ* 38 (1952): 399–413.

Sera, Beatrice del. *Amor di virtù.* Edited by Elissa Weaver. Ravenna: Longo editore, 1990.

Sherr, Richard. "Mecenatismo musicale a Mantova: Le nozze di Vincenzo Gonzaga e Margherita Farnese." *Rivista italiana di musicologia* 19 (1984): 3–20.

Skeris, Robert A. CHROMA THEOU: *On the Origins and Theological Interpretation of the Musical Imagery Used by the Ecclesiastical Writers of the First Three Centuries, with Special Reference to the Image of Orpheus.* Altötting: Verlag Alfred Coppenrath, 1976.

Slim, H. Colin. "Music and Dancing with Mary Magdalen in a Laura Vestalis." In *The Crannied Wall: Women, Religion, and the Arts in Early Modern Europe,* ed. Craig Monson, 139–60. Ann Arbor: University of Michigan Press, 1992.

Smith-Rosenberg, Carrol. "The Female World of Love and Ritual: Relations between Women in Nineteenth-Century America." *Signs* 1 (1975): 1–29.

Somigli, Costanzo, and Tommaso Bargellini. *Ambrogio Traversari monaco camaldolese: La figura e la dottrina monastica.* Bologna: Edizioni Dehoniane, 1986.

Stevens, Denis. *The Letters of Claudio Monteverdi.* Cambridge: Cambridge University Press, 1980.

Storia della cultura veneta. 6 vols. Vicenza: Neri Pozza, 1976–85.

Strocchia, Sharon T. "The Politics of the Pen: Literacy and Social Exchange in Florentine Convents, 1450–1530." Paper delivered at Annual Meeting of Renaissance Society of America, Stanford, March 1992.

Surtz, Ronald E. *The Guitar of God: Gender, Power, and Authority in the Visionary World of Mother Juana de la Cruz (1481–1534).* Philadelphia: University of Pennsylvania Press, 1990.

Tega, Walter, ed. *Storia illustrata di Bologna.* 5 vols. Milan: AIEP editore, 1989.

Thurston, Herbert, S.J. *The Holy Year of Jubilee: An Account of the History and Ceremonial of the Roman Jubilee.* St. Louis: B. Herder, 1900.

Tomlinson, Gary. *Monteverdi and the End of the Renaissance.* Berkeley and Los Angeles: University of California Press, 1987.

[Traversari, Ambrogio]. *Ambrosii Traversarii generalis Camaldulensium aliorumque ad ipsum, et ad alios de eodem Ambrosio latinae epistolae,* vol. 2. Edited by Pietro Cannetti and Laurence Mehus. Florence: Typographio Caesareo, 1759. Repr., Bologna: Forni editore, 1968.

————. *Hodoeporicon.* Edited by Vittorio Tamburini. Florence: Felice le Monnier, 1985.

Trexler, Richard C. *Public Life in Renaissance Florence.* Ithaca, N.Y.: Cornell University Press, 1991.

Varni, Angelo. "Il periodo napoleonico." In *Storia illustrata di Bologna,* ed. Walter Tega, 2: 341–60. Milan: Nuova editoriale AIEP, 1989.

Vecchi, Giuseppe. *Le accademie musicali del primo seicento e Monteverdi a Bologna.* Bologna: A.M.I.S., 1969.

Vigorelli, Giancarlo, ed. *Vita e processo di suor Virginia Maria de Leyva, monaca di Monza.* Milan: Garzanti, 1985. 3d ed., 1986.

Vitali, Carlo, ed. *Il Faramondo.* Vol. 9 of *Drammaturgia musicale veneta.* Milan: Ricordi, 1987.

Weaver, Elissa, "Canti suoni e balli nel teatro delle suore toscane." In *Letteratura italiana e musica: Atti del xiv Congresso dell'A.I.S.L.L.I, University of Odense, Denmark, 1–5 July 1991.* Forthcoming.

———. "The Convent Wall in Tuscan Convent Drama." In *The Crannied Wall: Women, Religion and the Arts in Early Modern Europe,* ed. Craig Monson, 73–86. Ann Arbor: University of Michigan Press, 1992.

———. "Spiritual Fun: A Study of Sixteenth-Century Tuscan Convent Theater." In *Women in the Middle Ages and the Renaissance,* ed. Mary Beth Rose, 173–205. Syracuse, N.Y.: Syracuse University Press, 1986.

Wernli, Andreas. *Studien zum literarischen und musikalischen Werk Adriano Banchieris (1568–1634).* Publikationen der Schweizerischen Musikforschenden Gesellschaft, 2d ser., vol. 3. Bern and Stuttgart: Paul Haupt, 1981.

Wilkinson, Christopher. "Gabriele Fattorini: Rival of Viadana." *ML* 65 (1984): 329–36.

Wright, Anthony David. *The Counter-Reformation: Catholic Europe and the Non-Catholic World.* New York: St. Martin's Press, 1982.

Yardley, Anne Bagnall. "The Marriage of Heaven and Earth: A Late Medieval Source of the *Consecratio virginum.*" *Current Musicology* 45–47 (1990): 305–24.

Zarri, Gabriella. "Istituzioni ecclesiastiche e vita religiosa a Bologna (1450–1700)." In *Storia Illustrata di Bologna,* ed. Walter Tega, 2: 161–200. Milan: Nuova editoriale AIEP, 1989.

———. "I monasteri femminili a Bologna tra il xiii e il xvii secolo." *Deputazione di storia patria per le province di Romagna: Atti e memorie,* n.s., 24 (1973): 133–224.

———. "I monasteri femminili benedettini nella diocesi di Bologna (secoli xiii–xvii)." In *Ravennatensia ix: Atti del convegno di Bologna nel xv centenario della nascita di S. Benedetto (15–16–17 settembre 1980),* 333–71. Cesena: Badia di Santa Maria del Monte, 1981.

———. *Le sante vive: Profezie di corte e devozione femminile tra '400 e '500.* Turin: Rosenberg & Sellier, 1990.

———. "Orsola and Catherine: The Marriage of Virgins in the Sixteenth Century." In *Creative Women in Medieval and Early Modern Italy: A Religious and Artistic Renaissance,* ed. E. Ann Matter and John Coakley, 237–78. Philadelphia: University of Pennsylvania Press, 1994.

———. "Monasteri femminili e città (secoli xv–xviii)." In *Storia d'Italia: Annali,* 9: *La chiesa e il potere politico dal Medioevo all'età contemporanea,* ed. Giorgio Chittolini and Giovanni Miccoli, 359–429. Turin: Giulio Einaudi, 1986.

———. "Recinti sacri: Sito e forma dei monasteri femminili a Bologna tra '400 e '600." In *Luoghi sacri e spazi della santità,* ed. Sofia Boesch Gajano and Lucetta Scaraffia, 381–396. Turin: Rosenberg & Sellier, 1990.

———. " 'Vera' santità, 'simulata' santità: Ipotesi e riscontri." In *Finzione e santità tra Medioevo ed età moderna,* ed. Gabriella Zarri, 9–36. Turin: Rosenberg & Sellier, 1991.

Zucchini, Roberta. "Santa Cristina della Fondazza: Storia architettonica e storico artistica." Tesi di laurea, Università di Bologna, 1987–88.

INDEX

Accademia degli Oziosi, 18

Accademia dei Floridi, 65, 68

Acciaioli, Cardinal Niccolò, 232, 317n20

Adda, Cardinal Ferdinando [Borromeo] d', 200, 206, 212, 219, 223

Adoramus te dulcissime Jesu Christe (Banchieri), 53, 62

Ælred of Rievaulx, Saint, 85

Agazzari, Agostino, 128

Agnes, Saint, 78–79, 195

Agostino, don (Camaldolese procurator general), 200, 201, 206–7, 306n2

Agucchi, Francesco, 207

Albergati, Msgr. Antonio, 186

Albertazzi family, 245

Aldobrandesca of Siena, Blessed, 99

Alexander VII, 192, 205

Allè, Maria Caterina, 207, 208, 212, 223, 224

Almirante, Margarita, 49

Altarpieces: commissioned by nuns, 32–33, 135, 182, 258n68; in convent cells, 29; in convent/parish churches, 259n76; female focus of, 33–34, 259n72; "Romuald's Dream" from, 77–78

Amalia of Brunswick, 219

Ambrose, Saint, 1, 3, 141

America: women's separation in, 11; women's work culture in, 8–9

Amo Christum (Vizzana), 76, 78–79, 80

Angela of Foligno, Blessed, 86, 99, 272n32

Angelici concentus (Vernizzi), 63

Anges, Jeanne des, 141

Anima mia perdona (Monteverdi), 66 (example)

Annales Camaldulenses, 132

Annunciation (Passerotti), 32–33, 34

Anthony of Padua, 4

Antico, Andrea, 127

Apocalypse *14:2,* 88

Arali, Emilia, 29, 30, 47, 60–61

Archivio Arcivescovile (Bologna), 13, 14

Archivio di Stato (Bologna), 14

Archivio Segreto Vaticano, 13

Arena del Sole, 244

Aretino, Pietro, 159, 287n46, 289n64

Ariosti, Monica Felice, 29, 30, 47

Armonia ecclesiasticorum concertuum (Vernizzi), 63

Arnold, Denis, 64

Artusi, Giovanni Maria, 65, 85–86, 269n25

Ascension of Our Lord (Carracci), 32, 33, 76

Associazione Leone XIII, 242, 243

Audi coelum: by Gabriele Fattorini, 54; by Ercole Porta, 54; by Claudio Monteverdi, 54

Augerau, Pierre-François-Charles, 239

Augustine, Saint, 86, 108, 123, 272n32

Augustinian order, 4, 240

Ave stella matutina: hymn text by Peter the Venerable, 95, 125–26; motet by Agazzari, 127; motet by Brumel, 126; motet by Maistre Jahn, 126; motet by Vizzana, 95, 119, 124–25, 128–30, 281n39; motet by Weerbecke, 126

Azzoguidi, Girolamo, 219

Azzolini, Maria Elisabetta, 229, 231, 236, 316n19

Compositor:	Impressions
Text:	10/12 Baskerville
Display:	Baskerville
Printer and Binder:	Edwards Brothers, Inc.